INTEGRATED RISK MANAGEMENT

Techniques and Strategies for Managing Corporate Risk

NEIL A. DOHERTY

McGRAW-HILL, INC.

New York   San Francisco   Washington, D.C.   Auckland   Bogotá
Caracas   Lisbon   London   Madrid   Mexico City   Milan
Montreal   New Delhi   San Juan   Singapore
Sydney   Tokyo   Toronto

Library of Congress Cataloging-in-Publication Data

Doherty, Neil A.
  Integrated risk management : techniques and strategies for reducing
  risk / by Neil A. Doherty.
    p. cm.
  Includes bibliographical references.
  ISBN 0-07-135861-7
  1. Risk management. 2. Corporations—Finance. 3. Insurance, Business. I. Title.

HD61 .D643 2000
658.15'5—dc21

99-088282

McGraw-Hill

A Division of The **McGraw·Hill** Companies

1 2 3 4 5 6 7 8 9 0 DOC/DOC 9 0 9 8 7 6 5 4 3 2 1 0 9

ISBN 0-07-135861-7

The sponsoring editor for this book was Catherine Schwent, the editing supervisor was John M. Morriss, and the production supervisor was Charles Annis. It was set in Palatino by Pro-Image Corporation.

Printed and bound by R.R. Donnelley & Sons Company.

McGraw-Hill books are available at special quantity discounts to use as premiums and sales promotions, or for use in corporate training programs. For more information, please write to the Director of Special Sales, Professional Publishing, McGraw-Hill, 2 Penn Plaza, New York, NY 10121-2298. Or contact your local bookstore.

This publication is designed to provide accurate and authoritative information in regard to the subject matter covered. It is sold with the understanding that neither the author or the publisher is engaged in rendering legal, accounting, or other professional service. If legal advice or other expert assistance is required, the services of a competent professional person should be sought.

> —*From a Declaration of Principles jointly adopted by a Committee of the American Bar Association and a Committee of Publishers.*

This book is printed on recycled, acid-free paper containing a minimum of 50% recycled de-inked fiber.

C O N T E N T S

Chapter 16

A Case Study: The Securitization of Catastrophe Risk 593

PREFACE

This book is really a sequel to an earlier one, *Corporate Risk Management: A Financial Exposition*. When the earlier book was published in 1985, the term "risk management" had a more precise, but narrower, meaning than today. Some risks facing firms, such as property and liability risks, are known as "pure" risks. These are risks that only have a downside potential and are often insurable. But there was increasing recognition that insurance was not the only way to manage pure risks. Alternatively, risks could be reduced by investing in safety and quality control, or they could be retained, which often involved setting up a funding mechanism, such as a captive insurance company. "Risk management" was the name given to the formulation of strategy from this tool set to address this limited set of pure risks. There was little recognition that the tools of corporate finance could be used as a framework for this exercise. The aim of my earlier book was to provide such a financial economic framework and to show that risk management strategy could be expanded beyond "pure" risk.

Times have changed. Now, few would question the value of financial analysis for risk management. Indeed, risk management has become part of the mainstream of finance. The intervening decade and a half has seen remarkable developments. The derivatives market has blossomed and with it, financial engineering has provided sophisticated tools that can be used to hedge risks such as interest rate risk, foreign exchange risk, and commodity risk. And, unlike the early 1980s, we now a have a respectable theory that shows how risk destroys corporate value and how value can be created from its management. In this new environment, insurance companies are selling financial risk management products, and insurance substitutes are being placed directly in capital markets. Risk assessment and mapping models are in increasing use, and the vendors of new risk management products are increasingly being required to demonstrate their contribution to shareholder wealth.

This book takes a "value creation" approach to risk management. The book starts by reviewing some of the basic economics, finance, and statistics that are needed to develop the value created approach. But the real foundation for the development of risk management strategies is to understand why risk is costly to the firm in the first place. The book reviews the various theories on the cost of risk and the supporting evidence. The idea is that, if we understand why risk is destroying value, we cannot only measure the damage but formulate strategies to recoup shareholder value.

Simply knowing that risk can reduce shareholder value provides a rationale for hedging the risk (transaction costs permitting). The approach here delves deeper to examine the structural features of the firm that cause risk to be a problem. This approach allows us to identify which firms are most vulnerable to risk and therefore have the most to gain from its management. More importantly, this approach allows us to develop strategies by changing those structural features and making the firm more robust to risk. For example, for firms with high financial leverage, risk can cause high expected bankruptcy costs, can lead to costly incentive conflicts between creditors and shareholders and, if something bad happens, can cause a situation in which the firm is unable to finance future investment opportunities. This reasoning leads to an examination of simple and compound leverage strategies for managing risk, as well as contingent financing. The book also addresses the use of limited liability to manage risk and deals with some of the thorny welfare problems of such a strategy. And, of course, also considered are hedging products (such as derivatives and insurance) and analyses are made of some of the newer insurance products that are appearing. The book not only outlines new risk management strategies and products that are appearing on the market, but shows how new products can be designed for particular needs. The book closes with a case study of the securitization of insurance risk.

The material for this book has been developed from my teaching notes used for undergraduate, MBA, and executive education courses at the Wharton School. I would like to express my thanks to the numerous students and colleagues who have offered specific inputs or who have stimulated and honed my interest in risk management over the years.

Neil A. Doherty

Background Analysis

CHAPTER 1

The Convergence of Insurance Risk Management and Financial Risk Management

This book is about corporate risk management. It is concerned with the use of both insurance and financial instruments to control the costs of corporate risk. The name nowadays given to a comprehensive risk management strategy is "integrated risk management" or sometimes "enterprise risk management."

This comprehensive approach to risk management echoes recent shifts of practice both in Wall Street and in the insurance industry. From the capital markets side, the rapid growth of the derivatives and related markets, together with the emergence of financial engineering, have led to a emphasis on risk management as one of the key functions in corporate finance. From the insurance side, policies are being redesigned to bundle protection from a number of insurance risks and even to encompass financial risks. This reflects a growing awareness of the indivisible nature of risk in corporate value and an increasing focus of insurers on the financial needs of their corporate clients. But insurers and banks have not been timid in approaching each other. Indeed, they are becoming increasingly engaged in each other's business. Banks are now nesting insurance coverage into bond issues and insurers are issuing policies that hedge against financial risks such as interest rate and foreign exchange volatility. For the firm, the risk management industry from which they can obtain risk services is expanding as financial institutions of all types are starting to deliver a broad array of risk management products.

INSURANCE AND RISK MANAGEMENT

The term "risk management" gained currency in the 1960s and 1970s by those interested in exploring broader options for managing "insurable risk." Insurance has long been used by corporations to manage property, liability, and related insurable risks. Insurable risks expose the firm to volatility, but the volatility is all in one direction. Damage to property, or liability settlements, offer chance of loss, not of gain. The defining characteristic of such insurable risks is that they are downside in direction. Such risk is often called "pure risk."

Of course, insurable risks can be managed by insuring them. But the advent of risk management reflected a recognition that this was not the only possible strategy. Insurance provides a source of finance to pay for losses. But losses could be paid from the firm's cash or the firm could borrow or raise new equity to pay for losses. Moreover, if the firm did not insure its losses, it could set up an internal funding mechanism. This funding approach is often formalized by setting up a subsidiary, or captive, insurance company. In this way, the risk could be priced, premiums paid to the captive, and a formal loss settlement process implemented.

A second characteristic of insurable risks is that they are often under the control of the policyholder. The firm can influence the probability that its property will be damaged by fire or flood as it can influence the probability that it will be sued for defective products, environmental contamination, or the tortuous activities of its directors and officers. Recognition of this control suggests another risk management strategy: risk can be reduced or avoided. By investing in safety, quality control, hazard education, the firm could reduce the expected value of such losses (and possibly the volatility). Thus, loss reduction could complement insurance and other risk management strategies.

This *insurable risk management* was structured in the work of Robert Mehr and Bob Hedges in the 1960s in the following way.

FIGURE 1–1

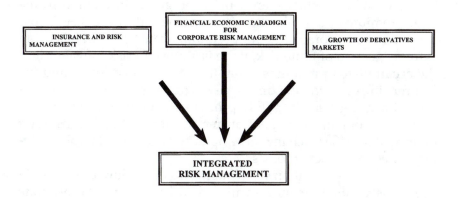

Risk can be

* *transferred* to a counter-party by purchase of an insurance policy or financial hedge.
* *retained* in either an active or passive way. Simply not insuring is retaining risk. But the firm can mimic the insurance process by self insuring with internal pricing, reserving, and loss settlements.
* *reduced* by investing in sprinklers, smoke alarms, inspections, and other safety measures.
* *avoided* by not undertaking activities that were risky or by substituting less risky processes.

The conceptual work of Mehr and Hedges was matched in practice by the evolution of the "insurance manager" of the firm into the broader role of "risk manager." Thus, health and safety might come under the risk manager's control or at least be coordinated with his or her activities. Moreover, the risk manager would normally operate the firm's captive or other internal funding schemes. But the office of the risk manager was rarely so broad as to address noninsurable risk faced by the firm.

Innovation in the management of insurable risk did not flow one way. Insurers for their part have been quietly active. Three key innovations reveal their trajectory. One is the introduction of finite risk programs. These programs are partly insurance and partly debt financing. A finite risk policy typically covers a number of years and offers a level of coverage set in relation to the total premiums paid over the coverage period. Moreover, if loss experience is favorable, some premiums can be returned. In an extreme version of finite risk, there is almost no risk transfer, since the accumulated premiums equal the accumulated losses and the insurer simply funds the timing risk. This extreme version is simply a financing vehicle. While programs usually are not this extreme and contain some risk transfer, this innovation is significant because it signifies a change in emphasis away from simply hedging losses to financing losses.

A second innovation for insurers was to follow the banks in use of asset liability management to deal with their own corporate risk exposure. This technology stresses a portfolio approach to risk management. Insurers hold both risky assets (bonds, stocks, real estate, etc.) and risky liabilities (insurance policies). The overall risk to the insurer, and therefore to its policyholders, depends on the combined performance of the asset and liability portfolio. What if the insurer had abnormal claims on its policies and the bond market collapsed at the same time? Such questions have caused many insurers to seek out assets that have low correlations with insurance liabilities and to examine carefully their investment risk when planning reinsurance needs. This is an integrated approach to managing insurer risk.

And what is good for the goose may be good for the gander. Insurers have started to offer integrated coverage to their clients. In the 1990s, insurers started bundling risks into policies that offered common coverage against a number of perils. The novelty of such bundled coverages is that the insurance payment is determined by the total loss of the insured; thus it is truly a coordinated coverage rather than several separate policies sold under one document. More recently, these bundled policies have included financial risks (such as interest rate and foreign exchange risk) as well as traditional insurance risks (such as property and liability risk). The barriers between insurance and capital markets are being breached.

THE GROWTH OF DERIVATIVES MARKETS

The 1980s and 1990s were a period of rapid financial innovation. Perhaps the defining mark of this period was the growth of the options, futures, and related markets. The increasing availability of derivative instruments on corporate shares, interest rates, commodity prices, and foreign exchange rates armed investors with instruments to take speculative positions on these underlying values. But it also armed firms with tools to hedge their preexisting exposure to these risks. For example, the exposure of a bank to interest rate risk could be hedge with a plethora of interest rate derivative instruments such as futures, swaps, and caps. The firm that imports raw materials could hedge against changes in the exchange rate through forwards and futures, and the oil company could hedge against falls in oil prices with oil futures. Amongst the new and hybrid derivatives a particularly interesting new one, insurance derivatives, emerged in the 1990s. These were introduced on the Chicago Board of Trade, and their payout and exercise price is related to the insurance industry's catastrophe losses. Thus, investors can speculate on storms and hurricanes, and insurance companies can use these instruments to hedge their preexisting exposure to these events.

Whether the supply of new instruments created a demand for hedging or the reverse is not critical here. The 1970s and 1980s did witness high levels of volatility in many financial indicators and in some basic commodity prices. The impact of OPEC on oil prices in the 1970s was dramatic; the late 1970s and early 1980s saw extreme volatility in interest rates, and this period also was one of exchange rate volatility following the collapse of the Bretton Woods, which had previously stabilized exchange rates. The 1980s were also a period in which litigation for product liability, environmental damage, and related harms was racheting up by orders of magnitude. Superfund had created enormous retroactive liabilities, and class actions from asbestos and other latent injuries were bankrupting large firms. Thus, it was a time of uncertainty, and the volatility could be attributed to quite specific causes. For financial risks, the new demand for hedges matched a explosion of supply of new derivatives instruments; for liability risk, the increased demand was met initially by a collapse of the insurance market, which only gradually reemerged, although with new contract designs.

The growth of the derivative market in the 1980s was also facilitated by another development. Before the 1970s techniques for pricing these complex instruments were inadequate. But in the early 1970s the work of Fisher Black and Myron Scholes and others yielded working option pricing models. Such models provided confidence to investors on both sides of an option trade that pricing was no longer guesswork, and this removed a major impediment to the growth of this market.

The growth of derivatives markets provided the grist for the hedging mill, but it also provided the material for other risk management strategies. Derivatives could be used by the firm to hedge specific risks, but they could also be embedded in the firm's debt and equity. This had long been done with convertible and callable debt, which package normal debt with an option to convert or call. These forms of debt have been shown to have risk management benefits. For example, callable debt has an embedded interest rate hedge because the exercise of the call option will be determined in part by the behavior of interest rates. Convertible debt also has been shown to reduce the incentive conflicts arising from leverage and therefore to reduce the need for hedging. More recent innovations have been directly motivated by risk management considerations. For example, recent catastrophe bond issues have a built-in hedge in the form of principal or interest forgiveness should a defined event (such as a hurricane or an earthquake) occur. Other recent innovations include convertible debt in which the firm, rather than the bondholder, has the option to convert, and the issue by a firm of put options on its own stock such that it may recapitalize after some painful event that causes its stock value to tumble.

In the late 1980s and early 1990s the term "risk management" started being heard in capital markets. Its use was not very restricted. One application was simply the management of portfolio risk for the investor. Increasingly, however, risk management referred to the process of managing a corporation's exposure to financial risks. And now a chapter, or even a whole section, on risk management is standard fare in finance books.

THE INTELLECTUAL CLIMATE

The genesis of integrated risk management also is intellectual. The 1980s and 1990s saw an emerging paradigm on the role of risk in determining corporate value. A comfortable traditional explanation for risk management had been (and for many continues to be) that shareholders are risk-averse and their interests are well served if the firm manages risk on their behalf. This was fine with older models of asset pricing, and in the new explanation of asset pricing that emerged in the 1960s and 1970s, the capital asset pricing model (CAPM) risk also played a central role. If risk could not be diversified by investors, it would be priced. If corporate risk could be diversified, it imposed no costs on investors and would not be priced. Probably the first serious attempt to explain risk management in the CAPM world was a 1976 paper by David Cummins in which the author showed how a firm could maximize its value by insuring risk. But a reinterpretation of his results shows that insurance can only add value if the policy is underpriced. This new view of things seemed to leave no role for corporate risk management if markets were functioning efficiently. There was no value in hedging diversifiable risks, since they were irrelevant for shareholders. And as for undiversifiable risks, the firm would end up giving up any gain from hedging to the insurer as the latter's price for accepting the risk. There would be no net gain. So why bother to manage risk?

The search for a reconciliation between asset pricing theory and corporate risk management really began in the early 1980s. The most influential early paper was that by Mayers and Smith (1982) from which a newer theory of corporate risk management began to coalesce based on the frictional costs associated with corporate risk. Risk will tend to increase taxes and will increase the prospective costs of financial distress. Moreover, when a firm's cash flows are risky, conflicts of interest arise between shareholders and creditors. Unless constraints are imposed on managerial actions, this incentive conflict can lead to dysfunctional investment decisions. The related prong stressed in my 1985 book is that risk management is concerned with the financing of the firm's investment activities and can promote efficient investment decisions. Hedging complements other sources of financing, internal and external, to replace destroyed assets and new investments. Later attention focused on the role of managers in controlling corporate risk: did managers take risk postures to further their own interests or to maximize firm value, and how did the managers' compensation structure influence this process? Moreover, if managers could be induced to control risk, would this make them more effective decision makers?

This frictional or transaction cost approach to risk management is a value added one. A firm seeks to add value by its investment and financing decisions, but risk can interfere with these decisions. This line of reasoning arms the risk manager with a broad array of risk management strategies. Of course, if risk leads to problems and thereby reduces value, one can remove the risk. Insurance and financial hedges do just that. But this is only one side of the coin. One can also adapt the organizational and financial structure of the firm to make it more resilient to risk. For example, if more volatile cash flows increase the risk of bankruptcy or the incentive conflicts between shareholders and creditors, the effect should be more severe for the more highly levered (higher debt to equity ratio) firm. Accordingly, one can mitigate this problem by reducing leverage. Risk reduction and leverage reduction become complementary risk management strategies in this value added risk management world.

With each of the frictional cost explanations of why risk is a problem, there are two generic strategies: to remove the risk or to adapt the financial or organizational structure to increase the firm's tolerance to risk. Thus, the costs of financial distress can be reduced by removing risk or changing leverage, as shown in the last paragraph. Similarly, the additional taxes imposed by volatile cash flows can be reduced by risk management and tax management, and the problems that risk causes for compensation design can be mitigated by managing the risk or redesigning the compensation. Under this approach, risk management is a story about insurance and hedging, but it is also a story about investment financing: about leverage management, about managerial compensation design, and about tax management.

INTEGRATED RISK MANAGEMENT

From this mixing of ideas and market changes is emerging an approach to corporate risk management. This new approach uses the technology of both finance and insurance to address the whole range of corporate risks—financial, insurable, operational, and business risk. In its coverage, this new approach is comprehensive. Where risk comes from is of secondary importance. Insurable and financial risks are both able to disrupt earnings, create funding problems for new investments, or bankrupt the firm. Moreover, the contributions of each source of risk cannot be conveniently isolated. Risk does not simply "add up." The ability of a firm to tolerate any one risk is determined by its current exposure to other risks. These considerations call for a comprehensive, or integrated, strategy in treating risk. The characteristics of this new integrated approach are:

- ♦ *It is diagnostic.* The starting point for the current treatment of risk management is a diagnosis of the corporate costs of risk. This approach has a medical analogy. An individual with hay fever caused by an allergy to dust can relieve the condition by removing himself from the source of the trouble: the dust. But this remedy often is impracticable. Other treatment options become available if one understands the mechanisms by which exposure to dust causes the hay fever symptoms. Antihistamines and other drugs thus have been developed that enable the individual to tolerate the dust but avoid the uncomfortable symptoms. Similarly, risk can be managed by removing the risk, that is, by contracting with a counter-party such as an insurance firm to assume the risk. But this is often an expensive or unavailable option. The range of risk management strategies can be extended if one understands how risk destroys corporate value. This understanding has led to a number of complementary risk management strategies that complement or substitute for risk transfer. Risk management becomes more efficient with a wider range of available strategies.

- ♦ *It is designed to support optimal investment.* The new risk management is based largely on the proposition that, when the firm is exposed to risk, it may be unable to make optimal investment decisions. This can occur in two ways outlined above. First, risks impose the possibility that the firm will run out of cash and be unable to finance new and replacement investment. Second, the risk may give rise to opportunistic behavior as shareholders and managers seek investments that maximize their welfare at the expense of creditors. With these problems recognized, risk management strategies are designed to ensure that the firm makes optimal post-loss and pre-loss investment decisions. These financing strategies include post-loss financing and contingent financing.

• *It is transaction cost based.* Other costs of risk arise because risk enhances certain transaction costs. Risk can increase expected taxes. As seen above, risk increases bankruptcy costs and can promote frictional costs between shareholders and creditors, thereby increasing the cost of debt. Risk management is concerned with reducing these frictional costs. This can be done by removing risk, by tax management, or by changing the financial structure of the firm.

• *It is inclusive.* The reasons why risk is costly to the firm do not depend much on where the risk came from. Losing a billion dollars might bankrupt a firm regardless of whether the loss arose from a liability suit, a sudden change in exchange rates, a loss of a key contract, or a turn in the economy. Thus, the new risk management usually embraces all types of risk: financial risk, organizational risk insurable risk, etc.

• *It is coordinated but discriminating.* The need for coordination arises from the basic feature of risk: that individual risks cannot be isolated. Many cash flows can be volatile. But the combined risk from all these cash flows is not simply the sum of the parts. Risk does not simply "add up." The ability of a firm to tolerate any one risk is determined by its current exposure to other risks. Even if risks are independent of each other, they combine to impose less total risk than the sum of their parts. This is the virtue of diversification. Thus, if I have 1 risky cash flow, it can make sense to insure it. But with 50 similar risky cash flows, their combined relative risk can be low and the need for insurance of each minimal.

There are other reasons for coordination than simple diversification. Sometimes cash flows have negative correlation and, in combination, impose almost no total risk. Hedging one of these risks while ignoring the other would actually ADD risk to the firm since it undoes a natural hedge. Failure to coordinate can lead to such dysfunctional risk management decisions. But coordination does not necessarily mean equal treatment. Some risks can be particularly expensive to hedge because the market is thin or because hedging can alter incentives for efficient behavior. For example, hedging away the very entrepreneurial risks that are core to all business will throw away the profit that comes with such risk taking. But the presence of such core risk, even if not hedged, can affect how one deals with risks that are incidental to the firm's core activities.

PLAN OF THE BOOK

The plan of the book is laid out in Figure 1–2.

Integrated risk management is "integrated" in more than one way. Not only does it address multiple sources of risk in a coordinated strategy, but it brings to bear a number of underlying disciplines to that task. The task of Part I of the book (chapters 2–6) is to serve as a primer on these various background disciplines. This part of the book does not get into the meat of corporate risk management at all. Rather, it introduces the underlying economics, statistics, and finance that will be used in the main part of the book. Part I can serve as introduction to those unfamiliar with the underlying economics of utility, the statistics of diversification, and the basics of investment and corporate finance. It will serve as a review for those who are a little rusty on the basics. But for those familiar with the basic ideas, Part I can be skipped in part or entirely.

The substance of the book is in Part II. The starting point is an analysis in Chapter 7 of why risk is important and how it can destroy firm value. From this emerges a set of generic strategies for dealing with risk as outined above. This is the subject of Chapter 8. Much of the potential to add value comes in ensuring that random events do not sap the firm's financial resources and prevent the firm from undertaking its optimal investment decisions. We first need to know what these preferred post-event investment decisions are and thereby assess the need for financing. This is the subject of Chapter 9. We then move into post-loss financing in Chapters 10 and 11. These two chapters look at ways of funding investments through debt and equity after a loss occurs. We set up a valuation model to compare financing methods and address

F I G U R E   1–2

PART 1
A PRIMER ON ECONOMICS, STATISTICS AND FINANCE

BASIC ECONOMICS: HOW INDIVIDUALS DEAL WITH RISK

MORE ECONOMICS: MORAL HAZARD AND ADVERSE SELECTION

BASIC STATISTICS: DIVERSIFICATION OF RISK - HOW INSURANCE WORKS

BASIC FINANCE: HOW RISK IS TREATED IN THE CAPITAL MARKET

BASIC FINANCE: OPTIONS FUTURES AND OTHER DERIVATIVES

PART 11
INTEGRATED RISK MANAGEMENT

WHY IS RISK A PROBLEM TO FIRMS?

HOW SHOULD WE MANAGE RISK?

ADDING VALUE BY POST-LOSS FINANCING

ADDING VALUE BY CONTINGENT FINANCING

LEVERAGE AND CONTINGENT LEVERAGE STRATEGIES

HEDGING AND INSURANCE STRATEGIES

USING LIMITED LIABILITY TO MANAGE RISK

A CASE: INNOVATION IN THE MANAGEMENT OF CATASTROPHE RISK

some of the problems that arise with post-loss funding; particularly whether the firm will have sufficient value to be creditworthy after a big loss. Chapter 12 looks at proactive ways of financing post-loss investment activities, such as contingent financing. The instruments examined here range from a simple contingent financing device (a line of credit) to more complex instruments that give the firm access to new equity after a loss on terms set in place before the loss.

The cost of risk is closely related to the financial leverage of the firm. Accordingly, leverage management becomes an important part of risk management (and vice versa). Chapter 13 looks at simple and contingent leverage strategies. Simply changing the current debt to equity mix can lower the costs of risk. But more innovative are contingent leverage strategies in which the firm's debt can be called on advantageous terms, converted to equity, or even forgiven should a major loss event occur. Chapter 14 examines hedging strategies, which can include insurance and the assembling of financial hedges. The hedging strategies include simple hedges and basket strategies, which span a number of risks and which give the book its title. Chapter 16 considers how the firm may use limited liability as part of its risk management program. The strategies considered here include spinning off risky activities, and the ways in which limited liability affects the firm's optimal choice of insurance and safety. Moreover, this chapter will examine some of the social welfare issues involved with use of bankruptcy as a risk management strategy; surprisingly, these are not always adverse. The book then concludes with an examination of one marketplace in which innovation has been dramatic, the management of catastrophic natural hazard risk (earthquakes and hurricanes) for insurance firms. Many of the devices and strategies considered in earlier chapters have been appearing on this market, and the innovations are starting to migrate as non-insurance firms adopt similar instruments to address other types of risk.

REFERENCES

Black, Fisher, and Myron Scholes. 1973. "The Pricing of Options and Corporate Liabilities." *Journal of Political Economy* 81:637–54.

Cummins, J. David. 1976. "Risk Management and the Theory of the Firm." *Journal of Risk and Insurance* XLIII:587–609.

Doherty, Neil A. 1985. *Corporate Risk Management: A Financial Exposition.* New York: McGraw-Hill.

Mayers, David, and Clifford W. Smith Jr. 1982. "On the Corporate Demand for Insurance." *Journal of Business* 55:281–96.

Mehr, Robert I., and Bob A. Hedges. 1963. *Risk Management in the Business Enterprise,* Homewood, Ill.: R. D. Irwin.

CHAPTER 2

Risk and Utility: Economic Concepts and Decision Rules

Risk is present when the outcome of some defined activity is not known. Given the financial economic approach of this text, the outcomes with which we are concerned can be directly or indirectly measured in money. Risk refers to the variation in the range of possible outcomes; the greater the potential variation, the greater the risk. In the economic sense, risk does not refer to the adverse quality of some outcomes (losses instead of profits), but rather to the lack of knowledge about which of several outcomes may prevail. Risk is implied by our inability to predict the future. If risk were not present, many of our decisions would be trivial; we would simply choose the course of action that had the highest certain payoff. However, when chance intervenes in the selection of outcomes, decision making becomes both more complex and more personal. Even though we may reasonably assume that everyone prefers more money to less, people differ in how they respond to risk. The differences in personal preferences may relate to our personalities and our economic circumstances. Accordingly, if economics is to provide us with a useful framework for making decisions under conditions of risk, it must help us to process and compare the potential outcomes on terms dictated by our personal preferences and circumstances.

Our task in this chapter is to specify decision rules that will help us to come to terms with the nature of risk and its effect on decision making. The so-called expected-utility hypothesis will be used to analyze simple risk management decisions. To start, we will discuss simple risk-management decisions faced by an individual rather than a corporation. The individual must make decisions on financing or take steps to prevent events that might prove catastrophic to him or her. When we come to look at corporations later, the separation of ownership and control will call for considerable modification of the decision procedure. Ownership of a corporation is presented by financial claims (shares of stock). We must then determine how the risk prospects facing a firm affect the ownership claims and how risk management decisions can best protect the welfare of a firm's owners. This will require some development of statistical measures of risk, an understanding of the process of diversification, and some rudimentary awareness of how capital markets function. These are the subjects of the following chapters. For now, we will concentrate on an individual who must make decisions concerning risky events that may profoundly affect his or her personal welfare.

DERIVATION OF DECISION RULES

Simple Risky Prospects

A convenient starting place for our exploration of risky decision rules is an analysis of choices in which no risk is present. The decisions to be made in this simple and safe world turn out to be trivial if outcomes can be specified in money terms. Of course, some events bring payoffs that are not directly specified in money values, but we assume that money equivalents can be assigned by the decision maker. For example, consider a choice between action A and action B. Action A is simply "do nothing" and has a zero payoff. Action B involves working for 10 hours for a fee of $200. To make a comparison, the decision maker must place a money-equivalent value for the labor involved in action B. If he decides that he is indifferent between each hour's work and receiving $18, then 10 hours' effort has a negative money value of $180. The comparison between actions A and B is now presented in the following terms:

Action		Payoff ($)
A (Do nothing)		$ 0
B (Work 10 hours)	Fee	$200
	Value of effort	−$180
	Net value	$ 20

As long as the decision maker is confident that he has correctly valued his time and effort at $18 per hour, the decision is quite mechanical. Action *B* has a higher payoff than action *A* and should be preferred.

To stretch our assumption of a certain world, consider a "gamble" between two people who have the unnerving facility to predict the future. The gamble involves the slip of a coin, the outcome of which, for us mortals, is certainly a risky activity, but for our prophets is never in doubt. Prophet *A* will pay prophet *B* $10 if the coin turns up heads; otherwise prophet *B* will pay prophet *A* $10. Since both know that the coin will turn up tails, a meaningful transaction will never take place; prophet *B* will never agree. Possibly prophet *A* might be willing to pay prophet *B* $10 to induce him to make the "bet," but the activity is pointless because both break even. If we descend from Mount Olympus, the transaction will have quite different implications since the outcome from tossing a coin is quite risky. Neither party will, in reality, know the outcome in advance, and the gamble exposes both parties to a risky future. The payoff to the parties depends on chance, as follows:

Decision	Payoff
A's Decision:	
1. Gamble	$10 or −$10
2. Do not gamble	$ 0
B's Decision:	
1. Gamble	$10 or −$10
2. Do not gamble	$ 0

To help *A* and *B* decide whether to gamble with each other, they might each make use of further information they have at their disposal. Neither knows whether the coin will land heads or tails, but each, believing the coin to be unbiased, assumes that the coin is equally likely to land on heads and tails. In other words, A and B believe that the probabilities of heads and tails are each one-half. We will represent this information, together with the payoffs, in the following format (the alternatives available to each decision maker are prospects V (gamble) and W (do not gamble):

$$V \text{ (gamble)} = \begin{cases} \$10; & 0.5 \text{ probability} \\ -\$10; & 0.5 \text{ probability} \end{cases}$$

$$W \text{ (do not gamble)} = \begin{cases} \$0; & 0.5 \text{ probability} \\ -\$0; & 0.5 \text{ probability} \end{cases}$$

The dollar value on each line represents the payoff, and the associated probability follows.

In this choice, risk is present in the spread of values for the first alternative, but it is absent from the second alternative. With the gamble, the outcome cannot be predicted; it can take a range of values. Risk is inherent in this range or spread. If no gamble is selected, the outcome is the same, regardless of the toss of a coin. However, risk is a relative term. Consider the preceding gamble V along with the following:

$$X = \begin{cases} \$10; & 0.99 \text{ probability} \\ -\$10; & 0.01 \text{ probability} \end{cases}$$

$$Y = \begin{cases} \$10; & 0.01 \text{ probability} \\ -\$10; & 0.99 \text{ probability} \end{cases}$$

$$Z = \begin{cases} \$20; & 0.5 \text{ probability} \\ -\$20; & 0.5 \text{ probability} \end{cases}$$

X has the same range of outcomes as V, but the probabilities have changed. Certainly the odds have been altered in favor of the gambler, but the degree of predictability has also changed. Winning comes close to being a "sure thing." Chance has less opportunity to be unkind. Although the range of possible outcomes remains unchanged, the degree of "variability" has changed significantly. Y simply reverses the probabilities from X. Now the odds are biased against winning, and undoubtedly, this reduces the attractiveness of gambling. However, the degree of "predictability," or variation in outcomes, remains similar to that for X. Our concept of risk will take account of probabilities. When Z is compared with V, the probabilities are the same, but the range of outcomes has increased. The increase in the range of outcomes contributes to an increase in risk. Risk is a quality that reflects both the range of possible outcomes and the distribution of respective probabilities for each of the outcomes.

The Expected-Value Rule, EV

Let us now set up a decision rule that can help us to choose between risky alternatives. Consider, for example, a choice between the following (outcomes in dollar values, followed by probability):

$$A = \begin{cases} 10 & 0.5 \\ 10 & 0.5 \end{cases} \quad D = \begin{cases} 0 & 0.4 \\ 20 & 0.6 \end{cases}$$

$$B = \begin{cases} 0 & 0.5 \\ 20 & 0.5 \end{cases} \quad E = \begin{cases} 0 & 0.6 \\ 20 & 0.4 \end{cases}$$

$$C = \begin{cases} 5 & 0.5 \\ 15 & 0.5 \end{cases} \quad F = \begin{cases} 1 & 0.5 \\ 21 & 0.5 \end{cases}$$

Each set will be called a prospect; outcomes B, C, D, E, and F may be further described as "risky" prospects. Outcome A is clearly a non-risky prospect.

The decision rule will focus on the "average" of the possible outcomes. More precisely, we will select the alternative with the highest expected value EV, defined as follows:

$$EV_j = \sum_i p_i X_i$$

where:

EV = expected value of prospect j
p_i = probability of outcome X_i
X_i = outcome in money value

Thus, for alternative B, the expected value is:

$$EV_B = 0.5(\$0) + 0.5(\$20) = \$10$$

One interpretation of this value is as follows. If an individual accepted a large number of such risky prospects, he or she would win $20 on some and nothing on others. The average outcome would be very close to $10 per prospect if the number of prospects were sufficiently large. Thus, $10 is the long-run average value of repeated B gambles. If the individual paid $10 for each bet of type B, he or she would break even in the long run.

If we use this expected-value rule, a single value can be assigned to each prospect, and this, hopefully, will aid in decision making. The respective values are:

$$EV_A = EV_B = EV_C = \$10$$
$$EV_D = \$12$$
$$EV_E = \$8$$
$$EV_F = \$11$$

Consequently, our ranking should be (the sign ">" means "preferred to" here):

$$D > F > (A \text{ or } B \text{ or } C) > E$$

If this rule works, testing a group of decision makers should confirm the ranking. Testing on a class of students reveals some problems. Preference of D over E appears to be virtually unanimous for all subjects. So far, so good; this is exactly what the rule predicts. However, preferences tend to appear between A, B, and C, and according to the rule, they should rank equally. Most students prefer A to B (or C) and C to B. One stubborn approach to such problems is to assert that students do not know what is good for them and that we should continue to believe the rule. However, the rule must serve preferences, not be a master to them. Other problem rankings tend to arise. The expected value rule asserts that F should be preferred to A, but many students (not all) prefer A. Several other choices do not correspond with the expected-value rule. Such experiments are not laboratory controlled, and differences between group responses appear. However, such simple tests do reveal that individuals have strong preferences that cannot obediently be classified by such a simple rule. Having preferences different from those predicted by the expected-value rule does not imply irrationality. Rather, it reveals that the "rule" does not capture the preferences.

The St. Petersburg Paradox

A more dramatic illustration of how such a rule may break down was formulated some two centuries ago by Daniel Bernoulli. Bernoulli, an 18th century Swiss mathematician and physicist and one-time professor of mathematics at the Russian Academy in Saint Petersburg, posed the following problem, which has come to be known as the St. Petersburg paradox:

> *Consider a game in which one player flips a fair coin. If the coin reveals heads, this player will pay the other player 2 dollars (or ducats or whatever), and the game is over. If the coin lands on tails, it is tossed again. If the second toss lands heads, the first player pays ($2) dollars to the second, and the game is over. If the second toss lands tails, the coin is flipped again. Thus, the game continues until the first head appears, and then the first player pays the second $(\$2)^n$, where n signifies the number of tosses required to reveal the first head. Since a head will turn up eventually, the second player wants a long preceding run of tails. The problem is: how much will the second player be willing to pay to enter the game? Of course, individuals vary in their responses, but seldom will anyone be willing to pay more than $10 to enter such a game.*

The nature of the paradox can be seen by considering the expected value of such a game. We will represent the risky prospect in the following form, showing the sequence of tails and heads required to produce each outcome:

The St. Petersburg Paradox

Outcome	Probability	Sequence Required to Produce Outcome
$2	$\frac{1}{2}$	H
$\$2^2$	$(\frac{1}{2})^2$	TH
$\$2^3$	$(\frac{1}{2})^3$	TTH
$\vdots$	$\vdots$	$\vdots$
$\$2^n$	$(\frac{1}{2})^n$	TT . . . $(n-1)$ times . . . H

The expected value of the game is:

$$\sum_i P_i X_i = 2(\tfrac{1}{2}) + 2^2(\tfrac{1}{2})^2 + 2^3(\tfrac{1}{2})^3 + \ldots 2^n(\tfrac{1}{2})^n$$

$$+ \ldots \text{continue indefinitely}$$
$$= 1 + 1 + 1 + \ldots \text{etc.}$$
$$= \infty$$

Why is it that people will typically only pay a few dollars to participate in a game that has an infinite expected value? Clearly, the expected-value rule has broken down dramatically.

What causes the expected-value rule to fail in the earlier simple choice experiments and in the St. Petersburg paradox? The answer is that risk is ignored. Returning to the simple prospects, $10 with certainty (prospect A) is clearly very different from a 50–50 gamble for $20 or $0 (prospect B). The general preference for A over B and the small entry price to the St. Petersburg game indicate that the quality of variability in outcomes is an adverse factor for the decision maker given equality in expected values. Most people prefer choices with less risk rather than more. This does not mean that people will never choose risk when it can be avoided. The expected value of one prospect may be so advantageous in comparison with a competing prospect that aversion to risk is overcome. It is easy to construct such choices. Consider the following:

$$G = \begin{cases} 10 & 0.5 \\ 10 & 0.5 \end{cases} \qquad H = \begin{cases} 9 & 0.5 \\ 20 & 0.5 \end{cases}$$

G may be seen as the entry to gamble H; by not gambling, the individual retains $10 with certainty. If I were to make a general public offer of such a gamble, I imagine that I would be killed in the rush (I hasten to add that idle speculation does not constitute such an offer). The next question, therefore, is: How can attitudes toward risk be considered in an appropriate decision rule? One useful answer lies with the concept of utility.

The Expected-Utility Rule, EU

There are two related ways of trying to resolve the St. Petersburg paradox. One approach, suggested by Bernoulli, is to place some weighting on money outcomes; later, this approach led to the concept of utility of income or wealth. A second approach is to recognize explicitly that risk *per se* has a cost and to use risk as a parameter in the decision. This second approach will be examined later when we discuss the mean-variance rule. We will now present the utility approach and show that this copes with risk.

Utility is a scale of measurement of the satisfaction derived from money. To represent utility, let us make some fairly innocuous assumptions. First, we will order levels of satisfaction with the statement that "more wealth is preferred to less wealth." Second, we will make a further statement that has the effect of ordering differences in wealth. The incremental utility, or satisfaction, from unit increases in wealth decreases as wealth increases. Thus, if I am poor, an addition of $1000 to my wealth will make a considerable impact on my level of welfare. If I am rich, the extra $1000 will still increase my satisfaction, but only marginally. These concepts are known in economics as the *law of diminishing marginal utility,* and the law is represented by utility function *OA,* shown in Figure 2–1. Of course, different individuals will scale different levels of wealth in different ways. Thus, two other utility

FIGURE   2–1

Utility Functions and Risk Aversion

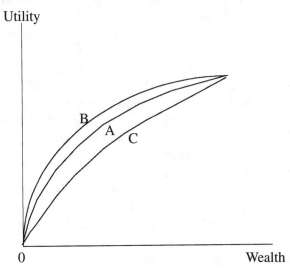

functions, *OB* and *OC,* are also shown in the figure. The *positions* of these functions have little significance because they apply to different people. We are unable to make direct comparisons of different individuals' capacities for enjoying wealth. However, we can compare the *shapes* of different peoples' utility functions. The function *OB* seems to be less concave than *OA,* whereas *OC* appears to change its slope more rapidly than *OA* as wealth increases. In other words, individual *B* (with curve *OB*) appears to value increases in wealth almost as highly at high levels of wealth as at low levels of wealth. In contrast, the satisfaction curve *OC* of individual *C* flattens out very quickly, indicating that individual *C*'s capacity for enjoying additional wealth tails off quickly as wealth increases. These features, as we shall see, reveal differences in attitudes toward risk.

What is the connection between utility and risk? Consider a simple gamble. The choices are (1) to keep our current wealth and not gamble or (2) to enter a fair gamble in which we win or lose $10. Put another way, the gamble substitutes for our current wealth of $10 a 50–50 chance of wealth $0 or wealth $20. Should we enter the gamble? Let us represent the choices on the wealth scale of Figure 2–2, which also shows a utility function conforming to the preceding assumptions. If the gamble is not undertaken, wealth is $10, which has a utility value shown on the vertical axis as $U(\$10)$. For an income of $10, the slope of the utility curve is neither very steep nor very flat, showing an intermediate value on changes in wealth. Now consider a very small gamble in which we either win or lose $1. If we win, wealth increases to $11, which naturally has a higher utility than $10. If we lose, our wealth falls to $9, which has a lower utility than $10. However, notice the respective sizes of these prospective changes in utility. Because the utility curve becomes flatter as wealth increases, the loss of utility from the fall in wealth exceeds the increase in utility from an equal gain in wealth. This differential valuation of the gain and loss from the gamble causes a bias against taking such a risky decision. Now consider the larger gamble. Losing reduces wealth drastically to position $0, where marginal dollars have a very high value, as indicated by the steep slope of the utility curve at this level of wealth. However, winning takes us to $20, where the utility curve is pretty flat, showing that marginal dollars have relatively low utility value. If the utility curve is of the form shown,

Risk Aversion and Gambling

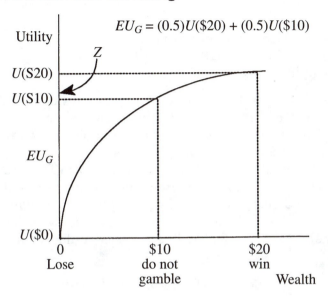

gambles represent a trade-off in which the individual sacrifices dollars that are highly valued (because they coincide with low wealth) in exchange for contingent dollars that have a low utility value (because winning will transport the individual to a higher wealth level, where the marginal utility of wealth is low). At face value, this prospect does not appear very attractive. Diminishing marginal utility creates a bias against gambling.

The relationship between utility and risk is now presented in a more precise fashion. The expected-utility rule represents a revised decision rule that substitutes utility values for money values in risky prospects in order to select among risky alternatives. The rule was developed by John von Neumann and Oskar Morgenstern (1944) and has proved to be a very powerful technique for analyzing risky choices. The rule is based on a set of formal axioms that will not be examined here; however, we will show that it can be used to provide some very useful preliminary insights into risk-management problems.

An expected utility EU is assigned to a risky prospect in accordance with the following expression:

$$EU_j = \sum_i P_i \, U(X_i)$$

where:

EU_j = expected utility of prospect j
P_i = probability of outcome X_i
$U(X_i)$ = utility value of outcome X_i

Notice how similar this rule is to the expected-value rule. Whereas expected value is the weighted average of the money outcomes, expected utility is the weighted average of outcomes when those outcomes are expressed in utility values.

The application of the rule is illustrated in Figure 2–2. The utility values of winning and losing are shown on the vertical axis as $U(\$20)$ and $U(\$0)$, respectively. Since the odds on winning and losing are each 0.5, the weighted average of the two utility values is the halfway point; that is, the expected utility of the gamble EU_G is:

$$EU_G = (0.5)U(\$20) + (0.5)U(\$0)$$

The position is shown on the vertical axis. Now consider the alternative choice, which is to avoid the gamble and keep current wealth with certainty (i.e., a probability of unity). Writing the expected utility from not gambling as EU_{NG}, we have:

$$EU_{NG} = (1.0)U(\$10) = U(\$10)$$

In the diagram, the expected utility from not gambling is higher than that from gambling. Therefore, according to the decision rule, the gamble should be avoided.

There is no indication from this analysis that one should never gamble, but it does imply that gambling should not be undertaken at such odds. The preceding example reveals fair odds; that is, the entry price is equal to the expected payoff. There is an entry price for the gamble of zero and the expected payoff is also zero, as shown:

$$EV = 0.5(-\$10) + 0.5(\$10) = 0$$

It is possible to play with the odds until the gamble becomes attractive. For example, at 0.9 probability of winning, the expected utility is recalculated at point Z on the vertical axis. This is higher than the utility of not gambling. From these results, we can make some general statements that apply to an individual who has a utility curve of the concave shape shown in Figures 2–1 and 2–2:

1. These individuals would not rationally gamble at fair odds.
2. The odds would have to be loaded in the individual's favor in order to induce him or her to gamble.

Accordingly, we will state a very important conclusion. If an individual has a concave utility function of the form shown in Figures 2–1 and 2–2, that individual is averse to risk. As we shall soon see, aversion to risk implies the willingness to pay a premium to avoid risk. Before proceeding, the interested reader may try constructing a utility function that is convex, that is, slopes upward at an increasing rather than a decreasing rate. The same gamble can be represented and the expected utilities recalculated. From such an exercise, it can be concluded that an individual with a convex utility function derives positive value from risk and would gamble at fair odds. Such a person may be described as a "risk lover."

INSURANCE AND THE EXPECTED-UTILITY RULE

An insurance policy has the opposite risk effect to a gamble. A gamble involves the sacrifice of certain wealth in order to acquire the possibility of an increase in wealth. An insurance policy involves the sacrifice of certain wealth in order to avoid the possibility of a loss of wealth. With a gamble, one pays to acquire risk; with an insurance policy, one pays to avoid risk. The insurance strategy can be valued using the expected utility rule in an identical manner to gamble.

Suppose you wish to insure your home. To simplify the issue, your total wealth is $120, of which $100 is the value of your home. The house may or may not burn down, but assuming any loss to be a total loss, a fire would reduce your wealth from $120 to $20. The probability of a fire is 0.25 (this does not reflect pathologic tendencies in your children; it is simply a convenient value for

purposes of illustration). Since your final wealth will be either
$120 or $20, with respective probabilities of 0.75 and 0.25, you can
represent your utility in contemplating this insecure prospect as:

$$EU_{NI} = (0.75)U(\$120) + (0.25)U(\$20)$$

where the subscript "*NI*" indicates that "no insurance" has been
purchased. What is insurance is available? The expected value of
the loss is:

$$EV = 0.25(\$100) = \$25$$

Ignoring transaction costs, an insurer charging a premium equal
to expected loss would break even if it held a large portfolio of
such policies. This premium could be called a fair premium or an
actuarially fair premium, denoting that the premium is equal to
the expected value of loss (sometimes called the actuarial value of
the policy). The term *fair* is not construed in a normative sense;
rather it is simply a reference point.

   If you are offered insurance at a fair premium, in this case
$25, should you insure? Consider Figure 2–3 which shows a utility

F I G U R E   2–3

Expected Utility & Insurance

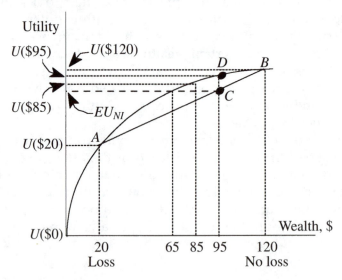

curve revealing aversion to risk. The horizontal axis shows possible values of terminal wealth. The positions \$20 and \$120 represent possible wealth positions if you do not insure, and the respective utility values are revealed on the vertical axis. Insurance at a premium of \$25 will remove the financial impact of a chance fire, but you must sacrifice \$25 of certain wealth to pay the premium. Thus, with insurance, your wealth position will be \$120 − \$25 = \$95 with a corresponding probability of unity. The expected utility values for insurance, EU_I, and no insurance, EU_{NI}, are constructed as follows:

$$EU_I = (1.0)U(\$95) = U(\$95)$$

$$EU_{NI} = (0.25)U(\$20) + 0.75U(\$120)$$

Both positions are clearly shown on the vertical axis of Figure 2–3. As shown, $EU_I = U(\$95)$, is greater than EU_{NI}, suggesting that insurance should be purchased. Is this ranking accidental? In fact, it is not.

A geometric technique to find the expected utility of two wealth levels is shown in Figure 2–3. A chord AB is drawn from the two positions on the utility curve corresponding to the alternative wealth levels. The position at which this cord intercepts the expected money value of wealth (position C) traces out expected utility. The reason this trick works is that the same probability weights are used for expected value and expected utility. Clearly, if the utility curve is concave from below, point C, which traces out the expected utility of not insuring, will always be below point D, which identifies the expected utility of insuring. Thus, we can state the following preliminary ideas:

1. A concave utility curve implies aversion to risk, in confirmation of our earlier result.
2. A rational, risk-averse individual will choose to insure if the premium is equal to the expected value of loss.

This second statement is very important. Often known as the Bernoulli principle, it provides a powerful rationale for insurance and will help condition our thinking for more complex corporate risk management problems.

Before introducing more realistic problems, let us dwell for a little while longer on risk aversion and stress the equivalence between the shape of the utility function and attitude toward risk by considering exceptional cases. Figure 2–4*a* shows a utility function that is convex, implying that, for this individual, the marginal valuation of wealth increases as wealth increases (the more money she gets, the more money she wants). The attitude toward insurance is quite different from that revealed by a concave utility function. Since the marginal valuation of wealth is high when we pay the premium but low when we receive a loss settlement, insurance is unattractive. The same geometric construction is undertaken, using the same notation as in Figure 2–3, to show the respective positions of EU_I and EU_{NI}. Notice that EU_{NI}, derived from position C, is now higher than EU_I, from position D, showing that insurance should not be purchased. It takes little imagination to show that if the utility curve is linear, as shown in Figure 2–4*b*, the individual is neither averse to risk nor does she like risk; she is risk-neutral. Now the expected utility from insuring is exactly equal to that from not insuring. The risk-neutral individual will choose purely on the basis of expected values of alternative risky prospects; the risk *per se* has no value.

SOME RISK MANAGEMENT PROPOSITIONS FOR INDIVIDUALS

Insurance with Premium Loadings

The Bernoulli principle provides a useful starting point for a treatment of risky decision making. It reveals that risk has a cost and that this cost is neglected in a decision rule that uses expected value alone. However, for practical risk management, the Bernoulli principle addresses a problem that is not very interesting. Rarely is an insurance premium equal to the expected or actuarial value of the policy payment. Even if the insurance market is highly competitive, such that all excess profit is removed from insurers, the transaction costs of writing insurance must be covered and the capital employed in the insurance industry must make a normal return. Typically, transaction costs of writing insurance are high, both for the insurer and for the agent or broker. Can we use the expected-utility rule to say anything about optimal insurance decisions with these more realistic premium structures?

Consider Figure 2–3 again, but suppose that the premium charged by the insurer is $35 instead of $25. The effect of purchasing insurance would be to give the insured a certain wealth

F I G U R E   2–4

(a) Insurance and the Risk Lover (b) Insurance and
Risk Indifference

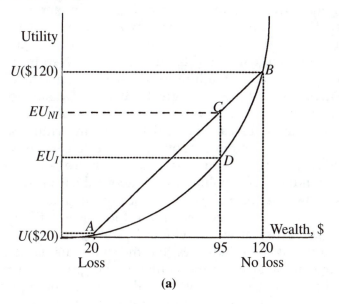

(a)

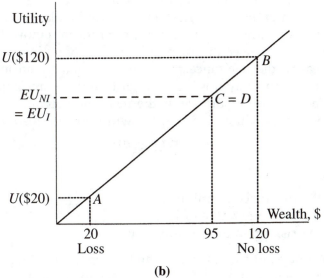

(b)

of $85 (that is, $120 − $35 = $85). The utility from insuring can be ascertained by using the utility curve to plot the corresponding value, $U(\$85)$, on the vertical axis. Clearly, this value lies between $U(\$95)$ and EU_{NI}; therefore, insurance is still preferred to no insurance. If the premium were $55, it would turn out that insuring would give the same utility, $U(\$65)$, as not insuring. At this premium, the individual would be indifferent between insuring and not insuring. At any premium lower than $55, insurance would be desirable; at any premium greater than $55, insurance would be undesirable.

This example reveals that a risk-averse individual would be willing to pay a premium above the expected value of loss in order to remove risk by purchasing an insurance policy. The maximum an individual is willing to pay above the expected value of loss is known as the *risk premium* (not to be confused with the insurance premium, which is simply the price of the insurance policy). The fact that an individual is willing to pay a risk premium to remove risk indicates that the individual is risk-averse. The more risk-averse the individual is, the greater the risk premium that he or she will pay. Thus the risk premium provides a measure of an individual's attitude toward risk.

Risk premiums will differ among individuals. A risk-averse individual is willing to incur a risk premium to remove the riskiness of his or her wealth prospect by means of an insurance policy. In reality, the insurance premiums charged by an insurance company may or may not be too high to induce any given individual to purchase insurance. If the insurance premium satisfies the following condition, individual i will purchase insurance:

$$P - E(L) < RP_i$$

where:

P = the insurance premium
$E(L)$ = the expected value of loss
RP_i = the risk premium for individual i

The left-hand side of the inequality represents the portion of the insurance premium allocated to transaction costs and insurer's profit. This is known as the *premium loading* or *markup*. If we know the loss distribution and the insurance premium, we can calculate the left-hand side of this condition, but the right-hand side is a subjective value that will differ among individuals. At any given premium loading, some people will purchase insurance and others will not. The best we can say is that, other things being equal, the higher the premium loading, the smaller the number of people who will wish to buy insurance.

From this discussion, it seems that the expected-utility rule can help to discipline and organize our thinking about the purchase of insurance or similar hedging behavior. We can use the rule to make general statements about the decision process and the tradeoffs an individual has to make. However, to correctly predict the actual decision made by an individual requires knowledge of that individual's utility function—not just its general shape (such as concave), but its exact form. We can never look inside people's heads, nor are people usually able to articulate and quantify a concept as abstract as utility. Despite these operational limitations, the rule does yield important insights. It focuses attention on the types of costs and benefits that are involved in the decision, and it will often enable us to narrow down the set of alternative choices so that we focus only on those solutions which are compatible with our general attitude toward risk. Some further general propositions are now appropriate.

Gambling at Unfair Odds

The preceding proposition asserted that a risk averter would be willing to pay a risk premium (i.e., pay an insurance premium in excess of the expected value of loss) in order to purchase an insurance policy. The risk premium is really the price to the insured for converting a risky wealth prospect into a riskless wealth prospect. With this reasoning, it would appear that a risk averter would want to be paid a risk premium in order to induce him to voluntarily accept risk. Put another way, a risk-averse individual would have to be offered odds that were in his favor in order to induce him to gamble. First, we will demonstrate this proposition; then we will try to resolve the difficulty it creates for us in explaining why people actually gamble at unfair odds.

Figure 2–5 depicts a gamble that is, initially, identical to that shown in Figure 2–2. The individual starts with a wealth level of $10. The individual can choose to keep the $10 or gamble. The gamble might involve rolling a die. If the resulting number is

F I G U R E   2–5

Gambling at Unfair Odds

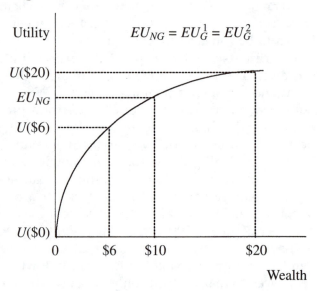

even, the gambler wins $10; if the resulting number is odd, the gambler loses $10. Assuming the die is unbiased, the odds of winning and losing are each 0.5 and the expected value of the gamble is:

$$0.5(-\$10) + 0.5(510) = 0$$

The expected wealth is the same for both the gamble and the no-gamble alternatives, that is, $10. The expected utilities differ significantly. Respectively, the expected utilities of not gambling, EU_{NG}, and gambling, EU_G, are as follows:

$$EU_{NG} = U(\$10)$$

$$EU_G = (0.5)U(\$0) + (0.5)U(\$20)$$

The respective positions are shown on the vertical axis, revealing that the individual will prefer not to gamble.

What will induce this risk-averse person to gamble? Two possibilities spring to mind: (1) keep the stakes the same, but change the odds in the gambler's favor; or (2) keep the 50–50 odds, but change the stakes in the gambler's favor. For solution 1, consider that the probability of winning is 0.85 and losing is 0.15. Therefore:

$$EU_G^1 = (0.15)U(\$0) + 0.85U(\$20)$$

These odds have been engineered such that $EU_{NG} = EU_G^1$, revealing that the individual is indifferent between not gambling and gambling at these favorable odds. So, in Figure 2–5, the position of EU_{NG} is an 85%–15% weighting of $U(\$20)$ and $U(\$0)$. If the odds are further improved in the gambler's favor, she would definitely prefer to gamble.

Much the same result can be achieved by changing the stakes instead of the odds, i.e., solution (2). Consider the gamble to involve a win of \$10 with a probability 0.5 and a loss of \$4 with a probability of 0.5. The expected utility of gambling is now:

$$EU_G^2 = (0.5)U(\$6) + (0.5)U(\$20)$$

which, again, has been engineered to give the same utility value as not gambling, as shown on the vertical axis of Figure 2–5.

In each of these cases, the expected value of the gamble has been increased in order to make the gamble more attractive relative to the no-gamble choice. Expected wealth without gambling is \$10. In contrast, the expected values, respectively, of (1) and (2) are:

$$EV(1) = 0.15(\$0) + 0.85(\$20) = \$17$$

$$EV(2) = 0.5(\$6) + 0.5(\$20) = \$13$$

This increase in expected value is necessary in order to induce a risk averter to gamble and it is analogous to the risk premium discussed in connection with insurance.

Resolution of the Insurance and Gambling Paradox

This analysis of gambling leaves us with a problem in explaining why people, in reality, choose to gamble. Even more puzzling is the fact that the same people often gamble and insure. The weekend visitor to Las Vegas or Atlantic City will return home and promptly pay the insurance premium for her home or life policy. Let us first address the simpler issue of why an individual might choose to gamble. The difficulty in explaining gambling is enhanced when we consider that most gambling is undertaken at unfair odds; after all, the bookmaker and the casino must come out ahead to stay in business.

1. One explanation of gambling is simply that gamblers are not risk-averse; their utility curves are convex rather than concave. For such individuals, gambling is rational behavior. However, we observe many people who gamble but otherwise appear to behave in a risk-averse manner. Some possible explanations of gambling that do not upset the notion of risk aversion are as follows.

2. Gamblers act on subjective rather than objective probabilities. Gamblers often believe they have a system or that they can read the cards or have a superstitious belief in "Lady Luck."

3. The attraction of gambling is not confined to the money outcomes; other forms of consumption also arise. A weekend in Las Vegas may be considered to be good entertainment, and any loss in gambling is the "price" of that entertainment. The unfair odds are comparable with the price of a theater ticket or the cost of a football game.

4. Another explanation, associated with the British economist G. L. S. Shackle (1938), is that individuals do not respond mathematically to the odds, but instead focus their attention on particular outcomes that exert an undue influence on their decision. For example, with gambling, we might be blinded by the thought of winning; with insurance, we might be consumed by the image of our house reduced to ashes.

5. The previous explanation offered a possible resolution of why people might simultaneously gamble and insure. A more direct attack on this paradox was undertaken by Friedman and Savage (1948) and by Markowitz (1952), who suggested that the utility function may not be uniformly concave. A brief examination of the Friedman–Savage analysis follows.

Figure 2–6 shows a utility curve that is concave over most of its length, but it also exhibits a convex section over part of its range. It is important that the point at which the curve changes

F I G U R E   2–6

The Friedman–Savage Hypothesis

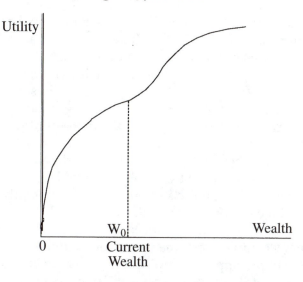

its curvature from concave to convex is current wealth W_0. Thus, for any reduction in wealth, the relevant section of the curve is concave (i.e., in the range 0–W_0). Insurance relates to events that will reduce wealth from W_0, and since this range is concave, the individual responds in a rational risk-averse manner by purchasing insurance. For wealth increases (i.e., above W_0), the relevant section of the curve is convex. Since gambling offers us the prospect of wealth increases, this section of the utility curve is relevant in analyzing such decisions. The curve reveals risk preference in this range, and accordingly, it predicts that gambling will be undertaken at fair or even unfair odds. Subsequent debate on this issue has centered on whether the curve will eventually return to the concave form at very high wealth levels and on what form of gambling would appear to be rational from this model (high odds and high stakes or low odds and small stakes).

Some experimental evidence by Shoemaker and Hershey (1980) suggests that the context in which a decision is presented may affect the decision. For example, consider the following choices:

$$A = \$100 \text{ with certainty} \qquad B = \begin{cases} \$120 & 0.8 \text{ probability} \\ \$\ 0 & 0.2 \text{ probability} \end{cases}$$

The selection might represent the choice about purchasing insurance. Current wealth is $120, but there is a 20% chance that it will be totally destroyed. For a premium of $20, insurance can be purchased that gives the individual $100 with certainty. The same prospects could be presented as a speculative business opportunity. The individual can invest $100. There is an 80% chance that this will earn a return of $20, giving the investor a final wealth of $120, but there is a 20% chance that the investor will lose everything. Although these two stories are very different, the mathematical descriptions of the two problems are identical. Laboratory evidence reveals that subjects often respond differently when the context of the decision is changed.

The ideas discussed here reveal that actual decisions may be a little more complex and may have other dimensions than revealed by simple application of the expected-utility rule. Nevertheless, many of these ideas represent attempts to describe actual behavior, which may not always be rational or which may reflect unusual risk preferences, rather than attempts to identify rational optimizing behaviors. Our task is to prescribe a decision rule that will assist in identifying rational risk management decisions, and for this purpose the expected-utility rule provides keen insights. Thus, our main interest lies in the prescriptive value of the rule rather than its descriptive value.

Partial Insurance

In the insurance decisions presented earlier, the choice was of an all or nothing nature. Insurance was purchased or it was not. More useful is a consideration of intermediate solutions. Various devices are currently available through which risk can be shared between insurer and insured. One common practice is to write an insurance policy with a deductible that assigns liability for the first k dollars of each loss to the insured, the insurer picking up the residual. Alternatively, the insurer may cover an agreed proportion of each loss, leaving the residual proportion to the insured. Other policies place an absolute limit on the insurer's liability. With such devices, the risk may be shared by the parties to the insurance contract, and the appropriate decision is one of degree. The question How much insurance should be purchased? replaces the question Should insurance be purchased?

Consider here that the risk is divided on a proportionate basis. The individual has an initial wealth of $120, of which $20 is non-risky and $100 represents some asset that is subject to possible destruction with a probability of 0.25. Only total loss is assumed in this example. The reader will recognize this example (see Figure 2–3). In the earlier discussion, only full insurance was available, and it could be purchased at a premium of $35, the expected value of loss being $25. Let us view full insurance as the purchase of $100 of compensation in the event of (total) loss. However, we might have insured half the loss (i.e., purchased $50 compensation in the event of (total loss) or a quarter of the loss (purchased $25 of compensation), etc. We can think of the degree of coverage as variable, the relevant issue being: How many dollars of protection should we purchase for the contingent $100 loss?

To promote this example, the premium is scaled according to the number of dollars of protection purchased. If the premium is scaled according to the expected value of the insurer's claim payment, it will be 25 cents per dollar of compensation purchase, reflecting the 25% probability of loss. Full coverage would cost $100 × 0.25 = $2, 50% coverage would cost $50 × 0.25 = $12.50, etc. However, in the example given earlier, there was a premium of $35 for full coverage, reflecting a premium rate 35 cents per dollar of insurance purchased. What is the optimal level of insurance to be purchased?

This problem will be tackled using a rather different diagram. Figure 2–7 shows individual wealth in the event of a loss and in the event of no loss. Each possible event is called a state of the world. State 0 refers to "loss" and state 1 refers to "no loss." The respective axes show the wealth levels, and the initial contingent wealth position with no insurance is shown at position A. If the actuarially fair premium were to be charged, full insurance could be purchased for $25. With such full insurance, the individual will have $95 regardless of whether a loss occurs or not. This position is represented as B. The 45° line shows equal wealth in both states and, as such, plots out full insurance positions. Only if full insurance is purchased will wealth be independent of which state arises. However, the actual premium is 35 cents per dollar of insurance purchased and will be scaled according to how much insurance is purchased. Thus, starting at position A, each 35 cents

F I G U R E   2–7

Expected Utility and Partial Insurance

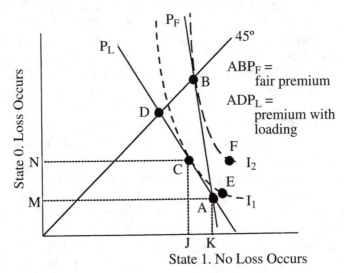

State 1. No Loss Occurs

of income sacrificed in state 1 in insurance premium will purchase $1 of compensation in state 0 (loss payment from the insurer). The insurance possibilities are shown on line ADP_L. Full insurance is shown at position D (in which case wealth would be $85 with certainty), but the individual can select partial insurance along segment AD. Position C represents a partial insurance solution because it reveals greater wealth in the event of no loss than in the event of loss. In other words, compensation would be insufficient to provide full indemnity for the loss.

Now let us establish what level of insurance would be optimal at different premium rates. The solution of this problem requires some knowledge of the individual's risk preferences. These are represented by a set of curves such as I_1 and I_2, which are indifference curves. To understand these curves, consider two points such as B and F in Figure 2–7. These are on the same curve, I_2, indicating that our subject is indifferent between the wealth combinations represented by these points. Notice the tradeoff involved in a move such as that from position F to position B. Maintaining the same level of utility (i.e., indifference) requires that loss of income in the state 1 be compensated by increasing income in the state 0. Despite such tradeoffs at a constant utility level, more wealth in both states is preferred to less wealth in both states; thus, position F is clearly preferred to position E. Therefore, E must offer a lower satisfaction level than F, and consequently E is on a lower indifference curve, that is, I_1. To summarize, all positions on a given indifference curve represent the same level of utility, but any point on an indifference curve, such as I_2, is preferred to any point on a lower indifference curve, such as I_1. Indifference curves denote increased satisfaction as they move away from the origin. The convexity of the curves to the origin indicates aversion to risk. Thus, a set of indifference curves can represent the same concepts as a utility function.

We know from the Bernoulli principle that a risk averter will choose to fully insure at an actuarially fair premium. Thus, at premium rate ABP_F. the subject chooses position B over partial insurance solutions on the segment AB. The preference for position B is shown by the fact that it is on the highest possible indifference curve that can be obtained given the opportunities along AB. The higher premium rate of 35 cents per dollar is shown by the line from ADP_L. However, the subject can no longer achieve the satisfaction level denoted by indifference curve I_2. The best that can be achieved is just to reach I_1, which offers lower satisfaction than I_2. This is the highest indifference curve that can be reached, as indicated by the tangency point C. Thus, point C is the optimal position. Notice that point C is below the 45° line, indicating that less than full insurance is purchased. In fact, the insured pays JK dollars in premiums to receive MN dollars in compensation should the loss occur. Notice that the subject could have chosen not to insure (position A) or to fully insure at this premium rate (position D). However, both these positions are below indifference curve I_1, indicating lower utility than position C.

This diagrammatic approach illustrates an idea that was proved mathematically some years ago by Mossin (1968) and Smith (1968): that a risk averter will normally choose to partially insure if the insurance premium includes a loading factor that is positively related to the expected claim payment. Since premiums are usually structured in this way, we would expect that most rational people will not choose to insure everything in sight, but will retain part of the risk themselves. As with most other goods, it appears that as price increases, we choose to purchase less.

The Design of an Insurance Policy

The expected-utility concept predicts that, in the face of premium loading, a rational risk management strategy for an individual is to partially insure rather than to fully insure. We can use the same ideas to say something about how such a partial insurance arrangement may be constructed.

As mentioned earlier, various devices are commonly used to structure a risk sharing arrangement between an insured and an insurer. A *deductible* policy covers only the surplus above a stated value. Losses below this value are not covered, and the value of the deductible is subtracted from the insurer's payment if the loss exceeds the deductible. A proportionate *coinsurance* policy simply pays a stated proportion of all losses. With an *upper limit* policy, the insurer's claim payment is limited to an upper value; that is, the insurer pays the value of loss or the policy limit, whichever is the lower. Each of these policies will be illustrated in the following example, and we will show that the risk-averse insured will have definite preferences for the different types of policies. The preferences are demonstrated in the example using the expected-utility rule. (A more general proof of these rankings can be derived mathematically, although this goes a little beyond the current text; see Arrow, 1963; Raviv, 1979; and Doherty, 1981).

Consider an individual with an initial level of wealth of $200, which is tied up in physical assets, such as a home and furniture. In addition, she has $60 in cash. The physical assets are subject to the possibility of damage or destruction, the appropriate information being given in the first two columns of Table 2–1. Thus, there is a:

50% chance of no loss
10% chance of a loss of $20
20% chance of a loss of $40, etc.

The expected value of loss is $40. If the subject were fully insured, at a premium of $60, she would receive an insurance payment equal to the value of loss, as shown in the third column. The final wealth (i.e., after any loss has occurred and the insurance payment is made) is shown in the fourth column. Final wealth is calculated as the initial wealth ($260) minus the premium ($60) minus the

TABLE 2-1

Different Ways of Sharing Risk

| Probability | Loss | Full Insurance | | $20 Deductible | | 75% Coinsurance | | $100 Upper Limit | |
		Insurance	Wealth	Insurance	Wealth	Insurance	Wealth	Insurance	Wealth
0.5	0	0	200	0	215	0	215	0	215
0.1	20	20	200	0	195	15	210	20	215
0.2	40	40	200	20	195	30	205	40	215
0.1	100	100	200	80	195	75	190	100	215
0.1	200	200	200	180	195	150	165	100	115
Expected Value	40	40	200	30	205	40	205	30	205

loss plus an insurance payment. Since the subject is fully compensated, the final wealth does not vary from $200. However, our problem here is to choose between the different partial insurance strategies shown in the remaining columns of the table. Respectively:

1. The deductible policy pays the value of the loss minus $20, or $0, whichever is the higher. Thus, with a loss of $20, nothing is paid; with a loss of $40, the policy pays $20. The expected policy payment is $30, and the final wealth shown has an expected value of $205.

2. The proportional coinsurance policy simply pays 75% of loss, irrespective of size. The insurance payments and final wealth are shown accordingly. Notice that this policy has been designed so that the expected value of the policy payment is again $30 and, accordingly, the expected value of final wealth is again $205.

3. The upper limit policy pays the value of loss or $100, whichever is lower. Again, the respective values of policy payment and final wealth are $30 and $205.

For each partial coverage policy, the premium is $45, which is 150% of the expected policy payment. Which of these policies is preferred? On the face of it, they appear to give equal value for money, since the policies have the same actuarial value and the same premiums. The expected utility formula will now be used to arrive at a ranking. To do this will assume a particular form for the utility function that ensures the shape concurs with the risk-averse, concave form illustrated earlier. The chosen form is:

$$U(X) = X^{0.5}$$

To calculate the expected utility of wealth EU, we see that:

$$EU = -\sum_i P_i U(X_i)$$

The calculations are as follows:

1. Deductible:

$$EU_D = 0.5(215)^{0.5} + 0.1(195)^{0.5} + 0.2(195)^{0.5}$$
$$+ 0.1(195)^{0.5} + 0.1(195)^{0.5}$$
$$= 14.314$$

2. Coinsurance:

$$EU_c = 0.5(215)^{0.5} + 0.1(210)^{0.5} + 0.2(205)^{0.5}$$
$$+ 0.1(190)^{0.5} + 0.1(165)^{0.5}$$
$$= 14.307$$

3. Upper limit:

$$EU_{UL} = 0.5(215)^{0.5} + 0.1(215)^{0.5} + 0.2(215)^{0.5}$$
$$+ 0.1(215)^{0.5} + 0.1(215)^{0.5}$$
$$= 14.269$$

A definite ranking appears. The deductible policy is preferred to a coinsurance policy having equal expected policy payment. In turn, the coinsurance policy is preferred to an upper-limit policy having the same expected policy payment. This preference reveals that the deductible policy is a more effective instrument for containing the riskiness in the insured's final wealth. Certainly, the deductible exposes the insured to some risk, but an upper value is placed on her loss. In contrast, the upper-limit policy limits the insurer's payment, leaving the insured's potential loss quite open ended. If we compare the final wealth columns under the respective policies, the final wealth under the deductible policy exhibits the lowest degree of risk and the final wealth under the upper-limit policy is the most risky. A cautionary note: the expected utilities are rather close in value. It should not be concluded that differences in utility are marginal. The expected-utility rule is a ranking device only.

This example also can be used to illustrate that partial coverage is often preferred to full coverage. In the previous section we demonstrated that if the premium loading is positively related to the expected value of claim payment, some degree of partial coverage is optimal. We have not tried to ascertain what level of risk sharing is optimal; thus, the $20 deductible may be inferior to a $30 deductible. However, it is of interest to see whether the various forms of partial coverage are preferred to the full insurance policy. The respective premiums for each of the policies are set at 150% of the expected policy payment; thus, in each case the loading is 50% of the expected payment. This satisfies our premium criterion, since the loading is positively related to the expected payout. The utility index for full coverage is established easily, since final wealth is $200 with certainty. Expected utility is:

$$EU_{FC} = 200^{0.5} = 114.147$$

Clearly, each of the partial insurance strategies is preferred to full insurance. This is quite comparable with our previous result, although it is still possible that some other levels of partial insurance may prove even better.

DEALING WITH ONE RISK WHEN FACED WITH ANOTHER

So far we have been dealing with decisions in isolation from each other. Consider the following three decisions that might face a person:

1. Purchase automobile insurance or do not purchase automobile insurance
2. Purchase home insurance or do not purchase home insurance
3. Purchase risky shares of stock or put money in riskless bank account

Traditionally, expected utility has normally been applied to each choice as though it were independent of others. We have looked at the optimal decision on automobile insurance without referring to background decisions that must be made on home insurance and on financial investment. It would be surprising if our tolerance for risk bearing insurable risk were to be independent of our investment choices and vice versa.

In the early 1980s attention on optimal hedging decisions began to take a portfolio approach (Mayers and Smith, 1983; Doherty and Schlesinger, 1983a, 1983b; and Turnbull, 1983). What is the optimal hedge on one source of risk when faced with other risk in our portfolio? This work took its cue from portfolio theory, which, as we shall see later, suggests that as more and more risky assets are added to a portfolio, the overall risk in the portfolio increases by less than the standalone risk of the added assets. Thus, the risk in a portfolio containing a large number of independent assets will be very low relative to the size of the portfolio. The reason is that, while some assets will turn out to make money through the luck of the draw, others will lose. While one does not know which particular assets will win and lose, the overall effect is for the gains and losses to largely cancel each other out. Similarly, an insurance company insuring a large number of cars or homes can expect that a fairly predictable proportion will have claims and that its overall financial results will vary relatively little.

Now let us take this property of portfolios and see what it implies for individual hedging decisions. First, consider that you have a large number of assets (your home, your health, your job, your car, your money, etc), each of which could be subject to some degree of risk. Or you can be a firm with many different properties spread over the country, each of which is subject to risk. Now, the fact that you own so many assets means that the chance of having losses on all of them, or even a substantial proportion of them, is extremely low. Thus, it is not quite so important to hedge the risk in any one. Your tolerance for self-insuring risk on any asset will be increased the more independent assets you have. Second, suppose the risks are correlated: if a loss occurs on one, it is more likely that another asset will have a loss. This correlation will tend to increase your demand for insurance and hedging since it is like having a run of bad luck. You might have been able to stand the cost of damage to your car, but if you have to pay medical bills at the same time, your finances are stretched. If losses on assets were negatively correlated (a loss on one asset reduces the chances of having a loss on another), this would tend to reduce the overall risk in your portfolio and you could afford to reduce your insurance protection on each of the assets.

These brief results only scratch the surface of the literature on how background risk affects individual hedging decisions. However, they do serve as a lead-in to portfolio theory, which will be discussed in Chapter 4. The idea of portfolio risk will become very important later in the book for two reasons. Most corporations do indeed have a portfolio of risks, and, depending on correlations, it is unlikely that a number of things could all go wrong at the same time. Thus, diversification is an important mechanism for controlling risk. Less directly, many firms are owned by investors who individually own many different assets. Investors too can control their investment risk through diversification. We need to understand this process in order to see whether risk management by a firm's managers will be rewarded by the capital market in terms of higher stock prices. This issue will be examined in

Chapter 5. But to close this chapter, we will mention some of the limitations of expected utility as a tool for aiding risky decisions and discuss briefly some other decision aids.

ALTERNATIVE DECISION RULES

Problems with the Expected-Utility Model

The expected-utility model rule is a very useful device for helping to condition our thinking about risky decisions because it focuses attention on the types of tradeoffs that have to be made. Furthermore, the results it generates are useful as first approximations in the search for risk management solutions. Certainly, it makes sense to transfer risk if there is no sacrifice in terms of expected return. When the transfer of risk is costly in terms of expected return, somewhat lower insurance purchases appear to be justified. However, the expected-utility rule does have limitations:

1. To calculate the expected utility, we need to know the precise form and shape of the individual's utility function. Typically, we do not have such information. Usually, the best we can hope for is to identify a general feature, such as risk aversion, and use the model to identify broad types of choices that might be appropriate.

2. Much corporate risk management has developed on the simplistic assumption that a firm can be treated as a risk-averse individual that can be represented as having a utility function. However, a firm is a coalition of interest groups, each having claims on the firm: shareholders, bondholders, managers, employees, customers, agents, etc. The description process must reflect the mechanisms with which these claims are resolved and how this resolution affects the value of the firm.

We will briefly outline alternative decision rules that can be used for risky choices. The first of these, the mean variance rule, will occupy a central role in the following chapters. The second rule, stochastic dominance, is more complex but is presented in sketchy form because it is more difficult to apply. Some readers may choose to skip the stochastic dominance section, and this will not destroy continuity.

The Mean Variance Rule

The mean is the expected value. Expected value already has been used as a simple decision rule. Its drawback is that it ignores the riskiness of different alternatives, as dramatically illustrated by the St. Petersburg paradox. Instead of developing the subtle and indirect treatment of risk implied by expected utility, we could instead find a direct measure of risk and then make our choice using *both* expected value and risk.

Consider the alternatives shown in Table 2–2. Assume that people are risk-averse but prefer a higher expected value to a lower expected value. Under such conditions, most (probably all) of us would feel A is better than choices B, C, or D; choice C is better than B; and choice D is better than B. In each of these rankings, the preferred alternative scores higher on at least one of the two criteria, but it does not score lower on either criteria. For example, choice A is preferred to D on expected value, but they score equally on risk. Notice, however, that the risk/expected-value rule does not rank all alternatives. Choices C and D cannot be ranked. Choice D is preferred to C on the risk criterion, but on the basis of expected value, C has a better result. The risk/expected-value rule will not always work.

In order to make this approach operational, we need to be able to measure risk. Various measures of risk are available. Consider a risky prospect such as:

$$A = \begin{cases} \$10; & \tfrac{1}{3} \text{ probability} \\ \$20; & \tfrac{1}{3} \text{ probability} \\ \$30; & \tfrac{1}{3} \text{ probability} \end{cases}$$

The risk is implicit in the spread of possible values. One measure is simply the range of values, for example, from $10 to $30. The range is the highest possible value minus the lowest possible value. Clearly, this gives some idea of spread, but it ignores probabilities. Amongst the various alternative contenders for a risk measure, the one with the most convenient properties is standard deviation (or its square, the variance). Standard deviation is defined as:

T A B L E   2–2

Choice	Risk	Expected Value
A	Low	High
B	High	Low
C	High	High
D	Low	Low

$$\sigma = \left[\sum_i P_i (X_i - E(X_i))^2 \right]^{1/2}$$

where P_i is the probability of outcome X_i and $E(X_i)$ is the expected value of X.

The expected value, EV, of prospect A is:

$$E(A) = \tfrac{1}{3}(\$10) + \tfrac{1}{3}(\$20) + \tfrac{1}{3}(\$30) = \$20$$

and the standard deviation is:

$$\sigma = \{\tfrac{1}{3}(\$10 - \$20)^2 + \tfrac{1}{3}(\$20 - \$20)^2 + \tfrac{1}{3}(\$30 - \$20)^2\}^{1/2} = \$8.165$$

The variance σ^2 is $\$8.165^2 = \$66.67$.

These measures, expected value, standard deviation, and variance, will be used in later chapters. For the moment, we will simply examine one or two general properties of the mean variance rule. Consider the choices outlined in the previous table. We can represent each of these as a probability distribution, showing the range of possible values on the horizontal axis and the associated probabilities on the vertical axis. The four choices are represented in this way in Figure 2–8. Choices A and D have the same shape or spread, indicating a low level of risk; in each case the possible values are closely clustered around a central value. The central, or expected, values of the two distributions are different. The expected value of A is high, whereas the expected value of choice B is low. Alternatives B and C have the same shape, the wide spread indicating high risk. However, whereas B is centered on a low expected value, choice C centers on a high

F I G U R E   2-8

Mean Variance Analysis

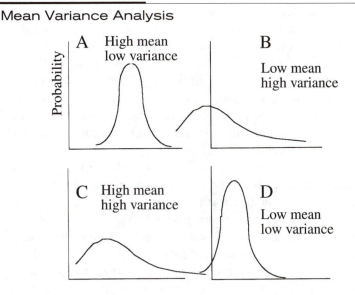

expected value. Comparison of different pairs of these alternatives will confirm the rankings we derived earlier.

Both the expected-utility rule and the mean variance rule require the decision maker to be able to estimate the possible outcomes and their respective probabilities. Such measures are feasible in principle and often in practice. However, this is the only input required for the mean variance rule, in contrast with the expected utility, which also requires specification of the utility functions. This operational advantage is achieved at some cost, since we find that not all risky choices can be ranked. We derive a limited ranking that applies to all risk-averse individuals. This rule has proved very useful in analyzing investor behavior and, in consequence, in valuing the firm.

Stochastic Dominance

Like mean variance, stochastic dominance describes a decision procedure that is applicable for risk averters and does not require specification of the individual utility function. As with mean variance, it can rank some, but not all, choices. However, it has one particular advantage over mean variance. Expected value and standard deviation (or variance) describe only certain features of a prospect. Often a risky prospect cannot be represented by a smooth or symmetric curve, such as those shown in Figure 2–8, but rather the curve will be irregular and asymmetric. Such features may be relevant to an individual's choice, but they are ignored by the mean variance rule. Stochastic dominance is designed to overcome such problems, although it is more difficult to use and may sometimes fail to produce clear rankings, even where mean variance succeeds.

Stochastic dominance is really a set of decision rules that applies to progressively more restrictive pairings of distributions. A full mathematical specification is beyond our scope. However, an intuitive understanding is easily presented.

Consider distributions A and D shown earlier in Figure 2–8. These are represented in the left side of Figure 2–9 on the same diagram, and the respective cumulative distributions are presented immediately below. The cumulative probability distribution shows the probability that any outcome will be equal to or less than a given value. The preference of A over D is pretty clear.

FIGURE   2–9

Stochastic Dominance Analysis

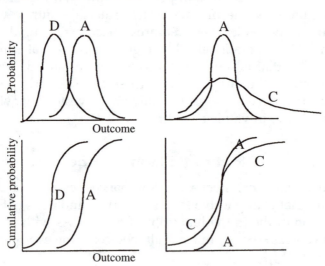

Both have the same shape, indicating the same variance, but distribution A clearly centers around a higher expected outcome. The cumulative distributions reveal that distribution A is always equal to or below distribution D. In essence, prospect D "exhausts probabilities" at low levels of the wealth. In A, the probability is allocated at higher wealth levels; thus, the distribution appears to be shifted to the right. This reveals the first rule for stochastic dominance:

If the cumulative distribution of A *is equal to or below that for* D *for every level of wealth, then prospect* A *dominates (is preferred to) prospect* D.

This rule is not restricted to those who are averse to risk, but it does apply to all who prefer greater wealth to lesser wealth. This probably describes us all, and the rule is quite general.

Now look at the right side of Figure 2–9. Distributions for A and C are extracted from Figure 2–8 and are presented on a single graph. The distributions have the same expected value, but C exhibits considerably more risk. Choice A should be preferred to C. The appropriate stochastic dominance rule is developed from the cumulative distribution. It will be seen that the cumulative distribution for choice A starts below that for C, the distributions intercept, and then at higher wealth levels choice C is lower than choice A. The lower level of risk in A is revealed by the much steeper slope in the cumulative distribution. This is anticipated in the second stochastic dominance rule, which applies only to risk-averse decision makers.

If the cumulative distributions of A *and* C *intersect one or a greater number of times,* A *is preferred to* C *if*

$$\int_{-\infty}^{x} [C(x) - A(x)]dx \geq 0 \text{ for all } x \text{ with inequality for some } x$$

where $C(x)$ and $A(x)$ are the cumulative distributions for prospects C and A.

The application of this rule is a little complex, although in Figure 2–10 an example appears of how it might apply to a simple risk management problem. If full insurance is purchased, the resulting distribution of wealth for an individual will exhibit no risk; wealth level W_0 will be achieved with certainty. An appropriate

F I G U R E   2–10

Insurance versus No-Insurance

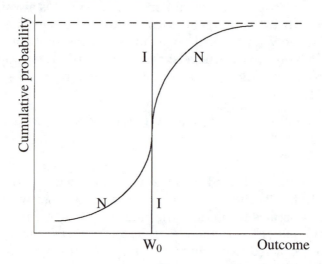

cumulative distribution is shown as I in Figure 2–10. If no insurance is purchased, wealth will be risky and an appropriate distribution is shown as N. The distributions intersect just once. Under such circumstances, second-degree stochastic dominance will apply if the premium for insurance is actuarially fair. The full-insurance distribution is preferred to the no-insurance distribution. This is compatible with the Bernoulli principle.

The treatment of stochastic dominance is sketchy and will not be developed. The interested reader might consult the literature review provided by Bawa (1982) for further applications, including insurance applications.

Non-Expected-Utility Analysis

Expected-utility analysis is derived from a set of axioms about preferences and behavior that may be considered as minimal and reasonable. For example, preferences are assumed to be transitive (if A is preferred to B and B is preferred to C, then A should be preferred to C) and there are certainty equivalents (for a risky prospect A there is a certain sum B such that the individual is indifferent between A and B). However, other decision rules have been constructed using rather different, but still minimal and reasonable, axioms about preferences and behavior. These alternatives have been generated largely because experimental behavior has revealed that individuals often violate the axioms of expected utility. For example, experimental studies often find that subjects violate the transitivity axiom and are heavily influenced by the framing of tasks.

The non-expected-utility models, while built on different axioms, nevertheless result in mathematical formulae that resemble expected utility, the main difference being in how risk enters the decision. Expected utility differs from expected value by transforming wealth according to the individual's preferences. The more concave the utility function, the more risk-averse the individual. Other functions allow transformations of wealth and/or probability to model the effect of attitude to risk. Perhaps the simplest and starkest contrast to expected utility is Yaari's "Dual Theory." In this model, the wealth enters the function directly rather than being transformed. However, the probability of achieving a wealth level W_i, which is p_i, is transformed by multiplying by a value g that depends on the cumulative probability. The comparison is seen in the following three formulae:

Expected value $= \Sigma\, p_i W_i$

Expected utility $= \Sigma\, p_i\, U(W_i)$

Dual theory $= \Sigma\, g(P_i) p_i\, W_i$

I will not go into detail here, but the general effect of transforming probabilities, instead of wealth, to allow for risk is as follows. Most of the results about optimal insurance described in this chapter still hold. This does not mean that people will buy exactly the same amount; still, it is optimal to buy full insurance if the price is fair, and when premiums are increased above expected loss, the preferred form is sharing is a deductible. However, there is a difference. Yaari's formula is more likely to result in "all or nothing" answers. Whereas expected utility leads to a smooth result (the optimal amount of insurance falls smoothly as the premium is increased), with dual theory the optimal insurance coverage remains at full insurance as the premium is increased by small increments. However, if the premium gets too large, there can be a sudden shift to partial coverage or no coverage at all.

The real value of these alternative models is that they seem to do a better job of describing how information is processed and how decisions are made. Some of these models do seem to outperform expected utility in laboratory experiments in which non-repeated decisions are made. However, it is not clear that they do any better when the decision is made in a market setting in which people can learn over time and in which decisions are repeated. For example, how the *average* person makes a decision is of little interest if one is trying to describe how products are priced in a market setting where the *marginal* buyer is critical. Moreover, for all the evidence favoring alternative models in laboratory situations, there is much more evidence in which economists have constructed predictive models of economic activity such as price behavior, the nature of contracts, market structure, business strategy, etc., using expected utility and have tested these models using actual market data.[1] There is no question but that expected utility is the model of choice in this positive economic setting.

CONCLUSION

The task of this chapter has been to present decision rules that can be used to rank competing risky choices. From these rules, we have derived a set of preliminary insurance or hedging strategies for individuals that will help focus our thoughts when we tackle more complex corporate risk management decisions.

The simplest decision rule considered is to choose the alternative with the highest expected value. There is some long-run virtue in this rule. Its repeated use over many separate decisions will ultimately lead to expected wealth maximization. However, the rule fails to account for differences in the riskiness of competing prospects, as dramatically illustrated by Bernoulli's St. Petersburg paradox.

The expected-utility rule requires that the decision maker select the prospect with the highest expected utility. Under this rule, the possible outcomes are weighted according to their respective

---

1. Such models allow tests of joint hypotheses. One hypothesis relates to the institution being modeled and the other relates to expected utility upon which individual decisions are based.

probabilities and according to the utility scale of the decision maker. The substitution of outcomes measured in utility terms for money outcomes ensures that individual risk preferences can be impressed on the decision process. This rule has been widely used in economics and is used here to compare some simple risk management choices.

The expected-utility rule can be used in conjunction with the assumption of aversion to risk to reveal a propensity to insure or hedge at fair prices (premiums are equal to the expected value of loss) or even at unfair prices. There is an equivalent aversion to gambling. This is not to assert that people will never gamble and will always insure, since both activities can be priced to encourage or deter demand. Under realistic pricing assumptions, partial insurance often appears more attractive than "all or nothing" attitudes toward insurance purchase. For insureds, deductibles appear to provide a more attractive mechanism for risk sharing than other devices, such as coinsurance or policy limits.

While the rule establishes generalized patterns of behavior that are useful in guiding individual decisions, corporate risk management is more complex and requires a study of the interactions between stakeholders such as creditors, shareholders, and managers. To do this, we need to know what information the parties have, what their economic stake is in the firm, who can control decisions, and how these decisions are influenced by their economic self interest. To start examining information and incentive issues, we address two problems that arise when risk is transferred between parties as in insurance and other hedge contracts; moral hazard and adverse selection.

REFERENCES

Arrow, K. J. 1963. "Uncertainty and the Welfare Economies of Medical Care." *American Economic Review* 53:941–73.

Bawa, V. J. 1982. "Stochastic Dominance: A Research Bibliography." *Management Science* 28:698–712.

Borch, K. 1968. *The Economics of Uncertainty.* Princeton Studies in Mathematical Economics. Princeton, N.J.: Princeton University Press.

Doherty, N. A. 1976. *Insurance Pricing and Loss Prevention.* Lexington, Mass.: D. C. Heath.

――. 1981. "Stochastic Ordering of Risk Insurance Exchanges." *Scandinavian Actuarial Journal* no. 4: 302–08.

Doherty, N. A., and H. Schlesinger. 1983*a*. "Optimal Insurance in Incomplete Markets." *Journal of Political Economy* 91:1045–54.

――. 1983*b*. "The Optimal Deductible for an Insurance Policy when Initial Wealth Is Random." *Journal of Business* 56:555–65.

Eeckhoudt, L., and M. Kimball. 1992. "Background Risk, Prudence and the Demand for Insurance." In *Contributions to Insurance Economics*, ed. Georges Dionne. Boston: Kluwer Academic Publishers.

Friedman, M., and L. J. Savage. 1948. "The Utility Analysis of Choices Involving Risk." *Journal of Political Economy* 56:279–304.

Hirshleifer, J., and J. G. Riley. 1979. "The Analytics of Uncertainty and Information—An Expository Survey." *Journal of Economic Literature* 17:1375–1421.

Karni, E. 1992. "Optimal Insurance: A Nonexpected Utility Analysis." In *Contributions to Insurance Economics*, ed. Georges Dionne. Boston: Kluwer Academic Publishers.

Markowitz, H. 1952. "The Utility of Wealth." *Journal of Political Economy* 60:151–58.

Mayers, D., and C. W. Smith. 1983. "The Interdependence of Individual Portfolio Decisions and the Demand for Insurance." *Journal of Political Economy* 91:304–11.

Mossin, J. 1968. "Aspects of Rational Insurance Purchasing." *Journal of Political Economy* 76:553–68.

von Neumann, J., and O. Morgenstern. 1944. *Theory of Games and Economic Behavior.* Princeton, N.J.: Princeton University Press.

Raviv, A. 1979. "The Design of an Optimal Insurance Policy." *American Economic Review* 69:223–39.

Shackle, G. L. S. 1938. *Expectations, Investments and Income.* London: Oxford University Press.

Shoemaker, P. J. H. 1982. *Experiments on Decisions under Risk.* Amsterdam: Kluwer Nijhoff.

Shoemaker, P. J. H., and J. C. Hershey. 1980. "Risk Taking and Problem Context in the Domain of Expected Utility Analysis." *Journal of Risk and Insurance* 47:11.

Smith, V. 1968. "Optimal Insurance Coverage." *Journal of Political Economy* 76:68–77.

Turnbull, S. 1983. "Additional Aspects of Rational Insurance Purchasing." *Journal of Business* 56:217–29.

Zeckhauser, R. 1970. "Medical Insurance—A Case Study of the Tradeoff between Risk-Spreading and Appropriate Incentive." *Journal of Economic Theory* 2:10, 26.

CHAPTER 3

Moral Hazard and Adverse Selection

Insurance transfers risk from one party for whom the risk is particularly costly to another who can bear that risk more lightly. As we get into risk management for firms, insurance will be seen as only one of a number of instruments for hedging risk. As risk is transferred from one party to another, so incentives for behavior are changed. This is the subject of this chapter.

The first set of incentive problems is generally known as principal–agent problems and more specifically as moral hazard. These problems arise because one party makes a decision and someone else picks up the tab. In insurance this problem arises because, once having transferred risk to an insurer, the policyholder has little incentive to take actions that might reduce the probability of, or severity of, a future loss. This is important because the policyholder can influence a loss: it is his or her property that is insured, it is his or her actions that can result in a liability claim from a third party. In some other hedging contexts this may be less of a worry. For example, fuel costs might be an important part of a firm's production costs and the firm might be able to transfer this risk to another by buying a derivative based on oil prices. However, that single firm is far too small to be able to influence fuel prices, and so the counter-party in this derivative trade is not worried that the firm's behavior will be an important factor in determining the payoff. In other risk management situations, the incentive fears return. For example, firms (i.e., share-holders) appoint managers to make decisions but the shareholders bear the consequences of those decisions. Thus, how a firm makes decisions in managing risk may reflect the manager's preferences over risk rather than those of shareholders.

The principal agent or moral hazard issue has two parts: first, how does an agent behave, and second, how can the principal write contracts that induces the agent to make decisions that favor the principal. This problem is one of self-interested behavior and contract design, which is examined in the first part of this chapter.

The second issue examined in this chapter is adverse selection. The parties to a contract in which risk is transferred will probably have different information about the potential payoffs. This asymmetry can affect behavior in strategic ways. For example, if policyholders know more about their risk potential than insurers, the latter will not be able to set prices that are appropriate for each individual. Low-risk types will end up subsidizing high-risk types. Insurance will be a good buy for the high risks and a bad buy for the low risks. Thus, insurers will find their portfolios crowded with the policyholders with high loss potential.

Adverse selection arises from an information asymmetry. How can insurers come up with strategies to deal with this issue? We will see in this chapter that there are sometimes ways of resolving these problems by offering a menu of options designed to induce people to reveal their private information in the way they make these choices. We will see later in the book that information asymmetry has other risk management implications. For example, information asymmetry between managers and investors (insiders and outsiders) leads to problems of finding appropriate prices for firms' securities, and this issue is more severe when cash flows are risky. It is sometimes possible to design risk management strategies to be able to signal important (usually favorable) inside information to the capital market.

MORAL HAZARD

Moral hazard has somewhat different meanings in insurance industry parlance and in microeconomics. In either case, the problem arises because the insured typically has a degree of control over the probability that an insured event will occur, or the size of the loss if it does arise. The motorist can drive more slowly, or with more care. The property owner can install smoke alarms and make sure inflammable wastes are cleared up. The firm buying worker's compensation insurance can choose to educate its workers in safety techniques. The same firm can minimize worker's compensation claims after the fact through occupational therapy. The insured who has suffered a fire can often minimize the loss by removing and protecting undamaged goods. I will refer to such actions, or inactions, of the insured as the chosen "level of care" or the chosen "investment in safety."

In insurance, the term "moral hazard" refers to the tendency for those with insurance to relax their level of care or their investment in safety and loss prevention. It is sometimes used with ethical overtones. Some people are given to take advantage of their insurance protection by failing to take care. Others, of more upright character, behave impeccably (from the insurer's viewpoint) despite their insurance coverage. Thus, moral hazard describes a behavioral characteristic of the insured that is used in the underwriting decision.

In microeconomics, the focus is on information, incentives, and rational behavior. Insurance and other hedges do relax incentives to take care or invest in safety. The expected loss is not fixed. Rather, the expected loss can be expected to increase as a result of the insurance protection. This would present little problem to the insurer if the behavior of the insured could be monitored perfectly; the insurer could simply make coverage, or price, conditional on the level of care or safety chosen by the insured. The problem arises when the level of care is hidden to the insurer. The policyholder may be tempted to choose a low investment in safety once the insurance is in place. It would seem that the best the insurer can now do is to anticipate that the insured will reduce his chosen level of safety and take this into account in the price. This will make insurance more expensive because the insured will be required to pre-pay for the anticipated increase in expected loss. The insured is hoisted on his own petard.

The moral hazard problem is not unique to insurance. It is an illustration of a wider set of *principal–agent* problems. A principal–agent problem arises when one party, the principal, employs another, the agent, to perform a task on the principal's behalf.

Unless the principal can monitor all actions of the agent, the agent may be tempted to act in his own interest. For example, a lawyer acting on behalf of the client may favor the publicity and challenge of a trial, whereas the plaintiff, the agent, could be better off with a settlement. Another common example is the relationship between shareholders and managers of a firm. The managers are there to act in the interest of shareholders, which implies maximizing the value of the shareholders' investment. However, the manager might be tempted to work with less vigor, consume perquisites, choose projects that minimize the risk of job loss, and engage in relationships that maximize the manager's marketability for a new job. The more difficult it is to monitor these actions, the more likely it is that managers will undertake such actions. The problem is that one party chooses a set of actions but another party gets the rewards of those actions, or picks up the pieces. One party chooses the meal, but someone else pays the bill. There is a separation of ownership and control. Similarly, in insurance the policyholder pays for the protection, but the insurer pays the losses if the protection fails.

Moral hazard can be divided into *ex ante* and *ex post*. If wealth is insured against some event, the policyholder will have little incentive to undertake actions *before the event* that will reduce the expected cost, nor will he or she have incentive to take actions *after the event* that can minimize its impact, and therefore the payout under the policy. For example, the firm may be little inclined to spend a lot on product safety if it is insured against liability; nor will it have a great incentive to deny liability if considers that a legal fight would have an adverse effect on product demand and the insurer was paying for the settlement anyway. These are *ex ante* moral hazard and *ex post* moral hazard. We will first look at *ex ante* moral hazard.

EX ANTE MORAL HAZARD

Optimal Safety for the Insured

Insurance gives rise to a classic principal–agent problem: the insured chooses safety and thereby determines the expected loss, but the insurer pays the loss. To see the basis of the insurance problem, we will first consider that an individual must choose some level of care or safety. For example, the person must choose how much to invest in sprinklers, smoke detectors, fire doors, and other forms of fire safety. The insured faces the cost, $c(s)$, which says that the cost, c, is a function of the level of safety, s, chosen. One would expect this cost to increase the higher the chosen level of safety, that is, c is an increasing function of s. On the other hand, the individual receives a benefit. Because safety reduces the expected value of loss (either by reducing the probability or the size), then the expected cost of fires will fall. Let us consider a fall in probability. The probability of a loss of size L depends on the chosen level of s, that is, probability is $p(s)$ where p falls as s increases. Consider first that the person is indifferent to risk. The level of safety that will maximize expected utility is that which equates the marginal cost and marginal benefit of safety. In Figure 3–1, the rising curve is the marginal cost of safety, $c(s)$. The marginal benefit, assuming no insurance, is shown as the steepest falling line denoted "no hedge." The optimal choice is where the cost of any incremental improvement (marginal cost) just matches the incremental reduction in expected losses (marginal benefit). This is shown as position A.

F I G U R E   3–1

Value Maximizing Safety and Insurance

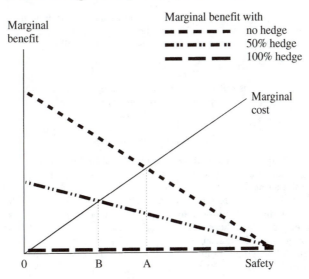

To see what is going on here, let us first consider that the person's expected wealth, W, is some initial level, W_0, minus the cost of safety, $c(s)$, minus the expected cost of paying for accidents, $p(s)L$:

$$W = W_0 - c(s) - \Sigma\, p_i(s)\, L$$

Let us simplify a little to start and assume that the person in indifferent to risk. The task is to choose the level of s that maximizes expected wealth. This can be done by taking the derivative of wealth with respect to s and setting this derivative to zero to derive the maximum:

$$\frac{\partial W}{\partial s} = -\frac{\partial c}{\partial s} - \Sigma\, \frac{\partial p_i}{\partial s}\, L = 0$$

This leads to the straightforward interpretation, marginal cost, $\partial c / \partial s$, equals marginal benefit, $-\Sigma(\partial p_i / \partial s)L$.[1]

Now suppose that insurance is purchased. The marginal benefit is zero if the loss is fully insured; the insurer pays for all damage. Thus, the marginal benefit to the insured is zero, regardless of the level of safety. This is shown in Figure 3–1 as the line that coincides with the horizontal axis, labeled "100% hedge." The point where marginal cost and marginal benefit are now equal

---

1. If the person is averse to risk (why, after all, would she wish to buy insurance?), the analysis can be adapted by looking at the utility of wealth, $U(W)$, and taking the derivative with respect to s. Formally this will look as follows:

$$U(W) = \Sigma\, p_i(s)\, U(W_0 - c(s) - p_i(s)L_i)$$

The derivative turns out to be a little messier, and one can ignore this step and move straight to the interpretation at the end of the paragraph.

$$\frac{\partial U(W_i)}{\partial s} = -\Sigma_i \left(\frac{\partial U}{\partial W_i} \left[\frac{\partial c}{\partial s} - \frac{\partial p_i}{\partial s}\, L \right] + \frac{\partial p_i}{\partial s}\, U(W_i) \right) = 0$$

This is still equating marginal costs and marginal benefits of safety, but now everything is stated in utility terms. The term involving $\partial c / \partial s$ is the marginal cost and all the terms involving $\partial p_i / \partial s$ comprise the marginal benefit. The marginal cost is the utility loss from paying for safety, and the marginal benefit is the utility gain from reducing the probability of paying any potential future loss. While the actual level of safety chosen will depend on the shape of the utility funciton (and will not generally be the same as the case of risk neutrality), the risk-averse person will still be willing to invest more in safety, the greater is the saving in potential future losses.

is where $s = 0$. the interpretation is straightforward. The policy-holder pays the costs of safety but gets none of the benefit. Consequently, the policyholder invests nothing in safety. An intermediate case is also shown where 50% of the loss is insured. Here the policyholder pays all the costs but gets half the benefit (the full benefit being shared with the insurer).[2] The chosen level of safety is shown at the intermediate level B.

The problem with insurance can be shown as follows. Some proportion of the loss, α, is insured and the remaining portion, $1 - \alpha$, is paid by the policyholder. For this insurance there is a premium, αP, which is scaled according to the portion of the risk insured. Thus, wealth is now the starting level, W_0, minus the cost of safety, $c(s)$, minus that portion of the expected loss that is not insured, $(1 - \alpha)p(s)L$, minus the premium, αP:

$$W = W_0 - c(s) - (1 - \alpha)p(s)L - \alpha P$$

The task for the policyholder is still to choose the level of s that maximizes expected wealth. Setting this derivative to zero to derive the maximum:[3]

$$\frac{\partial W}{\partial s} = -\frac{\partial c}{\partial s} - (1 - \alpha) \sum \frac{\partial p_i}{\partial s} L = 0$$

Now the marginal cost is set equal to $(1 - \alpha) \times$ the marginal benefit. The effect is to scale down the level of safety chosen by the policyholder.[4]

The Optimal Insurance Contract, Given That Safety, s, Is Not Observed by the Insurer

Now consider the problem from the insurer's point of view. The insurer has to design and sell an insurance policy knowing that

---

2. The utility benefit may not be exactly half that for no insurance. However, the marginal utility benefit will lie between the full-insurance and no-insurance cases.
3. Or, with utility:

$$\frac{\partial U(W_i)}{\partial s} = -\sum_i \left(\frac{\partial U}{\partial W_i} \left[\frac{\partial c}{\partial s} - (1 - \alpha) \frac{\partial p_i}{\partial s} L \right] + \frac{\partial p_i}{\partial s} U(W_i) \right) = 0$$

4. Notice that the insurer could not monitor the chosen level of s. If this were not the case, the insurer could have set the premium relative to s and there would have been no problem.

the policyholder will select s (or at least can change s) after the policy has been sold. One way the insurer can go is to scale back on the level of coverage. This will at least give the policyholder some stake in future losses and encourage him to take an interest in preventing or containing them.

Suppose that the expected loss was independent of the level of coverage; there was no moral hazard issue. Now imagine that the insured can choose some proportion, α, of the loss to insure. Apart from any fixed transaction costs, it seems plausible that the premium would be proportional to α. Figure 3–2 shows such a premium schedule as the straight upwards sloping line labeled "price without moral hazard." Because the vertical axis measures price (which is undesirable to the insured) and the horizontal axis shows coverage (which is desirable), the policyholder's utility will be higher the farther to the southeast. Thus, indifference curves for the policyholder are shown with $I(1)$ having higher utility than $I(2)$ because it is further to the southeast. The individual chooses the level of coverage that attains the highest indifference curve, $I(1)$. This coverage is shown as A in the diagram.

With moral hazard, the policyholder's chosen level of s will likely decline the more coverage is purchased. Thus, the expected

F I G U R E 3–2

Moral Hazard and Optimal Hedging

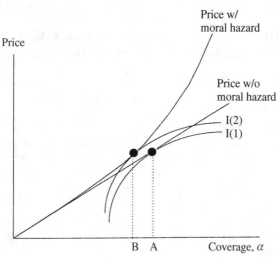

loss, $p(s)L$, will increase as more coverage is purchased. This means that the price charged by the insurer just to break even will not be proportional to α but will increase in greater proportion than α. More insurance means that the policyholder is getting a larger proportion of an increasing expected loss. This double whammy makes the premium rise steeply to cover the increasing moral hazard effect. The new price line is that marked price with moral hazard." With the increased cost from the moral hazard, the original level of utility, $I(1)$, is no longer attainable. The highest utility that can be achieved by the policyholder is shown by the indifference curve $I(2)$. The result shows that less insurance is purchased.[5]

The optimal level of insurance can be solved with moral hazard along the lines shown in the previous paragraphs. But that is not necessarily the optimal insurance contract that can be arranged between the policyholder and insurer. Solving the optimal *level* of insurance assumes the structure of contract is fixed. For example, one can assume that the form of the insurance coverage is such that a proportion of the loss is covered by the insurer and the choice is what proportion. Alternatively, one could assume that the structure is one with a deductible and the choice is what level of deductible. There are many other potential structures for insurance coverage. The questions are what the optimal structure is and, given that structure, what the optimal parameters are.

While the formal solution of this problem is a little messy, the solution is quite accessible. Consider another agency problem with a similar structure. The board of directors of a firm must decide how to structure the compensation of the CEO. The issue is not simply the level, but on what factors compensation will depend. Two sets of issues are clearly relevant. One is risk sharing. Shareholders can diversify risk at low cost in how they form portfolios of assets. Managers cannot diversify the risk surrounding their employment, since it typically represents a large portion of their wealth. Accordingly, it would appear to make sense that any risk attached to the firm's earnings or value is best allocated to shareholders, who have a comparative advantage in bearing that

---

5. In these models it is usually the case that moral hazard reduces the level of insurance that the individual would choose. However, a formal proof does require certain assumptions. Winter (1992) has a nice review of the economics of moral hazard.

risk. If one were to require managers to take part of that performance risk (say by rewarding them with profit-related bonuses) the
managers would require a risk premium. This can be avoided by
paying flat compensation that is unrelated to profit.

The other factor to consider in designing compensation is
incentive. Managers, as argued above, have an incentive to work
in their self interest if they cannot be monitored. Accordingly, one
would like to make compensation related to the quantity and
quality of effort exercised on behalf of the firm's owners; the
greater the effort, the higher the pay. In this way, the interests of
the managers would be aligned with those of the shareholders.
Accordingly, such contracts are often referred to as *incentive compatible*. But shareholders cannot observe effort and therefore cannot make a feasible contract conditional on effort. If they tried to
do so, they would have to rely on the managers' own statements
on effort, and, since these could not be independently verified,
managers could not be penalized for lying.

The solution to the compensation design problem relies on a
relationship existing between effort and something the managers
can observe. If managerial inputs cannot be observed, the fruits
of those inputs can. Shareholders can observe the price at which
shares are traded. They can and do observe periodic earnings.
Even though profit reports rely on information provided by management, this is independently audited. So if pay is related to such
value or profit measures, managers will have an incentive to take
those actions (supply more effort) that are likely to increase profit.

Notice that the effectiveness of this compensation scheme in
increasing shareholder wealth does depend on a positive relationship existing between effort and share value or earnings. But it
does not rely on this relationship being deterministic. Earnings are
not determined solely by managerial decisions and effort. The
best-laid plans can go astray. Thus, profits will be influenced by
factors outside the manager's control, such as the state of the economy, interest rates, changes in exchange rates, and technical problems of production that could not have been foreseen. Thus, profits will partly reflect managerial talent and effort and partly reflect
chance. It is sometimes said that there is "signal and noise." Profit
levels reflect both the signal (of managerial effort) and the noise
(exogenous factors outside management control). If managers are

given incentive compensation, then there is a problem they could be rewarded, or punished, due to factors outside their control. This is simply a problem of being unable to monitor effort. The point is that, prospectively, managers will tend to supply greater effort if it increases the *likelihood* that their bonuses will increase.

With these two ideas in conflict (optimal risk sharing favors flat compensation whereas incentive compatibility favors output related compensation) we have a tradeoff. As in many economic dilemmas, there is a tradeoff between risk sharing and efficiency. The optimal arrangement is often one that has a little of both. So compensation is often a mixture of fixed salary and a bonus related to profit or share value.

Now consider insurance. Insurers wish policyholders to take those actions that reduce expected loss, but the actions cannot be observed. But actual losses are observed—indeed, the insurer has to pay them—and there is a probabilistic relationship between care/safety and losses (just as there is a probabilistic relationship between managerial inputs and profit). Thus, the insurance contract will have its price related to actual loss experience. This does court the risk that the insured can be penalized for bad luck. For example, an automobile policy might increase premiums if there are two or more accidents within a space of three years. There is a chance that even the best driver could have had two accidents simply due to ill fortune. But if you do not know whether the driver is good or bad, the fact of two accidents may appear to lend more support to the view that the driver is bad (and the record is representative of a bad driver) than that the driver is really good (but that the experience is not representative). There is a scene in Oscar Wilde's *The Importance of Being Earnest,* where a young man is trying to explain that he is an orphan, only to be told that losing one parent is bad luck but losing two seems like carelessness.

Premiums can be related to losses in two ways: one is an experience-rated premium and the other is a retrospective premium. Experience-rated premiums are calculated with reference to the loss experience of prior periods. If I know my premiums in the future are to be experience-rated and I anticipate buying insurance in the future, then I will be encouraged to take care even though the insurer will pay for losses. The second method is to treat each year's premium as conditional on the losses that occur in the year. Usually this is done in two stages. A provisional premium is paid up front. At the end of the insurance period (often with some delay because claims take some time to evaluate) the provisional premium will be adjusted to reflect the loss experience. At the extreme, the adjustment could be the difference between the provisional premium and the actual losses. But this would undo the insurance protection. The insured would end up paying for his own loses and would receive, effectively, a short-term loan to pay for those losses. Short of this extreme, the adjustment would normally be some portion of the difference between the provisional premium and actual losses. Thus, there is part risk sharing and part an incentive-compatible contract.

ADVERSE SELECTION

One of Groucho Marx's often quoted remarks is that he would not like to belong to any club that would have him as a member. Groucho here captured the essence of adverse selection. Adverse selection can arise in any marketplace where people trade with different information. If one party has better information about some relevant features of the trade, that party may use that knowledge to his or her advantage and often to the disadvantage of the trading partner. The way the partner reacts to this potential disadvantage can act as a barrier to trading and can lead to market inefficiencies. While moral hazard has been described as a problem of hidden actions, adverse selection has been defined as a problem of hidden information: one party has access to material information that is denied to the other. It is a problem of information asymmetry.

An appealing illustration of this concept was used some years ago by George Akerlof, and since his example was the market for secondhand cars, adverse selection is often referred to as a "lemons" problem. The sellers of secondhand cars have better information about their quality than the buyers. They know of any prior accidents, they know the service and repair record, and they know of any chronic problems with the vehicle. The buyer may be able to uncover some, but not all, of this information. Thus, there is an information asymmetry with (in the language of political correctness) the seller being informationally advantaged and the buyer informationally challenged. Cars coming onto the secondhand market will vary in quality, some being better than average and some worse than average. The seller will know the quality of the particular vehicle, but the buyer will know only the average quality of cars of this type. Not being able to verify individual quality, the buyer is only willing to offer a price suitable for a car of average quality. If the seller knows her car to be better than average, this price is unlikely to be acceptable and she may well withdraw her vehicle from the market. But for the seller with a worse than average car, a price based on average quality is more than the car is worth and he will gladly sell. The trade in this market will be made up mostly of worse than average cars.

But the problem gets worse. Buyers can now anticipate that mostly poor-quality cars will be offered for sale, and this will lower further the price they are willing to pay. This will make any remaining sellers with high-quality cars even less willing to sell. As this dynamic process continues, we will be left with few, if any, good secondhand cars for sale. Good cars are "driven out" of the market.

Ah! but why does the seller of a high-quality car simply not say to the buyer, "My car is better than average and therefore should command a high price." The problem is that because the buyer cannot verify this statement, the sellers of lemons will also straighten their faces and say that their cars are also wonderful, and so buyers will be denied meaningful information. Cheap talk like this is simply not convincing. We will see later that there may be mechanisms to separate the good and bad cars, but they will need to be more subtle. For these mechanisms to work, the seller of the high-quality vehicle must be able to send some credible signal of quality that will not be replicated by the seller of the low-quality car.

To see how adverse selection can arise in insurance markets, consider the case of automobile insurance. To keep things simple, drivers can be grouped into two classes: those with a high expected value of loss and those with low loss expectancy. If the insurer can distinguish drivers according to their respective loss characteristics, each can be charged a premium that reflects his or her expected value of loss. Thus, insurers may use observable characteristics, such as automobile type, location, or age, to distinguish different risk groups of automobile policies. In this way, the insurer will have many categories of policyholders, each category containing drivers that are similar in observable features. But even after this classification there may still be considerable variation within each class; not all 22-year-old males driving sedans in Philadelphia have the same loss potential. The skill levels and behavioral characteristics can vary substantially. Thus, there will be an effective subsidy from low-risk drivers to high-risk drivers within each class. This subsidy can be destabilize the insurance market and reduce insurance supply, as shown below.

In Figure 3–3 we consider a category of drivers who are similarly classified on the basis of observable characteristics. However, there is hidden variation in loss potential, some drivers being worse than average and others better than average. We will simply call these "high"- and "low"-risk drivers. Each insured starts with a wealth level of $125, but a loss can reduce the wealth to $25. The groups differ in the probability of loss. For the high-risk group, the probability of loss is 0.75, resulting in an expected loss of $75. For the low-risk group, the probability loss is 0.25, resulting in an expected loss of $25. If the insurer can distinguish between

F I G U R E   3–3

Adverse Selection

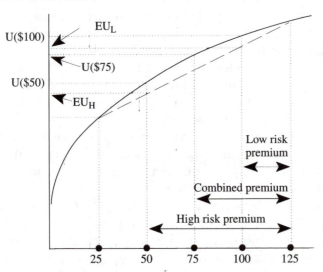

the two groups, respective competitive premiums of $75 and $25 can be charged (ignoring transaction costs). With premiums set at the expected value of loss for each insured, the Bernoulli principle asserts that each would fully insure. For the low-risk group, the utility of insuring and having wealth of $100 with certainty (that is $U(\$100)$) is higher than the expected utility of not insuring EU_L. Thus:

$$U(\$100) > EU_L = (0.75)U(\$125) + (0.25)U(\$25)$$

and, for the high-risk group:

$$U(\$50) > EU_H = (0.25)U(\$125) + (0.75)U(\$25)$$

The respective positions are shown on the vertical axis of Figure 3–3.

Now suppose that the insurer is unable to distinguish between high- and low-risk drivers. If there are equal numbers in each group, the break-even premium will be $50. However, at this premium the low-risk group will not insure because the utility of not insuring, EU_L, is greater than the utility of insuring and having a wealth level of $75 for certain, that is:

$$EU_L > U(\$75)$$

Conversely, the high-risk group will find insurance to be a bargain and will choose to insure, that is:

$$U(\$75) > EU_H$$

Consequently, the portfolio composition will change as low-risk drivers cancel their policies, leaving a portfolio of high-risk drivers (each having an expected cost of $75) and an inadequate premium.

In practice, there may be several risk groups, and coverage may be arranged on a partial basis. The insurer that averages premiums over a number of risk groups will find that it tends to lose the good risks as they cancel or reduce their coverage. The resulting change in the composition of the portfolio will cause the average premium to be inadequate, forcing the insurer to raise the premium. This aggravates the flight of low-risk drivers, and so the process continues until only bad risks are left. This process is usually attributed to information deficiency on the part of the insurer, but the same effect can result from regulation designed to

prevent insurers from using classification variables that are polit-
ically sensitive, such as sex or race (see Dahlby, 1983; Crocker and
Snow 1986; and Hoy, 1989).

Competition between insurers may help reduce problems of
adverse selection. Information on loss expectancies of individual
drivers is of economic value to an insurer. Armed with such information, an insurer can selectively attract low-risk drivers from
a rival that is unable to discriminate simply by offering a lower
price and admitting only low-risk drivers. Thus, competition will
induce insurers to seek and compile information that will enable
them to use premium structures that discriminate to some extent
between risk groups. Of course, information will never be perfect,
and adverse selection will never disappear. But in an actively competitive market, adverse selection will be reduced to a level that
reflects the cost of information.

The Rothschild–Stiglitz Model

While competition may stimulate insurers to use information that
is observable to classify insureds, there will always be some information asymmetry between insureds and insurers. Insofar as
insureds are better informed, the problems of adverse selection
remain. But there are ways in which insureds can be induced to
reveal private information in a credible way. The principle works
as follows. Suppose I, the insurer, offer a pair of contract to an
individual without knowing whether that person is a high or low
risk. The person receiving this offer, however, does know his or
her risk type. Now the contracts are designed such that one contract would only be appealing to those who knew they were a low
risk and the other contract would be appealing to those who knew
they were a high risk. The person receiving such an offer will
select according to his or her private information about his or her
loss type. Accordingly, if he or she chooses the contract that would
only be appealing to high (low) risks, I can safely conclude that
he or she is indeed a high (low) risk. By making a contract choice,
the person reveals his or her hidden identity. It works because of
the clever design of the two contracts. This is essentially the Rothschild–Stiglitz (R/S) model. This concept is known as *self selection*.
By their own choices, the different types will separate into their
respective groups.

Consider Figure 3–4. The axes show the wealth of the individual under two different circumstances: first if he or she does not have a loss and second if he or she has loss. A "loss" in this context means some event that would affect the individual's net worth. The 45° line traces out equal values on both axes. On this line, the person's wealth is unaffected by whether a loss occurs; it can only mean that the person made some arrangement to protect himself or herself from the financial impact of the event. In other words, the person is fully insured, or fully hedged. Call the 45° line the "full insurance line." Point A is the starting position. This is the wealth combination if no insurance is purchased, so that, at A, wealth is much higher if the person has no loss than if a loss is suffered. The difference in wealth on the two axes is the size of the loss. Now look at line A–P_L. This line shows the opportunities for buying insurance at a premium rate that is equal to the expected value of loss for the low-risk type. If we ignore transaction costs, and insurers could sell only to low risks at this price, the insurers would break even. For example, if the low risk had a probability p_L of suffering a loss of size D and insures for a percentage α of the loss, the premium would be $\alpha\,p_L\,D$. The line shows the wealth combinations after different levels of insurance

F I G U R E   3–4

Rothschild–Stiglitz Separating Equilibrium

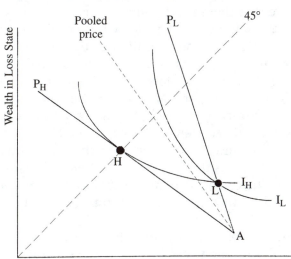

are bought. Thus, if α is one, there is full insurance and the person is on the full insurance line. The reduction in wealth in the no-loss state is simply the premium paid, and the increase in wealth in the loss state is the insurance payout net of the premium. Similarly, the line $A–P_H$ shows the insurance possibilities based on a high-risk premium. This line is much shallower, signifying that a higher premium must be paid to approach the 45° line.

We know from Chapter 2 that if anyone is offered an insurance contract in which the premium equals the expected loss, they would fully insure. If high-risk types could be identified and offered insurance at premium rate $A–P_H$, they would fully insure and buy contract labeled H. This is shown by the point of tangency of the price line and the high-risk indifference curve I_H. Similarly, if low risks could be identified and offered a policy priced according to their risk level, they would buy a contract at the point where the 45° line intersects $A–P_L$. Of course, these contracts cannot be offered, since the types cannot be identified.

Suppose the insurer offers everyone a choice between contract H and L. Notice H is full insurance at the high-risk price and L is partial insurance at the low-risk price. Who would buy which contract? The high-risk type is indifferent; both contracts are on the same high-risk indifference curve, I_H. If contract L is defined as marginally below this indifference curve, then the high risk will prefer contract H. Now the low-risk type will have indifference curves of different slope. The low risk, knowing his or her risk type, therefore that there is a smaller probability of having a loss than the high-risk type, will be less wiling to give up money in the no-loss state to gain compensation in the loss state. This implies that, at any point in the diagram, the low-risk indifference curves will be steeper. I_L is a low-risk indifference curve through the point L, which is steeper than I_H at point L. The curve I_L passes to the right of contract H, implying that the low risk strictly prefers contract L to contract H. Here is the separation. The high risk will choose contract H and the low risk will choose contract L. They each reveal themselves by their contract choices. This is a *separating equilibrium* in which there are no cross subsidies between the risk types; each is paying a price appropriate to his or her risk type.

Despite the separating equilibrium shown, adverse selection is not resolved without a cost. To derive the separation, low risks must choose less than full insurance to signal that they are not high-risk types. Low risks must therefore sacrifice some desired insurance protection in order to avoid being pooled with, or misclassified as, high-risk types. The separation works because the cost of giving up some insurance protection is lower for low risks because they know they are less likely to need the insurance protection than the high risks.

The Rothschild–Stiglitz model was very influential in changing idea about adverse selection, but it is not without problems. One criticism is that there may be no equilibrium. However, the work was followed by many other studies that refined and extended the original model. Some of these studies changed the notion of equilibrium, and this is discussed briefly in the Appendix. Another limitation was that the model assumed that the parties trade just once and then go their separate ways. Accordingly, multiperiod models of adverse selection were then developed.

Multiperiod Contracts and Adverse Selection

The Rothschild–Stiglitz model and others discussed in the Appendix are single-period models. The problem is set up as though insurance is traded just once and then the parties go their separate ways. This may be suitable for some markets, such as life insurance, but for other situations the parties can and do do repeated business over many years. This multiperiod setting offers other possibilities for resolving adverse selection. We will not go into the various models in detail but will draw out one or two of the interesting possibilities.

There is a problem of trying to take a single-period model, such as Rothschild–Stiglitz, and applying it at a situation in which contracts are written in successive periods. If a Rothschild–Stiglitz menu of policies is offered in the first period, people can choose which contract to take. If all the low risks take the low-priced partial insurance policy and all the high risks take the full-insurance high-priced one, then each has revealed his or her type at the beginning of the first period. When the second period starts, insurers will know exactly who is who and will simply offer everyone an appropriately priced full coverage policy. But then high risks might anticipate that if they choose the policy designed for low risks in the first period, they will be mistaken for low risks in the second period and offered full insurance at a low price. Thus, the Rothschild–Stiglitz approach may not make sense.

A series of papers, including Kunreuther and Pauly (1985), Cooper and Hayes (1987), Hosios and Peters (1989), Doherty and Dionne (1994), and Nilssen (1990), have examined such multiperiod insurance situations. Perhaps the most interesting thing to emerge is the ability to lower the costs of adverse selection by conditioning the terms of a contract in one period (the price and level of insurance coverage) on the loss experience in prior periods. This *experience rating* can be used in several ways.

For example, suppose that long-term contracts can be written that are binding on both parties. At the beginning one can ask people their type and set a contract for each person priced as though he or she answered truthfully. Over time, people will accumulate records of loss experience. After a period, one can ascertain, at a given level of confidence, whether the loss experience is compatible with what type the person initially said he or she was. For example, someone who claims to be a low-risk driver and has five accidents in four years has little credibility. One with no accidents in a four-year period has a record that is consistent with his or her claimed type. If the accident record is not consistent (say worse), then the individual is not only reclassified as a high risk but also given a severe premium penalty. This additional penalty is calculated such that it will more than offset any expected gain to a high risk from initially lying about risk type. The deterrent penalty works like a criminal punishment: you may be better off for a while lying, but you will ultimately be much worse off.

Another way of using experience rating is to include it as part of a menu. An insurer offers all policyholders a choice of two plans. The first plan is a sequence of policies over successive periods that will all have a relatively high price (appropriate to high risks), but the premium will not be adjusted according to loss experience. The second plan starts with an even higher premium but is experience-rated. The high initial premium will drop drastically in the future if the policyholder has few or no losses. Any policyholder can choose either plan, and the insurer again does not know who is of which type. Think it through from the viewpoint of each type. If you know you are high risk, the first plan is better (no use starting with an even higher premium if you believe that you are likely to have accidents and the premium is therefore unlikely to drop). If you are low risk, you are willing to start with a high premium, knowing that your low risk type will most likely be revealed in your accident record and the premium will then drop drastically. This system can work without committing the policyholders to a long-term contractual relationship, since it focuses on rewards rather than punishments.

CONCLUSION

To set the background for upcoming analysis, the economic concepts introduced this chapter, moral hazard and adverse selection, were used to illustrate two important issues that arise in insurance markets and constrain the supply of insurance services. Moral hazard refers to the adverse incentives that insurance may convey to the insured to reduce the prospect of future loss. This becomes a problem if the insurer is unable to monitor the insured behavior. Similar information problems may lead to adverse selection. If the insurer is unable to correctly discriminate between insureds in its pricing structure, there will be an effective subsidy to higher risks. This will lead to disproportionately high demand from high-risk groups, causing a deterioration in the risk composition of the insurer's portfolio and escalating loss experience.

Insofar as moral hazard and adverse selection attach to insurance, they are an important part of the risk management problem. Other factors being equal, they increase the cost of insurance and create a bias in favor of alternative methods of handling risk. But these are special cases of more general economic problems that afflict many other activities. As we will see later, the principal–agent problem complicates relationships between shareholders and creditors and between owners and managers of firms. These complications are important to any explanation of why risk is a problem to firms and will be studied in some detail in Chapter 7 and later. Moreover, it is the need to address these particular types of problems that helps us to identify alternative risk management strategies.

REFERENCES

Akerlof, George. 1970. "The Market for Lemons: Quality Uncertainty and the Market Mechanism." *Quarterly Journal of Economics* 84:488–500.

Arnot, Richard. 1992. "Moral Hazard in Competitive Insurance Markets." In *Contributions to Insurance Economics*, ed. Georges Dionne. Boston: Kluwer Academic Publishers.

Arnott, Richard, and Joseph Stiglitz. 1988. "The Basic Analytics of Moral Hazard." *Scandinavian Actuarial Journal* 90:383–415.

Bond, Eric W., and Keith Crocker. 1991. "Smoking, Skydiving and Knitting." *Journal of Political Economy* 99:177–200.

Cooper, Russell, and Beth Hayes. 1987. "Multi Period Insurance Policies." *Journal of Industrial Organization* 5:211–31.

Crocker, Keith, and Arthur Snow. 1986. "The Efficiency Effects of Categorical Discrimination in the Insurance Industry." *Journal of Political Economy* 94: 321–44.

Dahlby, D. B. 1983. "Adverse Selection and Statistical Discrimination." *Journal of Public Economics* 20:121–130.

Dionne, Georges, and Neil Doherty. 1992. "Adverse Selection in Insurance Markets: A Selective Survey." In *Contributions to Insurance Economics*, ed. Georges Dionne. Boston: Kluwer Academic Publishers.

———. 1994. "Adverse Selection, Commitment and Renegotiation: Extension to Evidence from Insurance Markets." *Journal of Political Economy* 102:209–35.

Dionne, Georges, and P. Lassere. 1988. "Dealing with Moral Hazard and Adverse Selection Simultaneously." Working Paper, University of Montreal.

Grossman, Sanford, and Oliver Hart. 1983. "An Analysis of the Principal Agent Problem." *Econometrica* 1:7–45.

Hosios, A., and M. Peters. 1989. "Repeated Insurance Contracts with Adverse Selection and Limited Commitment." *Quarterly Journal of Economics* 2:229–54.

Hoy, Michael. 1989. "The Value of Screening Mechanisms under Alternative Insurance Possibilities." *Journal of Public Economics* 39:177–206.

Kunreuther, H., and M. Pauly. 1985. "Market Equilibrium with Private Knowledge: An Insurance Example." *Journal of Public Economics* 26:269–88.

Lambert, R. 1983. "Long Term Contracts and Moral Hazard." *Bell Journal of Economics* 8:441–52.

Marshall, J. M., 1976. "Moral Hazard." *American Economic Review* 66:880–90.

Nilssen, T. 1990. "Consumer Lock-in with Asymmetric Information." Working paper, Norwegion School of Economics and Business.

Pueltz, Robert, and Arthur Snow. 1994. "Evidence on Adverse Selection: Equilibrium Signaling and Cross-Subsidization in the Insurance Market." *Journal of Political Economy* 102:236–57.

Rubinstein, A., and M. E. Yaari. 1983. "Repeated Insurance Contracts and Moral Hazard." *Journal of Economic Theory*, 30:74–97.

Shavell, S. 1979. "On Moral Hazard and Insurance." *Quarterly Journal of Economics* 93:541–62.

Winter, Ralph. 1992. "Moral Hazard and Insurance Contracts." In *Contributions to Insurance Economics*, ed. Georges Dionne. Boston: Kluwer Academic Publishers.

A P P E N D I X

SOME PROBLEMS WITH THE ROTHSCHILD–STIGLITZ MODEL

Unfortunately, the Rothschild–Stiglitz model does not always produce a separating equilibrium. This problem can be shown in Figure 3–5, which reproduces some of the essentials from Figure 3–4 but also has a "pooled price" line. Suppose that a contract could be offered to everyone (high and low risk) that would just break even for the insurer. The pooled price would obviously be somewhere between the high and low price lines; just where in this space would depend on the relative numbers of high and low risk. For example, with equal numbers of high and low risks, the pooled price would be halfway between the high and low price lines. In this way, the deficit to the insurer on each high-risk policy would be covered by an equal subsidy from the low-risk policy. With more high than low risks, the pooled price would have to

F I G U R E   3–5

Rothschild–Stiglitz—No Equilibrium

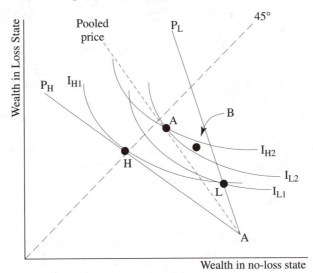

extract large subsidies from each of the few low risks to cover the small deficits to the insurer on each of the many high-risk policies. Thus, the pooled price would lie closer to the high-risk price line.

Figure 3–5 depicts a situation where there is a sufficiently large proportion of low risks that the low risk indifference curve, I_{L1}, intersects the pooled price line. In this situation a second insurer could come along and offer a policy such as A that would be preferred by both types to a choice from the menu of H and L; high risks prefer A to H and low risks prefer A to L. Thus, the menu of H and L would not survive in a competitive market. It would seem that the market would settle down to a *pooled equilibrium* in which both types bought a contract such as A. But this situation is not stable. Imagine that a third insurer now offers a single contract such as B. This is situated between the indifference curves I_{H2} and I_{L2}. Notice that low risks will prefer B to A but that high risks will prefer A to B. Thus, all low risks would cancel their A policy and buy B from the rival insurer. B is profitable because it attracts only low risks but is priced higher than the fair low risk price P_L. But the second insurer stuck with A is now in trouble. The contract A was priced to break even *if* it was bought by both high and low types. But only highs are left, and the second insurer will lose money and withdraw the coverage. Without the choice to buy A, the low risks will now flock to B, which will not become unprofitable if bought by both types, since it lies above the pooled price line (indicating that it is priced below the pooled break-even price). Thus, the third insurer is now losing money and *there is no equilibrium.*

Let us summarize the messages coming out of this analysis. Whether a separating equilibrium exists or not depends on the relative numbers of high and low risks. Unless there are too many low risks, a separating equilibrium can exist in which low risks select partial coverage at a low price and high risks take full coverage at a high price. Low risks signal their type by accepting a policy with partial coverage. Knowing their type, high risks are not willing to sacrifice some insurance protection to obtain the lower price, since they know there is a high probability they will have a loss and need the coverage.

OTHER ADVERSE SELECTION MODELS

The main insight of Rothschild and Stiglitz was that hidden information can be signaled by offering a contract choice in which the contracts will have different appeal to those with different (but hidden) characteristics. Later models have refined the nature of the equilibrium or have examined different signals. In the 1980s attention was focused on different types of equilibrium. Perhaps the most influential approach was that coming from the separate works of Wilson, Spence, and Miyazaki. Riley formulated an equilibrium concept in which only contracts that would at least break even, after other firms' anticipated reactions to the introduction of these contracts, would remain. With this equilibrium, Spence and Miyazaki showed that a separating equilibrium always existed but might require that some subsidy be paid from low to high risks. Figure 3–6 illustrates their model. Policies H and L are the Rothschild–Stiglitz equilibrium. These policies separately break even for an insurer, and thus an insurer offering both policies would obviously break even. Policies H^* and L^* are another pair, with H^* offering full insurance and L^* offering partial coverage but over which high risks are indifferent. This pair differs from H and L in that H^* is cheaper than H (makes a loss for the insurer) but L^* is more expensive than L (and makes a profit for the insurer). However the combination of H^* and L^* breaks even. The

F I G U R E   3–6

Wilson-Miyazaki-Spence Equilibrium

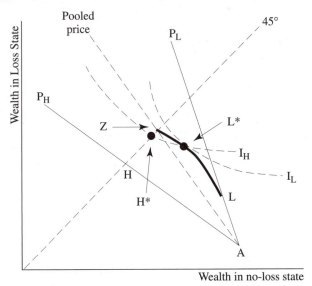

Wealth in no-loss state

subsidy on L^* just covers the deficit on H^*. The line LZ denotes pairs of contract matching this joint break-even criterion. For any point on LZ there is a policy L', with a corresponding full insurance policy H', such that high risks are indifferent between H' and L' and the pair of policies breaks even for the insurer. H^* and L^* is the pair of such policies that offers highest utility to low risks, which satisfies the self-selection constraint. In this equilibrium, both types might be better off than under Rothschild–Stiglitz, but at least we are assured that an equilibrium exists. Notice that the low risks are signaling their type now by their willingness to accept partial insurance and to pay a subsidy to the high risks. There is still a price to resolve adverse selection, and this price is borne by the low risks.

CHAPTER 4

Portfolio Theory and Risk Management

The essence of portfolio theory is captured in such well-known sayings as "Don't put all your eggs in one basket" and "You will gain on the swings what you lose on the roundabouts." The intuitive logic of these statements warns us not to bet all our money on one horse or purchase a single stock with all our capital. It tells us that single-engined aircraft are inherently more dangerous than multi-engined aircraft and informs us that we should take a large (random) sample if we wish to measure popular support for competing presidential nominees. Diversification, it seems, helps us to avoid, or at least minimize, the probability of extreme outcomes. The same mechanism helps to explain how insurance functions and can be put to work to identify strategies for corporate risk management. More formally, these mechanisms have been analyzed under the heading of portfolio theory.

The growth and evolution of portfolio theory can be illustrated in three subject areas. In *statistics* the properties of samples and their relationship to the population from which they were drawn have been intensively studied. The properties of the sample, which is simply a portfolio of observations drawn from a parent population, enable us to make statements about the population and evaluate the degree of confidence we can place in such statements. For example, if we choose a suitably large sample of female Americans in a random fashion, not only can we estimate the average height of all female Americans, but we can also place a confidence interval around our estimate. This permits us to make a statement such as "The estimated average height of American females is 5 feet 4 inches plus or minus inches at the 95% confidence level." Subject to proper sampling techniques, the larger the sample, the more we can narrow the range of error. More loosely speaking, the larger the portfolio, the more we cut down the risk of being wrong.

A second area in which portfolio theory has been developed and successfully put to work is *security analysis*. The rate of return on securities of all kinds is rarely, if ever, free of risk. In the case of common stocks, the variance of the return is usually fairly large. Thus, it is not uncommon for a stock to lose or gain a large proportion of its initial value over a short period. The investment risk can be partially controlled by a number of securities. Over a given period, some security prices may fall while others rise. Even this diversified stock portfolio can suffer a large loss in value if there is common movement in stock prices. Most stocks do tend to track movements in a representative price index (e.g., the Dow Jones Index or the Standard & Poors Index) to a greater or lesser degree, and this element of risk is not amenable to simple diversification. The common movement or correlation between such variables as stock prices is of concern to us and will be considered in some detail presently. Moreover, the analysis of security markets is also important to our treatment of risk management. Investor behavior determines the value of a firm. Since our financial approach to risk management requires that decisions be appraised in terms of their contribution to the value of a firm, we must set our decision criteria with reference to investor behavior.

The third area that has provided a fertile field for the application of portfolio theory is *actuarial science*. Its roots lie in the study of mortality rates, typically classified by age and sex groupings of the population. For large samples of individuals, such as portfolios of insureds underwritten by life insurance companies, the actual mortality rates usually show little deviation from the expected rates calculated from large banks of mortality data. While the insurance company knows little of the time and place of death for any individual, its prediction of average mortality is fairly accurate. Consequently, it can budget for claims liabilities with reasonable confidence. The life insurer has diversified and has accordingly reduced risk. More recently, attention has been paid to the portfolio properties of other forms of insurance, and a sophisticated branch of mathematics, risk theory, has been developed. The initial focus of risk theory was on the probability (or risk) that aggregate claims liability will exceed the insurer's reserves. Risk theory now encompasses a wider study of the risk properties of a diversified insurance portfolio.

The study of diversification within an insurance portfolio provides a useful starting point for our analysis of portfolio theory in risk management. However, the terms of reference of risk management go beyond the study of insurance. The same basic relationships that explain risk spreading in an insurance fund can be used to show how the individual exposure units under a corporate umbrella combine to form the aggregate loss distribution for the firm. Knowledge of the properties of the corporate portfolio of risk exposures is essential to the formation of proper risk management strategy.

DESCRIPTION OF AN INSURANCE PORTFOLIO

In an insurance fund the basic units that are insured are usually called "exposure units." These are not synonymous with the policies in an insurance portfolio. A policy might provide insurance coverage on several automobiles, but for practical purposes each automobile is a unit of coverage. Each vehicle is insured along with many other vehicles, and each is assumed to introduce its own risk properties to the portfolio. It would be convenient to define exposure units as independently exposed to the prospects of damage or loss by the perils covered. Because each is independent of the other, it may be introduced to the portfolio with predictable and acceptable risk effects. However, the assumption of independence is too restrictive. Instead, we will think of the exposure units as being separately exposed to the possibility of loss or damage. Thus, individual houses may be considered exposure units within a homeowners' insurance portfolio. However, if two homes are condominiums separated by a non-fireproof party wall, it may be convenient to consider these as a single risk from a fire insurance viewpoint, since a single fire could easily destroy both homes. A home a block or two away may be considered as a different exposure unit, even though common factors could jointly affect the probability of loss in each (examples are a local arsonist, local weather conditions, construction hazards since both were erected by the same contractor, etc.). The relevant criterion is the degree of independence, although no hard and fast rule can be applied.

Each exposure unit insured by an insurance company represents a liability of the insurer for potential claims that may arise. At the inception of the policy, the value of this liability is not known, but over time its value will be revealed. For most policies the eventual liability turns out to be zero because no loss arises and therefore no claim is filed. However, for some policies a loss does arise, and the insurer will be faced with a set of claims that will vary in size according to the intensity with which the peril struck, the inherent protection, the value at risk, etc. If we include the "zero" cases, we can represent the final set of outcomes for the insurer having "n" exposure units as:

$$L_1 \; ; L_2 \; ; L_3 \ldots L_n$$

where $L_i \geq 0$ is the revealed liability of the insurer under exposure unit i. The total liability of the insurer is therefore:

$$L = L_1 + L_2 + L_3 + \cdots + L_n = \sum_{i=1}^{n} L_i$$

For our purposes, it is useful to think of the insurer's liability on a per risk basis. This is determined by dividing L by the number of exposure units n:

$$\frac{L}{n} = \frac{1}{n} \sum_{i=1}^{n} L_i$$

This will be called the mean or average loss, and we will refer to the distribution of average loss. Most policies run for a year, but the value of L may not be known for some considerable time after the expiration of the policies. Liability claims in particular can take an extremely long time to settle, and it may be many years before

F I G U R E   4–1

Individual and Aggregate Distributions

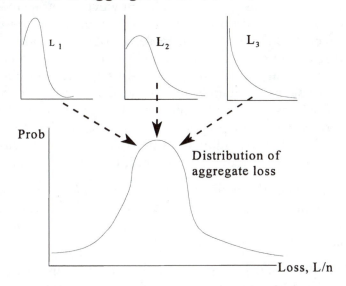

final values are known.[1] At the time of underwriting the policies, the insurer knows none of the outcomes L_i. Each liability is a random variable that may assume one of a range of values.[2]

The professional interest of the insurer focuses on the properties of the variable L/n. The component values L_i may be of intense interest to the policyholders, but the interest of the insurer arises solely from the insurance contract. The financial performance of the insurer rests on the distribution of average claim payments. However, the distribution of L/n is determined by the distributions of L_i. Schematically, this interdependence may be represented as shown in Figure 4–1. The exposure units are represented on the top row by a set of probability distributions from

1. Recent litigation on asbestos claims suggests that policies written 30 or more years ago may still carry liabilities for cases of asbestos-related disease that are currently being diagnosed.
2. An alternative notation is to use tildes, ˜, to denote random variables. Since most of the discussion in this book relates to random variables, we can conveniently omit the tilde, taking care to point out particular cases in which we refer to a realized value from a random distribution.

which the values L_1, L_2, . . . , L_n will eventually be revealed. The probability distribution for losses on individual exposure units will generally be skewed to the right. However, their shapes may differ considerably according to size, value, degree of peril, and related factors. In combination, these distributions form the average distribution L/n, as shown by the arrows. The process of aggregation accomplishes one very interesting and useful result if the individual exposure units are statistically independent of each other. We will assume for the moment that this condition strictly holds. The very useful property that emerges is that the distribution of the mean loss value will approach a normal distribution. The result is stated by the Central Limit theorem, which states:

The distribution of the mean value of a set of n *independent and identically distributed random variables each having mean* μ *and variance* σ^2 *approaches a normal distribution with mean* μ *and variance* $\sigma^2/$n *as* n *tends toward infinity.*

To apply this theorem to insurance, consider an insurer writing n automobile policies in some homogeneous rating category, such as male urban drivers over 25. These policies can be viewed as a sample of the total population of drivers in this category, the others being insured by other companies or self-insuring. We assume that the risks are sufficiently similar that they can be seen as identically distributed, each having the same expected loss $E(L_i)$ and the same variance $\sigma^2(L_i)$. Our task is to find out what happens to the riskiness of the insurer's portfolio as the insurer increases the number of risks it insures. To undertake this task we consider two different definitions of risk:

1. The variance or standard deviation of the distribution of $\Sigma L_i/n$. This is a conventional measure of the spread of the distribution.
2. The probability that $\Sigma L_i/n$ exceeds some critical value. The critical value can be set at the level of the insurer's total reserves plus surplus averaged over all policies. If average losses turn out to be below this value, the insurer is able to discharge its claims liabilities. However, should average losses exceed this value, the firm will fail in its obligations and will be insolvent. The probability that such an eventuality will arise is known

as the *probability of ruin* and is considered to be an important risk measure for the insurer.

In order to examine how these risk measures are affected by the size of the insurance fund, it is necessary to define the relationships between the individual loss distribution and the average distribution. Consider a portfolio formed just be adding two random variables, L_1 and L_2. The aggregate distribution will have the following properties:

$$E(L) = E(L_1) + E(L_2)$$

and

$$\sigma^2(L) = \sigma_1^2 + \sigma_2^2 + 2\sigma_{1,2}$$

where:

$\sigma^2(L) =$ the variance of the portfolio L
$\sigma_1^2 =$ the variance of L_i
$\sigma_{1,2} =$ the covariance of L_1 and L_2

Although variance is useful, the more useful summary description of risk is standard deviation, which is simply the square root of the variance:

$$\sigma(L) = \sqrt{\sigma^2(L)}$$

Covariance is a measure of the common variations between L_1 and L_2 and is defined by

$$\Sigma p_i(L_{1i} - E(L_1))(L_{2i} - E(L_2))$$

where p_i is the probability of the joint occurrence of L_1 and L_2.

Examination of covariance reveals that it looks very much like the formula for variance, which is

$$\Sigma p_i(L_{1i} - E(L_1))(L_{1i} - E(L_1)) = \Sigma p_i(L_{1i} - E(L_1))^2$$

In effect, variance is simply covariance of one variable with itself.

If there are more than two variables, the formulas for mean and variance are

$$E(L) = E(L_1) + E(L_2) + E(L_3) + \cdots + E(L_n) = \sum_i E(L_i)$$

and

$$\sigma^2(L) = \sigma_1{}^2 + \sigma_2{}^2 + \sigma_3{}^2 + \cdots + \sigma_n{}^2 + \cdots$$

$$+ 2\sigma_{1,2} + 2\sigma_{1,3} + \cdots = \sum_{i=1}^{n} \sigma_i^2 + \sum_i \sum_{j \neq i} \sigma_{i,j}$$

Or first task is to calculate the risk in a portfolio of identically distributed independent exposure units. Because the risks are independent, the covariances are equal to zero. The variance of the distribution of average loss is therefore

$$\sigma^2\left(\frac{L}{n}\right) = \text{var}\left(\frac{L_1 + L_2 + L_3 + \cdots + L_n}{n}\right)$$

$$= \text{var}\left(\frac{L_1}{n}\right) + \text{var}\left(\frac{L_2}{n}\right) + \cdots + \text{var}\left(\frac{L_n}{n}\right)$$

$$= \sigma^2\left(\frac{L_1}{n}\right) + \sigma^2\left(\frac{L_2}{n}\right) + \cdots + \sigma^2\left(\frac{L_n}{n}\right)$$

since the covariances are zero. Now,

$$\sigma^1\left(\frac{L_i}{n}\right) = \sum p_i \left(\frac{1}{n} L_i - \frac{1}{n} E(L_i)\right)^2$$

$$= \frac{1}{n^2} \sum p_i \, (L_1 - E(L_i)^2 = \frac{\sigma_i^2}{n^2}$$

Thus,

$$\sigma^2\left(\frac{L}{n}\right) = \frac{1}{n^2} \, (\sigma^2 \, (L_1) + \sigma^2(L_2) + \cdots + \sigma^2(L_n))$$

Because all risks are identically distributed, they all have the same variance, that is,

$$\sigma_1^2 = \sigma_2^2 = \cdots = \sigma_n^2$$

Therefore:

$$\sigma^2\left(\frac{L}{n}\right) = \frac{1}{n^2} \, n\sigma_i^2 = \frac{\sigma_i^2}{n}$$

This is the result stated by the Central Limit theorem.

To put some meat on these bones, let our automobile portfolio with male urban drivers over 25 be made up of exposure units that each have an expected loss of $500 and a standard deviation of $800. The variance of each unit is $\sigma_i^2 = (\$800)^2 =$

T A B L E   4-1

Risk Reduction in Portfolios of Independent Risks

n	$\sigma^2(L/n)$	$\sigma(L/n)$
1	640,000	800
10	64,000	253
100	6,400	80
1000	640	25
10,000	64	8
∞	0	0

$640,000. The variances and standard deviations of the insurer's liability per exposure unit are given in Table 4–1. In general, the effect of portfolio size on portfolio risk is shown in Figure 4–2. As n gets larger and larger, the risk of average loss gets smaller and smaller, eventually approaching zero.

Diversification does benefit the insurer because it reduces risk. However, a word of caution is needed. It is the measure of risk per policy that is reduced. The standard deviation of the absolute dollar liability of the insurer increases. As a simple exercise, consider an increase in size of the insurer's portfolio from 100 to

F I G U R E   4-2

Portfoio Risk Reduction

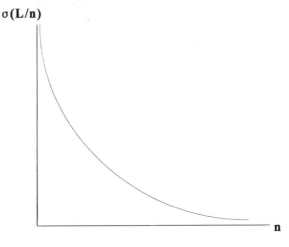

$\sigma(L/n)$

n

1000 exposure units. The standard deviations of absolute dollar liability before and after the increase in portfolio size are, respectively,

$$\sigma_p = \sqrt{100(800)^2} = 8000 \qquad \text{when } n = 100$$

$$\sigma_p = \sqrt{1000(800)^2} = 25{,}298 \qquad \text{when } n = 1000$$

However, it will be noticed that the standard deviation has increased at a much smaller proportionate rate (just over 3 times) than has the portfolio size (10 times). This less than proportionate increase in aggregate total risk explains why the riskiness per policy falls.

Our result on diversification can be summarized graphically. Figure 4–3 shows possible distributions of L/n at different portfolio sizes As n increases, not only does the distribution exhibit a smaller standard deviation, but it becomes more symmetrical, approaching a normal distribution. This last feature becomes important for our examination of the probability of ruin. Figure 4–3 reveals that as n increases, the distribution of L/n huddles closer

FIGURE   4–3

The Law of Large Numbers

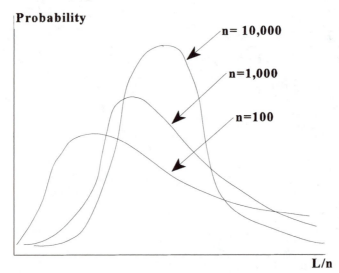

and closer around the mean value μ. This property is known as the *law of large numbers*.

The second measure of riskiness we wish to examine is the probability that the distribution of the average loss will exceed the financial resources of the insurer. This is the so-called *probability of ruin*. When the insurer receives the premium on a policy, it is allocated to a reserve fund for unearned premiums (after deduction of expenses). Funds in this reserve are held to match liabilities developing on the maturing policies. At the end of the accounting period, funds may be reallocated to other reserve funds, such as outstanding claims and claims incurred but not reported. Procedures also govern the allocation of any residual values to surplus, which can be either distributed to shareholders or retained. Thus, an insurer can meet aggregate claims up to the total value of its reserves plus surplus. If this total value is denoted L^*, the insurer will be able to pay a maximum of L^*/n per policy. We wish to know the probability that the average claims liability will exceed L^*/n per policy. This is the probability of ruin. Figure 4–3 depicts such a critical value. The probability of ruin is depicted by the area of the tail to the right of L^*/n. Apparently, this is systematically related to the size of the portfolio, although it behooves us to demonstrate this effect.

As a rule of thumb, when a portfolio is formed of more than 30 independent random variables, the distribution of the mean value is considered to be sufficiently close to normal that statistical tests based on the normal distribution can be used. The normal distribution has the convenient property that the total probability (or area under the curve) can be segmented symmetrically if we know the mean and the standard deviation. We know, for example, that the probability that a randomly selected value will be above $\mu_p + \sigma_p$ (that is, one standard deviation above the mean) is 0.1587, as shown in Figure 4–4. Similarly, the probability that a randomly selected value will be below $\mu_p - \sigma_p$ (one standard deviation below the mean) is also 0.1587, since the distribution is symmetric. Consequently, there is a $1 - 0.1587 - 0.1587 = 0.6826$ probability that a randomly selected value will lie within the range of one standard deviation on either side of the mean. We can work out the probabilities in any other segments, and they are described in terms of multiples of standard deviations from the mean. Thus,

F I G U R E   4–4

The Normal Distribution

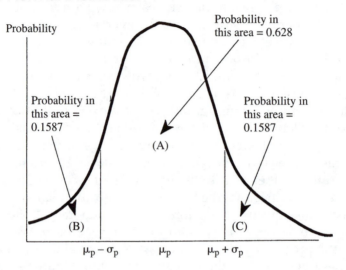

the probability that a randomly selected value is greater than (or less than) μ plus some multiple of σ is as follows:

Probability that $L > \mu + (1.5)\sigma_p = 0.0668$

$$\mu + (1.96)\sigma_p = 0.025$$

$$\mu + (2.33)\sigma_p = 0.01 \quad \text{and so forth}$$

These and other values are conveniently tabulated in z tables, which are available in many statistics textbooks. A segment of such a table is reproduced at the end of this text. Given this pattern, and the tendency of the portfolio toward a normal distribution, we can easily calculate the probability that the insurer's average claim liability exceeds the ruin value L^*/n simply by defining this value as a multiple of z standard deviations from the mean. The value L^*/n will be defined to be z standard deviations above the mean:

$$\frac{L^*}{n} = \mu_p + z\sigma_p$$

or

$$z = \frac{L^*}{n} - \frac{\mu_p}{\sigma_p}$$

Values can now be calculated using the automobile portfolio example considered earlier. Recall that each exposure unit had an expected value of $500 and a standard deviation of $800. The expected loss per policy is:

$$\mu_p = E\left(\frac{L}{n}\right) = \frac{E(L_1) + E(L_2) + \cdots + EL_{(n)}}{n} = \frac{n(500)}{n} = 500$$

The portfolio standard deviation has already been calculated:

$$\sigma_p = \sigma\left(\frac{L}{n}\right) = \frac{\sigma_i}{\sqrt{n}} = \frac{800}{\sqrt{n}}$$

Substituting these values into the equation for z gives

$$z = \frac{(L^*/n) - 500}{800/\sqrt{n}}$$

Now suppose that the insurer's reserves and surplus permit it to pay up to a maximum of $660 per policy. We have

$$z = \frac{660 - 500}{800/\sqrt{n}} = 0.2\sqrt{n}$$

Thus, if $n = 9$, $z = 0.6$. Reading from the table of z values, the probability that $L/n > L^*/n$ is 0.2743. This value is recorded in Table 4–2 alongside values calculated for other n.

The results in Tables 4–1 and 4–2 confirm the pattern in Figure 4–3 that diversification reduces risk, both in the sense of reducing variance per policy and by reducing the probability of ruin. We will now try to apply these ideas to more complex portfolios.

RISK REDUCTION IN AN INSURANCE PORTFOLIO OF INDEPENDENT, HETEROGENEOUS RISKS

The second type of portfolio preserves the assumption that risks are independent of each other, but relaxes the restriction that all units are homogeneous in the sense of having identical probability

T A B L E   4–2

Ruin Probabilities in Portfolios of Independent Risks

n	z	Probability that $L/n > L^*/n$
1[a]	0.2	0.4207
9[a]	0.6	0.2743
50	1.41	0.0793
100	2.0	0.0228
1000	6.3	negligible
10,000	20.0	neglibible
∞	∞	0

[a] These sample values are too small for reasonable approximation with the normal distribution.

distributions. The heterogeneous portfolios we have in mind here could be made up of policies of different types, such as a mixture of fire, automobile, and liability policies, or of comprise policies of the same type but having different risk levels, such as a fire insurance portfolio drawn from different industries. The portfolio could also combine a firm's exposure to insurable risk, financial risk, and market risk. In order to measure the effects of size on this type of portfolio, it is important to distinguish between two possibilities, one relating solely to the size of the portfolio and the other combining both size and composition effects:

1. Growth of a portfolio might arise without change in the mix of the various types of exposure units. The firm might simply write different types of new policies in the proportions that those policy types represent in the existing portfolio.

2. Conversely, the insurer might grow through acquisition of new policies that are different from existing business. For example, an insurer with a heavy automobile portfolio might acquire another company with a predominantly fire portfolio. Such growth changes the mix of business.

Our main concern is with the effect of size on portfolio risk; thus, we will consider size changes that preserve composition. The combined size and mix effects will be examined presently.

Insurers typically subdivide their insurance portfolios into risk classes that are fairly homogeneous internally. Fire, automobile, marine, and liability policies are primary subdivisions. In turn, these lines are subclassified by insured characteristics relating to hazard level (e.g., by age and sex in life insurance, by industry, protection, and location in fire insurance, or by vehicle type, driver age and sex, location, etc. in automobile insurance). The number of homogeneous categories can be very large, but the purpose is to group units that are *a priori* similar in order to aid the rating and underwriting decision process. For our purposes, let us suppose that there are three categories, labeled R, S, and T. The total number of policies is n, where $n = r + s + t$, and r, s, and t are the numbers of R, S, and T policies, respectively. Within each group, units are identically distributed, having the same mean and variance, and they are subscripted by the group code, for example, $E(L_R)$, $E(L_T)$, σ_S, etc. Let us combine the policies to examine the risk-return characteristics of the portfolio (L/n).

Recalling the calculations of expected value and variance of the distribution of mean loss, we have

$$\mu_p = E\left(\frac{L}{n}\right) = \frac{1}{n} \sum_{t=1}^{n} E(L_i)$$

and, since the covariances are zero,

$$\sigma_p^2 = \sigma^2\left(\frac{L}{n}\right) = \sum_{i=1}^{n} \sigma_i^2 + \sum \sum_{i \neq j} \sigma_{i,j} = \frac{1}{n^2} (r\sigma_R^2 + s\sigma_S^2 + t\sigma_T^2)$$

To put flesh on this skeleton, consider the following portfolio:

R refers to fire policies each with $E(L_R) = 300$ and $\sigma_R = 400$
S refers to automobile policies each with $E(L_S) = 400$ and $\sigma_S = 350$
T refers to liability policies each with $E(L_T) = 200$ and $\sigma_T = 300$

The portfolio includes the following numbers of policies in each category:

$$r = 0.5n; \quad s = 0.3n; \quad t = 0.2n$$

This permits us to examine the effect of growth in n without change in the composition of the component units. Now,

$$\mu_p = E\left(\frac{L}{n}\right) = \frac{0.5n(300) + 0.3n(400) + 0.2n(200)}{n} = 310$$

$$\sigma_p^2 = \frac{1}{n^2}\left(0.5n(400)^2 + 0.3n(350)^2 + 0.2n(300)^2\right)$$

$$= \frac{0.5(400)^2 + 0.3(350)^2 + 0.2(300)^2}{n} = \frac{134{,}750}{n}$$

giving

$$\sigma_p = \sqrt{\frac{134{,}750}{n}} + \frac{367}{\sqrt{n}}$$

The forms of the variance and standard deviation clearly reveal that riskiness of the portfolio will fall in the pattern depicted in Figure 4–2 for the portfolio of homogeneous risks. Futhermore, the standard deviation will tend toward zero as the number of exposure units tends toward infinity. Some values for n and the corresponding variances and standard deviations are shown in Table 4–3.

The reader might experiment with other portfolios that shown different initial compositions. However, caution must be exercised to ensure that the proportionate mixture of units does not change. This will reveal that the law of large numbers continues to apply for all portfolios of independent risk units, regardless of proportionate mix, as long as diversification does not affect the relative composition.

T A B L E   4–3

Risk Reduction: Independent Heterogeneous Risks

n	$\sigma^2(L/n)$	$\sigma(L/n)$
1	134,750	367
10	13,475	116
100	1348	36.7
1000	135	11.6
10,000	14	3.7
∞	0	0

The second measure of risk is the probability of ruin. We can apply this is an identical manner to that shown for homogeneous portfolios. The reason is that the normal approximation continues in view of the independence of the risk units. To illustrate the process, let us assume that the insurer's reserves and surplus permit it to meet claim liabilities up to a limit of $400 per policy. We now have sufficient information to calculate ruin probabilites for different portfolio sizes. Using the formula for z and the previously calculated values for μ_p and σ_p, we have

$$z = \frac{L^*/n - \mu_p}{\sigma_p} = \frac{400 - 310}{\dfrac{367}{\sqrt{n}}} = 0.245\sqrt{n}$$

Values for ruin probabilities at different levels of n are given in Table 4–4.

The ruin probability behaves in a fashion similar to that for the portfolio of independent and homogeneous risks; it diminishes as n increases, approaching zero when n approaches infinity. Combining this with the result for the behavior of standard deviation, diversification achieved by increasing the size of the insurance portfolio reduces portfolio risk. This result is valid if exposure units are independent, regardless of whether the units are identical, as long as the portfolio composition remains unchanged. To see how important this last assumption is, we will consider an

T A B L E   4–4

Ruin Probabilities: Independent Heterogeneous Risks

n	z	Probability that $L/n > L^*/n$
1	0.25	0.4013
9	0.74	0.2296
10	0.77	0.2206
100	2.45	0.0071
1000	7.75	negligible
10,000	24.5	negligible
∞	∞	zero

example in which the portfolio size grows but the composition also changes. Independence is retained in this example.

EXAMPLE: CHANGING PORTFOLIO COMPOSITION

Consider an initial portfolio of say, 10,000 automobile policies, each with a standard deviation of $300 and an expected loss of $300. To calculate the ruin probability, assume the insurer can pay claims up to $400 per policy. The mean, standard deviation, and ruin probability of the insurer's portfolio are

$$\mu_p = E\left(\frac{L}{n}\right) = \sum_{i=1}^{n} \frac{E(L_i)}{n} = \frac{300n}{n} = \$300$$

$$\sigma_p = \sqrt{\sigma^2(L/n)} = \left(\frac{1}{n^2}\left(\sum_{i=1}^{n} \sigma_i^2 + \sum_{i\neq j}\sum \sigma_{i,j}\right)\right)^{1/2}$$

$$= \left(\frac{1}{10,000^2}(10,000)(300)^2\right)^{1/2} = \$3$$

and

$$z = \frac{L^*/n - \mu_p}{\sigma_p} = \frac{400 - 300}{3} = 33.33$$

Reading from Table 4–3, the probability of ruin is negligible (less than 0.001).

Now suppose that this insurer also writes a set of fire insurance policies in order to diversify its line base. The firm writes 1000 fire policies, each covering fairly large industrial risks. Each risk has an expected loss of $10,000 and a standard deviation of $15,000. The firm estimates that its reserves and surplus permit it to meet claims up to $1300 per policy. Now the portfolio mean, standard deviation, and ruin probability are

$$\mu_p = \frac{10,000(300) + 1000(10,000)}{11,000} = \$1,181.8$$

$$\sigma_p = \left(\frac{1}{11,000^2}[10,000(300)^2 + 1000(15,000)^2]\right)^{1/2} = \$43.21$$

and

$$z = \frac{1300 - 1181.8}{43.21} = 2.74$$

Hence, the probability of ruin is 0.0031.

In this case diversification has increased the portfolio risk both in terms of the standard deviation averaged on a per policy basis and in terms of the ruin probability. A little reflection will reveal what has gone wrong. Originally, the insurer had written a book of automobile risks that each had a small expected value and a small level of risk. In diversifying, the insurer changed the composition of the portfolio to include a significant number of high value, high-risk policies. The impact is to "swamp out" the already diversified risks of the automobile portfolio. The mean and variance of the sub-portfolio of fire policies alone is

$$\mu_p(\text{fire}) = \$10,000 \text{ and } \sigma_p(\text{fire}) = \$474.3$$

Thus, diversification means that an automobile portfolio having a standard deviation of \$3 per policy is combined with one having a standard deviation of \$474.3 per policy. Not surprisingly, the fire policy risks dominate the portfolio, increasing overall portfolio risk.

MEASURING CORRELATION BETWEEN RISK UNITS

With independence, the covariance terms between risk units are defined to be zero. Now we consider portfolios in which there is correlation between exposure units. Consider some examples:

1. Close proximity of buildings implies that a fire in one structure immediately increases the probability of a fire in each of the remaining buildings, since the natural progress of the fire or the blowing of burning embers may cause the fire to spread. The probabilities of loss in each are interdependent.

2. Bad weather conditions increase the probability that any one vehicle may crash, but the same conditions increase the accident probability for each other vehicle in the same meteorological region. Thus, the probabilities are interdependent.

3. Many types of losses, such as fires, industrial accidents, collisions, and burglaries, may bear some relation to the

economic cycle. For example, arson increases during
recession; people drive more miles during peak periods
in the cycle, increasing exposure to loss, etc. These sorts
of effects may lead to relationships between the loss
probabilities in different types of portfolios. For example,
fire losses might be correlated with automobile losses.

4. A non-insurance firm has the risk of liability of directors
   and officers from shareholders lawsuits. Such lawsuits
   are more likely when the firm's stock price is depressed,
   and the stock price is related in part to financial and
   business conditions. Thus, the firm considers its
   directors' and officers' liability risk to be correlated with
   its business and financial risk.

Whether such relationships do exist or not is an empirical matter.

To illustrate the operation of covariance, consider the loss
experience on two fire policies for industrial risks. The historical
record for a 16-year period is given in Table 4–5. The data are
expressed in real terms to remove the effect of inflation.

The formula for covariance was given earlier, but the following form will make the computation somewhat simpler:

$$\sigma_{1,2} = \sum p_i(L_{1i} - E(L_1))(L_{2i} - E(L_2)) = E(L_1 L_2) - E(L_1)E(L_2)$$

$$= 19{,}373{,}125 - 6550(1569) = 9{,}096{,}175$$

The relationship is positive. Large losses on exposure unit 1
tend to arise at the same time as large loses on exposure unit 2;
small losses similarly coincide. Intuitively, we might expect that if
all units in a portfolio exhibited such positive relationships, the
portfolio risk would tend to be high. Bad weather, or depressed
economic conditions, would bring a flood of claims. "It never rains
but it pours." However, good weather or a strong economy might
reverse the flow of claims. This correlation could cause large fluctuations in the insurer's total claims experience, even if the insurer
holds a large number of policies. The impact of covariance on
portfolio risk depends on the relative strength of the covariance.
Unfortunately, the measure $\sigma_{i,j}$ does not directly reveal the
strength of the relationship; it is an absolute number that is not
placed on any scale. Certainly, the number 9,096,175 seems a large

T A B L E   4–5

Sample Fire Loss Data

Year	Total losses per exposure unit, in dollars 1	2
1985	5000	500
1986	300	600
1987	6200	3200
1988	7000	2900
1989	—	1500
1990	500	—
1991	5300	—
1992	25,000	5600
1993	5000	2000
1994	7000	1800
1995	200	—
1996	—	—
1997	1000	500
1998	8000	—
1999	32,000	3000
2000	2300	3500
μ	6550	1569
σ	8831	1625

number, but a casual inspection of Table 4–5 shows the relationship to be less than perfect. If covariance were very strong, we
always find that above-average losses on unit 1 are associated
with above-average losses on unit 2. This is clearly not so; witness
1987, 1993, 1998, and 2000. The good news is that a convenient
measure of the strength of the relationship is available. This is the
correlation coefficient, which is defined as

$$r_{i,j} = \frac{\sigma_{i,j}}{\sigma_i \, \sigma_j}$$

Thus, for the information in Table 4–5, the correlation coefficient
is

$$r_{i,j} = \frac{9{,}096{,}175}{8831(1625)} = 0.634$$

The correlation coefficient is defined on a scale of minus unity to plus unity. Negative values show a negative relationship, with -1 suggesting a "perfect negative correlation." A perfect negative relationship of this form means that there is an inversely proportional relationship between the variables; if one variable falls to half its previous value, the other variable doubles in value. A correlation coefficient of zero indicates that there is no association between the variables. Positive values denote a positive relationship, with $+1$ indicating a "perfect positive correlation." A perfect positive relationship is a directly proportional relationship between the two series. The example in Table 4–5 reveals a reasonably strong positive relationship. Insurers would worry about this strong relationship because it implies that there is a fire conflagration hazard. In a diversified insurance portfolio, it would be expected that correlations would average much lower values.

If we use the correlation coefficient instead of covariance, the variance of a portfolio is

$$\sigma^2(L) = \sum_{i=1}^{n} \sigma_i^2 + \sum \sum_{i \neq j} \sigma_{i,j} = \sum_{i=1}^{n} \sigma_i^2 + \sum \sum_{i \neq j} r_{i,j} \sigma_i \sigma_j$$

Thus, the standard deviation of the mean loss is

$$\sigma^2\left(\frac{L}{n}\right) = \left[\frac{1}{n^2}\left(\sum_{i=1}^{n} \sigma_i^2 + \sum \sum_{i \neq j} r_{i,j} \sigma_i \sigma_j\right)\right]^{1/2}$$

This is the expression we must now use to calculate the variance of the insurance portfolio. This task will be more complex in view of all the correlation terms that had previously dropped out. To perform such calculations, it is helpful to know how many terms there will be in this expression and, in particular, how many covariances or correlations.

The variances and covariances in a portfolio can be represented schematically, as shown in Figure 4–5. All the shaded terms in the leading diagonal are the variances; for example, the pair L_4, L_4. The remaining expressions represent all the possible covariances; for example, L_3 and L_7. In total, the matrix must have $n \times$

F I G U R E   4-5

A Variance-Covariance Matrix

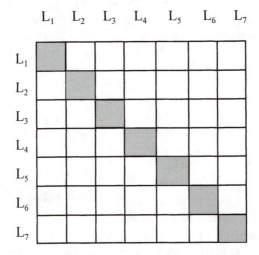

n elements, since it is square (in this picture n is 7). Of these elements, there are n variances, leaving $(n_2 - n)$ or $n(n - 1)$ covariances. The double summations sign in the previous variance formula contains $n(n - 1)$ terms. This will be very convenient to remember. The behavior of a portfolio having correlated exposure units can now be examined.

RISK REDUCTION IN AN INSURANCE PORTFOLIO OF INTERDEPENDENT RISKS

For a portfolio of n identical exposure units in which the correlation coefficient between any pair i and j is $r_{i,j}$, the mean and standard deviation are

$$\mu_p = E\left(\frac{L}{n}\right) = \sum_{i=1}^{n} \frac{E(L_i)}{n} = E(L_i)$$

$$\sigma_p = \sigma^2\left(\frac{L}{n}\right) = \left[\frac{1}{n^2}\left(\sum_{i=1}^{n} \sigma_i^2 + \sum \sum_{i \neq j} r_{i,j}\sigma_i\sigma_j\right)\right]^{1/2}$$

$$= \left[\frac{1}{n^2}\left(n\sigma_i^2 + n(n - 1)r_{i,j}\sigma_i\sigma_j\right)\right]^{1/2}$$

$$= \left[\frac{\sigma_i^2}{n^2} + \left(\frac{n - 1}{n}\right) r_{i,j}\sigma_i\sigma_j\right]^{1/2}$$

If $r_{i,j} > 0$, then portfolio risk will not converge on zero when n approaches infinity because the term $(n - 1)/n$ approaches unity as n approaches infinity. Thus, the second term in the bracket will approach the positive constant $r_{i,j}\sigma_i\sigma_j$ as n approaches infinity. This can be seen in the following example.

Consider a portfolio with n policies that each have

$$\mu_i = 500 \quad ; \quad \sigma_i = 650 \quad ; \quad r_{i,j} = 0.1$$

$$E\left(\frac{L}{n}\right) = 500$$

$$\sigma_p = \left[\frac{650^2}{n} + \frac{n-1}{n} 0.1(650)(650)\right]^{1/2} = \left[\frac{380{,}250}{n} + 42{,}250\right]^{1/2}$$

Values for the mean, variance, and standard deviation are shown in Table 4–6 for different portfolio sizes.

Consequently, the portfolio risk is seen to converge on some positive value, that is, 205.5, as n approaches infinity. Diversification brings some risk reduction, but there is a limit to this process. This limit is determined by the size of the correlation coefficient. The higher the correlation coefficient, the higher the lower limit on portfolio risk. In Figure 4–6 we show how the correlation coefficient affects diversification. We assume the same portfolio of units that each have $\sigma_i = 650$, but we allow the correlation coefficient to assume the values 0.1, 0.2, 0.5, and 1.0. The calculation follows the previous case. For each correlation coefficient, the portfolio standard deviation asymptotically approaches the value shown. There is a clear scope for risk reduction as long as units

T A B L E   4–6

Risk Reduction: Interdependent Risks

n	$\sigma_2(L/n)$	$\sigma(L/n)$
1	422,500	650
10	80,275	283
100	46,052	214.6
1000	42,630	206.5
10,000	42,288	205.6
∞	42,250	205.5

F I G U R E   4–6

Risk Reduction with Correlated Risk

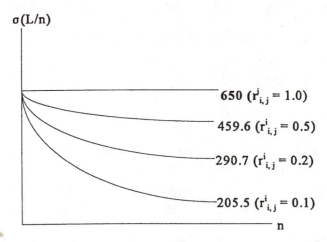

$\sigma(L/n)$

650 $(r^j_{i,j} = 1.0)$

459.6 $(r^i_{i,j} = 0.5)$

290.7 $(r^i_{i,j} = 0.2)$

205.5 $(r^i_{i,j} = 0.1)$

n

are not perfectly correlated. However, the risk-reducing benefits become more pronounced as the correlations get lower.

The second aspect of risk that has been explored is the ruin probability. When risks are independent, the combined distribution approaches normal as the number of risks approach infinity. The distribution cannot be assumed to be exactly normal, but the approximation is sufficiently close for reasonable estimation when n exceeds, say, 30. *The assumption that the portfolio distribution approaches normal does not hold when the exposure units are correlated.* This means that use of the normal distribution to estimate ruin probability is not appropriate for correlated exposures even when n is very large. The degree of error in using the normal approximation for such cases depends on the degree of correlation. If the correlation coefficient is close to zero, the normal approximation may be reasonable if n is fairly large. However, when the correlation coefficient diverges widely from zero, the error may be very substantial. Our purpose here is not to give accurate estimates of ruin probabilities; rather, it is to show how diversification reduces the risk of ruin. This will be illustrated on a portfolio with fairly low correlations, and we will use the normal distribution as a crude approximation. However, we recognize that the results may contain a significant error factor, and we will therefore supplement with alternative calculations based on Chebyshev's inequality. The Chebyshev method enables us to establish an upper boundary for the ruin probability without actually providing a direct calculation.

The normal approximation is calculated as before, recognizing the additional error:

$$z = \frac{L^*/n - \mu_p}{\sigma_p} \quad : \quad \text{probability that } \frac{L}{n} > \frac{L^*}{n}$$

Chebyshev's inequality states:

For any random variable x, *the probability of realizing an outcome above* k *standard deviations above the mean is at most* $1/k^2$.

This implies that an upper limit can be set on the ruin probability for any critical value L^*/n. The actual ruin probability will be lower than this value. However, unlike the calculation from the normal approximation, the upper-limit calculation is valid for any distribution. Given this generality, the upper limit calculated by the Chebyshev method tends to be conservatively high. Nevertheless, we will observe how the estimated ruin probabilities behave as the number of items in the portfolio increase. To simplify the calculation, we will specify the Chebyshev inequality in the following terms:

$$\text{Probability} \left(\left| \frac{L^*}{n} \right| > \mu_p + k\sigma_p \right) \leq \frac{1}{k^2}$$

Verbally, the probability that the absolute value of L^*/n is greater than $\mu_p + k\sigma_p$ is at most $1/k^2$. Therefore, an upper limit on the ruin probability, given some maximum payout L^*/n, is given by α in the following expression:

$$\frac{L^*}{n} = \mu_p + \sigma_p \sqrt{\frac{1}{\alpha}}$$

Rearranging gives

$$\alpha = \frac{1}{\left(\dfrac{L^*/n - \mu_p}{\sigma_p} \right)^2} = \frac{1}{z^2}$$

where z is defined as earlier for the normal distribution. The Chebyshev method will only provide meaningful answers (probabilities below unity) if $k > 1$.

T A B L E   4–7

Ruin Probabilities: Interdependent Risks

n	z	Normal Approximation	Chebyshev Upper Limit ($1/z^2$)
1	0.462	0.3228	a
10	1.059	0.1446	0.892
100	1.398	0.0808	0.512
1000	1.453	0.0735	0.474
10,000	1.458	0.0721	0.470
∞	1.460	0.0721	0.469

a value exceeds unity.

Now consider the portfolio discussed earlier with $\mu_i = 500$, $\sigma_i = 650$, and $r_{i,j} = 0.1$, to which we will add the information that the insurer can pay losses up to maximum of \$800 per policy. Calculating rough ruin probabilities with the normal approximation gives:

$$z = \frac{800 - 500}{\sqrt{380,250/n + 42,250}}$$

Table 4–7 shows sample calculations using this expression and the z tables.

Both the normal-approximation values and the Chebyshev upper limits reveal that ruin probabilities decline as the number of exposure units increases. Furthermore, both the normal approximation values and the Chebyshev upper limit converge on positive values, revealing no tendency for the ruin probability to approach zero as n approaches infinity. This may be contrasted with the portfolio of independent units that does converge to zero risk.[3] In view of the latent error in the normal approximation and the severe conservatism of the Chebyshev method, these results are not as strong as we would like.[4] However, they may be interpreted as providing some support for the claim that diversification

---

3. For independent exposures, it is easily verified that the Chebyshev upper limit on ruin probability also approaches zero. Tables 4–2 and 4–4 showed that, for such portfolios, $z \to \infty$ as $n \to \infty$. Since the Chebyshev value α equals $1/z^2$, then clearly $\alpha \to 0$ as $n \to \infty$.
4. There are many other methods of estimating the tails of distributions. One of the newer methods is extreme value theory (see Embrechts et al., 1997).

will still provide limited benefits in the form of risk reduction even when exposure units are positively correlated. The reduction in risk arises in all cases in which the correlation coefficient is less than unity.

RISK REDUCTION WITH CORRELATED RISKS

For completeness, we should show that limited risk reduction can be achieved in heterogeneous portfolios of positively correlated risk units as long as the correlation coefficients are less than unity. The method of tackling this should be well established by now, and we will content ourselves with a quick example showing the calculation of portfolio standard deviation.

Let us consider a mixed portfolio of fire and automobile policies in which there are s fire policies and t automobile policies. To preserve the portfolio mix, we assume that s and t bear a constant ratio to each other. The total number of policies is $s + t = n$. In order to calculate the portfolio standard deviation, we need to know how many terms will be present in the formula. Clearly, there are $s + t$ variance terms for individual policies. In addition, there will be:

$s(s - 1)$ correlations between different fire risks

$t(t - 1)$ correlations between different automobile risks

$2st$ correlations between fire and automobile risks

The respective correlation coefficients for these groups are

$$r_{F,i,j} = 0.1 \quad \text{for fire policies}$$

$$r_{A,i,j} = 0.1 \quad \text{for auto policies}$$

$$r_{A,F} = 0.05 \quad \text{for fire and auto policies}$$

Further information for the portfolio is

$$s = 20{,}000 \quad \mu_F = 500 \quad \sigma_F = 700 \quad \text{for all fire risks}$$
$$t = 10{,}000 \quad \mu_A = 300 \quad \sigma_A = 400 \quad \text{for all automobile risks}$$

The standard deviation of the distribution of mean loss can now be calculated in the usual manner:

$$\sigma_p = \sigma^2\left(\frac{L}{n}\right) = \left[\frac{1}{n^2}\left(\sum_{i=1}^{n} \sigma_i^2 + \sum \sum_{i \neq j} r_{i,j}\sigma_i\sigma_j\right)\right]^{1/2}$$

$$= \{1/30,000^2 \, [20,000(700)^2 + 10,000(400)^2$$

$$+ \, (20,000)(19,999)(0.1)(700)(700)$$

$$+ \, (10,000)(9,999)(0.1)(400)(400)$$

$$+ \, 2(20,000)(10,000)(0.05)(700)(400)]\}^{1/2}$$

$$= 29,789^{1/2}$$

$$= 173$$

The interested reader might experiment with different values of s and t (but retaining the ratio of $s = 2t$) to confirm that risk does indeed fall as n increases and that it converges on a positive value as n approaches infinity.

A final word in this section concerning negative correlations. Within a real insurance portfolio there may be a large degree of heterogeneity between risks and a wide diversity in the correlations between individual pairs of risks. Some of these correlations might be negative. The incremental effect of including a policy that is negatively correlated with other policies already in the portfolio is to reduce risk substantially. Therefore, negative correlations should be valued by the insurer.

THREE APPLICATIONS

To highlight the process of diversification, three examples are now given below in which common risk management types of activities take advantage of diversification.

EXAMPLE 1: MERGERS AND ACQUISITIONS
An insurer with some 80,000 industrial fire policies acquires a second firm writing 20,000 automobile policies. The respective policies will be subscripted F and A and details of individual policies are given as follows:

> **Fire policies:** *Each policy has mean $\mu_F = 1000$ and standard deviation $\sigma_F = 1500$. The correlation between any pair is $r_{F,i,j} = 0.1$*

Automobile policies: Each policy has mean $\mu_A = 500$ and standard deviation $\sigma_A = 700$. The correlation between any pair $r_{A,i,j} = 0.1$

Fire and auto policies are uncorrelated.

The standard deviation of the distribution of mean loss of each insurer before acquisition is

$$\sigma_{p,F} = \left[\frac{1}{n^2}\left(\sum_{i=1}^{n} \sigma_i^2 + \sum \sum_{i \neq j} r_{i,j}\, \sigma_i\, \sigma_j\right)\right]^{1/2}$$

$$= \{1/80,000^2[80,000(1500)^2$$

$$+ (80,000)(79,999)(0.1)(1500)(1500)]\}^{1/2}$$

$$= 474$$

and

$$\sigma_{p,A} = \{1/20,000^2[20,000(700)^2$$

$$+ (20,000)(19,999)(0.1)(700)(700)]\}^{1/2}$$

$$= 221$$

And, after the merger, the acquiring insurer will have a portfolio with standard deviation

$$\sigma_{p,(F-A)} = \{1/100,000^2[80,000(1500)^2 + 20,000(700)^2$$

$$+ (80,000)(79,999)(0.1)(1500)(1500)$$

$$+ (20,000)(19,999)(0.1)(700)(700)]\}^{1/2}$$

$$= 382$$

This reduction in risk has been accomplished by two effects. First, the acquiring company has obtained a group of policies with significantly lower risk (standard deviation) per policy. Second, the initial fire portfolio and the acquired automobile portfolio are uncorrelated; thus, diversification is achieved simply by combining two uncorrelated portfolios.

It might be objected that the reduction in risk calculated on a per policy base is misleading. The original portfolio consisted only of fire policies, but the combined portfolio averages over the "chalk and cheese" of fire and automobile policies. To avoid this problem, consider what

*happens to total risk (that is, not averaged over policies). This is calcu-
lated in a similar fashion to σ_p, except that we do not divide by $1/n^2$.
The before and after values are*

$$\sigma_p \text{ (total)} = 37{,}949{,}466$$

$$\sigma_{p,A} \text{ (total)} = 4{,}428{,}184$$

$$\sigma_{p,(F-A)} \text{ (total)} = 38{,}206{,}947$$

*Not surprisingly, total risk increases. However, the combined value is
significantly less than the sum of the parts. In fact, total risk hardly
increases at all, despite the fact that insurer has increased its portfolio
by some 20,000 policies.*

EXAMPLE 2: REINSURANCE

*Two insurers have identical portfolios that are each made up of 10,000
identical policies with $\sigma = 400$ and $r_{i,j} = 0.1$ for any i and j. The
correlation between any policy of insurer A and any policy of insurer B
is also 0.1. The insurers establish a reciprocal reinsurance treaty in which
A receives half the premium on each policy written by B and vice versa.
In return, A pays B half the cost of each and every claim suffered by B,
and vice versa. That is, each pays half its premiums to the other in return
for reimbursement on half of each claim. Before the treaty, each insurer
had a portfolio risk of*

$$\sigma_p = \left[\frac{1}{n^2} \left(\sum_{i=1}^{n} \sigma_i^2 + \sum \sum_{i \neq j} r_{i,j} \sigma_i \sigma_j \right) \right]^{1/2}$$

$$= \{1/10{,}000^2 [10{,}000(400)^2 + (10{,}000)(9{,}999)(0.1)(400)(400)]\}^{1/2}$$

$$= 126.5$$

*To calculate standard deviation after the treaty, consider that the agree-
ment has produced two relevant effects. Whereas each insurer previously
had an interest in only 10,000 risk units, it now has an interest in
20,000. Second, each insurer will pay only half the loss on each policy;
thus, the standard deviation per risk unit will be smaller. Both effects
should reduce the portfolio standard deviation. The standard deviation
per exposure unit can be calculated as follows:*

Before reinsurance:

$$\sigma_i = \left[\sum_i p_i \, (L_i - E(L_i))^2 \right]^{1/2} = 400$$

After reinsurance:

$$\sigma_i = \left[\sum_i p_i \left(\frac{L_i}{2} - \frac{E(L_i)}{2} \right)^2 \right]^{1/2} = \frac{1}{2} \left[\sum_i p_i \, (L_i - E(L_i))^2 \right]^{1/2}$$

$$= 200$$

Then the portfolio standard deviation for each insurer after the treaty is:

$$= \{1/20{,}000^2[20{,}000(200)^2 + (20{,}000)(19{,}999)(0.1)(200)(200)]\}^{1/2}$$

$$= 63.26$$

The reduction in risk is dramatic. Generally, the smaller the correlation coefficients between the portfolios of the participating insurers, the greater the risk reduction achieved by reciprocal reinsurance arrangements of this nature.

EXAMPLE 3: RUIN IN A SELF-INSURANCE FUND

A grocery retailer has 100 stores that are located in several states. In view of the geographic separation and similar size and risk of the stores, the firm decides to self-insure. The administration of this program involves the establishment of a fund into which "premiums" are paid and from which losses are financed. Each store has an expected loss of $1000 and a standard deviation of $1500. The risks are assumed to be independent. Ignoring any administrative expenses, how much should the firm contribute to the fund for each store in order to restrict the probability to 10% that the fund's resources will be inadequate to meet losses?

Since there are 100 units and they are independent, we can assume that the normal approximation applies. Recall that z tables record the probability that any revealed value from a normal distribution will be more than z standard deviations from the mean. The z value corresponding to a 10% probablity is 1.28. Thus,

$$z_{10} = \frac{F - \mu_p}{\sigma_p} = 1.28$$

where F is the cutoff contribution that leaves a 10% chance of ruin. Therefore,

$$1.28 = \frac{F - 1000}{1500/\sqrt{100}}$$

giving F = 1192.

Since the assumptions for the use of the normal approximation are met in this particular case, the result is fairly accurate (not strictly accurate, since the portfolio distribution only approaches normal as n approaches infinity). Had there been significant correlations, this method would not have produced reliable answers. However, we would generally expect that the required contribution to maintain any given ruin probability would be higher with positive correlation because the portfolio distribution would exhibit higher risk.

DIVERSIFICATION AND THE DISTRIBUTION OF AGGREGATE LOSSES FOR THE (NON-INSURANCE) FIRM

Example 3 provides a bridge between the use of portfolio theory to explain risk reduction in an insurance fund and its application to risk management in other types of corporate organizations. All firms face a variety of risks, and each type of risk can affect the firm's financial performance and indeed its valuation. For some purposes it may be useful to identify and treat these risk units individually. A narrow focus on individual units provides a starting point in estimating an aggregate loss distribution, or at least summary measures. Furthermore, attention to individual units may reveal possibilities for reducing loss costs by safety and preventive activities. However, in the determination of the financial performance of a firm, it is the aggregate impact of these risk units on the earnings and value of the firm that is of importance. Because the properties of a portfolio are somewhat different from the sum of its parts, we must derive risk management strategies with reference to these aggregate effects. In the meantime, we consider the properties of the portfolio of exposure units that is owned or controlled by a firm.

All firms are exposed to multiple risks. In addition to the risks inherent in business activity (such as market risk, financial risk, and regulatory risk) there are multiple pure risks (such as fires, liability suits, and weather-related perils). Even a very small single-plant firm can consider itself to have a portfolio of risk exposures, and each exposure pertains to a different type of risky event. Just how diversified such a portfolio will be depends on how the risk units are defined and what correlations exist between them. We have already argued that the identification of separate exposure units is a matter of judgment relating to the degree of correlation between risks. However, it should be clear from the preceding discussion that we cannot usefully define exposure units as statistically independent. Thus, for a one-plant firm, the risk of fire to the plant may exhibit a "small" correlation with the probability that the firm's truck will collide, leading to the common-sense judgment that they are separate exposure units.

For larger more diversified firms, the portfolio of risk units is more obvious. Firms such as Safeway, Ford, and IBM own many plants, stores, warehouses, offices, etc., and each can be considered a separate exposure unit, even when we are contemplating a single peril such as fire. Again, we are not asserting independence. It may be that due to the quality of management, corporate protection policies, the effect of economic cycles on corporate activity, etc., there is interdependence between the loss distributions for separate exposure units. Nevertheless, these firms do achieve some degree of diversification, since the correlations between units will fall far short of unity. The same general principles of diversification apply to the risk management issues facing a firm and to the formation of an insurance portfolio. Therefore, it is important to examine the properties of a firm's portfolio of exposure units in order to properly measure risk management costs and derive appropriate risk management strategies.

Although the general principles of portfolio theory can be transferred to risk management problems for industrial, commercial, and service firms, the resulting portfolio may not display such convenient properties as those for the insurance portfolio. The main differences that do arise are:

1. Many firms are made up of only a small number of risk units. Consequently, portfolio risk will not substantially disappear even if risk units are not correlated.

2. However, risky events may be correlated. Risk units within a firm may be exposed to common influences that imply statistical dependence. For example, financial and insurable risks may be commonly related to the level of business activity for the firm. Common management strategies, labor relations, and safety programs may give rise to interdependence. Physical proximity of some units may give rise to conflagration hazard (although at some stage conflagration hazard may be so severe that risks may be combined into a single exposure unit).

3. A third difference is that risk exposures may differ vastly in terms of value and expected loss. Insurance portfolios are usually far from homogeneous, although insurers do try to group exposures into fairly homogeneous classes. The device of "averaging" risk over exposure units was useful in illustrating the nature of risk spreading. For risk management purposes, the main focus of attention is on the distribution of aggregate losses. It is this distribution that determines the risk costs to the firm, and it is this distribution that becomes a primary focus in formulating risk management strategy. We will now show how the distribution can be affected by diversification within the firm's portfolio of exposure units.

These conditions (if present) imply that the degree to which risk is reduced by diversification is limited. Nonetheless, risk can always be reduced to some extent if exposure units are not perfectly correlated. To illustrate the range of possibilities, consider three firms that differ with respect to the degree of diversification. Details of assets held by the firms and summary measures of the fire loss distributions are as follows:

Firm A: Operates 30 fast-food restaurants. The restaurants are similar style and have equivalent value and are exposed to identical risk from fire:

Value of each restaurant	$ 300,000
Total value	$9,000,000
Expected loss, each restaurant	$ 1500
Total expected loss	$ 45,000
Standard deviation, each restaurant	$ 2500
Exposure units are independent	

Firm B: Manufactures plastic goods. Its business premises are constructed on a fairly large site with sufficient physical separation of buildings to limit fire conflagration hazard. The building values and summary loss measures are:

	Value	Expected loss	Standard deviation
Factory	$5 million	$30,000	$50,000
Warehouse	$2 million	$10,000	$16,667
Distribution	$1 million	$ 3000	$ 5000
Office	$1 million	$ 2000	$ 3333
Total	$9 million	$45,000	

The correlation coefficient between exposure units is $r_{i,j} = 0.1$

Firm C: Also manufactures plastic goods. Manufacture, storage, and related office works are all housed in a single building, which is considered a single exposure unit from a fire viewpoint.

Value of premises	$9,000,000
Expected loss	$ 45,000
Standard deviation	$ 75,000

The three firms described are comparable in terms of the value at risk and the risk characteristics. Each firm has assets at risk valued at $9 million. The total expected loss in each case is $45,000, indicating comparable degrees of hazard. Furthermore, the variability of risk for each exposure unit, measured as the ratio of standard deviation to expected loss, assumes the same value (≈ 1.67). The three firms differ only with respect to the degree of diversification on the riskiness of the firm's *aggregate* loss distribution. Using the standard deviation formula,

$$\sigma(L) = \left[\sum_{i=1}^{n} \sigma_i^2 + \sum \sum_{i \neq j} r_{i,j}\sigma_i\sigma_j \right]^{1/2}$$

For firm A:

$$\sigma_A(L) = [30(2500)^2]^{1/2}$$

$$= \$13{,}693$$

For firm B:

$$\sigma_B(L) = [(50{,}000)^2 + (16{,}667)^2 + (5000)^2 + (3333)^2$$
$$+ 2(0.1)(50{,}000)(16{,}667) + 2(0.1)(50{,}000)(5000)$$
$$+ 2(0.1)(50{,}000)(3333) + 2(0.1)(16{,}667)(5000)$$
$$+ 2(0.1)(16{,}667)(3333) + 2(0.1)(5000)(3333)]^{1/2}$$
$$= \$55{,}633$$

For firm C, the standard deviation of aggregate losses is already given, since there is only one exposure unit:

$$\sigma_C(L) = \$75{,}000$$

Although the expected loss is the same, the variability in losses differs considerably. This difference may substantially affect the type of risk management strategy adopted by each firm. Consider, for example, whether the firms should purchase insurance. The need for insurance is normally considered to arise from the variability of the loss distribution. Insurance certainly does not reduce expected loss cost (in view of transaction costs and insurer's markups, the expected cost of an insurance policy usually exceeds the expected value of the loss). However, insurance does reduce, or ideally eliminate, variability. One might therefore suppose that firm *A* has the least to gain from insurance and firm *C* has the most to gain. We should not be surprised to find firms with a wide spread of exposure units choosing not to purchase insurance and firms with a high concentration of value in a small number of exposure units choosing extensive insurance protection.

CONCLUSION

This chapter examines the pooling process that permits insurance companies to diversify much of the risk in their portfolios. Current interest in the insurance process arises, first, because insurance is an important risk management device, and second, because a similar pooling process arises within the portfolio of risk units held by the non-insurance firm. The interaction between these risk units is important in determining the total level of risk facing a firm. An insurance portfolio is a collection of insurance policies, each of which represents a separate contract with an external party. Whether claims arise under each policy and the size of such claims are random processes. The insurer's interest lies in the aggregate claims to be paid under the portfolio, for it is upon this aggregate that the insurer's financial performance depends. Aggregate claims also follow a random process that is determined by the risk and return characteristics of the individual policies. However, as we have seen in this chapter, this insurer's risk is not equal to the sum of the individual policy risks.

When insurance contracts in a portfolio are independently and identically distributed, the riskiness of the portfolio, as measured by the standard deviation of the average loss, tends toward zero as the number of policies in the portfolio tends toward infinity. Furthermore, by the Central Limit theorem, the distribution of average loss tends toward a normal distribution as the number policies increases. This last tendency makes possible the use of the normal approximation method to estimate the probability of ruin. The probability that the average loss for the portfolio will exceed some critical value (determined by the insurer's reserves) in excess of the mean falls as the number of policies increases. As n approaches infinity, the ruin probability approaches zero. Thus, both risk measures, the standard deviation and the ruin probability, reveal that portfolio risk is related inversely to size in a portfolio of independent and identical policies.

Broadly similar results prevail when the insurer's portfolio is made up of heterogeneous but independent policies. Risk tends to disappear as the number of policies becomes very large. However, this conclusion is qualified, since it assumes that the relative composition of the portfolio is independent of its size.

When policies are not independent, the conclusions on portfolio diversification require substantial modification. First, with correlated policies, the distribution of average loss does not tend toward normal as the number of policies increases. This implies that use of the normal approximation to estimate ruin probability is not strictly appropriate. Even more significant, the riskiness of the distribution of average loss does not tend toward zero as the number of policies approaches infinity. Such portfolios exhibit an irreducible minimum level of risk that cannot be diversified away. The size of the remaining risk depends positively on the correlations between the policies. An example of this problem is earthquake insurance. It is not so much the high expected value of loss that makes insurers nervous about insuring this risk, but rather the high degree of geographic interdependence between individual policies.

The same process of diversification arises with the portfolio of exposure units possessed by a non-insurance firm. The riskiness of the rim's distribution of aggregate value is derived from the characteristics of individual cash flows. But risk does not add up in a simple way. The aggregate risk is less than the sum of its parts. Thus, as part of the firm's risk management strategy, it might well consider the natural risk pooling that arises within the firm. A good example of such pooling is an oil company that owns several hundred service stations. The aggregate loss from, say, fire might be fairly predictable, even though the loss to any individual station is highly uncertain. Another example is a firm that does business in many countries but accounts in dollars. It is subject to foreign exchange risk in many transactions. Suppose each transaction were hedged. This would certainly remove risk, but the transaction costs of all these hedges would be enormous. However, a closer look reveals that many of the exposures might have low or even negative correlations. For example, one branch might be long in sterling and short in dollars, whereas another division is short in sterling and long in dollars. These two positions offset each other (i.e., have a negative correlation). Thus, it might be that the overall portfolio risk to the firm from foreign currency fluctuations is low. Further opportunities for internal pooling arise when it is considered that the business risk of a firm often exhibits low correlation with risk management risk.

The process of diversification is also important in understanding how investors behave and in determining the value of a firm. Similar concepts will now be put to use to help derive sensible financial criteria for evaluating risk management strategies.

REFERENCES

Beard, R. E. 1977. *Risk Theory: The Stochastic Basis of Insurance.* New York: Halstead Press.

Beard, R. E., T. Pentikainen, and E. Pesonen. 1969. *Risk Theory.* London: Methuen.

Breiman, L. 1968. *Probability.* Reading, Mass.: Addison-Wesley.

Cramer, H. 1946. *Mathematical Methods in Statistics.* Princeton, N.J.: Princeton University Press.

Embrechts, Paul, Claudia Klüppelberg, and Thomas Mikosch. 1997. *Modelling Extremal Events for Insurance and Finance.* Applications of Mathematics: Stochastic Modelling and Applied Probability, vol. 33. New York: Springer.

Feller, W. 1966. *An Introduction to Probability and Its Applications,* vol. 2. New York: John Wiley & Sons.

Friefelder, L. R. 1976. *A Decision Theoretic Approach to Insurance Ratemaking.* Huebner Foundation Monograph no. 4. Homewood, Ill.: R. D. Irwin.

Gerber, H. 1979. *An Introduction to Mathematical Risk Theory.* Huebner Foundation Mongraph no. 8. Irwin, Homewood, Ill.: R. D. Irwin.

Houston, D. B. 1964. "Risk, Insurance and Sampling." *Journal of Risk and Insurance* 31:511–38.

Markowitz, H. 1959. *Portfolio Selection: Efficient Diversification of Investments.* New York: John Wiley & Sons.

Spurr, W. A., and C. P. Bonini. 1973. *Statistical Analysis for Business Decisions.* Homewood, Ill.: R. D. Irwin.

CHAPTER 5

Capital Market Theory

The corporate objective assumed for this book is that a firm wishes to maximize the value of its owners' equity. This is equivalent to maximizing the value of the firm's shares. To derive risk management strategies in pursuit of this objective requires some knowledge of how stock prices are determined. In particular, we must examine how the capital market functions and what motivates investors in their decisions to purchase securities. In the conclusion of the previous chapter, we examined the possibility for diversification across the various risky activities undertaken by a firm. The effect of pooling the various risky cash flows is to reduce the total level of risk in a firm's earnings. These earnings accrue to the owners of the firm, and the owners must absorb any remaining risk. How does this remaining risk affect the welfare of the shareholders? Presumably the shareholders' main concern is with the value of their shares. Thus, we may restate the last question: How does the remaining risk in the firm's earnings affect the share values? It is tempting to reply that shareholders are risk-averse and therefore risk will simply reduce share value. Therefore, any reduction in risk, perhaps by risk management strategy, will increase share value. This straightforward total-risk approach is widespread in the traditional risk management literature. However, we will see that it is an oversimplification that results in misleading and sometimes incorrect conclusions. The possibilities for diversification have not yet been exhausted.

A CAPITAL MARKET IN WHICH INVESTORS HOLD ONLY ONE SECURITY

It is common, and probably not unreasonable, to assume that most people are averse to risk and that this attitude is reflected in many forms of economic behavior. The most obvious *prima facie* evidence in support of this assumption lies in the widespread demand for personal insurance protection. Most of us appear willing to convert the uncertain prospect of a large loss of wealth through the destruction of our home or our life into a regular payment of an insurance premium, even though insurance is costlier in the long run, since premiums typically exceed the expected value of loss. There is considerable evidence that investors (if indeed they form a separate group from homeowners) typically are averse to risk and that this attitude influences their investment strategies and thereby helps to determine the prices of securities.

Investors prefer higher returns on their investment holdings to lower returns, other things being equal. A slightly stronger assumption is that investors prefer less to more risk, other things being equal. Together, these assumptions are broadly acceptable as a general statement of investor motivation. It is conventional to measure return and risk as the expected value of the rate of return and its standard deviation. The rate of return yielded on an investment in a share of stock is the sum of the dividend payment and the capital gain, expressed as a ratio of the price initially paid for the stock. Thus, the actual rate of return is

$$r_t = \frac{d_{t+1} + (P_{t+1} - P_t)}{P_t}$$

where:

r_t = the return from time t to $t + 1$
d_{t+1} = the dividend payable at $t + 1$
P_t = the share price at t
P_{t+1} = the share price at $t + 1$

The expected rate of return for any period t is denoted

$$E(r_t) = \sum_i p_i r_{i,t}$$

where p_i is the probability of return r_i in period t. The standard deviation is

$$\sigma(r_t) = \left\{ E[r_{i,t} - E(r_t)]^2 \right\}^{1/2}$$

Now consider an investor who is faced with a choice between alternative investments and who seeks to base his or her decision on expected return and standard deviation. For our example, we will consider just three possible stocks from which to choose, and, to keep things simple, we will further assume that the expected return and its standard deviation can be estimated from recent past experience. More specifically, the mean annual rate of return over the recent 10 time periods, and its standard error, are used as estimators for future returns.

As shown in Table 5–1, an examination of the three stocks reveals that stock C has the highest mean return and therefore is estimated to have the highest expected return. Stock B has the lowest expected return, with stock A having an expected return roughly halfway between stocks B and C. In terms of risk, stock B clearly performs badly, having a much higher standard deviation than stocks A and C. Stock C is a little riskier than stock A.

Our intrepid investor must now make his or her choice. If the investor has to choose one stock, he or she will clearly avoid stock B because it has the lowest return and highest risk. So the choice is between stocks A and C. Stock C exhibits higher return and higher risk than stock A. If the individual is highly risk-averse, he or she will probably choose stock A, being more impressed by its lower risk and being willing to sacrifice a little in terms of expected return. However, if the investor is not so intensively averse to risk (although still risk-averse), he or she may decide that stock C offers a distinct improvement in expected return over stock A, with only a small increase in risk. Under such circumstances, stock C is preferred to stock A. Thus, the ranking of the three stocks, using the symbol > to denote preference, is

$A > C > B$ for highly risk averse
$C > A > B$ for less risk averse

T A B L E 5–1

Actual Rates of Return on Specimen Stocks

	Period	Stock A	Stock B	Stock C
	1	0.06	0.03	0.13
	2	−0.03	0.03	−0.07
	3	0.00	0.23	0.13
	4	0.06	−0.12	0.13
	5	0.20	−0.22	0.18
	6	0.13	−0.15	0.13
	7	0.10	0.19	0.08
	8	−0.06	0.24	−0.10
	9	0.05	0.16	0.10
	10	0.23	0.00	0.18
Mean return, $E(r)$		0.074	0.069	0.081
Standard error, $\sigma(r)$		0.089	0.179	0.091

Figure 5–1 shows the risk-return characteristics of the stocks. Stock C has the highest return and stock B the lowest. Stock B has the highest risk and stock A the lowest. In the space shown in the figure, the investor wishes to be as far in a "northwesterly" direction as possible, since movement in this direction signifies increasing return and falling risk. On this criterion, stock B is clearly dominated by both stocks A and C, but stocks A and C cannot be ranked unambiguously because they fall in a "southwest–northeast" array with respect to each other.

Let us now see how the capital market would function to determine the price of securities. If investors were only allowed to hold one stock, nobody would wish to hold stock B and all investors would seek stocks A or C. Those already holding stock B would try to sell, thereby driving down its price. Simultaneously, investors would seek to purchase stocks A and C, thereby driving up the price. Since the rate of return for a security is based on its price, a fall in price will push up the expected rate of return,

F I G U R E   5-1

Return and Risk for Stock in Table 5-1

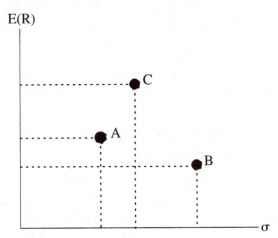

assuming no change in the firm's expected earnings. Conversely, an increase in price will lead to a fall in expected return, *ceteris paribus.* This supply–demand pressure will restructure the risk–return characteristics of the three stocks, perhaps until each of the stocks matches the preferences of some subgroup of investors. The final position might look like that shown in Figure 5–2, which

F I G U R E   5-2

Risk and Return after Price Adjustment

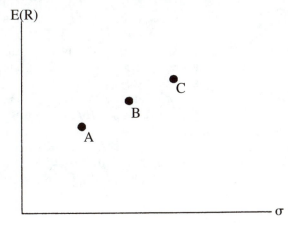

reveals that expected return is positively related to standard deviation.

Some of the older theories of capital markets did indeed produce results like those displayed by Figure 5–2. This pricing structure certainly is based on risk aversion, but modern capital market theory recognizes that the assumption of risk aversion also leads the investor to hold a portfolio rather than a single security, and this radically affects the capital market equilibrium.

CAPITAL MARKET EQUILIBRIUM WITH DIVERSIFICATION

Simple Diversification

Table 5–2 reproduces the information concerning stocks A, B, and C, but it also includes a fourth asset, D. It is seen immediately that D dominates stocks A and B in terms of risk and return and that it compares favorably with stock C. In fact, asset D delivers

T A B L E   5–2

Actual Rates of Return

	Period	A	B	C	D
	1	0.06	0.03	0.13	0.097
	2	−0.03	0.33	−0.07	0.063
	3	0.00	0.23	0.05	0.11
	4	0.06	−0.12	0.13	0.047
	5	0.20	−0.22	0.18	0.047
	6	0.13	−0.15	0.13	0.037
	7	0.10	0.19	0.08	0.116
	8	−0.06	0.24	−0.10	0.013
	9	0.05	0.16	0.10	0.120
	10	0.23	0.00	0.18	0.120
Expected return		0.074	0.069	0.081	0.077
Standard error σ_n			0.089	0.179	0.091	0.038
Covariance,	$\sigma_{A,B} = -0.0117$;	$\sigma_{A,C} = 0.007$;	$\sigma_{B,C} = -0.0131$		
Correlation coefficients	$r_{A,B} = -0.8$;	$r_{A,C} = 0.86$;	$r_{B,C} = -0.73$		

Note: $D = 0.33\,B + 0.67\,C$

an expected return that is only slightly lower than that for stock C, but asset D has a much lower standard deviation. Therefore, most moderately risk averse or highly risk-averse investors prob- ably would prefer asset D to stock C. Where did asset D come from? Asset D is a portfolio containing securities C and B.

Let us return to the problem of selecting from securities A, B, and C without the constraint that the investor hold only one security. Suppose two securities can be held, thereby forming a portfolio. It is tempting to return to the ranking derived earlier, which showed stocks A and C to be superior to stock B, although the ranking between stocks A and C was unclear. From this ranking, it appears that no rational investor would ever choose stock B.

However, this view ignores one important dimension. When risky cash flows are combined into a portfolio, the riskiness of the portfolio depends not only on the individual variances or stan- dard deviations of the component stocks, but also on their covar- iances or correlations. Negative covariances can have a dramatic effect by reducing portfolio risk, even if the items concerned each exhibit a high level of risk. Reexamination of stocks A, B, and C reveals that stock B has the attractive property that it appears to vary inversely with both stocks A and C. When stocks A and C deliver high returns, stock B tends to deliver low returns, and vice versa. However, stocks A and C appear to vary in the same direc- tion, suggesting positive correlation. Although stocks A and C ap- pear to be attractive when each is considered in isolation, a port- folio containing these two securities would not be effective in reducing portfolio risk. A portfolio containing stocks B and C would contain securities whose returns tended to vary in oppo- sition, thereby producing a fairly stable portfolio return. Asset D is such a portfolio, and it is formed by permitting the investor to invest one-third of his or her capital in stock B and two-thirds in stock C. The resulting portfolio has an expected return between that of stocks B and C, but a standard deviation that is much lower than that of either stock B or stock C.

The behavior of security portfolios closely parallels the port- folio behavior identified in the previous chapter. It is necessary to modify the formulas used there to calculate the portfolio mean and variance, for here we are dealing not with dollar values but with rates of return. The expected return, the variance of that rate of return, and its standard deviation for a portfolio of n securities are as follows:

$$E(r) = \sum_{i=1}^{n} w_i \, E(r_i) \tag{5.1}$$

$$\sigma^2(r) = \sum_{i=1}^{n} w_i^2 \, \sigma_i^2 + \sum_{i \neq j}\sum w_i w_j \sigma_{i,j} \tag{5.2}$$

$$\sigma(r) = [\sigma^2(r)]^{1/2} \tag{5.3}$$

where:

w_i = the weight of security i in the investor's portfolio
r_i = the rate of return on security i
σ_i = the standard deviation of the rate of return on security i
$\sigma_{i,j}$ = the covariance between the returns on securities i and j

Often, it is more useful to use the correlation coefficient instead of the covariance. This is easily accomplished by recalling that the correlation coefficient $r_{i,j}$ is defined by

$$r_{i,j} = \frac{\sigma_{i,j}}{\sigma_i \sigma_j}$$

Substitution into previous equation for portfolio variance is straightforward.

$$\sigma^2(r) = \sum_{i=1}^{n} w_i^2 \, \sigma_i^2 + \sum_{i \neq j}\sum w_i w_j r_{i,j} \sigma_i \sigma_j \tag{5.2a}$$

The means, standard deviations, covariances, and correlation coefficients are shown at the bottom of Table 5–2. Consider portfolio D, made up of one-third of capital invested in stock B and the two-thirds invested in stock C. The expected return and standard deviation can be confirmed by Equations (5.1) and (5.3):

$$E(r_D) = 0.33(0.069) + 0.67(0.081) = 0.077$$

$$\sigma(r_D) = [(0.33)^2 \, (0.179)^2 + (0.67)^2 \, (0.091)^2$$

$$+ \, 2(0.33)(0.67)(-0.0131)]^{1/2} = 0.038$$

The means and standard deviations of stocks B and C are now plotted in Figure 5–3a. By forming the portfolio from stocks B and C, the investor can also choose the risk–return combination shown as D on the graph. However, these possibilities do not exhaust the investor's choice. The investor could have invested 50% in each of stocks B and C, or perhaps 75% in stock B and 25% in stock C, and so on. The various options are plotted along the broken line that travels through B and C but that is convex to the vertical axis. The fact that the line is convex clearly illustrates possibilities for reducing risk by forming a portfolio.

From earlier analysis, it should be clear that the facility for reducing risk depends on the covariance between the securities. Suppose a portfolio, labeled E, was formed by combining stocks A and C. Since these stocks are positively correlated, there should be no dramatic reduction in risk. Figure 5–3b shows, on a diagram similar to Figure 5–3a, a broken line giving the risk–return combinations for portfolios of stocks A and C. Position E shows weights of 0.5 on each of stock A and stock C, with $E(r_E)$ and $\sigma(r_E)$ calculated as follows:

$$E(r_E) = 0.5(0.074) + 0.5(0.081) = 0.0775$$

$$\sigma(r_E) = [(0.5)^2 (0.089)^2 + (0.5)^2 (0.091)^2 + 2(0.5)(0.5)(0.007)]^{1/2} = 0.087$$

Figures 5–3a and b illustrate the effect of correlation on the potential for risk reduction through portfolio formation. The more pronounced convexity in Figure 5–3a indicates much greater risk reduction than that shown in Figure 5–3b. The limiting cases are given by perfect positive correlation (the correlation coefficient is unity) and perfect negative correlation (the correlation coefficient is minus unity). Although none of the pairs of securities in our example meets these criteria, Figures 5–3c and d show what the portfolio possibilities would be. Notice that with perfect positive correlation there is no curvature in the portfolio line at all. This is consistent with the analysis in the previous chapter, which revealed no prospect for diversification under these circumstances. With perfect negative correlation, the portfolio line actually touches the vertical axis, showing that one portfolio exists that will remove all risk. (It might be pointed out that with securities such as stocks, this very attractive perfect negative correlation is rarely found.)

FIGURE 5-3

Portfolio Risk Reduction: The Effect of Correlation

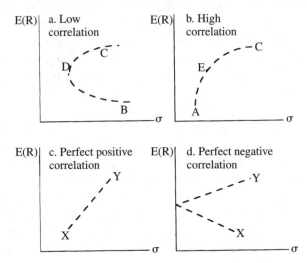

Derivation of the Efficient Frontier

So far, the portfolios have only been formed using pairs of securities. Relatively little imagination is needed to realize that further possibilities for diversification might exist if three or more securities are combined into a portfolio. The equations given for calculating expected return and variance are not restricted to any number of securities, and we could search through the wide selection of stocks and other financial assets available to us until we found our preferred risk–return combination. This may prove to be a long search, but it is quite simple to represent what might happen.

In Figure 5–4 a set of stocks is represented, each by its expected return and standard deviation. For any pair of stocks, we could construct portfolio lines such as those shown in Figure 5–3, and the shape of each line would depend on the correlation coefficient. Only two such portfolio lines are shown to avoid congestion. However, portfolios could be formed with three or more stocks. These can be represented as "portfolios of portfolios." Thus, the thin solid line joining the broken lines *AB* and *CD* rep-

F I G U R E   5-4

The Efficient Frontier

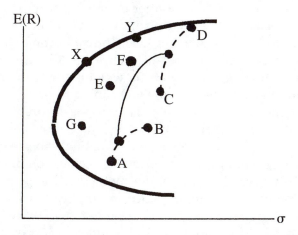

resents some of the portfolios that can be formed by combining securities *A, B, C,* and *D.* It is clear that portfolios along this line would not be attractive, since there are still other securities offering higher return and lower risk, such as stocks *E* and *F.* However, even further prospects for improvement arise from combining stocks *E* and *F* into a portfolio and perhaps including stock *C* and/ or stock *D.* When all such possibilities are exhausted, the resulting envelope curve, that is, the curve enclosing all the portfolio lines, will look like the thick solid line. The upper left portion of this envelope is known as the *efficient frontier* because it represents the most efficient portfolios that can be formed. The portfolios represented along this line deliver the minimum level of risk for each given level of expected return.

The various positions along the "northwest" segment of the efficient frontier represent portfolio choices that are efficient in mean–variance terms. Apparently, there is no optimal portfolio along this line (a statement that will be revised in due course). The more risk-averse investors presumably would choose portfolios, such as *X,* that exhibit relatively little risk but have a corresponding low level of expected return. More speculative investors would accept more risk to deliver higher expected return, such as portfolio *Y.* According to individual preference, each investor would locate at a position reflecting his or her degree of risk aversion.

To derive the efficient frontier in practice would appear to be an enormous task. There are hundreds of securities to choose from, and we have to consider every possible combination. Bearing in mind that the number of securities to be assembled into portfolios is not fixed and that the weights for each security can assume any value (subject to their summing to unity), the number of possible portfolios is infinite. This implies a pretty long game of trial and error; in fact, the proverbial three monkeys might well randomly type out the complete works of Shakespeare earlier than trial and error would lead to complete specification of the efficient frontier. However, there are easier methods. One possibility is to use quadratic programming, since its application is straightforward with a personal computer. Another possibility is to solve mathematically, since an analytical solution has been derived by Merton (1972). Thus, the technology to solve the efficient frontier is now routinely available.

The efficient frontier solution to the problem of portfolio selection was presented in 1952 by Markowitz. This work represented an important turning point in capital market theory because it offered a usable quantitative solution to the issue of portfolio selection. Its implications have proved to be far-reaching, leading to a revolution in the way we view the workings of the capital market.

The Market Portfolio

The efficient frontier turns out to be a misnomer, for there may be ways of improving investment performance as measured by risk and expected return. Let us suppose that, in addition to the various risky securities that are used to derive the efficient frontier, there is also a riskless security. This may be represented as debt that is free of default risk and has a fixed yield. As a rough approximation, a Federal Treasury Bill may be considered to be risk-free. Given the absence of risk, we would expect such a security to bear a fairly low yield, which is denoted r_f in Figure 5–5. The diagram also reproduces the efficient frontier.

F I G U R E   5-5

The Capital Market Line and Market Portfolio

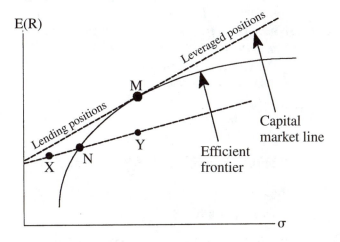

The rate r_f is the risk-free rate, and we will assume that un-limited borrowing and lending take place at this rate.[1] With bor-rowing and lending available at r_f, the investor may chose not to invest all his or her capital in risky securities. Instead, he or she may choose some portfolio, such as N, and invest half of the cap-ital in N and the remainder in the risk-free security yielding r_f. This composite position will yield an expected return and stan-dard deviation shown as X on the straight line connecting r_f and N. Indeed, any other position on the line is also available by var-ying the proportions of capital invested in N and r_f. A more ag-gressive investor may choose to borrow money at r_f, thereby per-mitting him or her to invest more than the initial capital in portfolio N. This leveraged investor will achieve some position on the broken line such as Y.

---

1. The reader should not get nervous about simplifying assumptions here. Indeed, sev-eral more simplifying assumptions will soon be made to proceed with the analy-sis. These assumptions are necessary to construct a predictive model, and this model should be appraised on its predictive power rather than on the accuracy of its assumptions. The assumptions can be relaxed, causing some modification of the model; however, the basic insights of the simple model are still preserved.

These two investment strategies are illustrated quite easily by considering a lending investor who lends half her capital at the risk-free rate and a leveraged investor who borrows an amount equal to half his initial capital to invest in a risky portfolio. In this example, the risk-free rate is 0. 1; the expected return on the risky portfolio is 0.15, with a standard deviation of 0.2. The covariance between r_f and the risky portfolio must be zero, since the former has no risk.

Lending Investor

$$E(r) = 0.5(0.1) + 0.5(0.15) = 0.125$$

$$\sigma(r) = [(0.5)^2(0)^2 + (0.5)^2(0.2)^2 + 2(0.5)(0.5)(0)]^{1/2} = 0.1$$

Leveraged Investor

$$E(r) = -0.5(0.1) + 1.5(0.15) = 0.175$$

$$\sigma(r) = [(-0.5)^2(0)^2 + (1.5)^2(0.2)^2 + 2(-0.5)(1.5)(0)]^{1/2} = 0.3$$

In this example, the investor generated new opportunities not available with the efficient frontier. Portfolios along the segment $r_f N$ may well be chosen over positions on the efficient frontier. However, a leveraged position such as Y clearly is suboptimal, since there are positions on the frontier offering higher expected return for the same level of risk.

By choosing another risky portfolio on the efficient frontier and then lending or leveraging, the investor can do even better. This portfolio is defined by a point of tangency between the efficient frontier and a straight line going through r_f. The tangency point defines a risky portfolio that is denoted M. Lending positions are defined along the segment $r_f M$, and leveraged positions are defined along the segment MZ. The line $r_f MZ$ is known as the *capital market line*. Notice that the capital market line dominates the lending/leveraged positions that could be attained holding portfolio N. For every position on $r_f NY$, there are corresponding positions on $r_f MZ$ offering higher returns for the same risk or, equivalently, offering lower risk for the same level of expected return. It is also fairly obvious that the tangency portfolio M is optimal in the sense that it offers lending/leverage opportunities that dominate those offered by any other risky portfolio on the efficient frontier.

This analysis leads to the conclusion that there is a single portfolio of risky securities that is optimal for all investors regardless of personal attitude toward risk. This portfolio is M. Investors who are risk-averse are better served by holding part of their capital in M and lending at the risk-free rate to achieve a position on the lending portion of the capital market line than by holding a portfolio such as N that is fairly low in risk. Similarly, investors who are more speculative are better off borrowing at r_f and investing the proceeds, together with initial capital, in risky portfolio M. This leads to a position on the leveraged part of the capital market line that is superior to holding a risky, high-return portfolio such as Y. Consequently, all investors, regardless of risk preference, would choose the same portfolio of risky assets, but they would differ in their financing decisions. On the latter decisions, some investors will achieve lending positions and others will achieve leveraged positions to match their individual risk preferences. This conclusion can be given as a *separation theorem*:

The selection of a portfolio of risky stocks is independent both of the financing decision and of individual risk preference given the assumptions of the analysis.

If all investors are predicted to hold the same portfolio of risky stocks, then all stocks represented on the market must find their way into that portfolio. The portfolio can be none other than the *market portfolio*, which includes all traded stocks, with each stock being held in the proportion its market value bears in relation to the total market value of all stocks. This is quite a dramatic conclusion, and it leads to interesting conclusions about the way in which securities are priced. This pricing process will now occupy our attention.

Systematic and Unsystematic Risk

Some assumptions have been necessary to get this far in the examination of capital markets. Further assumptions are necessary in order to continue. These assumptions are now collected together, and from these a model of asset pricing will be constructed:

1. Unlimited borrowing and lending can take place at a single risk-free interest rate. The Federal Treasury Bill rate usually is used as a proxy for this rate.

2. All assets can be bought and sold immediately in any quantity at the prevailing market price.

3. Assets are perfectly divisible; the investor can buy or sell any quantity, including fractions, of assets and short sales.

4. There are no taxes or transaction costs.

5. All investors base decisions only on the expected return and its variance (or standard deviation) and seek the minimum variance for any given level of return.

6. The planning horizon for investment decisions is one period. Note that the return during this period includes the terminal value of the asset.

7. Investors share identical expectations about the probability distributions of available assets.

These assumptions clearly do not accurately describe the real world. However, the relevant question is whether the predictions of the model correspond with the actual performance of the capital market. We will comment on the relaxation of these assumptions later.

These assumptions describe a frictionless market in which rational economic men and women conduct their business. In this market, investors would indeed hold the market portfolio, as described earlier, and the market would reach equilibrium when all investors reached the market portfolio position. How would assets be priced in such a market?

The rational investor in our assumed world is concerned with the expected return and variance (or standard deviation) of his or her investment portfolio. Any individual security that is purchased will affect the return and risk of the investor's portfolio, and the attractiveness of that asset to the investor therefore depends on these portfolio effects. Since the equilibrium portfolio is the market portfolio, each asset will be priced according to its contribution to the risk and return of the market portfolio. Since the expected return of a portfolio is simply the weighted average of its component securities, an individual asset will increase the portfolio expected return if that asset has a higher expected return than the portfolio. A lower expected return will pull down the portfolio return. However, the incremental risk the asset brings to the portfolio rests not so much on the riskiness of the asset as on its covariance with the portfolio. This leads to the partitioning of risk into *systematic* and *unsystematic* risk.

Consider two securities that have comparable expected returns and, according to past experience, have displayed similar levels of risk. However, the securities have exhibited very different correlations with returns on the market portfolio. As seen in Figure 5–6a, security A has tended to deliver high returns during periods when returns on the market portfolio were high and correspondingly low returns when returns on the market portfolio were low. Each dot in the diagram represents the pair of returns for the security r_A, and the market portfolio r_M during a given period. There is not a perfect correlation, which suggests that there is a random, or unexplained, component to the return of stock A. Nevertheless, there is a strong correlation, and the relationship is represented by a straight line. This line is constructed by fitting a simple regression as follows:

$$r_{A,t} = \alpha + \beta(r_{M,t}) + e_{A,t} \tag{5.4}$$

where:

F I G U R E   5–6

Positive and Negative Betas

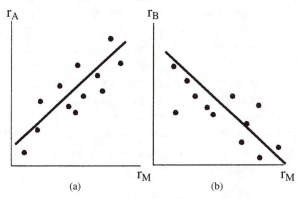

(a)   (b)

$r_{A,t}$ = the return on A in period t
$r_{M,t}$ = the return on the market portfolio in period t
α and β = estimated regression coefficients
$e_{A,t}$ = the residual error in period t

The term β shows the sign and sensitivity of the relationship that exists between A and M. In the case illustrated in Figure 5–6a, r_A moves upward on average as r_M moves upward; thus β has a positive slope. However, the slope is rather less than 45°, indicating that a percentage movement in r_M would be associated with rather less than a 1% movement in r_A. Thus β would have a value of something less than 1. In Figure 5–6b, a negative β security is shown. With this security, rates of return have tended to move in the opposite direction to the return on the market portfolio. It is clear that β is really measuring a similar relationship to that represented by the covariance. In fact, β is nothing more than a scaled version of covariance:

$$\beta_A = \frac{\text{cov}\ (r_A\ r_M)}{\sigma^2(r_M)}$$

where:

cov $(r_A r_M)$ = the covariance between r_A and r_M
$\sigma^2(r_M)$ = the variance of the return on the market portfolio

Examination of Equation (5.4) and Figures 5–6a and b reveals that the riskiness of the security is divided into two components. Part of the risk is explained by the relationship between the security's returns and the return on the market index. This risk is transmitted through the sensitivity coefficient β (or covariance). Thus, as the market moves up or down, there are sympathetic movements in the individual stock's returns. For stock A, the explained movement is in the same direction as the movement in returns on the market portfolio; for stock B, the movement is in the opposite direction. This explained component of risk is labeled *systematic risk* (otherwise known as *market risk*) because it is systematically related to movement in the market portfolio. The higher β is, the more sensitive the stock's returns are to changes in the market portfolio.

The second component of risk also is apparent from examination of Equation (5.4) and Figure 5–6. The distribution of security returns in Figures 5–6*a* and 6*b* is not fully explained by movement in the market portfolio. The various dots in the diagrams show some random variation about the correlation line, revealing that there is an unexplained variation in security returns. The unexplained variation in security returns is also shown by the error term $e_{A,t}$ in Equation (5.4), and the unexplained component of risk is known as *unsystematic, or non-market, risk.*[2]

The Security Market Line and the Capital Asset Pricing Model

The market portfolio is, by definition, highly diversified. Consequently, the unsystematic component of risk will be almost "diversified out." The unsystematic risk of each security will have little or no effect on the overall riskiness of such a diversified portfolio. As a result, the investor should be indifferent to the degree of unsystematic risk exhibited by an individual security, and this will have no effect on the price of the security.

Systematic risk is an entirely different matter. If the covariance with the market portfolio is high (that is, β is high), the addition of the security to the investor's diversified portfolio will have an adverse effect on the portfolio risk. Conversely, if β is low, the addition of the security will have a beneficial effect on portfolio risk. In the somewhat unusual case that the covariance (and therefore β) is negative, the inclusion of the security can bring a big reduction in portfolio risk. Thus, it is the covariance with the market portfolio, or β, that determines the incremental

---

2. The partition of risk can also be seen as follows:
$$r_A = \alpha + \beta r_{M,t} + e_{A,t} \quad \text{from Equation (5.4)}$$
However, the expected return on security A is
$$E(r_A) = \alpha + \beta E(r_M)$$
Therefore, $\sigma^2(r_A) = E[r_A - E(r_A)]^2$
$$= E\{[\alpha + \beta r_{M,t} + e_{A,t}][\alpha - \beta E(r_M)]\}^2$$
$$= E\{\beta [r_{M,t} - E(r_M)] + e_{A,t}\}^2$$
$$= E\{\beta^2 [r_{M,t} - E(r_M)]^2 + 2e_{A,t} [r_{M,t} - E(r_M)]\beta + e_{A,t}^2\}$$
$$= \beta^2 \text{ var } r_M + \text{var } e_A \quad \text{since } E(e_{A,t}) = 0$$
or $\sigma^2(r_A) = $ systematic risk + unsystematic risk

contribution of each security to the riskiness of the typical investor's portfolio, and consequently β exerts an important influence on the security price.

The capital asset pricing model (CAPM) embodies a linear relationship, in equilibrium, between the expected return of a security and the security's β value. This relationship is known as the *security market line* (SML) and is shown in Figure 5–7. The security market line reveals that price is determined by systematic risk alone. Unsystematic risk does not affect price, and thereby does not affect the expected return, because this element of risk is substantially eliminated by simple diversification.

In Figure 5–7 two stocks are represented that do not lie on the SML. For stock X, the expected return is high relative to its p value. The returns on stock X will be viewed as abnormally high relative to β and it will be viewed as being underpriced. Investors will seek to purchase this security, thereby bidding up its price. The price rise will result in capital gain to existing holders, but, for those buying at the higher price, the expected return (based on the new price) will be correspondingly lower. In this manner, the expected return will fall until the equilibrium relationship is restored. Conversely, security Y is overpriced according to market expectation. Excessive selling pressure will drive the price down, causing expected return to be restored to its equilibrium level.

F I G U R E   5–7

The Capital Asset Pricing Model

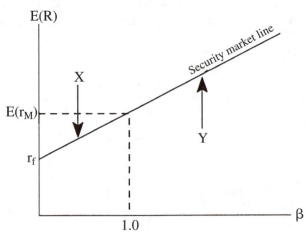

Two positions on the SML may be pointed out. The market portfolio must have a value of unity because β measures the correlation with itself. The expected return on the market portfolio is therefore illustrated at $\beta = 1.0$. The intercept on the vertical axis shows the expected return for a security that is uncorrelated with the market portfolio. Such a security will have a return of r_f (i.e., the risk-free rate), if one keeps in mind that a risk-free security also must have no systematic risk. Comparing these two rates reveals that the market portfolio commands an additional return for systematic risk of:

$$E(r_M) - r_f = \text{market risk premium} \qquad (5.5)$$

Securities with β values in excess of unity will command higher returns, and thus a higher risk premium, than the market portfolio. When β is lower than unity, the risk premium will be less than that for the market portfolio. Some securities may even have negative β values. These securities would be in high demand because of their facility for counteracting portfolio risk. Consequently, expected return would be very low, even lower than the risk-free rate. The risk premium on securities with negative values is negative.

The capital asset pricing model (CAPM) was derived independently in the mid-1960s by Sharpe (1964), Lintner (1965), and Mossin (1966)[3] and represented a natural evolution from Markowitz's portfolio theory of the 1950s. We now present the CAPM more formally to reveal the structure of security returns. The security market line is stated by Equation (5.6):

$$E(r_j) = r_f + \beta_j[E(r_M) - r_f] \qquad (5.6)$$

where:

r_j = return on security j
β_j = β value for security j

The first component of any security's return in Equation (5.6) is simply the riskless interest rate. The second component is the

---

3. Though, in fact, Karl Borch had already published in 1962, a model of reinsurance markets that was identical in all relevant respects to the CAPM and that he argued could be applied to capital asset markets. It is thus arguable that Borch should receive credit for the CAPM.

risk premium, which is the β value times the market risk premium. Notice that Equation (5.6) shows the expected return in equilibrium to be a linear function of the security's β value. Consistent with the earlier analysis, the equation does not contain any reward for unsystematic risk because this is irrelevant to the security price.

Relaxing the Assumptions of the Model

Clearly, the assumptions used to develop the capital asset pricing model represent an oversimplification of reality. Again, we emphasize that it is not appropriate to reject the model on the basis of its assumptions; rather, we should test whether its predictions correspond with observed behavior. However, we will illustrate how changes in the assumptions affect the predictions. The treatment is illustrative rather than exhaustive, since this is peripheral to our main purpose and an extensive literature exists on the subject.

One assumption that clearly does not hold up is that there exists a single risk-free interest rate for borrowing and lending. Clearly, intermediaries have transaction costs and wish to make some profit. Therefore, borrowing rates typically are higher than lending rates. This implies that there is not one tangency portfolio on the capital market line, but two; one corresponding to the borrowing rate and one corresponding to the lending rate. Labeling these portfolios M_B and M_L, respectively, yields two expressions for the security market line:

$$E(r_B) = r_{f,B} + \beta[E(r_{M,B}) - r_{f,B}]$$

$$E(r_L) = r_{f,L} + \beta[E(r_{M,L}) - r_{f,L}]$$

where $r_{f,B}$ and $r_{f,L}$ are the respective borrowing and lending rates. These security market lines are shown in Figure 5–8a. The result is that there is no unique equilibrium price for each security. For some investors, trade in a given security will be in the context of a lending portfolio; for others, trade will be supported by a borrowing portfolio.

Consider another assumption: that there are no transaction costs. Without this assumption, investors may observe small differences in expected returns (and therefore prices) from their estimated equilibrium values without being induced to trade. Divergence from equilibrium must be sufficient to cover transaction costs before trading occurs. This suggests that the SML may not be a single line but a band, as shown in Figure 5–8b. The width of the band will depend on the size of transaction costs: the smaller the transaction costs, the narrower the band. Differences in expectations among investors may also produce a range of expected returns for a given β value, also producing a band rather than a unique security market line. The resulting band is shown in Figure 5–8c.

Changes such as these produce a pricing relationship that is not as sharp as that shown in the simple model but still has the same general properties. Thus, in Figure 5–8d a fuzzy upward-sloping area is shown in place of a well-defined equilibrium pricing line. The fuzziness reveals some range of uncertainty in the

F I G U R E   5–8

Imperfections and the Capital Asset Pricing Model

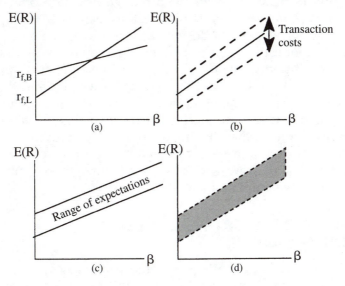

equilibrium price, but this is insufficient to destroy the main insight of the model: that expected returns in equilibrium bear a positive relationship to systematic risk.

Relaxing the assumptions of a unique borrowing/lending rate and no transaction costs implies that investors may hold different portfolios. However, this does not destroy the valuable insight of the model that much risk reduction can be achieved by diversification. The extent of risk reduction depends on the covariances of the securities in an individual's portfolio. Strictly speaking, the use of β values to measure these covariances is appropriate only if investors actually hold the market portfolio. However, if individuals hold portfolios that are highly correlated with the market portfolio, β serves as a useful proxy for these covariances. Most diversified portfolios are highly correlated with the market portfolio, and consequently β serves as a useful measure of systematic risk.

Some modifications of the capital asset pricing model (CAPM) have been formulated in response to some of its stronger assumptions. For example, Merton (1973) formulated a multiperiod asset pricing model, Gonedes (1976) formulated a capital asset pricing model with heterogeneous expectations, and Mayers (1972) formulated a model with some nonmarketable assets. Perhaps one of the more interesting developments has been the introduction by Ross (1974) of the arbitrage pricing model, which, *ceteris paribus,* measures systematic risk in relation to multiple factors. These developments do represent improvements in our understanding of capital markets. However, they have not displaced the CAPM but have qualified and fine-tuned it. They all preserve the basic insight of CAPM, that investors diversify and that only risk that is undiversifiable is priced. However, most of the newer models predict that more than one factor explains the variation in asset prices. Rather than having a single beta, many of the derivative models explain asset returns with respect to several macroeconomic variables. We will now see whether the predictions of the CAPM have empirical support.

TESTING THE CAPITAL ASSET PRICING MODEL

Many tests have been conducted on the capital asset pricing model and its various derivatives. It is difficult to summarize this literature and to arrive at an unqualified conclusion as to whether the

CAPM is supported or rejected by the evidence. I will suggest that the mainstream opinion among academics and practitioners is that, while earlier tests of the simple single-beta CAPM provided some support, later empirical work favors the more complex derivatives of CAPM in which multiple common factors explain much of the variation in asset returns.

As pointed out by Miller and Scholes (1972), and Roll (1977) many of the earlier tests of CAPM had been plagued by statistical problems. One of the landmark studies designed to overcome these problems is that of Fama and MacBeth (1973), who showed that portfolios formed (and reformed) according to the rankings of the stock betas, did indeed exhibit rates of return that were linearly related to the portfolio betas as predicted by the CAPM. Contrary evidence on the single factor CAPM also exists (e.g., Levy, 1978) and, more recently, in a series of studies by Fama and French (1993, 1996a, 1996b) and there is still disagreement as to whether the simple CAPM is "alive or dead." However, even if we accept the negative results on the single-factor CAPM, Fama and French are amongst a number of people who have shown that asset returns can be well explained by a small number of common factors, say three–five. A full analysis of these issues is not appropriate here. However, the message that is relevant is as follows. We do not know whether the undiversifiable risk is adequately measured by a single factor (the stock beta) as predicted by the simple CAPM or by a small number of common economic factors as in the derivative versions of the CAPM or the arbitrage pricing theory. But this distinction is not really important for our purposes. Empirical work does lend support to the view that some risk is idiosyncratic to each firm and can be diversified if investors hold a number of assets in their portfolio. This risk is not priced, and returns on financial assets should be independent of this diversifiable risk. But other risk is common to most firms, and this risk is not diversified away simply by adding more stocks to your portfolio. This undiversifiable risk is priced and is reflected in rates of returns on financial assets.

IMPLICATIONS FOR FINANCIAL MANAGEMENT

It is now time to draw attention inward to the decisions made within a firm to see how these are influenced by activity within the capital market. The obvious connection is that financial management is assumed to be directed toward the goal of value maximization, and the value of a firm's securities is determined by investor preferences as expressed in their trading activity. The equilibrium rate of return given by the CAPM for a stock with a given β value is the return required by investors to compensate for the systematic risk of that stock. This required rate of return provides a guide for the firm's capital budgeting decisions.

The expected rate of return delivered by a stock depends on the expected future earnings of the firm. Indeed, the equilibrium price of the stock is otherwise defined as the expected value of future earnings of the firm discounted at the equilibrium rate appropriate to the β value. This price implies that the expected return is at its equilibrium rate. With this in mind, consider a new company that has just been floated with a particular investment program in mind. The criterion commonly used to decide whether such a project should be accepted is that the expected cash flows should yield a positive present value when discounted at an appropriate rate. The appropriate rate is simply the equilibrium rate corresponding to the level of systematic risk in the cash flows. This requires calculation of a β value for the cash flows by estimating their correlation with the market portfolio. If the net present value criterion is satisfied, the firm will yield an expected return to the stockholders that exceeds the equilibrium return. Consequently, the stock of the firm will acquire a value in excess of the capital raised by the original flotation. In this way, value is created in satisfaction of the assumed corporate goal.

The preceding paragraph describes the well-known capital budgeting framework. The capital budgeting criteria apply to the decision to float a new firm, but they also can be used to evaluate new projects contemplated by an existing firm. The rules can be applied separately to individual projects as long as the correct risk-adjusted discount rate is used. The expected return and β value for a firm can be represented as the weighted average of the expected returns and β values of the various component activities of the firm, that is,

$$E(r) = \sum_i E(r_i)$$

$$\beta = \sum_i w_i \beta_i$$

where:

$E(r)$ = expected return from all the firm's activities
$E(r_i)$ = expected incremental return on component activity i
  β_i = systematic risk for r_i
  w_i = weighting of activity i

The implication of this weighting procedure is as follows: Consider a firm that is currently offering an expected return of, say, 15% to its shareholders, which is the equilibrium rate given the estimated β of 0.8. The equilibrium is illustrated at position A in Figure 5–9. A new project is contemplated for which the expected cash flows represent a 20% return on new capital to be raised. The β value for these cash flows is estimated at 1.4, and the equilibrium return for this β value is 18%. Clearly, the expected return on this new project, position B, is above the equilibrium return shown by position D. If the new activity accounts for 50% of total activity (that is, $w_i = 0.5$), the above equations show that the firm should have an expected return and β value of:

$$E(r) = 0.5(0.15) + 0.5(0.2) = 0.175$$
$$\beta = 0.5(0.8) + 0.5(1.4)\ \ = 1.1$$

This position, C, is definitely above the equilibrium value shown

F I G U R E   5-9

Creating Wealth through Project Selection

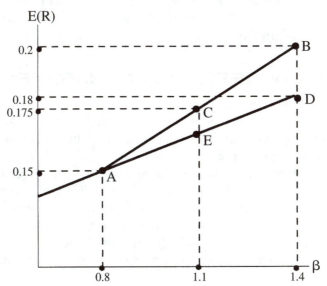

by position *E*. This excessive return will cause investors to seek to purchase the stock, thereby bidding up its price. In this way, acceptance of the project will increase the share price in satisfaction of the corporate objective.

The relationship between capital market theory and financial management can be summarized as follows. The equilibrium rate of return is the return required by investors given the level of systematic risk. Since this rate is required by investors to supply capital to the firm, it may be considered to represent the cost of equity capital to the firm. This rate reflects the effect of risk on investors' personal portfolios given that they have the facility for diversification. The rate does contain a risk adjustment, but this only relates to systematic risk. Since the corporate objective is assumed to be value maximization, it follows that any investment project accepted by a firm that delivers an incremental return above its equilibrium rate will add value to the firm's stock. This condition will be satisfied if the estimated incremental cash flows from the project yield a positive net present value when discounted at the equilibrium rate of return relevant to the project's systematic risk. Alternatively, the condition for value creation is satisfied if the internal rate of return exceeds the cost of capital. Notice that the new project is not assessed on the basis of its total risk, since part of that risk will disappear when combined with the risk of other activities of the firm and when combined with the risk of other stocks held by the shareholder in his or her investment portfolio. These implications carry over to our consideration of risk management.

IMPLICATIONS FOR RISK MANAGEMENT

The capital asset pricing model is as interesting in what it does not imply for risk management as in what it does. Let us start with the negative. Suppose a firm has a risky cash flow that is uncorrelated with the market portfolio. In other words, this cash flow has a zero beta. Whether the firm retains or hedges this cash flow should be of little concern to the firm's shareholders. Since investors can diversify zero beta risk in the formation of their personal investment portfolios, then the corporation does them no favor by hedging the risk itself. If a firm hedges, the shareholder's portfolio will face a given risk and return which depends on the weight of that firm in the portfolio and upon the composition of the rest of the portfolio. If the firm does not hedge, the investor can replicate the original portfolio risk and return simply by changing its composition, such as by reducing the weight of that security. Shareholder diversification is a substitute for corporate hedging.

Let us take another case, where the risky cash flow is correlated with the market portfolio. Under this condition, will corporate hedging add value? The answer depends on the price of risk. Suppose that all insurance policies (or other hedges) are bought for a premium that reflects the beta of the risky cash flow being hedged. Hedging will certainly affect the risk of the firm, and it will certainly affect the beta of the shareholders' portfolios. But investors will neither be better off nor worse off, since the changes in the portfolio are made at exactly the same terms the investors could have obtained by buying and selling stocks. Shareholders could have duplicated the effects of the corporate hedge by trading shares.

But insurance can be mispriced. If the firm can transfer risk to another party at a price that does not reflect the risk (i.e., the price of the risky cash flow is its present value when discounted at a risk-free rate), there can be real gains and losses from the transfer. For example, suppose insurable losses are high when capital market returns are high. Since losses are a negative cash flow, this reverses the sign of the beta, which will be negative. Such losses have the attractive property that they will stabilize a broad portfolio. Thus, they *should* sold at a price which discounts the expected loss at *less than* the risk-free rate to reflect the negative beta. This price will be high because the discount rate is low. Thus, if the firm pays a price that is discounted at the risk-free rate, then the price is too low and is a bargain. A firm that buys such mispriced insurance is adding value, not so much by changing the risk as by buying a policy at a bargain price. The gain is the difference between the equilibrium price and the actual price. Thus, the capital asset pricing model guides us on what the equilibrium market price should be for hedge products.

But notice how little the capital asset pricing model tells us about why we should hedge. If anything, it says that if hedges are priced to reflect beta, corporate hedging is irrelevant and will not benefit shareholders. All it says is that if we do hedge, we should look carefully at the price, and that the CAPM provides a benchmark. This is an important point; it warns us against a misleading, but widely held view, about why firms should hedge risk. The idea that firms should hedge because shareholders do not like risk carries little credibility in the CAPM world. Either the risk is diversifiable and can be controlled by shareholders through their own portfolio management, or the risk is undiversifiable, in which case it will carry a price that reflects the beta. In the last case, the effect on shareholders could be replicated by shareholders simply by trading stocks. *The CAPM does not tell us why firms should manage risk; rather, it tells us something about the prices at which insurance and other hedges should sell.*

Thus, we are badly in need of an explanation of how firms can create value through risk management. This will come in Chapter 7. However, it is important to note that the CAPM does not argue against hedging. What the CAPM and derivative asset pricing models tell us is that the prices of residual cash flows that filter through to investors should strike a balance between systematic risk and expected returns. The above argument is that hedging will do little in the risk dimension that will make investors better off. The irony is that the hedging story is more about changes to the expected value of returns to shareholders. What we will show in Chapter 7 is that if the underlying cash flows of the firm (not the residual claims of shareholders on these cash flows) are risky, this risk will induce opportunistic behavior, increase taxes, or produce other inefficiencies that will lower their expected value. This lowering of expected cash flows is a real cost to shareholders. Thus, the role of risk management is not to change the risk–return balance to investors but to reduce the inefficiencies associated with risky cash flows.

The financial management and risk management implications of the capital asset pricing model that are drawn here apply to firms whose ownership is traded. By contrast, consider a family-owned firm whose owners are concerned not solely with value maximization, but with other objectives, such as maintenance of family control. Furthermore, family members may work in the business, thereby combining their ownership interest and their employment interest. For such firms, total risk, not just systematic risk, may be especially important. Family owners probably have not diversified away the joint risk of ownership and employment in the family business. Under such circumstances, ownership interest cannot be separated from employment interest. Indeed, cross subsidization may arise between these separate interests. The value of ownership claims may not be maximized in order to protect family control and promote the employment interests of family members. For this firm, financial management and risk management will be differently motivated, and sole concentration on systematic risk is inappropriate. Investment projects and risk management proposals may be assessed according to their impact on the total risk of corporate earnings. Although we will concentrate on the more widely held firm in the remainder of this book, we will admit the occasional example in which concentrated ownership dictates the use of more substantial risk premiums.

CONCLUSION

If the value of a firm's equity is to be used to guide risk management decisions, the process by which the capital market values securities merits examination. For risk management in particular, the examination of capital markets is essential because risk and the potential for reducing risk through diversification are at the heart of the valuation process.

The capital asset pricing model rests on the propensity for an investor to hold a portfolio. The risk of a security may be divided into systematic and unsystematic components. Systematic risk is that which is explained by the correlation of the security returns with returns on the market portfolio. The unexplained, or residual, risk is labeled unsystematic risk. The systematic risk measures the incremental contribution of a security to the riskiness of the market portfolio. Because investors are predicted to hold the market portfolio, it is this measure of risk that is relevant to the pricing of the security. Unsystematic risk is not relevant for security pricing, because it is easily diversified away. This reasoning leads to a model of security pricing that asserts that expected returns are linearly related to the security's β value and are independent of unsystematic risk. This relationship is known as the capital asset pricing model.

The capital asset pricing model is based on several restrictive assumptions, thereby tempting the reader to reject it as unpractical. However, the main insights of the model do survive relaxation of these assumptions. Furthermore, the acid test of the model is not whether its assumptions are realistic, but whether its predictions are confirmed by real-world behavior. Evidence does lend some support for the model in a modified form in which there is a not a single factor, or beta, but several common economic factors that jointly explain variations in asset returns.

The capital asset pricing model and its variants have important positive and negative implications for risk management. In the assessment of the cost of capital to appraise risk management (or any other) risk management projects, the relevant measure of risk is the systematic risk of the project, not its total risk. Throughout the book, we will need to discount future cash flows, and we will look to the CAPM either explicitly or implicitly to provide the appropriate cost of capital. The second important implication is a negative one. Reduction of risk for a firm may not by itself add value, since shareholders themselves can reduce risk in the management of their personal portfolios. Thus, it is unconvincing to argue that firms should manage risk simply because their owners are risk-averse. We are lacking a clear motivation for risk management. As we will see in Chapters 7 and 8, we must look beyond asset pricing to how risk affects the transactions costs of a firm in order to explain how value can be created through risk management.

REFERENCES

Black, Fisher. 1972. "Capital Market Equilibrium with Restricted Borrowing." *Journal of Business* 45:444–55.

Borch, Karl. 1962. "Equilibrium in a Reinsurance Market" *Econometrica* 30:424–444.

Fama, E. R., and J. MacBeth. 1973. "Risk Return and Equilibrium: Empirical Tests." *Journal of Political Economy* 71:607–36.

Fama, E., and K. R. French. 1993. "Common Risk Factors in the Returns on Stocks and Bonds." *Journal of Financial Economics* 33:3–56.

Fama, E., and K. R. French. 1996a. "The CAPM Is Wanted, Dead or Alive." *Journal of Finance* 51:1947–58.

Fama, E., and K. R. French. 1996b. "Multifactor Explanations of Asset Pricing Anomalies." *Journal of Finance* 51:55–84.

Gonedes, N. 1976. "Capital Market Equilibrium for a Class of Heterogeneous Expectations in a Two Parameter World." *Journal of Finance* 31:1–15.

Levy, H. 1978. "Equilibrium in an Imperfect Market: A Constraint on the Number of Securities in the Portfolio." *American Economic Review* 68:643–58.

Lintner, J. 1965. "Security Prices, Risk and Maximal Gains from Diversification." *Journal of Finance* 20:587–615.

Markowitz, H. 1952. "Portfolio Selection." *Journal of Finance* 7:77–91.

———. 1959. *Portfolio Selection*. Cowles Monograph No. 16. New York: John Wiley & Sons.

Mayers, D. 1972. "Nonmarketable Assets and Capital Market Equilibrium under Uncertainty." In *Studies in the Theory of Capital Markets*, ed. M. C. Jensen. New York: Praeger.

Merton, R. C. 1972. "An Analytic Derivation of the Efficient Portfolio Frontier." *Journal of Financial and Quantitative Analysis*. 2:1851–72.

———. 1973. "An Intertemporal Capital Asset Pricing Model." *Econometrica* 41: 867–88.

Miller, M., and M. Scholes. 1972. "Rates of Return in Relation to Risk: A Reexamination of Some Recent Findings." In *Studies in the Theory of Capital Markets*, ed. M. C. Jensen. New York: Praeger.

Mossin, J. 1966. "Equilibrium in a Capital Asset Market." *Econometrica* 34:768–83.

Roll, R. 1977. "A Critique of the Asset Pricing Model Theory's Tests: Part 1. On Past and Potential Testability of the Theory." *Journal of Financial Economics* 4:129–76.

Ross, S. 1974. "Risk Return and Arbitrage." In *Risk and Return in Finance*, ed. I. Friend and J. S. Bicksler. Lexington, Mass.: Lexington Books.

———. 1978. "The Current Status of the Capital Asset Pricing Model." *Journal of Finance* 33:885–901.

Sharpe, W. F. 1964. "Capital Asset Prices: A Theory of Market Equilibrium under Conditions of Risk." *Journal of Finance* 19:74–80.

CHAPTER 6

Derivatives and Options

In later chapters we will examine various instruments for managing risk. Among the most apparent risk management devices will be hedging tools or insurance. These permit the party holding some risky asset to transfer that risk to another, a counter-party. Risk can be stripped from the asset value and sold separately for a price. Risk is a traded commodity. The two most familiar hedging products are insurance and options. Insurance has been available as a risk management tool for centuries. Options, though the idea has been around for a long time, have been used widely only in the past couple of decades. Options are one of a class of instruments called derivatives; the class also includes futures, forwards, and swaps, and various complex combinations of these basic types. All these derivatives have a vital role in risk management. This chapter will serve as an introduction, not to their risk management function but to their basic features.

There is transparency in the naming of derivatives. This is not Alice's Wonderland; things are very much what they seem to be. Derivatives are just that: they are instruments that are *derived* from other instruments. Options are what they claim to be, that is, *choices;* futures and forwards are simply devices for trading some asset in the *future,* and swaps are the *exchange* of one thing for another. This chapter will serve as an introduction to derivatives and as a preparation for some of the uses of derivatives in risk management.

FORWARDS AND FUTURES

Perhaps the simplest derivatives are forwards and futures. These are similar in their overall structure and differ in the details of trade and execution. We will defer discussion of these differences and start with, say, a forward. For the most part, one is free to purchase or, if you own it, sell any asset. This is the nature of a free market. The price at which you are able to buy or sell the asset will depend upon market conditions. The price for immediate transactions is known as the *spot* price. If, when you wish to sell, spot prices are high, you will do well; but someone else will have to buy at a similar high price. If spot prices are low, you will get a better deal on the buying side and a worse deal on selling. The terms at which you trade are subject to the vagaries of the market; the more volatile the prices, the more you can gain or lose by delaying your transaction. This situation provides opportunities and risks. A buyer facing high prices has the opportunity of waiting in case the spot price falls, and a seller can hold out hoping for spot prices to rise. Figure 6–1 shows such a possibility. Imagine you are a farmer and you own wheat that you wish to sell. Or a slight variation: it is spring, but you will have wheat to sell in the fall when you harvest. If the prices remain as they are in the spring, you will make a given amount of profit. If prices rise between spring and fall, you will make more profit. Your graph is the upwards-sloping line through the origin. Increases in prices show an increase in profit, and falling prices show a decrease in profit.

Enter the forward contract. For a farmer, the profitability of the coming season will depend on whether prices rise or fall from their present level. The forward contract enables you to lock in to a price. You can agree with a counter-party to sell the wheat in the fall at a price that is fixed today in the spring. The agreement is one to sell an asset at some future date, but at a price to be fixed now (known as the *forward* price). Thus, the contract will be immune from changes in the spot. For the moment, let us say that the forward price is the current spot price. The forward contract will, in fact, yield a profit or loss, depending on which way spot

F I G U R E   6–1

Gain or Loss from Price Change

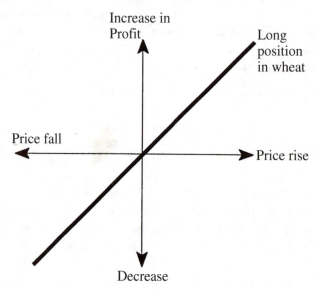

prices change. This is shown in Figure 6–2. Suppose the farmer buys the forward contract and prices rise by an amount shown as *R*. Had the forward not been purchased, the farmer would have been able to sell at the higher price and her profit would have increased by an amount *S*. But, the forward contract now means that she has to sell at the forward price and will lose all the profit she would have made had she sold at the higher fall spot price. So a loss, −*S*, is made on the forward contract. The overall position of the farmer is thus to have all profit that would have been made from the price rise wiped out. Why would the farmer do this? Because in the spring she does not know whether prices will rise or fall. Suppose prices do fall by an amount *F*. Had the future not been in place, the farmer would have lost an amount *G* from selling at the lower fall spot price. Thus, the forward contract enables the farmer to sell at the current price rather than the lower fall price and thereby to avoid a loss of *G*. In other words, the forward contract makes a profit of *G*.

   If we look at this from the spring, the farmer will have a profit that is the flat line shown as the horizontal origin. The

F I G U R E   6–2

Hedging with Future Contract

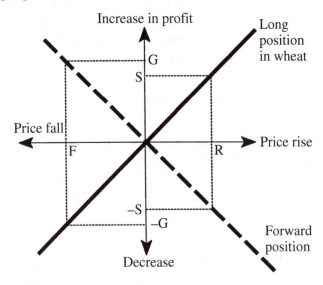

farmer gives up possible gains from price rises in exchange for avoiding losses from price falls. The same transaction can be seen by the other party. The person buying the wheat forward will lock in the purchase price. Thus, the forward buyer is protected from rising spot prices but sacrifices potential gains from falling spot prices. This can be useful for a baker who will need to purchase wheat anyway. By buying forward, the baker is able to hedge against price increases, just as the farmer is able to hedge against the risk of price falls.

So far we have assumed that the forward buyer and seller have some preexisting interest in the underlying asset and are exposed to risk from future price changes. This need not be the case. The forward contract can be used purely for a speculative purpose. You may have no interest in the underlying asset; you simply believe that prices are more likely to move in one direction than another. If you believe that prices will fall, then selling the asset forward will gain you a profit *if* your prediction is correct. You have locked in to the current high price and, if prices fall when you have to deliver (when the contract matures), you can simply buy at the lower spot price to complete the transaction. If you believe that prices will rise, you can buy forward. If you are correct, you will pay the forward price to complete the transaction, which will be higher than the spot price at maturity. If you do not wish to own the commodity, but simply buy the forward for speculation, you can simply resell the good at the spot price and clear the difference between that and the forward price.

Forward Prices

Forward prices are set in relation to spot prices by the following formula. The equilibrium forward price, FW, is:

$$FW = SP(1 + c)^n$$

where:

SP = current spot price
c = carrying cost
n = number of years to maturity

The carrying cost, c, requires a little explanation. If you sell forward, rather than now, you will face certain opportunity costs. By holding the asset, you lose the income you could have earned from investing the proceeds of a current sale. For some assets, such as commodities, you might have direct costs of storage. On the other side, there can be gains from holding the asset. For example, holding wheat provides an inventory that provides a buffer against supply shortages. The benefits of holding are known as convenience yields. The net carrying cost (after deduction of convenience yields) is the opportunity cost of holding the asset and will be reflected in price. Because this cost is denominated at an annual rate, the total cost is determined by the length of time the asset is held, and thus the carrying cost rate is compounded over the n periods to maturity. Because the opportunity cost can be positive or negative, the forward price can be either greater or lower than the current spot price.

Forward contracts are not traded on exchanges and are not standardized; they are "over-the-counter" contracts. These are often undertaken with banks and can be tailor-made to match a particular need for hedging or speculation. Forward contracts are common on commodities, currencies, and interest rates.

Futures contracts are similar in their underlying structure to forwards but with three differences. First, futures are standardized, exchange traded contracts. This makes the contract liquid and will tend to lower transaction costs. Thus, a party holding or writing a future can liquidate his or her position fairly easily. The second two differences address the credit risk associated with this type of contract. With a forward, there is a risk that the buyer (or the seller) will not be able to perform. Suppose the buyer simply does not have the money to buy the asset at maturity; for example, the buyer is bankrupt. To guard against this risk, futures contracts adopt, first, a device known as "marketing to market" or "cash settled." Each day the balance on the futures contract is settled between the parties. As the futures price changes daily, so the change is settled between the parties. This limits the amount of "debt" between the parties to no more than a single day's change in the forward price, and, at maturity, the buyer simply has to come up with the change in the futures price on the final day. The second device is that the buyers and sellers are required to post a performance bond known as a "margin." This is adjusted with cash settlements, but must never fall below an agreed floor. This collateralizes the transaction and minimizes credit risk.

Futures contracts are in effect a sequence of rolling daily forward contracts. Each day a forward contract is closed at the prior day's forward price and a new one opened at the current day's forward price. In this sense, the forward contract is a more primitive instrument and becomes a basic building block for more complex derivatives.

OPTIONS

A forward or future is an *obligation* to buy or sell some asset at a future date at an agreed price. An option is a *choice* to buy or sell the asset at an agreed price at some future date. In a forward or future, both parties agree to perform (to buy or sell) as they contracted. In an option, one party, the *option holder* (i.e., with the *long position* in the option) has the choice to buy or sell under the agreed terms. The choice may be exercised or not; there is no obligation. However, the counter-party who *writes* the option (i.e., who has a *short position* in the option) is obligated to sell the underlying asset if the option holder chooses to buy, or buy if the option holder chooses to sell.

There are many types of options: options to buy and options to sell (respectively calls and puts), options with a single exercise time and options that can be exercised over a time period (respectively European and American), options with cash distributions and options without, etc. We will cover just the basic forms, call and put options, and we will illustrate simple European options.

A *call option* is an option to buy an underlying asset. I will illustrate using options on shares of stock. The holder of the call has the option to purchase so many shares of the stock at some future date at a fixed price known as the *exercise price* or *striking price*. The exercise price is denoted E here. If the price of the underlying asset, the stock price M, at maturity exceeds the exercise price, then the person having the long option position, the holder, can exercise the option and buy the stock for E even though it is worth M ($>E$) at maturity. Thus, the holder makes a gain of $M - E$. However, the option was purchased up front for some price C and therefore the net profit from the long position in the call is $M - E - C$. But suppose that M was less than E at maturity. This would mean that if the option was exercised, the holder would be buying a stock for E when it was worth the lower amount M. The option holder would simply not exercise the option; he would let it expire worthless, in which case the option holder makes zero at maturity, and netting out the cost of the option, his net profit is $0 - C$, which is negative. This profit pattern is illustrated in Figure 6–3 by the line marked "long call."

The person holding the short position in the call option has no choices to make at maturity; she has sold the choice of purchase of the stock to the option holder. If the holder of the option exercises his choice to buy, the person writing the same option is obligated to honor that choice and sell the stock at the exercise price. With a price rise, the option will be exercised by the holder and the writer will be forced to sell the stock at E, making a negative amount of $E - M$. But the option was not given away free. The holder had to buy the call option at C, and this amount is kept by the writer whether or not the option is exercised. The net profit of the writer, if the option is exercised, is $C + E - M$. If the

F I G U R E   6–3

Call Options

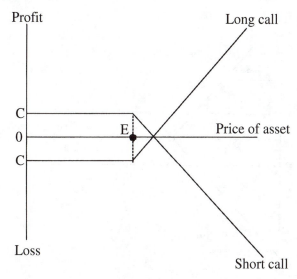

stock price at maturity rises only a little, the writer can still be up on the deal because the price will more than offset any small loss on exercise. For a larger rise in the stock price, the writer will lose money. But if the stock price is below E, the holder will not exercise and the writer will walk away with a profit of C. Thus, while the holder of a call can make money if the price rises and lose money if the price falls, the profit profile of the writer is exactly the opposite. The profit from the writer of the call option also is shown in Figure 6–3 as "short call."

The other main class of options is the put option. As a call option is the option to buy an underlying asset, a put option is the option to sell. The option holder, with a long position, buys the right to sell an underlying asset at some future date for a price agreed upon now. The agreed price is again the exercise, or striking, price. The counter-party, the option writer, sells the right to the put holder to be able to sell the asset to the option writer. Therefore, if the holder exercises her right to sell at maturity, then the writer is obligated to buy the asset at the exercise price. Figure 6–4 illustrates the profits to the two parties at different maturity values for the underlying asset. The exercise price is E. If the value

F I G U R E   6-4

Put Options

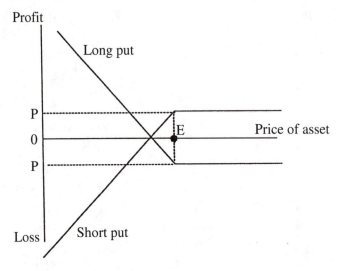

of the asset at maturity is above E, the holder will not exercise. There is simply no point in selling the asset at the exercise price E if the spot price is above E, and therefore the option expires worthless. If the spot price at maturity is below E, then the holder will exercise and clear the difference between the exercise price and the spot. If we bear in mind that the holder had to buy the put option for a price P, the net profit for the holder is $E - M - P$ if $M < E$ and $-P$ if $M \geq E$. Because the profit to the holder is a loss to the writer, and vice versa, the writer's profit is $P - E + M$ if $M < E$ and P if $M \geq E$.

Hedging and Speculating with Options

Options can be used to hedge a position in an underlying asset. Figure 6-5 shows the profit profile for a short position in a call option on an asset; together with the value of the asset, denoted "long asset." The value of the asset depends on its price and is therefore shown as the 45° line. Notice that, for values of the asset less than E, the asset value slopes upwards but the call profit is horizontal. Thus, any variation in the asset value in this range will

F I G U R E   6–5

Hedging Asset Position with Short Call

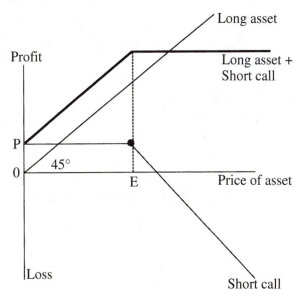

not change the value of the call. But if the asset value finishes in the range above *E*, any variation in the asset value will be matched by an offsetting variation in the call value; one slopes up at 45° while the other line slopes down at 45°. The combined position is shown by the thick line marked "long asset + short call." The effect of adding the short call to the long asset position is to provide a fixed "bonus" (the call premium) to the asset holder for low values of the asset, but in return the asset holder sacrifices the upside risk. The asset holder is left with most of the downside risk but has hedged the upside.

Figure 6–6 shows another hedge strategy for the holder of an asset: combining the long asset position with a long put position. Notice that now the long put increases in value as the underlying asset falls in value. The combination of these two positions is shown as the thick line. The downside risk from the asset position is hedged, but the upside potential of the asset is retained (minus of course the option premium). This seems a more natural type of hedge; the investor removes the downside risk but preserves upside potential. But options also can be used speculatively. A

F I G U R E   6–6

Hedging Long Asset with Long Put

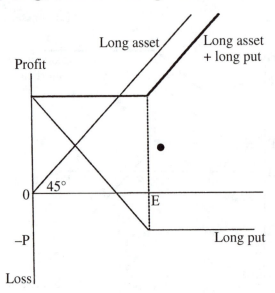

"naked" option position (holding the option without the under-lying asset) means that the holder of the option can make a lot of money if the asset price moves in the right direction, but will lose money if the option is not exercised. The call holder is speculating on a price rise and the put holder is speculating on a price fall. The writer also can speculate. Writing a call is speculating on a downward price movement and writing a put is speculating on an upward movement.

Equilibrium Pricing and Put–Call Parity

A call option is said to be "in the money" if the current asset price is above the exercise price and "out of the money" if the current asset price is below the exercise price. Conversely, a put option is in the money if the current price is below the exercise price and out of the money if the current price is above the exercise price. thus, either type of in the money option would be profitable to the holder if it could be exercised at the immediate stock price. If the option is in the money at maturity, then it is exercised and the holder makes money. If the exercise price is exactly the same as the current price of the asset, the option is said to be "at the money."

This gives us our first clue about how options are valued and therefore priced. In the money options are more valuable than out of the money options. Even if the option cannot be exercised immediately, the fact that it is in the money now bodes well for it being so at maturity since it does not require a big price change to make a profit. Consider a call option. Given any exercise price, the call is more likely to be in the money at maturity, the higher the current price and the lower the exercise price. The value of the call increases as the current price of the asset increases and as the exercise price decreases. These relationships are shown in the following table. The table shows the effect of the asset price on the value of a call option as a + and the effect on a put as a −; that is, an increase in the asset price increases the value of the call and reduces the value of the put. Similarly, increases in the exercise price reduce the value of the call and increase the value of the put. Other factors also affect the option values. For our purposes, the most important of these is the volatility of the price of the underlying asset (Figure 6–7).

Factors Determining Option Prices

	CALL	PUT
Price of Underlying Asset	+	−
Volatility or Risk of Asset	+	+
Interest Rate	+	−
Time to Maturity	+	+/−
Exercise Price	−	+

Imagine a call option where the current price of the asset on which it is written is 50 and the striking price is 55. If the asset price is perfectly stable, the option will never come in the money and is bound to expire worthless. With zero risk to the asset, the call option would have zero value. The same can be said of an out of the money put option; with zero risk to the asset, the option will remain "out of the money. Some risk is necessary to give these

FIGURE   6-7

Call Option Values and Current Stock Prices

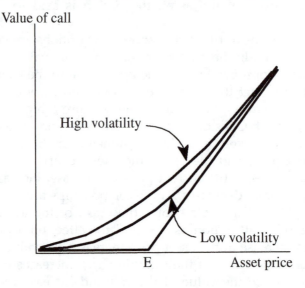

options value. The greater the risk that is introduced to the asset, the deeper the option can go into the money. Of course, risk works in two directions, up and down, but when looking at options we are only interested in one side of the risk. With a call option, the important thing is the upside risk in the asset. Increasing the downside movement in the asset price will have no effect on the call payoff; any out of the money position at maturity yields a zero payoff. But as upside risk increases, this does increase the possible payoffs to the call option. With puts the reverse is true. Increasing risk to the asset will increase the downside, which will increase the value of the put and will increase the upside, which will have no effect on the put value. Thus, increasing risk increases the value of both call and put options, as shown in the table.

A SIMPLE PRICING MODEL FOR OPTIONS
We will show a simple binomial pricing model *to demonstrate how options are priced. The trick in valuing the option is to find "something else" that has exactly the same payoffs as the option. If we know the price of that "something else," then it should sell for the same price as the*

option. If the option were to sell for any different price, then arbitrage would quickly bring the prices together. So, being mysterious about the something else, let us proceed with an example. The example will simplify the price volatility by assuming the price of the underlying asset can only be one of two values at maturity. Wharton stock[1] currently sells for 50 but it could rise to 77 or fall to 23. Let us find the value of a call option written on Wharton with a striking price of 52 and that can be exercised in one year. First, consider the potential payoffs to the option at maturity.

	Wharton price = 23	Wharton price = 77
Call option value (exercise price = 52)	0	25

Now consider what the something else might be. Imagine you were to purchase 0.46296 of a share of Wharton stock and borrow 9.68, which had to paid back with 10% interest in exactly one year. This "portfolio" containing the stock and the debt would have the following value at year end.

	Wharton price = 23	Wharton price = 77
0.46296 of share of Wharton stock	10.648	35.648
Repayment of loan of 9.68 plus 10% interest	(10.648)	(10.648)
TOTAL	0	25

The portfolio has exactly the same payoffs as the option and therefore must sell for the same price. Thus, the value of the option must be:

$$Value\ of\ call = hedge\ ratio\ (asset\ price)$$
$$- present\ value\ of\ loan\ repayment$$
$$= 0.46296\ (price\ Wharton\ share) - 9.68\ loan$$
$$= 0.46296(50) - 9.68 = 13.468$$

Because the payoffs to the option can always be replicated by combining a risk-free position (lending or borrowing) with a position in the underlying asset, this formula enables you to value the option. The trick to

---

1. Letting Wharton go public is a very interesting, but remote, prospect to contemplate.

*doing this is to find how much of the underlying asset needs to be in-
cluded in this portfolio. This proportion is known as the hedge ratio of
the option delta (δ). It is calculated as follows:*

$$\text{hedge ratio } (\delta) = \frac{\text{spread of option payoffs}}{\text{spread of asset prices}} = \frac{25 - 0}{77 - 23} = 0.46296$$

*Let us now value a put option on the same stock where the exercise
price is, say, 50 (at the money). The payoff at maturity to the holder of
the put option is:*

	Wharton price = 23	Wharton price = 77
Put option value (exercise price = 50)	27	0

*Now the hedge ratio, or δ, is $(0 - 27)/(77 - 23) = -0.5$. But the
portfolio positions are reversed. Now you will take a short position in
0.5 shares of Wharton stock and lend 35 at 10% interest. The terminal
value of this portfolio is:*

	Wharton price = 23	Wharton price = 77
Short 0.5 of share of Wharton stock	(11.5)	(38.5)
Repayment of loan of 35 plus 10% interest	38.5	38.5
TOTAL	27	0

*The portfolio has exactly the same payoffs as the put option and therefore
must sell for the same price. Thus the value of the put option must be:*

$$\text{Value of put} = -0.5 \ (\text{price Wharton share}) + 35 \ \text{loan}$$
$$= -0.5(50) + 35 = 10$$

The same general principles of option pricing can be used
where the asset prices does not simply fall out as one of two values but can, at maturity of the option, be spread over a very large
number of values. The insight is the same: one must establish a
portfolio that has the same payoff structure as the option (i.e., for
each possible value of the underlying asset, the payoff to the portfolio is exactly the same as the option). This key insight is the

meat of the Black–Scholes option pricing model. The formula is a little opaque, but the important thing is to note the variables and how they affect value:

$$C = SN(d_1) - Ee^{-rt}N(d_2)$$

$$\text{where } d_1 = \left(\frac{\log\left(\frac{S}{E}\right) + \left(r + \frac{1}{20}\sigma 2\right)t}{\sigma\sqrt{t}}\right); d_2 = d_1 - \sigma\sqrt{t}$$

The two terms in the formula for C are essentially the same as those in the binomial formula. Recall that the binomial pricing formula had two terms: the first was the hedge ratio times the current asset price and the second was the present value of a loan. The same is true here. The first term, $SN(d_1)$ is the stock price times the hedge ratio. The second term $Ee^{-rt}N(d_2)$ is really the present value of a loan. The hedge ratio, $N(d_1)$, is rather complicated to calculate since the stock price is changing constantly over time. The expression $N(.)$ is the cumulative normal distribution, reflecting that the final value will follow some distribution. The relevant variables are the current price of the underlying asset, S, the exercise price, E, the discount rate, r, the time to maturity, t, and the volatility of the asset price, σ. These are all the variables noted in the above table, and their effects on price can be worked through the formula to show the signs in the table. The call price increases as the S, σ, r, and t increase, and the call value decreases as E increases.

An important relationship is that between the price of a call and a put. This relationship is called "put–call parity." The relationship is an equilibrium one. If prices do not bear this relationship to each other, a possibility for arbitrage exists. Therefore, in equilibrium, the prices of call and puts will gravitate to this relationship. Put–call parity assets the following relationship between the price of a put option and a call option that has the same exercise price:

$$C - P = S - PV(E)$$

The difference between the price of a call option and a put with the same exercise price is equal to the difference between the price of the underlying asset and the present value of the exercise price. In the above example, the value of a put with an exercise price of 50 on a stock with a current value of 50 was 10. Let us now consider what the value of the call would have been had the exercise price been 50 rather than 52. The hedge ratio, or δ, would now be $(27 - 0)/(77 - 23) = 0.5$. A loan of 10.4545 would be needed to make up the portfolio with the same payoff structure as the call. Thus, the call would be priced at

Value of call = hedge ratio (asset price)

$\qquad\qquad$ − present value of loan repayment

$\qquad\qquad$ = 0.5 (price Wharton share) − 10.4545 loan

$\qquad\qquad$ = 0.5(50) − 10.4545 = 14.5455

So, using put–call parity, we have

$$14.5455 - 10 = \frac{50 - 50}{1 + 0.1} = 4.5455$$

Had they been priced any differently, money could have been made by arbitrage.

SWAPS

Swaps are private agreement in which parties exchange cash flows. The exchange is usually one of different currencies or different interest payments. In the swap, the parties are obligated to the exchange, and in this sense the swap is like a forward or future but not like an option. But, unlike the forward and future, the swap involves the exchange of a number of different cash flows at various future dates. For example, a currency swap might be sought by a U.S. firm with debt raised in Germany for which it must meet Deutschmark interest payments. Another firm might be in the opposite position of having to meet an interest obligation denominated in dollars. If these obligations are of roughly equal value (adjusting by exchange rate), then a swap of these interest obligations is feasible. In this way, each firm can replace an obligation denominated in one currency with an obligation in another, more suitable currency. Thus, the U.S. firm with some foreign operations might prefer to have all its obligations denominated in dollars, and the swap is often a convenient and economical way of achieving this.

The other common type of swap is the interest rate swap in which a payment stream of floating rates is exchanged for one in fixed rates. In this type of arrangement, two firms with different needs can agree to exchange the interest payments on some notional principal. For example, one of the firms may have income that is positively correlated with interest rates but have its debt obligations fixed. This firm would be able to hedge its asset risk if it could rearrange to have its debt interest to be floating. Another firm may find itself with income that is interest-insensitive but have debt obligations that float with interest rates. This firm could avoid the interest risk by replacing its floating interest payments with fixed. Thus, the two firms have a mutual basis for an exchange of interest payments. More subtly, firms may wish to match the duration of their assets and liabilities, and this may call for periodic readjustments that can be achieved through the use of swaps.

The needs of firms vary considerably, and you can imagine trying to find an appropriate swap partner whose needs exactly mirror yours. Thus, swaps are usually arranged with intermediaries who may act as guarantors or who may make a market. This involves a fee for the intermediary to cover the risk in the guarantee and the risk attached to mismatches in the dealer's overall position.

AN ILLUSTRATION OF AN INTEREST RATE SWAP

A car manufacturer has an expected income stream that has a present value of 100 million. This value is calculated by discounting expected income at the current interest rate of 5%. However, if interest rates change over the next year, this will affect the present value of this cash stream to (values in $ millions):[2]

$$V(A) = \frac{5}{r} = \frac{5}{0.05} + \Delta V(A) = 100 - \frac{5}{r^2} \Delta r$$

The firm also has floating rate debt with a value of $40m. Note that the value of this debt will not change as interest rates change.

---

2. Note that the change in $V(A)$ in the formula is $-(5/r^2)\,\Delta r$. This is derived from the total derivative of $dV(.) = \{dV(.)/dr\}\Delta r$; where $V(.) = 5/r$.

$$V(D_1) = r(40)/r = 40$$

In addition, the firm has $40m of fixed debt paying a fixed interest of $2m (5%). Notice that the value of this debt is sensitive to changes in interest rates ($m).

$$V(D_2) = \frac{2}{0.05} + \Delta V(D_2) = 40 - \frac{2}{r^2} \Delta r$$

The TOTAL FIRM VALUE is

$$V(A) = 100 - (5/r^2) \Delta r$$

minus $V(D_1) = \quad 40$

minus $V(D_2) = \quad \underline{40 - (2/r^2) \Delta r}$

Net Worth $\qquad 20 - (3/r^2) \Delta r$

Now suppose that the floating debt was exchanged for fixed rate debt. The difference is

$$V(D_1) = 40 - (2/r^2) \Delta r$$

$$V(D_2) = 40$$

Difference $\qquad \underline{} \\ -(2/r^2) \Delta r$

So the firm should be able to buy a swap, exchanging the floating payments on a notional debt of $40m for fixed payment of $2m for a cost c and now assume a liability of $-(2/r^2) \Delta r$. The net worth of the firm is now

$$V(A) = \quad 100 - (5/r^2) \Delta r$$

minus $V(D_1) = \quad 40$

minus $V(D_2) = \quad 40 - (2/r^2) \Delta r$

Plus $SWAP = \quad \underline{-c + (2/r^2) \Delta r}$

Net Worth $\qquad 20 - c - (1/r^2) \Delta r$

which is much less sensitive to interest rate changes than before the swap.

Notice that if the firm had undertaken the swap on a notional amount of $60m for a price of

$$1.5(-c + (2/r^2)\, \Delta r)$$

the firm would have been perfectly hedged.

$$V(A) \quad = \quad 100 \quad - (5/r^2)\, \Delta r$$

$$minus \quad V(D_1) \; = \quad 40$$

$$minus \quad V(D_2) \; = \quad 40 \quad - (2/r^2)\, \Delta r$$

$$Plus \quad SWAP = - \quad 1.5c + (3/r^2)\, \Delta r$$

Net Worth $\qquad\qquad\qquad 20m - 1.5c$

One can see how that the hedged value of the firm is independent of r. *The firm has used the swap to remove all risk that arises from changes in interest rates.*

SOME APPLICATIONS OF OPTIONS

Debt, Equity, and Bankruptcy: The Default Put Option

Debt is a fixed obligation for a firm. In return for borrowing money, the firm commits to a series of interest payments plus repayment of principle. These payments take priority over payments to shareholders; equity is the residual claim. How do we value these claims on the firm? In principle, we can take the capitalized value of the future expected cash flows. Let us simplify this idea in order to show that the financial structure of the firm has clear option characteristics. One of the decisions the firm makes constantly, though often by default, is whether to continue or to liquidate its operations. The decision to continue is rational if the ongoing value exceeds the liquidation value. If this is the case, the firm could be sold for its ongoing value. The sale value is the capitalized value of investors' expectations of future cash flows. This line of thinking enables us to streamline the relationships between debt and equity by compressing the future into a single time period. The present value of the firm is the present value of the maximum of the (a) liquidation value or (b) sale as an ongoing concern value in one period's time. If the firm is liquidated or sold, the value of the equity in one period's time is the residual after accounting for the value of debt.

These relationships are shown in Figure 6–8. The firm has debt with a face value shown as D. The firm can discharge its debt liability by repaying debt for this amount, and the value of the debt is shown as its face value D if the firm is solvent. Suppose the total value of the firm, labeled $V(F)$, is less than D. The firm simply does not have sufficient value to discharge its debt obligation. Under the absolute priority rule of bankruptcy, the equity is now worthless and the whole firm essentially belongs to the creditors. Consequently, the value of debt is the 45° line when $V(F) < D$, and D when $V(F) \geq D$. The value of equity is the residual; zero when $V(F) \leq D$; and $V(F) - D$ when $V(F) > D$. The equity value is shown by a line coincident with the horizontal axis up to point D and sloping up at 45° thereafter.

The relationships between debt and equity can be seen as option positions. First, notice that the payoff line to equity shown

FIGURE   6–8

Values of Debt and Equity

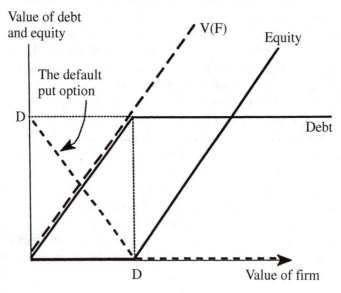

in Figure 6–8 is the same as that for a call option. If we consider that debt and equity are simply claims on the value of the firm, we see them immediately as derivatives. Moreover, notice that equity is zero when the underlying asset (the value of the firm) is less than D, and equity is worth the firm value minus D otherwise. Thus, *equity emerges as a call option on the underlying firm value with an exercise price equal to the face value of debt*. This relationship is denoted:

$$V(E) = C\{V(F), D\}$$

This says the value of equity, $V(E)$, is the same as a cell option, $C\{.\}$, on the value of the firm, $V(F)$, where the exercise price is the face value of debt, D. Figure 6–9 shows the intuition behind thinking of equity as a call option. Start with the 45° line shown as a thin solid line labeled $V(F)$; this is the value of the firm. If we subtract the face value of debt, D, from $V(F)$ we are left with the dotted line $V(F) - D$. The downwards arrow shows the effect of deducting D from $V(F)$. Also drawn on the diagram is a put option with a striking price equal to the face value of debt. This put option is shown as a dashed line and labeled *the* "default put

F I G U R E   6–9

Values of Equity

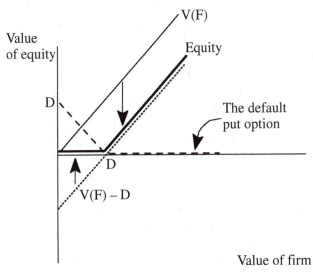

option" for reasons that will become clear. If this put option is added to $V(F) - D$ as shown by the upwards arrow, we are left with the bold solid kinked line, which is the equity payoff shown in Figure 6–8; that is, we have shown how the equity call option is related to other firm values. These mathematical operations can be shown as follows:

$$V(E) = C\{V(F), D\} = V(F) - D + P\{V(F), D\}$$

where $P\{V(F), D\}$ denotes a put option written on asset $V(F)$, with an exercise price D. Does this look familiar? Let us reassemble the relationship as follows:

$$C\{V(F), D\} - P\{V(F), D\} = V(F) - D$$

This is simply put–call parity. Recall that the original notation was $C - P = S - PV(E)$. The right side is simply the difference between the value of a call and put written on the same underlying asset with the same exercise price. The underlying asset here is $V(F)$ (compared with the share price S with stock options), and the exercise price is D. Thus, the only difference is that in the original put–call parity we used the present value of the exercise price on the right side. The reason this was not done in the firm values was simply that we did not think of the time dimension and thus the need for discounting.

Debt can also be seen in terms of options. We can write the same put–call parity relationship in the following form:

$$V(D) = D - P\{V(F), D\} = V(F) - C\{V(F), D\}$$

This says that the value of debt is the difference between the face value of the debt, D, and a put option, $P\{V(F), D\}$. Despite the face that creditors are formally promised a repayment of D, the value of the debt is somewhat less than D; it is D less the value of the default put option. The other side of this coin is that the shareholders have the long position in the default put. They have the right to "put" the firm to the creditors; that is, the right to exchange the firm for their obligation to pay D to the creditors. It makes sense for the shareholders to exercise this option when the value of the firm is lower than D. Thus, saying that shareholders have limited liability and that share prices cannot go negative is the same as saying that shareholders own the default out option.

Let us now work through an example to show how the default put option is valued and therefore how debt is valued. To do this we will use the binomial pricing model. It is also useful to reintroduce time and discounting into the model. So let us start by restating the put–call parity relationship with the time value of money shown:

$$C\{V(F), D\} - P\{V(F), D\} = V(F) - PV(D)$$

Consider the value of a default put option for a firm that is currently worth 132 but may be worth 100 or 200 in one year's time. The firm has outstanding debt with a face value of 120. We will assume a 10% interest rate on riskless debt.

	Terminal value of firm $V(F) = 100$	Terminal value of firm $V(F) = 200$
Terminal payoff on default put (face value = 120)	20	0

Now we can calculate the hedge ratio, or δ, using the binomial pricing model considered earlier. The ratio is that of the spread in the option payoff to the spread in V(F) i.e., $(0 - 20)/(200 - 100) = -0.2$. Now consider that an investor is to take a short equity position in 20% of the firm value and lend 36.36 at 10% interest. The terminal value of this portfolio is:

	$V(F) = 100$	$V(F) = 200$
Short 0.2 of $V(F)$	(20)	(40)
Repayment of loan of 36.36 plus 10% interest	40	40
TOTAL	20	0

The portfolio has exactly the same payoffs as the put option and therefore must sell for the same price. Thus the value of the put option must be:

$$\text{Value of default put} = -0.2(V(F)) + 36.36 \text{ loan}$$
$$= -0.2(132) + 36.36 = 9.96$$

The value of the various claims on the firm can now be calculated. Debt is valued as the value of riskless debt (PV(D) = 120 discounted at 10% = 109.09) minus the value of the default put. And equity is the residual claim.

$$Debt:\ V(D) = 120/1.1 - 9.96$$
$$= 99.13$$

$$Equity:\ V(E) = 32.87$$

Let us finish where we started, with put–call parity:

$$C\{V(F),\ D\} - P\{V(F),\ D\} = V(F) - PV(D)$$
$$32.87 - 9.96 = 132 - 109.09 = 22.91$$

The default put options is at the heart of the corporate risk management story. The various stakeholders will behave strategically to manipulate the value of the put option to their respective advantages; the shareholders to increase value and the bondholders to reduce it. In seeking advantage at the expense of other stakeholders, shareholders are lulled into decisions that are not value-maximizing from the view of the firm as a whole, and the overall level of efficiency of the firm declines. The private but dysfunctional temptations depend on the level of risk. Thus controlling risk can eliminate this opportunistic game playing and make everyone better off. We shall see in Chapter 7 that much of the rationale of corporate risk management is about jointly controlling risk and leverage and thereby about managing the value of the default put.

The Option to Abandon an Investment Project

The default put option is the option for shareholders to abandon the firm and pass ownership to creditors. As we have just seen, shareholders will rationally exercise this option when the firm is worth less than the face value of the debt. The same principle applies to individual projects undertaken by the firm. One might suppose that a project is undertaken because its NPV is positive at when the project is first evaluated. But things can change over the project life. At any point in time the firm can reassess the value of incremental future cash flows. Of course, the initial capital costs are by gones. But the remaining life of the project will generate expected cash flows, and new estimates can be more or less optimistic than those held at inception. Moreover, there are other potential cash flows that can be gained by closing down the project. The firm can sell off capital equipment, licenses, and maybe even goodwill. There may be close-down costs as well as revenues. The firm may have to make severance payments to workers and incur demolition costs. Call the net proceeds of the sale of assets, after deduction of any closedown costs, K^S. Finally, call the future expected cash flows, C_t, for future year t. With a discount rate k, the following formula can be used to determine whether to close down or continue the project.

$$NPV = -K^S + \frac{C_t}{(1 + k)^t}$$

The formula shows the NPV from continuing the project, losing the close-down sale value and preserving future cash flows. If this value is negative, the firm will add value by closing down the project. If the value is positive, value will be added by continuing.

To show how the option value plays a part, consider a simple example. A project initially costs 1000 and generates cash flows of 400 per year for three consecutive years. Cash flows are realized at the end of each year. The firm could decide to close down the project immediately after inception and would recover 900. The firm could also choose to abandon the project and sell off assets at the beginning of year 2 and recover either 700 or 400, each with a 0.5 chance. Similarly, the firm could see off assets at the beginning of year 3 and realize either 500 or 200 with 0.5 each with chances. The discount rate is 5%. What is the value to the firm from being able to choose to abandon the project at various stages?

Year	Initial Capital Cost (beginning of year)	Close-Down Value (beginning of year)	Cash Flow (end of year)
1	1000	900	400
2		0.5(700) + 0.5(400)	400
3		0.5(500) + 0.5(200)	400

First, consider the NPV of the project assuming there is no possibility of abandoning it midstream

$$NPV = -1000 + \frac{400}{(1 + 0.05)} + \frac{400}{(1 + 0.05)^2} + \frac{400}{(1 + 0.05)^3} = 89.3$$

Consider what would happen if the firm closed down at the beginning of year 3. If the firm could close down at this time and recover 200, it would not do so. Continuing operations into year 3 gives the firm a cash flow of 400, which is worth $400/(1 + 0.05) = 381$ at the beginning of year 3. If the close-down value is 500 at the beginning of the year, then it makes sense to close down at the beginning of the year rather than wait till year end for 400 (which is worth 381 at the beginning of year 3). Thus, the option to close down at the beginning of year 3 is worth $500 - 381 = 119$, if the beginning of year close-down value is 500. Given the 0.5 chance of this close-down value, the expected value of the option at inception of the project is $0.5[119/(1 + 0.5)^2] = 54$. The expected value of the project at the beginning of year 3 is $0.5(500) + 0.5(381) = 440.5$.

Now look at the beginning of year 2. At this point the value of continuing the project is:

$$NPV_{year2} = \frac{400}{(1 + 0.05)} + 0.5 \left(\frac{400}{(1 + 0.05)^2} \right) + 0.5 \left(\frac{500}{(1 + 0.05)} \right)$$
$$= 800.45$$

Because this exceeds either close-down value (700 or 400), it is always better to continue with the project at the beginning of year 2. It is also apparent that the firm would not take advantage of closing the project immediately after inception when the close-down value is 900 (since we know the continuing value is at least 1089.3). Thus, the only potential close-down opportunity that can add value arises at the beginning of year three if the close-down value equals 500.

Now let us reevaluate the project accounting for the close-down values.

$$NPV = -1000 + \frac{400}{(1 + 0.05)} + \frac{400}{(1 + 0.05)^2}$$
$$+ 0.5 \left(\frac{400}{(1 + 0.05)^3} \right) + 0.5 \left(\frac{500}{(1 + 0.05)^2} \right)$$
$$= 143.3$$

Thus, the NPV increases from 89.3 to 143.3, an increase of 54, when account is taken of the abandonment option. As a cross check on what *is going on, notice also that the value of the abandonment option at project inception is $0.5[119/(1 + 0.5)^2] = 54$ as calculated before.*

Abandonment options will play an important role in the risk management story. Consider a couple of examples. First, imagine that the firm is exposed to the possibility of a large product liability suit if it introduces a new product line. If the suit occurs, there is a further chance that, in addition to having to pay damages, the adverse publicity from the suit will dampen future demand for the project. Should this happen, the firm will have the opportunity to abandon the project and sell off project assets. Given that the event has occurred and affected demand, the option to abandon cannot make the firm worse and may well help it to limit the extent of the loss. Thus, an important part of the risk management function is how to reevaluate existing investment projects after a risky event. As a second illustration, consider that a firm can lose a productive assets through its physical destruction (e.g., by fire). The fact the asset was in use before the fire does not imply that its replacement by a new asset will be an automatic positive NPV project. The firm might well choose to use the loss as a reason for abandoning the activity altogether. These issues will be discussed in great detail in later chapters, especially in Chapter 9.

Insurance Policies as Options

An insurance policy can be thought of as a derivative instrument. Consider the value of your home. Now it is worth some amount determined by its condition and by the market for comparable homes. If the condition deteriorates, other things being equal, the value will fall. At the end of the year the condition might very well have changed; your house may have burned down. Thus, an insurance policy is really like a forward policy on the future value of your house. This needs a little qualification. The policy does not normally cover you for changes brought about by economic trends, only for changes due to insured perils such as fire, storm damage, and earthquake. Similarly, you can think of an index that records how much you owe to third parties in liability suits. At any point in time this index is, for most of us, zero. But if we get sued for a traffic accident, the index will suddenly shoot up. An insurance policy is a forward contract on this index where the insurer agrees to assume the index value (a liability) in exchange for an upfront premium.

The terms of insurance contracts are often modified to make them look more like options than forwards. For example, a typical car insurance policy will cover losses incurred above a given amount: the deductible. The deductible may be, for example, $500. If losses are less than $500, the policyholder covers the cost; if loses exceed $500, the insurers pays the loss minus $500. The payout structure that can be seen in Figure 6–10 displays the option-like feature of the deductible policy. The vertical axis shows how much the insurer will pay based on any loss size recorded on the horizontal axis. The deductible is shown as D. The insurer pays zero for losses less than D and pays the loss minus D for losses in excess of D. This payoff structure is shown by the thick line, which is zero to the left of D and rises at 45° to the right of D. If we change the labels, this is exactly the same structure as the payout on a call option with an exercise price of D. Conveniently, the payment for the insurance, just like the payment for the option, is a "premium."

F I G U R E   6–10

Insurance as an Option

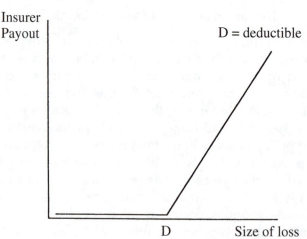

There is one big difference between the insurance policy with a deductible just described and an option such as shares of stock. The latter is an option on another financial asset that is (normally) traded and whose market value can be fairly easily determined. This makes this type of option fairly easy to value and explains the use of the term "derivative." With normal option pricing formulas, the option price is determined in relation to that of the underlying asset; notice that the price of the underlying stock enters the Black–Scholes price formula. With an insurance policy, the underlying value on which the option is written may not be a traded financial asset. The value of a fire loss or a liability suit being examples. This becomes all-important for various technical reasons. Suffice it to say that it would be inappropriate to price the insurance policy using Black–Scholes, because the probability distribution that underlies insurance losses is unlikely to be the same as that which is assumed to specify the movement of stock prices (the lognormal).

CONCLUSION

To many people, the terms "financial risk management" and "derivatives" are inseparable. The rise of financial risk management in the late 1980s and 1990s was largely a movement of using derivatives to hedge interest rate, foreign exchange, and commodity risk. But many risk profiles turned out to be complex, and simple instruments could not offset the risk. For example, some cash streams were non-linearly related to interest rates or commodity prices, or cash flows could be jointly determined by several exogenous factors. This created a demand for more complex hedge instruments, and financial engineers began to combine basic instruments to form new securities. Derivatives, whether used separately or combined into complex instruments, have become tools of the trade in risk management.

Even for insurable risk, derivatives have become important. Insurance contracts themselves are like derivatives; they can have a "forward-like" or an "option-like" structure. Actuarial techniques used for pricing insurance are being used to improve the pricing of financial derivatives, and economic techniques used for pricing financial derivatives are being employed in insurance pricing. New types of instruments are being derived that can be used to hedge both insurable risk and financial risk, and these are being sold in both capital markets and insurance markets. Indeed, insurance and derivatives are becoming increasingly interchangeable and their respective market places increasingly integrated.

But our interest in derivatives goes further. As we will see in the next chapter, the reasons that risk is costly to firms are not widely understood. Only recently have credible theories been advanced and tested on how the management of risk can enhance corporate value. A big part of this story is related to the potential for risk to bankrupt the firm. This prospect can set the interests of the firm's stakeholders, creditors, and shareholders on a collision course. To understand these conflicts, and how they can be mitigated by the management of risk, it is important to understand the option-like characteristics of the stakeholder claims. In particular, the option of the shareholders to default on their obligations is the source of the trouble. The management of corporate risk has become, in part, the management of the default put option.

REFERENCES

Black, Fisher, and Myron Scholes. 1973. "The Pricing of Options and Corporate Liabilities." *Journal of Political Economy* 81:637–54.

Brys, Eric, Mondher Bellalah, Huu Minh Mai, and Francois De Varenne. 1998. *Options, Futures and Exotic Derivatives.* Chichester: John Wiley & Sons.

Doherty, Neil, and Steven D'Arcy. 1987. "The Financial Theory of Pricing Insurance Contracts." S. S. Huebner Foundation Monograph. Homewood, Ill.: R. D. Irwin.

Hull, John. 1993. *Options, Futures and Other Derivative Securities.* Englewood Cliffs, N.J.: Prentice Hall.

PART TWO

Risk Management Strategies

CHAPTER 7

Why Is Risk Costly to Firms?

Finance theory leaves us with a risk management puzzle, for it seems to imply that reducing or removing risk (especially insurable risk) has no value for the publicly traded firm. The story can be told in various ways. Suppose a firm faces the prospect of an uninsured or unhedged loss. This introduces risk to the firm's value. However, this risk is spread over the firm's shareholders, each of whom will bear only a small part of the risk. Moreover, many shareholders (especially institutional shareholders) are highly diversified. Thus, the effect of the risk from the uninsured firm on the portfolio risk of each shareholder is minimal. This is especially true if the uninsured risk is uncorrelated with the remaining risk in the shareholders' portfolios. The risk of loss to a single firm is essentially diversified across the capital market. In effect, it is insured by the capital market. Just as insurance spreads the effect of loss across a population of policyholders similarly exposed to risk, public ownership spreads corporate loss across investors, who each assume a small portion of the risk of each firm. But the story gets better. Normally uninsured losses are tax deductible. With a 34% tax rate the loss is deductible and is diversified across all the nation's taxpayers. Thus, an uninsured or unhedged loss is diversified in a very complete sense: about one third is diversified across all taxpayers and the other two thirds is diversified throughout the capital market. Surely no insurance market could achieve a better spreading of the effects of risk.

The capital asset pricing model tells the story in a more precise way. Suppose first that the unhedged loss is uncorrelated with aggregate wealth or the market portfolio, that is, the risk has zero beta. In this case the risk can be borne effectively at no cost by shareholders, who can diversify the unhedged risk simply by their choice of investment portfolio. Accordingly, hedging the risk has no value to shareholders and will not affect the stock price *ex ante*. Shareholders will not reward management for hedging a risk that they could hedge themselves at little or no cost. Now consider that the unhedged risk is correlated with the market portfolio. In this case leaving the risk unhedged does affect the investor's portfolio risk and will command a price. Leaving the risk unhedged will change the firm's beta, which will affect the equilibrium price of its stock. However, selling the risk to a risk bearer, such as an insurer, will normally command a risk premium related to the beta of the transferred risk. Thus, when the firm hedges the risk the effect on the investor is twofold: first the risk of the investor's portfolio is reduced, and second the earnings of the investor will fall by the risk premium paid to the insurer. It is identical to the effect that could have been achieved by the investor simply by switching a little of her portfolio between stocks with different betas. Again, why would the shareholders wish to reward the firm's management for hedging when they could achieve the same effect simply by readjusting their portfolios?

It seems we have something of a conundrum. Shareholders apparently should have no interest in managing risk, according to conventional finance theory. The purpose of this chapter is to tell a different story about why risk is costly. The basic message of this story is rather surprising. It turns out that risk is important to shareholders, not because the risk *per se* is a problem to the firm's owners, but because risk can have indirect effects that will reduce *expected* shareholder income. Moreover, we need to understand these disruptive effects of risk because appropriate risk management strategies can be formed effectively only if we understand the precise effects of risk. Indeed, some risk management strategies need to target the precise disruptions caused by risk. In the remainder of this chapter we examine why risk is costly to firms. We explore a set of ideas that have gained currency since the early 1980s. We will show that unhedged risk can increase expected taxes; cause agency conflicts between various classes of corporate stakeholders that result in dysfunctional investment decisions; deprive the firm of funding for new investments; and interfere with the design of effective compensation plans for managers. But first we will examine in more detail the counter case that risk can be handled simply by shareholders and that its retention has little direct cost to the firm's owners.

RISK AND SHAREHOLDER DIVERSIFICATION

Before considering *why* risk is costly to firms, first consider *why not*. Consider the following rationale for corporate risk management: *Investors typically do not like risk; therefore value will be created for shareholders if the firm hedges risk.* Two levels of argument will be advanced below. The first addresses the question under the assumption that the risk is diversifiable to investors; in capital asset pricing model terms, the earnings have a zero beta. The second argument addresses the question when the beta is not zero.

Risk Is Diversifiable in the Capital Market

Consider insurable events such as fires and liability suits. Most insurable losses appear to have little or no correlation with capital market indices. Does it matter to investors whether firms insure such risks or not? To pursue this, take an investor that has $1000 invested, allocated in equal weight, w_i, over 10 different assets (so $w_i = 0.1$), each having an expected return, $E(r_i)$, of 0.1 and a standard deviation, $\sigma(r_i)$, of 0.1. Each of the firms has purchased some insurance, and the remaining risk is simply unhedged. The risks of the firm are uncorrelated. Clearly, the overall expected return for the investor is 0.1 and the investor's risk is calculated by the following formula:

$$\sigma(r) = \sqrt{\sum_i w_i^2\, \sigma^2(r_i) + \sum\sum_{i \neq j} w_i w_j\, r_{ij}\, \sigma(r_i)\, \sigma(r_j)}$$

$$\sigma(r) = \sqrt{(10) \left(\frac{1}{10}\right)^2 (0.1)^2} = 0.032$$

Now, suppose one of the firms (firm 10) cancels its insurance policy. This increases the standard deviation of that firm's return from 0.1 to 0.3. However, since the insurable risk was independent of market risk, this will not affect the typical correlation between this firm's return and those of other firms. The correlations remain the same; in this case zero. But ask what the cancellation of the insurance will do to the expected return. Under our assumptions, the insurable risk would not have commanded a risk premium from the insurers (the insurer's shareholders could easily diversify this zero beta risk, so they would not demand a risk premium). So, apart from any transaction costs in the insurance premium, firm 10's expected earnings would remain unchanged, and so would its expected rate of return. The risk to the shareholder who has invested 1/10 of his capital in this firm has now increased as follows:

$$\sigma(r) = \sqrt{(9)\left(\frac{1}{10}\right)^2 (0.1)^2 + \left(\frac{1}{10}\right)^2 (0.3)^2} = 0.0424$$

However, suppose the investor accommodates this change in risk in firm 10 simply by increasing the number of securities in his portfolio from 10 to 15 (each has a weight of 1/15):

$$\sigma(r) = \sqrt{(14)\left(\frac{1}{15}\right)^2 (0.1)^2 + \left(\frac{1}{15}\right)^2 (0.3)^2} = 0.032$$

If we ignore some minor rounding error, this is the same level of risk that he had before the tenth firm canceled its insurance.

The point of this exercise is to show that while firms can change their level of risk by hedging, investors can change their level of risk in the choice of the portfolio. If there were on transaction costs either for the firm to buy insurance or for investors to buy and sell assets, then it would make no difference to owners whether the firm bought insurance or not. If firm do hedge, investors can achieve desired risk–return levels by holding fairly small portfolios. If firms do not hedge, investors can achieve the same risk–return level simply by holding more assets. Investor diversification is a substitute or corporate hedging and insurance. One would not expect the capital market to reward those firms buying hedges by bidding up the values of their stocks.

We did ignore transaction costs. These become relevant at two points. First, insurance will attract some transaction costs. This will include administration costs and costs of settling claims, as well as frictional costs that arise from moral hazard. But it is also costly for investors to diversify. First, transaction costs tend to increase as a given capital sum is subdivided over more securities, costs on smaller lots being proportionately higher. Thus, the issue of hedging seems to rest on which transaction costs are higher; will the saving of insurance transaction costs outweigh the additional costs to investors of adjusting their portfolios to contain more securities?

But the second issue is probably more important. In the example given, the investor need not adjust to the cancellation of the insurance by holding more assets in his portfolio; he could simply sell shares in firm 10 and purchase shares in other firms with lower risk profiles (i.e., similar to that of firm 10 before it canceled its insurance). This argument speaks more to *changes* in hedging behavior than to the optimal *levels* of those hedges. If the firms choose *stable* risk management strategies, investors can structure their portfolios once and will not have to incur transaction costs in adjusting their personal portfolios to offset changes in corporate risk profiles.

Risk Is Not Diversifiable in the Capital Market

Consider Figure 7–1, which shows the capital asset pricing model. A firm's stock is valued according to expected earnings and systematic risk (β), thus yielding the relationship between expected return and β. This firm's beta and expected return are shown at point A. The firm buys insurance. In this case, assume that insurable losses are less likely when the market index is high. Since losses are cash outflows, including such losses in a diversified portfolio will tend to increase systematic risk (holding a negative beta liability has the same effect on portfolio risk as holding a positive beta asset). Thus, when the firm insures this risk, this is like ridding itself of a positive beta asset, and the firm's beta will fall. If the insurer were naive enough to sell this insurance for a premium equal to the expected value of loss, then the policyholder firm's expected income would not change, but its beta would be lowered. This is shown as position B in the diagram. Clearly this

FIGURE 7-1

Hedging a Systemmatic Risk

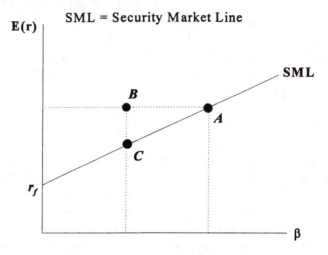

is an attractive position for any investor; beta has been lowered without giving up any expected return. The stock is now under-priced. This stock would be in high demand, bidding its price up and therefore, the expected return would fall to position C. This rise in price would be a capital gain to existing shareholders and would signal a reward for insuring the risk.

Now consider where the reward comes from. The firm rids itself of a negative beta liability (like a positive beta asset), and it is assumed the insurance firm did not charge a risk premium (over expected loss) for insuring the beta risk. Naturally, the insurance company's beta will be affected by this transaction; as the insuring firm's beta falls, so the insurance company's beta will rise. So the insurer's shareholders would naturally want this additional sys-tematic risk to be priced in the insurance premium. If this is the case, the insurance transaction simply shifts the policyholder firm from A to C in the diagram. The firm's shareholders would find the firm correctly priced before the transaction, given the initial beta. The insurance policy would reduce expected earnings (since now the insurer demands a risk premium) and reduce the beta so that they are once again in balance. Let us contrast the two situ-ations:

1. *If insurers do not charge a risk premium:* insurance reduces the firm's beta without reducing expected earnings. Consequently, the stock is underpriced and the price rises, yielding a capital gain to shareholders.
2. *Insurers do charge a risk premium:* insurance reduces the beta and reduces expected earnings. Thus, the stock is still correctly priced and no price adjustment occurs in the firm's stock.

Back to the question, does hedging risk benefit shareholders? The answer is no, if the party assuming the hedge prices it correctly. Of course, shareholders can benefit if the insurer underprices the insurance policy. But this is hardly a justification for risk management; it is a justification for buying underpriced assets. It is really no different from the firm's buying a building or machine, or license, for less than its market value. We can generalize this argument from the simple capital asset pricing model to later-generation pricing models that also assume that diversifiable risk is not priced in the capital market.

Having agreed why risk should not be a problem for publicly held firms, we will now address why risk is a problem.

WHY IS RISK COSTLY TO FIRMS?

Tax Effects—Risk Reduction and Convex Tax Schedules[1]

The tax functions facing firms typically are convex. Higher levels of corporate earnings usually encounter higher rates off marginal taxation. The convexity may not be uniform, but this is nevertheless a typical pattern in many countries. To some degree this convexity is built into the tax schedule; initial corporate earnings, like the first dollars of individual earnings, are untaxed at the federal level. Above this threshold, earnings pass through several marginal rates, settling on a constant rate. But convexity also arises from other features of the tax code. Firms are allowed deductions

---

1. For ideas presented in this subsection, see Smith and Stulz (1984), Scholes, et al. (1990), and others.

for certain expenditures such as depreciation and loss carrybacks. The effects of such deductions is to increase the range of income which attracts a zero marginal rate. The effects are graphed in Figure 7–2.

This nonlinearity in tax functions gives rise to a interesting relationship between risk and expected tax liability. The intuition is straightforward. Consider a firm with expected earnings of $B. If it earns exactly B dollars, then the firm's tax liability can be read straight off the tax schedule as illustrated in Figure 7–2. The tax liability for this firm is shown as $T(B)$ (read this notation as the tax, T, appropriate to income B). Now consider a second firm that also has possible earnings of A or C, as shown in Figure 7–2. If there is a 50% chance of either A or C, then the expected earnings are B (the same as for the first firm). This firm will incur a tax liability of either $T(A)$ or $T(C)$, each with a 50% chance. The expected tax is the weighted average of $T(A)$ and $T(B)$, shown as "E(tax)." Notice that the expected tax for the second firm is considerably higher than for the firm with certain income of B, despite the fact that the expected earnings of the two firms were identical at B.

F I G U R E   7–2

Non Linear Taxes and Risk

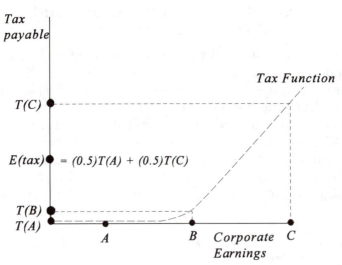

This story can be translated into one of risk management, starting with the second firm, whose risky income can be either A or C. For example, C is the earnings of the uninsured firm if it does not suffer loss. A loss of assets or an uninsured liability could reduce income to A. The probability of this loss is, say, 50%. The expected earnings of the firm are at point $B(B = 0.5C + 0.5A)$. If an insurance firm were to sell a policy covering a loss of AC with a 0.5 probability, it would have to charge a premium at least equal to the expected loss. An insurance policy bought at a premium of BC (the expected value of the loss which is $0.5 \times AC$) would give the firm a certain income of B.[2] Consider the tax effect of the insurance. If insurance is purchased, the firm's certain income is B and it will pay an appropriate tax of $T(B)$. If the firm does not insure, it will have a tax liability of $T(C)$ if it has no loss, and a tax of $T(A)$ if it does have a loss. The firm's expected tax is $E(\text{tax})$ as shown in Figure 7–2. The level $E(T)$ is calculated as the $(0.5)T(A) + (0.5)T(C)$. Thus, the expected tax is higher without insurance. Insurance reduces expected tax from $E(\text{tax})$ to $T(B)$.

Consider a simple example. A firm has earnings that follow the distribution.

Earnings	Probability
0	0.2
100	0.3
200	0.3
300	0.2
EXPECTED VALUE = 150	

The firm faces a 34% marginal tax rate but, due to progressivity of the code and to tax shelters such as depreciation, the first 120 of earnings is free of tax. The firm's expected after-tax income is (E denotes before tax earnings and S denotes the value of the earnings shielded):

---

2. The insurance premium normally will be somewhat higher than BC, and the certain income of the firm will be slightly lower than point B, when transaction costs such as profit allowance, reserves, and commissions are also factored into the premium.

$E - \text{MAX}\{0.34(E - S); 0\}$	After-Tax Earnings
0 − 0	=
100 − 0	= 100
200 − 0.34(200 − 120)	= 172.8
300 − 0.34(300 − 120)	= 238.8
	EXPECTED VALUE = 129.6

Now consider that the firm can hedge this risk by a derivative instrument that will replace the risky earnings stream by its expected value which is 150. The firm's after tax income will be

$$150 - 0.34(150 - 120) = 139.8$$

This represents a gain of 10.2, without any change in the expected value of before-tax earnings.

The representation of the tax code above is rather simple. One important omission is the ability of the firm to carry forward losses to future tax periods; that is, negative income this year can be used as a deduction against future earnings. Suppose that the firm could carry forward each dollar of losses with interest and was absolutely certain that it would have sufficient future income to avail itself of the deductibility. The *expected present value* of each $1 carried forward would be a tax relief (a negative tax liability is a tax benefit or refund) of:

$$-\frac{\$1(1 + r)}{1 + r} = -\$1$$

With this assumption, all income is either taxed at the marginal rate or is forgiven at the marginal rate. Thus, the tax function would not be convex (kinked) as shown in Figure 7–2, but would just be a straight line (shown as a short dashed line in Figure 7–3). Expected tax of positive and negative income would be symmetric with this linear tax function, and there would be no gain from hedging.

Now suppose that the probability that future earnings will be sufficient to use the carryforward is p, which is less than unity,

F I G U R E   7–3

The Effect of Carry Forwards

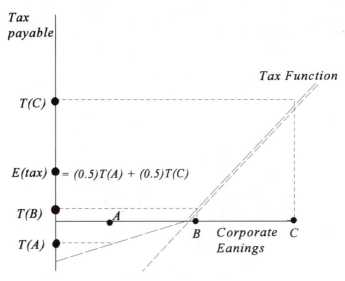

and that the loss cannot be carried forward with interest. The expected present value of each $1 of carryforward would be

$$- \frac{(p) \times \$1}{1 + r}$$

This is a benefit of less than $1. This situation is depicted in Figure 7–3 as the wide dashed line. Notice that this line is convex, which implies that the expected tax liability from hedging, $T(B)$, is lower than that for the unhedged position, $E(\text{tax})$. Thus, even with carryforwards, there is still a tax advantage to reducing the riskiness of earnings.

The tax gain described above, and illustrated with insurance, is not a specific tax preference built into the tax code for insurance (e.g., a specific deductibility for insurance premiums). Rather, it is a general tax benefit that can be secured by reducing the riskiness of earnings, whatever the source of the risk of the nature of the hedge used. Finally, notice that the tax advantage from hedging is jurisdictional. The gain comes about from reducing the riskiness

F I G U R E   7-4

Risk and the Probability of Bankruptcy

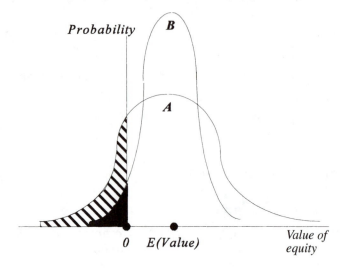

of earnings within a given tax jurisdiction, not necessarily from reducing the risk of global corporate earnings.

Risk Management and the Costs of Financial Distress

Direct Costs of Financial Distress

If a firm becomes bankrupt, then according to the absolute priority rule, shares expire worthless and the firm transfers to the creditors. Consequently, any transaction costs,, such as legal fees, court fees, and accounting costs, will be borne *ex post* by the creditors. In addition to direct costs of bankruptcy, there may be indirect costs, or opportunity costs, that also will fall on creditors. For example, when a firm is administered by the court, the normal incentive structure that leads managers to perform efficiently may be disturbed. This may happen in two ways. Most directly, there are contracts written with managers, agents, employees, and others that often have rewards and penalties associated with performance. During a bankruptcy, these contracts are sometimes challenged, especially if they seem retroactively generous given the firm's current plight. Moreover, new contracts written during such a peirod are written under court influence. Will these contracts written under court supervision carry the same incentive provisions as contracts written during a normal period under which the firm is monitored continuously by the capital market? To the extent that incentive compatibility is sacrificed during bankruptcy, the performance of the firm will suffer. The forgone value will be lost to the creditors who now "own" the firm. Similarly, value may be lost if the selection of investment projects is affected by court supervision. For example, during solvent operations, and capital market accountability, the firm may be aggressive in its project selection and earn the appropriate premium associated with such entrepreneurial activity. If the bankrupt firm is less entrepreneurial in its project selection, any loss of value will fall on the creditors.

The various transaction costs of bankruptcy (known simply as "bankruptcy costs") theoretically fall *ex post* upon the creditors since equity claims expire worthless. In practice, distressed firms may not be reorganized according to the absolute priority rule. Many distressed firms are reorganized in out-of-court settlements or "workouts." These settlements invariably leave the shareholders with some value, and the usually lower transaction costs associated with workouts will fall jointly (according to negotiation) on both classes of stakeholder. Thus, the transaction costs associated with bankruptcy fall, *ex post*, on the principle stakeholders. *Ex ante*, these costs will be anticipated in the vlaue of the bonds (and perhaps the stocks). The discount in bond values will reflect investor expectations as to the prospective size of the bankruptcy costs, together with investor expectations about the probability of bankruptcy. Accordingly, any strategy that reduces the probability of bankruptcy (or persuades investors that the probability has been reduced) will enhance the value of the firms bonds.

The value of a firm, $V(F)$, is the capitalized value of its expected future cash flows, CF, discountted at a rate r:

$$V(F) = \sum_{1} \frac{E(CF_t)}{(1 + r)^t} \tag{7.1}$$

This value is divided between the vairous stakeholders; that is, the shareholders and the bondholders. To see how bankruptcy costs affect value, consider some different possibilities. First, suppe that bankruptcies do not result in liquidation, and consequently the firm can potentially have multiple bankruptcies over its future lifetime. Equation (7.2) gives an idea of how the firm value will be reduced. In this equation P_t is the probability the firm will become bankrupt in year t and BC is the associated bankruptcy cost. Notice that the second term in Equation (7.2) did not appear in Equation (7.1), and it is this second term that captures the expected value of the bankruptcy cost. Under the absolute priority rule, this loss of value would fall wholly on creditors.

$$V(F) = \sum_t \frac{E(CF_t) - (P_t)(BC)}{(1 + r)^t} \qquad (7.2)$$

Now consider that bankruptcy results in liquidation of the firm. In this case the loss due to bankruptcy includes not only the transaction costs of the bankruptcy as described, but also loss of future earnings as the firm ceases to operate. This is captured in Equation 3. To see this, imagine that in any future year s there is a probability $1 - P_s$ that the firm will survive and a corresponding probability P_s that the firm will become bankrupt and liquidate conditional on having survived to that year. We assume that bankruptcy occurs at the end of the year. Thus, if one knew thta the firm would survive to year s and then be bankrupted and liquidated in that year, the present value of earnings would be:

$$V(F) = \sum_{t=1}^{s} \left[\frac{E(CF_t)}{(1 + r)^t} \right] - \frac{(BC)}{(1 + r)^s}$$

Now, bearing in mind the probability that the firm will survive to year t, then be liquidated, is $(1 - P_1)(1 - P_2) \cdots (1 - P_{t-1})$, then the value of the firm becomes:

$$V(F) = \sum_{t=1}^{\infty} \left[\prod_{i=1}^{t-1} (1 - P_t) \left((1 - P_t) \frac{E(CF_t)}{(1 + r)^t} - \frac{P_t(BC)}{(1 + r)^t} \right) \right]$$

$$(7.3)$$

Notice that in all of the above formulas the value of the firm will increase if the probability of bankruptcy can be reduced. This will reduce the expected value for bankruptcy costs in both Equations (7.2) and (7.3). Additionally, in Equation (7.3), reducing P also will reduce the probability that the firm will liquidate and thereby lose access to all future revenues.

To see the risk management implications, consider Figure 7–4. Distribution A shows the distribution of *equity* value for a firm with significant risk. If the equity value falls below zero, the firm becomes insolvent and will undergo bankruptcy proceeding or some out-of-court settlement. The probability of bankruptcy is the area to the left of the zero and under curve A, as indicated by the diagonal shading. Recall that the total area under a distribution is unity, and thus the area shaded will translate directly into a probability that is less than unity. If risk can be reduced, as shown by the more compressed distribution B, the probability of bankruptcy can be reduced, as shown by the smaller solid shaded area to the left of zero and under curve B.

Agency Costs and Dysfunctional Investment: Underinvestment and Asset Substitution

Apart from the transaction costs associated with financial distress, the prospect of future financial distress causes a number of other problems. These transaction costs are agency costs known as "underinvestment" and "set substitution."

Agency problems arise between shareholders and creditors. Shareholders have some control over the decision-making processes within the firm through their ability to appoint and compensate the management team. Creditors lend their money to the firm without such control over its decision making. Thus, the shareholders are in an agency relationship with respect to the bondholders. This relationship generates opportunities for shareholders to exploit bondholders by choosing investment projects with risk characteristics that selectively favor shareholders at the expense of creditors. This exploitation arises from the different patterns of payoffs to the different classes of investors. These distortions in project selection can even cause shareholders to pass up profitable investment opportunities.

To start, we will consider the nature of the payoffs to shareholders and creditors and develop the illustrations by assuming that creditors are bondyholders. Bondholders receive a fixed payoff of principal and interest if the value of the firm is sufficient to cover this obligation. Shareholders receive the residual claim; they are paid dividends after interest and principal have been met and receive the residual in a liquidation after all priority claimants have been paid. This can be represented simply in a one-period setting. Figure 7–5 shows the value of the firm on the horizontal axis, and the vertical axis shows the values of the main classes of

F I G U R E   7-5

Leverage and Dysfunctional Investment

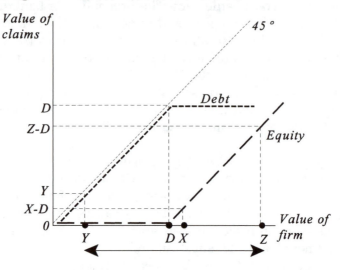

securities, debt and equity. We ignore taxes in tis example for simplicity. The face value of the debt is D. If the value of the firm is worth less than D, the firm is insolvent. In this case the equity is worthless and the debt is worth whatever remaining value is left to the firm. Thus, the debt claim is the full value of the firm (i.e., follos the 45° line) and the equity claim is zero (i.e., on the horizontal axis). If the firm value exceeds D, the firm is solvent and the debt claim is worth its full face value D and the equity is worth whatever is left (i.e., the firm value, $V(F) - D$).

Now consider a firm that faces no risk and has a certain value of X, as shown in Figure 7–5. It can now choose a new project that will have an expected value of zero, but a downside risk of $X - Y$ together with an upside potential of $Z - X$. The range of risk from the project is shown by the arrowed line underneath the diagram. If the firm undertakes the new project, the firm value would be a lottery over points Y and Z but still have an expected value of X. With the project, the upside and downside risk are borne unequally by the shareholders and bondholders. All the upside risk benefits the shaeholders whose claim increases from ($X - D$) to ($Z - D$) if the project is successful. On the other hand, if the project fails, the shareholders claim only falls from $(X - D)$ to zero. The shareholders benefit from all the upside but bear little downside. The bondholders fare less well. If the project succeeds, they receive no additional benefit as fixed stakeholders; their value stays at D. On the other hand, if the project fails, they do not receive their promised value D but rreceive only the remaining value Y. Thus, the bondholders face o potential gain from the project, but they face a potential loss of $D - Y$. In summary, the projects offers the shareholders a chance of substantial gain, but little loss, as they can deflect any loss to the bondholders. In effect, the shareholders are playing a *"heads I win, tails you lose"* game with the bondholders. Naturally such games are very attractive to the shareholders and unattractive to bondholders.

This attraction of shareholders to high risk investment can lead to "asset substitution." The firm raises debt, promising to undertake a low-risk project. but having secured the funds, it then substitutes a high-risk investment causing a wealth transfer from bondholders to shareholders. However, there is a catch for the shareholder. Bondholders anticipate that shareholders will be tempted to seek out such risky investment projects, and accordingly, when bonds are issued, they are discounted to reflect this potential expropriation. This hurts shareholders, for it increases the cost of debt. Shareholders are hoisted on their own petard; when they secure funds from bondholders, they are tempted to risk those funds in highly uncertain ventures. This *ex post* temptation hurts shareholders *ex ante* because it reduces the amount bondholders are willing to pay for new debt. Prospectively, shareholders would be better off if they could send bondholders some credible signal that they would not engage in such expropriatory behavior.

Underinvestment arises also from the asymmetry in the payoffs to bondholders and shareholders. We can again use Figure 7–5 to begin our illustration of underinvestment. Suppose a firm already has considerable risk; for example, the value is a lottery over points Y and Z with an expected value of X. The shareholders will either get 0 (if the firm value is Y) or $Z - D$ (if the firm value is Z). Bondholders will get either Y or D, depending on whether firm value is Y or Z. If the respective probabilities of Z and Y are 0.5, then:

$$\text{Value of the firm} = V(F) = \tfrac{1}{2}(Y) + \tfrac{1}{2}(Z)$$

$$\text{Value of equity} = V(E) = \tfrac{1}{2}(0) + \tfrac{1}{2}(Z - D)$$

$$\text{Value of debt} = V(D) = \tfrac{1}{2}(Y) + \tfrac{1}{2}(D)$$

Now suppose the firm faces a new riskless investment opportunity that has a small positive NPV. The cost is C, which is paid for up front by shareholders. The present value of future cash flows from the new investment is N, giving an NPV of $N - C$. I will assume here that the NPV is not sufficient to pull the firm out of bankruptcy ($N - C < D - Y$). After this investment, the values are:

NEW value of the firm

$$\tfrac{1}{2}(Y + N) + \tfrac{1}{2}(Z + N) - C = V(F) + N - C$$

NEW value of equity
$$\tfrac{1}{2}(0) + \tfrac{1}{2}(Z - D + N) - C = V(E) + \tfrac{1}{2}N - C$$

NEW value of debt
$$\tfrac{1}{2}(Y + N) + \tfrac{1}{2}(D) = V(D) + \tfrac{1}{2}N$$

Although the value of the firm rises by the full NPV ($N - C$), this benefit is split unevenly between the stakeholders. Shareholders here pay the full cost of the project but only get back one-half of the income N. The reason is that the firm was already risky and, due to limited liability, shareholders could default on debt if the firm value was Y (paying only Y instead of the full face value of debt D to bondholders). With the project, shareholders increase the amount they pay to bondholders in the event of bankruptcy from Y to $Y + N$. Thus, half of the benefit of the project goes to shoring up the debt should the firm default. The shareholders pay the full cost of the project but benefit only if the firm does not become bankrupt. Thus, shareholders are likely to pass up this project despite its positive NPV.

Like the asset substitution problem, underinvestment ultimately hurts shareholders. Bondholders can anticipate that the firm is likely to forgo positive NPV projects when it is insolvent and this will harm bondholders. The greater the risk of the firm, the more likely that such underinvestment will occur and the less attractive are the bonds to investors. But if the firm can lower the risk, it can make the bonds more attractive and thereby lower the cost of the firm's debt. Thus, both asset substitution and under-investment raise the cost of debt. However, reducing risk will mit-igate these distortions and thereby lower the cost of debt capital. In this way, risk management can add value to the firm and to its shareholders.

Costly Access to Capital and the Crowding Out of Investment Projects (or Cash Flow Hedging)

After a firm suffers a loss of assets, such as through fire damage to a plant, it is presented with an investment opportunity. The firm has the opportunity to reinvest in the construction of a re-placement plant. Like any other investment opportunity, reinvest-ment will add value to the firm only if the net present value is positive.[3] Reinvestment can be financed in two ways. Under *post-loss* financing, the funds are secured (from internal or external sources) after the loss has occurred. Funds may be either debt or equity, but the opportunity cost of raising this money is met after the funds are raised. If money is borrowed, it must be repaid after the loss; if equity is raised, dividends will be payable after the loss. Unless the firm is sufficiently liquid, the firm must go to external sources to secure the reinvestment funds, and this in-volves significant costs. *Pre-loss* financing occurs if the funds to reinvest in future prospective losses are secured and paid for be-

---

3. This decision is not trivial. Just because a firm continues to operate with productive assets does not imply that it makes economic sense to replace those assets should they be destroyed. The decision to continue to operate with assets in place in-volves a comparison between the *disposal* value of the assets in place and the earnings that they are expected to generate. If the projected earnings capitalize to a value greater than the disposal value, it adds value to continue production. If the assets should be destroyed, the replacement value becomes the appropriate ba-sis for measuring the return. Only if the projected earnings capitalize to a value greater than the replacement value does it make sense to reinvest. For example, imagine a steel mill with disposal value of 300, generating annual earnings of 80. There is an effective rate of return of 26.7% from continuing production. But should the mill be destroyed in an explosion and cost $1000 to replace, the rate of return will be only 8%. With a cost of capital of, say, 12%, reinvestment would not be appropriate.

fore the loss occurs. Insurance is such a source. Premiums are paid in anticipation of possible losses, and the insurance proceeds can be used to finance reinvestment. In this fashion, insurance may be seen as a source of financing for insurable losses, in much the same way as debt and equity are sources of financing.

Some financing is necessary for the firm to capture the net present value of reinvestment, and the financing source that adds most value is the preferred one. Thus, the decision to purchase insurance involves a comparison between the transaction costs associated with insurance (such as commissions, overheads, and moral hazard frictions) with the transaction costs of more conventional capital sources such as debt and equity, which we will discuss later. It can be seen that one of the benefits of hedging or insurance is that it permits the firm to undertake value adding reinvestment opportunities, which might be lost if post-loss financing is not forthcoming or is too costly.

The analysis of the previous two paragraphs was developed[4] to analyze insurance and reinvestment decisions. These ideas have been generalized by Froot, Scharfstein, and Stein (FSS) into a broader rationale for hedging, which I will call the "crowding out" hypothesis, or what is sometimes called "cash flow hedging." The first element of this idea is that capital sources have different costs. FSS evoke the work of Myers and Majluf to argue that external capital is more costly than internal capital. This is obvious in the case of direct costs. External capital encounters issue costs and underwriting costs that are avoided when retained earnings are used to fund projects. More important are the costs of information asymmetry. Managers will normally have greater knowledge of their firms and their firm's investment opportunities than external investors. This information asymmetry gives rise to the sort of expropriatory behavior we analyzed previously when discussing the underinvestment problem. Such behavior either forces the firm to adopt costly controls (e.g., restraints included in bond issues, costly reporting and monitoring) or it is anticipated by investors and lowers the amount raised in new issues and thus increases the cost of capital. The additional costs associated with external

---

4. See Doherty (1985).

funding, lead to the so-called pecking order hypothesis: firms have a ranking of sources of financing with internal funds beings preferred, followed by external debt and then external equity.

The differential costs associated with capital are used by FSS to develop their rationale for hedging. First, firms derive value from identifying and undertaking new investment projects. A healthy and growing firm may be investing in research and development, developing new products and rationalizing existing operations. Such firms face a continuing need for capital to fund their investment opportunities. Given the pecking order of the costs of financing, one would expect such firms to adopt a financial strategy (e.g., a capital structure and dividend policy) to fund as much as feasible of the new investments from internal sources. Now suppose that such a firm takes a sudden loss in liquidity from an uninsured fire or liability suit, a sharp deterioration in exchange rates, or an unanticipated rise in the price of a commodity that is used intensively in production. The loss in liquidity compromises the firm's ability to undertake its desired investment projects. Some projects that were attractive given internal funds are not so attractive now that they have to be paid for from costly external sources. Thus, the firm may defer (until sufficient internal funds have accrued) or cancel some investment projects. This results in a real loss of value to the firm. In contrast, hedging these losses preserves internal funds so that they can be used to finance new investments in a cheap and orderly manner.

The crowding out hypothesis can be summarized as follows. In the face of costly access to external capital, hedging preserves internal funding sources and avoids the loss of positive NPV projects. This loss of value can be high. FSS quote sources that suggest that for every \$1 of sudden capital loss, firms reduce their investment budget by approximately 35 cents. More direct support for this hypothesis is given in recent work by Géczy, Minton, and Schrand (1997). They examine a sample of Fortune 500 nonfinancial firms that are exposed to currency risk and find that firms that have high R&D, low quick ratios, and highest foreign exchange exposure (i.e., the firms that face the highest opportunity cost from unhedged losses) are indeed the firms that are most likely to use currency hedges.

Managerial Utility Maximization and Risk Aversion[5]

Here we will examine two separate but related issues. First, we are concerned with why risk is costly and how a firm can add value by avoiding risk. In this vein, we wish to see how firms can achieve more effective job performance from managers by design of their compensation. In the examination of this issue, a central point is whether managers bear risk and how much they need to be compensated for doing so. The second issue arises because managers actually make decisions that determine both the productivity of the firm and the amount of risk it accepts. We are facing another type of agency cost. Will managers make decisions to serve their own interests or to serve the shareholders? Moreover, if we accept that managers are self-interested, then can shareholders design compensation systems to influence the risk management choices made by managers?

Typically, corporate decisions are made not by a firm's owners but by employed managers. We now show that managers may choose to adopt risk postures that are not in the interests of shareholders; this decision making depends very much on how managers are rewarded. Presently, we will show how value can be added for shareholders by the adoption of risk management strategies that recognize managerial utility maximization. We will start with the explanation of risk management serving manager self-interest.

Managerial Self-Interest and Risk Taking

Suppose that managers serve their own self-interest, which may or may not coincide with others, such as shareholders. Further assume that managers are risk-averse, which we capture by the function which shows manager utility to be the square root of wealth.

$$U = W^{0.5}$$

where:

---

5. See Smith and Stulz (1985).

U = utility
W = manager wealth

The manager's wealth includes his earnings from employment and other wealth. If other wealth were very large relative to employment income, then one might suppose the risk of employment income to be of little interest. But this is not true for most managers for whom employment income is a major, or even dominant, source of wealth. For these managers, risk in employment income is important. Accordingly, if employment income is risky, the manager will find it distinctly less attractive

To develop the example, the firm's value (i.e., the present expected value of its future cash flows) can be either $500m or $1000m, each with 0.5 probability. The risk can be hedged and, bearing in mind any transaction cost associated with the hedge and any efficiency gain from hedging,[6] value can be stabilized at $780 m. Would a manager choose such a hedge? We consider three cases.

Flat Salary First, consider a manager with a flat salary of $300,000. Assuming job security is not affected by the purchase of the hedge, the manager should be indifferent, even though shareholders gain from the hedge. The manager's utility is

$$U = (300,000)^{0.5} = 547.72$$

regardless of whether the hedge is purchased or not. One might suppose that the tie would be broken, since the board of directors would favorably assess the manager's job performance if the hedge were purchased.

Incentive Compensation Now suppose the manager is paid some proportion x of the value of earnings. Such a scheme can be labeled "incentive compensation" or "performance-related

---

6. Note that the certain value of profit with the hedge exceeds the expected value of profit without hedging. This implies either that the transaction costs of the hedge are negative or, more likely, that transactions costs are positive but are more than offset by an efficiency gain from hedging. The efficiency gain could come from resolution of asset substitution, underinvestment, or the crowding out problem.

earnings." If there is a competitive labor market, the value of x should be sufficient that the manager is no worse off with incentive compensation than with flat salary (the previous case shows the manager's utility is 547.72 with flat salary). Thus, the utility of earnings with incentive compensation (either $x \times \$500m$ or $x \times \$1000m$) must be no less than 547.72.

$$547.72 \leq 0.5(500,000,000x)^{0.5} + 0.5(1,000,000,000x)^{0.5}$$

$$1095.45 \leq (500,000,000^{0.5} + 1,000,000,000^{0.5})(x)^{0.5}$$

$$1095.45 \leq 53983.46 \, (x)^{0.5}$$

$$0.02029 \leq x^{0.5}$$

$$x \geq 0.000412$$

Having established the competitive compensation level, let us now examine the manager's utility level with and without the hedge.

With the hedge:

$$U = \{0.000412(\$780m)\}^{0.5} = 566.89$$

Without the hedge:

$$U = 0.5(500,000,000 \times 0.000412)^{0.5}$$
$$+ 0.5(1,000,000,000 \times 0.000412)^{0.5} = 547.72$$

Now utility is higher with the hedge than without. Thus, the manager now has a direct monetary interest in that decision which favors shareholders; that is, hedging.

Stock Options   The third compensation system considered is a stock option plan. Suppose the manager receives neither salary nor shares of stock, but has call options on the stock. The firm's value is either $500m or $1000m, and you now know there are 10 million shares outstanding. The firm has no debt, so firm value can be divided over the number of shares; each share will be worth either $50 or $100. Suppose each call option is the right to purchase a share at a price of $80 (this price is known as the "exercise price" or the "striking price"). The share is worth either

$50, in which case the option to buy at $80 is worthless and the option expires, or $100 and the option to buy at $80 yields a clear profit of $20 per share. The probability of each share value is 0.5, and the *expected profit* from holding one option on one stock is:

$$E(\text{profit})_{\text{per option}} = 0.5(\$0) + 0.5(\$20)$$

and the *expected utility* from holding options to purchase some number y shares is:

$$EU = 0.5(\$0 \times y)^{0.5} + 0.5(\$20 \times y)^{0.5}$$

Notice that the option will be worth money only if the stock price can rise above the exercise price of $80. Thus, if the firm were to hedge and stabilize its value at $780m, each share would be worth $78 and the option to purchase a share at $80 would be without value.

It should be becoming clear that if the manager is rewarded with stock options, then hedging is unattractive; the manager will receive no income. What is the good of holding options with an exercise price of $80 on stocks that are certain to be valued at $78? In fact, the expected utility of the manager is the square root of zero, which is zero. If, on the other hand, the manager held 60,000 stock options and the firm did not hedge, then the expected utility of the manager would be:

$$EU = 0.5(\$0 \times 60{,}000)^{0.5} + 0.5(\$20 \times 60{,}000)^{0.5} = 547.72$$

The manager is clearly better off if the firm does not hedge. If the manager is to make the decision, he will clearly prefer not to hedge. You will notice that I have given a number of 60,000 options so that the manager receives the same utility as if he had a flat salary of $300,000 or received 0.00412 of the firm's value. Thus, I am comparing compensation systems that are comparable and competitive with each other.

The above analysis suggests that we should be able to predict what type of hedging policies are adopted by firms by examining the compensation package offered to their managers. Firms offering incentive compensation that is directly related to value (both upside and downside), such as stock ownership plans, are very likely to hedge risk because managers will reduce their own risk and secure any efficiency gains from the hedge. Firms that offer flat salary may still hedge, but the likelihood is weaker. Managers have no direct money interest in hedging, but may benefit indirectly if it affects job security or performance evaluation. In contrast, managers rewarded mainly with stock options are less likely to hedge, since it can lower the value of their options. There is some recent evidence supporting this pattern. Peter Tufano (1996) recently examined hedging behavior in the gold mining industry. Here firms face an easily identifiable risk, that of fluctuations in gold prices. However, there is an active market in gold price hedging instruments. Tufano found clear differences in hedging patterns that seemed to be explained only by differences in management's holdings of securities of their employer. Firms whose managers held large equity holdings tended to hedge, but firms whose managers held large option positions were much less likely to hedge gold price risk.

Risk and the Efficiency of Compensation Design

Now consider a firm that faces no risk. Managers can affect productivity, and thereby profitability, by their effort. High effort will lead to high (certain) profit and low effort will lead to low (certain) profit. The problem is that managers would, other things being equal, prefer not to work hard, and thus there is an incentive conflict. This conflict could be resolved if directors could observe the effort level of managers and simply reward them conditional on effort, but effort is not easily observable. In this example, however, there is another simple solution. The firm can simply pay the managers according to profit: high profit receives high compensation and vice versa. As long as the additional compensation for high effort (a) exceeds the manager's disutility from supplying high effort and (b) is less than the additional profit generated by the high effort, then this compensation system will add value without making managers any worse off. Notice that profit becomes a perfect *ex post* signal of the manager's effort, and thus compensation will be directly related to effort.

We can now add risk to the mix. High effort from the managers will lead to a higher likelihood of high profits, and low effort will likely cause lower profits. If the manager is paid incentive compensation in the form of a proportion of profits, then it becomes likely (but not certain) that the manager will be paid more the higher his level of effort. But the risk of the profit stream will be reflected in the manager's compensation. Because employment income typically is a large portion of the manager's wealth, this risk significantly reduces the manager's welfare. Thus, incentive compensation typically is higher than flat salary; incentive compensation has to compensate for both the disutility of high effort and the inherent risk.

The gain from hedging risk can now be seen in two different ways. If profit risk is hedged, then incentive compensation becomes riskless and thus the level of compensation can be lowered. The firm need no longer pay managers a risk premium. Another way of approaching this issue is to address the tradeoff involved in performance-related earnings compared with flat salary. Performance-related earnings induce higher effort but are more costly because of the risk imposed on managers. This risk usually results in managers being paid hybrid compensation, part salary and part bonus. The firm forgoes some efficiency gain in order to avoiding loading managers with too much risk. If risk is hedged, the compensation scheme can focus solely on productivity and pay only bonuses. This means higher productivity. In more general terms, hedging affects the optimal mix in the compensation system; less risk will favor a higher proportion of performance-related compensation.

Risk and Signaling

A variation on the managerial utility maximization model uses risk management as a signal of managerial ability (DeMarzo and Duffie, 1995, and Breeden and Viswanathan, 1996). In these models investors are unable to tell from performance measures (quarterly profit, stock price, etc.) to what extent the result is due to the ability of the manager or to exogenous factors. This makes it more difficult for managers of high ability to command appropriate rewards. Consider the following simple example. A well-managed airline will on average command higher profits than a poorly managed one. The term "well-managed" might encompass effective pricing policies, effective choice of routes, effective marketing, appropriate safety policies, and so on. However, profits will still be adversely impacted by factors outside management control, such as rising fuel prices, changes in the demand for travel, or chance accident that occurred despite effective safety policy. Imagine that the annual profits of the well-managed firm and the poorly managed firm are as follows:

Profit $ million	Probability Well Managed	Probability Poorly Managed
100	01	0.4
200	0.2	0.3
300	0.3	0.2
400	0.4	0.1
Expected profit	300	200

Investors, unfortunately, never get to see *expected* profit. They can make some estimates of what they expect profit to be for the coming year. But this will depend on how much information they have about investment opportunities, managerial practices and a whole host of other factors, and they are unlikely to have the same quality of information as the firm's own management. All the investor gets to see at the end of the year is the actual profit. Suppose this turns out to be 100. Does the investor know whether the firm is well managed or poorly managed? The investor might infer that such a low profit is more likely to be indicative of poor management than good management, but she cannot be sure. Using the table, we can see that an observation of 100 would have a 40% chance of occurring with bad management but only a 10% chance with good management. Similarly, a result of 400 would have a 40% chance with good management but only a 10% chance with bad management.

This idea is sometimes known as a "signal-to-noise ratio." Consider a radio signal: you wish to listen to the British Broadcasting Corporation on your short wave radio. A signal is transmitted from London, but what you hear on your radio in Philadelphia is a combination of the broadcast signal and a lot of static interference or noise. Reception is good when the signal is strong and the interference low: a high signal-to-noise ratio. Reception is poor when the signal is weak and the static loud: a low signal-to-noise ratio. Profit performance combines in a single measure (a) management quality (the signal) and (b) random events (the noise). What effective managers would like (though not ineffective managers) is a strong signal and low noise.

The good managers may wish to signal quality by removing the noise. If the risk is hedged, observed profit will be 300 (minus any transaction cost for the hedge). However, if a poorly managed firm hedges, the actual profit will turn out to be 200 (minus transaction cost). Thus, with complete hedging, the result would reveal fully the quality of management; the actual profit performance is all signal and no noise. In this way, efficient management managerial compensation could be more accurately tied to performance. Complete hedging of all corporate risk is rarely possible, but some hedging can remove risk. Thus, the game played by high-quality management would now be to increase the signal-to-noise ratio so that actual performance is more likely to be indicative of high-quality management.

Comparative Advantage in Risk Bearing

Two of the stories about why risk was costly were "moral hazard" tales. Managers are agents of the firm's owners and, if left to their own devices, will make self-interested decisions. Recognizing this, owners usually arrange compensation systems to align interests of shareholders and managers. One of the design choices is how to trade off risk sharing (favoring flat compensation) with efficiency (favoring performance-related pay). Hedging can lighten this tradeoff by providing incentive compensation and lowering the risk premia demanded by managers. Similarly, the underinvestment phenomenon arose because of the agency function of shareholders with respect to money provided by creditors. The opportunity for owners to default on debt leads to the selection of abnormally risky projects. Anticipating such excessive risk taking leads investors to discount the value of corporate bonds. Hedging removes the advantage to shareholders of such high-risk activity and can provide a credible signal that such expropriatory behavior will not be undertaken. Both these arguments suggested that the level of risk and the potential losses the firm faces are dependent on how the firm's value is divided between stakeholders. Another argument will also show that the level of hedged cash flows depends on how rights to earnings and value are divided.

Consider the following situation. A firm (call it the main contractor) designs and builds a telecommunication satellite. This is a complex product, and the main contractor subcontracts with other firms who supply subsystems that are then assembled into the final product. The final product is then sold to a telecommunications firm that uses the satellite for telephone communications. Of course, the satellite has to be launched by a rocket into an appropriate orbit before it can fulfil its function. Suppose something goes wrong and the customer fails to acquire a functioning satellite in the correct orbit. Who should pay? You are the main contractor, and you seek advice from your corporate lawyers. No doubt they will try to persuade you that contracts should be written so that someone else (anyone else) is responsible. Is this a desirable solution?

Now consider just a sample of the things that can go wrong:

The rocket can blow up during launch, destroying the satellite.

The satellite can be delivered to the wrong orbit.

The satellite can get to the correct orbit but fail to function through an assembly fault.

The satellite can get to the correct orbit but fail through a subsystem failure.

If the accumulation of all these risks is too high, the customer is simply going to say, "@?#!$ satellites. I will use fiber optic instead because it is more reliable." Clearly, then, to retain your market you will wish to offer the customer a reliable and economic product. Now the question is, who should bear the risk of losses and how does this decision affect the final price and reliability of the product?

This answer depends on an idea elaborated by Calibresi (1970), which is to make that party responsible who can avoid the loss at least cost.[7] So, consider failures from subsystem faults. Subcontractors produce these subsystems, and through their effort they can improve quality control. It makes sense to make the subcontractors liable for these type of failures. If they are not liable,

---

7. This discussion is related to the Nobel Prize-winning work of Ronald Coase (1960), who explored optimal rules for property rights and legal liability accidents. Coase's contribution was to suggest that liability rules would not affect investments in safety if contracting costs were zero. Regardless of the initial allocation of liability, the parties could enter contracts or bargains in which the person who made the safety decision had a financial incentive to make one that was socially optimal.

they will simply pay less attention to quality control. Similarly, it is sensible to make the rocket manufacturer or the launch contractor responsible if the rocket fails to deliver the satellite to correct orbit, and the main contractor responsible for faults stemming from overall design and assembly. In this way each party has a strong financial incentive to see that the operations over which it has control function without hitch.

You may object to this reasoning and claim that everyone has an incentive to competent work anyway, since otherwise they will obtain a poor reputation and will not be asked to do future work. Certainly reputation is important. The point here is that there is simply an additional, and more immediate, incentive to perform.

CORE RISK AND INCIDENTAL RISK

The idea that firms can have a comparative advantage or disadvantage in risk taking has recently been given a slightly different flavor. When an oil company explores for oil, it acquires risk. When an insurance company issues policies, it takes risks. When a bank lends to a startup firm, it takes risk. Firms are in the business of taking risk; indeed, that is how they earn profit. Consider first the oil company. The oil company takes the risk that its exploration will not result in a finding of oil or that the finding might be small and uneconomic. The firm is banking on its superior exploration technology and geological knowledge to increase the odds in its favor. This is a core competency of the firm, and in exploiting this competency the firm expects to earn economic profit. The risk is more than compensated by the expected profit; in short, it is a positive net present value opportunity. The firm is rewarded for its particular and scarce skills. Indeed, the organization of business is centered around the ability of specialist firms to identify and exploit positive NPV investment opportunities within their areas of competence. Investment opportunities are, by nature, risky. Those same opportunities might not be identified, and could not be exploited at a similar profit, by others without those skill sets. Thus, the specialized firm is rewarded for adopting risk. The scarcer the skills and the greater the value created by the investment, the higher the reward-to-risk ratio (i.e., the higher the risk-adjusted NPV).

However, in taking this risk, the oil company acquires incidental risk. Profit can be depleted if its engineers are killed in an air crash, or if the currency rate between the country of exploration and the head office domicile changes. These are risks that are not core and that the firm has no special advantage in handling. Consequently, the oil company can gain no special reward in retaining these risks. Like core risks, these risks are costly. They can increase agency costs, taxes, etc. But the firm can expect no extra profit from bearing the noncore risks as it does from bearing core risks.

The insurance firm can dichotomize its risks in a similar fashion. Assuming risk through insurance is a specialty for which the firm expects profit. The core competencies of the insurer include the abilities to diversify this risk through the structure of its portfolio, underwrite successfully (i.e., discriminately accept those policyholders who are better than average), price the risk, and settle claims effectively and cheaply. However, the insurer acquires incidental risks. For a small insurer without a full investment department, this could include investment risk, risk of suits against the company's officers and catastrophe risk. There are others better equipped to handle and assume these risks. A portfolio manager's core competency is to handle the investment risk, and a reinsurer's is to handle the catastrophe risk. These risks might well be transferred to outsiders who have greater expertise in handling them.

The point is not to assert that an insurer's core competency does not include investment management (larger insurers would indeed claim such expertise). The point is that for any firm there will be some risks that are core (its very business is the exploitation of these risks for profit) and some risks that are incidental. How this carves up will vary from firm to firm. An important idea developed and tested by Schrand and Unal (1997)[8] concerns the composition of risk and how it might be managed. If risk is costly, then one will wish to control overall risk in a way that maximizes profit relative to the risk assumed. If one has a choice over which risk to assume, it makes sense to assume the risks with the highest reward ratio. Thus, in managing risk, the idea is to transfer the incidental risk (they use the label "homogeneous

---

8. See also the much earlier work of Kenneth Arrow (1964, ch. 5), who also considered comparative advantage in risk bearing.

risk") to outsiders in order to free up capacity to assume more core risk. This idea is called "coordinated risk management."

WHICH FIRMS BENEFIT FROM MANAGING RISK?

The various explanations of why risk is costly suggest that the cost of risk will differ between firms in a predictable way. This is important when it comes to testing these theories as well as for those charged with managing risk. We will take each theory in turn and isolate the firm characteristics that determine whether risk is important and, by implication, whether hedging the risk can add value.

The tax nonlinearity rationale rests on the firm's tax function being convex. If taxes are linear in income, then expected taxes are unrelated to the riskiness of income. The more convex the tax function, the more expected taxes will increase with risk. But this relationship is compounded when we consider the distribution of earnings. Convexity is important over the range of earnings that are most likely. Consider a firm whose tax function is convex over a low range of earnings, then becomes linear as earnings increase (i.e., the marginal tax rate is constant over medium to high earnings). If a firm's earnings are most likely to lie in the medium to high range, convexity in the low range has little effect on expected taxes. The issue then is whether the range of probable earnings spans the kinks in the tax schedule. Firms with high probable earnings and low investment tax credit and carryforwards are unlikely to secure much tax benefit from managing risk. Firms with higher tax shields and a high variation of earnings about the level of tax shield can reduce their expected taxes most through hedging. Roughly, this means those firms whose tax shields are roughly equal to expected earnings.

The financial distress rationales for risk management carry a clear implication. Firms with higher leverage will bear a higher cost of risk. If two firms have the same level of risk, the higher-leverage firm will have a higher probability of bankruptcy and therefore the higher expected bankruptcy costs. Moreover, the indirect agency problems also will be higher for the more leveraged firm. The indirect cost of financial distress model also relies on the firm having opportunities for growth; it is in the selection of new investment projects that principal–agent distortions can occur. Leveraged firms with available investment opportunities will gravitate towards high-risk projects. The anticipation of this by bondholders can increase the cost of debt and lead to underinvestment. This is not as important for firms with no growth potential. Leverage and growth also are relevant firm characteristics when crowding out costs are considered. Unhedged losses crowd out new investment only for firms with investment opportunities. The greater these growth opportunities, the greater the opportunity cost of risk.

The managerial utility maximization model also has clear predictions, but these predictions are not so much about which firm's shareholders are likely to gain most from hedging as about which firms are likely to hedge because the managers choose to do so. Firms whose management compensation systems focus on share ownership are more likely to engage in hedging activities. Firms that make intensive use of options in rewarding managers are more likely to engage in risky activities and less likely to hedge.

Firms Most Likely to Hedge

Tax Nonlinearity	Ratio—Tax Shield: E(earnings) ≈ 1
Financial Distress—Direct	High leverage
Financial Distress—Indirect	High leverage High growth High R&D
Crowding out	High leverage High growth High R&D
Managerial Utility Maximization	Managers hold few options/many shares
Stakeholder Risk Aversion	Creditors/warranties

SOME EVIDENCE ON THE COST OF RISK AND FIRM VALUE

Various people have tested the theories of why risk is costly. A selection is summarized here. It would be difficult to measure the costs of risk directly, and these research tests do not usually attempt to do so. Rather, the reasoning is that the higher the cost of risk to a firm, the more it has to gain from hedging and therefore the more likely it is to hedge. The trick is then to find the firm characteristics that indicate that risk is more or less costly. For example, with the tax nonlinearity model, firms with a tax shield to expected earnings ratio close to 1 would gain more than firms whose range of earnings does not span different marginal tax rates. With the underinvestment model, firms with more leverage and higher growth opportunities would have the most to gain from hedging. However, the crowding out model suggests that hedging behavior would be explained by similar firm characteristics. Thus, a finding that hedging behavior was positively associated with leverage and growth would be supportive of both models. It is not necessary to come up with a winner. Many academics believe that all of these models have something to say about the cost of risk.

There have been some tests of hedging of insurance firms purchase of reinsurance. Mayers and Smith (1990) take an interesting approach that tests several of the models considered. The various models presented earlier in this chapter asked why risk was costly to a firm whose owners could diversify easily in their portfolio choices. Mayers and Smith consider this issue and argue that different ownership structures of insurance firms present different opportunities for diversification. The greater the fraction of the owners' wealth accounted for in the insurance firm's equity, the greater the demand for reinsurance. Thus, a ranking of ownership structures according to their demand for reinsurance would be headed by Lloyd's associations, followed by single-family, closely held, and widely held firms. They do find evidence consistent with this hypothesis. In addition, their results show that demand for reinsurance is negatively related to credit standing (Best's rating), which is consistent with the financial distress hypothesis. Other results concern the effects of size and, more importantly, geographical diversification. The latter result is taken to support the hypothesis that reinsurers offer real service efficiencies that are more valuable to the smaller, more geographically diversified insurer. Although not stressed by Mayers and Smith, this result also can be explained by insurers developing core competencies and being more willing to assume risk in such areas.

Another insurance result tests the cost of risk hypotheses indirectly. Kleffner and Doherty (1996) look at the supply of catastrophe insurance in California. Instead of examining whether firms offload risk, they look at whether firms assume risk in a way that is systematically related to firm characteristics that reveal the cost of risk bearing. Consider the financial distress and crowding out hypotheses and the significant degree of undiversifiable risk assumed by insurers offering earthquake insurance. These factors suggest that insurers would be more willing to offer earthquake coverage the lower their leverage, the greater their reinsurance, and the more diversified (geographically and by line of business) their portfolios. These results are consistent with the costs of financial distress hypothesis. They failed to find evidence of tax-motivated risk assumption, though there were difficulties in finding good proxies for tax convexity.

A study of another industry, gold mining, by Peter Tufano (1996) comes up with different results. Gold mining firms can hedge their exposure to fluctuation in the price of gold by using various instruments; such as forward sales, loans, and put and call options. However, these instruments could be used for both risk management and speculative purposes. To separate these different uses of derivatives, he uses the concepts of *delta*, the sensitivity of the value of a portfolio to a small change in the price of an underlying asset, and *delta percentage*, the percentage of gold production accounted for by the portfolio delta. He then tests the various hypotheses of costly risk bearing and finds strong support for the managerial utility maximization model but little support for the other models that suggest that hedging can increase the wealth of shareholders. The variables that proxy for financial distress and tax convexity have no significant power in explaining delta percentages. However, Tufano finds that firms whose management holds more stock engage in more risk management but firms whose managers hold more stock options manage less risk. Managers of gold mines, it seems, pay more attention to their own welfare than to that of their shareholders in managing risk.

Another empirical test by Schrand and Unal (1997) supports the managerial utility maximization hypothesis but also provides support for other theories. These authors look at the issue of core versus incidental risk—their "coordinated risk management" concept. This test is a little subtle because they examine firms that *increased* their levels of risk. They look at thrift institutions that differ according to organizational form; some are stock firms owned by investors and some are mutuals owned by depositors. A fundamental difference is that stocks can access new capital markets, by issuing equity, to fund new projects. The inability of mutuals to do so implies that they are more exposed to risk. The conversion of a mutual firm to a stock form of organization removes this constraint and effectively increases its risk-bearing capacity. This enables the demutualized firm to assume more core risk. This can still have all the frictional costs we have identified, but because the risk is core, it can be rewarded. Their evidence does confirm that demutualizing firms tend to assume more risk. However, recall that risk is still costly, and so such firms tend to switch between core and incidental risk; that is, they hedge non-rewarded incidental risk to release capacity to absorb more core risk.[9] This is what one would expect from the crowding out hypothesis (or indeed from the financial distress theories). But the story gets more interesting. Demutualization enables firms to reward managers with shares and options. Demutualizing firms that go on to focus on compensation-based share ownership decrease total risk following conversion, whereas converting firms whose managers are rewarded with options increase total risk. This difference is statistically significant.

Further indirect support for one of the theories is provided in the patterns of executive compensation. There has been an ongoing debate about whether executive pay is related to performance. Following an important paper by Jensen and Murphy in 1990, various people have addressed this topic, but the results on this relationship have been mixed. But a recent paper by Aggarwal and Samwick helps resolve the puzzle and bring the subject squarely into the risk management field. They find that the sensitivity of pay to performance is significantly positive if one controls for the volatility of stock prices. Firms with highly volatile stocks are least willing to offer performance-related pay because it imposes large risk on managers; the reverse is true for firms with more stable stock prices. Thus, it is difficult for firms with volatile stocks to motivate managers and one might expect that performance would suffer. However, the clear implication is that,

---

9. Credit risk is a core activity and interest rate risk is incidental.

insofar as the management of risk reduces stock price volatility, it becomes easier to write performance-related compensation and thereby boost efficiency.

Some evidence to support the crowding out hypothesis also is available. Empirical evidence cited by Froot et al. (1993) suggests that for each dollar of unhedged loss, project budgets will be cut by about 30 cents. More recent evidence from Minton and Schrand (1999) also supports this opportunity cost. They show that capital expenditure for firms with high cash flow volatility is about 19% below the mean and expenditures for those with low volatility is about 11% above the mean. Hedging avoids this loss and protects the ability of the firm to fund its investment program.

CONCLUSION:
A TRANSACTIONS COSTS EXPLANATION
OF CORPORATE RISK MANAGEMENT

The various theories as to why risk affects corporate value have a common base: they all arise from the frictional costs (or, as they are known by economists, "transactions costs") faced by a firm in doing its business. Firms have to pay taxes, and the expected value of these taxes is affected by risk. Firms bring together various stakeholders, and frictions between these stakeholders affect the quality of its decisions. For example, firms typically raise money in the form of both equity and debt. But creditors and shareholders are affected differently by future risk. Insofar as shareholders control investment decisions, they are likely to favor risky projects because they can keep the upside and default on the downside. This propensity for risk taking is anticipated by creditors and therefore increases the cost of debt capital. Firms can reduce this transaction cost, the cost of debt capital, by hedging risk.

We also saw how hedging can facilitate the financing of new investments after a loss. Firms may wish to hedge to preserve their liquidity so that new investment can be funded internally. Failure to hedge courts the possibility that a loss will absorb internal funds and expose the firm to the costly external capital market to finance new investment. Given the higher hurdle of external capital costs, some new investment will be lost.

Another theory examined in this chapter looked at how hedging can be used to write more effective compensation contracts with managers. Managers are typically risk-averse and relatively undiversified, whereas outside shareholders are typically diversified. Thus, from a risk-sharing view it makes sense for managers to be paid flat salary and for risk to be borne by shareholders. But from an incentive view it makes sense to align interests of shareholders and managers in the form of performance compensation. This tradeoff can be largely avoided if firm risk is hedged. This permits firms to use incentive compensation without burdening managers with risk that is outside their control.

Finally, we examined signaling theories. Insider managers can use hedging to signal private information to outsiders. This inside information can pertain to the quality of investment opportunities or to the underlying quality of the managers. For example, when a firm hedges risk that is outside the managers' control, the profit of the firm is purged of noise and becomes a more pure signal of the productivity of the managers. Thus, managers of high productivity may choose to hedge in order to command higher compensation.

As risk increases these various transactions costs, so hedging or insurance reduces these costs and adds value to the firm. In the next chapter we will return to each of these transactions costs and illustrate how hedging can create. But hedging will be only one of several risk management strategies examined in the following chapters. For each transaction cost examined, we will show that value can be created either by reducing risk or by redesign of the firm's financial, organizational, or contract structure so that it can tolerate the risk without imposing high cost.

REFERENCES

Aggarwal, Rajesh K., and Andrew A. Samwick. 1999. "The Other Side of the Trade-off: The Impact of Risk on Executive Compensation." *Journal of Political Economy* 107:65–105.

Aiuppa, Thomas A., Robert J. Carney, and Thomas M. Krueger. 1993. "An Examination of Insurance Stock Prices Following the 1989 Loma Prieta Earthquake." *Journal of Insurance Issues and Practices* 16:1–14.

Arrow, Kenneth. 1964. *Essays in the Theory of Risk Bearing.* Amsterdam: North Holland.

Babbel, David F., and Anthony M. Santomero. 1996. "Risk Management by Insurers: An Analysis of the Process." Working Paper, Financial Institutions Center, Wharton School, University of Pennsylvania.

Breeden, Douglas, and S. Wiswanathan. 1996. "Why Do Firms Hedge? An Asymmetric Information Model." Working Paper, Duke University.

Calibresi, Guido. 1970. *The Costs of Accidents.* New Haven: Yale University Press.

Cambell, Tim S., and William A. Krakaw. 1990. "Corporate Risk Management and the Incentive Effects of Debt." *Journal of Finance* 45:1673–86.

Coase, Ronald H. 1960. "The Problem of Social Cost." *Journal of Law and Economics* 3:1–44.

DeMarzo, Peter, and Darrell Duffie. 1995. "Corporate Incentives for Hedging and Hedge Accounting." *Review of Financial Studies* 8:743–72.

Doherty, Neil A. 1985. *Corporate Risk Management: A Financial Analysis.* New York: McGraw-Hill.

——. 1996. "Corporate Insurance: Competition from Capital Markets." In *Universal Banking,* ed. A. Saunders and I. Walter. New York: New York University. Salomon Center.

Doherty, Neil, and Seha Tinic. 1981. "A Note on Reinsurance under Conditions of Capital Market Equilibrium." *Journal of Finance* 36:949–53.

Froot, Kenneth, David Scharfstein, and Jeremy Stein. 1993. "Risk Management: Co-ordinating Investment and Financing Problems." *Journal of Finance* 48: 1629–58.

Garven, James R., and Henri Louberge. 1996. "Reinsurance, Taxes and Efficiency: A Contingent Claims Model of Insurance Market Equilibrium." *Journal of Financial Intermediation* 5:74–93.

Géczy, Minton and Schrand (1995, 1996).

Géczy, Christopher, Bernadette A. Minton and Catherine Schrand. 1997. "Why Firms Use Currency Derivatives." *Journal of Finance* 52:1323–1356.

Jensen, Michael C., and William H. Meckling. 1976. Theory of the Firm: Managerial Behavior, Agency Costs and Ownership Structure." *Journal of Financial Economics* 3:305–60.

Jensen, Michael C., and Kevin J. Murphy. 1990. "Performance Pay and Top-Management Incentives." *Journal of Political Economy* 98:225–64.

Kleffner, Anne E., and Neil A. Doherty. 1996. "Costly Risk Bearing and the Supply of Catastrophe Insurance." *Journal of Risk and Insurance* 63:657–71.

Lamb, Reinhold P. 1995. "An Exposure Based Analysis of Property Liability Insurer Stock Values Around Hurricane Andrew." *Journal of Risk and Insurance* 62:111–23.

Leland, Hayne E. 1998. "Agency Costs, Risk Management, and Capital Structure." *Journal of Finance* 53:1213–43.

Lew, Keun-Ock. 1991. "Reinsurance and The Firm Value: Theory and Evidence." Ph.D. Dissertation, Wharton School, University of Pennsylvania.

Major, John A. 1996. "Index Hedge Performance: Insurer Market Penetration and Basis Risk." Paper presented at National Bureau of Economic Research Conference, Palm Beach, Florida.

Mayers, David, and Clifford W. Smith Jr. 1983. "On the Corporate Demand for Insurance." *Journal of Business* 55:281–96.

————. 1987. "Corporate Insurance and the Underinvestment Problem." *Journal of Risk and Insurance* 54:45–54.

————. 1990. "On the Corporate Demand for Insurance: Evidence from the Reinsurance Market." *Journal of Business* 63:19–40.

Minton, Bernadette A., and Catherine Schrand. 1999. "The Impact of Cash Flow Volatility on Discretionary Investment and the Costs of Debt and Equity Financing." Working Paper, Wharton School, University of Pennsylvania.

Myers, Stewart C. 1977. "Determinants of Corporate Borrowing." *Journal of Financial Economics* 5:147–75.

Myers, Stewart C. and Nicholas S. Majluf. 1984. "Corporate Financing and Investment Decisions When Firms Have Information That Investors Do Not Have." *Journal of Financial Economics,* 13: 187–221.

Nance, D. R., C. W. Smith, and C. W. Smithson. 1993. "On the Determinants of Corporate Hedging." *Journal of Finance* 48:267–84.

Schrand, Catherine, and Haluk Unal. 1997. "Hedging and Coordinated Risk Management: Evidence from Thrift Conversion." Working Paper, Wharton School, University of Pennsylvania.

Shapiro, Alan C., and Sheridan Titman. 1985. "An Integrated Approach to Corporate Risk Management." *Midland Corporate Finance Journal.* 3(2):41–56.

Shavell, Stephen. 1979. "Risk Sharing and Incentives in the Principal and Agent Relationship." *Bell Journal of Economics* 10:55–73.

Shelor, Rober M., Dwight C. Anderson, and Mark L. Cross. 1992. "Gaining from Loss: Property-Liability Insurer Stock Prices in the Aftermath of the 1989 California Earthquake." *Journal of Risk and Insurance* 5:476–88.

Smith, Clifford W. Jr., and Rene Stulz. 1985. "The Determinants of Firms' Hedging Policies." *Journal of Financial and Quantitative Analysis* 28:391–405.

Stiglitz, J. 1983. *Risk, Incentives and Insurance: The Pure Theory of Moral Hazard.* Geneva Papers on Risk and Insurance, vol. 8, no. 26, 4–33.

Stulz, Rene. 1984. "Optimal Hedging Policies." *Journal of Financial and Quantitative Analysis* 19:127–40.

Tufano, Peter. 1996. "Who Manages Risk? An Empirical Examination of Risk Management Practices in the Gold Mining Industry." *Journal of Finance* 51: 1097–1137.

————. 1998. "Agency Costs of Corporate Risk Management." *Financial Management* 27:67–77.

Risk Management Strategy: Duality and Globality

In the previous chapter we examined why risk was important to firms. If a firm is publicly owned then its shareholders can diversify risk in their choice of portfolio. Even if risk is not diversifiable within the capital market, its sale will command an appropriate risk premium. Therefore, hedging the risk at this price will not add value but will merely change the risk–return combination available to investors. This reasoning suggests that, if risk is costly, it is not because that risk causes a problem for the firm's investors directly. Rather, it is because it gives rise to a set of transaction costs that lower the *expected value* of the firm's cash flows. These transaction costs include increased tax burden from risky cash flows, increased expected costs of bankruptcy, agency costs that arise from potential financial distress and lead to inefficient investment decisions, crowding out of new investment by unhedged losses, and inefficiencies that arise from managerial risk aversion.

In this chapter the task is to lay out generic risk management strategies. In deriving risk management strategy, we must start by understanding why risk management is a problem, in order to know how to address it. Consider a medical analogy. Suppose you have an allergy which is triggered each time you are exposed to common dust. You can, of course, manage that allergy by removing yourself from dust. So you vacuum your home with great frequency and refurbish it with surfaces that do not retain dust.

This may be an effective solution, depending on your degree of sensitivity. But it may not be an ideal solution, since it can be very time-consuming and costly. Moreover, some people may respond to trace amounts that cannot be removed practically. But there is another way of dealing with the problem. If one understands why dust triggers the allergic reaction, then it may be possible to break the link between the exposure to dust and the allergic reaction. Thus, to manage the condition, one can either remove the exposure or one can accommodate the dust but break the link between the exposure and the reaction with a treatment such as an antihistamine. This accommodation strategy is an important part of the treatment menu. Indeed, for many with allergies it is impractical to remove every environment stimulus, and the only practical treatment is an antihistamine or similar drug.

Consider the parallel between the allergy problem and the corporate risk management problem. To manage the allergy, one can remove the dust or one can accommodate the dust and remove the cost caused by the dust. One can address the cause or one can address the effect. Thus, the physician must have a good understanding of the physiology and chemistry of the body. Similarly with risk. If risk causes costs to firms, one can either remove the risk or one can accommodate the risk and arrange the affairs of the firm so that the risk does not cause a problem. But to do this, one must understand exactly why risk is a problem. This is the principle of *duality*, which assets that for every type of cost that risk imposes on the firm, there are two generic risk management strategies: either remove the risk or accommodate the risk but reduce its cost.

This chapter will begin by exploring duality and using this concept to derive a basic risk management menu. We will then establish some general principles for assembling a risk management strategy from this menu. In particular, we will examine to what extent the strategy should be integrated or holistic.

DUALITY IN RISK MANAGEMENT STRATEGY

The essence of duality is that one can address the cause or the effect. One can remove the risk if one can adapt the firm so that the risk is not a problem. Table 8–1 lists the various reasons why risk is costly to publicly owned firms. The table also shows that

T A B L E   8-1

Duality of Risk Management Strategies

Type of Risk Cost		Strategy
nonlinear taxes	hedge	tax arbitrage
expected bankruptcy costs	hedge	change leverage
		contingent leverage
agency cost:	hedge	change leverage
dysfunctional investment		contingent leverage
crowding out new investment	hedge	contingent financing
		contingent leverage
managerial risk aversion	hedge	change compensation scheme
stakeholder risk aversion	hedge	change stakeholder contracts

for each type of risk cost there are two potential strategies. First, the cause of the problem can be removed; risk can be hedged. Second, the risk can be retained but the firm or its activities can be structured so that the risk causes less of a problem; this strategy is labeled "accommodate." This dual principle is important for identifying the menu of strategies available for dealing with risk. The task now is to take each risk cost in turn and flesh out the types of hedging and accommodation strategies that are available.

Duality and Nonlinear Taxes

To explore the principle of duality, consider the following simple example. A firm purchases a capital asset at a cost of $1 billion, which will generate an income stream over a five-year period. The annual income stream is risky, with:

0.5 chance of $132 million

0.5 chance of $532 million − expected annual earnings = $332m

The firm is allowed to depreciate the asset in equal installments over its five-year life. Thus, the firm can shield $200m from tax each year. The tax rate is 34%. The expected tax liability (in $m), and, if we note that if earnings are $132m no tax will be paid, is:

$$0.5 \times 0.34(532 - 200) + 0.5 \text{ times } (0) = 56.44$$

And the expected value of this investment opportunity (at a zero discount rate for simplicity) is:

$$\text{expected net present value} = -\$1,000\text{m} + 5(\$332\text{m} - \$56.44\text{m})$$
$$= \$377.8\text{m}$$

The example is depicted in Figure 8–1. If earnings turn out to be $532m, the tax liability is $112.88m, as shown. If earnings are only $132m, then taxes will be zero. If we bear in mind the 50–50 chances of the two earnings levels, expected taxes are $56.44m.

Notice that the firm gets the full benefit of depreciation if earnings are $532m (i.e., taxes fall by 0.34 × $200m). But if earnings are only $132m, then the depreciation has no effect on taxes. Thus, the depreciation allowance can be wasted (this lost deduction can sometimes be partly recovered with carryforwards, but this is uncertain and does not accrue interest).

Hedge Strategy
Suppose the firm can hedge its earnings to fix earnings at the expected value of $332m. Expected tax is now reduced to:

F I G U R E   8–1

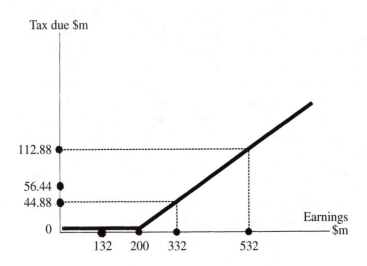

$$0.34(332 - 200) = 44.88$$

And the expected net present value of the investment opportunity is now increased to:

$$\text{expected net present value} = -\$1000m + 5(\$332m - \$44.88m)$$
$$= \$435.6m$$

compared with the unhedged value of \$377.8m. Note that expected taxes have changed even though expected earnings have not. How this hedge strategy would be achieved would depend on the source of the risk. For example, if the risk were insurable, then an insurance policy might be purchased. If the risk stemmed from the effects of interest rate fluctuations on demand for the product (as is common for consumer products that are financed, such as cars), an interest cap or future might hedge the risk. Similarly, if the risk stemmed from exchange rate fluctuations, an appropriate forward or future contract could hedge the risk.

Tax Arbitrage Strategy

Consider that there is another firm, whose expected earnings are either \$1 billion or \$2 billion. The precise amounts do not matter; the point is that this other firm can always expect to earn more than \$200 million. Therefore, if the second firm were to buy the same asset and receive an annual \$200m depreciation allowance, it would always have more than enough income to receive the full benefit of the deduction (0.34 times \$200m = \$68m). Ignoring the time value of money (simply to make the issues transparent), the annual cost (after tax) of buying this machine is (\$200m − \$68m = \$132m). Consequently, the second firm could buy the machine and lease it back to the first firm at an annual charge of \$132 without losing any money. Suppose firm 2 did just that. Let us now reexamine firm 1's expected after-tax income with this lease instead of the purchase of the asset. Expected pre-tax income is \$332m. Expected taxable income is now:

$$0.5(\$532m - \$132m) + 0.5(\$132m - \$132m) = \$200m$$

If the firm is able to deduct the cost of the lease (\$132m) as an ordinary expense, expected taxes are now:

$$0.5(\$532m - \$132m)0.34 + 0.5(\$132m - \$132m)0.34 = \$68m.$$

The expected net present value of the investment (bearing in mind there is no upfront capital cost) is now:

$$5(\$200m - \$68m) = \$660m$$

which is even higher than when the firm hedges (compare with $435.6m above). The reason for the extra gain is that the depreciation has been given a double tax advantage in this treatment (firm 2 deducts the full $200m annually, then firm 1 deducts the lease cost, which here is the after-tax cost to firm 1). Note that if firm 1 were unable to deduct the lease cost, its annual after tax income would be:

$$0.5(\$532m - \$132m) + 0.5(\$132m - \$132m)$$
$$- 0.34\{0.5(\$532m) + 0.5(\$132m)\} = \$87.12m$$

and the expected net present value project would be $5 \times \$87.12m = \$435.6m$, which is identical to that in which firm 1 buys the asset and hedges the earnings risk. Thus, the lease and the hedge are equivalent ways of securing the full tax advantage of depreciation.

This example is naturally oversimplified. The tax code is more complex than shown here. For example, there are carryforwards to consider, and the example should also consider the time value of money. I have also not allowed any profit for the leasing company but assumed that all tax advantage for depreciation is passed to the lessee. These effects will modify the numbers, but they will not destroy the main concept illustrated. Differences in marginal tax rates between firms do present arbitrage opportunities, and these can be used as a substitute for more conventional risk management strategies. One firm needs to purchase equipment but faces a large probability that its potential tax shield will go unused. Another firm does not need to make such a capital investment for production purposes, but its earnings profile is such that it could nearly always fully use any depreciation. This configuration yields opportunities for the latter to take full tax advantage of capital expenditures and then lease the equipment to the firm that needs to use it. The tax advantage afforded to the leasing company can be shared with the lessee in the price of the lease.

Other forms of tax arbitrage might be used in conjunction with risk management. A particularly interesting one is reinsurance. Insurers routinely purchase reinsurance as a means of limiting their portfolio exposure on the book of insurance policies they have sold to their clients. Thus, reinsurance is clearly used as a hedging strategy. However, there is some evidence suggesting that reinsurance is also used as a form of tax arbitrage. Insurers can deduct additions to loss reserves from taxable income. The value of this deduction to an insurer depends upon how much taxable income that insurer has that determines its marginal tax rate. Work by Keun-Ock Lew (1991) sought to explain patterns of reinsurance between firms. If firms were using reinsurance to hedge, then one would expect the patterns of trade to be explained by differences in risk between insurers and differences in the financial capacity bear risk. This indeed was found, but these factors did not fully explain reinsurance activity; there was considerable "unexplained" variation. It was found that differences in marginal tax rates between insurers explained much of the remaining variation. Insurers with low marginal tax rates (and who therefore gained little from more deductions) were transferring business to insurers with higher marginal rates. This suggests that reinsurance is being used for both hedging and tax arbitrage.

Duality and Bankruptcy Costs

We can also use an example to show the effect of hedging on expected bankruptcy costs and how a dual strategy can achieve the same effect. A firm has an expected value (the discounted value of future earnings) of $500m, but this is not certain. The effect of risk can be picked up by considering the following distribution (all figures are in $ million)

Value	Probability
100	0.1
300	0.2
500	0.4
700	0.2
900	0.1

Now we add that the firm has debt with a face value of 200. Let us now consider the value of this firm simply as its expected value. Since the firm owes 200, but there is a 10% chance firm value could fall to 100, there is a distinct chance of bankruptcy. Moreover, bankruptcy costs are assumed to be 50, which will fall upon the bondholders because equity will be worthless in this situation. If the firm does go bankrupt, bondholders receive only 50 (i.e., 100 − 50), but in all other situations they receive the full face value of 200.

value of debt

$$0.1(100 - 50) + 0.2(200) + 0.4(200) + 0.2(200) + 0.1(200) = 185$$

value of equity

$$0.1(0) + 0.2(300 - 200) + 0.4(500 - 200)$$
$$+ 0.2(700 - 200) + 0.1(900 - 200) = 310$$

total value of firm[1] = 495

Hedge Strategy

Suppose the firm is now able to hedge and compress the firm value to its expected value 500 − T, where T is the transaction cost associated with the hedge. This transaction cost could be the loading required by the insurer on the purchase of a policy or a similar cost from another hedge.[2] Unless T is very large (over 300), the firm will always have enough to pay off its debt and the probability of bankruptcy falls to zero. Consequently, the expected bankruptcy cost is also zero. Let us suppose $T = 2$. The value of

---

1. Notice that the total value of the firm, 495, falls short of the expected value of the cash flows in the table, 500, by 5, which is the expected value of the bankruptcy costs (0.1 × 50).
2. For example, the firm might have a value of 900 if no insurable loss occurs. But there is a 0.2 chance of an insurable loss of 200, leaving firm value of 700; a 0.4 chance of a loss of 400, leaving firm value of 500; a 0.2 chance of a loss of 600, leaving firm value of 300; and a 0.1 chance of loss of 800, leaving firm value of 100. These would explain the numbers in the table. Notice the no–loss value is 900 and the expected value of insurable loss is 400, giving an expected firm value of 500. One would expect an insurer to charge at least 400 to insure this loss. But the insurer would also charge a loading above the expected loss, explaining the value T. Thus, if the premium is 410, then $T = 10$.

the firm with the hedge is thus 498, divided between 200 value of debt and 298 value of equity. On these numbers, there is a overall gain from hedging; the firm values has *risen* from 495 to 498; the value of debt has *risen* from 185 to 200; but the value of equity has *fallen* from 310 to 298.

It seems as though we have something of a problem. Shareholders seem to be better off if the firm does *not* hedge. To sort this out we must look at the issues from two different time perspectives.

Ex Post Analysis First, imagine that bondholders had already purchased bonds at a price of 200. In this case the shareholders would prefer not to hedge, since equity is worth 310 without the hedge and only 298 with the hedge. The reason for the extra value in the unhedged situation is that risk is attractive to the shareholders. Without a hedge, if things go well, shareholders reap all the benefit. If things turn out poorly, shareholders can simply default on the debt. Thus, shareholders keep the upside risk and pass the downside on to the bondholders. This is a "heads I win, tails you lose" strategy.[3]

Ex Ante Analysis Rationally, bondholders will recognize that they will be taken for a ride; they recognize that once shareholders have their money, the latter will be tempted to adopt the unhedged strategy. Anticipating this choice, bondholders believe that there is a real chance of default and that the bonds are only worth the unhedged value of 185. Now consider the situation from the shareholders' perspective. If shareholders can commit to a hedge strategy and convince bondholders that they will not deviate from this strategy, then bondholders would be willing to pay 200 for the bonds. Thus, shareholders benefit by receiving an additional 15 in proceeds of the bond issue, whereas the share price is 298 compared with 310. The additional proceeds of the bond issue more than outweigh the fall in share price. There are various devices the shareholders could use to reap this value. For example, they could distribute the additional 15 of proceeds from the bond issue as a dividend or use it to fund new investment without

---

3. Notice the operation of the default put option considered in Chapter 6.

having to dilute equity. Thus, shareholders gain if they can send a credible commitment to bondholders that they will hedge risk.[4]

Leverage Strategy

Another simple strategy can achieve the same ends. Suppose that the firm simply funded its operations at a lower level of leverage. In this case imagine that debt has a face of value of only 100. Now the lowest value of the firm is sufficient to pay off debt in full and there is no possibility of default. In this case, the value of the firm is divided as follows:

value of debt

$$0.1(100) + 0.2(100) + 0.4(100) + 0.2(100) + 0.1(100) = 100$$

value of equity

$$0.1(100 - 100) + 0.2(300 - 100) + 0.4(500 - 100) + 0.2(700 - 100) \\ + 0.1(900 - 100) = 400$$

value of the firm = 500

Now the firm has avoided expected bankruptcy costs altogether. In practice this might be a little fanciful since one can never really reduce the probability of bankruptcy to zero. But one can reduce the expected value of bankruptcy costs effectively by lowering the level of debt in the capital structure.

Contingent Leverage Strategy and Post-loss Financing

There are other, more subtle strategies that do not change current leverage but entail a plan that will change leverage in the future should some specified event arise. I will mention such ideas now simply to complete the portfolio of risk management strategies.

---

4. In the example given, the value of the firm is higher with a hedge (if credibly signaled to bondholders) only if the transaction cost of the hedge ($T = 2$) is lower than the expected value of the bankruptcy costs (here 5). An unhedged strategy would appear to be better were the transaction costs reversed. However, remember that this is only a partial analysis. We have listed several potential efficiency gains that can arise from risk reduction, not only reduction in expected bankruptcy costs. So, even if $T = 10$, it may still be preferable to hedge if other efficiency gains from hedging (reduced taxes, reduced agency costs, etc.), together with the reduction in expected bankruptcy costs, exceed 10.

Some of these ideas may seem a little opaque (indeed, they include some rather exotic financial instruments), so you may simply note their presence and wait till later chapters where they will be explained more completely.

One of the problems with changing leverage to reduce expected bankrupt costs is that leverage is chosen to balance out a number of costs and benefits. The costs of debt and equity differ. As we will see in the next section, leverage influences agency costs between various stakeholders. Also, there are tax effects arising from the differential tax treatment of debt and equity. The CFO will normally choose the firm's leverage to balance these costs and benefits. Thus, it is unlikely that the firm's risk manager could steal control of the firm's capital structure from the CFO simply by arguing that leverage is an important risk management tool. Another approach is to keep the firm's current capital structure but put in place some facility or plan so that the capital structure changes should some predetermined event occur (an uninsured liability or property loss, a foreign exchange hit, etc.). Some simple examples are:

- An insurance policy or other hedge. Here, somebody else funds the loss so that the post-loss capital structure will revert to its pre-loss value.
- The firm may simply plan to issue new stock should a loss occur. These would be issued at whatever price the market would bear after the loss.
- The firm could issue put options on its own stock that could be exercised only after the defined event. Such options have been issued by insurers as a method of recapitalizing the firm after a major loss.
- The firm could issue current debt, with the provision that it be forgiven or that it convert to equity should a major loss occur.

Duality: Agency Cost: Asset Substitution

Consider a firm which has an existing product line that exposes the firm to some risk. Future earnings have an expected present value (PV) of either 100 or 200, each with a 0.5 probability. This risk could reflect different possible scenarios about consumer demand, commodity price risk, or the prospect of some uninsured property or casualty loss. The value of the firm is the expected value of 150. The firm has existing senior debt with a face value of 100. Since the debt is covered even under the worst-case scenario (firm value is 100), its value is 100 and the value of equity is the residual value of 50 (i.e., firm value of 150 minus the value of debt of 100). We assume all risk is diversifiable.

The firm now faces this choice; it can select one of the following new investments:

	Capital cost	PV of earnings	E(NPV)
Project A	200	220	20
Project B	200	20; probability 0.5 or 310; probability 0.5	−35

The capital cost of each project is 200. Project A generates an earnings stream with a certain present value of 220, which leaves a net present value of 20. Project B generates a risky earnings stream that has a present value either 20 or 310, each with a 0.5 probability, resulting in an expected value of 165. The expected NPV of project B is therefore $-200 + 165 = -35$. The earnings from the projects are independent of those from existing operations.

The firm issues new (junior) debt with a face value of 200 prior to making its project selection with a (dubious) hope of financing the project, which has a capital cost of 200. Finally, we assume that the transaction cost in the event of bankruptcy is 100. We now value the firm's claims, bearing in mind the permutations of earnings that can arise from existing operations and from whichever new project is chosen. We also net out bankruptcy cost where total value of earnings is insufficient to pay both senior and junior debt. If we note that the value of the firm will be the sum of the PV of existing operations and the PV of value generated by the project (less bankruptcy costs of 100 if firm value falls short of the total debt obligation of 300), the various claims can be valued under the alternative assumptions that A is chosen and that B is chosen.

The following tables show the overall cash flows to the firm from the original operations and from each new project. The left table shows overall value when project A is chosen, and the right table shows value if *B* is chosen. In each table the rows show the possible value of the existing operation (either 100 or 200) and the columns show the value from the project (200 for project *A* and either 20 or 310 for project *B*). The terms in parentheses are probabilities. The cells that are shaded show bankruptcy situations. In each of these cells the total value is lower than the amount owed of 300. Accordingly, the firm must pay the bankruptcy cost of 100. We can use these values and probabilities to value the firm and its constituent claims.

New Project ⇒	A	← B →	
Original Operations ⇩	200 (1.0)	20 (0.5)	310 (0.5)
100 (0.5)	300 (0.5)	120 −100 = 20 (0.25)	410 (0.25)
200 (0.5)	400 (0.5)	220 −100 =120 (0.25)	510 (0.25)

Value of the firm if project A *is chosen:*

Value of the firm	0.5(320 + 420)	= 370
Old debt	0.5(100 + 100)	= 100
New debt	0.5(200 + 200)	= 200
Equity	0.5(20 + 120)	= 70

Value of the firm if project B *is chosen:*

Value of the firm	0.25(20 + 120 + 410 + 510)	= 265
Old debt	0.25(20 + 100 + 100 + 100)	= 80
New debt	0.25(0 + 20 + 200 + 200)	= 105
Equity	0.25(0 + 0 + 110 + 210)	= 80

This illustrates the classic asset substitution problem. Since project selection is made after debt has been issued, shareholders favor project B, which offers an equity value of 80 compared with 70 for A. If bondholders anticipate this choice, they would only be willing to pay 105 for the new debt issue even though the face is 200. Since the capital cost of project B is 200, the amount raised from the debt issue would be insufficient to fund the project. In this example, there is insufficient gain to shareholders to make good the shortfall of 95 (i.e., 200 − 105) required to fund project B, since the value of equity is 50 with neither project and is only 80 if B is undertaken. Thus, the firm is simply unable to finance project B. Does that mean that A will be chosen? Suppose indeed that the firm announced its intention to choose A. Unfortunately, investors buying the new debt issue would still rationally assume that if they subscribed 200 for the issue, the shareholders would have an incentive to change the minds and use the 200 to fund project B. Thus, investors would still only subscribe 105 for the new bond issue. The firm is snookered. It is unable to accept either project. Because bondholders anticipate the firm's retroactive temptation to choose the risky negative NPV project, the firm is unable to fund either project. It is forced to sacrifice not only the expropriatory project B but also a project with a genuine positive NPV.

Hedge Strategy
Suppose that the firm can commit itself in some credible way to hedge any risk that arises from new projects. Since there is no risk in A, the commitment to hedge the project risk is meaningless and the values of debt and equity are exactly the same as shown above. But project B is risky and, with a costless hedge, the firm could replace a lottery of 10 and 310 with a certain value of 165. It is straightforward to show that the shareholders would never select a project with cost 200 and certain PV of 165 over an alternative with cost 200 and certain PV of 220. The various calculations to support this conclusion are now shown.

Value of the firm if project A *is chosen:*

Value of the firm	0.5(320 + 420)	= 370
Old debt	0.5(100 + 100)	= 100
New debt	0.5(200 + 200)	= 200
Equity	0.5(20 + 120)	= 70

Value of the firm if project B *is chosen:*

Value of the firm	0.5(165 + 365)	= 265
Old debt	0.5(100 + 100)	= 100
New debt	0.5(65 + 200)	= 132.5
Equity	0.5(0 + 65)	= 32.5

Since the project yields a certain 165, the firm will be unable to pay off all debt if existing operations yield only 100. Thus, there is still a potential for bankruptcy despite the hedge of the new project risk. With the hedge, equity will be worth 70 if A is chosen against only 32.5 if B is chosen. Thus, if a credible hedge is in place, bondholders will find it rational to anticipate that shareholders will choose project A and will be willing to pay the full 200 for the debt. Now the firm can pay for the new project since the proceeds of the bond issue are sufficient to meet the capital cost of the new project A.

Notice that the gain in value, and the ability to finance and undertake the positive NPV project A, do not come from the hedge *per se*. Rather, the value added comes from convincing bondholders that the project risk will be hedged. This creates an interesting issue as to how to give such a credible signal. This was exactly the same issue that was raised above when the hedging of firm risk a method of reducing expected bankruptcy costs was considered. A commitment can be made to hedge risk in the bond indenture agreement. Suppose that the firm binds itself to insure all risk that may arise from any project chosen. Insofar as this agreement is effective and binding, it should serve the present purpose. The effectiveness of such a commitment is enhanced by the prospect of *ex post* sanctions on directors and managers who violate it. The pervasiveness of directors' and officers' lawsuits, not only by shareholders but by other corporate stakeholders, speaks to this issue. On the other hand, effective hedges may not always exist. For example, it is possible, and indeed common, for a bond agreement to require insurance against fire and liability, but hedges for the risk of variations in the demand for the product are not easily constructed and it would be impractical to require such hedges.

Leverage Strategy
The asset substitution problem can be solved in another way. If the new project were to be financed with equity, project A would

be chosen. This follows because the total debt is now only 100 (old debt) and there is no chance that firm value would fall below 100 whatever project is chosen. Since the probability of bankruptcy is zero, shareholders bear all risk with either project and will select the project with the higher NPV. In fact, it is not necessary to fund the whole project with equity. Suppose that the firm chooses to raise 100 in new equity and 100 in new debt. The following calculations will show that the incentive conflict will be solved and the shareholders will opt for project A, which yields an equity value of 170 compared with 135 for B. Moreover, bondholders will anticipate the choice of A and will subscribe the full 100 for the new debt. Thus, there is no problem in funding the project and capturing its NPV of 20:

Value of the firm if project A *is chosen:*

Value of the firm	0.5(320 + 420)	= 370
Old debt	0.5(100 + 100)	= 100
New debt	0.5(100 + 100)	= 100
Equity	0.5(120 + 220)	= 170

Value of the firm if project B *is chosen:*

Value of the firm	0.25(20 + 220 + 410 + 510)	= 290
Old debt	0.25(20 + 100 + 100 + 100)	= 80
New debt	0.25(0 + 100 + 100 + 100)	= 75
Equity	0.25(0 + 20 + 210 + 310)	= 135

Contingent Leverage Strategy and Post-loss Financing

In the discussion of duality and bankruptcy costs, the idea of contingent leverage strategies was introduced. Such strategies also can be useful in addressing agency costs. These will be discussed in more detail later; the present purpose is simply to stake a claim. However, the idea is simple enough. Increased leverage will lead to incentive conflicts between bondholders and shareholders. These problems become especially severe when the firm loses value and approaches financial insolvency. If the firm's stock value is very low and bankruptcy is imminent, shareholders are much more likely to engage in high-risk activities that could hurt bond-holders. When the firm is on the verge of failing, the shareholders have little more to lose but everything to gain. If the high-risk investment fails, it was the creditor's money at stake; but if the high-risk investment succeeds, the upside goes to the sharehold-ers. Accordingly, one can imagine that a device that automatically unlevers the firm or refinances after a major fall in share value would remove this temptation to "bet the firm" on such high-risk investments.

Duality: Agency Cost: Underinvestment

Asset substitution can lead to the failure of the firm to undertake a positive NPV project, as shown in the previous example. Because bondholders anticipate the substitution of an asset with greater default risk, the amount they subscribe for the debt is insufficient to enable the firm to fund its desired investment. In this sense there is an underinvestment issue; the firm has failed to invest, even though faced with at least one positive NPV project. And even if the desired (by shareholders) project, B in this case, could be funded, this will not maximize value, since A has a higher NPV. We now address a more direct underinvestment problem that arises because the riskiness of *existing* operations causes the firm to pass over new positive NPV investment opportunities.

Ex Post Analysis

The underinvestment problem arises from the same conditions as asset substitution; the fact that the shareholders can default on their obligation to pay debt in full if the firm is bankrupt. The remedies are similar to those for asset substitution. Consider a banking firm with operations that generate a value of either 50 or 200, each with a 50% probability. The variation depends on inter-est rates. The firm has debt of 140. A new investment opportunity exists that will cost 100 to shareholders and will generate a cash flow with a present value of 120; thus, the NPV is 20. Let us sup-pose first that the firm will make its decision on the new project *after* it knows what the interest rate will be.

Existing Value	Potential Decision	Value of Firm	Value of Debt	Value of Equity	Decision
200	accept	220	140	80	*accept*
	reject	200	140	60	
50	*accept*	*70**	*140**	*−70**	
	reject	*50*	*50*		*reject*

It is clear that the firm would accept the project if the original value turns out to be 200 as shown by the first two rows. The new project increases the firm value by the NPV of the project, that is, 20, and all the increase goes to shareholders because the firm is not in default on its debt.

To see what happens when the original firm value is 50, consider the starred items in the third row. There is little point to the shareholders putting up an additional 100 when the firm is already insolvent. Recall that the investment decision is made *after* the firm value is revealed, and shareholders invest 100 such that the firm then receives 120. The firm therefore has this 120 plus the original value of 50, but owes 140 to bondholders. This leaves only 30 shareholders who have just paid 100 to invest in the new project. Shareholders are down a net of 70. Clearly, shareholders would not undertake the investment when the original value was only 50.

Hedge Strategy

The following table shows what happens if the interest rate risk is hedged, thereby fixing the firm value at 125. Clearly, the firm will undertake the project since the absence of downside risk does away with the bankruptcy problem that was causing the distortion of investment incentives.

Existing Value	Potential Decision	Value of Firm	Value of Debt	Value of Equity	Decision
125	accept	145	140	5	*accept*
	reject	125	125	0	

Another interesting point here is how the hedge affects the value of debt. In the original, unhedged, situation the potential for default on debt would be anticipated into the price of the debt. When debt is issued, bondholders can anticipate the uncertainty in interest rates and the likely investment decision. Therefore they estimate that the firm will be worth $\frac{1}{2}(200) + \frac{1}{2}(50) = 135$ and that their debt will be worth $\frac{1}{2}(140) + \frac{1}{2}(50) = 95$. Thus, the firm will receive only 95 for debt issued with a face value of 140. After hedging of the risk, the debt will be worth its full face value of 140. There is a definite gain to the shareholders from hedging. Not only does the hedge lead to the full capture of the NPV of the new project, but it also yields a higher price for the issue of debt.

Leverage Strategy

The following table shows that a reduction of leverage also will lead to the correct investment decision. The example shows the same investment choice for the firm with no debt.

Existing Value	Potential Decision	Value of Firm	Value of Debt	Value of Equity	Decision
200	accept	220	0	220	*accept*
	reject	200	0	200	
50	accept	70	0	70	*accept*
	reject	50	0	50	

Ex Ante Analysis

The underinvestment problem can also be examined in a different time sequence. Suppose that the details are the same as given above when debt was 140, with the exception that the investment decision is made *before* interest rates are known. This can be done by reconfiguring the numbers in the original table above to get the following (these values are *prospective* based on the *anticipated* investment decision and using the probabilities of 0.5 that interest rates will be low and 0.5 that they will be high).

Undertake project:

$$
\begin{array}{lll}
\text{Value of firm} & \frac{1}{2}(200 + 20) + \frac{1}{2}(50 + 20) = 145 \\
\text{Value of debt} & \frac{1}{2}(140) + \frac{1}{2}(140) & = 140 \\
\text{Value of equity} & \frac{1}{2}(80) + \frac{1}{2}(-70) & = 5
\end{array}
$$

Do not undertake project:

Value of firm	½(200) + ½(50) = 125
Value of debt	½(140) + ½(50) = 95
Value of equity	½(60) + ½(0) = 30

Again the positive NPV investment is lost, since should the firm go bankrupt, a very large portion of the 120 cash flow generated by the new project would go towards reducing the degree to which the firm defaults on its debt. You can also work through yourself to see whether the firm does in fact undertake the project when the original risk is hedged or when the firm unlevers.

Duality and the Crowding Out of New Investments

Recall that firms typically prefer to finance new investments from retained earnings because this is cheaper than external financing. If a sudden loss absorbs internal funds, then new investment can only be funded by more expensive external capital. Accordingly, unhedged losses tend to crowd out some new investment.

We will examine alternative generic strategies with a simple example. The firm identifies five investment opportunities, each having a capital cost of 10 but having different net present values as shown in order in the following table. We will suppose that the firm has available liquid funds of 50 and can therefore undertake all five projects. Clearly, all five projects will add value to the firm and should be undertaken.

Project	Capital Cost	NPV	NPV less Cost External Capital
1	10	3	0.5
2	10	2	0.5
3	10	1	−0.5
4	10	1	−0.5
5	10	1	−0.5

Now suppose that the firm takes a sudden hit to liquidity from an unhedged loss of 30, reducing cash from 50 to 20. The firm can now only fund two of the projects from internal sources and must go to the external capital market to fund the remaining three. If the transaction cost associated with external capital is 1.5 for each 10 raised, then the adjusted NPV shown in the final column reveals that projects 3, 4, and 5 will be lost.

Hedge Strategy

Had the risk been hedged, there would be no loss of internal capital; the sudden loss of 30 would have been paid for by an insurer (or other counter-party); the 50 in liquid funds would have been available to pay for all five new projects; and the total NPV of 3 from projects, 3, 4, and 5 would have been secured. Thus, the expected value of hedging is a gain of 3 multiplied by the probability that the loss will occur.

While hedging can create value, it too has transaction costs. For example, insurance encounters direct costs, moral hazard costs, and adverse selection costs. These transaction costs must be balanced against the costs of *ex post* financing that give rise to the crowding out idea. In the above illustration, suppose that there is a 0.1 chance that a liquidity loss of 30 will occur. We know that the loss of NPV will be 3 if such a liquidity loss actually occurs, so the *expected loss of NPV* from an unhedged position is 0.3. Suppose now that an insurance (or other) hedge can be purchased but the transaction cost of the hedge is 0.5 (note that the hedge cost arises whether or not the loss occurs). In this case the hedge will not add value prospectively. The optimal hedging policy involves a balance between the *actual* (i.e., certain) transaction cost incurred with the hedge and the *expected* loss of NPV from the displacement of investment opportunities.

Leverage and Contingent Leverage Strategies

The cost of external funding is not constant; it can vary according to the leverage of the firm and its financial strength. The relationship between leverage and cost of capital is considered in more detail in later chapters. For the moment, we can simply accept that leverage is material. Accordingly, by changing leverage, one can manipulate the conditional cost of external capital. For example, suppose that the firm lowered its leverage before any loss occurred. Lowering fixed obligations from earnings will raise retained earnings to, say, 80. Now the firm can absorb a loss of 30 and still have available the 50 internal funds needed to finance all five investment projects.

More radically, the firm may set in place some contingent financing facility that is triggered by the unhedged loss. Above, we discussed the idea that a firm may issue put options on its own stock that are exercised at a given price, but only when a defined loss occurs. In such a scheme the firm is effectively lowering the cost of external capital should an unhedged loss occur. Of course, there will be an upfront price for this facility, and this needs to be compared with the expected loss of value from projects that otherwise would be sacrificed.

Duality and Managerial Utility Maximization

In keeping with earlier discussions of duality, the issues will be developed with an example. You own a small firm. The profitability of this firm depends jointly upon the level and quality of work supplied by the manager and upon the state of demand for your product, which is related to general economic conditions. This second determinant of profit introduces risk. You must decide whether to pay the manager a flat salary or incentive (profit-related) compensation. If you pay a flat salary of 100, the manager's productivity will be such that the firm's profit is either 500 or 1500, each with a 0.5 probability. Call the profit before deduction of compensation V. Alternatively, you can pay the manager performance-related compensation at a level $x \times V$, in which case productivity is expected to improve by 60% such that V is either 800 or 1800, each with 0.5 probability. The manager, being risk-averse and undiversified, is interested in the expected utility of hear wealth, which includes only her employment compensation. The manager's utility function is $U = W^{0.5}$, where W is wealth. However, utility also reflects the effort provided, and we assume that high effort lowers utility. To capture this, the utility function is:

$$\text{utility with low effort} \quad = \quad U = W^{0.5}$$

$$\text{utility with high effort} \quad = \quad U = W^{0.5} - 1$$

The "$- 1$" is the monetary equivalent of the loss of utility of high effort, since people usually do not like to work hard, other things being equal. You, as owner, are more diversified and are interested in the expected value of the profit (after deduction of the manager's compensation). Some questions will need answering:

1. If you pay performance-related compensation, what must the value of x be to compensate the manager for risk?

2. Given that performance-related compensation must include a risk premium, which compensation schedule (flat salary or $x \times V$) would you choose to pay the manager?

3. Suppose that you can insure or hedge the riskiness of V (i.e., replace $0.5(500) + 0.5(1500)$ by 1000 and replace $0.5(800) + 0.5(1800)$ by 1300). What is the gain from the hedge to you as the owner?

Consider question 1. If the manager is paid a flat salary of 100, her expected utility[5] is $100^{0.5} = 10$. For the manager to be compensated for the risk and hard work inherent in performance-related compensation, x must be set such that her expected utility is no lower than under a flat salary ($100^{0.5} = 10$). I will use an equals sign in the calculation to derive the minimum level of x:

$$EU(\text{flat salary}) = EU(\text{compensation at } x \times V$$
$$\text{and assuming high effort})$$
$$(100)^{0.5} = (0.5)(800x)^{0.5} + (0.5)(1800x)^{0.5} - 1$$
$$11 = (0.5)(800^{0.5} + 1800^{0.5})x^{0.5}$$
$$x = 0.0968$$

The expected earnings of the manager under performance pay are $0.0968(1300) = 125.84$, compared with 100 under flat pay. The difference, 25.84, reflects two things. First, incentive compensation is risky (compensation will either be $0.0968 \times 800 = 77.44$ or $0.0968 \times 1800 = 174.24$), so the manager requires a risk premium.

---

5. Notice that this utility is calculated anticipating that the manager will choose high effort. This should be clear. Expected utility with low effort is $100^{0.5} = 10$, whereas the expected utility with high effort is $100^{0.5} - 1 = 9$. Consequently, low effort offers higher utility and would be chosen.

Second, if the manager is providing high effort, this also requires compensation.[6]

As owner, you face a tradeoff. You can pay on a performance basis, which will mean that you pay more on average to managers, but the incentive effects will improve profitability. Which schedule is better? Compare expected profit (you are risk-neutral in this example) net of compensation.

| flat pay | $0.5(500 + 1500) - 100$ | $= 900$ |
| performance pay | $0.5(800 + 1800) - 125.84$ | $= 1174.16$ |

Clearly, the improvement in productivity far outweighs any additional payment to the manager to compensate her for risk and for disutility of high effort in this example. Performance pay is better.

Hedge Strategy

Can you alleviate the tradeoff (i.e., avoid paying managers risk premium but still keep them motivated) by hedging the risk? Suppose you hedge the risk but can still manage to motivate managers by paying some fraction y of V. With such motivation, expected profit will be $0.5(800) + 0.5(1800) = 1300$ (ignoring transaction costs). What does y have to be so that compensation is competitive and motivates the manager to high effort? You can pay managers some amount yV, where, to make this acceptable to managers, yV must satisfy (remember to deduct 1 for the disutility of high effort and recall that the competitive level of utility is $100^{0.5} = 10$):

$$(yV)^{0.5} - 1 = (y1300)^{0.5} - 1 = 10$$

$$y = 0.09308$$

Because of the hedge, managers will not face risk and will end up

---

6. It is important to verify that if the manager is paid a portion 0.0968 of value, she will indeed supply high effort. To verify this, recall that with low effort value will be either 500 or 1500. Therefore the expected utility of the manager will be

$$EU = (0.5)(500 \times 0.0968)^{0.5} + (0.5)(1500 \times 0.0968)^{0.5} = 9.503$$

which is less than the utility from high effort of 10. Thus, the manager will choose high effort with this compensation schedule.

with certain compensation of 121.004 (i.e., 0.09308 × 1300). Without the hedge, the expected compensation was 125.84; the savings of 4.836 is the risk premium, which is no longer necessary. However, here the manager does not contract for 121.004 flat salary. Rather, the contract is to pay 0.09308 of value V, which will turn out to be 121.004 *only if she works hard*. If the manager were to slacken her effort such that production fell to 500/1500 (which is hedged at 1000), her income would fall to 0.09308(1000) = 93.08[7] Thus, hedging and paying by performance maintains managerial effort but enables the firm to avoid the risk premium to the manager.

Alternative Compensation Strategy
The generic alternative to the hedge strategy is a risk accommodation strategy. The task here is to find some way the firm can live with risk while still motivating managers to high effort and avoiding paying the risk premium. To see one way this can be tackled, look back on the hedging example we have just considered. By hedging risk and paying the manager 0.09308 of value, the firm avoided paying a risk premium of 4.836 but still managed to keep the manager motivated to supply high effort. What drove the gain in value was not the hedge *per se*, but that the compensation was based on a hedged value. So can we create a "phantom hedge?" This can be achieved by defining an accounting definition of profit or value that is purged of risk and basing compensation on this accounting number.

AN ILLUSTRATION OF HEDGING AND LEVERAGE STRATEGIES
To see some of these strategies (hedging, simple and contingent leverage) set in a single context, imagine a firm that is developing and producing new drugs. The current earnings are $300m, from which $100m interest (8% interest on debt of $1250m) must be paid, leaving

---

7. Just verify here that the manager will work hard if paid 0.09308 of earnings when earnings are hedged. Thus, check that $(0.09308 \times 1300)^{0.5} - 1 > (0.09308 \times 1000)^{0.5}$.

$200m. Of the remaining $200m, half is reinvested in research and de-velopment (R&D), and this continues to generate a stream of new in-vestment opportunities. Because of these opportunities, earnings remain-ing to shareholders (i.e., the $100m) expected to grow at an average of 5% per year.

Total earnings (current year)	$300m
Interest	$100m
R&D	$100m
Residual (dividend) for shareholders	$100m
	but expected to grow at 5% annually

The firm's cost of equity capital is 10%, and it has 200 million shares outstanding. How much would an income stream starting at $100m but growing at 5% per year be worth? To anticipate some analysis which will be developed later, a simple formula for finding the market value of the equity, MVE, of a firm is to divided the current earnings, E_0, by the difference between the cost of equity capital, k_E, and the expected growth rate, g:

$$\text{MVE} = \frac{E_0}{k_E - g} = \frac{\$100m}{0.1 - 0.05} = \$2 \text{ billion}$$

Each share would be worth $2 billion ÷ 200 million = $10.

Let us pause and take a look at some of the risk management issues facing this firm.

- *The firm faces some probability of bankruptcy. If some set of events occurred that reduced annual earnings below $100m per year, it would be unable to pay its debt.*

- *The firm has investment opportunities that are generated from prior investments in R&D. Investing in R&D is risky. Much R&D does not result in any product that can be brought to market; some results in marginal and high-risk project opportunities; some results in much more solid project opportunities. The willingness of the firm to undertake marginal high-risk projects will be increased by the presence of debt because the shareholders get to keep the upside risk and pass much of the downside to bondholders. We have the sort of agency problems discussed above.*

♦ *Suppose some unhedged loss occurs that causes a continuing loss of earnings. This firm must still service its debt. The firm would have less in retained earnings to pay for its R&D. To some extent the firm can continue to fund new projects by cutting down on dividends (i.e., from retained earnings). There is the prospect that it would be forced to:*

Raise new equity and/or debt capital to continue to fund its new projects, and/or

Cut down on its new investment projects.

Now consider what would happen if the earnings were reduced from $300m to $150m by some sudden event (fall in currency value, an uninsured property loss, a loss of a government contract, etc.). The firm still has the $1,250m in debt, on which interest still has to be paid. There is correspondingly less left, only $150m, to invest in R&D and to pay shareholder dividends, and the firm must decide how much it can continue to invest in R&D when shareholders still demand dividends. Thus, there will be:

Less money to pay dividends.

Less money to invest in R&D.

Less money to invest in new projects generated from R&D.

Increased cost of external financing; the loss will have increased financial leverage, which in turn will increase the cost of raising new debt or equity.

In terms of the above formula ($MVE = E_0/(k_E - g)$, all three terms will deteriorate, E_0 will be smaller, k_E will be larger, and g will be smaller. The loss will cause a fall in the stock price. For example, if only $75m were now paid to shareholders ($E_0 = 75$), k_E increased from 10% to 11%, and growth fell from 5% to 3%, then the market value of equity would be reduced to:

$$MVE = \frac{75}{0.11 - 0.03} = \$937.5m$$

and each of the 200 million shares would be worth only $4.69.

One can now think of the risk management issues as protecting the interests of the shareholders in preserving the share value. Think of how the share value can fall:

- *A direct loss (through E_0) can occur simply because the ability to continue to earn revenues has been reduced.*
- *A set of indirect losses (through k_E and g) can arise because the firm could lose its ability to secure future growth:*
  - *Because the earnings are lower*
  - *Because of the prior claim of debt on those reduced earnings.*
- *Indirect losses will arise because debt and risk give rise to agency costs and bankruptcy costs.*

Thus, risk management can potentially create value by:

- *Protecting the earnings from sudden loss*
- *Relieving the burden of debt so that reduced post-loss earnings can be allocated to R&D and new investments rather than to paying off debt*
- *Relieving the burden of debt so that the probability of financial distress is reduced and with it the expected bankruptcy costs and agency costs*

These can be accomplished by:

- *Avoiding the earnings loss; i.e., hedging the loss.*
- *Reducing the amount that has to be paid from post-loss earnings to service debt. This in turn can be accompanied by:*
  - *Reducing current leverage so that there will be less debt in place if and when a loss occurs*
  - *Having an automatic arrangement for debt to be forgiven should a loss occur*
  - *Having an arrangement for debt to be converted to equity should a loss occur.*
- *Having an arrangement for new equity to be issued to fund R&D and investments after loss.*

CLASSIFYING RISK MANAGEMENT STRATEGIES

From the discussion of duality, it should be clear that the same risk management strategy can address several different types of risk cost. The riskiness of a potential product liability imposes costs in the form of additional taxes, additional bankruptcy costs, additional agency costs, loss of value from crowded out investments, and loss from inefficiencies in compensating and motivating managers. The purchase of an insurance policy will provide relief from all these costs; the relief is not specific. Reducing leverage will provide relief from the agency costs, bankruptcy costs, and crowding out losses. On the other hand, redesigning compensation relieves only the specific risk costs of efficient motivation of managers. Tax arbitrage is another specific risk management strategy in that it focuses on only one type of risk cost. Table 8–2 shows the various strategies and their domain.

It is clear from looking at the various risk management strategies that there is an issue of boundaries. Some of the strategies clearly wander into other areas of management, including financial management, corporate governance, and tax management. For example, determining the capital structure is a central issue in financial management, and this function is usually assumed by

T A B L E   8–2

Risk Management Strategies

Strategy	Risk Cost Addressed
Hedging	Tax nonlinearities
	Bankruptcy costs
	Asset substitution and underinvestment
	Crowding out of new investments
	Managerial risk aversion
	Stakeholder risk aversion
Tax arbitrage	Tax nonlinearities
Changing leverage	Bankruptcy costs
	Asset substitution and underinvestment
	Crowding out of new investments
Contingent leverage and post-loss financing	Bankruptcy costs
	Asset substitution and underinvestment
	Crowding out of new investments
Re-design executive compensation	Managerial risk aversion
Design of other stakeholder contracts	Stakeholder risk aversion

the firm's chief financial officer or treasurer. But risk management is becoming an increasingly important part of financial management. Contrarily, leverage management is becoming an increasingly important part of the risk manager's function. In short, risk management and financial management are becoming increasingly hard to keep apart. Consequently, in the remainder of this work, capital structure strategies will be considered in some detail. Other strategies will receive less emphasis. Compensation design for managers is a highly specialized area and will be given some limited attention because it is managers who formulate risk management policy and any principal–agent conflicts here are of great practical concern. Nevertheless, compensation design is complex and specialized and we will do little more than scratch the surface. Tax management and tax arbitrage is an even more highly specialized area of study and give rise to very focused strategies that exploit the detailed structure of the tax code. Here the coverage will be limited to very general issues. Thus, in what follows, hedging, leverage, and contingent leverage strategies will be the prime focus, with coverage of compensation and tax issues somewhat secondary.

Hedging Strategies

A hedge is a *focused* risk management tool in that it addresses a specific form of risk. Hedge instruments usually are paired with specific forms of risk. Consider the following types of risk that face many firms: risk of liability suits, risk of damage to property; changes in demand over the business cycle, and the effects of interest rate changes and foreign exchange rate changes on firm profits. For each source of risk there may or may not exist a specific hedge instrument. For the liability risk there is a liability insurance policy, for the property risk a property insurance policy, and there are interest rate and foreign exchange futures that can hedge these risks. For some risks, finding an appropriate hedge instrument is difficult. For example, inflation can be difficult to hedge.

An important distinction as we proceed is that between *asset hedges* and *liability hedges*. Think of a hedge instrument as the pairing of two cash flows with offsetting risk. It is useful to start with some preexisting asset owned by a firm or individual; for example, a home. The value of this asset is risky because it can be damaged or burn down. The risk to this asset can be hedged on both sides of the balance sheet.

Asset Hedge

An asset hedge can be defined as an asset that provides a hedge against the risk in some other asset. A portfolio including the basic asset and the hedging asset has little or no risk. The asset hedge can be represented in a portfolio F in which an amount \$ is invested in two assets. The first basic asset has a payoff of A_B for each dollar invested. The second asset, the hedging asset, has a per dollar payoff of A_H. The capital \$ is allocated over the two assets in the ratio $\{1:h\}$, and the correlation coefficient r_{BH} is negative (in the limiting approaching negative unity).

asset hedge $F = \$(A_B + hA_H)$ where $0 > r_{BH} \geq -1$

If $r_{BH} = -1$, then some *hedge ratio* h^* can be chosen such that the portfolio is riskless; that is, the variance, *VAR*, is zero:

$$VAR\ \{\$(A_H + h^*A_H)\} = 0$$

The obvious asset hedge for a home is a homeowner's insurance policy. The policy was purchased at a price, the premium, and yields a potential payoff if your house burns down. Other examples are the purchase of a future contract by a farmer to hedge the risk of grain price movements; a reinsurance policy is a traditional form of asset hedge for the insurer who wishes to control risk in its direct insurance portfolio. A newer instrument used by insurers is the catastrophe option, which is an option written on the value of an index of insurance company claims that yields a payoff when the index triggers a pre-set value (the striking price).

Liability Hedge

A hedge can be achieved on the opposite side of the balance sheet. Instead of the hedging asset, the portfolio includes a liability L_H as follows:

liability hedge $F = \$(A_B - hL_H)$ where $0 < r_{BH} \leq 1$

If $r_{BH} = 1$, then some hedge ratio h^* can be chosen such that the portfolio is riskless; i.e.,

$$VAR\ \{\$(A_B - h^*L_H)\} = 0$$

Instead of owning an asset that pays off when you have a loss of the basic asset, you now have a liability that will be reduced when you have a loss on that basic asset. Consider the ownership of a home again. A liability hedge would exist if the bank holding the mortgage agreed to forgive the debt if the house were destroyed by fire, storm, or earthquake. An investor could hedge a long position in a stock by a short position in a call option on that stock. Some insurers have recently issued debt with the provision that it be forgiven if the issuing insurer suffers catastrophic losses on its direct insurance portfolio.

Leverage and Financing Strategies

Leverage Management

We will use terms such as "simple leverage management" and "leverage" to describe a reduction in leverage in anticipation of a possible future loss. This reduces the agency cost between creditors and residual claimants and reduces the expected value of bankruptcy costs. Moreover, if a sudden loss arises, the firm will find itself in a stronger position to approach capital markets for new funding (either to reconstruct destroyed assets or to fund new investment projects). Alternatively, dividend policy may be used to address directly the crowding out problem. Lower dividend payouts will enhance the ability of the firm to fund future projects from internal funds and reduce the probability that projects will be lost for lack of access to low cost capital.

Post-loss Financing

In several of the above examples, it was shown that issuing new equity after some event such as an insurable loss can partly address some of the costs of risk. This action enables the firm to finance and undertake investment opportunities that still exist despite the sudden event or loss. We refer to the raising of funds after a loss, on terms that are available after loss, as "post-loss financing" or "post-event financing." It is recognized that sometimes the event may have such a seriously depressing effect on the firm's value that it will be unable to raise sufficient money for its needs, or the terms will be penalistic. For example, the chemical discharge at Bhopal depressed Union Carbide's share price and made it more expensive to raise new money. Whatever money can be raised, and at what terms, depends on the severity of the event, the franchise value of the firm, and how the circumstances are received by financial markets. There may be two issues here: one concerning having money available for investment needs, the second concerning the post-loss leverage. Equity financing addresses the need for new funds without increasing post-loss leverage. Debt addresses the need for funds but increases leverage.

A particular situation in which post-loss financing can be very valuable is if the firm has significant franchise value but faces a liquidity crunch as a result of the loss. For example, an insurer may suffer a catastrophic loss that drains liquid assets. It may have considerable long-term assets that can only be liquidated in a fire sale. Recapitalization is essentially a tool to release illiquid assets and permits the firm to continue operating and preserve its franchise value.

Contingent Financing

If it is recognized that post-loss financing can add value, then contingent refinancing takes the idea one step further. The terms under which new money is raised can be agreed upon in advance of any possible loss. A simple example is a line of credit that can be drawn down on some prespecified event. There could be a simple commitment fee or, in addition, the interest rate could be fixed in advance so that the borrower is hedged from market fluctuations.

A more radical form of contingent refinancing is for the firm to issue put options for new issue of its own stock. One can imagine two forms of this strategy. First, simple put options are issued to a counter-party at an agreed striking price. Since a major adverse event, such as a product liability suit, is likely to depress the share price, there is a potential for the option to be "in the money" and to be exercised as a result of the event. If so, the firm will refinance at a price above the post-event market equity price. The difference between the exercise price and the post-event share price amounts to a partial hedge of the loss. Of course, there is a consideration in the form of the price of the put option, which is, in effect, an insurance premium for that part of the cost of refinancing that is borne by the counter-party.

A variation on this theme is a device that has been used by insurance firms to provide contingent capital in the event of suffering catastrophic claims experience on its insurance portfolio. Here, the firm issues put options on its own stocks, as before at a stated exercise price. But now there is an added trigger. In addition to the stock price falling below the exercise price, a certain predefined event must occur. In this case the insurer's own claims must lie within a range of values. These new instruments have recently been assembled for insurance firms under the trade name "CatEPuts."

Other Contingent Leverage Strategies

The same general objective of unlevering the firm after an event and partly offsetting the cost of the event can be achieved by converting the debt into equity. There is always a market option of buying back equity and issuing new stock. Insofar as this transaction takes place at market values, there is no direct value added. An alternative is to embed a conversion option in the debt and to make this option exercisable at the discretion of the firm. Because the firm will exercise the option only if it benefits shareholders, that is, if the equity has fallen below some critical value such that the shares offered have a lower value than the debt they replace. This has two effects. First, the firm unlevers (by exercise of the option) whenever the value falls sufficiently. Second, insofar as the firm exchanges less valuable shares to retire more valuable debt, there is a partial hedge. This instrument is known as "reverse convertible debt," and it differs from normal convertible debt in that the option to convert into equity is given to the firm rather than to the bondholders.

Other Strategies

Compensation Management

As seen above, risk management decisions can be made to further the self-interest of managers. This raises the issue of designing compensation systems to align the interests of owners and managers. A risk management formula for compensation design can be envisioned that balances the need to incentivize managers with performance-related pay and the risk premia needed in such compensation schedules.

Tax Management

Given a nonlinear tax schedule, we have seen that expected tax liabilities increase as the risk of the firm's earnings increases. Tax management strategies to reduce this cost can be derived that in effect linearize the tax schedule; these strategies include leasing and reinsurance. In addition to these general tax features, other very specific tax features may influence risk management decisions. For example, at times the tax code has contained features that encourage the formation of captive insurance firms. Moreover, this tax benefit has changed over time with legal challenges by taxpayers to broaden its scope and by the Internal Revenue Service to narrow it. Thus, many captives were located in offshore domiciles (notably Bermuda), and to distinguish them from self-insurance plans (which were less tax favored), captives often sold insurance to outside policyholders in addition to their parents.

Tax issues call for a particular skill set and detailed knowledge of the tax code. Accordingly, they will not be afforded a treatment in this book that is proportional to their financial importance.

INTEGRATED/HOLISTIC RISK MANAGEMENT

In this chapter there has been extensive discussion of the cost of risk but little discussion of the source of the risk. Risk has simply been considered to be a mathematical phenomenon: the variability of some basic economic number such as corporate earnings or corporate value. Variability causes problems that were identified without saying much about the cause of that variability. Earnings could vary because demand for the product was uncertain, the income from foreign sales was subject to the effects of currency fluctuation, there was variability in the annual cost of self insured worker's compensation liability, and so on.

Various attempts have been made to classify corporate risk. For example, Babbel and Santomero (1997) classify the risks facing insurers as:

Actual risk, which arises from the estimating and pricing of insurance products, including the risk that it will receive an inadequate rate of return on the policies sold or it pay too much for the funds it receives.

Systematic risk or market risk, which cannot be effectively eliminated by the owner holding a diversified investment portfolio. This may arise because either assets or liabilities are correlated with the market portfolio. This risk includes interest rate risk and inflation risk.

Credit risk because borrowers can default on obligations.

Liquidity risk, which relates to the prospect that the insurer will be unable to meet short-term obligations for lack of liquid assets.

Operational risks, which arise from the systems and processes that are necessary to run an insurance business. Examples would include the cost of a computer system failure or the cost of resolving regulatory conflicts.

Legal risk, which can arise because the legal system in which insurers operate is subject to change as new court precedents, legislation, and regulation can amend the rules under which insurers operate and liabilities are established.

While this classification is obviously designed for insurance firms, similar categories can be derived for noninsurance firms. For example, a manufacturing firm encounters:

Operating risk, which arises from failures in the basic processes that are the core of its business, such as plant breakdown of power supply failure

Financial risk from changes in the cost of capital that affect the firm's value directly, and indirectly if product demand is sensitive to capital market rates

Economic or market risk as changes in the level of economic activity or structural economic changes affect product demand or the cost of doing business

Pure or insurable risk, which is the downside risk from loss or damage to corporate assets or sudden claims on those assets

Classifications such as these are a little arbitrary and often have overlaps or gaps, but they are useful for several purposes. First, they are helpful in conducting a risk survey; the structure helps identify where to look for risk so that no stones can be left unturned. Clearly, such an exercise is an essential early step in the risk management process. Second, classification can be useful in designing an organization structure to manage risk. Different professional skills are needed for dealing with different types of risk.

For example, handling insurable risk calls for skills in understanding the liability system, settling claims with third parties, and investing in loss control. Handling risk caused by fluctuations in interest rates and other financial market numbers calls for skill in financial economics.

However, these are not our main concerns here. Risk is by nature largely indivisible. The whole process of diversification tells us that one risk cannot be separated from others; their impact is communal. And even if risks were separable, is there any reason to think that the corporate tolerance for risk would differ according to the source of the risk? If not, then risks presumably should be handled in a coordinated fashion. This lead us to an issue that has become an article of faith for many concerned with risk management: should risk management be holistic or global? Should one grand strategy encompass all corporate risk?

To set the stage for the discussion of integrated risk management, consider Commonwealth Petroleum Co. To simplify as far as possible, CPC has annual earnings as set out in the attached matrix:

	Oil Price Low chance 0.5	Oil Price High chance 0.5
No Liability Loss chance 0.5	500	1000
Liability chance 0.5	250	750

One can interpret this in the following way. CPC faces two types of risk:

1. *Earnings can be impacted by a potential liability suit for environmental damage. Such a loss could cost the firm 250. There is a 0.5 chance that such a liability will arise.*
2. *There is an additional risk that earnings can vary through changes in oil prices—this accounts for a plus/minus fluctuation of 250. Thus, without environmental liability, earnings can be 750 + 250 = 1000 or 750 − 250 = 500. With liability, the values are either 500 + 250 = 750 or 500 − 250 = 250. There is an equal probability of each price*

regime. The liability risk is assumed to be independent of the oil price risk.

First, let us calculate the stand alone standard deprivation for each source of risk.

Oil price risk: *Expected earnings are either 750 or 500 (depending on liability), but in either case the standard deviation is 250. The calculations are:*

$$\sqrt{0.5(500 - 750)^2 + 0.5(1000 - 750)^2} = 250$$

$$\sqrt{0.5(250 - 500)^2 + 0.5(750 - 500)^2} = 250$$

Liability risk: *Expected earnings are 0.5(500) + 0.5(250) = 375 or 0.5(1000) + 0.5(750) = 875. Either way, the standard deviation is 125, calculated as follows:*

$$\sqrt{0.5(500 - 375)^2 + 0.5(250 - 375)^2} = 125$$

$$\sqrt{0.5(1000 - 875)^2 + 0.5(750 - 875)^2} = 125$$

Now that the expected earnings and standard deviation for the firm as a whole are:

$$E(earnings) = 0.25(500) + 0.25(1000) + 0.2(250) + 0.2(750) = 625$$

$$\sigma(earnings) = \sqrt{\begin{matrix} 0.25(500 - 625)^2 + 0.25(1000 - 625)^2 \\ + 0.25(250 - 625)^2 + 0.25(750 - 625)^2 \end{matrix}} = 279.5$$

Clearly, the overall risk of the firm, 279.5, is not the sum of the two standard deviations for each risk type, 125 + 250, because of the independence of the two sources of risk.

A nonintegrated approach. *A simple illustration of a nonintegrated approach would be that the manager in charge of oil hedges is told that the firm cannot tolerate a standard deviation above 125, and the manager in charge of insurance is told the same tolerance level. The oil hedge manager then purchases oil futures such that half the fluctuation is hedged. Assuming no transaction cost, this ensures that earnings can only fluctuate downwards by 125 and upwards by 125 (instead of the up and down fluctuation of 250).[8] The insurance manager buys no*

---

8. You can recalculate the standard deviations for the effect of oil price changes, given each liability outcome, to verify that the standard deviations are 125, i.e.,

$$\{0.5(625 - 750)^2 + 0.5(875 - 750)^2\}^{0.5} \text{ and } \{0.5(375 - 500)^2 + 0.5(625 - 500)^2\}^{0.5}$$

insurance, since the standard deviation is already 125. The earnings matrix now looks as follows:

	Oil Price Low chance 0.5	Oil Price High chance 0.5
No Liability Loss chance 0.5	625	875
Liability chance 0.5	375	625

Now the overall return and risk are:

$$E(\textit{earnings}) = 0.25(375) + 0.5(625) + 0.25(875) \quad = 625$$

$$\sigma(\textit{earnings}) = \sqrt{\begin{array}{l} 0.25(375 - 625)^2 + 0.5(625 - 625)^2 \\ + 0.25(875 - 625)^2 \end{array}} = 176.8$$

The dangers of this approach are:

1. *The firm is not controlling the overall level of risk and does not pay attention to the interaction of risk. Focusing on each source of risk on a standalone basis means that the possibility of accumulation is not given attention, i.e., it ignores the possibility of a low oil price and a liability loss both occurring. Notice that despite informing both managers to achieve a risk level of 125, this risk is not attained at the firm level.*

2. *It does not help the firm achieve overall risk reduction in the most economical way. For example, here corporate risk falls from 279.5 to 176.8 and all the burden of reducing falls on the oil hedge manager. This may be desirable if the transaction costs of oil hedging is less than that of insurance. But if the reverse were true, might it not make sense to make marginal risk reduction through insurance?*

A simple integrated approach. *Suppose instead that the firm focuses on its overall level of risk and fixes this at a standard deviation of 150. There are still two ways of hedging risk available; oil hedges and insurance. An oil hedge can be bought that will reduce the price risk. Without the hedge, the risk is ± 250. We use the term* n *to denote the hedge ratio, which is the proportion of the oil price risk that is transferred to an outsider (the seller of the hedge instrument). Thus, the retained variation can be reduced to:*

expected income $\pm (1 - h) \times 250 = 750 - (250(1 - h)$

Thus, if h = *0, no oil hedge is purchased; if* h = *0.5 then half the variation is hedged;* h = *1, then all risk is hedged. With insurance some portion (hedge ratio)* i *of the risk will be insured for a premium of 0.5* $\times$ *250* $\times$ i *(that is, the probability of loss)* $\times$ *the size of the loss* $\times$ *the proportion of the loss insured). Notice that this premium is actuarially fair insofar as it does not include any transaction costs. If a loss happens, the firm loses 250 but is repaid* i $\times$ *250, which results in net loss of* (1 − i)250. *With these two hedges in place, the earnings of the firm are now*

	Oil Price Low chance 0.5	Oil Price High chance 0.5
No Liability Loss chance 0.5	$750 - 250(1 - h) - 0.5(250)i$ $= 750 - 250(1 - h) - 125i$	$750 + 250(1 - h) - 0.5(250)i$ $= 750 + 250(1 - h) - 125i$
Liability chance 0.5	$750 - 250(1 - h) - 0.5(250)i$ $- 250 + 250i$ $= 500 - 250(1 - h) + 125i$	$750 + 250(1 - h) - 0.5(250)i$ $- 250 + 250i$ $= 500 + 250(1 - h) + 125i$

The problem now becomes to select two hedge ratios h *and* i *so that the overall standard deviation of the firm's earnings is 150. It is easier to work with the variance, which is the square of standard deviation; i.e.,* VAR = 150^2 = *22,500. You may also note that since there are no transaction costs, expected earnings are still 625. Considering that each of the four cells in the matrix has a 25% probability, the problem is now to choose* h *and* i *to satisfy:*

$$0.25(750 - 250(1 - h) - 125i - 625)^2$$
$$+ 0.25(750 + 250(1 - h) - 125i - 625)^2$$
$$+ 0.25(500 - 250(1 - h) + 125i - 625)^2$$
$$+ 0.25(500 + 250(1 - h) + 125i - 625)^2 = 22,500$$

Solving this needs a little trial and error. However, with some checking you can verify that any of the following combinations of h *and* i *will result in the firm having its target level of overall risk:*

$$h = 0.668 \quad \text{and} \quad i = 0$$
$$h = 0.6 \quad \text{and} \quad i = 0.104$$
$$h = 0.5 \quad \text{and} \quad i = 0.3365$$
$$h = 0.45 \quad \text{and} \quad i = 0.437$$
$$h = 0.4 \quad \text{and} \quad i = 1.0$$

*This example shows the interdependence of the hedging policies in achieving an overall risk target. In this simple example the hedges had no transaction costs. This is unrealistic; those selling oil futures would do so at some spread, and insurance premiums would include some markup over expected costs to cover expenses and a risk premium. Flexibility in achieving this target is particularly useful if the availability or prices of hedges differ. For example, suppose that insurance encounters very high transaction costs relative to oil hedges. It may be preferable to select a combination in which no insurance is purchased but oil hedges are used intensively (*h = 0.668 *and* i = 0*). In this way the firm can choose to achieve its risk target at the lowest possible cost.*

Integrated risk management can now be considered in the light of the reasons given why risk was costly. Certainly none of the reasons given suggests that risk from one source (oil price changes) has any different cost to the firm than risk from another source (product liability). Each source of uncertainty creates variation in the bottom line, and this variability gives rise to a set of costs (higher expected taxes, higher expected bankruptcy costs, higher agency costs, etc.). A dollar of additional expected tax liability has the same depressing effect on net income whatever the risk source that spawned it. Moreover, shareholders will be just as willing to exploit creditors, whether the downside risk stems from interest rate fluctuation or from currency fluctuation. In short, the basic rationale for why risk imposed cost on the corporation did not differentiate according to the source of that risk. Accordingly, there is no apparent reason to differentiate in the treatment of risk. The various sources of risk have a combined and inseparable effect on overall corporate risk, and this calls for a combined risk management approach. As the example shows, this means not that the hedge ratio needs to be identical, but that the effect of risk on corporate value should be determined jointly and the strategies for dealing with each of the risks formulated jointly. The solution could be choosing an intensive hedge of one risk, $h = 0.668$, and not hedging the other, $i = 0$; or the solution could be a lower hedge on the first risk, $h = 0.4$, and a full insurance on the second, $i = 1$. The point is not that the hedge levels are the same, but that they are determined jointly for their combined effect on corporate risk.

Commonwealth has two divisions: Products and Refining. The products division produces and sells oil and oil products. The refining division does as the name suggests, refining oil, including oil of the products division, for which it charges a fee. However, the bulk of the refining is for oil owned by others, and again there is a fee. These external contracts account for the bulk of refining income. The profit of the product division, II_D, is related to oil prices, p, but there also is a random fluctuation, q̃, which is simply noise. Note also that profits are denoted in $ millions whereas the oil price is denoted in $ per barrel. The noise term has an expected value of 0 and a standard deviation of 25. Note that the price term has a positive sign indicating that as prices change by $1, profits will increase on average by 30 million dollars.

$$II_D = 100 + 30\tilde{p} + \tilde{q} \qquad E(\tilde{q}) = 0; \qquad \sigma(\tilde{q}) = 25$$

Refinery profits, II_R, also are determined by two factors. These profits also are influenced by oil prices, p̃. But here the sign is negative, showing that for every dollar rise in oil prices, refinery profits will fall by 25 cents.[9] The second influence on refinery profits is the random noise term, r̃, which has an expected value of 0 and a standard deviation of 10.[10]

$$II_R = 300 - 25\tilde{p} + \tilde{r} \qquad E(\tilde{r}) = 0; \qquad \sigma(\tilde{r}) = 10$$

The firm's total profit, II, is simply the sum of the profits of the two divisions:

---

9. The story here is that the refining becomes highly competitive when oil prices rise. The elasticity of refining fees to oil prices is sufficiently high (in absolute terms) that refining profits fall as oil prices rise.

10. The noise terms q̃ and r̃ are uncorrelated with each other and with the oil price p̃.

$$II_D = 100 + 30\tilde{p} + \tilde{q}$$
$$+ \ II_R = 300 - 25\tilde{p} + \tilde{r}$$
$$II = 400 + 5\tilde{p} \ + \tilde{q} + \tilde{r}$$

The risk facing the firm arises partly from the two noise terms that affect each division's profit, and partly from the fact that oil prices, which affect both divisions' profits, are also risky. The expected value of the oil price is $20, but this is surrounded by a standard deviation of $10.

$$E(\tilde{p}) = 20; \qquad \sigma(\tilde{p}) = 10$$

Now suppose that each division decides to buy oil futures and thereby hedge oil price risk. An oil hedge is an instrument that pays the amount $\tilde{h} = -\{\tilde{p} - E(\tilde{p})\}$. Notice that the expected payment under each unit of the hedge is:

$$E(\tilde{h}) = E(\tilde{p} - E(\tilde{p})) = E(20 - 20) = 0$$

Without transaction costs, the price of the hedge would be the expected value of zero. However, we assume a transaction cost of 2 for each unit of h *bought or sold. The standard deviation is:*

$$\sigma(\tilde{h}) = \sigma(\tilde{p} - E(\tilde{p})) = \sigma(\tilde{p}) = \$10$$

and, since we are discussing the hedge instrument, the correlation coefficient between $\tilde{h}$ *and* $\tilde{p}$ *is:*

$$r_{h,p} = -1$$

Integrated risk management solution. *To lay the ground for what can go wrong, first consider that the firm coordinates its hedging strategy. Overall profits are:*

$$II = 400 + 5\tilde{p} + \tilde{q} + \tilde{r}$$

which has an expected value of

$$E(II) = 400 + 5(20) + 0 + 0$$
$$= \$500m$$

and the risk level is (recall zero correlations between p, q, *and* r*):*

$$\sigma(II) = \{(5)^2 \ \sigma^2(\tilde{p}) + \sigma^2(\tilde{q}) + \sigma^2(\tilde{r})\}^{1/2}$$
$$= \{(5)^2 \ 10^2 + 25^2 + 10^2)^{1/2} = \$56.79m$$

If this risk is hedged by the purchase of 5 units of the hedge $\tilde{h}$ *(each unit of* $\tilde{h}$ *has an expected payment of 0 and a price of 2), then the expected profit is:*

$$E(II) = 400 + 5(20) - 5(2) + 0 + 0$$
$$= \$490m$$

The reduction on $10m in expected profit reflects the price of buying 5 units of the hedge each at a price of 2. The risk level is:

$$\sigma(II) = \{(5)^2 \ \sigma^2(\tilde{p}) + (5)^2 \ \sigma^2(\tilde{h}) + \sigma^2(\tilde{q}) + \sigma^2(\tilde{r})$$
$$- 2(5)(5)r_{h,p} \ \sigma(\tilde{p})\sigma(\tilde{h})\}^{1/2}$$
$$= \{(5)^2 \ 10^2 + (5)^2 \ 10^2 + 25^2 + 10^2 + 2(5)(5)(-1)(10)10))^{1/2}$$
$$= (25^2 + 10^2)^{1/2}$$
$$= \$26.93m$$

Because the oil price risk is completely hedged, the remaining risk, $26.93m, arises solely from the noise terms $\tilde{q}$ *and* $\tilde{r}$.

Nonintegrated snafu #1 (undoing a natural hedge). *Suppose risk management decisions are made separately by the divisions and the product division decides to hedge but the refinery division does not. The profits of the respective divisions are respectively:*

$$II_D = 100 + 30\tilde{p} + 30\tilde{h} - 30(2) + \tilde{q}$$

which shows the hedge in place, and

$$II_R = 300 - 25\tilde{p} + \tilde{r}$$

which shows no hedge. Total profits are thus:

$$II = 400 + 5\tilde{p} + 30\tilde{h} - 30(2) + \tilde{q} + \tilde{r}$$

which has an expected value of

$$= 400 + 5(20) + 30(0) - 30(2) + 0 + 0$$
$$= \$440m$$

and the standard deviation is

$$\sigma(II) = \{(5)^2 \ \sigma^2(\tilde{p}) + (30)^2 \ \sigma^2(\tilde{h}) + \sigma^2(\tilde{q})$$
$$+ \sigma^2(\tilde{r}) - 2(5)(30)r_{h,p} \ \sigma(\tilde{p})\sigma(\tilde{h})\}^{1/2}$$

$$= \{(5)^2 \ 10^{2+} + (30)^2 \ 10^{2+} + 25^2 + 10^2 + 2(5)(30)(-1)(10)10))^{1/2}$$

$$= \$251.45m$$

Look what a disaster this strategy has turned out to be. With no hedging, expected profit is 490 and risk is $56.79m. With the products division hedging, expected profit falls to 440 and risk increases to 251.45. What went wrong? The problem was that, even if no hedge is purchased, a natural hedge exists. Price affects the two divisions in the opposite direction. Price rises benefit the product division but hurt the refinery division, and vice versa. When the product division went off and bought 30 units of the hedge to insure its divisional risk, it not only spent 60 but disassembled the natural hedge across the divisions. Essentially this strategy reintroduces risk that was already hedged. Lufthansa has been reported as making this mistake.[11] Ordering jets from Boeing under a contract denominated in dollars, it was concerned that an increase in the value of the dollar would increase the Deutschmark cost of the planes. Accordingly, it hedged this currency risk. What went wrong was that its overall demand was closely related to the value of the dollar and that a natural hedge already existed. The currency hedge simply undid the natural hedge.

Nonintegrated snafu #2 (overkill). *The second blunder is that a nonholistic approach can lead to overkill. Suppose that both divisions independently decide to hedge their risk. The product division buys 30 units of the hedge and the refinery division sells 25 units. Because each unit is fully hedged against price risk, it will only have the noise term left. Thus, the overall risk level is the same as with the previous complete hedge, $26.93m. However, to achieve this overall level of risk reduction, the firm trades a total 55 units of the hedge (30 buys and 25 sells) for a cost of 110. Thus, expected profit is reduced to 390. This is simply a waste. Since there was a natural hedge, it was unnecessary to buy so many units. All that was necessary was to hedge the net price exposure to price risk shown in the total profit equation (i.e., buy only 5 units of the hedge).*

Focused and Global Strategies— Rifles and Blunderbusses

The various strategies identified turn out to have interesting domains. Some strategies are inherently holistic, whereas others are specific to a type of risk. Consider an insurance policy covering

---

11. This is reported in *The Economist*, February 10, 1996, Corporate Risk Management
    Survey, p. 16.

product liability risk. This is a hedge instrument targeted at a very specific source of risk: it covers only product liability risk. Similarly, a currency hedge achieved by buying pounds sterling forward covers only the risk that the exchange rate between dollars and pounds will change in a way that affects the firm's value. The forward contract covers only this risk. Similarly, one can think of focused hedges of property risk, interest rate risk, and risk from changes in other macroeconomic indicators that affect the firm's profitability. These hedges are "rifle shots;" each hedge targets only a single risk.

One can certainly imagine a holistic risk management strategy making use of rifle shots. Each source of risk is identified and matched with a particular hedge instrument (if one is available). The appropriate hedge ratios for each instrument are then determined jointly to meet an overall risk–return target. As in the Commonwealth Petroleum example, this does not necessarily mean the same hedge ratio for each instrument. Rather, the particular hedge ratios will depend on the relative cost and availability of the instruments. Now, it may not be possible to hedge all types of risk by focused hedge instruments. For example, pollution liability insurance has been difficult to obtain in the United States in recent years, and what is available is very costly and has low limits of coverage. More generally, liability coverage has been available, but limits of coverage rarely exceeds a few hundred million dollars, which offers incomplete protection for the Fortune 500 firm facing the possibility of multi-billion dollar suits. Thus, the attempt to assemble a holistic risk management program through focused hedges may well result in something of a patchwork.

Now contrast these rifle shot hedges with the use of a leverage strategy. For example, the firm has high leverage and its earnings and value are very risky. This leads to high expected bankruptcy costs, a severe discounting of bond values because investors believe the firm will overvalue high risk projects (ignoring the default put), and an expectation that post-loss financing will be extremely costly. Accordingly, the firm lowers its leverage by repurchasing debt and decides that instead of borrowing to fund a new plant, it will finance entirely with equity. It does not matter where the risk came from; the value added by reducing leverage accrues across all types. This strategy is by nature holistic. Now, a rifle shot can pick off one bird at a time, but a blunderbuss can down a whole flock at short range (blunderbusses are a little more colorful than shotguns). So too can the leverage strategy address all types of risk.

In Table 8–3 a number of sources of risk are listed in the columns. This table is not exhaustive, and more columns could be added. Strategies are shown in the rows. These fall into two distinct groups. In the top half of the table, specimen hedge instruments are paired with the corresponding risk. In the bottom part of the table, strategies such as simple leverage, contingent refinancing, and compensation design are shown to address risk regardless of cause.

CONCLUSION

In this chapter we looked again at the reasons why risk was costly to firms, and from these costs derived several generic risk management strategies. Deriving strategies directly from the costs of risk led to a dual, or shadow, classification of strategies. If risk is costly, these costs can be reduced by removing the risk; that is, hedging. Alternatively, if we know why risk is causing loss of value, the dual strategy lies in restructuring the firm so that it can accommodate the risk. We can remove the risk or remove its effect. Some of the risk management strategies derived by this approach will be a secondary focus in the remainder of the book; not because they are unimportant, but because they require specialized skills outside the financial economics paradigm. These strategies include tax management and design of managerial compensation systems. Other strategies will receive more attention, including hedging, leverage, contingent leverage, post-loss financing, contingent financing, limited liability, and organizational design. Each of these strategies will be examined in detail in later chapters.

In earlier chapters we examined how diversification can reduce risk. Combining risk exposures will cause the relative risk to fall. This process suggests that risk management strategies should be coordinated. This view was strengthened by the observation that many of the costs of risks were related to the overall risk to the firm, rather than to the risk to a specific division of the risk from a specific source. In the final part of this chapter we looked at integrated risk management strategies. The strategies derived fall into two distinct groups. The hedge strategies focus on a specific risk that is reduced or removed by being transferred to another party. One expression of integrated risk management is the

T A B L E   8–3

Rifle Shots and Blunderbusses–Focused and Global Strategies

Tool → Source ↓	Property Damage	Liability Loss	Interest Rate Risk	Foreign Exchange Risk	Industry Risk	Market Risk
Property Insurance	●					
Liability Insurance		●				
Interest Rate Cap or Floor			●			
Foreign Exchange Forward				●		
Short Industry Index					●	
Market Derivative						●
Simple Leverage	●	●	●	●	●	●
Contingent Refinancing	●	●	●	●	●	●
Contingent Leverage	●	●	●	●	●	●
Compensation Renegotiation	●	●	●	●	●	●
Tax Arbitrage	●	●	●	●	●	●

current trend to bundle insurance coverages into a single product that hedges across a number of sources of risk. However, the various dual strategies are usually not specific to source of risk and are naturally integrated. This discussion will prepare us for later chapters. We finished the chapter by illustrating that integrated risk management does not imply that we should hedge everything in sight, or design equal levels of protection against different types of risk. Rather, managing one risk has implications for other risks and strategy is best coordinated.

REFERENCES

Babbel, David F., and Anthony M. Santomero. 1997. "Financial Risk Management by Insurers: An Analysis of the Process." *Journal of Risk and Insurance* 64: 231–70.

Binder, Barrett F. 1991. "Integrated Risk Management Vital for Surviving Banks." *Journal of Commercial Bank Lending* 73(5):13–20.

Christine, Brian. 1995. "Environmental Risk Management: Integrated Risk Management Approach for Environmental Issues." RIMS Educational Course. *Risk Management* 42(1):62.

Froot, Kenneth A., and Jeremy C. Stein. 1998. "Risk Management, Capital Budgeting, and Capital Structure Policy for Financial Institutions: An Integrated Approach." *Journal of Financial Economics* 47:55–82.

Lange, Scott. 1997. "Moving Forward: Risk Management Meets the Information Age." *Risk Management* 44(9):43–47.

Lew, Keun-Ock. 1991. "Reinsurance and the Firm Value: Theory and Evaluation." Ph.D. Dissertation, Wharton School, University of Pennsylvania.

McGinn, Carol. 1998. "The New Risk Management." *Wall Street & Technology* 16(7):88–90.

Miller, Kent D. A. 1992. "Framework for Integrated Risk Management in International Business." *Journal of International Business Studies* 23(2):311–31.

Miller, Kent D. 1998. "Economic Exposure and Integrated Risk Management." *Strategic Management Journal* 19:497–514.

Nottingham, Lucy. 1996. "Integrated Risk Management." *The Canadian Business Review* 23(2):26–28.

Porter, Anne Millen. 1998. "Companies Integrate Risk Management, Appoint CRO's.'" *Purchasing* 125(1):59–69.

Santomero, Anthony M. 1997. "Commercial Bank Risk Management: An Analysis of the Process." *Journal of Financial Services Research* 12(2-3):83–115.

Schrand, Catherine, and Haluk Unal. 1998. "Hedging and Coordinated Risk Management: Evidence from Thrift Conversions." *Journal of Finance* 53:979–1013.

Shapiro, Alan C., and Sheridan Titman. 1985. "An Integrated Approach to Corporate Risk Management." *Midland Corporate Finance Journal* 3(2):41–56.

CHAPTER 9

Post-loss Investment Decisions and the Measurement of Loss

This chapter will address the impact of a risky event, such as a property loss, liability suit, or demand shock, on the firm. The effects may be direct (the firm needs to pay for a liability settlement or rebuild a damaged plant) or indirect (the loss can affect future product demand or costs of production). The firm has both the value of its current operations and its franchise value at risk. We will first address the determinants of corporate value and show how these sources of value can be affected by the risky event. Risky events will be classified into asset loss, transfers of wealth, and shocks to costs and demand. This classification aids in tracing the effects of the loss and also in examining post-loss investment decisions.

Following a loss, the firm faces a number of investment decisions. If productive resources are affected, the management must decide whether to repair or replace those assets. In addition to the reinvestment decision, the firm also faces a set of decisions on new investments. These opportunities might have been available before the loss, but the loss can change both the costs and expected cash flows. Accordingly, these new investments need reappraisal. The firm will minimize the impact of the loss if post-loss value-maximizing investment decisions are made.

The remainder of this chapter deals with some related issues in tracing the impact of a loss and in making optimal post-loss investment decisions. In particular, we will look in more detail at the decision whether to replace or abandon assets that have been destroyed or damaged. We will examine how this decision is affected by salvage and disposal values, properties of the production technology, business interruption loss, and by the Tobin's q ratio.

WHERE DOES THE VALUE OF A FIRM COME FROM?

Existing Assets

First, a firm will typically have assets in place that are generating, and will probably continue to generate, cash flow. Call these assets K_0, the subscript zero revealing the current time. For a manufacturing firm these assets will include plant, buildings, inventory, distribution channels, and the value of firm-specific capital embodied in its management and workforce. Let us suppose that in any future year t these assets in place are expected to generate cash flows of $K_0\, r_0$. The term r_0 shows the expected rate of return on assets K_0.[1] Many of these assets will have a lifespan of several years and will continue to generate earnings for a number of years before they are exhausted. But use will diminish and exhaust the assets and, unless renewed, the earnings stream will decline and disappear in time. Accordingly, we consider the return in any year t from current asset to be net of the cost of renewing and repairing and replacing these assets in year t. We are deducting not the cost of *new* capital investments, merely the cost of preserving the existing assets. Thus, the expected cash flow in year t from the existing capital stock K_0 is

$$E(E_t)^t = K_0\, r_{0,t}$$

These cash flows are available to pay debt and equity claims of the firm. It is useful to isolate the value of the equity owned by current shareholders since the risk management task will be to maximize this value. To value equity, the value of current debt, D, will be deducted from the firm value. The firm may also hold liquid assets (cash), L, and this will be included in the value of

---

1. For simplicity, the expected rate of return is assumed to be constant.

current assets. If the earnings stream from current assets has a lifetime of n_0 years and is discounted at the appropriate cost of capital k_t, the present value of equity is:

$$V(E) = \sum_{i=1}^{n_0} \frac{K_0\, r_0}{(1 + k)^t} + L - D = V_0(K_0 : r_0) + L - D \quad (9.1)$$

where $V_0\,(K_0\,;\,r_0)$ is the present value, at time 0, of the cash flows generated.

Future Investments

We will introduce the possibility that the firm will make future investments beyond maintenance of current assets. At some future date t the firm makes investments, K_t, in new assets, and each of these new investments makes a subsequent expected annual rate of return of $r_{t,i}$. The lifetime of each investment is n_t years. Thus, the net cash flow generated in some future year t, from investments made from assets not currently in place, is:

$$-K_t + V_t\,(K_t\,;\,r_t)$$

where $V_t\,(K_t\,;\,r_t)$ is the present value, at time 0, of the cash flows generated.

Total Firm Value (Internal Funding)

First, let us assume that future investments are made from retained earnings. The firm value is now the combination of the value from existing assets and the value generated by future investments, as follows:

$$V(F) = V_0\,(K_0 : r_0) + \sum_{t=1}^{n_0} \frac{-K_t + V_t\,(K_t\,;\,r_t)}{(1 + k)^t} \quad (9.2)$$

The three terms in Equation (9.2) can be written more compactly as:

$$V(F) = V(A) + V(R) + L \quad (9.3)$$

The two items in square brackets in Equation (9.3) are *the value of existing operations*, $V(A)$, and *the franchise value*, $V(R)$. The final term, L, is the liquid asset, cash.

Total Firm Value (External Funding)

Now let us do the same valuation exercise under the assumption that future new investments will be funded externally by debt or equity. This can soon get complex, but fortunately we can use a little theory to simplify things immensely. Imagine a firm that has existing equity value of 100 and an investment opportunity that will cost 50 but generate an earnings stream valued at 70. The NPV of the project is 20. The firm must sell some new security, debt or equity, to raise the 50. However, it will do so at a price that reflects the required rate of return to investors subscribing to a security with similar risk characteristics. Thus, the value to *current* equity holders will be the

100	from existing operations
$+70$	from new investment
$-N$	expected value of the payment stream to new security holders
$+T$	transaction cost of new issue

But if the new security is to offer a competitive risk-related return to investors, this payment stream, N, must have a present value of 50. Thus, the present value of the payment stream N must be the sum raised in the issue of 50. Another way of saying this is that the current shareholders will issue new securities at a price that offers new investors a fair rate of return. Thus, the net present value of the new investment is preserved for existing shareholders, net of any transaction costs from the issue.

We can now adapt Equation (9.3) to the case with external funding,

$$V(F) = V(A) + V(R) + L \qquad (9.3)$$

The only difference between the value for current owners with internal and external funding arises from the transaction costs, T, of the new security issue. Recalling the discussion above, these costs can represent direct costs of the new issue, such as underwriting costs, and any other frictional costs, such as costs associated with information asymmetry or moral hazard.

HOW VALUE CAN BE LOST AND RECAPTURED

Having seen how value is composed, consider how it can be lost in the types of events risk managers worry about. Consider the following risky events:

- Destruction of existing productive assets: e.g., fire, storm, earthquake
- Transfer of value to third party: e.g., liability loss, credit loss
- Shock to the cost function: e.g., currency change, interest rate change, regulatory change
- Shock to demand: e.g., change in taste, currency change, interest rate change, regulatory change, new entrant to market, change in economy

For each of these types of risky events, we can trace how it impacts firm value using Equations (9.3) and (9.4).

Destruction of Existing Assets

The plant of the firm is partially destroyed, so that the firm cannot produce and sell the same level of output. Several consequences are possible that can be identified with the help of the valuation Equation (9.3) and Table 9–1. We will consider each of the con-

T A B L E   9–1

Direct and Secondary Effects of Loss

Effect ⇒ Risky Event ⇓	K_0	r_0	K_t	$r_{i,t}$	L	T
Loss of asset	√	×	×	×		×
Transfer of value	×	√	×	×	√	√
Cost shock	×	√	×	×		×
Demand shock	×	√	×	×		×

Key: √ is direct effect
    × is secondary effect

sequences separately by looking at the rows of Table 9–1 one at a time.

Effect ⇒ Risky Event ⇓	K_0	r_0	K_t	$r_{i,t}$	L	T
Loss of asset	√	×	×	×		×

Key: √ is direct effect
× is secondary effect

1. The value of the existing assets is depleted. This is the direct effect; thus, K_0 falls.
2. A potential secondary effect is that the fall in K_0 can affect the earnings rate, r_0. There can be several types of effect. First, suppose there are diminishing returns to investment. For example, if the price elasticity differs across customers, the contract terms may vary and also the profitability. If this is true, the firm may respond to the loss of productive assets by supplying only the more profitable customers. Consequently, the average rate return on assets will increase, and this will partly make up for the loss in the asset base. Contrary effects also are possible. For example, if the production process is vertically integrated, then a partial loss or productive assets can bring a much larger proportionate reduction in output. Such would be the case if a computerized production line lost its computer and the whole line came to a standstill. Another possible effect on the earnings rate, r_0, is that the asset loss might cause a demand change. For example, customers might question the quality of a product, or the reliability of supply, made in a depleted plant.
3. Insofar as cash flows, $K_0\, r_0$ are reduced, the firm has lower internal earnings from which to fund new investments. This will either cause K_t to fall as the firm abandons investment opportunities that are marginal or cannot be financed externally, or the firm to resort to

external sources to finance new investment, thereby incurring transaction costs T.

4. If K_t are reduced, there may be secondary effects on the rates of return generated by these investments. For example, given diminishing returns as described in 2 above, there would be an increase in r_t as K_t falls.

EXAMPLE: PROPERTY LOSS

Plastique makes plastic beads that are sold to several manufacturing firms who make plumbing supplies, toys, casings for computers and televisions, etc. The firm makes two different formulas, and these are manufactured separately at two plants, A and B. The projected pre-loss outputs of these two plants are 100 and 140 units for 10 years respectively. The values (the replacement cost) of these plants are $5m and $7m respectively. The firm also has liquid assets, cash, of $5m. One of the plants, B, is totally destroyed in a fire. Plant A is operating at 90% capacity and thus can increase output to 111 units. The customer list is shown below with the number of units purchased and the profit (in $m).

Customer	Units Sold	Profit
1	76	1.2
2	35	0.5
3	50	0.6
4	29	0.3
5	50	0.4
TOTAL	240	3.0

We will assume that the cost of capital is 10%.

Before the loss, K_0 = $12m and the annual profit of $3m represented a 25% rate of return for 10 years (r_0 = 0.25).[2] After the loss

---

2. It can be argued that since current assets include the cash balance of $5m, K_0 = $17m and the rate of return on *total* current assets is $3m / $17m = 0.1765. Indeed, this does provide a more complete measure of investment return. However, it is more useful for current purposes to separate liquid assets from those directly involved in production. In this way we can their separate roles in the risk management process. Thus, it is important to note that r_0 does not provide a complete return on assets that investors have provided to the firm.

$K_0' = \$5m$ (primes are used to denote values after the loss). The after-loss return is calculated as follows. From the table, customers 1 and 2 offer a higher profit rate per unit sold than customers 3, 4, and 5. Thus, the entire capacity of the surviving Plant A, 111 units can be sold to the first two customers. The profit of $1.7m represents a 34% rate of return on $K_0' = \$5m$, i.e., $r_0' = 0.34$. The higher profit on the remaining customers 1 and 2 partly offsets the fall in K_0, thus limiting the fall in earnings.

Recall that the firm has $5m in liquid assets and can finance new investments with this and retained earnings. Before the loss, Plastique planned to build a new plant with a different product at the end of the current year at a cost of $8m with 10-year earnings of 16.875% ($K_1 = \$8m$; $r_1 = 0.16875$). Note that, without loss, there are expected to be sufficient funds to pay for this new investment ($5m in liquid reserves and $3m earnings). After the loss of plant B, the firm has an expected $6.7m in internal funds ($5m liquid reserve plus $1.7m earnings from customers 1 and 2 supplied by the surviving plant A). One choice the firm faces is to rebuild plant B and not undertake the new investment. Reconstruction would cost $7m, but there is only $6.7m in internal funds. Thus, $0.3m would have to be raised externally, which would incur transaction costs. Transaction costs on an issue of $0.3m are denoted $T(0.3)$. After the reconstruction of B the firm would have no internal funds left, $L' = 0$. This, and other choices are now summarized (the last is not exhaustive; for example, the firm could also sell off plant A).

Rebuild plant B (raising at least $0.3m externally) and forgo new investment:

$K_0' = 12m$; $r_0 = 0.25$ $K_1' = 0$; $T(\$0.3m)$; $L' = 0$

Forgo plant B, undertake new investment, and raise at least $1.3m externally:

$K_0' = \$5m$; $r_0 = 0.34$ $K_1' = \$8m$; $T(\$1.3m)$; $L' = 0$

Rebuild plant B, undertake new investment, and raise at least $8.3m externally:

$K_0' = \$12m$; $r_0 = 0.25$ $K_1' = \$8m$; $T(\$8.3m)$; $L' = 0$

Forgo plant B, forgo new investment, and raise nothing externally:

$K_0' = \$5m$; $r_0 = 0.34$ $K_1' = 0$; $T(0)$; $L' = \$5m$

Transfer of Value

The second type of risky event is typified by a liability suit or a default by a creditor. The productive capacity of the firm is intact, but either part of the earnings, or assets, of the firm is claimed by an outsider (a liability suit) or part of the earnings and value that was anticipated from current assets disappears (credit default).

Effect ⇒ Risky Event ⇓	K_0	r_0	K_t	$r_{i,t}$	L	T
Transfer of value	×	√	×	×	√	√

Key: √ is direct effect
× is secondary effect

In the extract from the Table 9–1 shown, there are three direct effects. Paying a liability claim will either absorb current earnings, $r_{0,t}$, deplete liquid assets, L, or require the firm to raise new money, thus incurring transaction costs, T. Clearly, these respective effects depend very much on the size of the claim. If we consider a credit default, the direct effect will be to reduce earnings.

A number of secondary effects are possible. First, the firm might sell off current productive assets, K_0, to raise money for the settlement. This is quite a desperate response, but there are two circumstances where this response is plausible. The first is where the liability claim is very large and can only be paid through selling off assets. The second is where the claim itself lowers the rate of return on those assets such that the assets have higher disposal value than value in use. This will occur if the return on the *salvage* value of existing assets falls below the return obtainable elsewhere from investments of similar risk. An illustration would be a product liability claim that shakes customer confidence in the product. For example, highly visible claims were brought against Ford after one vehicle type, the Pinto, was involved in explosions of gas tanks. Allegedly these fires were due to a design fault, and the publicity of these cases almost certainly had a depressing demand effect.

Other secondary effects can arise because the cost of settling a liability claim, or the depletion of liquid assets through credit default, can force the firm to forgo new investments or finance them from external sources, thus incurring transaction costs. As discussed above, any change in the level of new investment can affect the rate of return. Moreover, in the case of liability suits, the adverse publicity may have a chilling effect, not only on the demand for the affected product, but on the company image, thus depressing demand for all its products.

EXAMPLE: LIABILITY CLAIM

Instead of the fire that destroyed Plant B, Plastique's misfortune is that it has just had a $6m liability award made against it for defects in design that make its product fail in crucial applications. The post-loss evaluation reveals the following. The adverse publicity will dampen demand for its current product such that expected profit will fall from $3m per year to $2m. While the replacement cost of current assets is $12m ($5m + $7m), these assets would have a disposal value of only $8m. The intended new investment, K_1, is for a product that is unrelated to the existing product line and is not likely to suffer any demand contamination from the lawsuit. Notice that after paying the lawsuit Plastique has internal funds of $L + K_0 r_0 - $6m = $5m + $2m - $6m = $1m, which are insufficient to fund the new project. However, the firm could sell off existing assets for $8m and fund the new project internally. Figure 9–1 is a

---

F I G U R E   9–1

Choices Following Property Loss

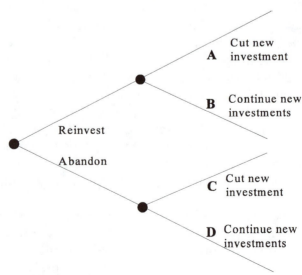

A   Cut new investment

B   Continue new investments

Reinvest

Abandon

C   Cut new investment

D   Continue new investments

decision tree that helps us to identify alternative decisions. The choices are represented as the branches of the tree and are now summarized (I have shown cases in which all existing assets are sold off, but not cases where the firm sells off one plant only):
    Retain current plant and forgo new investment:

$$K_0' = \$12m; \quad r_0' = 0.167 \quad K_1' = 0; \quad T(0); \quad L' = \$1m$$

Retain current plant, undertake new investment, raise new money for balance of settlement:

$$K_0' = \$12m; \quad r_0' = 0.167 \quad K_1' = \$8m; \quad T(7); \quad L' = 0$$

Sell current plant, undertake new investment, raise new money for balance of settlement:

$$K_0' = 0; \quad r_0' = 0 \quad K_1' = \$8m; \quad T(1); \quad L' = 0$$

Sell current plant, forgo new investment, and default (at $1m on the settlement):

$$K_0' = 0; \quad r_0' = 0 \quad K_1' = 0; \quad T(0); \quad L' = \$7m$$

Notice that the last option is liquidating up the firm. If the firm is liquidated before the current year's profit is earned, its liquidation value is only $7m, which is being the cash reserve of $5m plus the proceeds of the sale of assets of $8m minus the settlement of $6m. Bankruptcy is an ex post *risk management option.*

Shock to the Cost Function

For a firm that imports raw materials, a change in currency rates affects the cost function. Many other risky scenarios can have similar effects on cost. New regulations that impose more severe restrictions on the disposal of hazardous materials will tend to increase costs. The unionization of the labor force can change costs. Changes in interest rates can affect the cost of inventory and trade credit. Physical destruction of the plant (e.g., by fire) of a supplying firm that disrupts the flow of inputs and raw materials also can increase costs. These are a number of risky events that can cause random shifts in the cost function. In terms of the valuation model, the direct effect of these cost shifts is that earnings from current operations, r_0, will be randomly shocked. Such cost changes can be upwards or downwards, though the main concern in here is with the upwards cost shifts, and the illustrations follow accordingly.

Effect ⇒	K_0	r_0	K_t	$r_{i,t}$	L	T
Risky Event ⇓						
Cost shock	×	√	×	×		×

Key: √ is direct effect
× is secondary effect

The cost shift can cause a number of indirect effects. Given the earnings reduction, the firm will have smaller cash resources to finance new investments, and, if the effects are severe enough, will be forced to choose between cutting back or using external funding. As mentioned, changes in the level of investment activity can affect the rate of return if there are nonconstant returns to scale. Also, the cost shift for existing operations can carry over directly to the new investments. For example, the firm may import raw materials for its existing product line and for a new intended product, so existing costs and cost of the new product will both be adversely affected by a fall in the value of the home currency. Other indirect effects of an increase in costs can include the closing down of existing operations. As discussed in the case of claims on earnings, if the rate of return on salvage value of existing assets is reduced below a competitive level, shareholders gain by liquidating current activities.

EXAMPLE: SHOCK TO COST FUNCTION

The latest in the tales of misfortune of Plastique is that new regulations on the handling, transportation, and disposal of chemicals used in production cause a significant increase in costs, reducing profit from $3m to $1m, and therefore $r_{0,1}$ is reduced to 8.333%. (This is a return on replacement value of $12m; the equivalent return on salvage value of $8m is 12.5%.) Should new investment be undertaken, r_1 will be reduced to 8%. Plastique has internal funds of $L + r_{0,1} = \$5m + \$1m = \$6m$, which are insufficient to fund the new project. However, the firm could sell off existing assets for $8m and fund the new project internally.

Retain current plant and forgo new investment:

$$K_0' = \$12m; \quad r_0 = 0.083 \quad K_1' = 0; \quad T(0); \quad L' = 5$$

Retain current plant and undertake new investment (borrowing $2m):

$$K_0' = 12; \quad r_0 = 0.083 \quad K_1' = \$8m; \quad T(2); \quad L' = 0$$

Sell current plant and undertake new investment:

$$K_0' = 0; \quad r_0 = 0 \quad K_1' = \$8m; \quad T(0); \quad L' = 5$$

Sell current plant and forgo new investment:

$$K_0' = 0; \quad r_0 = 0 \quad K_1' = 0; \quad T(0); \quad L' = 13$$

Shock to Demand Function

Demand shocks can arise from many circumstances. Examples include shifts in tastes (either for the brand made by the firm or for the generic product), a downturn in the economy, a lowering of demand for consumer durables resulting from an increase in interest rates, changes in currency rates, and regulatory changes that affect the industry structure. Such changes directly affect the profit from existing operations, and the analysis follows along similar lines to those of cost changes.

Effect ⇒						
Risky Event ⇓	K_0	r_0	K_t	$r_{i,t}$	L	T
Demand shock	x	√	x	x		x

Key: √ is direct effect
x is secondary effect

MITIGATION AND OPTIMAL POST-LOSS DECISIONS: CRISIS MANAGEMENT

For an ongoing business, value maximizing involves a series of choices over a set of investment opportunities (not necessarily independent of each other) in the light of the cost and availability of funds. Risky event (such as property losses, liability suits, and currency losses) disturb the parameterization of this problem, and not surprisingly the optimal strategy can change as a result of the event. As we have seen, these events often change the rate of return on existing operations and new investment projects and change the availability and cost of financing.

The term "crisis management" is often used for the formulation of a response plan following some corporate trauma. Crisis management can involve many components. Following Union Carbide's accident in Bhopal, India, in which thousands were killed or injured by the release of a highly toxic gas, the company faced a set of decisions on how to mitigate the damage but not compromise its defense of any subsequent liability suit. For example, providing money for immediate medical expenses could relieve injury but might be later used by plaintiffs as indicative of Union Carbide's acceptance of responsibility. This is typical of many post-loss decisions facing firms. While the event cannot be undone, its effects can be mitigated by careful handling. The objective is to maximize post-loss firm value. We will concentrate on one set of decisions here. The event presents the firm with a set of investment decisions; what are the value-maximizing choices?

The optimal configuration of a firm at any point in time requires that the firm exhaust all opportunities for increasing its value. If there are opportunities for increasing value by changing the capital structure (by raising new money, changing dividends, repurchasing securities, etc.), these should be exhausted. If any investment opportunities are available that satisfy the investment criteria for increasing value, these should be undertaken. Potential investment opportunities include the addition of new projects and the retirement of existing operations. For a new project, the usual hurdle is that the net present value be positive. Whether it is so will depend on the projected cash flows that are estimated from projections of demand and cost. For existing operations, the firm faces the everyday choice of selling off assets and closing down those operations. If the disposal or salvage value of the assets used in production exceeds the capitalized value of the generated earnings, value will be added by selling off the assets. Thus, a value-maximizing configuration can be chosen that reflects all the available and estimated information on capital costs and future cash flows. If the parameters were to alter, then naturally the optimal configuration of the firm could change.

Optimal Post-loss Investment Decisions

The optimal post-loss investment decisions follow the normal capital budget procedure; that is, the net present value should be positive. Recall that the pre-loss value of the firm was given by Equation (9.2), which has been expanded (as in Equation (9.4)) to include transaction costs T:

$$V(F) = V_0 (K_0 ; r_0) + \sum_{t=1}^{n_0} \frac{-K_t + V_t (K_t ; r_t)}{(1 + k)^t} + L - T \quad (9.4)$$

Noting the various direct and indirect effects of a risky event, we can now rewrite Equation (9.4) to show the value of the firm after the loss. The primes denote values after the loss given such optimal decision making, and C denotes the cost of reinvestment in the destroyed or damaged asset.

$$V'(F) = -C + V_0' (K_0' ; r_0') \quad (9.5)$$
$$+ \sum_{t=1}^{n_0} \frac{-K_t' + +V_t' (K_t' ; r_t')}{(1 + k)^t} + L - T'$$

Post-loss investment decisions include both reinvestment in destroyed or damaged assets and decisions on new investments. For new investments the decision criterion is the usual capital budgeting rule, which is applied using after-loss information:

$$\text{NPV} = \left[\sum_{t=1}^{\infty} \frac{-K_t' - V_t' (K_t' ; r_t')}{(1 + k)^t} \right] - T_N \quad (9.6)$$

As we continue, we will assume that the firm's management responds to the loss in a value-maximizing way; they make the optimal decision on whether to replace assets destroyed in the loss and make decisions for new investments that are value maximizing in the post-loss environment. To consider the optimal reinvestment decision, let us expand the notation to three potential values for K_0 and r_0.

K_0 and r_0	value of current assets and the return on these assets, assuming no loss
$K_0'(N)$ and $r_0'(N)$	value of current assets and return with a loss but no replacement

K_0' and r_0' value of current assets and return with a loss and optimal replacement

The reinvestment cost, $C = K_0' - K_0'(N)$.

The post-loss reinvestment decision can now be made according to (where T' is the transaction cost for financing the reinvestment):

$$\text{NPV} = -C + V_0'(K_0' ; r_0') - V_0'(K_0'(N) ; r_0'(N)) - T' \qquad (9.7)$$

We will now illustrate the application of these rules for cases in which there is property loss and loss of value. We will also look at the effects of the transaction cost on these decisions.

Losses to Productive Assets

Plastique suffers the property loss described earlier; Plant B is destroyed in a fire. The issues facing the firm were summarized in the following choices:

Rebuild plant B (raising at least $0.3m externally) and forgoing new investment:

$K_0' = \$12m;$ $r_0 = 0.25$ $K_1' = 0;$ $T(\$0.3m);$ $L' = 0$

Forgo plant B, undertake new investment and raise at least $1.3m externally

$K_0' = \$5m;$ $r_0 = 0.34$ $K_1' = \$8m;$ $T(\$1.3m);$ $L' = 0$

Rebuild plant B, undertake new investment and raise at least $8.3m externally

$K_0' = \$12m;$ $r_0 = 0.25$ $K_1' = \$8m;$ $T(\$8.3m);$ $L' = 0$

Forgo plant B, forgo new investment and raise nothing externally

$K_0' = \$5m;$ $r_0 = 0.34$ $K_1' = 0;$ $T(0);$ $L' = \$5m$

Startup of Plastique. *The next task is to see which of these decisions maximizes the wealth of the current shareholders. Let us step back a little to see how Plastique came to be positioned as it was before the loss. A* *little more information is now added. Plastique was formed three years ago when it raised $15m in equity. This money was used to construct the two plants and for working capital. The investment parameters facing Plastique at inception were that it could make an estimated $3m per year for 13 years. Assume that the capital cost was incurred at the beginning of the first year and all cash flows occur at year end. The cost of capital is 10%. The net present value at startup was therefore:*

$$\text{NPV} = -15 + \sum_{t=1}^{13} \frac{3}{(1 + 0.1)^i} = \$6.309\text{m}$$

Pre-loss Value. *Shortly before the loss, Plastique had identified a new investment opportunity that would involve a capital outlay of $8m and generate an income stream of $1.35m (i.e., 16.875%) per year. This opportunity was to be undertaken at the end of the current year. At that time the firm was projected to have $3m income from the current year and $5m in cash. With the loss event, this would be just enough to finance the new project. The project is to be delayed for one year so that it can be financed internally. First, let us be sure that this new investment opportunity has a positive NPV. It will be undertaken in one year's time, when the cash flows will be:*

$$-8 + \sum_{t=1}^{10} \frac{8(0.16875)}{(1 + 0.1)^t} = \$0.296\text{m}$$

Since this is positive, the new investment makes sense. If we use the current cash (L = $5m) and end of year earnings of $3m to fund the project, the pre-loss value of the firm is (recall that existing assets now only have ten years of life left):

$$\left[\sum_{t=1}^{10} \frac{12(0.25)}{(1 + 0.1)^t} \right] - \left[\left(\frac{1}{1 + 0.1} \right) \left(8 - \sum_{t=1}^{10} \frac{8(0.16875)}{(1 + 0.1)^t} \right) \right]$$
$$+ 5 - 0 = \$23.705\text{m}$$

Post-loss Valuations. *To measure the post-loss value of equity, we need a little more information. Since the valuation depends on what actions the firm chooses, and some of these actions need external financing, we need to know the transaction costs, T, involved. Here the transaction cost will have two components. There will be a fixed cost of 0.3 for any issue, which reflects the cost of writing up and administering the new issue.*

However, we assume a second component that increases with the size of the issue.[3] Thus, the transaction costs will be:[4]

$$T = 0.3 + 0.005X^2$$

Choice 1: Rebuild plant B (raising at least $0.3m externally) and forgoing new investment:

We will include the $5m in cash and all the earnings stream, but recall that there is a capital cost of $7m for the rebuilding. The transaction cost on the new issue is $0.3 + 0.005(0.3)^2 = 0.30045$.

$$\left[-7 + \sum_{t=1}^{10} \frac{12(0.25)}{(1 + 0.1)^t}\right] - [0] + 5 - 0.30045 = \$16.13455m$$

Choice 2: Forgo plant B, undertake new investment, and raise $1.3m externally:

$$\left[\sum_{t=1}^{10} \frac{5(0.34)}{(1 + 0.1)^t}\right] - \left[\left(\frac{1}{1 + 0.1}\right)\left(8 - \sum_{t=1}^{10} \frac{8(0.16875)}{(1 + 0.1)^t}\right)\right]$$
$$+ 5 - 0.30845 = \$15.407m$$

Choice 3: Rebuild plant B, undertake new investment and raise at least $8.3m externally:

$$\left[-7 + \sum_{t=1}^{10} \frac{12(0.25)}{(1 + 0.1)^t}\right] - \left[\left(\frac{1}{1 + 0.1}\right)\left(8 - \sum_{t=1}^{10} \frac{8(0.16875)}{(1 + 0.1)^t}\right)\right]$$
$$+ 5 - 0.644 = \$16.06m$$

Choice 4: Forgo plant B, forgo new investment, and raise nothing externally (keep cash of $5m):

---

3. The reason for this increasing cost component is that external investors see a demand for substantial external funding as a negative signal. Recall that information asymmetry between insiders and outsiders creates possibilities for wealth expropriation. Outsiders may believe that high-quality projects are more likely to be funded internally so that insiders can appropriate all value. Thus, a demand for large external funding can be a signal that insiders have relatively little confidence. Alternatively, large external funding can be perceived as an attempt to expropriate all upside risk for insiders while sticking downside risk on new investors.

4. This formula produces reasonable levels of transaction costs for the values we are talking about; i.e., $0m to $20m. Clearly, for much larger levels the transaction costs get out of hand. For example, on new issues of $10m the transaction costs will be $0.3 + 0.05(10)^2 = \$0.8m$, which is 8%. This may seem high, but remember that we are including agency costs and the costs of information asymmetry as well as the direct costs of issue and underwriting.

$$\left[\sum_{t=1}^{10} \frac{5(0.34)}{(1 + 0.1)^t} \right] - [0] + 5 - 0 = \$15.446m$$

Now compare the choices. The best choice is the first one: rebuild Plant B but forgo the new investment opportunity. Now consider why the decision falls out like this. First, if we ignore the transaction costs from new issues, the firm has two positive net present value investment opportunities after the loss. First, rebuilding plant B costs $7m and yields an earnings stream of $1.3m per year for 10 years. You may check that the NPV is $0.988m. Second, the firm also has an opportunity to spend $8m in one year's time and receive an earnings stream of $1.35m per year for 10 years. We calculated before that this has an NPV of $0.296m in one year, which is $0.269m in today's value. Of the two projects, rebuilding plant B is more attractive, but both have positive NPV.

Had the loss not taken place, the new investment would not have required any external funding. Since there would have been internal funds of $8m in one year, the project would have been undertaken and entirely internally funded. With the loss, the firm only has $5m in cash plus $1.7m in year 1 earnings. Now let's take the post-loss projects incrementally, taking rebuilding of plant B first because this is clearly a more attractive project than the new investment opportunity. Rebuilding plant B alone creates an additional NPV of $0.988m, but since we must raise $0.3m in external money, there is a transaction cost of $0.30045. The NPV outweighs the transaction costs, and rebuilding adds value. Now look at what happens to value when, in addition to rebuilding the plant B, we add the new project. The NPV of this project is $0.268m, but transaction costs of external finance increase from $0.30045m to $0.644m, an increase of $0.34355m. The additional transaction costs from increasing external funding more than wipe out the gain in value. Thus, it does not make sense to undertake the new project, even though it would have been worthwhile before loss when it could have been funded internally. This is an illustration of the crowding out hypothesis at work.

A second important point arises from this example. The firm lost a plant in a fire. In one sense the loss was $7m, which is what it would cost to rebuild the plant. However, the value of the firm before the loss is $23.704m. After the loss the value is $16.13455m, a fall in value of $7.56945m. The firm loses more than the $7m even if it takes the value-maximized post-loss investment choices. The reason is that not only does the firm have to come up with the $7m replacement cost for the plant, *but it incurs a transaction cost of $0.30045m because external financing is needed. Moreover, the size of the transaction costs from a larger new issue is too high to justify financing the new investment opportunity. Thus, the franchise value is reduced by a further $0.268m as this opportunity is lost. Thus, the firm value lost as a result of the fire exceeds the cost of replacing the lost asset.*

Three important issues arise from this example:

1. The loss event poses a set of investment decisions. The first concerns replacement of the lost asset. In the previous example, replacement of the asset added value, but under different circumstances a value-maximizing strategy can be to abandon this asset. This can be so if the event significantly reduces earnings on the asset or if the replacement requires external financing that incurs large transaction costs.

2. The event can lead to reevaluation of decisions on new projects and a change in the franchise value. A change in investment plans can occur if the event changes estimated cash flows for new projects or if the depletion of internal funds and the costs of external financing crowd out marginal projects.

3. The loss of value depends on the post-event investment decisions but will not, in general, be equal to the cost of replacing the asset. Under ideal conditions the measure of lost value will be made under the assumption that value-maximizing post-loss decisions are made.

The Form of Transaction Costs: Crowding Out and Optimal Investment

We will explore further the post-loss investment decisions. Two extensions are worth exploring. First, in the example of Plastique given, the firm had a fairly marginal new investment opportunity (invest $8m for an NPV of $0.268m), and the transaction costs increased as the size of the new issue increased. The example was deliberately set up with the marginal decision to illustrate the crowding out process, and you can change the numbers modestly to reverse this result. But consider why the new investment was crowded out. If the firm simply rebuilt plant B, it needed some external funding and incurred some transaction costs. If the firm wished to go further and both reinvest in plant B and undertake the new project, more external funding was needed and the transaction costs increased. The problem was that the *increase* in transaction costs more than wiped out the incremental value added from the new project. You should be anticipating where this is going. What if the cost of external funding did not increase with the size of the new issue (or at least increased only moderately with size)? For example, consider that the transaction costs were simply a lump sum issue cost of $0.30045m (i.e., exactly the transaction costs for Choice 1, in which plant B was rebuilt but the new project was forgone). Then we would have reasoned as follows. It certainly pays to rebuild plant B, as the analysis of choice 1 showed. However, we would clearly add value by raising more external financing because this would not increase transaction costs but would allow us to capture the positive NPV of the new project. Thus, the new project would not have been crowded out. It seems that crowding out occurred only because the transaction costs increased with issue size. I will now show that crowding out can be related to the *frequency* of new external issues.

Elastique, a rival of Plastique, has a single plant producing 300 units of output for an annual expected cash flow of $2m per year indefinitely. Assume that, absent destruction of the plant by fire or similar peril, this income stream is stable and the firm has cash of $2m. The firm expects to reinvest $2m each year in a series of new investments in each of the next five years (cost technology improvements, improved new products, etc.). Each of these new investment projects will bring a cash flow of $0.22m per year in perpetuity. These project payoffs are independent of those for existing operations. Notice that each of these investments can be financed internally from earnings and, even if there is a small blip in earnings, the cash reserve of $2m will ensure internal funding. If external funding is required, there is a fixed issue cost of $0.3m.

Now the firm has a major fire. The plant is totally destroyed and will cost $8m to rebuild. The problem is this: reconstruction will take one year and, during this time, the firm will be unable to meet orders. The rival firms, including Plastique, are only too willing to use their *extra capacity to meet these orders and will probably win these customers indefinitely. Thus, even after one year, Elastique only expects an earnings stream of $1m per year.*

Pre-loss value. *Consider this in parts. The original cash flow of $2m per year in perpetuity has a present value of:*

$$\left[\sum_{t=1}^{\infty} \frac{2}{(1 + 0.1)^t}\right] = \frac{2}{0.1} = \$20m$$

Each of the new investments has an NPV of:

$$\left[-2 + \sum_{t=1}^{\infty} \frac{0.22}{(1 + 0.1)^t}\right] = -2 + \frac{0.22}{0.1} = \$0.2m$$

Each new investment has a positive net present value, and since they can be financed internally without transaction cost, they should each be undertaken. Thus, the total firm value is:

$$20 + \frac{0.2}{(1 + 0.1)} + \frac{0.2}{(1 + 0.1)^2} + \frac{0.2}{(1 + 0.1)^3} + \frac{0.2}{(1 + 0.1)^4}$$
$$+ \frac{0.2}{(1 + 0.1)^5} + 2 = \$22.758m$$

Post-loss choices. Reconstruction of the plant generates a post-loss cash flow of $1m per year, which has a present value of $10m. Since the reconstruction cost is only $8m, this is a positive NPV opportunity, even if new financing is used with a fixed transaction cost of $0.3m. Thus, it will clearly add value to rebuild. Notice that the firm does need to raise $6m externally (the $8m less cash of $2m). What about the new projects? After the fire the income stream is only $1m, which is insufficient to finance all of the new investment projects. The first opportunity occurs at the end of year 1. At that time the firm will already need to raise $6m to rebuild the plant, so it might as well raise another $2m for the new investment (making $8m in new financing), as the transaction cost is fixed at $0.3m. The second investment opportunity occurs in two years. At that time the firm only has $1m in second-year cash flows and cannot finance the project internally. Because the transaction cost of a second new issue, $0.3m, exceeds the NPV, $0.2m, this is not justified. For the third new investment opportunity the firm can use the combined cash flows of years 2 and 3, which sum to $2m (plus investment income), to finance internally. Thus, the third opportunity can be undertaken.

*Continuing in this mode, the fourth investment opportunity will be lost
and the fifth undertaken. Thus, the post-loss value will be:*

$$-8 + \frac{10 + 0.2 - 0.3}{(1 + 0.1)} + \frac{0}{(1 + 0.1)^2} + \frac{0.2}{(1 + 0.1)^3}$$

$$+ \frac{0}{(1 + 0.1)^4} + \frac{0.2}{(1 + 0.1)^5} + 2 = \$3.275m$$

*The loss in value is quite dramatic. Partly it occurs because some of the
new investment opportunities are lost. But most of the loss of value
occurs because the firm has to find $8m to reconstruct existing assets
but only receives half the earnings it had before the fire. But the main
point of this example was to show that even fixed transaction costs can
lead to crowding out when the firm has multiple future investment opportunities spread over time.*

*There are other ways to play this example. One possibility is to
argue that the firm could raise not $8m at the end of year 1 (to finance
reconstruction of existing plant and the first-year investment opportunity), but $10m (with some interest adjustment) and save $2m to finance
the second-year investment opportunity. In the meantime, the firm would
have a cash balance of $2m. This would salvage the second-year project,
but the fourth year project is still lost. Could the firm raise even more
at the end of year 1, anticipating that the fourth-year project also is
saved? The problem with pushing this reasoning too far is that the opportunity cost of cash can become high. Holding large cash balances to
fund projects in the distant future involves a sacrifice of rate of return
and may render the firm vulnerable to takeover as others seek to use
these balances more productively.*

Liability Losses and Other Risky Events

With destruction of or damage to existing productive assets, the
firm faces the decision of reconstructing those assets as well as
the reevaluation of new investment projects. For other types of
risk events, existing productive assets are not threatened directly;
rather the owners lose value as earnings are lost or as outside
stakeholders extract part of the wealth. The post-loss investment
decisions do not include a decision to rebuild assets, as they have
not been destroyed. But there can be a decision to liquidate existing assets if the event changes their value in use. In addition, the

event can change the parameters of new investment projects. We now return to Plastique, this time to consider its liability loss for a defective product instead of the fire loss to its plant.[5]

Return to the case of Plastique, in which there is a $6m product liability settlement, which is compounded by a dampening of expected profit from $3m per year for 10 years to $2m. The replacement cost of current assets is $12m, but their disposal value is only $8m. The firm also has a new investment project with a capital cost of $8m and a return of 16.875 for 10 years. There is no demand contamination of the new project from the lawsuit. After paying the lawsuit, Plastique has internal funds of $5m + $2m − $6m = $1m, which are insufficient to fund the new project. However, the firm could sell off existing assets for $8m and fund the new project internally. The transaction cost of new issues is the same as before, i.e., T = 0.3 = 0.005X². The firm value is now calculated under each of the choices identified.

Choice 1: Retain current plant and forgo new investment:

$$\left[-6 + \sum_{t=1}^{10} \frac{2}{1 + 0.1)^t} \right] - [0] + 5 - 0 = \$11.289m$$

Choice 2: Retain current plant, undertake new investment, raise new money, $7m, for balance of settlement:

$$\left[-6 + \sum_{t=1}^{10} \frac{2}{(1 + 0.1)^t} \right] - \left[\left(\frac{1}{1 + 0.1} \right) \left(8 - \sum_{t=1}^{10} \frac{1.35}{(1 + 0.1)^t} \right) \right]$$
$$+ 5 - 0.545 = \$11.014m$$

Choice 3: Sell current plant, undertake new investment, raise new money, $1m, for balance of settlement:

$$8 - 6 - \left[\left(\frac{1}{1 + 0.1} \right) \left(8 - \sum_{t=1}^{10} \frac{1.35}{(1 + 0.1)^t} \right) \right]$$
$$+ 5 - 0.305 = -\$6.964m$$

Choice 4: Sell current plant, forgo new investment, and default on the settlement (pay only $5m):

---

5. The classification of events included shocks to the cost function and the demand function. We will not consider examples of these risky events here, but the analysis of post-event investment decisions is essentially similar to that of liability losses.

$$8 - 6 - [0] + 5 - 0 = \$7m$$

The optimal post-event decision is Choice 1. The firm continues existing operations because they have considerable ongoing value ($12.289m) and pays for the liability settlement from cash and first-year earnings. However, the new investment is forgone because this would require external financing at a transaction cost that exceeds the NPV.

MEASURING LOSS

For various reasons it is important to be able to measure the cost of risky events. For example, an analyst wishing to value a firm that is subject to liability exposure needs to measure the impact of that exposure on the stock value. A risk manager knowing his firm is exposed to prospective property loss might seek to reduce the possibility of such loss by improving safety, such as by installing sprinkler systems. To subject this investment to the usual capital budgeting criterion requires that the value of the loss be established.

In the above examples we looked for the decision that maximized shareholder value after some risky event. The triggering event was a fire or a lawsuit or some shock to the cost function or demand function. Each of these events has an immediate effect on value, which can be called the "direct cost." For example, a fire involves the loss of an asset that has value in use or disposal value. The immediate loss is the cost of replacing the asset, the loss of earnings from the asset, or the loss of the opportunity of selling it. A liability suit has direct costs for settling or paying a court award as well as legal costs. A currency loss can be measured as the change in dollar (domestic currency) value of income earned in a foreign currency or the change in the dollar cost of goods bought abroad. But the impact on the wealth of shareholders is not confined to these direct losses. As seen, there are a number of indirect effects, and the final impact on shareholders is the change in the value of their shares, before and after the event. This change in value rests as much on the post-event decisions as on the direct cost.

Consider the after-loss value of the firm in Equation (9.5a). This is adapted from Equation (9.5), but the direct costs have been shown as DC and the primes denote after-event values of capital assets and returns.

$$V'(F) = -DC + V_0' (K_0' ; r_0')$$

$$+ \sum_{t=1}^{n_0} \frac{-K_t' + + V_t' (K_t' ; r_t')}{(1 + k)'} + L - T' \quad (9.5a)$$

If all of the Ks and rs are the same as before the loss (i.e., $K' = K$ and $r' = r$) and if there is no additional transaction costs for external financing, $T' = T$, then the post-loss value will differ from the pre-loss value only by DC.

The value lost as a result of the risky event is the difference between Equations (9.5) and (9.5a). This is shown as Equation (9.5b), where the deltas relate to the changes between the pre-loss and post-loss values of K and r.

$$\Delta V = -DC + \Delta V_0(.) + \Delta V_t(.) - \Delta T \quad (9.5b)$$

This measure of loss assumes that value-maximizing investment decisions are made after the loss. In Equation (9.5b) the terms other than DC are the various indirect costs that were described earlier in this chapter.

REINVESTMENT AND ABANDONMENT: SOME SPECIAL ISSUES

Abandonment Options

"Abandonment" refers to the decision to discontinue some activity, be it the firm itself or some project. Abandonment of the firm can mean either that the firm is abandoned by shareholders and passed on to the creditors or that the operations are liquidated. Passing the firm to creditors is an option that is implied by limited liability. On a smaller scale, a firm can choose to discontinue a product line and will add value from doing so if the ongoing value is less than the salvage value. These choices are illustrations of "real options." As financial options are instruments that allow investors the choice of trading in some security at prearranged conditions, real options are other choices that have similar structure. The decision by a firm to avail itself of bankruptcy law is such a choice. The conditions of the law are fixed in advance, and if the firm finds itself in a situation in which equity would assume a negative value, it can exercise the option to pass the firm to creditors. Shareholders have the right to "sell" their equity to creditors at a zero price even though the residual value of the equity is negative. In short, this right is an option to "put" the equity to creditors at a zero striking (or exercise) price. This is known as the "default put option."

Projects can be abandoned too. The project's cash flows are the difference between inflows and outflows. Under usual capital budgeting rules, the net present value is the discounted value of the future net cash flows given expectations at some point in time. The NPV at inauguration of a project is based on expectations at that time. But expectations will change over the project life. Demand may turn out to be lower than initially expected, or costs higher. NPV can then be recalculated for the remainder of the project life with revised expectations. Suppose the revised NPV is negative. The firm can choose to discontinue the project based on this new information. This choice to abandon is another real option.

Like financial options, real options have value. Consider the following simple illustration. A project has a capital cost of 35 and net cash flows for each of three years of either −10 or +30, each with a 0.5 probability. These net cash flows are perfectly correlated over time. Thus, if the first cash flow turns out to be −10, the remaining two also will be −10. At a zero discount rate, the NPV is −5, as shown:

$$-35 + 0.5\{(-10) + (-10) + (-10)\} + 0.5\{30 + 30 + 30\} = -5$$

It *appears* that this is not a value-adding project and that the firm should leave it alone.

But what if the firm undertakes the project anyway but can choose to walk away from the project at zero cost at the end of the first year? Naturally the firm would wish to do so if the first-year cash flow was −10 (since remaining cash flows also will be −10 because they are perfectly correlated). If the option to abandon is exercised, then the year 2 and 3 net cash flows will be zero. If this option is anticipated at the time the project is initially selected, the initial NPV is higher. In fact, the option to walk away changes this from a negative to positive NPV, as shown:

$$-35 + 0.5\{(-10) + 0 + 0\} + 0.5\{30 + 30 + 30\} = +5$$

It does make sense to undertake the project after all. The option to abandon the project increases the NPV from −5 to +5; that is, the value of the option itself is 10. One can think of the NPV of this project as its "raw" NPV of −5 plus the value of the abandonment option of 10, to give a project value of +5. In similar fashion, as we will see in later chapters, the value of equity is the raw value of the residual cash flows plus the value of the option to put the firm to the creditors.

In any project the option to walk away has potential value, which value arises because of new information. Having a fire, a liability suit, or a currency loss is new information. These events can change the remaining value of the firm or of a project. The option to abandon means that the firm can decide whether to continue an operation or wind it up. The firm must decide whether to replace or repair productive assets that have been destroyed or damaged. Moreover, the firm faced investment in new opportunities before the loss and must reevaluate these choices after the loss. We have not taken any of these decisions for granted. Just because the firm had working assets in place before the loss does not mean that these assets should be replaced if they are destroyed. Moreover, new investment opportunities with a positive NPV before the loss may not have a positive NPV after the loss. The loss can change everything.

In this section we will address some of the issues affecting post-loss decisions to replace destroyed assets. First, assets may remain in use because the firm compares the capitalized cash flows from those assets with the disposal value of the assets. When a loss occurs, the reinvestment decisions rest on a comparison of quite different numbers: the (revised) post-loss cash flows and the replacement cost of the asset. We will then examine the criterion for reinvestment decisions and show how salvage and disposal values enter the decision. Second, we will examine issues of scale and mix in production activities. Asset losses reduce the scale of operations and normally do not affect all assets equally. Accordingly, the mix of assets is affected. Part of the post-loss investment decision is about reestablishing an optimal post-loss scale and mix of productive assets. A third issue is interruption loss. The loss of wealth to a firm is not confined to the value of the productive asset destroyed. The destruction of the asset may have temporary or permanent effects on the sales and on future demand. This change in post-loss cash flows is material to the reinvestment decision and also presents new investment decisions. Finally, we will anticipate post-loss reinvestment decision by means of a statistic that compares market values of assets in use with the replacement cost of the assets: the Q ratio. We will show how that ratio and related ratios provide a rough guide to loss financing choices.

Abandonment and Replacement

The normal capital budgeting criterion for a new investment is presented in the following form:

$$\text{NPV(initial investment)} = E^0 \left(\sum_{t=1}^{n} \frac{C_t}{(1 + k_t)^t} - K^0 \right)$$

The decision is made at time 0 using expectations of future cash flows, C_t, at the time denoted E^0. The term K^0 refers to the initial (time 0) capital cost. At some later date the assets were in place, but a loss such as a fire has occurred. Did it make sense for the firm to have those assets in productive use just before the loss (which we will denote time $L-$)? Implicitly (maybe even explicitly), the firm must have made a decision not to sell off those assets for their resale value at that time, $K^{S,L-}$ (the first superior, S, refers to the resale value and the second, $L-$, means just before loss). This implicit decision can be summarized in the following adaptation of the capital budgeting rule, which simply compares the value of the assets in use with the resale or disposal value:

$$\text{NPV(pre-loss abandonment)} = E^{L-} \left(K^{S,L-} - \sum_{t=1}^{n} \frac{C_t}{(1 + k_t)^t} \right)$$

If the value NPV(pre-loss abandonment) is positive, then value is added by selling of the asset; otherwise there is greater value in use. Notice that even if the expected cash flows were to fall dramatically between time 0 and time $L-$, it might still make sense to continue production if the resale value, $K^{S,L-}$, were sufficiently small. On the other hand, it sometimes makes sense to abandon assets, as shown in the following illustrations.

If post-loss abandonment is selected, it would appear that important changes have arisen in the economic circumstances of the project. Some factors that might have changed since the original investment was undertaken are (1) appreciation of abandonment values, (2) revision of cash-

flow estimates, (3) revision of risk costs, or (4) phasing out of an old project. We will consider each in turn.

1. Appreciation of abandonment values. *London's gentlemen's clubs were part of a middle-class English tradition in which men could take refuge from the hustle and bustle of the city. Apart from "political correctness," the demise of many of the clubs is due to the fact that their premises, acquired in a quieter age in prime central London locations, became valuable sites for alternative city development. Thus, abandonment may arise not because of any failure of a project, but simply because it consumes resources that acquire higher value in alternative use.*

2. Revision of cash flow estimates. *Sharp Dealers operates an automobile showroom. Although the showroom was established only a few years ago, it has been severely hit by a slump in automobile sales, due partly to the subsequent high levels of interest rates. In trying to reach a decision as to whether to continue with the showroom, Sharp has prepared new estimates of future cash flows that differ considerably from those prepared originally when interest forecasts were optimistic.*

3. Revision of the cost of capital. *In revising the expected values of its future cash flows. Sharp has become acutely aware of the potential volatility of future interest rates and their effect on the automobile industry. Thus, in addition to downward revision of the expected cash flows, it has increased the risk premium in its discounting rate. This has led to further downward revision (NPV) of future cash flows. Such a revision in the discounting rate will often accompany a revision in the estimated cash flows, since the expected value of cash flows, the standard deviation, and the correlation with market indices may simultaneously be affected by changing market circumstances.*

4. Phasing out of old projects. *Many old projects using older technologies may still yield positive cash flows even though the equipment used in their production may have no alternative use and therefore little disposal value. If the disposal value is zero, any positive cash flows will add to the*

> *market value of the firm. In this case, abandonment before loss*
> *would not be called for, although abandonment after loss*
> *would be appropriate.*

The last of these illustrations takes us into post-loss analysis. Let us call the time immediately after loss $L+$. The following is the post-loss investment decision criterion. Reinvestment adds value if the after-loss expectations, E^{L+}, or the post-less cash flows, $C+$, exceed the post-loss replacement cost of the destroyed asset, $K^{R,L+}$.

$$\text{NPV(reinvestment)} = E^{L+} \left(\sum_{t=1}^{n} \frac{C'_t}{(1 + k_t)^t} - K^{R,L+} \right)$$

Salvage and Disposal Values

In the adaptation of this post-loss decision rule, an interesting issue arises in measuring the replacement cost of the asset. The idea has to do with "opportunity cost." Damage to a productive asset can generate salvage, or there may be disposal costs that must be undertaken by the firm if the damaged or destroyed asset is not replaced. Salvage arises if the remnants of the damaged asset have some market value. In some cases a loss will be total, leaving no remains (or at least no accessible remains). Examples are unrecovered thefts, the sinking of a ship in a deep oceanic trench, or the failure of a satellite in high earth orbit such that recovery of the wreck is not economically feasible. In other cases there are remains. A crashed vehicle has scrap values for its metal and perhaps for a secondhand trade in mechanical or electrical parts. In some cases the salvage values will be realized independently of reinvestment. It makes sense to sell damaged machinery for scrap if it is beyond repair, whether or not we choose to replace the machinery. In other cases, reinvestment may require that salvage be utilized, as in the case of a machine that has suffered lesser damage and can be economically repaired. Here, realization of salvage value depends on the reinvestment decision. Salvage is an example of a wider set of disposal values, which may be costs or benefits, and the treatment of these values depends on whether they are "avoidable" or "unavoidable" by the making of the reinvestment decision.

If a building is damaged beyond economic repair, the owner can be burdened with further costs to level the site in order to avoid a dangerous or unsightly ruin. A facility using radioactive or other highly toxic substances cannot simply be abandoned in the event of heavy damage. Again, the firm will probably be required to render the facility safe, thereby incurring disposal costs. If a production facility is to be abandoned following a loss, then workers may have to be laid off with severance compensation. Costs of this nature may or may not affect the reinvestment decision, depending on whether these costs can or cannot be avoided by reinvestment. Severance pay can be avoided if the firm chooses to reinvest. Demolition costs for a fire-damaged building constitute a more thorny case. If the existing shell cannot be used as a basis for reconstruction, the disposal costs cannot be avoided, and consequently it should not affect the decision.[6] However, if the shell can be used for rebuilding, it may still make sense to reconstruct, even though the costs of reconstructing exceed the price of erecting a new building. If, in reconstruction, the demolition costs are avoided, these considerations imply that the reinvestment rule requires modification. A firm should invest, therefore, if:

$$\text{NPV(reinvestment)} = E^{L+}\left(\sum_{t=1}^{n} \frac{C'_t}{(1+k_t)^t} + D^A - K^{R,L+}\right)$$

where D^A refers to avoidable disposal values. D^A is negative if we refer to a salvage value that can be earned if the asset is abandoned, and is positive if we refer to a disposal cost that is avoided by choosing to reinvest. Where disposal costs are unavoidable, they have no bearing on the reinvestment decision and can be ignored.

---

6. It may be argued that the firm can avoid disposal costs by walking away from the site, leaving the damaged building in its current state. This may be precluded by building regulations or the terms of a lease on the land. If the land is owned by the firm, its market value would diminish by the value of the disposal cost, and this cost would be internalized to the firm.

EXAMPLE: POLLY U THANE, INC.

Polly U. Thane, Inc. has its laboratory damaged by fire and subsequent explosion of volatile solvents. The two-story building is severely damaged, with complete collapse of the first floor and roof. The walls are of brick construction and are intact. Laboratory equipment in the building is mostly destroyed, although some salvage can be secured from items in one section that was less severely damaged. The firm's production and financial staff, together with an outside assessor, prepare the following financial estimates to assist the decision on reinvestment:

Building damage:
Cost of reconstruction from level site	*$25,000,000*
Cost of reconstruction from remaining shell	*$28,000,000*
Demolition costs	*$2,000,000*

Site:
Value of site after leveling	*$10,000,000*

Equipment:
Replacement costs:	*$30,000,000*
Salvage (some damaged equipment could not be reused by the firm because of contamination and lack of precision)	*$ 3,000,000*

Financial Penalties if No Reinvestment:
Severance compensation of workers laid off	*$ 4,000,000*
Nondelivery penalties on existing contracts	*$ 2,000,000*

Cash Flows from Reinvestment:
NPV future cash flows	*$65,000,000*

If the firm is to reinvest, it is apparent that the site should be leveled and an entirely new building erected. The cost of this option is $27 million (including demolition costs) against $28 million for rebuilding on the existing shell. The application of the reinvestment criterion can proceed as follows:

Reinvestment cash flow		*$65,000,000*
Plus avoidable disposal costs		
Sale of site	*(10,000,000)*	
Severance compensation	*4,000,000*	
Nondelivery penalties	*2,000,000*	*−$ 4,000,000*
Minus reinvestment costs		

Reconstruction	25,000,000	
Replace equipment	30,000,000	*$55,000,000*
		$ 6,000,000

Notice the inclusion of sale of site. This is a cash flow that is avoidable. In this sense, it is a disposal benefit. The inclusion of this item ensures that the use of this resource is properly considered as an opportunity cost of reinvestment. However, notice that demolition costs are not directly included in the reinvestment decision. In the firm does not reinvest, it will bear these costs. If it does reinvest, it has to level the site before rebuilding, which is cheaper than repairing the original shell. Demolition costs arise regardless of the reinvestment decision. A further point of interest is that the salvage of equipment did not enter the decision process, the reason being that the equipment was no longer usable by the firm and would be sold for salvage whether or not the reinvestment option was chosen. The benefit was "unavoidable."

The correct decision is to reinvest. However, notice that had the site value been $20 million, the decision would have been reversed because the opportunity cost of using the site for reconstruction of the laboratory would have been just too high.

The criterion for reinvestment following loss may be summarized as follows. Once a loss has occurred, the cash flows attributable to that loss are sunk costs and, as such, are irrelevant to the subsequent decision to reinvest. The only relevant cash flows are those that can be attributed to the decision to reinvest. These flows include direct cash flows, such as the reconstruction and equipment costs in the previous example, and opportunity costs or benefits, such as the forgone sale of the land and the avoidance of severance and nondelivery penalties.

Scale and Production Interdependencies

To look into these issues, it is helpful to step back into a little theory. In making its value-maximizing production decisions, a firm brings together inputs (labor, capital, raw materials, etc.) to produce some output that is then sold. Economic theory has some simple ways of representing the profit-maximizing decision. We will examine this decision at two levels: aggregated and disaggregated. At the aggregated level, scale is important for a number of reasons. Certain features favor larger scale. For example, the firm may get lower unit prices on large-scale orders, larger-capacity machines might be faster and cheaper per unit, or there may be training economies in a larger workforce. Other features favor smaller scale. For example, managing a large workforce can become complex and difficult, the demand function might be downward sloping over the relevant output range, or the firm might bid up the prices of scarce inputs if it grows too big. The optimal choice of scale will balance these competing influences to maximize value.

The firm makes an investment decision, K, and receives some future cash flows, C_t. If the discounted cash flows exceed the capital cost, the project will add value. We will present the discounted value of the cash flows as $C(K)$; this notation reveals that the present value of the cash flows, C, depends upon (is a function of) the initial investment K. But there may in fact be many mutually exclusive investment decisions to make. The initial investment can be on various scales, and we can use the term K to refer to the number of dollars invested or the *scale* of the project. The first choice the firm has to make is one of optimal scale. To look at this decision requires a little basic math.

The NPV is the difference between the present value of the cash flows and the capital cost.

$$V = C(K) - K$$

The task is to choose the level of K, the scale, that leads to the highest NPV. Now, it is often the case that there is an optimal scale, not too small and not too large. Figure 9–2 depicts this choice. The value of $C(K)$ increases with the scale K, but at a decreasing rate. The optimal value added is where the difference between $C(K)$ and K is greatest; that is, at K^*. Suppose that the function is $C(K) = 20\,K^{0.7}$, where K is measured in \$'000. We must now select the value of K that maximizes the following:

$$\text{MAX}_K \,(20K^{0.7} - K)$$

This is done by setting the derivative to zero. Note that the derivatives of aK^b with respect to K is abK^{b-1}. Thus:

FIGURE 9-2

Optimal Scale

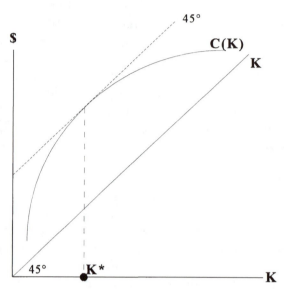

$$\frac{\partial V}{\partial K} = (20)(0.7)K^{-0.3} - 1 = 0 \quad : \quad K^{0.3} = 14 \quad : \quad K = 6{,}608 \ (\$'000)$$

Thus, the optimal scale of investment is $6,608,000.

Now suppose there is some destruction of the productive asset. If scale was set at a level that maximized profit before the loss, it will be suboptimal after the event. Consider two variations. First, the choice of scale is one of plant size, and, due to technology, plants come in discrete sizes. If the plant is damaged, it is still a plant of optimal scale; it just is not able to produce at capacity because it is impaired. The second possibility is that production choices are more continuous. For example, a car rental business can expand or contract output simply by increasing or reducing its stock of vehicles and its other, largely variable, inputs, such as clerical staff and salespersons. If one quarter of the stock of cars is destroyed in a depot fire, the other three quarters can be just about as productive as before.[7]

---

7. The distinction between variable and fixed inputs is not quite as clearcut as these examples suggest. For example, the car rental business will have some inputs that are fixed over certain ranges of output. These could include a repair facility or a computer installation to track activity.

The second production feature of importance concerns the mix of inputs. Production involves the combining of various inputs: labor, machines of different types, different raw materials, factory buildings and warehouses, and so on. Maximizing value requires not only the right choice of scale, but the right mix of inputs. Again, the problem can be addressed with a little economic theory. To maximize value, each input should be used until the point at which its *marginal cost* is equal to its *marginal revenue product.*

profit maximization ☞ marginal cost = marginal revenue product
or $MC = MRP$

To strip down the jargon, suppose I can add another unit to production, and this will increase the level of output of my final product. If the cost of that additional input (marginal costs) is lower than the additional profit I get from selling the additional output (the marginal revenue product), profit will go up. Adding more to revenues than to costs must increase profit. As long as opportunities for making such profit-enhancing decisions exist (i.e., when $MC < MRP$), profit cannot be at its maximum. If I keep on adding inputs until the point at which $MC = MRP$, profit will be maximized.

Now consider simple production processes. First, workers and machines are perfect substitutes in the sense that either can do a particular job. Many simple manufacturing processes have this quality; x people can produce output of similar quality and quantity to one machine. Figure 9–3 shows such a production process as a straight line depicting the combinations of the two inputs (in dollar costs), labor and capital, that produce a given level of output. The slope of the line shows the rate at which one can substitute capital for labor while holding production constant. A counter-case is where production requires inputs to be mixed in constant proportions. The right-angular line, denoted "complements," shows such a process. The optimal mix is shown at point A. Increasing either labor or capital from A will not change the level of output and is wasteful. For example, there is a fixed ratio of one worker per machine. An additional worker or machine will simply sit idle. Between these two extreme cases are those where there is some complementarity and some substitutability, shown as the dashed lines convex to the origin. If there is high complementarity, the most efficient input mixes will lie quite close to the

F I G U R E   9–3

Input Mixes for Given Output

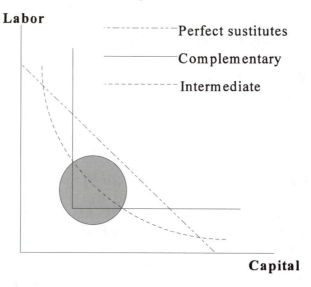

origin, as illustrated by the circle. If the input mix is outside this range, there is a begging opportunity to maintain production at lower cost by reducing the abundant factor and increasing the scarce factor.

Baker Corporation manufactures cookies. Its equipment includes dough mixers, ovens, and packing equipment. The production possibilities can be summarized by the production function, $C(K) = 16K^{0.75}$, where K is the dollar cost of the investment. Baker has determined that its optimal level of investment is $20.736, calculated as follows:

$$MAX_K \, (16K^{0.75} - K)$$

Setting the derivative to zero,

$$\frac{\partial V}{\partial K} = (16)(0.75)K^{-0.25} - 1 = 0 \quad : \quad K^{0.25} = 12 \quad : \quad K = 20{,}736$$

The optimal investment is $20,736, and at this scale the profit is $(16)(20736)^{0.75} - 20736 = \$27{,}648 - \$20{,}736 = \$6{,}912.

A fire occurs, destroying all packaging equipment. Baker can now make cookies but cannot pack them efficiently. It is true that packing can be done by hand, working current staff overtime, but this is costly and inefficient. Moreover, the slowness of hand packaging means that bottlenecks will occur, and either the other resources will be left idle or stockpiles of unpacked (and therefore unsold) cookies will build up. This inefficiency is reflected in the post-loss earnings function, which is reduced to $C(K)' = 16(K')^{0.5}$ The term K' refers to the capital in place after the loss, and the fall in the exponent reflects the inefficient mix of equipment. The replacement cost of this equipment is $3,600. The firm clearly faces an investment opportunity: to repurchase packaging equipment. What is the NPV of this reinvestment? Assume that if repurchased, the production and earnings will be restored to their pre-loss levels and therefore the firm repairs to its original earnings function, $16K^{0.75}$.

As a result of the loss, the value of the investment is reduced by $3,600 from $20,736 to $17,136. But this is not simply a scale effect; the mix of inputs has been unbalanced. The post-loss capitalized cash flows will now be $16(17136)^{0.5} = $2,094. The fall in earnings is dramatic. Two things have happened. First, the level of investment has fallen by some $3,600. Had the earnings function remained at $16K^{0.75}$, this would have produced a moderate reduction in capitalized cash flows (from $27,736 to $23,964). The much more dramatic effect occurs because the mix of equipment is thrown off balance, the effect picked by the change in the exponent.

Pre-loss capitalized earnings were $16(20736)^{0.75} = $27,648. Thus, for an investment of $3,600, the firm is able to increase the present value of cash flows by $25,554. This is an enormously attractive investment opportunity (the NPV is $25,554 − $3,600 = $21,954—some six times the capital investment).

The reason the reinvestment in the packaging equipment is so attractive is twofold. It restores the scale of the initial investment, which itself was optimal, but even more importantly, it restores the mix of equipment and thus removes the bottleneck in packaging.

Interruption Loss

The possibility that a risky event could disrupt the earnings stream of existing assets was mentioned above. We will now consider a special case that is particularly important in the case of insurable losses. If the productive assets of a firm suffer damage such that the production flow is disturbed, then the income stream also is likely to be disturbed. This may be true even if the assets are replaced. Many losses, especially large losses, cause some interruption of the trading of a firm, whether because its production flow is disturbed, because depleted inventory is insufficient to meet peak demand, or perhaps because the loss itself has an adverse effect on the demand for the firm's products. Some brief examples will help to clarify:

> *True Sincerity Greeting Cards sustains serious damages in its warehouse when a sprinkler accidentally discharges. The leak is undetected because the alarm fails, and large stocks of Christmas cards are destroyed. The loss arises in mid-November. The company's production strategy is to produce steadily over the year, building up inventory for the Christmas demand. Even though production is undisturbed, the peak demand cannot be met, resulting in severe loss of earnings.*
>
> *Fred Bear Carpets manufactures rugs that are sold by a major retailing outlet under its own trading label. A severe fire destroys the plant, and reconstruction takes some four months. Fred Bear carried no inventory, since all output was delivered immediately to its customer. The result is a severe interruption in trading, with substantial loss of earnings.*
>
> *A class action liability suit is brought against Michael Finn Pharmaceuticals after it transpires that the tranquilizers it manufacturers have produced serious side effects in a number of users, resulting in a state of coma. Even though the case has not been disposed of in the courts, the resulting alarm causes a slump in sales of the company's other products.*

In each of these examples the loss of earnings is independent of any decision to reinvest. True Sincerity will presumably wish to return to its inventory policy for future years, but immediate replacement of the destroyed cards is impossible. Similarly, Fred Bear will reconstruct its plant, but this will take considerable time. With Michael Finn, reinvestment is not really the issue, since production capacity has not been destroyed. The interruption may turn out to be temporary. Consumers may forget Finn's lawsuit, and Fred Bear's outlet may regain its former customers when production is reestablished. However, some permanent shift in trading can also result. When a firm is out of business for some time, competitors may steal into the market and capture a market share that may be extremely difficult to win back when production resumes. For example, Fred Bear's customer, desperate for supplies of carpets, may sign a long-term supply agreement with a competing supplier.

Strategies exist for dealing with business interruption loss. If the loss arises from damage to productive assets, then a prospective strategy is to carry inventory. If production is interrupted, customers can be supplied from inventory until production resumes. The greater the inventory, the longer the production stoppage that can be tolerated without supplies to customers being disturbed. Inventory can also play a role on the input side. Business can be interrupted through failure to secure inputs (for example, a major supplier has a fire that disturbs its production). Stockpiles of inputs will guard against this type of interruption. But the main concern in this chapter is with post-loss decisions. We will now focus on a particular form of post-loss investment decision, marketing to recapture lost business.

We will revisit Fred Bear Carpets and add some more detail. As a result of its fire, Fred Bear loses four months' sales. This is bad enough, but in addition its sole customer has established a new relationship (cemented with a one-year supply contract) with a rival firm and will now only take half the pre-loss level of production from Fred Bear. What will happen at the end of this year is up for grabs. The pre-loss annual expected cash flows for Fred Bear were 100, growing at 2% per year. The direct cost of rebuilding the plant is 600, and the following post-loss cash flows projections are prepared for the management:

Pessimistic: *No contract with major customer next year; some new business secured (probability 0.25):*

Current year	30
Next year	35
Subsequent growth	0.01
Probability	0.25

Most likely: *Limited contract with major customer is written next year; some new business secured (probability 0.5):*

Current year	30
Next year	50 + 35 = 85
Subsequent growth	0.015
Probability	0.5

Optimistic: *Full contract with major customer takes total capacity (probability 0.25):*

Current year	30
Next year	102
Subsequent growth	0.02
Probability	0.25

The post-loss cash flows have a discounted expected present value of 860, calculated as follows:

$$\frac{1}{1 + 0.1}\left[0.25\left(30 + \frac{35}{0.1 - 0.01}\right) + 0.5\left(30 + \frac{85}{0.1 - 0.015}\right)\right.$$
$$\left. + 0.25\left(30 + \frac{102}{0.1 - 0.02}\right)\right] = 860$$

The management is now presented with a marketing strategy that will cost 100 but will change the post-loss cash flows projections in two ways: it will increase business from new sources from 35 to 70, and it will increase the probability of a favorable contract with its traditional customer. The most optimistic outcome of this marketing strategy is that new business will be secured and it will restore its original contract. But the firm will not have the production capacity to meet all this demand. The following cash flows projections are based on the assumption that no new capacity is added.[8]

Pessimistic: *No contract with major customer; some new business secured (probability 0.15):*

Current year	30
Next year	70
Subsequent growth	0.01
Probability	0.15

If limited contract with major customer is written next year, some new business secured (probability 0.35):

Current year	30
Subsequent growth	0.015
Probability	0.35

---

8. You can develop the example as you see fit showing an investment in new capacity. You may also draw the conclusion that the firm might have considered developing new markets before the fire. But I have not considered these here.

Optimistic: *Full contract with major customer takes total capacity (probability 0.5):*

Current year   *30*

The post-loss cash flows now have a discounted expected present value of 1095, calculated as follows:

$$\frac{1}{1+0.1}\left[0.15\left(30+\frac{70}{0.1-0.01}\right)+0.35\left(30+\frac{102}{0.1-0.015}\right)\right.$$
$$\left.+0.5\left(30+\frac{102}{0.1-0.02}\right)\right]=1095$$

The cost of the marketing plan is 100. Because value is increased from 860 to 1095, the investment clearly adds value.

q Ratios and Related Numbers

The following chapters will be concerned with loss financing—paying for the costs of post-loss investments. Whether there is need for post-loss financing depends on whether the firm anticipates it will make positive post-loss investment decisions. The final topic here will provide a bridge between post-loss investment and financing decisions.

The q ratio was derived by Nobel Laureate James Tobin in 1969 and is otherwise known as "Tobin's q." This is the ratio of the market value of a firm over the replacement cost of its assets. The q ratio has various uses. It can be used as a measure of the management's stewardship of a firm's resources and therefore as a management evaluation tool; as a measure of the efficiency of alternative uses of capital (say in different industries); to identify targets for takeover. Notice also the close relationship to the net present value formula, which is the difference between the cost of an asset and the value of cash flows generated from its use. The differences between the two concepts are that Tobin's q is a firm-level relationship, whereas NPV can apply to individual investment projects; that q is a ratio of properties of assets in current use, whereas NPV is a relationship about assets in prospective use; and that q uses market values, whereas NPV embodies estimates of discounted expected future cash flows. The final difference is not so profound if one accepts that the market value of the firm reflects investor's capitalized expectations of future cash flows.

If we work off the similarities between NPV and q, a risk management application of q becomes apparent. Suppose that a firm lost all its assets in a fire or explosion. Would value be created by replacing all those assets and resuming the business as before? If we assume that resumption as before is possible, then Tobin's q gives a rough answer. For reinvestment, one would wish to compare the capitalized value of the income stream (the numerator in the q) with the replacement cost of the assets (the denominator in q). If the ratio is greater than unity, the NPV is positive and reinvestment is the optimal decision for the firm's owners. In this sense, q is a sort of prospective NPV rule for reinvestment should the firm's assets be destroyed. If the ratio exceeds unity, reinvestment will be warranted for some future calamity.

At this point I want to have my cake and eat it. I want to be able to point out some broad uses of q but also to draw attention to its limitations. Let me start with the limitations and then show that even with these, q still can be a useful risk management tool.

The limitations of q flow from the previous analysis of this chapter. Reinvestment decisions are based on the post-loss estimates of cash flows that might be affected by the loss event; q is based on current estimates. Post-loss reinvestment decisions usually address not a total loss of all the firm's assets, but some particular asset. The q is a rough average of the (imputed) market to replacement values of the firm's various assets, with allowance for synergies. Thus, the overall ratio may not be appropriate for any one destroyed asset. A further problem is that management may have an information advantage over outside investors in estimating the expected post-loss cash flows from a particular asset replacement. Finally, the reinvestment decision should include all cash flows that are affected by the decision, including salvage and disposal costs. It is not clear whether these would be included in the q denominator.

Subject to these comments, q does provide a rough guide to structuring a risk management strategy. For some firms q may be less than 1. This value should lead the firm's management to question whether it will ever need post-loss financing for destroyed assets, since it is unlikely to wish to replace many assets should they be destroyed. Conversely, where q is very high, the assets are in efficient use and their replacement is likely to be warranted should they be destroyed. Thus, q provides a convenient starting point in formulating a risk management strategy.

This line of thought can be pushed a little further. The q ratio is well known and, hopefully, understood. It is not designed for risk management purposes, but, as mentioned, it can provide some useful input into formulation of risk management strategy. But it is useful to think of divisional or asset q's that could be formulate specifically for risk management strategy. The idea would be to anticipate the likely reinvest choices that would be made were various assets destroyed and to use these anticipated choices to derive financing or hedging strategies. These micro-q's clearly would not use market value but would have imputed economic values. Moreover, the replacement costs could be explicitly designed to cover the full opportunity costs of anticipated reinvestments. With these thoughts, our attention is now focused on loss financing strategy, and we will move to this topic in the following chapters.

CONCLUSION

This chapter has been concerned with two main issues. The first is the identification and measurement of the changes in firm value following some risky event. To pursue this, events were classified into loss of productive assets, wealth transfers, and shocks to cost and demand. This classification was derived specifically because it focuses on the wealth consequences of the event and therefore helps us to measure the loss of value. Loss of productive assets leads to loss of production and interruption of trading; events such as liability suits transfer wealth to outsiders and can contain signals about future demand; cost and demand shocks have direct consequences for price, quantity, design, and production choices and therefore for future project.

The second issue examined was the optimal investment choices the firm faced after the loss event. While many events can lead to loss of value, this loss can be minimized by optimal post-loss investment choices. These choices were of two types. The first arose from destruction or damage to productive assets in use;

should those assets be replaced? This reinvestment decision had several dimensions: was there interruption loss, were there salvage and disposal values at issue, how was reinvestment conditioned by issues of production scale and mix? Nevertheless, the decision to reinvest ultimately rested on a positive NPV, and this could not be taken for granted simply because the assets were in use prior to loss. The second type of decision related to new investments, some of which might have been planned before the loss. The main issue here was that the loss event might have affected the demand and cost estimates and impaired the firm's ability to fund new investments.

Our attention to post-loss investment anticipates a potential need for financing. Moreover, the post-loss reinvestment decision may not be independent of the availability, cost, and source of funding; indeed, the crowding out hypothesis was based on such a relationship. In the following chapters we will examine post-loss investment decisions under different financing assumptions. After post-loss financing, we will consider schemes that secure contingent financing in anticipation of possible risky events. From there we will move to hedging strategies that simultaneously offer financing for post-loss investment and smooth out intertemporal value changes.

REFERENCES

Berger, Philip G., Eli Ofek, and Itzhak Swary. 1996. "Investor Valuation of the Abandonment Option." *Journal of Financial Economics* 42:257–87.

Brealey, R. A., and S. C. Myers. 1996. *Principles of Corporate Finance*, 5th ed. New York: McGraw-Hill.

Bonini, C. 1977. "Capital Investment under Uncertainty with Abandonment Options." *Journal of Financial and Quantitative Analysis* 12:39–65.

Gordon, M. J., and E. Shapiro. 1956. "Capital Equipment Analysis: The Required Rate of Profit." *Management Science* 3:102–10.

Kesinger, J. W. 1980. "Project Abandonment as a Put Option: Dealing with the Capital Investment Decision and Operating Risk Using Option Pricing Theory." Working Paper, Edwin L. Cox School of Business, Southern Methodist University, Dallas.

Leibowitz, M. L., and S. Kogelman. 1990. "Inside the P/E Ratio: The Franchise Factor." *Financial Analysts Journal* 46:17–35.

Miller, M. H., and F. Modigliani. 1961. "Dividend Policy, Growth and the Valuation of Shares." *Journal of Business* 34:411–33.

Myers, S. C., and S. Majd. 1990. "Abandonment Value and Project Life." *Advances in Futures and Options Research* 4:1–21.

Robichek, A. and J. Van Horne. 1967. "Abandonment Value and Capital Budgeting." *Journal of Finance* 22:577–90.

Williams, J. B. 1938. *The Theory of Investment Value*. Cambridge, Mass.: Harvard University Press.

CHAPTER 10

Post-loss Financing: Fundability and Dysfunctional Investment

This chapter examines the implications of recapitalizing the firm after it suffers a sudden risky event such as a fire, currency loss, or liability suit. This analysis follows quite naturally from that in Chapter 9. If a firm suffers a destruction of its productive resources, it faces a series of investment decisions. Should the firm reinvest in those productive assets, and should it undertake new investment activity? Can these investments add value, and can they be financed? If the investments add value, how should the firm raise money?

We will examine three generic sources of financing in the following chapters. In reverse order, we will consider hedging, contingent financing, and post-loss financing. Hedging can be considered a source of financing for post-loss investment opportunities. Because the cost of the risky event is borne by a counterparty, the firm retains its internal funds and its access to external funds so that it can fund post-loss investment as before. Hedging has other dimensions besides financing the post-loss investments, as we saw in Chapter 8; it addresses the asset substitution and underinvestment problems, reduces the probability of insolvency, permits more effective managerial compensation contracts, and may help reduce tax liabilities when tax functions are convex. But it also finances post-loss investments and thereby helps to resolve the crowding out problem.

The second generic approach to financing post-loss investment opportunities is to anticipate the potential events and set up a contingent financing source. The simplest way to do this is a line of credit. If financing is needed for any purpose, the line can be drawn upon. Anticipation has two advantages. First, the funds are available immediately and delays are avoided. Second, anticipating the possible need allows the terms of the funding can be fixed in advance. For example, the interest rate for a line of credit can be fixed in advance so that if a loss occurs, the firm is not subject to the risk of fluctuations in the cost of capital; in short, the firm is hedging risk in the future cost of capital. Other, more complex, forms of contingent financing also will be considered, such as put options issued by a firm on its own stock and debt that converts to equity when the firm falls on hard times.

The third generic approach to financing post-loss investment opportunities is to set up the financing after the event. This could involve withholding of dividends—if indeed earnings are still large enough after the loss—or raising new debt or equity after the loss. These activities will be referred to as post-loss financing. With post-loss financing, the amount that can be raised and the terms on which it is raised depend on the value and financial structure of the firm after the loss and upon the capital market conditions that prevail after the loss. The loss itself can change the value of investment projects in the pipeline, and can adversely affect the terms under which they can be financed. For example, losses that interfere with the continuity of output for a firm can lead to a restructuring of the product market in which it operates as we saw with interruption losses earlier. Liability suits can depress future product demand. Activities that might have added value before the event might not have it afterwards. Moreover, these and other sudden costly events will tend to absorb the firms liquid resources and increase its leverage. Thus, the terms under which the firm will seek financing for its investments can change as a result of the loss. These are issues we will examine in this chapter.

Before proceeding, let us first recognize that the issue we are addressing is not simply a risk management problem. We are discussing the capital structure the firm chooses after a loss. This is not a problem to be considered completely from scratch; indeed, it is one of the central issues in corporate finance. Thus, we will begin this chapter by reviewing the main themes in the capital structure puzzle. We will then consider the choice of financing in the post-loss environment.

A SKETCH OF THE CAPITAL STRUCTURE PROBLEM

Any analysis of corporate capital structure usually starts with the Modigliani–Miller hypothesis. This hypothesis was derived by Franco Modigliani and Merton Miller in 1958, and both authors were awarded Nobel Prizes on separate occasions partly on the basis of this model. What they show is that capital structure is irrelevant under certain strong conditions: when there are no personal or corporate taxes, all investors are symmetrically informed, there are no transaction costs, and the investment policy of the firm is already determined. With these assumptions, they showed that there is no advantage for a firm to manipulate its debt-to-equity ratio, since the effect of any particular leverage choice on investors can be replicated by the investors themselves in the management of their personal portfolios.

The importance of the Modigliani–Miller model is not that the prediction of capital structure irrelevance should be taken too seriously, but that their analysis changes our way of thinking about capital structure. Consider their prediction: capital structure is irrelevant under certain restrictive assumptions. Turn this statement on its head, and you have a set of reasons why capital structure might be important. If capital structure matters, it is because of taxes, information costs, transaction costs, or interdependence between the firms financing and investment policies. Following M&M, as the model is widely known, investigation of optimal capital structure has focused on the relaxation of these assumptions. Now the prevailing view is that the optimal capital structure of a firm is a compromise between the costs and benefits of the various sources of finance. And of course these costs and benefits include agency costs, costs of financial distress, tax effects, and costs of information asymmetry.

Corporate and Personal Taxes

Consider corporate taxes first. Interest income is a deductible expense, but dividends are not. This creates an advantage for debt financing; the cost of the firm's debt is partly paid for by the federal government. This leads to a simple relationship between the value of a firm without debt and one with debt. Debt will increase the value of the firm by the present value of the tax shield:

value of levered firm = value of all-equity firm
+ PV (tax shield)

To calculate the present value of the tax shield, consider the simplest example of a perpetual debt. The interest rate is k_E, and therefore annual interest is $k_E D$ and the tax benefit from deduction of interest is $t_c k_E D$, where t_c is the corporate tax rate. To establish the present value, we can divide the tax shield by the cost of debt, since this is an infinite series:

$$PV \text{ (tax shield)} = \frac{t_c k_E D}{k_D} = t_c D$$

Were the debt of shorter duration, the present value of the tax shield would be correspondingly smaller.

Deductibility of interest thereby increases the value of disbursements that can be made to the company's security holders. The size of the pie has been increased by using debt. But are investors necessarily better off? This depends on personal tax rates. The slices of the bigger pie still have to be taxed at the personal rate. It should be immediately apparent that if personal taxes on equity income are sufficiently smaller than on debt, investors could be better off without corporate borrowing. The personal rate on equity income is complicated by the fact that this income can be in the form of capital gains or dividend income. If all equity income were in the form of dividends, investors would pay the same tax rate on interest and dividends and corporate borrowing would be attractive. But equity income can be in the form of capital gains, which are taxed at a different rate from other income and can be deferred until realized. Call the personal tax rate on ordinary income t_p and the effective rate on equity income (reflecting its average composition between dividends and capital gains and the deferring of capital gains) t_E. Now the tax advantage of debt is:

$$\text{tax advantage of debt} = \frac{1 - t_p}{(1 - t_E)(1 - t_c)}$$

In the special case where $1 - t_p = (1 - t_E)(1 - t_c)$, the tax advantage of corporate deductibility of interest is exactly offset by the more favorable personal taxation of equity income. In this special case, capital structure is irrelevant.

But the story is more subtle. One interesting twist was added by Merton Miller in his well-known Debt and Taxes paper. Suppose that the personal and corporate taxes rates configure to give an advantage to corporate debt and that, as is the case, personal rates differ. As firms emphasize bonds, the cost of debt will increase and some investors with lower personal rates will switch. This will continue until the marginal investor is left with equivalent tax treatment, that is, when $1 - t_p = (1 - t_E)(1 - t_c)$. In this scenario firms will differ in their capital structures and each firm will have shareholders in different tax brackets. The model predicts only the aggregate debt to equity mix in the economy, and the optimal capital structure for any firm.

Another twist arises from tax shields. So far the corporate tax rate has been treated as a constant rate on all earnings. Firms do in fact have other tax shields from depreciation, carrybacks, and some employee benefit plans. Thus, firms will differ in their ability to use fully their interest deduction. Those with low expected income and large shields will not get the full advantage of the interest deduction, and the reverse is true for firms with low shields and high expected earnings. This and the prior issues have led many financial economists to conclude that for many firms there may be small tax advantage to debt. However, this is not uniform for all firms. Those with greater tax shields and lower income might be better off without debt. But for those firms that are able to get full benefit from tax shields, there is probably a moderate tax advantage to debt financing.

Cost of Financial Distress

This part of the capital structure puzzle has already been dealt with though under a slightly different guise, in Chapter 7. There we were concerned with the effect of risk on firm value. For given leverage, the more risky the firm's earnings, the more probable that it will become bankrupt and therefore the higher the expected value of bankruptcy costs. This argument is the mirror image of the usual financial distress argument in favor of equity financing. If the risk of the cash flows is fixed, then the higher leverage, the higher the probability of bankruptcy, and the higher the expected value of bankruptcy costs. Similarly, when considering the indirect costs of bankruptcy, shareholders may fail to undertake positive NPV projects that simply shore up the value of debt should the firm go bankrupt, and may undertake abnormally risky projects because the downside risk is largely transferred to creditors. In the language used earlier, there is "underinvestment" and "asset substitution," and risk can lead to dysfunctional investments. This is, of course, a capital structure issue, as was recognized at the time. Taking the various financial distress costs together, we can now extend the relationship between the values of the levered and unlevered firms:

value of levered firm = value of all-equity firm
$$+PV \text{ (tax shield)}$$
$$-PV \text{ (cost of financial distress)}$$

RECAPTURING VALUE THROUGH POST-LOSS REINVESTMENT

Suppose a firm has a loss of value from some risky event that is not hedged and has no contingent financing available. To undertake post-loss investments it must use internal funds available after loss or raise new money. Definitionally, it must use post-loss financing. Consider these questions. Does the use of post-loss financing to fund reconstruction of the destroyed assets, or to fund new investment, add value for existing shareholders? The question can be asked with a different emphasis. Do the terms on which new money is raised permit value to be created for existing shareholders? More pointedly, if a firm has just suffered a major setback, say a major liability suit, will investors have the confidence to buy newly issued securities and can the firm raise enough money for its investment needs?

In Chapter 9 a formula was presented to measure the value of existing equity before and after the firm undertakes post-loss investment activity. That formula did not consider that the firm had any existing debt. A streamlined version of that formula, which accounts for existing debt, is as follows:

$$\text{pre-loss} = V(E) = V_0 + L - K_t + V_t - D - T \quad (10.1)$$

This says that the value of equity before a loss is the sum of the present value of earnings from existing operations, V_o, and liquid assets, L, plus the value added from new investment, $-K_t + V_t$ (the first term here, K_t, is the present value of capital investments, and the second term, V_t, is the present value of earnings generated by these investments), minus the value of existing debt, D, and the transaction costs of any new issues required to fund new investments, T.

In deriving this formula, we took advantage of a simplifying assumption. The new investments will require financing. Suppose a new issue of debt or equity is made and the firm raises some amount S. New investors want some return, which can be interest payments or the expectation of dividends, depending on whether debt or equity is raised. Let us call the present value of expected dividends or interest payments R. The cost of the new investment is K_t. Now Equation (10.1) can be written as follows:

$$V(E) = V_0 + L + (S - R - K_t) + V_t - D - T \quad (10.1a)$$

However, this could be simplified in the following way. Since transaction costs of new issues, T, have been separated out, the term R represents a set of future payments expressed as the value raised, S, times the expected rate of return r. But if these new issues are competitively priced, the present value of these returns will be calculated using the discount rate r. Thus, $R = rS/r = S$. Therefore, R and S cancel out, leaving the original Equation (10.1).

Why this detour? The point is that if existing shareholders can attract capital in a competitive capital market, they need only offer a competitive rate of return on capital raised. They need not share any value added with new investors. Consequently, all NPV from new investments, less any transaction costs of the new issues, is captured by existing shareholders. I wish to apply the same principle now to post-loss financing. After a loss, the capital market is still competitive, and if the firm raises new capital, it will do so at a competitive cost of capital; that is, will offer investors an expected return that reflects the relevant risk characteristics. Will investors be willing to pay enough for these new security issues after a loss to fund the reconstruction of old assets, and possibly new investments?

First, look at the value of the original equity after a loss.

$$V'(E) = -C + V_0' + L - K_t' + V_t' - D - T' \qquad (10.2)$$

where the primes denote post-loss values and C is the direct cost of the risky event (capital cost of financing the reconstruction of existing assets, cost of settling the liability suit, credit loss, etc). Now rewrite Equation (10.2) showing the amount new investors pay for a post-loss security issue as ΔS. The present value of expected payments to shareholders is $r\Delta S/r$, if the new issue is competitively priced. Thus, the bracket in the following Equation (10.2a) should simplify to $-C$, and Equation (10.2a) will be identical to the previous Equation (10.2).

$$V'(E) = (\Delta S - r\Delta S/r - C) + V_0' + L - K_t'$$
$$+ V_t' - D - T' \qquad (10.2a)$$

IS POST-LOSS INVESTMENT FUNDABLE?

Fundability with Post-loss Equity Financing

How much would the new investors be willing to pay for new securities issued after a loss? Is the amount they are willing to pay, ΔS, sufficient to pay for the capital investment of C? For the moment, we will assume that outside investors have the same information about the firm's future earnings as insiders. Existing shareholders hold a total of m shares of common stock. Now consider a new equity issue in which n shares of stock are sold to new investors. The total number of shares is now $m + n$ and new shareholders receive a proportion $n/(n + m)$ of the total value of equity, which we will call E^T. Clearly, $E^T = V_o' + L - K_t' + V_t' - D - T'$, which is the post-loss value for the firm minus debt, $V' - D$. Thus, the aggregate sum paid in a competitive market for the new shares if $nE^T/(m + n)$. This will be sufficient to raise enough money to pay for the required post-loss capital needs, C, if:

$$\frac{n}{m + n} E^T \geq C \quad \text{which requires} \quad n \geq \frac{mC}{E^T - C}$$

We can make sense of this requirement only if E^T is greater than

C. If E^T were exactly equal to C, then mathematically n would have to be infinite to satisfy the inequality. The firm would have to issue an infinite number of shares so that all of the value E^T accrued to the new shareholders and old shares would be worthless. Notice also that if $E^T = C$, there is no value added from continuing to run the firm; the firm is right on the cusp of insolvency. If $E^T > C$, things are rather more comfortable. There is some (finite) number of shares the firm can issue to fund the post-loss investment, and any value created by reinvestment will accrue to old shareholders if the new issues are competitively priced. The greater is the value added (the greater is $E^T - C$) the smaller is the number of new shares required to finance the new investment C and the smaller the equity dilution.

The following general principle emerges. *As long as the cost of post-loss investment is less than the post-reinvestment value of total equity, it is always possible to finance the investment from a new equity issue* (subject to the assumption that outside investors are well informed about the firm's future earnings). This is an important principle because it establishes a potentially important role for post-loss financing. Notice that this principle is not equivalent to asserting that the post-loss investment will be value maximizing. To see this, consider a case where the only post-loss investment decision is whether to reconstruct existing assets; thus, K_t, L, V_t, and D are all zero. The reinvestment criterion is now that $(-C + (V_0^R - V_0^{NR}) - T') > 0$. The terms V_0^R and V_0^{NR} refer to the post-loss value of existing assets with and without reinvestment. The necessary condition for investors to fund the reinvestment (with the same assumptions about new investments) at a cost of C is weaker; that is, that $(-C + V_0' - T') > 0$. Because V_0^R is the same as V_0', the reinvestment criterion must be satisfied if the fundability condition is satisfied; but the reverse is not true. This should be pretty obvious. One can imagine a Fortune 500 company having a loss of a few thousand dollars to an asset that is redundant (a retired computer that is two generations old). The effect of this loss on its ability to raise new money is likely to be imperceptible. However, the fact that it can pay for a new computer does not imply that it should actually buy one.

The fundability of post-loss investment is thus a one-way hurdle. If post-loss investment is fundable, it does not follow that it should be undertaken. If it is not fundable, then clearly the firm should not even think of reinvesting.[1]

Chairs and Wares makes furniture and expects an earnings stream of 1000 (after deduction of costs of renewing plant) indefinitely from its current operations. The firm has an opportunity to reinvest both this year's earnings and next year's earnings in some product improvement and market development. If it does this, it expects the earnings stream to grow (after year 2) at a compound rate of 2%. The firm also has cash of 1000 and, even if some fluctuation in earnings occurs over the next two years, can still be certain of paying for the new investment from internal funds. The existing plant and other productive assets have a replacement cost of 8000 with a salvage value of 5000. The firm has existing debt of 5000; the cost of debt is 0.05. The firm's overall cost of capital (the weighted average cost of capital, WACC) is 0.1. The owners hold 1000 shares of stock.

First let us value the shareholder's equity with and without its undertaking the investment opportunity

Without New Investment

$$E = \frac{e}{k - g} - D + L = \frac{1000}{0.1 - 0} - 5000 + 1000 = 6000$$

where:

$e = $ *cash flow from current operations*
$g = $ *growth of this cash flow*
$k = $ *cost of capital*

---

1. An objection often raised to post-loss financing in insurance circles is that after-loss can be the worst time to go to the market for new money because the firm will likely be in poor financial condition; thus, there is a chance that the firm will be unable to raise the money it needs for reconstruction or planned new investments. This argument is then usually evoked to favor pre-loss financing such as insurance. Notice that there is a problem with this reasoning. If post-loss funding is unlikely to be feasible, it indicates that the reinvestment will probably not add value. In that case there is little point in setting up pre-loss funding such as insurance.

With New Investment

$$E = \frac{0}{(1 + 0.1)} + \frac{0}{(1 + 0.1)^2} + \left(\frac{1}{(1 + 0.1)^2}\right)\left(\frac{1000}{0.1 - 0.02}\right)$$
$$- 5000 + 1000 = 633$$

Thus, the new investment adds value (6331 beats 6000) and should be undertaken.

Suppose the existing plant suffers an explosion and is uninsured. The plant can still partly operate, and earnings are reduced to 300, but this figure is not expected to grow. However, an investment of 3000 will fully restore the plant, and earnings will return to the pre-loss level of 1000. The firm must raise new money for this reconstruction, but still plans to pay for the new investment in two years from retained earnings. Does the reinvestment add value to equity? What opportunities exist for raising new money by an equity issue after the loss? The transaction cost of a new issue is 200.

No Reinvestment

If we bear in mind that the firm will not have sufficient funds to undertake the new investments, the value is as follows:

$$V'(E) = \frac{300}{0.1 - 0} - 5000 + 1000 = \text{ZERO (limited liability)}$$

Notice that the value of the equation should be −1000. However, because of limited liability, the equity is worthless.

With Reinvestment

The firm can either raise 3000 to pay for the reinvestment and pay the transaction cost of 200 from cash (if there is any) or raise a total amount of 3200 from which to cover both the transaction cost and the cost of the reconstruction. In the final analysis, the results should be the same. I will take the latter route, and the transaction costs, T, are included in the capital reconstruction cost, C.

$$V'(E) = -3200 + \left(\frac{1}{(1 + 0.1)^2}\right)\left(\frac{1000}{0.1 - 0.2}\right)$$

$$- 5000 + 1000 = 3131$$

Thus, reinvestment is necessary for survival and raises the value of the original owners' equity from zero to 3131.

Look now at the new equity. How many new shares must be issued to fund the reconstruction? The firm will need to issue enough shares to raise the required amount of 3200 (3000 for reconstruction and 200 to cover transaction costs). The total value of all equity is 6331 (the firm raises 3200 in new equity and existing shares are worth a total of 3131). I will assert the answer here and justify it presently. The firm needs to issue 1022 new shares. This ensures that the total equity of 6331 is divided into a total of 2022 shares, each worth 3.131.

Let us cross check that the new shares are indeed worth what new investors paid for them. New shareholders buy 1022 shares at 3.131 each. In return, each shareholder holds 1/1022 of the total equity, or 6331, which works out fine at 3.131. Thus, the reinvestment is fundable and adds value to existing shareholders.

In the Chairs and Wares example the number of new shares to be issued was simply asserted and we then checked to see whether issuing this number of shares would fund the new investment. We can derive a formula to see where this number came from. The firm needs to issue a number of shares such that the price per share after issue, p, times the number of shares issued, n, is sufficient to finance the reinvestment of C. Thus, $C = pn$. We also know that the price, p, must equal the total value of equity after reinvestment, E^T, divided by the total number of shares, $m + n$ (m is the number of old shares). Thus, $p = E^T/(m + n)$. So, using basic algebra:

$$C = pn; \quad p = \frac{E^T}{m + n}; \quad \text{so}$$

$$C = \left(\frac{E^T}{m + n}\right)n; \quad \text{solving gives} \quad n = \frac{cm}{E^T - C}$$

In examining whether investors were willing to subscribe to

post-loss equity issues, we looked only at raising an amount C (plus transaction costs T). The firm also needs to finance any new investment activities available after the loss. The reasoning to resolve this should be fairly clear by now. If, in addition to financing the direct loss C, the firm needs further money to pay for new investments, and these new investments add value, then clearly it is feasible to finance them. The earnings stream increases by more than the expected dividend payments necessary to entice investors to buy the new equity.

Fundability with Post-loss Debt Financing

To see whether investors in a new debt issue would be willing to pay a sufficient amount for the firm's debt to pay for the direct cost, C, we will simplify the default assumption. The firm may become insolvent directly as a result of the risky event (i.e., the post-loss value of equity, even with reinvestment, is negative). But even if the post-loss equity value is positive, *future* risk could lead to insolvency and default on debt. For the time being we will simplify the analysis by considering only insolvency stemming immediately from the risky event. Another way of stating this is that after the loss, all future cash flows will be assumed to be certain. This is quite unrealistic, but it will get us started and then future risk will be introduced.

The firm needs an amount of C to pay for the direct costs. If debt is raised, the amount subscribed is ΔS, but the face value of the debt is C. The amount ΔS will be equal to C if the value of the firm, after payment for any senior debt, exceeds C. In Equations (10.1) and (10.2) the firm did have preexisting debt of D, so we will call the value of the firm after loss $V'(F) = V_0' + L - K_t' + V_t' - T'$. Furthermore, this value is risk-free because we have ignored future risk. If the existing debt is senior to any post-loss issue, the condition for ΔS to equal C is that $V'(F) - D - C > 0$. But notice that when discussing post-loss debt we had defined $E^T = V_0' + L - K_t' + V_t' - D - T'$. So clearly, $V = E^T + D$. Thus, the fundability condition that $V'(F) - D - C$ is positive is the same as $E^T - C$ is positive. This is exactly the same fundability condition we derived for post-loss equity financing. Whether debt or equity is used, investors will be wiling to subscribe a sufficient amount to fund the new investment if the post-loss value of the firm, minus any preexisting debt, exceeds the direct cost, C.

But this analysis of post-loss debt financing rests on the firm having no future risk after suffering the loss. This is simply unrealistic. If the firm continues its operations, it will be subject to the usual array of risks. Thus, even if the *expected value* of $V'(F) - D - C$ is positive (i.e., if $E(V'(F)) - C > D$), there is no guarantee that the firm will remain solvent into the future. We must consider future risk. To do this, we will return to the previous example of Chairs and Wares, but we will now consider paying for the reconstruction of the destroyed assets by borrowing.

Return to Chairs and Wares, only now consider post-loss debt financing. The post-loss values with reinvestment were calculated as follows:

No Reinvestment

$$V'(F) = \frac{300}{0.1 - 0} - 5000 + 1000 = \text{ZERO (limited liability)}$$

With Reinvestment

The firm borrows 3200 and undertakes the reconstruction. Also recall that the firm plows back the subsequent two years' earnings in growth-enhancing investment.

$$V'(F) = -3200 + \left(\frac{1}{(1 + 0.1)^2}\right)\left(\frac{1000}{0.1 - 0.02}\right) - 5000 + 1000$$
$$= -3200 + 10{,}331 - 5000 + 1000 = 3131$$

No Future Risk

It would seem that because the value of equity is positive after reinvestment, the firm has sufficient value to pay off all debt (senior debt of 5000 and junior debt of 3200) and still have a residual value of 3131. Suppose that the story was as follows. The firm takes the reinvestment and is then is immediately obligated to sell off the firm and discharge all claims to existing creditors. The firm would receive the full firm value, 11,331 (the earnings stream is worth 10,331 and there is cash of 1000), in a competitive market, and pay 5000 to senior creditors and 3200 to junior creditors, leaving 3131 to shareholders. Then investors would be willing to pay at par for debt with a face value of 3200. But now suppose there is no such obligation to sell the firm in this way. Can junior bondholders always be sure that they will paid in full in the future? If the earnings stream e of 1000, growing at 2%, were entirely risk-free, there would be no problem and the analysis of this paragraph would still apply; the junior debt would still be worth its face of 3200.

Since there is no future risk, the simple fundability condition for news investors to subscribe fully to new debt is fulfilled. The condition was $V'(F) - D - C > 0$, where $V'(F)$ is post-loss firm value after reinvestment, D is preexisting debt, and C is the capital cost. The condition fills out as $11,331 - 5000 - 3200 > 0$.

Future Risk

Suppose the earnings stream e is now risky. In this example the income stream has a capitalized value of 12,500 at the beginning of year 3, which discounts not the present value of 10,331. Suppose that the earnings stream looked like this:

Year 1	Year 2	Year 3	Year 4	Years 5, 6, 7, etc.
0	0	520 $p = 0.5$	530.4 $p = 0.5$	541 $p = 0.5$
all reinvested	all reinvested	1480 $p = 0.5$	1509.6 $p = 0.5$	1539.8 $p = 0.5$

The firm fully reinvests all earnings in the first two years. At year 3 the earnings settle either at 520 growing at 2% or at 1480 growing at 2%. The p's in the cells refer to the probabilities of each stream. One would know which path earnings would take at the beginning of year 3, and there would be no risk thereafter. Thus, all risk would be resolved at the beginning of year 3. If e took the lower value, then the PV of the earnings is $(520/(0.1 - 0.02))(1/1.1^2) = 6500/1.1^2 = 5372$ and the firm is valued at 6372 (including 1000 cash). If e takes the higher value, then the PV of the earnings is $(1480/(0.1 - 0.02))(1/1.1^2) = 18,500/1.1^2 = 15,289$, and the firm is valued at 16,289. Note that the expected value of the firm, if we use 0.5 probabilities, is 11,331 as before.

But what is the debt worth? Note that the firm owes 5000 plus two years' interest at 6% on senior debt, equal to 5618, at the beginning of *year 3. If one assumes a higher interest rate of 7% on the junior debt, then the firm would owe 3200(1.07)² = 3664 at the beginning of year 3. Thus, the firm will be bankrupt if value is less than 5618 + 3664 = 9282 at the beginning of year 3. Assume that there is a bankruptcy cost of 500.*

The following table plots the value of the firm at year 3 and shows how this value is allocated across stakeholders. (I will assume that the current cash balance grows at a rate of 10% to a value of 1210 in two years to keep things simple). First, senior creditors are paid 5618. If sufficient funds remain, junior creditors are paid up to 3664. Any residual goes to shareholders.

Value at Year 3	Senior Debt	Junior Debt	Equity
6500 + 1210 − 500 = 7210	5618	1592	0
18500 + 1210 = 19710	5618	3664	10,428

Now we can value the various claims on the firm at the present time.
value of senior debt

$$\frac{5618}{(1 + 0.06)^2} = 5000$$

value of junior debt

$$\left(\frac{1}{(1 + 0.07)^2}\right)(0.5(1592) + 0.5(3664)) = 2295$$

value of equity²

residual value of 3829

This gives a total firm value of 11,124 (note that this has been reduced from 11,331 by the expected present value of the bankruptcy cost).

You can now see the problem. Investors anticipate that there is a 50% chance that the firm will default on the new debt and are willing to pay only 2295 even though its face value is 3200. Thus, the firm is

---

2. The value of equity in year 3 is either 0 or 10,428, which has an expected value of 5,214. To discount this to year 0, one must use the cost of equity, which is not given. However, given a weighted average cost of capital of 10% and a cost of debt of 6% and 7%, one can deduce a cost of equity of 16.7%. Discounting 5,214 at this rate for two years gives the equity value of 3,829. Later in this chapter we will show the formula for the weighted average cost of capital.

short of 905 to finance the reconstruction. Is it still possible to salvage this example and allowing the firm to supplement this debt issue with an issue equity? A little thought will reveal that this is not a good idea. Issuing only equity and no debt to finance the reconstruction gave the original owners a value of 3131. Supplementing the new debt by an equity issue would result in a total equity value of 3892. However, that would involve some dilution to raise the shortfall of 905, and the equity of the original shareholders would be worth only 2987. In fact, the value would be lower because one would expect further transaction costs from a second new issue. The owners are better off sticking with all equity financing for the reconstruction.

This last example shows that the fundability conditions for post-loss debt financing are complex. It is not enough that the value of the firm after deduction of preexisting debt exceeds the cost of reinvestment. If we use this formula, we come up with $V'(F) - D - C > 0$, which comes out as $11{,}124 - 5000 - 3200 > 0$. Despite this, new investors will still not fully subscribe to new debt, because the values conceal future insolvency risk. Insolvency risk reduces the value of debt and enhances the value of equity.

As we saw in Chapter 6, one common way of describing this phenomenon makes use of option theory. Debt that is subject to default risk contains an implicit embedded put option. The creditors have an asset that is equivalent to default-free debt and a short position in a put option where the striking price is the face value of the debt. The firm's owners have a long position in this option. Consider Figure 10–1. The solid line shows the value of default-free debt. By definition, default-free debt does not depend on firm value, and it is shown as a horizontal line at the face value, F. The dashed line shows the payoff on a put option written on firm value with a striking price of F. If the firm value is above F, the owners of the put will not wish to "sell" the firm at F, and the option expires worthless. The option has zero value above F, but if firm value is below F, the option has a value equal to the difference between F and the actual firm value. This is shown as a 45° line from F on the vertical axis to F on the horizontal axis. The geometry should now be clear. Risky debt, shown by the bold dot-dash line, is the horizontal default free line minus the payoff

F I G U R E   10–1

The Default Put Option

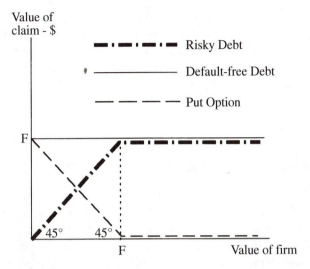

on the put option. When the firm has value less than F, the firm is insolvent and the payoff to creditors is the value of the firm (the 45° segment of this line). When the firm value is above F, the firm is solvent and the payoff is the promised face value F, shown as the horizontal segment of the bold dot-dash line.

This analogy with options is useful because we know a lot about the value (and therefore the pricing) of options. A put option is more valuable:

- The higher the risk (standard deviation) of the underlying asset
- The longer the term to maturity
- The higher the striking price
- The lower the current value of the firm

Because the value of debt embodies a *short* position in the put option (it is deducted from riskless debt), risky debt is worth less relative to risky debt:

- The higher the risk (standard deviation) of the underlying asset
- The longer the term to maturity

- The higher the striking price
- The lower the current value of the firm

This tells us a lot about fundability with post-loss debt financing. The firm will find it more difficult to finance the loss, the lower its post-loss (after reinvestment) value, the more risky its future value, the greater the leverage, and the longer the term of the debt. Post-loss debt financing is not for all. It is likely to be feasible following small losses for firms with modest leverage and stable future earnings.

DEBT OR EQUITY REFINANCING?

So far in this chapter we have shown that post-loss financing can enable the firm to capture value after some risky event. After such an event, the firm may well face a set of investment opportunities with positive NPV, yet not have internal funds to pay for them. Some of these investment opportunities arise solely because of the event: reconstruction of physical assets following their damage or destruction, or the rebuilding of reputation and therefore demand after a product liability suit. Other opportunities for new investments already existed but may now be compromised by the lack of internal funds. Post-loss financing potentially enables the firm to capture value embodied in post-loss investment opportunities.

Our second concern was to establish the conditions under which new investors would still be willing to lend money, or buy new equity, after a major fire, currency loss, liability suit, or fall in demand. This is the fundability issue. We showed that the firm could fully fund post-loss investment opportunities if the post-loss value of the firm, less any preexisting debt, exceeded the cost of those investments. The fundability criterion does not guarantee that post-loss investments add value. Correspondingly, it is a weaker condition than that the capital budgeting criterion required by existing shareholders to agree to post-loss investment activity.

We now turn our attention to the choice between debt and equity financing. Clearly, this is a particular application of the capital structure problem that faces firms continually. As discussed above, the optimal capital structure balances a number of effects.

There are tax effects, the direct and indirect costs of financial distress. The optimal capital structure after a loss must balance these just as it did before loss. But that does not mean the choice will be the same. The risky event can change the financial parameters. For example, after a loss of productive assets, a sudden loss of income, or a liability suit, the leverage of the firm will change. This loss of value will not fall equally on owners and creditors. Part of this loss of value may fall on creditors insofar as the lower value causes immediate default, or increases the probability of future default, on the debt. But in many cases the creditors are protected by their priority claim and most of the fall in value is a deadweight loss to shareholders. Thus, one would normally expect the leverage of the firm to raise after a loss.

Now consider a firm with low leverage, reasonable cash balances, and fairly secure earnings from existing product lines that is deciding how to pay for an expensive investment in the development of a new product. Given the low leverage, it may well conclude that the costs of distress (direct and indirect) are low and that a tax advantages of debt rule the day. Thus, it chooses debt financing. Now consider the same firm facing the same investment decision, with the difference that it has just settled a massive liability suit. Given the pre-loss conditions, the impact of the settlement will fall mainly on shareholders and leverage will jump substantially. In the post-loss decision on how to pay for the new investment, the costs of financial distress are going to play a more important role. From the high post-loss leverage position, the underinvestment and asset substitution problems are more prominent and the firm may therefore have difficulty in raising enough money in a debt issue.

The issues to be addressed are summarized in Figure 10–2a. The solid n-shaped line at the top shows how the value of the firm depends on the level of leverage. The value-maximizing capital structure is identified by the highest point on the curve and is shown as leverage A. The position and n shape to the value curve start with the unlevered value line shown as a dashed horizontal. Taxes reduce value and are shown in the negative quadrant. As shown here, the tax effect diminishes with leverage, and thus debt is tax-preferred. In contrast, costs of financial distress, including underinvestment and asset substitution costs, increase

F I G U R E   10-2

(a) The Effect of Loss on Leverage; (b) Loss of Productive Assets

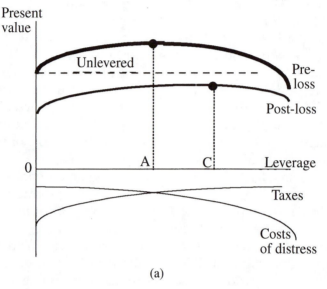

(a)

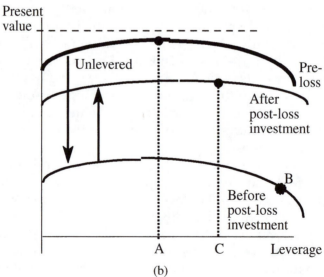

(b)

with leverage as shown. Combining the tax effect of leverage and costs of distress leads to the n shape in pre-loss value. Now suppose the firm has chosen its optimal capital structure A and then some risky loss occurs. There are two major effects:

1. The value curve now shifts down to the post-loss curve. The downward shift reflects the loss of value. The downward shift occurs in two stages, as shown in Figure 10–2b. If no post-loss investment is undertaken (i.e., destroyed assets are not replaced and/or new post-loss investment opportunities are not undertaken), then the loss in value will be severe. The downwards arrow shows the fall in the value curve. However, much of this lost value can be recaptured by post-loss investment, and the value curve shifts upwards again towards the original curve. As shown, not all pre-loss value is recaptured. There can be some permanent loss of value if the event shifts demand or leads to an increase in frictional costs.

2. The event itself will fall disproportionately on equity, probably increasing leverage to some point such as B. If no post-loss investment activity is undertaken, the firm is likely to be overlevered, and position B does indeed show this. Depending on what level of post-loss investment is undertaken and how it is financed, the post-loss leverage will resettle at some point such as C on the recaptured value curve. The post-loss optimal capital structure may not be the same as the pre-loss capital structure. As shown, the optimal post-loss leverage, C, is higher than pre-loss, B, but it could go the other way.

A couple of illustrations will show the effect of the increase in leverage following a loss on the post-loss financing decisions. In the first of these, MBA Startups, the firm suffers a fire loss that cuts earnings potential. This loss of value impacts both debt and equity. Debt value falls because there is now some chance of default, but the bulk of the loss of value falls on equity, and thus leverage increases. From the higher post-loss leverage position, we will see that reconstruction is fundable only if undertaken with equity. Post-loss debt financing now encounters such a severe agency problem that the proceeds of a debt issue would be insufficient to pay for the reconstruction.

MBA Startups is a new company that is set up to develop new businesses and then sell them. The first opportunity to present itself is to invest 1200 in a venture that will produce equatorial mounts and motors for astronomical telescopes. MBA will start the venture and sell after one year. Such new ventures are risky, and it is estimated that the value in one year will be either 1100 or 2200, each with 0.5 probability. MBA has borrowed 800 and is using 400 in its own money to fund the first project. The cost of debt is 0.05 and the cost of equity is 0.1. At this point the value of debt and equity, assuming MBA goes ahead with the project, is:

$$\text{value of debt} = (0.5(840) + 0.5(840)) \left(\frac{1}{1 + 0.05} \right) = 800$$

$$\text{value of equity} = (0.5(260) + 0.5(1360)) \left(\frac{1}{1 + 0.1} \right) = 736.4$$

Notice that the weighted average cost of capital (with minor rounding) is:

$$k = \left(\frac{800}{1536.4} \right) 0.05 + \left(\frac{736.4}{1536.4} \right) 0.1 = 0.074$$

When making this investment decision, the firm has cash of 1200. Of this, 800 is borrowed. Thus, if the firm were to decide not to undertake this investment, it could pay off the debt and pay a dividend of 400 to shareholders. The value of debt would be 800 and equity 400. Undertaking the project increases the value of the equity from 400 to 736.4 and the value of the firm from 1200 to 1536.4. Notice that the NPV of the project, discounting at the weighted average cost of capital, WACC, is:

$$(0.5(1100) + 0.5(2200)) \left(\frac{1}{1 + 0.074} \right) - 1200 = 336.4$$

which is equal to the increase in equity value and the increase in the value of the firm. It makes sense for the new project to be undertaken, and the firm does so.

A fire destroys half of the productive assets, and the estimated end-of-year value falls to half its prior value. Without replacement of those assets the end-of-year value will be either 550 of 1100, each with 0.5 probability. The assets can be replaced at cost of 600, and this will restore the value to the pre-loss level (i.e., either 1100 or 2200, each with 0.5 chance). Should this reinvestment be undertaken? Let us try debt financing first. The firm seeks to borrow the 600 at 6% interest. The firm will have senior debt of 800 and junior debt of 600, totaling 1400. Moreover, we will assume that if the firm goes bankrupt there is a bankruptcy cost of 50. There is also a transaction cost of 10 to float the debt.

First let us establish that the reinvestment opportunity does have a positive NPV. With reinvestment, the end-of-year value will rise either from 550 to 1100 or from 1100 to 2200. Thus, the expected change in year end value is {0.5(1100) + 0.5(2200)} − {0.5(550) + 0.5(1100)} = 825. The NPV is:

$$825 \left(\frac{1}{1 + 0.074} \right) - 600 = 168.2$$

Clearly, reinvestment can add value. But look at the values of the various debt and equity claims

Without Reinvestment

To calculate the value of debt and equity, note that the firm owes 840 (including interest) to bondholders. If the value is lower, the firm is bankrupt and will incur 50 bankruptcy costs

$$value\ of\ senior\ debt = (0.5(550 - 50) + 0.5(840)) \left(\frac{1}{1 + 0.05} \right)$$

$$= 638.1$$

To calculate the value of equity, we assume that the risk characteristics of the after-loss cash flows are similar to those pre-loss; that is, the beta has not changed. If so, the WACC will remain the same and the overall firm value will be a lottery over 500 and 1100 discounted at 7.4%, which gives a value of 744.9. This means that equity is worth 744.9 minus the value of debt, which leaves 106.8. The following shows that the cost of equity that results in this value is 21.7%. The large jump in the cost of equity is due to the large change in leverage. Before loss the leverage ratio was 800/1536.4 = 52%. After loss it is 638.1/744.9 = 86%.[3]

---

3. The Appendix shows how the cost of equity, the cost of debt, and the WACC are related to each other.

$$value\ of\ equity\ =\ (0.5(\text{ZERO})\ +\ 0.5(260))\ \left(\frac{1}{1\ +\ 0.217}\right)\ =\ 106.8$$

Reinvestment with Debt Financing

To make valuations, note that the firm is committed to pay 840 on senior debt, including interest, and 636 on junior debt, also including interest. Thus, the firm will go bankrupt if end-of-year value falls below 1476. If the firm performs badly, the firm will have 1100 minus bankruptcy costs of 50 minus 10 cost of new issue.[4] *The total amount to share is 1040, and this will go 840 to senior debt and 200 to junior debt. If the end-of-year value is 2200, there will be 2190 to distribute after transaction costs of the new issue, and this will be divided 840 to senior debt, 636 to junior debt, and 714 to equity. To show the present value of the firm, keep the WACC the same as before at 0.074, since we are showing the cost of changing the capital structure as direct charges on the cash flows. This means that the total value of the firm is an end-of-year value of (0.5(1040) + 0.5 (2190)), discounted at 0.074, which gives 1503.7.*

The value of equity is the residual value after deduction of junior and senior debt. The cost of equity is the discount rate, which equates the end-of-year value to the residual value calculated as just explained.

$$value\ of\ senior\ debt\ =\ (0.5(840)\ +\ 0.5(840))\ \left(\frac{1}{1\ +\ 0.05}\right)\ =\ 800$$

$$value\ of\ junior\ debt\ =\ (0.5(200)\ +\ 0.5(636))\ \left(\frac{1}{1\ +\ 0.06}\right)\ =\ 394.3$$

To value equity, note that the total firm value is 1503.7 and deducting

---

4. In this example I have inserted all transaction costs at the end of the year. This could require different treatment in other circumstances. For example, if the fire occurs at the beginning of the year and bankruptcy is instantaneous, the deduction of the bankruptcy cost should be immediate. A delay in bankruptcy proceedings would justify an end-of-year treatment. Similarly, if the new issue is made at the beginning of the year, to permit reconstruction and production throughout the year, then the issue cost should come at the beginning of the year. On the other hand, if the transaction cost of new issues is an agency cost that is felt in lower overall cash flows, then it is appropriate to deduct at the end of the year. These are issues that need to be addressed according to circumstance.

prior debt claims leaves a residual value of 309.4. The calculation below[5] shows that a cost of equity of 15.4% is necessary to capitalize the residual cash flows to value of 309.4.

$$value\ of\ equity\ =\ (0.5(ZERO)\ +\ 0.5(714))\left(\frac{1}{1\ +\ 0.154}\right)\ =\ 309.4$$

The value of equity certainly is higher than without reinvestment (309.4 compared with 106.8), and the value of the firm is higher (1503.7 compared with 744.9). However, the reinvestment cannot be financed in this way. If the firm raised new debt of 600, investors would see that they there is only a 50% chance they will be repaid the full face value plus interest of 636. There is a 50% chance the firm will become bankrupt and they will receive only 200. Anticipating this default, investors would be willing to pay only 394.3 for the debt, whereas the cost of reconstruction of the assets is 600. The firm is deficient 205.7 in the reconstruction cost.

Since equity is worth 309.4, the firm can supplement the new debt issue with an equity issue to raise the remaining 205.7. It should be apparent that if new investors are going to subscribe to a new equity issue (in addition to the debt issue) to raise the remaining 205.7, the discounted expected value of their payback also must be equal to 205.7. Thus, the original owner's equity must be worth a paltry 203.7 (i.e., 309.4 − 205.7).[6] This is less than the equity value without reinvestment, 106.8, and the original owners will be better off not even trying to rebuild the original asset.

Reinvestment with Equity

The alternative is to issue more shares to finance the 600 reconstruction cost. If this is undertaken, then the firm will have either a value of 1090 or 2190 (remember to deduct transaction costs of the new equity issue and note that there is no chance of defaulting on the original debt of

---

5. You may check with the formula used in the Appendix that weighing the cost of senior debt of 5%, the cost of junior debt of 6%, and the cost of equity of 15.4% by their respective values gives a WACC of 7.4%.

6. Note that the equity would probably be worth less. A second new issue of equity, in addition to the debt, would incur further transaction costs, which I have not shown.

800). Discounting these values at a cost of capital of 7.4% gives a total firm value of 1527. Since thee is no chance of default on the debt of 800, it will be worth its full face value. Thus, the equity will be worth 727. Part of that equity will represent new issues. Assuming a number m = *100 shares were already outstanding, then the firm needs to issue* n *new shares. Recalling the calculation earlier:*

$$n = \frac{Cm}{E^T - C} = \frac{600(100)}{727 - 600} = 472$$

Thus, the total number of shares is now 572, of which the original owners have 100 and new owners 472. The total value of equity is 727, and the value of the original shares is 100/572 × 727 = 127.1. Now things make sense.

value of original equity without reinvestment = 106.8

value of original equity with debt financing = 103.7
(and a supplementary equity issue of 205.7)

value of original equity with equity financing = 127.1

The optimal choice is equity financing. It is true that there is a large dilution of the equity. But reinvestment is a positive NPV project. The value created by reinvestment is 1527 − 744.9 − 600 = 182.1.

Who benefits by the gain in firm value from reinvestment? Without reinvestment, equity is worth 106.8 and increases to 127.1 for a gain of 20.3. The other gainers are the original bondholders, whose investment was worth 638.1 without reinvestment, and with reinvestment and equity financing this rises to 800 for a gain of 161.9. The bondholders gain because reinvestment has protected them against default through bankruptcy.

In MBA Startups the firm had raised debt to pay for most of start-up cost. After the loss its borrowing capacity is severely restricted and it is unable to pay for reconstruction with post-loss debt. A second example now illustrates a related point. Prime Autos was preparing to undertake a new investment in a new product line when it was hit by a large liability suit on its existing product. Like the fire loss in MBA Startups, the event mostly impacts equity and increases leverage. Thus, while Prime had planned to fiance the investment with debt before the loss, we will show that it is unable to do so thereafter.

Prime Autos has an existing product line that is generating a steadily growing earnings stream. Earnings for the coming year are expected to be 500, and this is expected to grow at 1% per year. The current cost of equity, k_E, is 0.09. The firm has existing debt of 2000 with cost of debt, k_D, of 0.06. The firm has the following investment opportunity. A sports car can be introduced, and there are two choices. The first is to use a conventional design that is sure to sell quite well. The cost of setting up production, distribution, and marketing is 5000, and the expected value of future sales is a certain 7000. The second idea is to introduce a radical design, both in technology and shape. This could be a great success or a failure. The present value future income will either be 1000 or 11000, each with a probability of 0.5. The capital cost of this project also would be 5000. For any new issue of debt or equity required to finance either investment, thee would be a transaction cost of 250. Should the firm become bankrupt, the direct value lost would be 750.

First, value the firm without introducing the new product. The value of the firm is:

$$V = \frac{e}{k - g} = \frac{500}{0.09 - 0.01} = 6250$$

Given the steady and growing earnings from the existing product, there is no possibility of default, the debt is worth its full face value of 2000, and equity would be worth the residual 4250.

This example has the structure of the asset substitution problem discussed in Chapter 8. However, here the parameters are such that there is no bankruptcy problem and the firm is not denied the choice of a positive NPV project even with debt financing. The analysis is as follows.

Value If Project A Is Undertaken

Note that the present value of total earnings, from existing products and the new project, is 6250 + 7000 = 13250. With debt financing, the total debt obligation would be 2000 + 5250 = 7250. Notice that the new debt includes the transaction cost of the issue, and thus the net proceeds will cover the capital cost of introducing the new design. Since the earnings are riskless, thee is no bankruptcy problem and the debt will be worth its full face value (senior debt 2000 and junior debt 5250). Equity will be worth 13250 − 7250 = 6000.

Value If Project B Is Undertaken

With project B the worst case is that the present value of earnings from the new project will be 1000, giving total value of 6250 + 1000 = 7250. This is still enough to cover old and new debt, which will both be worth face value: senior debt 2000 and junior debt 5250. The value of the firm is 6250 + {0.5(1000) + 0.5(11000)} = 12250. Thus, the value of equity is 12250 − 7250 = 5000. Shareholders are better off with project A, which results in an equity value of 6000.

PRIME AUTOS SUFFERS A LIABILITY LOSS

Before the firm commits to the new product, it is hit with a liability suit. This is settled in the following way. A trust fund is set up that will hold 60% of earnings from the existing product. Of the earnings of 500, some 300 will go into the trust, leaving only 200. The trust has priority over creditors and shareholders.[7] The firm now is faced with the decision of whether to undertake one of the new products, and if so, which.

Analysis with Equity Financing

Under this analysis the firm issues new shares to finance the new project. The firm raises equity for the full capital cost (5000) plus the transaction costs (250).

Project A Is Chosen

The existing operations are now worth a present value of 200/(0.09 − 0.01) = 2500. If the firm chooses project A, total value will be 2500 + 7000 = 9500. There is no possibility of default, debt will be worth its full face of 2000, and equity (old plus new) will be worth 7500. To ensure

---

7. Rather than get into a discussion over the priorities of stakeholders, imagine the following settlement. A holding company structure is established. The existing product line is put into a separate company in which the holding company shareholders hold 40% of the equity and the trust holds the remaining 60%. The new product is lodged in a separate subsidiary in which all equity is held by the holding company's shareholders.

that new investors will subscribe the full 5250, the new equity must be worth this amount and the old equity will be worth 2250. In other words, the new shareholders will hold a proportion (5250:7500) of the total number of shares.

Project B Is Chosen
In the worst case the firm will be worth 2500 + 1000 = 3500, which is still enough to pay the old debt of 2000. However the project performs, there is no bankruptcy and the old debt is worth its face of 2000. The total firm value is {0.5(2500 + 1000) + 0.5(2500 + 11000)} = 8500. Thus equity is worth 8500 − 2000 = 6500. If we use the same argument as above, the new equity is worth 5250 and the old equity is worth 1250.

With equity financing, project A would be preferred by the firm's original owners.

Analysis with Debt Financing

Under this analysis, the firm issues debt to finance the new project in an attempt to raise the full capital cost (5000) plus the transaction costs (250).

Project A Is Chosen
If the firm chooses project A, total value will be 2500 + 7000 = 9500. The firm has an old debt obligation of 3000 and a new debt obligation of 5250. There is no possibility of default, and debt will be worth its full face (2000 senior debt and 5250 junior debt). Equity will be worth 2250.

Project B Is Chosen
In the worst case the firm will be worth 2500 + 1000 = 300. Since the debt obligation is 7250, the firm will be bankrupt. After deducting bankruptcy cost of 750, there will be only 2750 to divide between creditors of which senior debt will get 2000 and junior debt 750. In the best case the firm is worth 2500 + 11000 = 13500, which is divided 2000 to senior debt, 5250 to junior debt, and 6250 to equity. The values of the various claims are now:

$$senior\ debt = 0.5(2000) + 0.5(2000) = 2000$$

$$junior\ debt = 0.5(\ 750) + 0.5(5250) = 3000$$

$$equity = 0.5(\ \ \ 0) + 0.5(6250) = 3125$$

The firm is truly locked into the asset substitution problem if it tries to finance the new project with debt after the liability loss. If creditors lent 5250, the firm would then wish to choose B since equity is more valuable under this choice. However, this gain in value comes about by a default on junior debt if the project turns out bad. Investors would anticipate the choice of B an subscribe only 3000 for the new debt. This is not enough to fund the project. An attempt to signal that will A will be chosen has the usual credibility problem because creditors can anticipate that shareholders have an incentive to switch their choice after the money is raised. The firm may be unable to undertake either project with debt financing.

Thus, the only feasible choice for the firm, after the liability suit, is to finance the project with new equity. In contrast, the firm could have used either equity or debt before the liability suit. The increase in leverage caused by the liability settlement has constrained the options for post-loss financing.

In the case of Prime Autos, the triggering loss was a liability suit. There was nothing peculiar to a liability loss that made this example work out as it did. The example could have been re-worked where the loss in value was the result of currency fluctuations depleting the value of exports of the existing product, or where the revenues from the existing product line were reduced because higher interest rates increased the costs of financing new cars and thereby reduced demand.

A MORE GENERAL FRAMEWORK FOR COMPARING POST-LOSS DEBT AND EQUITY FINANCING

The analyses in Chairs and Wares, MBA Startups, and Prime Autos each illustrated one main point. Chairs and Wares focused on the feasibility of raising sufficient funds to pay for the loss, and the example was constructed to show different fundability for equity and debt financing. The difference in fundabiilty arose from the increased bankruptcy risk with debt financing, which meant that new investors would not be willing to pay the face value for post-loss debt. MBA Startups was constructed to show some issues that arise in choosing how to pay for reconstruction of productive assets that have been destroyed. The problem illustrated was to show how leverage increased after loss and how this affected the choice between debt and equity financing to reconstruct the lost assets. In this case the possibility of default on new debt implied that debt financing was unfundable, but reconstruction using equity financing did add value. The Prime Autos example looked at the effect of a unhedged liability settlement. Prior to the settlement the firm had an investment opportunity that was not tripped up by the asset substitution problem. After the settlement the investment opportunity still stood, but the increase in leverage from the unhedged loss uncovered an asset substitution problem. The only was the firm could capture the net present value of this opportunity was to fund the project with equity.

The examples each really focused on a single issue and did not look too far into the future. Each example was introduced with all relevant information nicely summarized. Actual decisions are more messy. A property loss can present an opportunity for reinvestment and affect the parameters of many, as yet unspecified, future investment opportunities. Thus, the firm's management will face the post-loss investment decisions with less precise information. For example, the long-term influence of a product liability suit on product demand will depend on factors such as the size of the damage, the publicity of the suit, the visibility of the product label affected, and competition. Some degree of subjectivity will be involved in bringing these factors together to estimate future demand. On the other hand, the disruptive effects of such losses could be deduced from seeing how other firms have fared after major litigation and controlling for firm and market differences. Considering another example, the risk manager may well know that increased leverage can lead to los investment opportunities through underinvestment, but this is difficult to quantify because future investment opportunities are not yet known. Thus, estimation of this effect could take the form of a cross-sectional study of the effect of leverage on growth in other firms, with controls for industry, size, and similar features. The result would be a comparison of post-loss financing alternatives with different estimates of earnings growth for debt and equity.

Our task now is to present a more general framework for considering post-loss financing choices. The examples presented above used the equity valuation equations from the beginning of the chapter. The before-loss value of the equity is:

$$V(E) = V_0 + L + (S - R - K_t) + V_t - D - T$$
$$= V_0 + L - K_t + V_t - D - T$$

and the after-loss value of the original equity is:

$$V'(E) = (\Delta S - r\Delta S/r - C) + V_0' + L - K_t' + V_t' - D - T'$$
$$= -C + V_0' + L - K_t' + V_t' - D - T'$$

These formulae separated earnings from current operations and future earnings growth potential and showed how each might be affected by the risky event. We now present the valuation model in a different way that might be more convenient given the impression of actual decisions. The following table is designed to measure the value of equity, in particular the share value, and how this is affected by post-loss financing choices. The table starts with an estimate of future annual cash flows, labeled EBIT (earnings before interest and taxation). After deducting interest and taxes, we are left with net income that is potentially available to shareholders. Note that this is expected income for each period in the future; that is, it is an income stream. Thus, dividing by the difference between the cost of equity, k_E, and the expected growth rate, g, the market value of equity is calculated. Dividing the market value of equity by the number of shares gives the share price.

	Equity Refinancing	Debt Refinancing
Ebit	1	1
Interest	2	2
Tax	3	3
Net Income		
Cost of Equity, k_E	4	4
Growth Rate, g^N	5	5
Value of Equity, E	6	6
Value of the Firm, V	7	7
Of Shares, $m + n$	8	8
Share Price	9	9

In each cell of the table is a reference number. This key will be used to show how the various risk management issues described till now affect firm value.

Key

1. The choice of debt and equity post-loss financing will affect the future expected earnings. Insofar as the choice affects direct and indirect costs of bankruptcy, one would expect the value of EBIT to be lower with debt financing. Recall also that the event itself can affect earnings because productive assets can be destroyed and demand can be affected by such events as liability suits and interest rate changes.

2. Debt financing incurs an additional interest, but compare this with point 8, below which indicates that equity financing (unless retained earnings are used) leads to the issue of new shares and therefore to dilution. The choice of debt financing also affects the cost of debt. Additional leverage increases the cost of debt and, as shown below, the cost of equity.

3. Debt financing has a direct tax advantage because interest payments by the firms are tax deductible. But this does not completely pick up the tax effects. As we saw earlier in this chapter, the tax benefit from debt refinancing rests on both corporate and personal tax liabilities:

$$\text{tax advantage of debit} = \frac{1 - t_p}{(1 - t_E)(1 - t_c)}$$

4. The cost of equity will be affected by the level of leverage. However, the weighted average cost of capital will depend on the risk characteristics of the cash flows.

5. The growth rate also can be affected by the choice between debt and equity. In a purely mechanical way described in the Appendix, if EBIT is growing at a given rate, g, the growth of net earnings, g^N, will depend on the level of fixed interest deduction.

$$g^N = k_E - \frac{(k - g)(e - k_D D)}{(e - (k - g)D)}$$

More importantly, the additional direct and indirect bankruptcy costs from additional debt will affect future earnings. For example, the underinvestment problem will limit the rate of future growth.

6 & 8. The value of equity combines both the original holdings and, if any new shares are issued, the value of the new equity. There will be dilution with new issues, and the share price will reflect the relative values of debt versus equity financing to the firm's original owners.

7. The value of the firm provides a criterion for choosing between the two forms of financing. The relationship between the values of levered and unlevered firms is:

value of levered firm = value of all-equity firm

$$+ \; PV(\text{tax shield})$$

$$-PV \; (\text{cost of financial distress})$$

As laid out, this relationship should be partly reflected. The differences in earnings and growth rates between equity and debt financing are considered, and therefore the differences in the firm values will reflect the present value of the costs of financial distress. But the differences in value will only partly reflect the present value of the tax advantage to debt. The layout does show the effects of corporate taxes and will therefore show the corporate tax advantage, $t_c \, D$. But the personal tax issues are not reflected here.

9. The share price provides a measure of the residual value to the firm's original owners from the different forms of financing. Using the share price as a way of choosing between debt and equity financing is equivalent to comparing the value of the original owners equity as in Equations (10.1) and (10.2) above.

Ball LD makes bearings for vehicles and machinery. It has forecast that its coming year's earnings will be 120 and will grow at an annual rate of 2.5%. A failure of its product in a locomotive led to a crash, and in the ensuing suit a settlement of 400 has been reached. Ball's problem is how to pay for the settlement. Its retained earnings from last year are available in cash of 100 and the firm plans to pay this amount as a dividend. *Moreover, the adverse publicity has led to some concern about future demand, and its earnings forecast has been revised down from 120 to 100 and growth from 2.5% to 2.0%. The firm's cost of capital is 12%, and this is unchanged after the loss because the beta risk has remained unchanged. The firm has existing debt of 200 with a 5% coupon rate and has 100 shares outstanding.*

The firm can issue new shares or bonds to pay for the settlement. If new equity is issued, the probability of default on the existing debt is negligible and it is valued at its full face of 200. If the firm pays for the settlement with a new junior debt issue with a face value of 400, this will have a 6% coupon. Moreover, it is estimated that the additional leverage would cause future bankruptcy risk to increase. Direct bankruptcy costs would take the form of expected transaction costs and potential loss of new investment because of the more conservative administration of the firm under court supervision. The additional leverage would also increase potential conflict between bondholders and shareholders, leading to more severe asset substitution and underinvestment problems. The combined burden of additional direct and indirect bankruptcy costs would cause post-loss earnings to grow at a slower rate of 1.5%. It is estimated that given the default risk, investors would pay only 375 for the junior debt and the firm would have to use an additional 25 from cash to make up the settlement. It is not expected that the increase default risk would impact the senior debt.

	Equity Financing	Debt Financing
Ebit	100	100
Interest	10	10 + 24 = 34
Net Earnings	90	66
Growth Rate, g^N	0.025	0.0418
Cost of Equity, k_E	0.1375	0.2167
Value of Equity, E	800	377.4
Value of Firm	1000	952.4
Number of Shares, $m + n$	100 + 100 = 200	100
Share Price (plus dividend)	4 + 1 = 5	3.774 + 0.75 = 4.524

Equity Financing

If the firm had no prior debt, its value would be:[8]

$$V = \frac{e}{k - g} = \frac{100}{0.12 - 0.02} = 1000$$

On the assumption that existing debt is essentially default-free, the value of 1000 is divided between 800 equity and 200 debt. The cost of equity can be derived by backing it out of the weighted average cost of capital (see Appendix):

$$k_E = \frac{V_k}{E} - \frac{D}{E} k_D = \frac{1000}{800} 0.12 - \frac{200}{800} 0.05 = 0.1375$$

And the net earnings of 90 will grow at a rate (see Appendix):

$$g^N = k_E - \frac{(k - g)(e - k_D D)}{(e - (k - g)D)}$$

$$= 0.1375 - \frac{(0.12 - 0.02)(100 - 0.05(200))}{100 - (0.12 - 0.02)200}$$

$$= 0.025$$

We can now confirm the value of equity:

$$E = \frac{e - k_D D}{k_E - g^N} = \frac{100 - 0.05(200)}{0.1375 - 0.025} = 800$$

To pay for the liability loss, the firm will need to issue enough shares to raise the 400, or it could raise 300 and use the cash of 100 to make up the difference. I will do it the first way:

---

8. A word of explanation is needed here for those used to looking at the weighted average cost of capital to reveal optimal capital structure. The WACC is often assumed to be U-shaped, the minimum point on the curve being the optimal capital structure. This point represents the value-maximizing balance between the tax advantages of debt and the cost of financial distress. Implicitly, the tax effect and costs of distress are reflected, not as adjustments to cash flows, but as adjustments to the discount rate used to capitalize them. Alternatively, we can adjust the cash flows for the tax effects and distress costs, and then discount these at a WACC rate that is invariant with respect to capital structure. The important thing is not to double count the adjustment by doing it both in the numerator and denominator. Here we will use a WACC that is not affected by capital structure and then make explicit adjustments for distress costs and (in later examples) the tax effects of debt.

$$n = \frac{Cm}{E^T - C} = \frac{400(100)}{800 - 400} = 100$$

Thus, there will be a total of 200 shares and the share price will be 4. Because the whole 400 will be raised in an issue of 100 shares, the firm can pay the planned dividend of 100 (i.e., a value of 1 per share) to the original shareholders. Subsequently, the new issue can be floated and each share will now be worth 800/200 = 4. Thus, the value to the original owners is their dividend of 1 plus the share value of 4 = 5. You might confirm that, if the firm raised only 300 in the new issue and used the cash as part of the liability settlement, it would issue 60 shares and each would be worth 5. Thus, original owners should be indifferent as to which method is used to pay the liability.

Debt Financing

With debt financing, the total value of the firm is:

$$V = \frac{e}{k - g} = \frac{100}{0.12 - 0.015} = 952.4$$

Again, on the assumption that existing debt is essentially default-free but new debt is worth only 375, the value of 952.4 is divided between 200 senior debt and 375 junior debt and the residual of 377.4 is equity. The cost of equity can be derived by backing it out of the weighted average cost of capital (senior and junior debt is now denoted by the superscripts S and J):

$$k_E = \frac{V}{E} k - \frac{D^S}{E} k_D^S - \frac{D^J}{E} k_D^J = \frac{952.4}{377.4} 0.12$$

$$- \frac{200}{277.4} 0.05 - \frac{375}{377.4} 0.06 = 0.2167$$

The net earnings of 66 will grow at a net rate (here D is the total debt of 575 and $k_D D$ is the total interest of 34):

$$g^N = k_E - \frac{(k - g)(e - k_D D)}{(e - (k - g)D)} = 0.2167$$

$$- \frac{(0.12 - 0.015)(100 - 34)}{100 - (0.12 - 0.015)575} = 0.0418$$

We can now confirm the value of equity:

$$E = \frac{e - k_D D}{k_E - g^N} = \frac{100 - 34}{0.2167 - 0.0418} = 377.4$$

Because the firm was able to raise only 375 in the new debt issue, it must use 25 cash to make up the liability settlement of 400. Thus, the dividend will be a total of 75, or 0.75 per share. The share price is 377.4/ 100 = 3.774, and the total value, including dividend to each shareholder, is 4.524.

If we compare the welfare of the original shareholders, equity financing is preferred because the wealth per share is 5 compared with 4.524 with debt financing. We can get to the same conclusion by looking at the value of the firm under the financing alternatives. With equity financing the value was 1000, plus the firm could pay a dividend of 100. Under debt financing value was 952.4 and the dividend was only 75.

Are you surprised that Ball would choose equity financing? You should not have been; the game was rigged. The preference for equity was predetermined by the assumptions used. Let us go back to the relationship between the value of the levered and unlevered firm.

value of levered firm = value of all-equity firm
+PV(tax shield)
−PV(cost of financial distress)

If there are no taxes, the problem is a no-brainer; leverage simply increases costs of financial distress without any offsetting advantage. Leverage financing is doomed (unless we can find some other hidden advantages of debt). This formula can be adapted to compare the post-loss value with debt and equity financing. The relationship between the value of post-loss equity, $V(PLE)$, and the value with post-loss debt, $V(PLD)$, is as follows:

$V(PLD) = V(PLE)$
+PV(additional tax shield)
−PV(additional costs distress)
−(additional cash used for loss settlement)

With equity financing of the liability suit, the value of the firm is 1000 plus the 100 dividend, which can be paid in full. With debt financing, firm value falls by 47.6 (the additional costs of distress from this funding method) to 952.4 and the firm can only pay 75 dividend because the remaining 25 cash must help in the liability settlement. If we use the previous formula, the relationship between the debt value and the equity value is now:

$$1027.4 = 1100 + ZERO - 47.6 - 25$$

REINTRODUCING CORPORATE TAXES

The procedure we shall adopt is to reintroduce taxes in sequence. We will consider corporate taxes first; later we will introduce personal taxes. The reason for this sequential approach is that corporate taxes can be embodied quite easily into the valuation model we are using. This valuation model is quite transparent, and with a few assumptions, we can get clear answers. Inserting corporate taxes makes it marginally more complex, but we can still get clear caparisons. We will take this model as far as we can. Personal taxes are a different matter because they affect investors differently according to their income and portfolio choices.

We know from earlier in this chapter that corporate taxes will tilt the balance in favor of debt financing because interest is tax deductible but dividends are not. To do this we will rework the case of Ball Ltd. We will see that the value of the corporate tax shield is much more important than the costs of financial distress, and this tax treatment leads us to change out mind in favor of debt financing. In the next section we will reintroduce personal taxes.

Let us rework Ball Ltd with corporate taxes only. We will assume that all income is taxed at the rate of 35% and that if the liability settlement is paid for with a debt issue with a face value of 400, investors will only subscribe 375 because of default risk.

	Equity Financing	Debt Financing
Ebit	100	100
Interest	10	10 + 24 = 34
Tax	31.5	23.1
Net Earnings	58.5	42.9
Growth Rate, g^N	0.0469	0.1403
Cost of Equity, k_E	0.1594	0.3152
Value of Equity, E	520	245.25
Value of Firm	720	820.25
Number of Shares, $m + n$	100 + 333.3 = 433.3	100
Share Price (plus dividend)	1.2 + 1 = 2.2	2.45 + 0.75 = 3.2

Equity Financing

If the firm had no prior debt, its value would be:

$$V = \frac{e(1 - t_c)}{k - g} = \frac{100(1 - 0.35)}{0.12 - 0.02} = 650$$

However, this value will be enhanced by the tax shield on the debt; that is, by the value $t_cD = 70$. *Thus, the firm value is 720. On the assumption that existing debt is essentially default-free, debt is worth 200 and equity 520. The cost of equity is:*[9]

$$K_E = \frac{V_k}{E} - \frac{D}{E} k_D(1 - t_c) = \frac{720}{520} 0.12 - \frac{200}{520} 0.05(1 - 0.65) = 0.1594$$

To figure out the growth rate of net earnings note that a value, e − k_DD, *must grow at the same rate as a value, A × (e −* k_DD), *if A is a constant. Since we wish to establish the growth if (1 −t_c) (e −* k_DD), *this must be the same as the growth of e −* k_DD *if the tax rate is constant. Thus, we can use the no-tax formula for growth of net earnings. The net earnings of 58.5 will grow at a net rate:*

$$g^N = k_E - \frac{(k - g)(e - k_DD)}{e - (k - g)D} = 0.1594$$

$$- \frac{(0.12 - 0.02)(100 - 0.05(200))}{100 - (0.12 - 0.02)200} = 0.0469$$

We can now confirm the value of equity:

---

9. The normal formula for the after tax cost of capital uses the after-tax cost of debt; i.e., $k_D(1 - t_c)$.

$$E = \frac{(e - k_D D)(1 - t_c)}{k_E - g^N} = \frac{(100 - 0.05(200))(1 - 0.35)}{0.1594 - 0.0469} = 520$$

To pay for the liability loss, the firm will need to issue enough shares to raise the 400:

$$n = \frac{Cm}{E^T - C} = \frac{400(100)}{520 - 400} = 333.3$$

Thus, there will be a total of 433.3 shares and the share price will be 1.2. Because the whole 400 will be raised in an issue of 400 shares, the firm can pay the planned dividend of 100 to original shareholders before the nw issue. Thus, the value to the original owners is their dividend of 1 plus the share value of 1.2 = 2.2

Debt Financing

With debt financing, the total value of the firm is the unlevered value of

$$V = \frac{e(1 - t_c)}{k - g} = \frac{100(1 - 0.35)}{0.12 - 0.015} = 619$$

plus the value of the larger tax shield, t,D. Each of the two layers of debt offers its own tax shield, each with different interest rates but each discounted at a different rate. The value of the tax shield is now (using S and J as superscripts for senior and junior debt):

$$t_c D = t_c \frac{k_D^S D^S}{k_D^S} + t_c \frac{k_D^J D^J}{k_D^J} = t_c(D^D + D^J)$$

Thus, $t_c D = 0.35(200 + 375) = 201.25$ and the value of the firm is now $619 + 201.25 = 520.25$. You should be able to jump immediately to the conclusion that the firm is now better off with debt financing because of the large value of the debt tax shield. But before this is spelled out, the rest of the table can be completed.

The weighted average cost of capital (senior and junior debt is now denoted by the superscripts S and J:

$$k_E = \frac{820.25}{245.25} 0.12 - \frac{200}{245.25} 0.05(1 - 0.35)$$

$$- \frac{375}{245.25} 0.06(1 - 0.35) = 0.3152$$

And the net earnings will grow at a rate:

$$g^N = k_E - \frac{(k - g)(e - k_D D)}{(e - (k - g)D)} = 0.3152$$

$$- \frac{(0.12 - 0.015)(100 - 34)}{100 - (0.12 - 0.015)575} = 0.1403$$

We can now confirm the value of equity (with a very minor rounding error):

$$E = \frac{(e - k_D D)(1 - t_c)}{k_E - g^N} = \frac{(100 - 34)(1 - 0.35)}{0.3152 - 0.1403} = 245.27$$

Because the firm was able to raise only 375 in the new debt issue, it must use 25 cash to make up the liability settlement of 400. Thus, the dividend will be a total of 75, or 0.75 per share. The share price is 245.25/ 100 = 2.45 and the total value including dividend to each shareholder is 3.2. Clearly, the owners are better off with debt financing.

Look carefully at the differences between equity and debt financing to the Ball Ltd case when there is corporate tax. The total firm value (including remaining cash) is 720 + 100 = 820 with equity financing, and 820.25 + 75 = 895.25 with debt financing. The difference can be accounted for as follows. First, the value of the tax shield rose from 70 with equity to 201.25 with debt financing. Second, the basic (before value of tax shield is added in) firm value fell from 650 to 619 when we switched from equity to debt financing. This fall represents the additional distress costs. And third, the firm had to hold back 25 of the 100 it was planning to pay as a dividend to help pay for the liability settlement when debt was used. We can now state the relationship between the value of post-loss equity, $V(PLE)$, and the value with post-loss debt, $V(PLD)$, as follows:

$$V(PLD) = V(PLE)$$
$$+ PV(\text{additional tax shield})$$
$$- PV(\text{additional costs of distress})$$
$$- (\text{additional cash used for loss settlement})$$

$$895.25 = 820 + 13.25 - 31 - 25$$

You can now see the usual capital structure balancing coming into play. Use of debt increases corporate tax shields but leads to increased costs of financial distress. In this case the additional benefit from the tax shields completely outweighed the distress costs and debt financing was preferred.

There are some ways in which our analysis is approximate. We assumed that all corporate earnings after interest would attract a constant tax rate. This ignores other tax shields. If the firm can deduct depreciation of carryback earnings, the full interest deduction may not be used. In this case the method used overstates the value of the interest tax shield and therefore artificially biases in favor of debt. There are methods of valuing debt with other deductions. One such approach recognizes that nonlinear tax liabilities can be modeled as options. We will not explore that here, though it is a very useful tool in examining optimal capital structures. Instead we will look at the effects of personal taxes.

THE EFFECT OF PERSONAL TAXES ON POST-LOSS FINANCING

Recall from the beginning of this chapter that the combined effects of corporate and personal taxes can be summarized as follows:

$$\text{tax advantage of debt} = \frac{1 - t_p}{(1 - t_E)(1 - t_c)}$$

where t_p is the personal rate and t_E is the personal rate on equity income, having regard for the capital gains tax rate and the deferring of capital gains. Simply deducting interest from corporate taxes would be fine if individuals paid no tax, or even if individuals paid tax at the same rate on income from debt and income from equity. In that case the issue is clear: debt financing is tax preferred. But suppose that the rate of individual tax is lower for individuals on equity income. Given the ability to defer capital gains and the lower capital gains tax rate, this is indeed the case. It now becomes unclear whether corporate debt financing is tax preferred. If the personal rate on equity is sufficiently low, individuals could well prefer paying a low personal rate on disbursements of fully taxed corporate income rather than a higher personal rate on tax shielded disbursements of corporate income. If so, equity financing would be tax preferred. Recalling the special cases:

- If $t_p = t_E$, then only corporate tax t_c is relevant and we are back to the analysis of the previous section where debt is tax preferred.
- If $1 - t_p = (1 - t_E)(1 - t_c)$, the effects of corporate and personal taxes cancel out, leaving the capital structure unaffected by taxes. In this case the costs of financial distress would probably rule the day and equity financing would dominate.
- If $1 - t_p > (1 - t_E)(1 - t_c)$, the combined effect of personal and corporate taxes will favor debt financing. Consider the following example in which the corporate rate is 35%, the personal rate is 40%, which is paid on interest income, and a capital gains rate is 28% but the investor is able to reduce this to an effective rate of 10% by deferring capital gains. Moreover, all equity income is in the form of capital gains. Now consider two extreme forms of financing: all debt and all equity. The following table shows the net of (all) tax income flowing ultimately to the investor when the firm earns an income of 100.

	Debt	Equity
Ebit	100	100
Corporate tax @ 0.35	0	35
Earnings net of corporate tax	100	6.5
Personal tax	40	6.5
Personal income net of tax	60	58.5

- If $1 - t_p < (1 - t_E)(1 - t_c)$, equity financing is preferred. To illustrate, we can repeat the above example, changing only the personal tax rate paid by the investor on interest income. Suppose this is now increased from 40% to 42%. As the revised table now shows, this would just tip the balance in favor of equity financing.

	Debt	Equity
Ebit	100	100
Corporate tax @ 0.35	0	35
Earnings net of corporate tax	100	65
Personal tax	42	6.5
Personal income net of tax	58	58.5

Thus, the tax bias rests on how tax affects the net of tax income flowing to investors, not simply on the firm's net of tax earnings.

CONCLUSION

This chapter has addressed probably the two most important questions in corporate finance: should a firm undertake certain investment activity, and if so, how should it pay for these investments? These are the standard subjects of capital budgeting and capital structure. The difference here is that these questions are posed at a time when the firm is subject to stress, just after some shock by which the firm loses value. The investment options are, in part, recovery options. Can the firm recover from the shock of losing productive assets by reconstruction of those assets? Can the firm recover from some loss of value by undertaking investment projects that are identified before the loss? Can the firm recover from the adverse publicity of a liability suit by intensive marketing? These questions can be resolved with standard capital budgeting tools, but the parameters may change as a result of the loss. As we saw in Chapter 9, reconstruction of a productive asset that is accidentally destroyed is not a foregone conclusion; the post-loss replacement cost of the asset may simply be too high relative to post-loss estimates of future income. Even new, investment opportunities may come unstuck as a result of the loss if the event depresses future demand or inflates future costs. The point is that the loss changes the context in which these capital budgeting decisions are made.

The financing options for these post-loss investments may be very constrained. Losses will tend to fall disproportionately on equity and consume cash. The firm will face its post-loss financing decisions with less cash and more leverage (as well as possible reduced earnings potential). Even if post-loss investments can potentially add value, this value can be lost if the weakened financial condition increases the probability of future bankruptcy, distorts projects selection, and intensifies the asset substitution and underinvestment problems. If severe, these post-loss stresses may prevent the firm from raising external capital, especially debt. Moreover, the fact that shocks to value fall disproportionately on equity creates a bias in favor of post-loss equity financing to restore an optimal capital structure. But this equity preference is only a bias, not a foregone conclusion. The firm may have been underlevered before the loss. Moreover, there is no reason to expect that the optimal leverage will be unaffected by the loss. The post-loss financing decision still needs to balance the tax advantages of debt with its various frictional costs such as bankruptcy costs and distortions in project selection.

REFERENCES

Basin, J. 1989. "An Empirical Investigation of the Pecking Order Hypothesis." *Financial Management* 18:26–35.

Miller, Merton H. 1977 "Debt and Taxes," *Journal of Finance* 32:261–75.

Myers, S. C. 1984. "The Capital Structure Puzzle." *Journal of Finance* 39:575–92.

Myers, S. C., and N. S. Majluf. 1984. "Corporate Finance and Investment Decisions When Firms Have Information Investors Do Not Have." *Journal of Financial Economics* 13:187–222.

A P P E N D I X

PROBLEM 1

An cash stream of e dollars, growing at a rate g in perpetuity, will have a capitalized value of $e/(k - g)$, give a discount rate of k. For an unlevered firm k is the cost of equity and will be determined by the risk characteristics (i.e., the beta) of the earnings stream. The following variation on this valuation is necessary for some of the examples developed in this chapter. A fixed level of earnings, e, is reduced by a constant interest payment, $k_D D$, where k_D is the cost of debt and D is the value of that debt. The net payment, $e - K_D D$, needs to be valued using the cost of equity k_E (given the leverage) as the discount factor. The problem is that the net payment has an implicit growth rate, g^N, that needs to be calculated. Once this is known, the valuation equation is:

$$E = \frac{e - k_D D}{k_E - g^N} \quad \text{given} \quad V = \frac{e}{k - g}$$

PROBLEM 2

This is the well-known problem of relating the cost of equity and cost of debt to each other. The weighted average cost of capital averages the cost of equity, k^E, and the cost of debt, k^D, each weighted by their share of total value E/V and D/V:

$$k = \frac{D}{V} k_E + \frac{D}{V} k_D \quad : \quad k_E = \frac{V}{E} k - \frac{D}{E} k_D$$

To solve problem 1, since the earnings stream e is fixed (and taxes are not yet considered), the value of the earnings stream will be independent of how it is allocated across equity and debt; $V = V^N + D$. Thus:

$$\frac{e - k_D D}{k_E - g^N} + D = \frac{e}{k - g} \quad : \quad g^N = k_E - \frac{(k - g)(e - k_D D)}{(e - (k - g)D)}$$

Substituting from the weighted average cost of capital,

$$g^N = \frac{V}{E} k - \frac{D}{E} k_D - \frac{(k-g)(e-k_D D)}{(e-(k-g)D)}$$

Now suppose that the level of e changes from e_1 to e_2 and growth changes from g_1 to g_2 when debt is introduced. However the risk characteristics (i.e., the beta) are assumed to be unaltered and the value of the levered and unlevered firms both can be determined using the same discount rate k.

$$V(\text{unlevered}) = \frac{e_1}{k-g_1}$$

$$V(\text{levered}) = \frac{e_2 - k_D D}{k_E - g_2^N} - D = \frac{e_2}{k-g_2}$$

Thus, we can write the implicit growth rate g_2^N in the form:

$$g_2^N = k_E - \frac{(k-g_2)(e_2 - k_D D)}{(e_2 - (k-g_2)D)}$$

CHAPTER 11

Post-loss Financing: Liquidity and Debt Renegotiation

Post-loss investment sometimes offers the possibility that value lost from a risky event can be partly recovered. Destroyed assets can be replaced, increased future cost and reduced demand from the event may be repaired by remedial investment, and preexisting investment opportunities may still be present. But post-loss investment requires funding which, if not already in place, must be secured after the loss. Post-loss financing has to run the gauntlet of problems that were associated with financial distress. The possibility for bankruptcy can cause fundability issues; new investors may view the firm as not creditworthy after a loss has destroyed value and increased leverage. Moreover, potential future distress also causes distortions in project selection as existing shareholders have the chance to default on debt. In severe cases, this can cause dysfunctional investment decisions. In the low value, highly levered post-loss context, the underinvestment and asset substitution problems can be especially severe.

This discussion suggests that there are well-defined limits on post-loss financing and that it may neither be forthcoming nor desired after a very severe loss. For more moderate losses, post-loss investment may be both fundable and value additive. Implicit in the analysis is a liquidity issue. Firms awash in cash are not faced with such hard choices after a loss. Such firms can finance post-loss investments internally, without worrying about fundability and asset substitution and underinvestment. But cash has opportunity costs. Holding cash usually involves low returns, and its use for post-loss investment may involve the sacrifice of dividend payments.

In this chapter we will focus on liquidity issues. We will begin by reviewing capital structure and dividend policies of a firm and see how these policies are affected by random losses. We will show that sudden changes in dividends can signal a lowering of insider expectations about future earnings. Thus, it is important to be able to distinguish whether the risky event does indeed carry information about future earnings. When events carry negative information about earnings, management may wish to let dividends fall to "correctly" manage investor expectations. If so, maintaining dividends at high levels is not desirable and post-loss cash is not required for this purpose. However, we will show that post-loss financing can be used as a smoothing mechanism to avoid sending damaging signals when earnings are disturbed by uninformative events.

The chapter then switches to "liquidity crunches" for which the absence of liquid assets can threaten the firm's survival (or at least keep it solvent). We will show if, and how, post-loss financing can be used to avoid such problems. Finally, we will reflect on the hangover effect of debt. Many of the post-loss financing woes we have addressed arose because of high post-loss leverage. The loss of value from excess leverage is often shared by stakeholders, shareholders can lose franchise value through bankruptcy, and creditors can lose value in default. This gives an incentive to renegotiate debt obligations, and we will show how renegotiation can add value after risky losses.

INFORMATION ASYMMETRY—THE PECKING ORDER HYPOTHESIS

A Review of the Pecking Order Hypothesis

Another well-known theory of capital structure is known as the "pecking order hypothesis" (see Myers and Majluf, 1984, and Myers, 1985). We will briefly review this idea and then see why it can be relevant to post-loss financing. This hypothesis takes its cue from the prospect that insiders may have better information about what is happening within a firm and may therefore be able to forecast future earnings more accurately.

Think of a firm as having a number of "insiders" who can be managers and who have access to private information about the firm's activities. These insiders are clearly in an excellent position to forecast future earnings. Insiders often do own shares. Outsiders are other investors who own or might trade in the firm's shares but do not have access to inside information. Thus, insiders believe they are better informed than outsiders about factors that will affect future profit. Suppose this private information leads insiders to be optimistic. Not being privy to such good news, outsiders have no such reason to be optimistic. The firm needs to finance a new investment. How should it raise the money? Since outsiders are not so optimistic, they are unlikely to pay much for newly issued equity. Financing in this way would therefore cause a large dilution, and insiders would end up giving away all the privately expected profit to outsiders. It would be better to finance with external debt because the insiders would not have to share this anticipated upside. However, debt financing can still give away some of the cream because optimistic expectations imply that debt will have a low default risk. Better still, from the insider's view, is not to share the potential future profit with any newcomers but to pay for the new investment with inside funds. Thus, with optimistic inside information, there would be a ranking of ways of financing the investment: first inside funds, then new debt, and finally new equity.

Reverse the situation, and insiders now have negative information. One can now argue that since outsiders are likely to be more optimistic than insiders, selling new shares is a good idea; outsiders would be (in insiders' minds) overpaying for the new shares and thereby subsidizing the cost of the new investment. The reasoning would appear to reverse that in the last paragraph. However, now let outsiders be a little more sophisticated (if not directly informed). They should anticipate that when a firm issues new equity, it is quite likely that insiders have low expectations of future earnings. Investors are suspicious, and this is reflected in a low response. Insiders would not wish to share the promise of good news with new investors and any attempt to issue new shares is perceived as a bad signal. Thus, we begin to see an ordering appearing.

- Internal financing is most desirable.
- Debt financing is next best.
- Hybrid financing (e.g., convertible bonds) comes next.
- Equity financing is least desirable.

This is not the only theory of capital structure. If it were, we would never see firms issue new equity unless they had run out of all other possibilities. This theory must be placed alongside the costs of distress hypothesis (which tends to favor equity) and the tax reasoning (which tends to favor debt). It is just that on top of these effects the pecking order adds a tilt towards internal financing and towards external debt rather than equity. The pecking order becomes an additional factor to consider whenever investors have reason to believe inside information is important.

The Pecking Order Hypothesis and Post-loss Financing

In Chapter 7 we saw how the pecking order model explains why firms may wish to avoid risk. If internal capital is preferred to finance new investments, then unhedged losses can exhaust internal capital and expose the firm to the higher hurdle of outside capital. Here we will look directly at the post-loss investment decisions. The pertinent question here is whether inside information is likely to be an important issue following the occurrence of some risky event.
    Consider the following events:

- A U.S. firm trading in Europe suffers a moderate loss from currency fluctuation.
- A firm is being sued in a class action for defective products.
- A fire destroys one of two production facilities for a firm.

All three scenarios cause the firm to seek new financing. Are the respective financing decisions likely to encounter any peculiar problems from information asymmetry? In the currency loss the event is quite transparent: exchange rates are public information, and if investors have reasonable information about the geographical distribution of the firm's business, they can assess the likely impact on earnings from a given currency change. Moreover, with reasonable information about the firm's activities, they can roughly assess the continuing impact on the firm; for example, will the firm still be able to sell profitably in foreign markets? While we are not arguing there is perfect information, the loss itself is unlikely to give rise to any severe information asymmetry issues. For this loss the pecking order hypothesis may not be so important. Because the loss is quite transparent, raising new debt or equity may not present any peculiar problems.

For the liability suit there could be real information problems. In negotiating a settlement, the firm will be wary about information it reveals for fear it will compromise its ability to defend should the case come to trial. Moreover, insiders will have private documentation on the product, will know of any settlement offers, will know how adverse publicity is affecting current contract negotiations with other customers, and may well use the event to reexamine product quality and safety. In all, there is likely to be a lot of private information that is very important for forecasting the outcome of the settlement negotiations or trial, as well as for forecasting the impact of the suit on future profitability. Raising external funds, especially equity, could be problematic. If the settlement is not yet reached, a new equity issue might be interpreted as a signal that the management is pessimistic of the outcome. Additionally, a new issue could be read by investors to imply that the suit would adversely affect future earnings.

The fire loss is probably "in between." The fire itself, unless it is minor, will probably be public information. How much information outsiders will have on the disruption of production, the ability to meet current and future orders from the diminished production, the duration of the interruption, and so on, is unclear. Of particular importance is how the loss is affecting planned investment decisions. The loss is a disturbance of the normal course of business, and this does put outside investors, relying on public information, at a disadvantage in forecasting post-loss earnings.

These examples show that the loss events carry different information to outsiders. Events that are imperfectly observed and appraised by outsiders are, under the pecking order hypothesis, more costly to finance externally. Consequently, there is a bigger gain from preserving internal funds by use of hedges. We will now develop these ideas and look more closely at information effects of risky events.

LIQUIDITY PROBLEMS AND POST-LOSS FINANCING

Liquidity Headaches, New Investment, and Dividend Policy

Let us take stock for a moment. In the previous chapter we showed how large losses could deplete the value and disturb the financial structure of a firm. While post-loss reinvestment may lead to some recapture of value, post-loss financing does present serious challenges. The firm may find it difficult to raise new money, especially debt, if the loss is severe and the firm is already highly levered. If post-loss leverage is high enough, the firm may even find it difficult to raise new equity to finance positive NPV projects, for those investments will shore up old debt and shareholders will not be able to capture the full value added. Moreover, from the pecking order hypothesis, some large losses may widen the information gap between insiders and potential new investors. If so, financing post-loss investment with equity will be especially troublesome. But let us switch to the other end of the spectrum. There may be smaller losses, which are transparent to outsiders for which post-loss financing is especially suited. If the loss is small enough and the firm has some cash, there will be little problem. There are also intermediate losses that, while not threatening the firm's survival, do exhaust its liquidity and can derail post-loss reinvestment, displace new investment, or force the firm to change its dividends.

The formulas for the post-loss value of the original equity before and after loss, assuming no default risk, are:

$$V(E) = V_0 + L - K_t + V_t - D - T \qquad (11.1)$$

$$V'(E) = -C + V_0' + L - K_t' + V_t' - D - T' \qquad (11.2)$$

The firm needs C to pay for the loss and has cash L. If $L < C$, the firm is forced to consider new debt or equity or to give up some post-loss investment projects. But even if $L > C$, there are some real choices. Paying for the loss with cash may require that shareholders forgo a dividend payment. This gets us into a rather controversial topic. Does dividend policy affect firm value?

Arguments on dividend policy go both ways.[1] The traditional view, still held by many practitioners, seems to be that the market favors higher dividend payouts. But the Modigliani–Miller perfect market model, which implies the irrelevancy of capital structure, also implies the irrelevancy of dividend payouts. Adapting this model for taxes would seem to favor a low dividend payout insofar as capital gains taxes are lower than taxes on dividends. Yet this would leave a problem of why dividends are paid at all. A middle position sounds like revealed preference logic. Firms have adapted their dividend policies to meet the needs of clienteles (or investors have shopped around for their preferred dividend policy).[2] If so, one should not expect a cross-sectional relationship between dividend policy and firm value. The implicit stability of this idea is echoed in models that stress the information content of changes in dividends.[3] Changes in dividends may signal changes in expected earnings, and sudden changes do appear to be associated with stock price changes. This would suggest a case for dividend stability or for smoothing dividends in the face of random fluctuations in earnings. Let us adopt the middle-of-the-road view that value maximization is consistent with a wide range of dividend policies but that sudden changes in dividends can trigger stock price movements.

Now consider an unhedged loss and its potential effect on dividends and post-loss investment decisions. If the losses are paid for by varying dividends, dividends will become unstable. But would this affect value? If the losses are truly random, one could argue that they carry no information about future earnings. But this is too simple. Sudden unhedged losses are not the only source of variation in earnings. Short-run earnings changes can signal changes in cost efficiency or changes in product demand that affect long-run earnings. Such variations are real signals but are scrambled together with isolated losses caused by events such

---

1. For a summary see Brealy and Myers (1996, ch. 16), and Miller (1986).
2. See Miller and Scholes (1978).
3. See Bhattacharya (1979) and Miller and Rock (1986).

as changing currencies, uninsured fires, and liability suits. Even if unhedged losses do represent noise, it may be difficult for investors to isolate this noise from signals of changes in long-run value. Moreover, we should be a little skeptical of the view that unhedged losses contain no signals of future earnings. Liability losses can dampen future product demand, property losses can lead to interruptions of customers' orders and can affect future demand,[4] and unhedged losses can displace future investment, as we saw in the crowding out hypothesis.

Informative and Uninformative (Persistent and Transient) Events[5]

Taking our cue from the last paragraph, let us separate risky events into those that are informative of future earnings and those that are uninformative. Informative events can be defined as those risky events that influence future earnings expectations and uninformative events are those that do not influence expectations of future earnings. The former shocks have some degree of persistence in earnings, and the latter are transitory. The distinction between informative and uninformative may not always be clear-cut in practice. It is useful to make the separation because it can be shown that the information carried by a risky event is an important factor in deciding post-loss investment and financing (and later hedging). Describe earnings, then, in the current year, N_1, as some base level, $\underline{N}_1$, disturbed by some risky events: m, which is informative, and $\overline{u}$, which is uninformative:

$$N_1 = \underline{N}_1 + m + u$$

Now suppose that if we knew m, we could forecast expected earnings next year as follows:

4. It can be argued that it is not the fact that the losses are unhedged that affects product demand, but that the losses occurred at all. While this is true, the losses may be more transparent if they are unhedged and force a change in dividends.

5. Signaling models of risk management have been derived by Breeden and Wisvanathan (1996) and DeMarzo and Duffie (1995). The model outlined here is derived from one by Doherty (1999). See also Core and Schrand (1999) for a discussion of the valuation effects of informative and uninformative events.

$$E(N_2) = N_1 + am$$

where a is some parameter that reflects the degree of information carried by m. Notice that $E(N_2)$ does not depend on u precisely because it is uninformative and transitory.

A dividend signaling story can now be developed as follows. Insiders know the composition of earnings, they know $\underline{N}_1$, m, and u. But considers only observe N_1 (or maybe only the dividend d paid from N). Because insiders observe $\underline{N}_1$ and m they can make an earnings forecast, $E(N_2)$, as shown above. But outsiders see, at best, only N and must make an uninformed guess; for example, as follows:

$$E(N_2) = \underline{N}_1 + a\, E(m|N_1)$$

where $E(m|N_1)$ is the outsider's conjecture (conditional expectation) of the expected value of m, based only on having observed previous period earnings, N_1.[6] Because of this uninformed guess, outsiders are likely to underestimate next year's earnings (relative to insiders) if m turns out to be high, and overestimate if m turns out to be low.

You can see now why mangers might sometimes wish that outsiders were better informed. When information asymmetries arise, there are sometimes outcomes where those who are informed can send credible "signals" to the uninformed such that the market reaches an equilibrium with full information. This takes us into a rather technical economics literature on adverse selection, which was reviewed briefly in Chapter 3. A notion introduced there was the idea of a separating equilibrium. The idea is roughly as follows. Suppose that there are two (or more) firms that have similar *expected* earnings in year 1, but as it happens, firm 1 realizes a low level of m and firm 2 realizes a high level. The managers of each firm know the m for their firm and can therefore forecast next year's earnings with some accuracy. Outsiders do not see m and are handicapped in forecasting.

Can the manager of the high-m firm send a credible signal to investors to convince them that the earnings forecast for that firm

---

6. The value of $E(m|N_1)$ can be calculated by $\Sigma_i p(m = m_i|N_1)m_i$. We shall use this formula in the example of Overseas Trading below.

is high? "Credible" means that the signal is believable, and such a signal would only have rationally been sent by a firm that knew its m to be high. In other words, such a signal wound never be sent by a low-m firm. Paying a high dividend might be such a signal. What we have to show is that paying a high dividend imposes a higher cost on the management of the low-m firm than on the high-m firm.[7] The reasons a low-m firm may not wish to deceive its investors by paying a high dividend are:

1. It is more difficult to pay the dividend because lower m signifies lower earnings. This means that the low-m firm may have to raise costly external capital to fund the dividend payment of the forgo new investments and thereby lose its NPV.

2. If high dividends is paid despite low m, then next-year earnings will most likely be much lower than expected and the consequent revaluation of the stock price more severe. Large falls in price could threaten incumbent management.

3. Sending false signals can potentially result in civil action.

If it is more difficult, or more costly, for low-m firms to pay high dividends, there can be a separating equilibrium, and then investors will believe that dividends provide a reliable signal of future earnings.[8]

Overseas Trading Corp. has expected earnings of N = 100 + m + u. *The term* m *is an informative event that picks up earnings fluctuations due to variations in cost and demand. Call* m *a "systematic earnings fluctuation," meaning that the revealed value of* m *this year carries information about future expected earnings. The term* u *is a variable that picks up variations in earnings due to foreign currency changes. The term* u *is noise and is purely random; it carries no information about future earnings. The probability distributions of* m *and* u *are given in the following table.*

---

7. Showing that low-m firms face a higher cost from paying a high dividend is a necessary, but not a sufficient, condition for a separating equilibrium.

8. This reasoning is based on the Rothschild and Stiglitz (1976) model of adverse selection.

m	probability of	u	probability of u
−100	⅓	−100	⅓
0	⅓	0	⅓
100	⅓	100	⅓

The firm has cash of 100 and an opportunity to invest in a project that will cost 90 and has a present value of 120. In recent years earnings have averaged about 100 and the firm has paid a stable dividend of 50.

Information Available to Insiders and Outsiders

The firm's management can decompose earnings into its components $100 + m + u$. *They consider that the revealed value of* m *carries important information about future earnings, and they form the following adaptive expectation about earnings for next year and subsequent years* $E^M(N_{2+})$ *refers to expectations held by the management, and* N_{2+} *refers to earnings in years 2 and onwards):*

$$E^M(N_{2+}) = \underline{N}_1 + am_1 \quad \text{and} \quad N_1 = \underline{N}_1 + m + u$$

where m_1 *is the revealed value of* m *in period 1. The term* a *is a parameter with value 0.8, measuring the effect of period 1 shocks on period 2 earnings.*

In contrast, outside investors cannot observe the components of N, *only its total value. Consequently, their expectation of next year's and future earnings is (superscript* I *on expectations refers to outside investors):*

$$E^I(N_{2+}) = \underline{N}_1 + a\,E(m/N_1) = \underline{N}_1 + a\,\{\Sigma_i p(m_i/N_i)\,m_i)\}$$

where $p(m_i/N_1)$ *is the probability that the systematic variable* m *was some level* m_i, *given the observed level of overall earnings* N_1 *for the year. Now the conditional probabilities,* $p(m_i/N_1)$, *can be calculated from Bayes' rule as follows.*

$$p(m - i|N_1) = \frac{p(N_1|m_i)p(m_i)}{\Sigma_j\, p(N_1|m_j)p(m_j)}$$

Let us work out the adaptive expectations of future earnings for insiders and outsiders. First, consider the probability distribution of N_1. *The first table below shows all possible combinations of* m *and* n *and the corresponding value* N *together with the probability* (m *and* u *are assumed to be independent). The second table summarizes these combinations into a probability distribution for* N.

$N_1 = \underline{N}_1 + m + u$	Probability
100 − 100 − 100 = −100	1/9
100 − 100 + 0 = 0	1/9
100 − 100 + 100 = 100	1/9
100 + 0 − 100 = 0	1/9
100 + 0 + 0 = 100	1/9
100 + 0 + 100 = 200	1/9
100 + 100 − 100 = 100	1/9
100 + 100 + 0 = 200	1/9
100 + 100 + 100 = 300	1/9

N_1	Probability
−100	1/9
0	2/9
100	3/9
200	2/9
300	1/9

Bad News Scenario: N_1 turns out to be 0; $m = -100$ and $u = 0$

Insider observe all values, N_1, m, *and* u.
For insiders, calculating $E^M(N_2)$ *is easy:*

$$\text{insiders} \quad E^M(N_2) = (100) + 0.8(-100) = 20$$

Thus, insiders know the "bad news" (that the low level of N *is explained by a low* m*) and revise their earnings estimate way down to 20.*

Outsiders only see that N_1 *is zero but do not know its composition. This value could have occurred either because* m = −100 *and* u = 0 *or because* m = 0 *and* u = −100. *Since each pair has a probability of* 1/9, *the probability of* N_1 *being 0 is* 1/9 + 1/9 = 2/9. *If we use Bayes' rule, the conditional probabilities are:*

$$p(m = -100|N = 0) = \frac{p(N = 0|m = -100)(p(m = -100))}{\begin{aligned}&p(N = 0|m = -100)(p(m = -100)) \\ &+ p(N = 0|m = 0)(p(m = 0)) \\ &+ p(N = 0|m = 100)(p(m = 100))\end{aligned}}$$

$$= \frac{(\tfrac{1}{3})(\tfrac{1}{3})}{(\tfrac{1}{3})(\tfrac{1}{3}) + (\tfrac{1}{3})(\tfrac{1}{3}) + (0)(\tfrac{1}{3})} = 0.5$$

$$p(m = 0|N = 0) = \frac{p(N = 0|m = 0)(p(m = 0))}{\begin{aligned}&p(N = 0|m = -100)(p(m = -100)) \\ &+ p(N = 0|m = 0)(p(m = 0)) \\ &+ p(N = 0|m = 100)(p(m = 100))\end{aligned}}$$

$$= \frac{(\tfrac{1}{3})(\tfrac{1}{3})}{(\tfrac{1}{3})(\tfrac{1}{3}) + (\tfrac{1}{3})(\tfrac{1}{3}) + (0)(\tfrac{1}{3})} = 0.5$$

$$p(m = 100|N = 0) = \frac{p(N = 0|m = 100)(p(m = 100))}{\begin{aligned}&p(N = 0|m = -100)(p(m = -100)) \\ &+ p(N = 0|m = 0)(p(m = 0)) \\ &+ p(N = 0|m = 100)(p(m = 100))\end{aligned}}$$

$$= \frac{(0)(\tfrac{1}{3})}{(\tfrac{1}{3})(\tfrac{1}{3}) + (\tfrac{1}{3})(\tfrac{1}{3}) + (0)(\tfrac{1}{3})} = 0$$

Thus, the outside expectation is:

$$E^1(N_{2+}) = (100) - 0.8\{0.5(-100) + 0.5(0) + 0(100)\} = 40$$

Not surprisingly, insiders and outsiders have formed different expectations about future earnings. Informed insiders know there is bad news on m *and have lowered their expectations about future earnings down to 20. But outsiders only have observed that* N_1 *was very low at zero. They suspect that this might be bad news for the future (i.e., that the low* N_1 *was due to* m *being very low). But they can also reassure themselves that low* N_1 *could have been an aberration and is explained by a low, uninformative* u. *Thus, outsiders are not quite so pessimistic and form an expectations of 40 for future earnings.*

Now let us see how these differences in expectation affect investment and dividend decisions going forward. Recall that the firm has an investment opportunity that costs 90 and an NPV of 120. Moreover, the firm has maintained a dividend of 50 in recent years. Following this bad year, $N_1 = 0$, *the firm faces some touch choices about maintaining its*

*dividend and paying for the new investment. For example, if the firm
reduces its dividend to pay for the new investment, will outsiders see
the reduced dividend as a signal that insiders are pessimistic about the
future? First, let us consider that investors observe overall earnings, N_1
(but not m and u), and read nothing further into the dividend. We will
then consider the case when outside investors see the dividend as a signal
of the managers' inside knowledge.*

Investment and Dividend Choices

Investor Expectations Do Not Depend on Dividend

*The firm has zero earnings, 100 in cash, an investment opportunity that
will cost 90 and generate a value of 120. Two clear choices are:*

1. *Use cash for the new investment and pay dividend of 10. In
   this case, the value to shareholders can be calculated as the
   value of expected earnings from current operations plus the
   expected earnings from the project plus the dividend. Now the
   value of equity from current operations, cash, and investment
   opportunities will depend on whose expectations we use:
   insiders' or outsiders'.*

   insiders' estimated value $20/0.1 + 120 + 10 = 330$
   outsiders' estimated value $40/0.1 + 120 + 10 = 530$

2. *Sacrifice the project and pay a dividend of 50 and keep cash of
   50. The value of the shareholder stake is now:*

   insiders' estimated value $20/0.1 + 0 + 50 + 50 = 300$
   outsiders' estimated value $40/0.1 + 0 + 50 + 50 = 500$

*The better strategy is to withhold the dividend and invest in the new
project. Note that the difference in value between the choices is equal to
the NPV of the project.*

Investor Expectations do Depend on Dividend

*Now suppose that outside investors use the dividend payment of a signal
of insider information. Specifically, assume that if a dividend is paid at
its historic level of 50, investors interpret this to mean that the management is optimistic about future earnings (i.e., investors believe that
the current year's earnings of 0 are explained by m being 0 and u being
−100). This combination bodes well for future earnings, and thus they*

revise their expectation that $p(m_i = 0/N_1 = 0)$. *But if a dividend of 10 is paid, this is interpreted as a signal that managers believe future earnings to be low (i.e., investors believe that the current year's earnings of 0 are explained by* u *being 0 and* m *being* -100). *Thus, a dividend of 50 persuades outsiders that future expected earnings are 40, and a dividend of 10 persuades them that expected earnings are 20.*

The strategy choices concerning investment and dividends are the same as above, and the equity valuations are:

1. *Invest in project and pay 10 dividend:*

    insiders' estimated value $20/0.1 + 120 + 10 = 330$

    outsiders' estimated value $20/0.1 + 120 + 10 = 330$

2. *Pay dividend of 50 and sacrifice project:*

    insiders' estimated value $20/0.1 + 0 + 50 + 50 = 300$

    outsiders' estimated value $40/0.1 + 0 + 50 + 50 = 500$

What should management now choose to do? They could pay the dividend to keep outsiders (deceptively) happy, but management's belief is that the dividend level of 50 could not be sustained and the new investment would be lost. The equity would trade at 500, but insiders would believe this to be overvalued.

The firm may be able to borrow 90, undertake the new investment, and still maintain the dividend at 50. If priced at par, the new debt would pay for the reinvestment and the value would rise to 530. But again management believes this value to be unsustainable and would expect a future price collapse. It is true they could inflate investor expectations with the dividend, sell their shares and run, but there are moral and legal constraints on this behavior. Thus, a reasonable strategy would be to reduce the dividend to investors to 10 thereby sending a clear and accurate signal of future earnings, and undertake the investment. Management and outsiders would both believe the firm to be worth 330.

Better News Scenario: $N_1 = 0$; $m = 0$, and $u = -100$

Notice that "better news" does not refer to the level of earnings this year (which is still zero) but that it is explained by the transient effect of u $= -100$. *There is no adverse message for the future,* m $= 0$, *and therefore management's expectation of future earnings is more optimistic. We can use the same methodology to work through management's and outsider's earnings expectations.*

insiders $E^M(N_2) = (100) + 0.8(0) = 100$

To get outsider expected earnings, first calculate the conditionally ex-pected value of m *using Bayes' rule. But think for a moment. From the outsiders' perspective, nothing has changed. They still see earnings this year of zero, and so outsiders' expectations have to be the same as before. Formally,*

$$p(m_i = -100/N_1 = 0) = 0.5; p(m_i = 0/N_1$$
$$= 0) = 0.5; p(m_i = +100/N_1 = 0) = 0$$

Thus, the outside expectation is:

outsiders $E^1(N_2) = (100) + 0.8(0.5(-100) + 0.5(0)) = 40$

Now look at the choices for the new investment project and the dividend payment.

Investment and Dividend Choices: Investor Expectations Do Depend on Dividend

If investors do read dividend signals as indicative of future earnings, the respective choices pan out as follows:

1. *Invest in project and pay 10 dividend:*

insiders' estimated value $100/0.1 + 120 + 10 = 1130$
outsiders' estimated value $40/0.1 + 120 + 10 = 530$

2. *Pay dividend of 50 and sacrifice project:*

insiders' estimated value $100/0.1 + 0 + 50 + 50 = 1100$
outsiders' estimated value $100/0.1 + 0 + 50 + 50 = 1100$

On the one hand, the management does not wish to sacrifice the project, but it also would not wish to send a negative signal to investors by withholding the dividend. If the firm is able to borrow 90 to finance the project, it can get the best of both worlds: maintain dividends and un-dertake the project. Assuming little or no default risk, the issue is fund-able and the firm can capture the NPV of the new investment. With this post-loss financing strategy, the value is 1130 and insider and outsider expectations are in harmony.

Risk Management Strategy: Smooth Cash Flows from Uninformative (Transient) Events

The example of Overseas Trading and the analysis of dividend signals suggest a strategy for post-loss financing. Risky losses can be informative and uninformative. Both losses deplete current earnings, but they impose different costs and opportunities on the firm.

Negatively informative shocks not only deplete current earnings but will lead insiders to revise expectations about future earnings. The ability of the firm to maintain its dividend will be compromised. The firm may still be able to raise new money to make the dividend payment (since the information is not observed by outsiders), but to do so would send a false signal to investors about future earnings. If a separating equilibrium exits, the management will be better off reducing dividends and moderating investor expectations about the future. But informative losses also affect the value added from new investments. Most likely, an informative loss will be associated with a downward revision in expected future earnings and the payback from post-loss investment can be adversely affected. The earnings generated from nondamaged assets, replacement of damaged assets, and assets proposed in future investments all can be affected. Insofar as these paybacks are revised downwards, the incentive to commit new funds to reinvestment or new investment will be weakened. The need for post-loss financing will be reduced. There is little need to raise new money after informative losses either to maintain dividends (which would mislead investors) or fund investments (which have low NPV).

Positively informative shocks carry good news about the future. One can imagine counter-examples where informative losses increased expected earnings. For example, when insurers suffer major losses through natural disasters such as hurricanes or earthquakes, they sometimes experience increases in stock values. This is thought to reflect a potential increase in demand as the event educates consumers about the level of risk faced and thereby increases the demand for insurance. Moreover, such events deplete the capacity of all insurers to write new business and thereby contract the market supply curve. The shifting of the market demand and supply curves in this way will tend to cause price increases, which can increase future profitability. For such *positively* informative shocks, there is clearly a need for post-loss financing both to maintain dividends and to capture the attractive post-loss investment opportunities.

Uninformative (transient) shocks carry no adverse information about future earnings. If there is a forced dividend reduction following such losses, an incorrect signal will be sent to investors and the stock will be undervalued relative to management expectations. This generates a demand for post-loss financing to maintain the level of dividends. The demand for post-loss financing is reinforced by the post-loss investment and reinvestment opportunities. Uninformative losses do not dampen the need for new money for post-loss investment, since the payback to new investment is, by definition, unaffected. Thus, new money is needed both to maintain dividends and to fund new investments.

To show how post-loss financing can promote dividends that are consistent with inside expectations about future earnings, we will work with an example of Asymmetric Expectations Corp.

Asymmetric Expectations Corp. (AEC) sells military equipment, and its customers are overseas governments. Contracts are usually awarded following a competitive bidding process, and AEC will lose some auctions and win others. This process results in a variable flow of business, and the revenue earned in any year is somewhat risky. Against an expected earnings in year t of N_t, AEC can give or lose an additional amount u. As the notation suggests, the random adjustment u does not affect future earnings forecasts. However, AEC has production facilities in the U.S. and is subject to domestic environmental and labor laws. Regulatory and union activity creates considerable uncertainty in AEC cost function, and this variation in cost is picked up by a further profit fluctuation of m_t where m does have a carryover effect on future earnings (i.e., m is informative about earnings). The distributions of u and m are

u	Probability of u	m	Probability of m
−100	0.25	−100	0.25
0	0.5	0	0.5
+100	0.25	+100	0.25

The expected value of N for year 1 is 100. This is expected to grow at approximately 2% in any given year if the prior observation of m is zero. However, if m = −100, N for the next year is expected to fall by 10%. If m = 100, the following year's N is expected to be 10% larger. You will notice that since E(u) = E(m) = 0, the expected earnings for any year are $E(N_t/m_{t-1}) + E(u) + E(m) = E(N_t/m_{t-1})$. The firm desires to pay a dividend that reflects the revealed level of N_t since this is the level of earnings the management believes to be sustainable. With good or bad realizations of m, management is prepared to change dividends since this signals changes in future expected earnings. But it is afraid that random fluctuations from realizations of u will force it to change dividends and that this will be misinterpreted by investors as signaling permanent earnings shifts.

The following table shows the growth of earnings over a 10-year period, with m and u being drawn randomly from the above distributions. The value of N starts at 100 and changes as m changes according to the rule defined in the last paragraph. AEC starts by trying to build up cash of 100 and does not pay a dividend in the first year. The idea is to hold a cushion against which it can absorb fluctuations in u and still maintain dividends at the target level N_t. If the cushion runs out and the firm has insufficient earnings to pay a dividend of N_t, it simply pays its available cash. If the firm runs out of cash altogether and is unable to maintain its dividend, management believes that investors will revise expectations below sustainable earnings, and the share price will fall below its fundamental value.

Year, t	N_t	u_t	m_t	$N = \underline{N} + u + m$	Dividend	Balance
1	100	0	0	100	0	100
2	102	−100	−100	−98	2	0
3	91.8	0	100	191.8	91.8	100
4	101	−100	−100	−99	1	0
5	90.9	0	100	190.9	90.9	100
6	100	100	0	200	100	200
7	102	0	−100	2	102	100
8	91.8	100	0	−8.2	91.8	0
9	93.6	100	100	293.6	93.6	200
10	103	100	0	203	103	300
11					final dividend 300	
Total	total 976.1	0	0	total 976.1	total 976.1	

You can see from the table what happens. In year 1 AEC manages to build its cash balance of 100. But adverse values of u and m both occur in year 2, forcing the firm to pay an absolutely nominal dividend of 2. The firm does OK in year 3, paying its target dividend of 91.8 and building a cash balance again to 100. But similar lousy experience in year 4 forces to the firm to all but forgo its year 4 dividend payment. The firm does manage to survive the remainder of the 10-year period without lowering dividend below the target and finishes the period with a balance of 300.

In 2 of the 10 years, AEC has been unable to pay dividends at a level that management believes is compatible with its true earnings potential. If investors do receive dividend changes as signals of expected earnings, then in early years AEC would have been significantly undervalued. This example has not built in any new investment opportunities. If it had, AEC would have found it difficult, or costly, to finance new investments with such undervaluation. Furthermore, even though AEC finds it prudent to withhold the first year's dividend to build a cash reserve, at various times over the 10 years that cash reserve falls to zero in order that target dividends can be met. The cost of maintaining dividends in years such as 4 and 8 is that AEC completely runs out of cash. In these years the firm could not take advantage of any speculative investment opportunities, let alone absorb any unexpected and unpleasant surprises. Maintaining dividends as an earnings signal may have come at a high price.

Notice another problem. The example is closed after 10 years and a "final dividend" is shown. In practice the firm would probably continue operations into the future. But by year 10 the firm has built up a surplus of 300. The excess cash can have its own problems; if it is not productively used, the firm may become a takeover target, and excess cash can have an opportunity cost in terms of a low rate of return. The excess cash has built up because the firm has a somewhat stable dividend policy in the face of very unstable earnings. No mechanism has been provided for closing this mismatch.

A Smoothing Strategy

Now let AEC take a different strategy. It still desires to maintain dividends at the target level N_t and still withholds first-year earnings to *build a cash reserve of 100. However, it now plans to borrow money should it be unable to pay the desired dividend. If a poor m event occurs, funds are depleted, but this is partly offset by a reduction in the target dividend. But this is not a complete wash; a loss of $1 causes only a 10 cent reduction in target dividends, and m events can cause liquidity problems given the parameters of the problem. An even bigger danger is that poor u draws will also deplete cash and these will not be offset by a reduction in the target dividend. Thus, the particularly important time to borrow is when the firm has adverse draws on u, such as in years 2, 4, and 8. Years 2 and 4 are particularly bad because these are also poor m years and, as mentioned, there is not a full offset on the target dividend. In the following table AEC borrows the amounts, d_t, as follows:*

$$d_2 = 100 \text{ in year 2}$$
$$d_4 = 150 \text{ in year 4}$$
$$d_7 = 64 \text{ in year 7}$$
$$d_8 = 156 \text{ in year 8}$$

Each amount is repaid in four equal installments over the subsequent four years, though interest has been ignored for simplicity and transparency. Thus, debt raised in year t is repaid by four payments each of $r = (d_t)/4$, in years t + 1, t + 2, t + 3, and t + 4. In any year t, the total repayments will be:

$$R_t = \tfrac{1}{4}(d_{t-4} + d_{t-3} + d_{t-2} + d_{t-1})$$

Unpaid interest is all repaid in year 11 simply to close the example, though we could have continued indefinitely into the future.

   With this borrowing policy, the firm maintains dividends at the target ratio in all years and thus can manage investor earnings expectations consistently with internal expectations. The firm would not need to worry so much over its cash reserve being depleted and need not accumulate large cash balances when earnings turn out particularly favorable. Notice that the final cash balance here is only 100, compared with 300 in the prior example.

Year	N	$u_t + d_t - R_t$	m	$N = N + u + m$	Dividend	Balance
1	100	0 = 0	0	100	0	100
2	102	−100 + **100** = 0	−100	2	102	0
3	91.8	0 − 25 = −25	100	166.8	91.8	75
4	101	−100 + **150** − 25 = 25	−100	26	101	0
5	90.9	0 − 25 − 37.5 = −62.5	100	128.4	90.9	37.5
6	100	100 − 25 − 37.5 = 37.5	0	137.5	100	75
7	102	0 + **64** − 37.5 = 26.5	−100	28.5	102	1.5
8	91.8	−100 + **156** − 37.5 − 16 = 2.5	0	94.3	91.8	4
9	93.6	100 − 16 − 39 = 45	100	238.6	93.6	149
10	103	100 − 16 − 39 = 45	0	148	103	194
11		final repayment −16 − 78 = −94			final dividend 100	
	total 976.1	total 0	0	total 976.1	total 976.1	

In introducing the relationship between the information conveyed in risky events and post-loss smoothing, we assumed that risky events could be cleanly separated into transient (uninformative) and persistent (informative). This clean separation allowed us to keep the explanation simple, but it was not really necessary. The simplification did seem to lead to a stark contract: smoothing uninformative events removes all noise from earnings. Thus, earnings fluctuations reflect only the remaining informative shocks and thereby convey to investors a clear signal about future earnings. Events rarely fit into such a clean dichotomy; rather, they carry more or less information, and the information can be positive or negative. Moreover, even when shocks carry negative information, as in the example of Asymmetric Information Corp. above, they do influence the desired level of post-loss debt because they can interact with uninformative events in determining whether target dividends can be met. We can easily adapt the message to the continuous case. Smoothing becomes more important for events that are uninformative or carry positive information about future earnings. In such cases the event conveys information about positive NPV reinvestment opportunities and smoothing will reduce the prospect that the recovering firm will be undervalued. Conversely, smoothing adds less value when the risky event carries negative information about future earnings.

LIQUIDITY CRUNCHES

The post-loss financing examples considered so far have focused on the possibility that the firm's value will fall below its debt obligation, leaving shareholders with an incentive to walk away and default on the debt. We will now focus on the more immediate financial problems of having sufficient cash to pay bills and exploit new investment opportunities.

Figure 11–1 shows the value of debt and equity for given potential values of the firm. If the firm's value exceeds its debt obligation, D, the equity has positive value. Thus, at value, V, the value of the debt is apparently its full face value, D, and the equity is worth E ($= V - D$). However, suppose that the value, V, is made up of both assets that are tangible and liquid, L, and assets that

F I G U R E   11–1

Liquidity and Bankruptcy

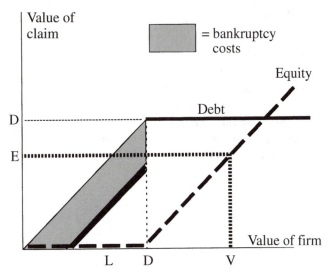

are intangible, $V - L$. The tangible assets could include cash, securities, and other assets that could be sold quite quickly. The intangible asset is the growth potential. Furthermore, suppose that the debt is due. The firm has a problem: how to repay the debt. The intangible asset cannot easily be sold to realize its value and make good the debt payment. The firm has a liquidity problem.

Liquidity problems can be more immediate. The issue may be that the firm is having trouble finding enough cash to pay its interest. To avoid bankruptcy court, the firm can sell off some tangible asset to make the interest payment. But this will have an opportunity cost. When an asset is sold, the return on that asset is lost. Another type of liquidity problem is one we have already considered. The firm has some cash and can meet its debt obligations. However, if there is some immediate claim on that cash to cover an unhedged loss, and external financing is costly, the firm may lose some future investment opportunity. This is the crowding out hypothesis discussed earlier.

Unhedged losses can bring about any of the above liquidity problems. In the following example of Tinky Toys, the firm suffers a currency loss and is able neither to meet its interest payment nor to fund a new investment.

Tinky Toys has earnings of 200 per year from existing operations. It has outstanding debt of 2000 with a 5% interest rate. The firm has 200 in cash and plans to use this for investing in a new product line that will generate further annual earnings of 21. Given the risk characteristics of these operations, the weighted average cost of capital is 7.5%. The firm has 100 shares outstanding. The first column in the following table values the firm. Total earnings, capitalized at 7.5%, give a firm value of 2947. Assuming default-free debt, debt is worth 2000 and equity 947, the latter being 9.47 per share. The cost of equity can be calculated as follows:

$$k_E = \frac{V}{E} k - \frac{D}{E} k_D = \frac{2947}{947} \, 0.075 - \frac{2000}{947} \, 0.05 = 0.1278$$

	No Loss	No New Financing	Post-Loss Equity Financing
EBIT	200 + 21 = 221	200	200 + 21 = 221
Interest	100	default	100
Tax	0	0	0
New Earnings	121	200	121
Cost of Equity, k_E	0.1278		0.1278
Value	947		947
Cash	200	200	200
Currency		−400	−400
New Equity Issue			420[a]
Cost of Investment	−200	cannot pay	−200
Value of Equity, E	947	217	947
Number of Shares, $m + n$	100	100	100 + 80 = 180
Share Price	9.47	2.17	5.26
WACC	0.075	0.075	0.075
Bankruptcy Cost		−250	
Value of Firm	2000 + 947 = 2947	200/0.075 + 200 −400 − 250 = 2217	2000 + 947 = 2947

[a]Includes 20 transaction cost.

Currency Loss and Bankruptcy

Tinky is hit with a 400 currency loss. Available cash of 200 is insufficient to cover this loss, and the firm is unable to meet interest and principal payments or pay for the new investment. Unless the firm raises new money, creditors threaten bankruptcy. The middle column shows the effects of bankruptcy. It is estimated that bankruptcy will involve a deadweight loss of 250. This represents direct costs of the bankruptcy proceedings and also includes an estimate of the loss of future earnings due to the managerial constraints imposed by court supervision. Because the risk characteristics are assumed to be unchanged, the earnings of 200 are capitalized at 7.5%, giving a value of 2667, which is adjusted to reflect cash of 200, the currency loss of 400, and the bankruptcy cost of 250, leaving a total firm value of 2217. If creditors extract exactly the face value of their debt, the value left to shareholders is 217, which averages to 2.17 per share. Other divisions of value are possible depending on the terms imposed by the court. As shown, the effect is a reduction in share value from 9.47 to 2.17 per share, a reduction of 7.3. The currency loss of 400 can account for a reduction of only 4 per share; the remaining reduction represents the effect of bankruptcy costs and the loss of the value of the new investment.

Post-loss Equity Financing to Restore Liquidity

Because the currency loss was unhedged, some loss of value is inevitable. However, the firm avoids its liquidity problem by raising new money. The firm has considerable value as an ongoing concern and sufficient residual value to shareholders to attract new investors. Suppose the firm now raises new equity. Raising a net amount of 400 will absorb the currency loss and allow Tinky to fund the new investment from its cash balances and pay interest due from earnings. Because new money is raised, I will assume a transaction cost of 20, and the firm thus needs to raise 420. Raising this amount will restore the overall value of equity, though there will be dilution. The number of new shares to be raised is:

$$n = \frac{Cm}{E^T} = \frac{420(100)}{947\ 420} = 80$$

There will now be 180 shares, and each will be valued at 5.26. By re-solving the liquidity problem, Tinky has been able to pay its interest (avoiding bankruptcy) and capture the present value of its new investment.

RENEGOTIATIONS OF DEBT AND POST-LOSS UNDERINVESTMENT

One of the specific post-loss investment opportunities to be evaluated is whether to reconstruct assets that have been destroyed. Examples in this and the previous chapter have shown how a positive NPV reinvestment opportunity can be unfundable if the firm finances the reinvestment through debt. We now consider a hangover problem from existing debt.[9]

Consider Equation (11.2) from early in this chapter, which shows the post-loss value of equity when the firm paid an amount C to reconstruct a damaged asset:

---

9. This problem is considered by Mayers and Smith (1986), who consider an insurance solution.

$$V'(E) = -C + V_0' + L - K_t' + V_t' - D - T' \qquad (11.2)$$

We can simplify things a little by assuming that L and T' are both zero and by assuming that the firm has no new investment opportunities to consider; K_t' and V_t' also are zero. However, we will expand one term, V_0', to show the present value of earnings, assuming the asset is not repaired, $V_0^{N'}$, plus the change in value from reinvestment, $\Delta V_0'$ ($V_0' = V_0^{N'} + \Delta V_0'$). One further change is a recognition that the firm has limited liability and that equity cannot have a negative value. We are left with an equation that says that equity is worth the maximum (MAX) of either ($V_0^{N'} - D + \Delta V_0' - C$) or zero:

$$V'(E) = MAX[(V_0^{N'} - D + \Delta V_0' - C); 0]$$
$$= MAX[(V_0^{N'} - D + NPV); 0] \qquad (11.2a)$$

where NPV is the net present value of the reinvestment (NPV = $\Delta V_0' - C$). If the asset is not repaired, the equation simplifies to

$$V'(E) = MAX[(V_0' - D); 0] \qquad (11.2b)$$

When we compare Equations 11.2a and 11.2b, two things are apparent. First, if $\Delta V_0'$ is greater than C, then reinvestment is a positive NPV opportunity and will add value to the firm as a whole. Second, suppose that the NPV of the reinvestment is positive, but $V_0^{N'}$ is less than D. If this is true, the firm will be insolvent if it does not reinvest and will default on the debt. If the firm does reinvest, the NPV will prop up the value of the debt and the shareholders will not reap the entire benefit from the reinvestment. The question is whether shareholders reap enough benefit from the reinvestment, after shoring up the debt, to make the reinvestment worthwhile. Consider the two possible cases:

1. If $V_0^{N'} - D + NPV > 0$, the shareholders will gain more than enough from the reinvestment to avoid default on the debt and leave the shares with some value. Reinvestment would be preferred.
2. But if $V_0^{N'} - D + NPV < 0$, the firm will be insolvent whether or not it reinvests. All the benefit from the reinvestment supports the debt, leaving nothing to entice the shareholders.

Let us work through an example and figure out how the firm might reorganize to address this issue. Consider that the firm will be worth 200 if the fire damage is not repaired and 1000 if it is required. $V_0^{N'} = 200$ and $V_0^{N'} + \Delta V_0' = 1000$; thus, $\Delta V_0' = 800$. The cost of reinvestment is 600 ($C = 600$ and NPV = 800 − 600 = 200). The firm has debt of 600, $D = 600$. We will add a couple of further features: if the firm goes bankrupt, there is a cost of 50. Consequently, if the firm does not reinvest, its net value will be 200 − 50 = 150. Finally, the shareholders own 100 shares (this will be needed later).

The following table presents the values of the firm and of its debt and equity under alternative post-loss decisions.

Decision	Firm	Debt	Equity
Reinvest	1000	600	400
Not reinvest	150	150	0
Gain	850	450	400

The value of equity will rise by 400 from reinvestment. But the cost of reinvestment is 600. If one tried to pay for the reinvestment by a new equity issue, it is clear that there is simply not enough value to persuade new investors to subscribe 600 for the new issues; the total value of all equity, old and new, would be only 400. The reinvestment is not fundable even with post-loss equity financing, nor is it desirable from the viewpoint of the original shareholders.

Reinvestment through Bankruptcy

In this case the natural outcome is for the firm to declare bankruptcy and be passed to the creditors. Let us suppose this is done. The original shares expire through bankruptcy and the new owners, the creditors, are now issued 350 shares. The ex-creditors (now the owners) can then decide whether to reinvest. They can issue 600 new shares, making a total of 950 shares.[10] Since the value of

---

10. You can calculate the number of new shares to issue from the formula previously used.

$$n = \frac{cM}{E^T - C} = \frac{600(350)}{950 - 600} = 600$$

the firm is 950 and there is no longer any debt, the new shares would be worth $600/950 \times 950 = 600$. Thus, the firm could finance the reinvestment with this issue. The following table now sets out the alternative decisions. The third column shows the equity position assumed by the ex-creditors, who are able to capture the whole 200 NPV of the reinvestment and would naturally choose to do so.

Decision	Firm	Equity ex-creditors	Equity new
Reinvest	950	350	600
Not reinvest	150	150	
Gain	800	200	

The creditors gain 200 from the reinvestment after the bankruptcy. The "correct" reinvestment decision is made, but it took a bankruptcy, with cost of 50, to get there. Can we get the firm to reinvest without going through the bankruptcy process?

Reinvestment through Debt Renegotiation

The original problem was that there was no reason for the original shareholder to reinvest, despite the positive NPV. But the creditors would have benefitted. Suppose now they all sit around a table and start negotiating. This is not a zero sum gain. One group of stakeholders, creditors, has something to gain from the reinvestment, and the other, shareholders, has nothing to lose. Surely it would pay the creditors to offer something to the shareholders to make it attractive to reinvest, without declaring bankruptcy and incurring the bankruptcy cost of 50. The creditors can offer to *renegotiate* their debt. Consider the following offer. Creditors agree to accept 700 shares in exchange for their bonds. Recall that the original shareholders hold 100 shares. After this renegotiation, all shareholders would benefit from reinvestment; the NPV of 200 would represent a gain of $200/800 = 0.25$ per share. The firm then decides to issue a further 120 shares to finance the cost of the reinvestment. Look now at the share ownership after all these transactions:[11]

Old shareholders hold	100 shares (5%)
Ex-creditors hold	700 shares (35%)
New investors hold	1200 shares (60%)
TOTAL	2000 shares

Now consider whether this reinvestment decision benefits the owners (original shareholders and ex-creditors). The following table shows the value of the holdings of the different investors

Decision	Firm	Equity ex-creditors	Equity original	Equity new investors
Reinvest	1000	350 (35%)	50 (5%)	600 (60%)
Not reinvest	200	175	25	
Gain	800	175	25	

Now the reinvestment does make sense to all post-renegotiation shareholders. Moreover, the firm can fund the reinvestment with the new issue; the new shares are worth 600 and new investors will therefore pay for the reinvestment cost.

Who has gained from the renegotiation of the debt? Clearly, the original shareholders have. Without the renegotiation the firm would have gone bankrupt and the original shares would be worthless. With renegotiation their share of the ownership is worth 50. Thus, despite a large dilution of ownership, the original shareholders gain. However, the creditors are no better off than if they had simply let the firm go bankrupt; their holding is worth 350 either way. Clearly they did not negotiate hard enough. Let us try again. Suppose creditors negotiated to replace their debt with 1500 shares. After the renegotiation the firm issues a further 2400 shares to finance reinvestment. The results come out as follows:

---

11. Since m now equals 800 (i.e., 100 + 700), the number of new shares to issue is:

$$n = \frac{cM}{E^T - C} = \frac{600(800)}{1000 - 800} = 1200$$

Old shareholders hold   100 shares (2.5%)
Ex-creditors hold   1500 shares (37.5%)
New investors hold   2400 shares (60%)
                 TOTAL   4000 shares

Decision	Firm	Equity ex-creditors	Equity original	Equity new investors
Reinvest	1000	375 (37.5%)	25 (2.5%)	600 (60%)
Not reinvest	200	187.5	12.5	
Gain	800	187.5	12.5	

Reinvestment will be chosen and the ex-creditors will hold shares worth 375 (compared with 350 after bankruptcy). Both classes of stakeholder gain from renegotiation of the debt. The overall gain from renegotiating the debt is the saving in bankruptcy cost of 50. How this gain is divided depends on the bargaining power of the creditors and original shareholders. The greater the share owner-ship negotiated by creditors, the greater their gain.

CONCLUSION

The previous chapter showed how post-loss financing could en-able the firm to capture the value of profitable investment oppor-tunities after a loss. This chapter looked at another risk manage-ment role for post-loss financing. A firm may simply run out of cash to meet current needs, and unless it can secure new sources of finance, it courts bankruptcy and loss of franchise value. Post-loss financing can be used to smooth earnings. But the smoothing role is complicated when there are information asymmetries be-tween the firm's management and outside investors. Information that is privately revealed to insiders may or may not be relevant in predicting future earnings. The problem arises when the firm suffers transient shocks that, in principle, carry no information for valuing the firm. But because outsiders are imperfectly informed, they can misinterpret these shocks as indicative of changes in fu-ture earnings that will lead to a misvaluation of the firm's equity. Particularly worrying is the prospect that negative shocks lead to an undervaluation of equity that makes it difficult to fund new, positive NPV, investment opportunities. Accordingly, we examined the effect of smoothing earnings from the effects of uninformative shocks so that the firm could maintain a dividend policy that was more in line with changes in the firm's fundamental value.

Earnings smoothing can also be used to avoid liquidity crunches. Firms sometimes are unable to meet current debt obligations when assets are illiquid. Unless cash is forthcoming, firms may be forced into bankruptcy despite having a healthy franchise value. Earnings smoothing can be used to avoid such problems.

We also examined problems that arise after a severe loss from the "hangover" or prior debt. A particular type of underinvestment problem is that the firm may fail to reconstruct assets that have been destroyed despite reconstruction having a positive NPV. Shareholders may prefer to let the firm go bankrupt rather than reinvest and let the proceeds from the reinvestment prop up debt that otherwise would have been in default. Thus, the firm must go through the bankruptcy process, with its associated costs, in order that creditors can take over the firm and undertake the reinvestment. The correct result on reinvestment is achieved at the expense of bankruptcy. The threatening costs of bankruptcy provide an incentive for creditors to renegotiate their debt by agreeing to a settlement that offers less than their face entitlement. The saving in bankruptcy costs enables deals to be struck in which the reinvestment is undertaken and both parties are better off.

Post-loss financing requires that the firm seek new funding after a loss. Contingent financing anticipates the post-loss funding needs of the firm and sets in place a dormant funding sources that will be activated if and when a loss arises. This is the next topic.

REFERENCES

Allen, Franklin, and Douglas Gale. 1997. "Financial Markets, Intermediaries and Intertemporal Smoothing." *Journal of Political Economy* 105:523–46.

Allen, Franklin, and Anthony Santomero. 1997. "The Theory of Financial Intermediation." *Journal of Banking and Finance* 21:1461–86.

Brealy, R. A., and S. C. Myers. 1996. *Principles of Corporate Finance.* New York: McGraw-Hill.

Breeden, Douglas, and S. Wiswanathan. 1996. "Why Do Firms Hedge? An Asymmetric Information Model." Working Paper, Duke University.

Core, John E., and Catherine M. Schrand. 1999. "The Effect of Accounting-Based Debt Covenants on Equity Valuation." *Journal of Accounting and Economics* 27:1–34.

DeMarzo, Peter, and Darrell Duffie. 1995. "Corporate Incentives for Hedging and Hedge Accounting." *Review of Financial Studies* 8:743–72.

Diamond, Douglas. 1997. "Liquidity, Banks and Markets." *Journal of Political Economy* 105:928–55.

Diamond, Douglas W., and Philip H. Dybvig. 1983. "Bank Runs, Deposit Insurance and Liquidity." *Journal of Political Economy* 91:401–19.

Doherty, Neil A. 1999. "Hedging, Compensation and Earnings Surprises." Paper presented at National Bureau of Economic Research Insurance Conference, February.

Mayers, David, and Clifford W. Smith Jr. 1986. "Corporate Insurance and the Underinvestment Problem." Journal of Risk and Insurance 54:45–54.

Miller, M. H. 1986. "Behavioral Rationality in Finance: The Case of Dividends." *Journal of Business* 59:451–86.

Miller, M. H., and K. Rock. 1985. "Dividend Policy under Asymmetric Information." *Journal of Finance* 40:1031–52.

Myers, Stewart C., Nicholas S. Majluff. 1984. "Corporate Financing and Investment Decisions When Firms Have Information that Investor Do Not Have," National Bureau of Economic Research; Working Paper #1396.

Rothschild, Michael, and Joseph E. Stiglitz. 1976. "Equilibrium in Competitive Markets." *Quarterly Journal of Economics* 90:630–49.

CHAPTER 12

Contingent Financing

$\mathbf{T}$he value of a firm derives from its future earnings. Risky events can disrupt this earnings streams by destroying productive assets, reducing the productivity of those assets, by reducing demand, diverting the value of the production to third parties, or increasing the cost of financing new investments. Some of this lost value can be recaptured by post-loss investment. Destroyed assets can be repaired or replaced, impaired demand may be recovered through advertising, and so on. In the previous chapter we looked at ways of securing money after the loss to pay for these post-loss investments. The loss itself sometimes proved to be a handicap in raising new funds because it usually weakens the firm's financial condition. The value of the firm is reduced by the loss, and usually leverage is increased. While this may impair the conditions under which new funds can be raised, post-loss investment can often minimize the loss of value.

But post-loss financing did encounter some problems. A particularly bothersome feature was that even if the post-loss investments offered a positive NPV, investors might still be unwilling to provide the necessary funding. This is particularly likely if the firm seeks to raise additional debt in its already highly levered post-loss state. Additional leverage simply intensifies distortions in project selection and increases the underinvestment and asset substitution problems. But even financing with new equity can be problematic. Existing debt may be sufficient to trigger post-loss underinvestment, and this can only be solved with a major reorganization such as bankruptcy or a workout.

Can these problems be avoided by setting up the financing in advance; that is, by setting up a financing vehicle that is triggered by the occurrence of a predefined loss? At the simplest level, contingent financing can be set in place and then activated by the loss event at terms appropriate the firm's post-loss condition. This simple option can be useful when post-loss investment is time-sensitive. But, more generally, our first task is to show that this simple contingent financing vehicle adds little or no value. A moment's thought will show why. This simple contingent financing is an option to raise money after loss on conditions that would have been available had that option not existed. It is like a call option to buy a stock at a future date at the market price on that date. We all have that option anyway; it is called an open market. This section of the chapter will be rather obvious, but it serves two purposes. First, it provides a formal review of post-loss financing, and second, it provides a nice starting point for developing contingent financing vehicles in which the post-loss financing terms differ from those that would have been available *ex post*.

COMPARISON OF POST-LOSS FINANCING AND SIMPLE CONTINGENT FINANCING

Let us set up the simplest possible contingent financing facility: a counter-party agrees to provide the firm with debt or equity financing conditional on some defined event occurring. Moreover, the financing will be available on terms appropriate to market conditions and the financial condition of the firm *after* the event. In other words, the contingent financing facility is a guarantee by a counter-party to make available what would have been available anyway.

With such a vehicle, the firm has gained nothing that it would not otherwise have. Moreover, the presence of such a vehicle should not affect investment decisions made after the loss event. The first statement is true by definition. One can object that setting up the facility in advance guarantees that financing will be available, but this is really playing with words. The facility only makes available what would have been available anyway. The second statement about post-loss investment also should be straightforward. The value-maximizing firm will make its post-loss investment decisions using normal capital budgeting techniques; the net present is value calculated using the opportunity cost of capital prevailing after the loss. The estimated cash flows from post-loss investment decisions are not affected, nor is the opportunity cost of capital affected, by the availability of contingent financing. Thus, all real investment decisions should be the same as with post-loss financing. Because no real value-creating decisions have changed, contingent financing will not add further value. We consider an exception later when investment is time-sensitive and delay is costly.

Post-loss Financing and Liquidity— Does a Line of Credit Add Further Value?

We will now go to perhaps unnecessary lengths to demonstrate these self-evident statements. The reasons for this indulgence are twofold. First, it provides an opportunity to reexamine, in a more formal way, when post-loss financing can add value. Second, it will give us a framework for showing how contingent financing can add value when the terms of the financing become predetermined. This somewhat inverted reasoning resembles that used in presenting the Modigliani–Miller theorem. They showed that, under restrictive assumptions, capital structure choices are irrelevant to firm value. The conclusion of irrelevancy is not of great interest by itself. The point is that if capital structure does matter, it does so because the restrictive assumptions have been relaxed.

Floating Rate Facility
Consider the post-loss value of equity under the assumption that there is no possibility of bankruptcy and default on the debt.

$$V'(E) = (\Delta S - r\Delta S/r - C) + V_0' + L - K_t' + V_t'$$
$$- D - T' \qquad (12.1)$$

When this equation was used to examine post-loss financing of investment decisions, the story was that the firm lost some value C in a currency change or liability suit or needed to spend the value C to reconstruct destroyed assets. Without default risk, the firm was able to raise ΔS (equal to C) after the loss and pay back an expected value of $r\Delta S/r$ ($= \Delta S$) in future interest or dividends. In doing so, shareholders could capture the NPV from replacing the destroyed assets and could preserve the franchise value ($K_t' + V_t'$) from future investments. Moreover, if liquidity, L, was limited, the firm could absorb the loss C and still maintain its dividend payments by using post-loss financing as a mechanism to smooth out random disturbances of long-run earnings.

What is the effect of contingent financing? Consider a simple line of credit, LOC. Suppose that some event can occur with a probability, p, that will cause a loss (and funding need) of C. Moreover, suppose that the market interest rate on debt fluctuates; it will be either r_1 with probability q or r_2 with probability $1 - q$ after the loss. These interest rates are appropriate given the financial condition the firm is expected to exhibit after a loss (e.g., they reflect any impact the loss may have on leverage). All we know in advance is that there is a p probability that the firm may need to borrow C and that, at that time, interest rates could be r_1 or r_2. Now, assume a counter-party, such as a bank, would be willing to lend an amount C after a loss at the prevailing post-loss interest rate, r_1 or r_2. The same counter-party should have no problem offering a line of credit for an amount C at the post-loss interest rate (r_1 or r_2), assuming transaction costs of the counter-party are covered.

Without the LOC:

> The bank would have pq probability responding to post-loss request for debt of C at rate r_1.
>
> The bank would have $p(1 - q)$ probability responding to post-loss request for debt of C at rate r_2.
>
> The bank would have $(1 - p)$ probability of receiving no post-loss request for debt.

With the LOC:

> The bank would face pq probability that the LOC would be drawn for an amount C at rate r_1.
>
> The bank would face $p(1 - q)$ probability that the LOC would be drawn for an amount C at rate r_2.
>
> The bank would face $(1 - p)$ probability that the LOC would be untouched.

The prospects for the bank are identical, and the investment decision of the firm should be the same whichever financing strategy is used.

Time-Sensitive Investment

Of course, this is oversimplified. First, there may be timing issues. If a loss occurs and no funding is arranged, there will be delays in floating a new equity or bond issue or in arranging a bank loan. These delays could result in loss of value. For example, if a loss occurred shortly before a dividend was due and the firm wished to avoid any unintended signaling from reducing the dividend, then having an LOC already set up would be valuable. Similarly, if productive assets are destroyed in a fire, there may be immediate salvage opportunities that could be lost if cash or immediate funding was not available. Thus, contingent financing can provide the firm with some timing benefits.

Fixed Rate Facility

Now change the assumptions a little. Suppose the LOC is secured by a fee, F, and the interest rate is fixed in advance at a rate, r, whereas market rates after loss could be either r_1 or r_2. We will assume that the fixed rate r is set such that $r_1 < r < r_2$. It now appears that the bank is insuring the firm against changes in interest rates in exchange for an insurance premium F. Can such a facility add value over post-loss financing? First, we must determine whether this arrangement would change post-loss investment choices.

> *Case 1: post-loss interest rate is* r_1, *and* $r > r_1$. In this case the firm would not draw its LOC, but would borrow at the post-loss market rate r_1. Post-loss investment decisions would be identical to those taken without the availability of the LOC.
>
> *Case 2: post-loss interest rate is* r_2, *and* $r < r_2$. The firm would rationally prefer to draw on its LOC rather than go the market for new money. But would this lower-than-market rate of interest change its investment behavior? The answer is no. If the LOC were unconditional on the loss, the firm could arbitrage at this rate differential. For example, it could draw on the LOC and lend at the market rate,

thereby profiting from the differential. Or it could use the lower rate to pay off its outstanding debt. After the loss these opportunities are still present in addition to the reinvestment opportunity. Thus, the firm would still condition it reinvestment decision on the post-loss market rate r_2 but use the lower LOC rate for arbitrage. The opportunity cost of investing is still the market rate of interest, not the LOC rate of r.

It is apparent that this fixed rate plus fee facility offers a partial and conditional hedge for the loss. If the loss occurs and post-loss rates exceed the LOC rate, then the facility offers the firm an arbitrage gain which will partly hedge its loss. But the hedge is conditional. If the post-loss rate is r_1, then no hedge exists.

From the bank's perspective, the LOC has an unattractive feature. The facility will be used when post-loss rates exceeds the LOC rate but will be left untouched if the reverse is true. So, from the bank's view, the facility looks as follows (note again that we are assuming that the LOC can only be used if there is a loss):

+ Bank would face $p(1 - q)$ probability that the LOC would be drawn for an amount C at rate $r < r_2$.
+ Bank would face $(1 - p)(1 - q)$ probability that the LOC would be untouched.

And the expected cost of offering this facility is:

$$-F + p(1 - q)C(r_2 - r) \tag{12.2}$$

Thus, the fee would have to satisfy $F \geq p(1 - q)C(r_2 - r)$ to be attractive to the bank. The fixed rate LOC can be viewed as containing an option. The firm may choose the exercise the option to draw on the LOC but will only do so when that action dominates direct access to the credit market. If rates in the credit market are lower than that for the LOC, the option will not be exercised.

In examining the fixed rate facility, we have gone beyond simple contingent financing. We have designed a hybrid instrument that is part financing and part a hedge. The limited hedging properties can themselves affect value in various ways, and we will explore this as we introduce other hybrids later in this chapter. In subsequent chapters we will look more directly at hedging instruments. In the meantime, the message so far is that a simple commitment to make funds available conditional on a loss, and at conditions that would have been available after the loss, does little to add value, other than providing immediacy. We will now look at whether such a commitment does anything to resolve the post-loss financing problems addressed in Chapter 11.

Review of Post-loss Financing and Fundability— Why a Line of Credit Fares No Better

To see why contingent financing does not resolve the fundability problem, return to the valuation equations in Chapter 10. Before and after loss, the value of original owner's equity was:

$$V(E) = V_0 + L - K_t + V_t - D - T \qquad (12.3)$$

$$V'(E) = (\Delta S - r\Delta S/r - C) + V_0'$$
$$+ L - K_t' + V_t' - D - T' \qquad (12.4)$$

But these equations ignore the default probability on the debt. As we saw later in Chapter 10, risky debt could be modeled as risk-less debt and a put option. If we consider D to be the face value of the debt, the value of risky debt is $D - P\{V(F); \sigma(F); D\}$ where $P\{V(F); \sigma(F); D\}$ is a put option, $P\{\ \}$, written on the value of the firm, $V(F)$, with risk $\sigma(F)$ and with a striking price equal to the face value of the debt, D.[1] The value of firm is $V(F) = V_0 + L - K_t + V_t - T$. This was shown in Figure 10–1.

The essentials of that diagram are reproduced here as Figure 12–1. Debt with a face value of D is shown without deducting bankruptcy costs. The default put option is shown as the payoff on a put option with a striking price D. The expected value of the firm is shown as $V(F)$. This is the expected value of future earnings. But the expectation is surrounded by risk, as shown by the probability distribution distribution 1 in the lower part of the figure. Only a small part of the distribution lies to the left of the striking price on the default put option. There is relatively little chance of the option being "in the money," meaning that the default risk is quite small and the put option is not very valuable.

---

1. Recall that the value of a put option will increase as the value of the underlying asset falls, the riskiness of the underlying asset increases, and the striking price rises.

F I G U R E   12—1

The Default Put Option

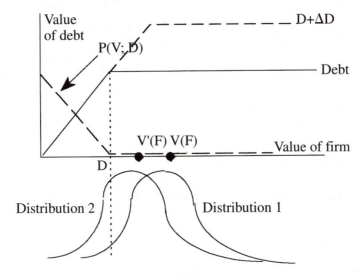

So let us rewrite Equation (12.3) as follows, showing that the value of debt is reduced by the value of the default put and the value of equity is increased by the same value.

$$V(E) = (V_0 + L - K_t + V_t - T) - D$$
$$+ P\{V(F); \sigma(F); D\}$$
$$= V(F) - D + P\{V(F); \sigma(F); D\} \qquad (12.5)$$

Now suppose a loss occurs that reduces the expected value of the firm from $V(F)$ to $V'(F)$ (reducing firm value without relieving debt will increase leverage). Some reinvestment may have limited the fall in value, but still $V'(F)$ is lower than the pre-loss value, $V(F)$. Moreover, assume for the moment that the reinvestment was financed by new equity and the debt stays at face value of D. Note that the riskiness of the distributions has not changed; the distribution has simply been shifted to the left to reflect the loss of expected value. You can see that the put option now has a much higher probability of being in the money because a much larger area of distribution 2 falls below the striking price, D. This means that the default option is more valuable, and the value of debt has decreased.[2] For shareholders, the increase in default probability on the debt partly offsets the fall in equity value. The default put option is now valued at $P\{V'(F); D\}$, which is higher than $P\{V(F); \sigma(F); D\}$ because of the reduction in $V(F)$. The value of debt is $D - P\{V'(F); \sigma(F); D\}$.

Now suppose that the reinvestment is financed with new debt and the face value of total debt (senior and junior) increases from D by ΔD to D'. The firm now has value $V'(F)$ and debt D'. There are now two effects increasing the value of the default put option and correspondingly reducing the value of the debt. Total debt now has a value of $D + \Delta D - P\{V'(F); \sigma(F); D + \Delta D\}$. Given priority, the junior debt would take the brunt of the default risk.[3] For example, assuming all default risk fell on junior debt issued after the loss, the values of senior and junior debt will be:

Senior debt D

Junior debt $\Delta D - P\{V'(F); \sigma(F); D + \Delta D\}$

and the value of equity would be:

$$V'(E) = \{\Delta S - \Delta D + P\{V'(F); \sigma(F); D + \Delta D\} - C\}$$
$$+ \{V_0' + L - K_t' + V_t' - T\} - D$$
$$= \{\Delta S - \Delta D + P\{V'(F); \sigma(F); D$$
$$+ \Delta D\} - C\} + V'(F) - D \qquad (12.6)$$

Rational and informed investors would pay a value of $\Delta S = \Delta D - P'\{.\}$, where $P'\{.\}$ is the abbreviated notation for the default put. Using this shorter notation:

$$V'(E) = \{\Delta S - \Delta D + P'\{.\} - C\} + V'(F) - D \qquad (12.7)$$

The post-loss financing problems arose because of changes in the value of the default put option. The post-loss investment of C

2. If the firm is able to recover all value through reinvestment and this is paid for with new equity, value will return to $V(1)$ and debt will remain at D. Thus, the default put will be unchanged and debt will remain as its pre-loss value.
3. If the senior debt and junior debt both had default risk after loss, their respective values would be:
Senior debt $D - P(V'(F); \sigma(F); D)$
Junior debt $\Delta D - P(V'(F); \sigma(F); D + \Delta D) + P(V'(F); \sigma(F); D)$

will not be fully funded with debt if $C > \Delta D - P'$. Note that debt will never be fully funded if the face value of new debt $\Delta D = C$ and the default put has any positive value. Thus, a necessary condition for full debt financing is that the face value of the debt ΔD exceed the amount raised C; that is, that the debt be issued below par.

Suppose one wishes to raise some value C_1, as shown in Figure 12–2. The amount investors will be wiling to pay is the face value ΔD minus the value of the default put P', that is, the value X in the figure that is less than c_1 and is insufficient to pay for the investment. To raise more money, the firm must increase the face value of the debt. But this is a double-edged sword. Increasing the face value is nice for creditors because each dollar increase is an extra *promised* dollar of payback, as shown by the 45° line labeled ΔD. But the additional face value increases the value of the default put option, as shown by the line P'. The net amount raised is therefore $\Delta D - P'$, as shown. Thus, the face value has to be raised to F_1 in order to raise an amount C_1 needed for the post-loss investment.

F I G U R E   12–2

Financing with Risky Debt

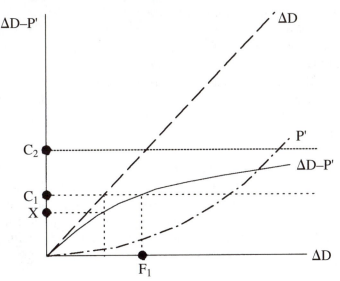

But say the firm needs to raise a larger amount, C_2. The problem is that one has to keep on increasing the face value above C_2 but that this starts backfiring because any additional promised repayment is more than offset by the increase in the default put. The firm simply cannot raise C_2 from rational and informed investors. This is the fundability problem.

Suppose the firm now anticipates that, for large future losses, it will not be able to raise sufficient funds in a post-loss bond issue to finance the reinvestment. So it secures a line of credit from a bank to draw C_2 in the event of a predefined loss. To agree to this, the bank must have an expectation that repayments must at least equal the present value of withdrawals. If the firm promises to repay ΔD, the bank can only realistically expect $\Delta D - P'$. Given a probability, p, that the loss will occur, the expected value of the facility is $p (\Delta D - P')$ which cannot equal pC_2 is $\Delta D - P' < C_2$.

The message coming out of this analysis is that contingent credit looks useful only for small losses. If post-loss credit will not raise sufficient funds to pay for large investment budgets, then rational investors will be unwilling to issue a LOC for such an amount.

Because contingent debt financing does involve the activation of the debt after a loss, our analysis should anticipate the features of post-loss financing. Return to the example of Chairs and Wares in Chapter 10. The firm's equity value, after 5000 existing debt is accounted for, and including the value of future investment opportunities, was 6331. The value could be reduced by damage to its productive assets. We considered what would happen if the firm suffered an explosion that reduced earnings and compromised its ability to fund the new investments internally. The firm needed to raise external capital of 3200 to replace the destroyed assets (including transactions costs of the issue). If the firm tried to raise new debt, post-loss leverage would impose considerable risk on this debt and it would be worth only 2295, which is insufficient to finance the reconstruction. In the terminology used, there is a fundability problem. It is possible to supplement the post-loss debt issue with a new share issue, but this would be less attractive than financing entirely with new equity. The values of the stakeholder positions of Chairs and Wares are now summarized:

No loss:

$$E = 6331; D_S = 5000$$

Loss: equity financing:

$$E^T = 6331 \text{ (old equity is 3131 and new equity is 3200)};$$
$$D_S = 5000$$

Loss; debt financing:

$$E^T = 3829; D_S = 5000; D_J = 2295 \text{ (905 short of}$$
cost of reinvestment)
(original shareholders equity worth 2924 after
issuing new shares for 905)

Suppose that investors are either naive or uninformed and, when the firm issued debt with a face value of 3200 to pay for reconstruction, new investors subscribed the full face value. In other words, investors were unaware that future risk of default meant the debt was only worth 2295. The total value of the equity would be 3829 in the example, and this would be a great deal for the shareholders. Post-loss debt on these terms would beat equity financing because the shareholders can keep the upside risk but stick the downside risk to creditors by defaulting on the debt. With naive creditors, post-loss debt financing is a wonderful deal for the shareholders.

Would Chairs and Wares be able to use debt to finance the reconstruction costs after future losses if the debt is set up in advance? Would an investor agree to issue a line of credit that would fully pay for the costs of reconstruction? Consider some probability, say 0.5, that the loss will occur. The line of credit is often secured by an up-front fee, but, for the sake of transparency, we will assume that a fee of 200 is charged if the LOC is activated; this fee compensates the bank for its transaction cost.[4] If drawn, the line of credit will have an interest rate of 7%, as in the ex post analysis. Thus, the details are the same as in the ex post analysis; the only thing that has changed is that the debt is set up in advance. Now suppose the extent of the LOC is 3200, which covers

---

4. Note that the 200 fee for drawing the LOC is exactly the same as the assumed transaction cost for post-loss financing when the example was first shown in Chapter 10.

reconstruction costs plus a transaction fee of 200. The investor advancing this line of credit can now anticipate:

0.5 chance that the LOC will not be activated

0.5 chance the LOC will be activated and the firm will draw the full 3200

We know from the analysis of the previous paragraph that if the firm can borrow 3200 at 7% after loss or issue new equity, the firm would prefer to borrow the 3200. But the firm may not pay back the full 3200. Future (i.e., after the loss) risk means that there is a chance the firm will default on repayment and the expected payback is only 2295. Thus, for the investor advancing the line of credit, the deal looks like this:

Expected value of credit advanced $0.5(3200) = 1600$

Expected value of pay back from borrower $0.5(2295) = 1147.5$

The rational and informed investor would not offer such a LOC. At most, the investor would agree that if the loss occurred, a sum of 2295 would be paid for a debt instrument with a face of 3200. Alternatively, the investor would require some higher interest rate on the 3200 to compensate for the considerable default risk. With rational investors, the LOC does not solve the feasibility problem, it anticipates it.

Is there any way of changing the design of the LOC to address the post-loss feasibility problem? To feel our way towards a solution, let us change our assumptions a little. We assumed that the LOC had no commitment fee but there was a transaction cost of 200 to draw on the facility. Suppose instead that the LOC had an up-front fee of 100 (which is the same expected value as the ex post fee given the loss probability is 0.5). I have reworked Chairs and Wares noting that cash is reduced from 1000 to 900 to pay the LOC fee and that the firm has to borrow only 3000 (instead of 3200) because there is no ex post transaction cost.

Loss; debt financing:

$E^T = 3829; D_S = 5000; D_J = 2295$ (905 short
      of cost of reinvestment)
      (original shareholders equity worth 2987 after issuing
      new shares for 905)

Loss; LOC Financing:

$E^T = 3881; D_S = 5000; D_J = 2143$ (857 short
of cost of reinvestment)
(original shareholders equity worth 3024
after issuing new shares for 857)

| *Expected value of credit advanced* | *0.5(3000)* | *= 1500* |
| *Expected value of pay back from borrower* | *100 + 0.5(2143) = 1171.5* | |

We have made the LOC a little less unattractive for the lender, but still no rational investor is going to offer this contingent debt. In order for the lender to be happy offering LOC, the expected payback must at least equal 1500. This means that either the debt must be free of default risk or there is some compensation, such as an up-front fee, to compensate for the default risk. In the latter case the arrangement is essentially a blending of a hedge and a LOC. We will look at this latter.

Post-loss Financing and Asset Substitution— Why a Line of Credit Fares No Better

The post-loss asset substitution problem can also be seen with this framework. Consider two mutually exclusive post-loss investment projects, labeled 1 and 2, each costing C and, for each, the firm attempts to raise ΔD (= C) in new debt. The following, derived from Equation 12.6 show the post-loss equity values with each project:

$$V_1'(E) = \Delta S_1 - C + V_1'(F) - (D + \Delta D)$$
$$+ P\{V_1'(F); \sigma_1(F); D + \Delta D\}$$

$$V_2'(E) = \Delta S_2 - C + V_2'(F) - (D + \Delta D)$$
$$+ P\{V_2'(F); \sigma_2(F); D + \Delta D\}$$

Suppose that project 1 has the higher value, $V_1'\{F\} > V_2'\{F\}$, and that project 2 adds considerably more risk to the firm, $\sigma_1(F) < \sigma_2(F)$. If the risk contributed by the second project is sufficiently high, the increase in value of the default put with project

2 more than compensates shareholders for the lower present value. Thus:

$$V_1'(F) + P\{V_1'(F); \quad \sigma_1(F); D + \Delta D_1\} < V_2'(F) + P\{V_2'(F);$$
$$\sigma_2(F); D + \Delta D_2\}$$

and E_2' is greater than E_1' despite project 1 having the higher NPV. If new creditors knew that the firm would select project 1, they would be willing to subscribe $\Delta S_1 = \Delta D - P\{V_1'(F); \sigma_1(F); D + \Delta D\}$ for the new debt issue. If they knew project 2 would be chosen, they would subscribe $\Delta S_2 = \Delta D - P\{V_2'(F); \sigma_2(F); D + \Delta D\}$. If investors do not know which will be chosen, they will anticipate that shareholders will choose project 2 and will only be willing to subscribe ΔS_2. If this is insufficient to fund project 1, there is a classic asset substitution problem that leads to underinvestment.

Would a line of credit of sufficient size to fund project 1 (ΔS_1) help resolve the asset substitution problem? The problem with obtaining post-loss credit was that the firm could not credibly commit itself to undertake project 1 if the funds, ΔS_1, were raised. If it is difficult to commit after the loss, then it would be no easier to obtain an enforceable commitment to use the LOC solely for funding project 1. As a result, a bank advancing a line of credit with face ΔD would anticipate that the firm would use the LOC to finance project 2. Accordingly, the bank's expected repayment is $p \, \Delta S_2$ (where p is the probability of loss), and it would limit the line to a value ΔS_2, which is insufficient to finance either project.

CONTINGENT FINANCING: SIZE, FUNDABILITY, AND TRIGGERS

If contingent financing is made available at market conditions, it anticipates post-loss decisions but does not fundamentally change them. The exception is time-sensitive investments. But when financing is made available on conditions that differ from post-loss market terms available to the firm, the firm may behave selectively and often quite dysfunctionally.

With post-loss financing the value of equity was given by Equation (12.7):

$$V'(E) = \{\Delta S - \Delta D + P'\{.\} - C\} + V'(F) - D \qquad (12.7)$$

This valuation assumes that the firm undertakes its value-enhancing post-loss investment opportunities. The value created for shareholders by such investment can be divided as follows:

$$\Delta V'(E) = \{\Delta V'(F) - C\} + \{\Delta S - \Delta D + P'\{.\}\} \qquad (12.8)$$

The first braces on the right-hand side show the NPV of the post-loss investment, which is the difference the increase in the value of the firm, $\Delta V'(F)$, and the cost of investment, C. The term in the second braces is the wealth redistribution from creditors to shareholders from the debt being underpriced. This second term is the difference between the amount lent to the firm, ΔS, and the economic value of the amount expected to be repaid, $\Delta D - P'\{.\}$.

In Figure 12–3 the components of Equation (12.8) are shown for different levels of loss C. For simplicity, the value added term, $\Delta V'(F) - C$, is shown as increasing proportionately with C. The redistribution term is shown as the lower line $\Delta S - \Delta D + P'$. This is zero for low levels of C (implying that the default put is zero and $\Delta S = \Delta D$). But as the loss gets higher, the value of the firm falls and the value of the default put rises. If $\Delta S = \Delta D$, this curve simply traces out the value of the default put option. The total of the two curves is shown as $\Delta V'(F) - C$. The diagram is showing the fundability problem. If money is raised *ex post*, new creditors

F I G U R E   12–3

Decomposing Value Created from Post Loss Investment

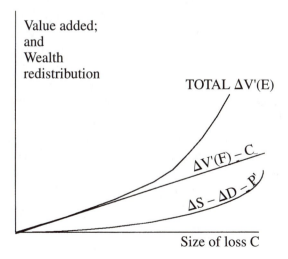

Value added; and Wealth redistribution

TOTAL ΔV'(E)

ΔV'(F) – C

ΔS – ΔD – P'

Size of loss C

would discount the value of a bond issue by the value of the default put. With the assumption that the value of the firm falls as the loss rises, the firm would find larger losses increasingly more difficult to finance.

Now suppose that the firm has a LOC where it can draw up to some limit amount ΔS. If the limit of the LOC is high, the bank must anticipate that when large losses occur it will be doubly attractive for the firm to use the LOC: first to finance reinvestment and second to redistribute wealth by means of the default put. This may cause the bank to limit the size of the LOC to some moderate value. Now suppose the limit is moderate. It is still possible for the firm with a moderate LOC to have moderate or massive losses. The firm with the moderate loss will be able to finance its loss with the LOC. But even though this will be insufficient to finance the massive loss, the firm may still be tempted to draw on the LOC simply to create shareholder value through the default put. For this reason the bank may wish to restrict the LOC by means of *triggers*.

Loss and Value Triggers

If a bank advances a LOC, it can assume that the firm will draw on the line to maximize shareholder value. I will assume that the LOC is designed to finance post-loss reinvestment and has an event trigger; that is, the line is activated when a described event occurs such as a fire or liability claim of a certain minimum value. The bank would therefore price the LOC on the assumption that it is drawn to maximize Equation (12.8). The bank may charge an up-front fee that is no lower than the expected value (using the probability of the triggering loss) of the default put option. Because this option increases with the borrowing limit, so too would the securing fee increase with the borrowing limit.

The danger with the LOC should now be apparent. If the default put option is priced into a post-loss debt issue, the firm will embody this option in its post-loss investment and financing decisions. If a post-loss underinvestment problem is caused by new debt, this disciplines the firm to switch to equity financing and, in doing so, to abandon a suboptimal investment choice. The shareholders would like to take risks and put the downside to creditors, but new creditors simply refuse to place their money behind this game. With a LOC, in which *the default put is anticipated and pre-priced,* the firm is no longer subject to the financing discipline (the pricing of the default put is a sunk cost). Consequently, shareholders are induced to take risky, and often suboptimal, investment choices with the option of putting the firm to the bank should adverse outcomes prevail.

To illustrate this dysfunctional aspect of fixed term LOCs, we will return to a case considered in Chapter 10.

In Prime Autos in Chapter 10, the firm had a choice between two mutually exclusive investment projects. Project A was a safe investment costing 5000 and yielding a riskless cash flow with a present value of 7000. Project B also cost 5000 but could yield a cash stream with a present value of 1000 or 11,000, each with 0.5 probability. The firm could fiance the chosen investment with debt or equity, and in each case there was a transaction cost of 250 that was financed from the new issue. The analysis showed that there was initially no underinvestment problem; the firm's shareholders would choose project A even if it were to be funded with a new debt issue for 5250. The analysis showed that the value of the equity would be 6000 with project A compared with 5000 with project B.

However, a liability loss hit the firm and increased its leverage. The analysis of the new investment choice, after the liability suit was settled, revealed an underinvestment problem. The following table summarizes the value of the claims of the various stakeholders with different options for post-loss financing the new project.

	Equity	Debt
Project A		
Senior Debt	2000	2000
New Debt/Equity	5250	5250
Equity	2250	2250
Project B		
Senior Debt	2000	2000
New Debt/Equity	5250	3000
Equity	1250	3125

The conclusion reached there was that if the firm could have raised

an amount of 5250 to pay for the project in a new debt issue, project B
*would have been chosen because old equity would have been worth 3125
as opposed to 2250 with project* A. *But if the firm tried to issue new
debt, investors would anticipate choice of project* B *and would subscribe
only 3000 for the new debt issue despite its face value of 5250. The firm
would not have sufficient money to pay for the project and would be
locked in the asset substitution trap. The resolution was to pay for the
project with a post-loss equity issue, in which case project* A *looks much
better to original shareholders (2250 compared with 1250 for project* B).
*Notice tht if the debt had been issued with a face of 5250, we could have
thought of its value as being the difference between its nominal value of
5250 and the default put of 2250, yielding a net value of 3000.*

   *Now consider what would happen if the firm had access to a line
of credit up to a value of at least 5250. After the loss, original shareholders would be better off by drawing on the LOC for the 5250 and
choosing project* B, *in which case the bank offering such a LOC would
anticipate this sort of behavior. If the probability of the liability loss were
0.5, then the bank would require a securing fee of 0.5 times the value of
the post-loss default put option; tht is, 0.5(2250) = 1125*

EX ANTE ANALYSIS OF LOC

Shareholder Value without LOC

*Now consider whether it would make sense to set up the LOC. If the
LOC is not set up we can figure out the value of the original owner's
shares as the weighted average of the value without the liability loss and
the value after the liability loss. Without the liability loss, the firm will
choose project* A *and equity will be worth 6000. With the liability loss,
the firm would choose to raise 5250 in a new equity issue and undertake
project* A, *leaving original equity worth 2250, as shown in the above
table.*

Ex ante equity value without LOC = 0.5(6000) + 0.5(2250) = 4125

Shareholder Value with LOC

*With the LOC the equity will be worth 6000 without the liability loss.
But if the liability loss occurs and the firm is free to draw the full 5250,
then* B *will be chosen and equity will be worth 3125, as shown in the
table. However, the bank anticipates the* ex post *choice of* B *and charges*

an up-front fee equal to the expected value of then-default put option (i.e., 0.5 × 2250).

Ex ante equity value $0.5(6000) + 0.5(3125) - 0.5(2250) = 3437.5$

What has gone wrong here is that the LOC has removed a discipline that spot capital markets impose on investment choice. With post-loss financing, the underinvestment aspect of debt financing prevents the firm from making the inferior project choice. The firm can finance a new investment only with equity financing, and if equity is used, project A looks superior to the shareholders, so it is chosen. With the LOC already in place when the loss occurs, the firm is able, if it chooses, to undertake projects that could not be funded with new post-loss money. Rationally, the bank will anticipate these dysfunctional and/or expropriatory decisions and charge "up front." Thus, the firm securing an LOC will be charged prospectively for behavior that it would not have undertaken had it relied on post-loss funding.

How can the dysfunctional aspects of LOCs be avoided? Our solution is to make the credit available on post-loss firm and market conditions. The firm drawing on the line would be able to draw only the risk-adjusted present value of the anticipated repayments; that is, the firm could draw only the face value of repayments minus the default put ($\Delta S = \Delta D - P'\{.\}$). This encounters the fundability risk, but fundability helps discipline post-loss investment decisions.

The other approach is to put other limits or triggers into the LOC. For example, we have discussed event-triggered LOCs where the line can be drawn if a loss event meeting a certain description occurs. The description can refer to the cause of the event (a liability suit, fire, interest rate loss, etc.). The trigger can refer to minimum size of loss, but it can also relate to the maximum size of the loss or to financial indicators of the firm's post-loss financial condition. For example, the LOC might offer borrowing capacity up to $0.5 billion that is triggered if the firm suffers a liability loss within a range of $0.5 to $1 billion. The upper limit would be fixed in relation to the firm's financial resources and leverage. The bank might consider that a loss over $1 billion would create sufficient default risk given the firm's leverage that the LOC is withdrawn when the loss exceeds this value.

This is a sort of "knock out" facility that disappears when a upper loss trigger is activated. The use of an upper loss trigger builds on an implicit relationship between the size of the loss and the firm's post-loss creditworthiness. An alternative would be to relate the trigger directly to post-loss financial ratios such as firm value and leverage. But this would be a cumbersome risk management tool because the firm would have only a vague idea of the availability of the LOC in the vent of any given loss.

Conclusion on Lines of Credit

Lines of credit may simply be a commitment to make credit available should a loss event occur, at the conditions under which the firm could secure new debt after the loss. As a risk management tool, this LOC offers the same advantages and disadvantages that post-loss debt financing does. Like a post-loss funding source, the LOC will help the firm to capture the NPV of post-lost investment opportunities. It will help the firm to smooth dividend payments and avoid sending misleading signals to investors that are not based on sustainable estimates of long-run earnings. However, like post-loss financing, the LOC will not resolve the problems of fundability and agency costs that results in dysfunctional investment decisions. Contingent financing simply anticipates these problems; it does not resolve them. Simple contingent financing essentially duplicates the features of post-loss financing with one exception. If the post-loss investment is time-sensitive, the immediate availability of funds is important. By setting up a financing facility in advance, contingent financing can avoid delays and thereby avoid compromising time-sensitive investment.

But contingent financing may go further. The terms on which money is available after loss can be fixed in advance and differ from those for the market might offer after loss. In this way a LOC can build in some degree of hedging. For example, the bank offering a LOC might anticipate post-loss credit risk and price this up front. This can be a mixed blessing. If money is available on terms that are more favorable than those the market would offer after loss, the firm might be tempted to use the easy post-loss LOC terms as the appropriate cost of capital in making post-loss investment decisions. This would understate the true opportunity cost of capital and lead to inefficient post-loss investment choices.

But we have introduced the possibility of hybrids: contingent financing instruments with some hedging built in. So far we have looked only at the effects of the hedge component on post-loss investment decisions. The partial hedge may also affect real pre-loss choices. We now turn our attention more formally to hybrids. The first of these will be contingent equity that takes the form of a put option issued by the firm.

CONTINGENT EQUITY – LOSS PUT EQUITY OPTIONS

Contingent debt is familiar in the form of the line of credit. Contingent equity is less common, though we can imagine it in several forms. One form is another security that will convert to equity in defined circumstances. Convertible bonds fall into this category, and we will examine a particular variant of this instrument later in Chapter 13. A second form of contingent equity can be envisioned in which the firm makes arrangements for a counter-party to provide equity capital under agreed terms and circumstances. For example, the firm can issue a put option on its own stock. In exercising this option, the firm can issue new shares and put these to the counter-party at the agreed striking price. Such instruments have recently started to appear for insurance firms, although these are options on preferred shares rather than on common stock. We will examine the risk management potential of using equity puts.

Design Choices for Loss Equity Put Options

To start, let us consider the general design of such instruments. Essentially, the idea is that a put option is issued by the firm on its own stock. However, there is an additional trigger that relates to some risky event of risk management concern. For example, the event could be a property or liability loss within a given range. Thus, the option can be exercised only when two triggers are activated: first, the option must become "in the money" (the stock price must fall below the striking price), and second, the activating event (property or liability loss) must occur. These two triggers are likely to be related to each other. An event such as a liability loss, property loss, or currency loss will normally result in a fall in the stock price. Thus, the probability that the option will be exercised is somewhat greater than the product of the probabilities of each trigger. Figure 12–4a shows the *expected* relationship between loss events and expected stock prices. There is no magic in the convex shape; the main thing is that the curve is upwards-sloping, meaning that losses result in an expected fall in share prices. Moreover, the relationship might not be deterministic. There may be idiosyncratic features of a loss that can cause its effect on stock price to be greater or less than depicted; the relationship is only an *expected* one.

Figure 12–4b shows the payoff to a normal put option where S is the striking price; this is the solid line kinked at S that shows the profit to the firm conditional on any given stock price. The price of the option has not been deducted, so this is a gross payoff. Now suppose the option has a second trigger, which is the loss event (for ease of discussion we will talk about a property loss, though we could have picked other events just as easily). Let us start with the current stock price as P_1 as shown in Figure 12–4b. At P_1 the option is "out of the money." Suppose now that a loss event occurs of sufficient size to satisfy the lower trigger shown by the arrow and marked Δ on the horizontal axis of Figure 12–4a. The same change in stock price is shown in part (b) also as an arrow marked Δ. Thus, starting with P_1, a loss event above the lower trigger is expected to push the stock price below the striking price S to point X, and the option is now in the money and can be exercised. Had the current stock price been P_2, the same loss event would have satisfied the event trigger but would not have been sufficient to depress the stock price, and the option would have been out of the money (point Y). Thus, the double trigger put option (like a normal put option) becomes more valuable the lower the stock price.

Let us continue to assume for illustration that the current stock price is P_1. We can imagine various designs for the double-trigger put option.

1. The option has two event triggers: the property loss must lie between the lower and upper triggers as shown in part (a) of Figure 12–4a and the striking price is S. Given current price P_1, the range of admissible loss events will result in expected stock values between points X and Z. Any loss outside the event trigger will

F I G U R E   12–4

Loss Events and Stock Price

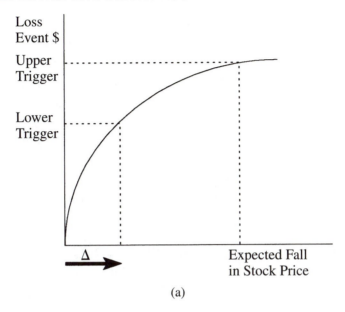

(a)

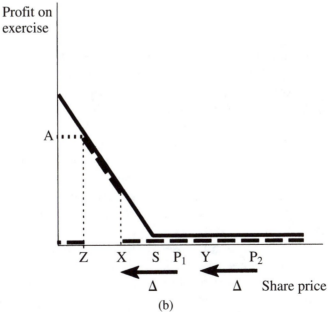

(b)

F I G U R E   12-4

Continued

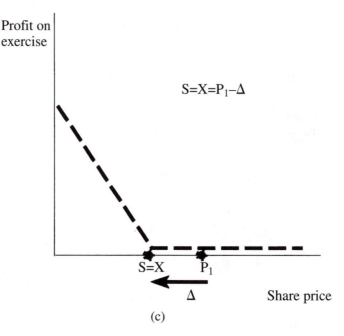

(c)

preclude exercise even if the option is otherwise in the
money. Note that points X and Z are not triggers in
themselves; rather, they are the expected stock values
that correspond to the real event triggers. The payoff
structure to this option is shown as the broken line
(payoff is zero for stock values below Z and above X
and follows the basic put payoff between X and Z).
Notice the discontinuities in the payoff. If the loss event
is a little smaller than the lower trigger, the firm will be
sitting with an apparently in the money put option but
be just unable to exercise it. There are some funny
incentives here. Suppose the firm has some control over
the loss trigger (e.g., in a fire loss the firm may be a little
sloppy in mitigating damage; in a liability suit the firm
may be a little more generous in settling; in a currency
loss the firm may be a little more pessimistic in
accounting for the value affected). The firm could

thereby exaggerate the loss in order to activate the loss trigger and exercise the option. Even worse incentives arise with the upper trigger (point Z) because the value at stake is even higher. Moreover, it may be easier for the firm to understate its loss than to overstate it. If the loss takes the stock price just below Z, the otherwise very valuable option is simply lost. This is known as a "knock out" option.[5]

2. Another design removes the adverse incentives surrounding the upper trigger. Instead of the option knocking out when the loss event exceeds the trigger, one can cap the option payout at value A shown in part (b) of the figure. A device for achieving this would be to combine the put option with a striking price of S and a call option with a striking price of Z. Thus, for values below Z the call option payoff would offset any increase in the payoff on the put option. In concert, these two options would create no incentives for the firm with a loss above the upper trigger to manipulate its size.

3. This still leaves the perverse incentives surrounding the lower trigger. A way of dealing with this is to design the loss put option with a floating strike price. The idea is to fix the striking price in relation to the value the stock would have taken immediately before the loss event. In doing this the goal is to avoid a situation in which the firm is holding an in the money option that cannot be exercised because the event trigger has not quite been activated. If the event is sudden and unanticipated, this is straightforward. For example, in a loss put option triggered by fire or earthquake loss, the strike price could be set relative to the stock price on the day preceding the event. For hurricane loss the lead time would have to be longer since the build-up of weather systems gives some advance warning of potential loss and this can be impounded in the stock prices of firms

---

5. In principle, the upper knock out feature can also be written directly on the stock value; for example, if the stock price falls below a value such as Z, the option is worthless.

at risk. Liability events also do not have such clear event times.

In Figure 12–4c a floating striking price is shown. The idea is to set the stroking price at the current price, P_1 minus the amount by which the stock price is expected to fall if an event just big enough to satisfy the event trigger is shown. This minimum change in the stock price is shown as Δ and marked with an arrow in parts (a) and (b) of the figure, and this same value is shown in part (c). Thus, the strike price is set at $P_1 - \Delta = X$. Doing this means that the option should just be at the money" when a loss just sufficient to satisfy the event trigger occurs. This avoids the problem of a discontinuous gain to the firm from manipulating the value of a loss event. In practice, there is still a problem since the effect of the loss event on the stock price is not deterministic. Thus, a loss just activating the event trigger produces only an *expected* change in stock price of Δ. The actual price change will be subject to some random error. Accordingly, this device will not eliminate the incentive problems, but it can be used to lower them.

With each of these designs the hybrid nature of the loss put can be seen. On the one hand, it provides a source of new money from which post-loss investment projects can be financed. However, it is also in part a hedge, since part of the cost of raising the new money is borne by the counter-party who buys the shares at a (striking) price in excess of their post-loss market value. The payoff in the diagrams can be thought of as partial insurance of the loss event, and the option premium correspondingly resembles an insurance premium.

Loss Put Equity Options on Preferred Shares

An alternative to common equity loss put options is to issue options on preferred shares. The idea is similar, though there may be some differences in the risk management effects. The issues of "CatEPut" options (designed by Aon and issued under this trade mark by insurance firms in conjunction with their exposure to

accumulated natural catastrophe claims) were preferred share issues and had features such as buy-back from the counter-party
within a fixed time period. Comments here will be limited to brief
comparison with common share loss equity put options.

- Because preferred shares are junior to debt, the benefits
  to existing creditors are similar to those with common
  share put options. The provision of new funds from the
  exercise will enable the firm to undertake post-loss
  investment projects, and the value created will shore up
  the value of existing debt.
- Moreover, the fact that the loss is partly hedged by the
  counter-party further secures the debt.
- However, preferred shares options may create somewhat
  different incentives for shareholders in choosing
  investment projects. On exercise, a senior claim is created
  rather than (with common equity options) an equity
  dilution.

Value Added through Loss Equity Puts

Let us recall some of the reasons that risk is costly for firms. First,
risk increases the possibility of bankruptcy and thereby increases
the expected value of bankruptcy costs. Second, risk increases indirect bankruptcy costs such as the loss of value from underinvestment. Third, because external financing is more costly than
internal capital, risk can lead to the crowding out of new investments as unhedged losses absorb available cash. Looking just at
these reasons, we can start building an argument why the issue
of put options by the firm, to be exercised after a loss event, can
add value.

It is straightforward to see that loss equity puts can reduce
the probability, and the expected direct costs, of bankruptcy. The
loss is partly hedged by the counter-party who agrees to buy the
firm's securities above their post-loss market value. Moreover the
equity injection after the loss permits the firm to capture value
through post-loss investment. In concert, these effects both increase the value of the firm and moderate the increase in leverage
that follows major loss events. In so doing, the put option reduces

the prospect of bankruptcy. It is also fairly straightforward that the loss equity put will address the crowding out problem. While the put option will be priced *ex ante*, the firm can finance post-loss investments without immediately facing the higher marginal costs of capital raised in external markets. However, the way in which these put options address underinvestment requires a little more explanation, and we will do this by way of illustrations.

Equity Put Options and Post-Loss Underinvestment

Let us return to an example of post-loss underinvestment that we looked at in Chapter 11. First, the example is summarized. Without a loss, the firm is worth 1000, debt is worth its full face value of 600, and the 100 shares each are worth 4. The firm has a fire that knocks out much of its productive capacity. The firm will be worth 200 if the fire damage is not repaired and 1000 if it is repaired. The cost of reinvestment is 600 and the NPV = 800 − 600 = 200. The firm has existing debt of 600. If the firm goes bankrupt, there is a cost of 50. Consequently, if the firm does not reinvest, its net value will be 200 − 50 = 150. Finally, though we did not use this information before, suppose that the prior chance the fire will occur is 0.1.

The following table presents the value of the firm and of its debt and equity under alternative post-loss decisions.

Decision	Firm	Debt	Equity
Reinvest	1000	600	400
Not reinvest	150	150	0
Gain	850	450	400
Cost of Reinvestment			600

The value of equity will rise by 400 from reinvestment. But the cost of reinvestment is 600. If one tried to pay for the reinvestment by a new equity issue, it is clear that there would simply not be enough value to persuade new investors to subscribe 600 for the new issues; the total value of all equity, old and new, would be only 400. To see this formally, we can use the formula that tells how many new shares, n, need to be issued to raise a given amount C if the total equity value, E^T, is known (m is the number of existing shares):

$$n = \frac{Cm}{E^T - C} = \frac{600(100)}{400 - 600} = \text{negative}$$

The formula gives us a silly answer; it is negative. Of course one cannot raise more money by issuing a negative number of shares. This is the formula's way of telling us that it does not work; we simply cannot raise the money by issuing more shares after the fire.

What would happen formally in this case is that the firm would go bankrupt and be passed to creditors. As seen in the section on debt renegotiation in Chapter 11, the creditors would then choose to reinvest, and, after bankruptcy costs, the value of their position would be 350 (i.e., 1000, less bankruptcy costs of 50, less cost of reinvestment, 600 leaves 350).

But suppose the firm holds put options to issue 300 shares of stock at a striking price of 2 per share. After the loss the firm could exercise its option and pay for the reinvestment; issuing 300 shares at 2 apiece would raise the 600 needed for reinvestment. After the option is exercised and the reinvestment undertaken, the firm is worth 1000, which, after debt of 600 is deducted, leaves the total value of equity worth 400. Since there are now 400 shares (100 original plus 300 issued under the option conditions), the shares are each worth 1. The counter-party on the other side of the equity put option has thus paid a total of 600 to purchase 300 shares that have a total value of 300. Naturally, the counter-party will anticipate losing money when the option is exercised, and this will be reflected in the option price. While we will not get into details of options pricing here, one can see that a loss of 300 to the counter-party on exercise, with a 0.1 chance that the fire would occur and the option be exercised, suggests a break-even option price of 30 (or 0.1 per share). *Ex post*, the firm has an effective hedge equal to 300, for which it paid an up-front premium of whatever the option price happened to be (e.g., 30).

The following table shows the value of the various claims after the put option has been exercised. The top row shows values after deduction of cost of reinvestment (i.e., the firm will have value 1000 plus the proceeds of the option, 600, less cost of reinvestment, 600, leaving 1000). The original shareholders gain 50 from reinvestment and the new shareholders gain 150, thus accounting for the reinvestment NPV of 200.

Decision	Firm	Debt	Counter-Party	Equity
Reinvest	1000[a]	600	300	100
Not reinvest	800	600	150	50
Gain	200	0	150	50

[a]After deducting cost of reinvestment.
[b]Including 600 raised on exercise of put option.

An interesting property of the equity put in this example is that the main gainers are the existing creditors. This reveals an intriguing possibility for embedding short put positions in the firm's debt. Consider that there is a 0.1 chance of loss that would cause the put to be exercised by the firm. We will also tentatively assume that the equity put price is 30. This assumed price is 0.1 times the amount the counter-party expects to lose if the option is exercised; that is, it is the expected loss to the counter-party.[6] Without the put in place, debt would be worth $0.9(600)$ + $0.1(350) = 575$ (note that the firm would go bankrupt and creditors would choose to reinvest in the positive NPV project).[7] With the put in place but held by some external investor, debt would be worth 600, as shown in the above table. Therefore, the put option increases the value of debt by 25, yet is only priced at expected loss of 30. However, the value of equity also increases. Without the put option, equity was worth $0.9(400) + 0.1(0) = 360$. With the put option, equity is worth $0.9(400) + 0.1(100) = 370$. There is an overall gain of 25 in debt and 10 in equity, totaling 35. If the cost of the put is 30, this represents a net gain of 5. Where does this gain come from? A little thought will show that the net gain is

---

6. Expected loss pricing is used only for simplicity here and is only a crude approximation. To develop this concept further requires more attention to option pricing technology.

7. See Chapter 11 for the original working of this problem. The value of 350 in the event of loss was derived as follows. If the firm becomes bankrupt and reinvests, the total value is 950 (1000 minus bankruptcy costs of 50). But to achieve this value, the new owners (ex-creditors) have to raise 600 for reinvestment. This leaves 350, as shown.

the expected value of the saving in bankruptcy cost ($0.1 \times 50 = 5$). Notice also, for later comparison, that the overall value of the firm with the put option is debt of 600 plus equity of 370 minus the cost of the put of 30, which leaves 940.

Embedding a Short Loss Put Option in the Firm's Debt

Now suppose that the debt had been issued with a short position in the put option built in; that is, the bondholder also is the counter-party to the equity put option. How much would the debt be worth? There is a 0.9 chance the option will expire without exercise and a 0.1 chance it will be exercised by the firm and then the firm will use the proceeds for reinvestment. If it is exercised, the bondholder has a claim of 600 that can be met, but only because he or she purchased shares worth 600 at an exercise of 300. Thus, the net position of the bondholder in the loss state is $600 - 600 + 300 = 300$. Weighing by the appropriate probabilities, the value of the debt with this embedded short equity put is $0.9(600) + 0.1(300) = 570$. Compare this with the value of 575 when the debt had no embedded short put. The debt is worth less with embedded short put option than without it. This should not be too surprising; bondholders have the additional liability of honoring the put option, and this should reduce value. Notice that the equity in this case is worth $0.9(400) + 0.1(100) = 370$, so the total firm value is 940.

But now repeat the whole exercise but change the conditions of the loss put option. Instead of issuing 300 shares to the creditors at a striking price of 2 to fund the 600 reinvestment, suppose that the option bought from the creditors was to issue 900 shares at a striking price of 0.6667. After the loss and the exercise of the option, creditors would now own 900 of the total 1000 shares; that is, 90% of the equity. The total equity with reinvestment is 400 (1000 minus the debt of 600), and the creditors would now own 90% of 400 = 360. Thus, the *ex ante* value of the debt with the embedded short loss put option is $0.9(600) + 0.1(360) = 576$. Ironically, debt is worth more with the short position in the loss put, 576, than without it, 575. And the equity would be worth $0.9(400) + 0.1(40) = 364$; thus, the total value of the firm is 576 +

364 = 940, which is the same as when 300 put options were shorted by creditors at a striking price of 2 in the previous paragraph. Thus, varying the conditions of the loss put option allows the gain in firm value (the saving in expected bankruptcy cost of 5) to be divided between creditors and shareholders.

This examination of the effect of embedding the short put option in the debt raises an interesting possibility. For events that are so large that they could bankrupt the firm, the main losers are the creditors, who must eat the bankruptcy costs or renegotiate with shareholders. Under these conditions the firm is passed to creditor, who will presumably make positive NPV investments. By embedding the short put option in the debt, we can replicate the passing of much of the firm to creditors without incurring the bankruptcy costs. Marrying the put option with the debt is a proactive way of dividing a distressed firm between stakeholders. Bondholders might well consider that this restructuring is better anticipated in the terms the debt is issued than by relying on *ex post* negotiation, where their bargaining position will be weaker and they will bear transaction costs.[8]

Equity Put Options and Future Underinvestment

The illustration in the previous section showed that equity put options can be used to correct underinvestment problems arising from existing debt. Shareholders could not capture the full gain from reinvestment because it shored up the value of existing debt, which might otherwise be in default. Equity put options can be used to correct this problem because they partly hedge the loss and provide funds for reinvestment. When short equity puts are embedded in debt, the *ex ante* value of the debt can actually increase, due both to the efficiency gain and to the fact that this arrangement prevents post-loss wealth shifting by shareholders. We will now turn to the second type of underinvestment problem. After the loss, future investments can be lost because the loss increases the leverage of the firm and the value of the default put. Thus, investment opportunities that might have been captured had the loss event not occurred are lost. We will return to an

---

8. Similar issues arise with reverse-convertible debt, considered in Chapter 13.

example from Chapter 10 to illustrate this process. To provide continuity, this is the Prime Autos example that was used a few pages back to show that a simple LOC will not resolve this asset substitution problem. The equity put option fares better.

The stakeholder values under the various post-loss investment and financing options in Prime Autos are summarized again in the following table:

	Equity	Debt
Project *A*		
Senior Debt	2000	2000
New Debt/Equity	5250	5250
Equity	2250	2250
Project *B*		
Senior Debt	200	2000
New Debt/Equity	5250	3000
Equity	1250	3125

Prime emerges from the liability loss with the need to pay for the loss and the opportunity for a new investment: either Project A or B. From previous analysis, we know that the best post-loss investment decisions would be to choose project A and pay for this with a new equity issue. Suppose that Prime paid for both the liability loss of 3750 and the new investment of 5250 with a post-loss equity issue. To do so, it needs to raise a total of 9000. "Paying for the liability loss" means that 3750 of the money raised in the post-loss equity issue is used as a cash settlement to the plaintiffs and all the firm's earnings are now captured by shareholders and creditors. If the firm did this, the present value of all cash flows available to shareholders and creditors would be 6250 + 7000 = 13,250 (figures from original working of this case in Chapter 10). Deducting 2000 for debt, the total value of equity would be 11,250. If PRIME has an original 1000 shares outstanding, it would need to issue 4000 shares, calculated as follows:

$$n = \frac{Cm}{E^T - C} = \frac{9000(1000)}{11{,}250 - 9000} = 4000$$

Since 4000 new shares are issued, the post-loss share price will be 11,250/

5000 = 2.25. Notice that this gives us the equity value of 2250 for original shareholders shown in the table above. Had the liability loss not occurred, one can check from the original working of this case that original equity would have been worth 6000 or 6 per share.

We will now examine the effects of financing the liability claim with an equity put option. To illustrate, the striking price of the option will be 5. Notice that relative to the "no-loss" equity price of 6, the put option is out of the money. To pay for the liability claim of 3750, the firm will exercise the put option and issue 750 shares. After the exercise of the option, the firm can now finance the new investment, A or B.

Post-loss Equity Financing of New Investment

Under this analysis, the firm issues new shares to finance the new project. The firm raises equity for the full capital cost (5000) plus the transaction costs (250). And the liability loss is financed through the exercise of the put option.

Project A Is Chosen

If the firm chooses project A, then total value will be 6250 + 7000 = 13,250. There is no possibility of default, debt will be worth its full face of 2000, and equity (old plus new) will be worth 11,250. To raise 5250 in new equity (and recognizing there are already 1750 shares: 1000 original plus 750 issued under exercise of the option), 1531 new shares must be issued:

$$n = \frac{Cm}{E^T - C} = \frac{5250(1750)}{11{,}250 - 5250} = 1531$$

There are now 1531 + 1750 = 3281 shares, each worth 3.4288. The original 1000 shares are worth 3429, and the 750 shares issued to the counter-party short on the put option are worth 2571. Notice that the counter-party has paid 3750 on exercise of the option to buy shares worth 2571. Thus, the counter-party has hedged part of the 3750 liability loss.

Project B Is Chosen

In the worst case the firm will be worth 6250 = 1000 = 7250, which is still enough to pay the old debt of 2000. However poorly the project performs, there is no bankruptcy and the old debt is worth its face of 2000. The total firm value is {0.5(6250 + 1000) + 0.5(6250 +

1000)} = 12,250. Thus, equity is worth 10,250. If we use the same argument as above, the new equity is worth 5250, the shares issued to the counter-party 2143, and the original shares 2857.

Analysis with Debt Financing

Under this analysis the firm issues debt to finance the new project in an attempt to raise the full capital cost (500) plus the transaction costs (250).

Project A Is Chosen

If the firm chooses project A, total value will be 6250 + 7000 = 13,250. The firm has an old debt obligation of 2000 and a new debt obligation of 5250. There is no possibility of default, and debt will be worth its full face (2000 senior debt and 5250 junior debt). The total equity is divided now between the 1000 original shares and the 750 shares issued to option counter-party, as shown in the table.

Project B Is Chosen

Even under the worst outcome of project B, firm value is 7250 and there is no default on the debt. The analysis should now be repetitive, and in the following table I have simply shown the values of the various claims under the assumption that the firm tried to raise the new 5250 with post-loss debt.

	Equity	Debt
Project A		
Senior Debt	2000	2000
New Debt/Equity	5250	5250
Put Counter-Party	2571	2571
Equity	3429	3429
Project B		
Senior Debt	2000	2000
New Debt/Equity	5250	5250
Put Counter-Party	2143	2143
Equity	2857	2857

The situation now is very different from the original presentation, in which the firm lost part of its income stream to the liability trust and *tried to fund the new investments by raising new money. Now the firm has exercised the put option to pay off the defendants directly. Accordingly, the income stream is available for all stakeholders (old shareholders, those having shares put to them, new investors funding the new investment, and old bondholders). You can see there is no longer an asset substitution problem. After exercising their option and paying off the liability defendants, the firm would rationally choose project A regardless of whether it was funded with debt or equity. The firm therefore has flexibility to choose its investment decision and its post-loss capital structure.*

Two mechanisms are at play here that explain the resolution of the asset substitution problem. First, paying off the liability is important. In the original example the liability claimants were first at the feeding trough of the company's earnings. The trust had priority access to the earnings generated by existing operations; it was like a senior debt and effectively increased the firm's leverage. In the reworking here, the liability claim is paid off in full by the proceeds of the new equity put to the counter-party. In return, the firm acquires a residual equity claim from the new shareholders. This has effectively unlevered the firm. But in addition to the unlevering by changing the form of the liability settlement, the put option provides a partial hedge, with the put counter-party effectively hedging part of the liability loss. This also mitigates the increase in leverage that normally follows loss events. The joint effect is to remove the post-loss asset substitution problem, and the firm can make its investment and financing decisions in much the same way as if no loss had occurred.

THE IMPACT OF HEDGED LOSSES
ON SHARE VALUE: FEEDBACK EFFECT

Consider the following scenario. A firm buys put options on its own shares from a counter-party in an attempt to protect its share value from the impact of some loss. A loss event occurs, such as a large fire or liability suit. What is the impact on share price? The direct impact of the loss event should be for the share price to fall, as we have seen extensively in this and prior chapters. For example, the event can destroy the firm's productive capacity and the earnings on that capacity are lost. However, the firm has hedged its shareholders' equity position by purchasing an instrument that will pay off when the share price falls, thus protecting the share price. We are left in the "apparadox" (this is a portmanteau word combining "apparent" and "paradox"[9]) that

- ♦ The share price has to fall to trigger the exercise of the put options, but
- ♦ If the share price falls, the options are exercised and the share price will be protected.

This section will examine this feedback effect. The loss affects the share price . . . but then the changing share price affects the payout on the hedge instrument . . . which in turn affects the share price . . . and so on *ad infinitum.* The section will illustrate the feedback problem with loss equity put options. However, the problem also arises with other hedge instruments that are triggered by changes in the share price. The same feedback effects would occur with reverse convertible debt, which is considered in the next chapter. Notice that the scenario outlined is very different from a standard insurance policy that pays for the loss directly. In that case the loss occurs and is paid by a third party. Thus, the share price is affected by the loss and the effect is limited by insurance. However, the fall in the share price does not affect how much the insurer will pay on the loss; there is no feedback from the changing share price to the insurance payout.

The Ability of Insurance to Protect Shareholders against a Reduction in Share Price

Consider an uninsured loss and an insured loss and their impact on share value. We will assume a liability loss, though the issue is not materially different with property loss or other sudden claims on wealth or earnings. Before a loss, the equity value is given by Equation (12.3) earlier in the chapter. However, for simplicity we will ignore post-loss investments and transaction costs and Equation (12.3) can be restated as:

---

9. Or it could be a Bostonian's description of two medical practitioners.

$$V(E) = V_0 + L - D \tag{12.9}$$

The after-loss value will depend on whether the loss is insured or not. If the loss is uninsured, the value of equity is given by Equation (12.4) earlier in the chapter (which has also been simplified to ignore new investments and transaction costs):

$$V'(E) = -C + V_0' + L - D \tag{12.10}$$

and the share price is $V'(E)/m$, where m is the number of shares. I am assuming here that the direct cost of the loss, C, is met by issuing new debt rather than by a new share issue. In contrast, the before-loss share price was $V(E)/m$. If we assume that the loss does not impact cash flows, $V_0' = V_0$, then the fall in the value of equity is exactly equal to the amount paid by the firm to settle the liability suit. Similarly, if one assumed property loss that was replaced at a cost, C, without any interruption in cash flows, $V_0' = V_0$, then again the fall in equity value is exactly equal to the cost of replacing the damaged asset. The fall in share price will be strictly proportional if debt is used to finance the loss. The change in share price as a result of the loss is:

$$\Delta P = \frac{1}{m}(V'(E) - V(E)) = \frac{1}{m}((-C + V_0' + L - D)$$

$$- (V_0 + L - D)) = \frac{1}{m}(-C + V_0' - V_0) \tag{12.11}$$

If the loss causes a fall in earnings, $V_0' < V_0$, the fall in equity will exceed the cost of paying for the loss. Although assumed away for simplicity, the same result will occur if there are transaction costs to financing the loss or if the loss adversely affects the return on future investments.

Now suppose that the loss is fully insured. By "fully" we mean that the insurer covers all costs, C. In that case we can represent the pre-loss and post-loss values as follows. the pre-loss value is:

$$V(E) = V_0 + L - D - p \tag{12.12}$$

where p is the insurance premium, and the post-loss value is:

$$V'(E) = -C + \$ + V_0' + L - D - p \tag{12.13}$$

where "$\$$" is the amount paid by the insurer to settle the loss. By definition of full insurance, $\$ = C$. If there is no interruption loss, $V_0' = V_0$, $V(E)$ will be equal to $V'(E)$, indicating that the value of equity will be unchanged by the loss. Insurance has protected the shareholders against a fall in the share price. The same result can be made with less restrictive assumptions if the insurance covers the all-interruption loss.

Stock Derivative Hedges and Share Price Feedback

Now consider that the firm tries to hedge its loss by buying some instrument that indemnifies the firm (not the shareholders directly) if the share value falls. For example, the firm holds a long position in put options on its own stock. If a loss occurs, there is a tendency for the share price to fall. If the share price falls to a point below the striking price of the put options, those options will be in the money and will pay the firm an amount equal to the difference between the post-loss market value and the striking price.

$$V'(E) = -C + \$ + V_0' + L - D - p \qquad (12.14)$$

where $\$$ can be reinterpreted as the payout on the option and p is now used to denote the price paid for the option. The fall in the share price, ΔP, as a result of the loss is now:

$$\Delta P = \frac{1}{m}\left(V'(E) - V(E)\right) = \frac{1}{m}\left((-C + \$ + V_0' + L - D - p)\right.$$

$$\left. - (V_0 + L - D - p)\right) = \frac{1}{m}\left(-C + (V'_0 - V_0) + \$\right) \quad (12.15)$$

The hedging strategy will be described by two parameters. The first is the striking price of the option, which we will refer to as a deviation of k/m dollars from the pre-loss share price $V(E)/m$; that is, the striking price is $(V(E) - k)/m$. If $k > 0$, the option would have been out of the money before loss, and if $k < 0$, the option would have been in the money. If $k = 0$, the option is on the money before loss. The second parameter will be referred to as the hedge ratio, which here means the number of options written on each share. This will be denoted by h, where $h = 1$ says that there is one put option purchased on each share. The values

k and h are equivalent to the deductible and coinsurance percentage in an insurance contract. Thus, the payout on the firm's option position is:

$$\$ = hm \left(\frac{V(E) - k}{m} - \frac{V'(E)}{m} \right) = h(V(E) - k - V'(E)) \quad (12.16)$$

When this is substituted into the change in value, the result is:

$$\Delta P = \frac{1}{m} (V'(E) - V(E)) = \frac{1}{m} (-C + (V'_0 - V_0)$$
$$+ h(V(E) - k - V'(E)) \quad (12.17)$$
$$= \frac{1}{(1 + h)m} (-C + (V'_0 - V_0) - hk)$$

To interpret what this means, consider a very simple case. The firm tries to "fully insure" by setting the striking price equal to the pre-loss share price $(k = 0)^{10}$ and by setting the hedge ratio equal to 1. Further assume that there is no interruption loss, so $V_0' = V_0$. Simplification now reveals that:

$$\Delta P = \frac{1}{m} (V'(E) - V(E)) = - \frac{1}{m} \left(\frac{C}{2} \right) \quad (12.18)$$

The stock price would fall by half the cost of the liability suit (property loss, etc). Thus, the shareholders are NOT fully hedged despite the firm's apparent attempts to do so. The problem is the circularity of the position. Since the stock was at the money before the loss, the stock price must fall for the option to be exercised. The more the stock price falls, the more valuable the firm's option position becomes, and this injection from external investors holding the short positions in the puts prevents the share price falling too far. Does this mean that this strategy could never provide a full hedge? To answer this, we must consider varying h and k to define other hedging strategies.

If $k > 0$, the share price must fall some discrete distance below the pre-loss share price, $V(E)/m$, before the put options will

---

10. This strategy would require continuous attention. Since the share price is constantly changing, so too would the striking price. This could be done periodically by changing the striking price each time the position is renewed, or by creating an instrument with a floating striking price.

be in the money. This implies that for many smaller values of the loss C, the option position will have a zero payoff. Conversely, if $k < 0$, the option will be in the money before a loss occurs. This means that the hedge position will pay something even if no loss occurs (unless C were to have the quite perverse effect of raising the share price), but the option position would yield a higher payoff the more the post-loss share price fell. These two striking price positions (together with $k = 0$) are shown in Figure 12–5 as the solid lines falling at a rate ½ or 22.5°. These lines all assume that the hedge ratio $h = 1$. In contrast, the hedge strategy can be changed by fixing k and varying h. We illustrate this by the broken lines, which show hedge strategies labeled $k < 0$; $h < 1$ and $k < 0$; $h > 1$. We could also have shown variations of h for different values of k, but the diagram would soon have become cluttered. The point is that the option position payoff can be increased for any given level of C by

+ Reducing the striking price by increasing k or
+ Increasing the hedge ratio h

F I G U R E   12–5

Hedging with Derivatives: the Effect on Share Price

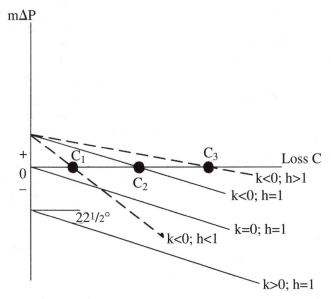

Hedging Strategies with $k \geq 0$

It is clear from Equation (12.10) and Figure 12–5 that when the striking price is at or below the pre-loss share price, the share price must fall for any loss event C (unless for some strange reason $V_0' > V_0$). Figure 12–5 shows the change in the total value of equity, $m\Delta P$, for any value of the loss C. A full hedge, $m\Delta P = 0$, is impossible for any positive C. Thus, at best, such strategies can only partly hedge shareholders from the effects of the loss event on the share value. Varying both k and h will vary the effects of the hedge; lower k and higher h will provide more robust hedges. Higher k and lower h provide a weaker hedge, but the up-front price should be cheaper. Notice that the *sensitivity* of $m\Delta P$ to changes is C (i.e., the slope of the hedge line in the diagram) and is controlled by the hedge ratio h. Thus, the firm wishing to keep the cost of the hedge down, yet provide protection to the share price from very large losses, could choose a low exercise price (k is large) and a high hedge ratio (h also is large).

Hedging Strategies with $k < 0$ and Double Triggers

You may have spotted a strange problem with the case in which the hedging strategy includes $k < 0$. One problem is that it appears that the firm is sitting on an in the money option before the loss occurs. Thus, while these strategies can yield good protection against large C losses, they also require that the firm buy an option that pays even if no loss occurs. Such in the money options are expensive. But there is another technical problem. The circularity problem implies that the pre-loss share value will reflect the payoff to the pre-loss in the money option. Thus, the pre-loss price will be bid upwards. To avoid these issues, we can design the option with a double trigger, as shown by our discussion of loss equity puts.[11] Now the payoff can occur only if the value of C exceeds some given value.

Suppose the trigger is C_1 as shown in Figure 12–5. Then a hedging strategy shown as $k < 0$; $h < 1$ would provide a complete hedge if the loss were exactly at the loss trigger C_1. But if the loss

---

11. Actually, we don't entirely avoid the problem with double trigger. the pre-loss share price will reflect the potential for fall in price should a loss event occur and the potential for this contingent fall in share value to be limited by the chosen hedging strategy.

exceeded the trigger, the share price would fall. If the loss were less than C_1, the trigger would not be activated and the option position would not yield any profit. Thus, with the double trigger, the positive portion of the diagram reverts to zero ($m\Delta P = 0$). Similarly, if the trigger were C_2, the hedge strategy shown as $k < 1$; $h = 1$ would give a full hedge only if the loss were exactly C_2. Larger losses would be undercompensated but would still provide more protection than with the C_1 trigger. And so on for the C_3 trigger. You will discern that no strategy exists that provides a full hedge for all levels of loss. Thus, even double-trigger strategies cannot provide across-the-board protection to shareholders from loss events.[12]

Direct Hedging by Shareholders

Contrast the following strategies. First, the firm hedges by purchase of put options on its own stock. Second, individual shareholders protect their position by purchasing put options *on their own account*. As we saw in the first case, hedging by the firm feeds into the share price, which feeds back into the option payout. In the second case, a loss event will put downward press on the stock price and will trigger the option. However, the option payouts are not fed directly to the firm and the fall in share price is not mitigated. Accordingly, by trading on their own account, shareholders could provide a complete hedge against falling stock values after a loss event.

Figure 12–6 shows the standard payout diagram for a put option. The striking price is S and the payout is shown before deduction of the purchase price of the option. The 45° slope indicates that one put option is held for each share. The payoff shows that the investor is fully hedged against falls in share price below the striking price.

---

12. You will note that it is still possible to have a revere hedge for which share prices rise when a loss occurs. For example, suppose that the loss trigger is C_1 and the hedge strategy is that labeled $k < 0$; $h = 1$ in the diagram. With this strategy, losses above C_1 but below C_2 would be overcompensated. This problem was discussed in the section on loss equity puts because it created perverse incentives for the firm to exaggerate smaller losses (i.e., below C_1).

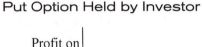

FIGURE   12–6

Put Option Held by Investor

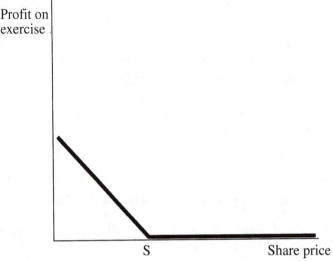

CONCLUSION

There is generally accepted wisdom that post-loss financing is risky because the terms at which funds are available after a significant loss can be penalistic. Accordingly, the belief goes, it makes sense to set up the funding in advance. This chapter shows that the ability of contingent financing to add value is limited. Simply arranging a line of credit, to be drawn after a loss under post-loss terms, does little more than anticipate the post-loss fundability issue. If the firm cannot fund an investment after loss, the terms under which the LOC will be available will simply also be restricted. Moreover, if the LOC is made available under terms fixed in advance, the post-loss investment decision is removed from the scrutiny of capital markets and may not reflect the true, post-loss, opportunity cost of capital. The only real value in lines of credit arises when investment are time-sensitive; the LOC makes money available immediately. This can be important for earnings smoothing.

We also looked at the possibility of raising contingent equity. A version that has recently appeared is the loss put option, in which the issuer sells to a counter-party the right to issue new shares at a fixed price after a loss to recapitalize the firm. These instruments partly hedge the firm, provide it with post-loss liquidity, and mitigate underinvestment and asset substitution problems. Because the bondholders receive a benefit from these instruments, a natural extension that was examined is the inclusion of such options into the firm's debt.

The final part of the chapter addressed an interesting conundrum related to the effectiveness of instruments that provide a hedge based on the firm's equity value. There is a circularity: the stock price must fall for the instrument to be activated. However, if activation is anticipated and a hedge is provided, the expected value of this hedge will be anticipated by investors and so prop up the stock price. We showed how these circular forces play out. The implication of this analysis is that full insurance is not possible for all losses. This discussion will set us up to examine other new device, such as convertible and reverse convertible debt, that are also activated by the post-loss equity value. These and other leverage strategies will now be examined.

REFERENCES

Berkovitch, Elazar, and Stuart I. Greenbaum. 1991. "The Loan Commitment as an Optimal Financing Contract." *Journal of Financial and Quantitative Analysis* 26:83–95.

Martin, J. Spencer, and Anthony Santomero. 1997. "Investment Opportunities and Corporate Demand for Lines of Credit." *Journal of Banking and Finance* 21:1331–50.

Snyder, Christopher. 1998. "Loan Commitments and the Debt Overhand Problem." *Journal of Financial and Quantitative Analysis* 33:87–116.

CHAPTER 13

Contingent Leverage Strategies and Hybrid Debt

Contrast the list of reasons why capital structure matters with the reasons why risk is costly, and they turn out to be remarkably similar. Capital structure matters if there are transaction costs, if agents are not fully informed, if there are tax distortions, and if the firm's investment policy is affected by the choice of financing. Risk is costly because of agency effects that can change investment policy, costs of financial distress, tax effects, and costs of information asymmetry that lead to loss of new investments when the firm suffers sudden losses that consume internal cash. The similarity should not be too surprising. We showed in Chapter 7 that the costs of risk depended heavily on the capital structure. And those who are interested in capital structure know the reverse to be true: the optimal capital structure is closely related to the riskiness of the firm. Accordingly, it was shown in that chapter that problems of asset substitution and underinvestment, costs of financial distress, and the crowding out hypothesis could be addressed either by reducing risk or by changing leverage.

In the previous chapters post-loss financing was addressed. This was addressed as a risk management exercise. Risky events lead to a change in value. In the case of insurable events, this is a loss of value and the events usually call into play a financing decision: how to pay for reinvestment or how to pay for a liability settlement. With other risky events, the event can change the ability of the firm to fund ongoing investment projects from preferred (often internal) capital sources. The problem is to mitigate the impact of the risky event by ensuring optimal post-event investment decisions and optimal funding of those investments. But the same problem can be couched in standard corporate finance terms. If one accepts the post-loss environment as given, the firm simply faces a set of investment and financing decisions that are amenable to normal financial economic analysis. What we add in the risk management treatment is a consideration of the impact of the risky event on the post-loss decisions and a framework for anticipating risky events and the prospective investment and financing decisions that might follow. This *ex ante* approach will allow us to compare debt and equity financing alongside insurance that is a hedge but also can be considered as a loss financing tool.

We will begin this chapter by examining *ex ante* leverage strategies. The perspective is as follows. Some risky event, such as a currency loss, commodity price change, liability loss, or change in the firm's stock price, can occur in the future. Whether it will occur, and/or its magnitude, are not known in advance. The chapter will look at debt instruments that are conditioned on such events. Such debt instruments are in fact combinations of normal debt and a derivative such as a future or option. The idea is to use the option feature to mitigate the costs that are associated with post-loss leverage. For example, the option can forgive the debt, or transform it into equity, should the defined event occur. This will lower the likelihood of financial distress and avoid some of the associated costs. Moreover, the fact that the firm might partially unlever in strained financial circumstances will affect incentives for investment decisions, and this might be used to redress the agency costs associated with high risk and leverage.

The chapter will examine some of the forms of hybrid debt that are encountered. These will be examined to show how they can redress some of the costs of risk. Many of these instruments were created to address specific risk management needs of an issuing firm. This "financial engineering" is a continuing business. As new needs arise, and as firms understand the nature of risk costs better, other instruments will undoubtedly appear. In this spirit, a new instruments, reverse convertible debt, is discussed to illustrate how this and existing hybrids address the various risk costs encountered by firms.

RISK MANAGEMENT AND CAPITAL STRUCTURE

Risk management and leverage, while not exactly different sides of the same coin, are nevertheless closely related. The previous two chapters exploited this relationship and considered *ex post* leverage approaches to risk management. In this chapter we will use *ex ante* leverage management strategies, which in turn can be subdivided into *immediate* and *conditional*. This chapter will focus on conditional leverage strategies, but before we go forward, it will be useful to summarize these three approaches.

Ex post Leverage—Post-loss Financing

The choice of how to finance post-loss investment is no different in principle from how to finance investment made at any other time; all the trade-offs made in capital structure decisions apply as usual. The risk management treatment given in the Chapters 10 and 11 is an expansion of the capital structure approach. It was expanded to account for the fact that post-loss investment decisions were not taken as given but were considered endogenously with capital structure. This was particularly important because the decisions followed in the wake of some risky event that could shake up the estimated returns from new investments or reinvestments. Thus, our treatment in one way echoes that of Froot and Stein (1998), who examine the joint determination of risk management, capital structure, and capital budgeting decisions.[1]

Ex ante Leverage—Immediate Leverage

Enough has now been said for us to conclude that management of the capital structure of the firm and risk management are inseparable. The agency and associated cost associated with the riskiness of future events can be reduced by changing the leverage,

---

1. Froot and Stein (1998) and Leland (1998) have recently examined the interdependence between risk management and capital structure in financial institutions.

and conversely, reducing the risk can change the firm's tolerance of increased leverage. By extension, we can also envision mixed strategies in which partial hedging is matched with an intermediate capital structure. Thus, hedging may permit the firm to secure any tax advantages to debt, without suffering from unusual agency cost and financial distress costs that normally accompany high leverage. It will also be recalled that the empirical studies cited in Chapter 7 lent some support to the view that more highly levered firms were more likely to hedge because the value added higher.

Ex ante Leverage–Contingent Leverage

The third leverage approach also anticipates the costs jointly associated with leverage and future risky events. But rather than change current leverage, it makes it contingent on the occurrence of a future shock. An instrument is put in place now that will unlever the firm if the defined risky event occurs. One such instrument was considered in Chapter 12, the equity put option written on the firm's own shares. Unlevering follows a loss if the option is shifted into the money. In this case, leverage is lowered by the issue of new debt (and by the value added from investing the proceeds in positive NPV post-loss investment projects). Here we will address contingent leverage strategies in which the burden of debt is reduced in some way, conditional on the occurrence of the risk event. The debt is designed to transform on the happening of the risk event by the operation of an embedded derivative. Such debt is called "hybrid debt."

CONTINGENT LEVERAGE STRATEGIES AND HYBRID DEBT

Hybrid debt is a package including conventional debt and a second (and perhaps even a third or fourth) instrument such as an option, forward, future, or swap. The inclusion of the second instrument can be used as a hedge or to mitigate some undesired leverage effect such as the shareholder/bondholder agency cost.

Hybrid debt is certainly not a new concept. Corporate bonds, though not government bonds, routinely embody call options under which the issuer can buy back the bond at the face value. If interest rates fall, the market value of a bond will normally rise.

This call provision gives the firm the opportunity to buy back the bond at face and reissue at a new coupon rate that reflects the lower interest rate. The exercise of this option provides a gain to the issuer, and there is a corresponding cost to the holder, who is forced to sell his asset at less than the value of the income stream it would have generated. Accordingly, the call option will be reflected in the bond price/interest rate. Callable bonds will sell at a lower price, or pay higher interest, to compensate the holder for "selling" to the firm the call option. An interesting feature of the callable bond is that it permits a transfer of wealth between the issuer and holder of the bond at the time a significant economic event occurs, i.e., when interest rates change. Suppose that one or other of these parties had a wealth position that was sensitive to changes in interest rates. If so, the callable bond could be used to hedge that interest sensitivity. But the value of the bond could also change as a result of a change in the credit risk of the firm; an improvement in credit risk would enhance the value of the bond, and this could lead the firm to exercise its call option. In this way, the firm is rewarded for an improvement in credit risk. This suggests a second type of benefit: that the inclusion of the option might change the operational and financial decisions of the firm in a way that more closely aligns the interests of shareholders and creditors. These two characteristics provide a useful starting point for looking at hybrid debt as a risk management tool.

Another feature that is often embedded in debt is a warrant. This enables the holder of the bond to purchase a number of shares of stock at an agreed price (the exercise or striking price). The warrant is simply an option held by the bondholder and sold in package with the debt. The bondholder can choose to exercise the option and will have an incentive to do so only when the share price exceeds the exercise price. From the issuer's point of view, it will be forced to sell shares when the option is exercised at a price lower than the prevailing market value. Accordingly, one would expect this provision to be accompanied by a lower rate of interest. The inclusion of the warrant lowers the interest cost to the firm. But this does not mean that it lowers the cost of debt capital. Something is given in return for the lower interest, namely the opportunity for the bondholders to participate in the upside fortunes of the firm. The lower interest rate is the price of this option, which is paid by the bondholders for this participation.

There are other longstanding examples of hybrid debt. Convertible bonds have been traced at least as far back as the 1850s (Tufano, 1997). The convertible bond combines a normal bond with an option to convert into a fixed number of shares. If the value of bond is lower than the n shares for which it can be exchanged, the bondholder will secure a gain. The firm is then forced to give up valuable equity in exchange for less valuable bonds. For example, suppose the bond has a value of $1000 and the conversion option allows the bondholder to trade in the bond in exchange for 10 shares. If the stock price is $80, 10 shares are worth $800. At the 10-to-1 ratio, it is not in the bondholder's interest to convert. If the stock price rose to $120, 10 shares would be worth $1200 and the bondholder would gain $200 exercising the conversion option.[2] This package is similar to that of a normal bond and a warrant, except that here the equity is acquired in exchange for the bond instead of buying for cash at a fixed price. The economic implications are, not surprisingly, similar to those for warrants, and these will be discussed later.

To compare these three common examples of hybrids bonds, they all contain an option feature, but they differ somewhat in the type of event which triggers the option. The warrant and convertible are tied the underlying economic value of the firm, whereas the call can be related to changes in credit ranking or to changes in an external economic indictor, interest rates. Starting in the 1970s, there has been a wave of debt hybrids tied to external economic indicators. This activity, like the growth of other derivative products, is associated with a dramatic increase in the volatility of interest rates, exchange rates, and, to some extent, commodity prices, following the collapse of the Bretton Woods agreement to peg interest rates. The new regime of floating rates has exposed many firms to the effects of this price volatility and has accordingly created a demand for hedging instruments. The

---

2. This simple illustration assumes that the bond price is independent of the stock price, which may not be too realistic. The point of the illustration is simply to compare the value of one bond and 10 stocks to see whether exercise generates a profit and thus whether the option would be exercised. Another complication is whether the option would be exercised under favorable conditions or whether it would be left open in the hope that it might be exercised under even better price ratios in the future.

wave of corporate hybrid debt instruments attached to these indicators, along with options, forwards, futures, swaps, and other instruments written on these variables, has responded to this demand.[3]

The various forms of hybrids can be classified in various ways. To illustrate the range, the performance of the debt can be linked to both internal or external variables and the type of transformation of the debt can be the inclusion of options, swaps, forwards, or futures.

Triggers

The conditions of the debt can be linked to:

* The financial performance of the issuer (stock price, credit rating)
* Some external economic indicator (commodity prices, interest rates, or exchange rates)
* Some noneconomic indicator (the occurrence of a political or natural event)

Transformation

The debt can:

* Be called (repurchased) at an agreed price by the issuer
* Be forgiven on the occurrence of the trigger
* Be sold back to the issuer at an agreed, exercise, price
* Be converted to equity under fixed terms
* Be linked with options to buy equity at an agreed price
* Have its interest linked to an internal or external economic indicator

Given the actual, and potential, variety of hybrid debt, a useful way of organizing our enquiry is to set out some risk management criterion and show how different forms of hybrid debt fare.

---

3. See Smithson and Chew (1998) and Rawls and Smithson (1989) for a description of the development of hybrid debt products and other risk management instruments.

REDUCING CONVEXITY OF THE PAYOFF

Figure 13–1 shows the values of conventional debt and equity, given different firm values. The face value of the debt is F. The diagram does not show transaction costs or the effects of taxes. The debt, D, can be thought of as default-free debt, D_{DF}, and a short position in a put option, $P(V(F), F)$ on the firm value, $V(F)$, at which the exercise price is the face value of the debt, D.

$$V(D) = D_{DF} - P(V(F), D)$$

The equity, $V(E)$, is the residual value. Thus:

$$V(E) = V(F) - V(D) = V(F) - D_{DF} + P(V(F), D) = C(V(F), D)$$

where $C(V(F), D)$ is a call option written on $V(F)$ with striking price D. These equations show that the equity can be thought of as the firm value minus a default-free debt obligation plus ownership of a put option that we have referred to earlier as the "default put." This residual payoff is similar in structure to a call option written on the value of the firm with a exercise price of D, as shown in both the equation and the diagram. In fact, the equation for equity value contains an implicit relationship between the

F I G U R E   13–1

Project Distortions under Leverage

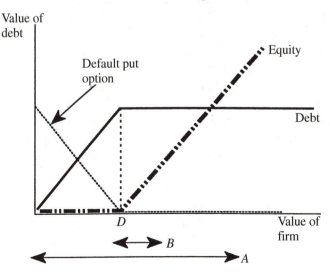

value of a put and the value of call option written at the same exercise price. This relationship is "put–call parity," which was shown in Chapter 6.

The difference in the shapes of the debt and equity payoff structures explains the principal–agent costs that were important in explaining why risk was costly to the firm. For example, consider the selection of a project that increases firm variability and leads to a spread of possible value the spans D, as shown at the bottom of the diagram by line A. There is now a considerable downside risk that falls exclusively on the creditors. Thus, shareholders are tempted to undertake such a project so that they reap the upside risk and avoid the downside. Ignoring the downside enhances the residual value of the project.

Another way of showing this same point is that the shareholder's position is a call option and such options increase in value as the risk of the underlying asset (i.e., firm value) increases. Shareholders are tempted to enhance their call position by choosing to increase risk. Or the same point can be made with put–call parity. Shareholders are tempted to increase risk because it enhances the value of the default put option that they hold. Consider the arrowed lines under Figure 13–1. Line A shows considerable fluctuation in value and line B shows a low-risk profile. These two value distributions have been drawn such that they are centered at about the same position, a little to the right of D. The expected value of the firm is the same in either case; only the risk differs. The value of the call option owned by the shareholders will be higher under profile A than under B. Potential values below D are irrelevant to the value of the call value. But to the right of D, profile A has a lot of upside potential whereas B has little. Thus, the call option and the equity value will be higher under the high-risk profile. In short, the value of the call option increases as the risk of the firm increases. The value of the debt position falls as firm risk increases. Also shown is the default put option. This also must increase as the risk increases, by the same logic. The increase in value of the default put option as the risk increases benefits the shareholders and erodes the value of the debt.

This principal–agent cost rests on the degree of risk and the nonlinearity of the residual claim. The kink around the point D is the source of the problem. Technically, the residual claim is convex (from below; or concave from above), and this convexity causes the conflict of interest between the main stakeholders. One way of straightening the equity curve is to unlever the firm entirely. If the debt goes away, the equity line is simple a 45° line sloping up from the origin. The shareholders will be exposed to the entire risk of the firm (upside and downside), and distortions in project selection will be avoided. Hybrid debt can be used to reduce the convexity of the equity function and thereby mitigate principal–agent conflict.

Convertible Debt

Figure 13–2 shows the payoffs under conventional debt and convertible debt. Ignoring, for the moment, the curve labeled "reverse convertible," look at the shape of the convertible debt value. There is some face value D_c. If the firm value falls below this point, the firm is insolvent, the bondholders become the residual claimants, and the payoff follows the 45° line. However, if the firm value rises, with a corresponding increase in share prices, we will eventually reach a point at which the creditors can benefit from exercising their option to convert. This point is shown as C. To the right of C, the value of the "creditors" claim increases at less than

F I G U R E   13–2

Payoff Structure to Bondholders from Debt Hybrids

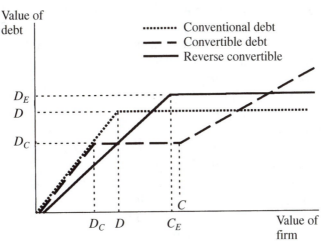

45°. Actually, when conversion takes place, the creditors are no longer creditors but share the ownership with the original shareholders. The slope of the line to the right of C indicates what portion of the total equity is owned by the former bondholders. For example, if the firm had 1 million shares and another 1 million were created on conversion, then former creditors would own half of the post conversion shares. Thus, for every $1 increase in share value, 50 cents would go to the old shareholders and 50 cents to the former bondholders who are the new shareholders. The line would slope at 22.5°. The greater the proportion of the overall equity owned by the former bondholders after conversion, the steeper would this line be.

An important feature of the convertible profile is that the point D_c is shown to the left of point D. When we introduced convertibles, we mentioned that the conversion option was a valuable feature for the bondholders and would lower the interest rate on the debt. Because we do not show interest rates in this diagram, we need to find another way of showing that the conversion benefit is appropriately priced. Suppose a firm needed to raise 0.9 million dollars and issued 1000 bonds, each with a face value of $1000 but issued at $900. The bonds carry a 10% coupon interest rate. The cost of capital is 11.1% ($100 of interest on each $900 raised). With a conversion option, the $1000 bond might sell at par because the option has value to investors. The interest payment of $100 would be a 10% return. Thus, the interest rate is lower, reflecting the benefit of the conversion option. The other way of looking at this is that only 900 such bonds would need to be raised to satisfy the $0.9 million capital requirement. Thus, instead of owing $1 million on conventional debt (1000 bonds each at $1000 face), the firm only owes $0.9 million (900 bonds at $1000 face). Thus, the conversion option will lower the amount owed to the bondholders. Other things being equal, this will lower the probability of bankruptcy.

Figure 13–3 shows how conversion affects the original shareholders. Below D_c, the firm is insolvent and the equity s worthless. Between D_c and C, the debt obligation is covered but share value is not sufficiently high that bondholders will use their conversion option. Thus, shareholders get all the incremental benefit of changes in firm value in this range and the slope is 45°. But above C, when conversion is exercised, the residual claim is shared. The

F I G U R E   13–3

Payoffs to Original Shareholders with Debt Hybrids

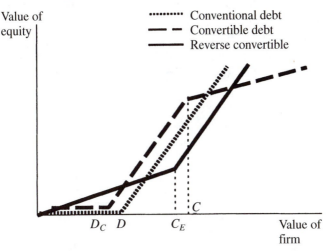

portion of equity not going to former bondholders accrues to the original shareholders. Notice that the slope of the equity line in Figure 13–3 and the slope of the debt line in Figure 13–2 must always sum to 45°.[4] Thus, if there were originally 1 million shares and another 0.5 million were issued to covering bondholders, the former bondholder would hold one third of the total equity and the original shareholder would hold two thirds. The slope of the debt line would be 15° and the slope of the equity line 30°.

Now comes the crux. Compare the equity value lines for conventional and convertible debt. Equity value is less convex under the convertible debt. The single kink in the nonconvertible case at D gives the equity curve its convex property. It is true that some sections are not convex (it is linear to the left of D and to the right). But if value spans D, the overall effect is convex. Equity under the convertible debt has changed in two ways. Reducing the debt obligation (lowering the interest rate) has pushed the kink to the left. Thus, we are less likely to push over the kink and the effect of convexity has been lessened. Second, we have added a concave section at point C.

---

4. This is true at any firm value because we have ignored other claims such as taxes.

But what does all this geometry mean? Shareholders now keep more of the downside risk with convertible debt. The default put options kicks in at a lower value, and thus shareholders will take more interest in downside risk when considering projects. On the other hand, the shareholders do not keep all the upside risk. If things go well, share prices will rise and bondholders will participate in the good fortune. In short, the interests of the bondholders and the shareholders are now not so far apart; their payoff structures are not so dissimilar. The incentive to select high-risk projects is now mitigated; they keep more of the low end and have to give up some of the high end. Risk is not so attractive anymore (see Greene, 1984).

Hood Down converts standard saloon (sedan) cars into convertibles. This enterprise has some risk, and future earnings have an expected present value of either 100 or 200 each with a 0.5 probability. The firm has 100 existing shares and existing senior debt with a face value of 100. Because the debt is covered in all states of the world, its value is 100 and the value of equity is 50.

Project Selection with Nonconvertible Debt (NCD)

The firm faces a new investment opportunity: to use its engineering facilities in boat construction. But there are two ways of doing this. It can acquire an existing small firm with its existing core market and build from there. This alternative, call it project A is low risk, and we will characterize it as riskless. The capital cost is 200 and the projected cash flows have a present value of 220. Thus, the NPV is 20. Alternative B is to use a revolutionary technique that is largely untried and build production facilities from scratch. The capital cost is again 200, but this is fraught with risk, on both the production and demand side. The PV of earnings could be either 20 or 310, as shown below, and the expected NPV is negative at −35.

	Capital Cost	PV of Earnings	E(NPV)
Project A	200	220	20
Project B	200	20; probability 0.5 or 310; probability 0.5	−35

The earnings from the projects are independent of those from existing operations. The firm issues new (junior) debt with a face value of 200 prior to making its project selection with the (dubious) hope of financing the project, which has a cost of 200. Finally, we assume that the transaction cost in the event of bankruptcy is 100. We now value the firm's claims, bearing in mind the permutations of earnings that can arise from existing operations and from whichever new project is chosen. We also net out bankruptcy cost where total value of earnings is insufficient to pay both senior and junior debt.

Value of the Firm if Project A Is Chosen

The ex post firm value will either be 320 (100 from existing operations plus 220 from project A) or 420 (200 from existing operations plus 220 from project A), each with 0.5 probability. This gives a present firm value 370, which is shown below with its allocation over debt and equity.

Value of the firm	0.5(320 + 420) = 370
Old debt	0.5(100 + 100) = 100
New debt	0.5(200 + 200) = 200
Equity	0.5(20 + 120) = 70

Value of the Firm if Project B Is Chosen

The ex post firm value will be one of the following values, each with a 25% probability:

20 (100 from existing operations, 20 from project B less bankruptcy cost of 100)

120 (200 from existing operations, 20 from project B less bankruptcy cost of 100)

410 (100 from existing operations plus 310 from project B); or

510 (200 from existing operations plus 310 from project B)

Therefore, the firm and its various stakeholders are valued as follows:

Value of the firm	*0.25(20 + 120 + 410 + 510) = 265*
Old debt	*0.25(20 + 100 + 100 + 100) = 80*
New debt	*0.25(0 + 20 + 200 + 200) = 105*
Equity	*0.25(0 + 0 + 110 + 210) = 80*

This illustrates the classic underinvestment problem. Since project selection is made after debt has been issued, shareholders favor project B, which offers an equity value of 80, compared with 70 for A. If bondholders anticipate this choice, then debt is valued only at 105, and thus the debt issue will not command a sufficient price to fund the project. In this example there is insufficient gain to shareholders to make good remaining 95 (i.e., 200 − 105) required to fund project B, since the value of equity is 50 with neither project and is only 80 if B is undertaken. Unless the firm can credibly signal to bondholders a commitment to undertake A, the firm is snookered and will be unable to undertake either project if it persists with debt financing.

Project Selection with Convertible Debt

Convertible debt should change the incentives of shareholders. Specifically, it should make the more risky project less attractive, even if it is funded with debt. To see this, suppose that the new debt can be converted into 200 shares at the option of the bondholders (senior debt of 100 is not convertible). If the bondholders choose to convert, the number of shares will rise from 100 to 300. First, we need to establish the value of the firm at which the conversion option will be exercised. Since the option is held by bondholders, it will be exercised at values for which the value of equity issued on conversion (which will then amount to two thirds of total equity) is greater than the nonconverted obligation of 200; i.e.:

$$\text{Convert if}: \tfrac{2}{3}(\text{value of equity}) > 200$$

$$\text{or if}: \tfrac{2}{3}(\text{value of firm} - \text{Senior Debt}) > 200$$

$$\text{which implies}: \text{value of firm} > 400$$

Value of the Firm if A Is Chosen

Value of the firm	$0.5(320 + 420)$	$= 370$
Old debt	$0.5(100 + 100)$	$= 100$
New debt	$0.5\{200 + \tfrac{2}{3}(420 - 100)\}$	$= 206.7$
Equity	$0.5\{20 + \tfrac{1}{3}(420 - 100)\}$	$= 63.3$

Value of the Firm if *B* Is Chosen

Value of the firm $0.25(20 + 120 + 410 + 510)$ $= 265$

Old debt $0.25(20 + 100 + 100 + 100)$ $= 80$

New debt $0.25\{0 + 20 + \frac{2}{3}(410 - 100) + \frac{2}{3}(510 - 100)\}$ $= 125$

Equity $0.25\{0 + 0 + \frac{1}{3}(410 - 100) + \frac{1}{3}(510 - 100)\}$ $= 60$

There is clear incentive to undertake project A, since the value of equity is higher than for B. Why would shareholders switch their choice from B to A? The main change that has taken place with the convertible is that the shareholders have to share much of the upside risk if they choose B (shareholders now get only one third of any value in excess of 400). Even though shareholders retain the default put option, a measly one third of the upside is no longer appealing enough to overcome the negative NPV of project B. With convertible debt, the intrinsic soundness (higher NPV) of project A *shines through.*

We argued earlier that convertible debt would reduce the probability of bankruptcy. We see this indirectly in this example as a consequence of the switch in the project choice. Since investors subscribing to the new debt issue can anticipate the choice of project A, which has low risk, they can be assured there is little (in this case no) risk of bankruptcy. Avoiding the expected bankruptcy cost does not directly enhance the equity value, since it would have been paid by creditors. But it does mean the debt is more attractive. In this case investors would be willing to pay 206.7 for the new debt despite the fact that its face is 200. This reflects both the absence of bankruptcy costs and their participation in the upside potential. This means that the firm could actually have lowered face amount a little and still have had investors pay an amount sufficient to cover the 200 capital cost.[5]

A related argument on why firms issue convertible debt has been offered by Brennan and Schwartz (1988). The value of non-

---

5. Lowering the face in this way would normally result in a further gain because it would reduce the probability of bankruptcy even further. However, we have no bankruptcy risk with *A* in this example, and this effect is not illustrated here. To make the example a little richer, you can introduce a very small possibility of extreme outcomes (say a 1% chance of a PV of zero and a 1% chance of a PV of 400 with a 98% chance of a PV of 200). This should still give similar results on project choice but will show this second bankruptcy effect from convertibles.

convertible is sensitive to firm risk because changes in risk affect the value of the default put option. The inclusion of the conversion option dampens this risk sensitivity. Because the conversion option also is sensitive to the risk of the firm, and this option is held by the bondholders, increases in risk will increase the value of this option. Thus, the two options being held by different parties have opposing risk effects. What bondholders lose on the default put with an increase in risk they largely get back through an increase in the value of the conversion option. Accordingly, the value of convertible is relatively insensitive to risk. Now consider a firm that wishes to issue debt, but the risk is difficult to estimate. Such would be the case in new and high-growth firms. The danger for the firm is that the management may be more optimistic about risk than outsiders. Moreover, investors may believe the firm will play games that increase risk and expropriate bondholder wealth. Accordingly, the cost of conventional debt will be high. But with convertible debt the difference in risk perceptions is not crucial because of the offsetting effects on the default and conversion options. Accordingly, firms with uncertain risk will find it cheaper to finance with convertible than with conventional debt.

Reverse-Convertible Debt, RCD

With loss equity put options, discussed in the previous chapter, a loss of sufficient size both to activate the event trigger and to drive the stock price below the strike price will give rise to a new equity issue. The debt remains, but the issue of new equity at a price above post-loss market price will cause some unlevering. In this way these options can be thought of as contingent leverage instruments. When considering loss equity put options, asset substitution, and underinvestment, we discussed the possibility that the option could be shorted by the firm's creditors; thus, creditors would hold a portfolio including the debt and the loss equity put. The short position in the put option was embedded in the firm's debt to create a hybrid security. We will now take that idea a step further and discuss a hybrid security in which the debt converts into equity when an appropriate loss occurs.

Reverse-convertible debt, RCD, is similar to convertible debt except that the long and short position in the conversion option are reversed. The firm has the option to convert the bonds into shares, and bondholders must accept the conversion if it is chosen by the firm. To use the same numbers as above to illustrate convertible debt: bonds are worth $1000 and can be converted into 10 shares *if the firm chooses*. At a share price of $120 the firm is not going to buy out of an obligation of $1000 by giving away assets worth $1200. The option will not be exercised. But if the share prices falls to $80, buying out of an $1000 obligation for $800 is a good deal for the firm. But it doesn't sound like a good deal for the bondholders. With regular convertible bonds, the bondholder can only gain; there is upside, but not downside, risk. With reverse convertible debt, the bondholder can only lose. If stock prices remain high, the bonds will remain and the bondholder will be just as well off as if the bonds were not reverse convertible. But if share prices fall, the bondholder will be forced to give up his fixed claim for an uncertain and lower value asset. *Ex post*, there are clear gainers and losers.

Reverse-convertible debt is illustrated in Figures 13–2 and 13–3 alongside convertible and conventional debt. In Figure 13–2 the payoff structure to bondholders with RCD is shown. For firm values at which the conversion option is in the money (i.e., below point C_R), the debt payoff is shown as a ray from the origin, indicating that the debt has reverted to an equity claim. At values at which the conversion option is out of the money (to the right of C_R), the value of the RCD is its face value D_R. The corresponding values of the residual claim of the original shareholders are shown in Figure 13–3. Note that below C_R the equity is convertible and the original shareholders share the equity with the ex-bondholders. However, above C_R the debt remains intact. Again, relative to the nonconvertible debt, there is some "linearizing" of the equity payoff, and this will change incentives for project selection.

Why are we interested in this unusual instrument for risk management purposes? And why on earth would bondholders wish to hold such an instrument when they can lose but not win? To answer these questions we must look at the *ex ante* prospects

for the parties. First, notice that this is a contingent leverage instrument; contingent upon the share price falling sufficiently that
the firm will unlever. With this in mind, consider the following
implications:

1. With RCD, the probability of bankruptcy will fall. When
   the share value falls, a firm with conventional debt will
   approach a financial distress condition. If share value
   continues to fall, the firm will become insolvent and
   bankrupt. But when the debt is reverse convertible, the
   fall in share value, which otherwise led to bankruptcy,
   will become the trigger for unlevering the firm. Thus, at
   the very time when debt becomes a problem, it converts
   into equity. If all debt were convertible, in theory, the
   firm would never go bankrupt. Short of that point,
   making some debt convertible will reduce the firm's
   obligations when it falls on hard times and thus reduce
   the probability of bankruptcy.

   Under the absolute priority rule, the equity of a
   firm expires worthless when the firm is bankrupt.
   Accordingly, all the costs of bankruptcy fall on the firm's
   creditors. Thus, if the probability of bankruptcy is
   reduced, so too is the probability that bondholders
   would have to pay those costs. This will enhance the
   value of the firm's bonds.[6]

2. The inclusion of the reverse conversion option changes
   the incentives of the firm to undertake new investments.
   With regular debt the firm will be tempted to ignore
   downside risk because, beyond the point at which shares
   become worthless, all downside falls on the creditors.
   This default put option increases the value of high-risk
   investment projects to shareholders and can lead to the
   asset substitution and underinvestment problems. With

---

6. Under workouts the parties negotiate a settlement in which the equity usually retains
   value and the debt is renegotiated. This makes the allocation of the costs of distress a little less clear; the allocation will depend in part on the *ex post* bargaining
   power of the parties.

RCD the default put is replaced by a conversion put option. In this way the shareholders do not get to walk away from all downside risk; rather, equity is diluted by exercise of the option and the original shareholders get to share the downside with the (ex-) bondholders. This leads to closer alignment of interests between shareholders and creditors and will improve the efficiency of project choices.

Who will gain from improved investment decisions? Potentially everybody. Bondholders gain because they already had downside default risk with regular bonds, which was enhanced by the propensity of the firm to select high-risk projects. With RCD the default risk is replaced by conversion risk, but with the benefit that the incentive effects will change project choice in a way that reduces the probability that the conversion option will ever be exercised.

3. The crowding out hypothesis focuses on the high costs of external financing due largely to information asymmetries. The costs will be higher the higher the leverage of the firm. Indeed, we have seen in many places how agency costs can increase with leverage. However, RCD will unlever the firm when it has a loss and thus will reduce the costs of post-loss external financing. This means not that crowding out is entirely removed, but rather that its effect is reduced.

Given these effects, it becomes feasible that bondholders are better off with the conversion option embedded in their debt than without it. While the *ex post* effect on bondholders is negative (the option is exercised only when it transfers wealth from bondholders to shareholders), the *ex ante* benefits (improved project selection and reduced probability of bankruptcy) might more than offset the *ex post* costs. Thus, RCD could command a higher price than regular debt. We will now show how these benefits can arise.

We will rework the example with HOOD DOWN but using reverse-convertible debt instead of convertible debt.

Project Selection with Nonconvertible Debt (NCD)

To recall from the section dealing with convertible debt, the values of the firm under the alternative project choices financed with nonconvertible debt were:

Value of the Firm if Project A Is Chosen

Value of the firm	0.5(320 + 420) = 370
Old debt	0.5(100 + 100) = 100
New debt	0.5(200 + 200) = 200
Equity	0.5(20 + 120) = 70

Value of the Firm if Project B is Chosen

Value of the firm	0.25(20 + 120 + 410 + 510) = 265
Old debt	0.25(20 + 100 + 100 + 100) = 80
New debt	0.25(0 + 20 + 200 + 200) = 105
Equity	0.25(0 + 0 + 110 + 210) = 80

Project Selection with Reverse-Convertible Debt

The advantages of RCD can be illustrated using the same example but changing the debt to reverse convertible. We will show that RCD will reduce the distortion, in this case leading to the value-maximizing decision. Moreover, we will show that the benefit to bondholders can be sufficiently large that reverse-convertible debt can actually have a higher value than nonconvertible debt, despite the fact that with RCD the option is exercised against the bondholders. In effect, the conversion option appears to have negative value. This gain in value stems from the fact that RCD reduces or removes expected bankruptcy costs and from the real effects of project choice on the value of the conversion put.

Now the new debt is assumed to contain an option for the firm to convert the debt into equity, the option being held by shareholders. The face value of the debt is the same, and the conversion ratio will permit the exchange of the bonds for 200 shares of stock. If the firm chooses to convert, the number of shares will rise from 100 to 300. The old senior debt is still assumed to be nonconvertible. First, we need to establish the values of the firm at which the conversion option will be exercised. Since the option is held by shareholders, it will be exercised at firm values for which the value of equity issued on conversion (which will then amount to two thirds of total equity) is less than the nonconverted obligation of 200; i.e.:

$$\text{Convert if} : \tfrac{2}{3}(\text{value of equity}) < 200$$

$$\text{or if} : \tfrac{2}{3}(\text{value of the firm–Senior Debt}) < 200$$

$$\text{which implies} : \text{value of firm} < 400$$

Since the firm will unlever its junior debt for all firm values less than 400, it can become bankrupt only if it is unable to pay the senior debt of 100. No matter which of the new projects is selected, there is always sufficient value from existing operations, and from the project, to pay the senior debt. Thus, there is no bankruptcy cost to consider.

Value of the Firm if *A* Is Chosen

Value of the firm	$0.5(320 + 420)$	$= 370$
Old debt	$0.5(100 + 100)$	$= 100$
New debt	$0.5\{\tfrac{2}{3}(320 - 100) + 200\}$	$= 173$
Equity	$0.5\{\tfrac{1}{3}(320 - 100) + 120\}$	$= 97$

Value of the Firm if *B* Is Chosen

Value of the firm
$$0.25(120 + 220 + 410 + 510) = 315$$

Old debt
$$0.25(100 + 100 + 100 + 100) = 100$$

New debt
$$0.25\{\tfrac{2}{3}(120 - 100) + \tfrac{2}{3}(220 - 100) + 200 + 200\} = 123$$

Equity
$$0.25\{\tfrac{1}{3}(120 - 100) + \tfrac{1}{3}(220 - 100) + 110 + 210\} = 92$$

Now there is clear incentive to undertake project A since the value of equity is higher than for B. Moreover, in anticipating the choice of A, bondholders will be willing to pay 173 for the new reverse-convertible debt. Notice that for nonconvertible debt (NCD), bondholders would only have paid 105. Thus, despite the fact that the conversion option is held by shareholders, RCD is much more valuable than NCD. The source of the gain in value is twofold. First, bankruptcy costs, which would have been borne by bondholders, are avoided with RCD. Second, because RCD disciplines the choice of project A, the conversion put under RCD has a much smaller value than the default put under NCD. Finally, it remains to show that the choice of A is feasible and will be funded. While project A costs 200, investors will subscribe only 173 for the new RCD. The remaining 27 needs to found from equity. Bearing in mind that the value of equity if neither project is undertaken is 50, and that this increases to 97 if project A is undertaken, the increase in equity value will permit the issue of new equity (to fund the remaining 27) and still leave old shareholders better off.

This example shows that RCD can discipline the firm to take the positive NPV project and that when it does so, the gain in value can be captured by the firm's current shareholders. To see this, notice that if neither project is undertaken, equity is worth 50. If RCD is issued and A is chosen, existing equity is worth 70 (97 minus the 27 needed to supplement debt of 173 in funding the project). The gain in the value of existing equity is exactly equal to the NPV of project A.

In this example and in that of convertible debt, the parameters were chosen to bring about the desired result; that is, project A is chosen by shareholders over project B. In particular, the conversion ratio of bonds into stock was selected carefully. There is no guarantee that, with different conversion ratios, project A would still be preferred. Think for a moment what this means. Had the conversion ratio been higher (more shares of stock given in exchange for each bond), the striking price for the conversion option would have been reduced. To see this, consider the formula used in the examples. If we use n for the number of shares exchanged for the RCD, m for the number of preexisting shares, $V(F)$ for the value of the firm, S for the value of senior debt, and D for the face value of RCD, the conversion will be exercised if:

$$\frac{n}{n+m}\left(V(F) - S\right) < D$$

Thus, the critical value of $V(F)$, call it $V^*(F)$, at which this holds as an equality defines the exercise price

$$\frac{n}{n+m}\,(V^*(F) - S) = D \quad \text{which gives} \quad V^*(F) = S + D\left(1 + \frac{m}{n}\right)$$

Thus, the higher is n, the lower is the exercise price $V^*(F)$. Now suppose that n is infinite. $V^*(F)$ then becomes $S + D$. Thus, if the terms of conversion are so generous that the whole firm is handed to the bondholders (i.e., the proportion m/∞, which approaches zero, is retained by the original shareholders), the firm will choose to convert when the value of the firm falls below the total value of all (senior and junior) debt. This should be familiar; it is identical to the absolute priority rule for nonconvertible debt. Thus, if the conversion ratio is increased indefinitely, RCD eventually turns into nonconvertible debt.[7] You can also go in the other direction. If n is very close to zero, the exercise price will be very high (approaching infinite). Since the firm holds the conversion option with an enormously high price, it is (almost) certain to be exercised. Although formally the new debt is RCD, in effect it is the same as raising new equity.

The foregoing discussion pushes the choice of the conversion ratio to the extreme. But short of this extreme there is flexibility in choosing conversion ratios. If the conversion ratio is high, the striking price for the conversion option is low, and vice versa. Since we know from the example that project B would have been chosen ex post with nonconvertible debt, it can be judged by approximation that project B also would have been chosen had the project been financed with RCD with a very high n. But had n been exceedingly small, the RCD would have been equity in all but name and project A would have been preferred. Thus, RCD will not automatically solve the project distortion problem. Choice of parameters is critical. For any particular firm facing given investment choices, there is a critical value and any conversion ratio below this critical value will resolve the project selection problem. Why not then choose a very low conversion ratio and be sure to solve the problem? The trouble with going too far is that the lower is n, the more likely that the debt will be converted and the more

---

7. You can do a similar exercise for convertible debt. As the conversion ratio $n/(m + n)$ gets close to zero, the striking price for the conversion option will approach infinity and the convertible debt become the same as nonconvertible debt.

the debt begins to look like equity. Recall that we are assuming there is an optimal capital structure that balances several effects. For example, insofar as there is a tax advantage to debt, the lower the conversion ratio, the more likely that conversion will be exercised and the more likely that the tax advantage will be lost. In fact, with a very low n, the IRS could even rule that RCD is not fundamentally different from equity *ex ante* and deny tax deductibility of interest even though the option is not yet exercised. The trick is to select a conversion ratio that is sufficiently low to influence project selection, but not so low as to negate all the cost advantages associated with debt financing.

A related issue is that the critical value of the conversion ratio that will resolve the project selection problem will not be the same for all firms. We can infer a rough relationship between the critical value of n and the underlying firm characteristics.

- The greater the riskiness of the firm value (derived from the risk of existing operations and proposed new projects) and in particular the greater probability in the lower tail of the distribution:
- The greater will be the value of the default put option, thus
- The greater the distortions in project selection
- The greater the offsetting value of the conversion option to remove this distortion
- The greater the conversion ratio; i.e., the higher the ratio $n/(m + n)$.

The problem is to choose the conversion ratio in light of the firm and project risk characteristics. But this leads to a second issue. Even insiders cannot specify and evaluate the whole set of future investment opportunities that will arise after debt is issued. The lines of the game are much fuzzier. We may know that the supermarket chain is likely to face a set of more predictable investment opportunities than the firm doing basic research in genetic engineering, but even the supermarket chain cannot foresee all opportunities that might present themselves in the next year or two. Thus, any chosen level of conversion ratio will not guarantee that all project choices will be made according to contribution to overall firm value. But for any firm, the lower the ratio, the more likely that the projects with low risk/high NPV will be selected over those high risk/low NPV.

Warrants

The inclusion of a warrant has a similar effect to convertible debt. The warrant offers the bondholder the option to purchase the firm's shares at a prespecified price. This hybrid is a combination of a regular bond and a call option on the firm's shares. The bondholder will naturally exercise the option to purchase the shares only if the value exceeds the striking price. Thus, the firm will be forced to share its upside with its bondholders. In return, the edge is taken of the downside because the firm pays a lower rate of interest. Thus, for the issuer this hybrid is very similar to a convertible bond. The difference is that the bondholder acquires shares for a fixed price rather than through the exchange of bonds.

Callable Debt

As discussed above, callable debt can be recalled by the issuer before maturity at a specified price. The advantage to the issuer is that should interest rates fall, the firm can call back the debt and reissue at the lower rates. Naturally, this will entail a cost in terms of higher interest to compensate bondholders for sitting on the short side of this call option. The sensitivity of callable debt to interest rates means that this option does offer some hedging potential against interest rate movements. We will return to this issue later under hedging.

The second advantage of the callable debt to the issuer is that if its credit standing improves, thereby enhancing the value of the bonds, the firm can secure the benefit by buying back at the exercise price. This feature does affect incentives for project selection. While debt does contain the implicit option to default, which will distort incentives in favor of selection of higher-risk projects, the inclusion of the call provision works in the opposite direction. Higher-risk projects will reduce the credit standing of the firm and thereby reduce the value of the bonds.[8] Reducing the value of the bond will reduce the value of the call option written on those bonds. Conversely, management decisions that enhance credit standing will increase the value of the call on the bonds. Thus, the call option will reward (penalize) shareholders for decisions that reduce (increase) firm risk.

Puttable Debt

Puttable debt includes a option held by the bondholders to sell the bonds back to the issuing firm for an agreed price, often the face value. Like other options holder, the bondholders will have an incentive to exercise their option if the value they receive on exercise is greater than the value of the asset they give up. Bond prices will typically fall with increases in interest rates or with a deterioration in the credit standing of the issuing firm. In the former case, the bondholders can sell back their debt and have the opportunity to relend at higher interest. From the firm's viewpoint, it will be forced by buy back debt when interests rates rise. This implies that a puttable bond issue would partially hedge a firm whose value is positively related to interest rates.

---

8. Be careful not to make the following mistake when working through the effects of increases risk on the value of callable bonds. *Increased risk will increase the value of a call option. Since shareholders hold a call option (to call the bonds), their wealth is increased by selection of high-risk projects. Thus, the call option works in the same way as the default put option in giving owners a vested interest in risk increases.*
The problem with this reasoning is that it confuses options written on the firm with options written on the bonds. The default put option is an option on the firm value that is embedded in debt. The shareholders have an obligation to the bondholders to pay the debt, plus an option to put the firm to the bondholders in which the exercise price is the face value of the debt. Increasing the risk of the asset underlying this option (i.e., increasing the risk of the firm) increases the value of the default put and thereby benefits shareholders. The same increase in risk penalizes bondholders who have effectively nondefaultable debt plus a short position in the default put. But the call option in callable debt is an *option on the bonds,* not an option on the firm. An increase in risk of the firm increases the value of the default put, but since bondholders hold a *short* position in the default put, the value of the bonds falls. As the bond value is decreased, the value of call option on the bonds also is decreased. The call option in the debt is an *option on an option* (a long position in a call option written on debt that includes a short position in a put option).

But the credit issue is of more interest here. With puttable bonds, bondholders can avoid the loss of value from a deterioration in credit. From the issuer's viewpoint, issuing such bonds does change incentives for investment decisions. As we have seen over and over, this *implicit* default put option in normal bonds increases the attractiveness to shareholders of high-risk investment decisions. A puttable bond effectively neutralizes the *implicit* default put held by the issuer by giving an *explicit* put option to the lender. If the firm's financial condition seems to be deteriorating, such that bond prices fall, the bondholders can sell back their securities at the agreed price. If things have not gone too far, the firm will buy back the bonds as obligated and the bondholders will avoid the looming downside risk. Prospectively, this changes the payoff structure from new investments for shareholders. They now face the prospect of being forced to buy out of any emerging downside risk by buying back the deteriorating bonds. High-risk investments are no longer as attractive to the shareholders.

Just as callable bonds will offer a higher interest rate to investors to compensate them for "selling" the firm the call option, so puttable debt will offer bondholders lower interest because they hold the option to put the debt back to the firm. The difference in interest rates between normal debt and callable/puttable debt represents the price or premium for the option feature. The price is paid by the party holding the option. If the option is not exercised, the party in the short position gains by receiving this option premium.

Liquid Yield Option Note, LYON

The coverage of forms of hybrid debt is not complete. Indeed, there is unlimited potential to combine different instruments to form different payoff structures. LYONs illustrate this potential. The LYON is a callable, puttable, convertible, zero coupon bond. Given our separate analysis of the call, put, and conversion features and their effect of corporate risk taking, one can project that the issuers of such complex bonds would have little incentive or ability to expropriate the wealth of bondholders by playing games of risk.

INCLUSION OF A LIABILITY HEDGE

Callable, Puttable, and Convertible Bonds: Interest Rate Hedges

Callable, puttable, and convertible bonds all offer some capability for hedging interest rate risk. Callable bonds allow the firm to take advantage of a reduction in interest rates to refinance debt. The fall in interest rates increases bond prices and, if sufficient, shifts the call option into the money. Thus, the firm (i.e., its owner) benefits when interest rates fall. If interest rates do not fall, the bonds will not be called. In such conditions the firm is worse off because it paid a higher interest rate to secure the call option in the debt issue and does not get to exercise the option. The firm whose value is positively related to interest rates would be able to use the call feature in the debt to hedge this position.

Contrarily, the puttable option will be exercised by bondholders when the bond price falls; that is, when interest rates rise. The rise in rates pushes the bond price below the exercise price and the firm is obligated to buy back the debt for the exercise price. The firm loses on its short put position when interest rates rise. If we bear in mind that the issuer is compensated for giving the bondholders the put option by paying lower interest, the firm will gain from its short put position if interest rates fall. Thus, like the call on the bond (held by the issuer) the put (held by the lender) offers the firm whose value is positively related to interest rates, a hedging instrument.

But the hedges are not identical. Figure 13–4 shows a firm with an underlying value that is positively related to interest rates. This is shown as the upwards-sloping dashed line. The figure also shows how the firm can hedge this position by options included in its debt. If rates rise, the firm has an open-ended loss on the short put option (which will offset its natural gain from rising interest). With the long call option, the firm's loss on the call from the interest rate rise is capped at the call premium. If interest rates fall, the firm can make an open-ended gain from its call provision, but the put provision offers a gain that is capped at the option premium. Combining the payoffs on the option embedded in the debt with the firm's underlying position shows the firm's final hedged sensitivity to interest rates. This is shown in Figure 13–5. With callable bonds, the firm keeps its upwards risk from interest

F I G U R E   13-4

Interest Rates with Callable and Puttable Bonds. Payoffs to Equity from Option Positions

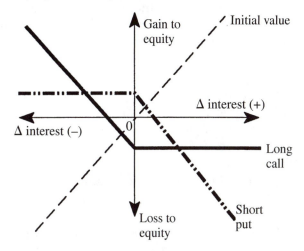

F I G U R E   13-5

Hedged Positions with Callable and Puttable Bonds

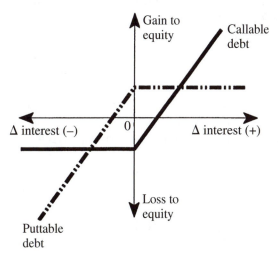

rate rises but is hedged against interest rate falls. With puttable bonds, the firm is capped on the upside and has an open-ended downside.

It is worthwhile comparing the hedging capacities of callable and puttable bonds with insurance policies. Suppose that an insurance policy were available to cover interest rate changes with a deductible provision. Recall that we are discussing a firm whose value is positively related to interest rates. Thus, a flat premium is paid and, when rates fall below some value, the loss of firm value from the change in interest rates is reimbursed by the insurer. The policy puts a floor on firm values from interest rate changes for a flat fee. In fact, only the callable bond has this insurance-like feature; the puttable bond leaves an open-ended downside exposure. Indeed, the only downside protection the firm has is that it *receives* a premium from a counter-party should interest rates fall. This is rather like insuring your house with the following transaction. You sell to the insurance company a policy in which you are obligated to pay the insurance company the value of your house (i.e., give your house to the insurer) if it does not burn down. On the other hand, you will be paid a premium for this transaction. And since the probability of the house not burning is very high, the premium will be huge.

If the desire is to "insure" against (remove the downside risk from) adverse interest rate movements, then callable debt is appropriate. It may also be appropriate if the firm is tempering its need for a hedged position with a belief that an interest rise is more likely than a fall. With callable bonds, the firm retains much of its upside sensitivity to rising interest rates that are considered likely.

Convertible bonds turn out to have similar hedging properties for the firm whose value is positively related to interest rates. The reasoning is follows. A fall in interest rates reduces the underlying value of the firm and will thereby reduce share value. But the same interest fall will cause bond prices to rise. With the combination of a fall in share price and a rise in bond values, bondholders will not wish to convert. A rise in interest rates will increase underlying firm value and increase share prices. With lower bond prices, conversion is attractive. Thus, the exercise of the conversion option will limit the gain to the firm when interest rates rise. But with falling interest rates, the conversion does not occur and the firm walks away with the option premium (i.e., the lower interest rate from offering the conversion option). This option premium mitigates the negative affect of the interest fall.

Floating Rate Notes and Inverse Floating Rate Notes: Interest Hedges

Thus, puttable, callable, and convertible bonds all have desirable hedging properties for the firm whose value is positively sensitive to interest rates. Suppose that the firm is in the construction industry and its value is negatively related to interest rates. How can this firm hedge its interest exposure? First, note that the firm has available a set of interest hedging instruments that can be used independently of its debt. These include interest futures, caps and floors, options on bonds and options on bond futures, and exotics such as captions and swaptions. But hedges can be built into the debt. One such example is an inverse rate note. First, a brief description of a floating rate note is required. This is simple debt in which the interest payment is related to current interest rates. Thus, the interest rate risk is borne by the lender, not the borrower.

An inverse floating rate note is a combination of a floating rate note with a bullet repayment and an interest rate swap for twice the notional principle of the note. Under the note, the issuer pays a random interest rate of $\tilde{r}$. Under the swap, the issuer exchanges a fixed rate of $\bar{r}$ for a floating rate of $\tilde{r}$ on twice the principal. Thus, the interest payment is $\tilde{r} - 2\tilde{r} + 2\bar{r} = 2\bar{r} - \tilde{r}$. With this coupon payment, as interest rates rise, the net coupon payment falls. The issuer benefits when rates rise and loses when rates fall. In this way, the construction firm can issue debt that hedges its natural negative position with respect to interest rates.

Hybrid Debt, Commodity Hedges, and Foreign Exchange Hedges

Bonds with options and warrants have been used to build to hedge against commodity and FX risk. For example, the inclusion of options on gold prices allow investors a share in the issuer's (e.g., a gold mining company) revenues. The inclusion of the warrant lowers the issuer's interest payment and thus provides some protection against falling price of gold. In this way the issuer is able to reduce its sensitivity to varying gold prices.

Principal indexed bonds have a principle that is linked to some external economic indicator such as oil prices, gold prices, or some foreign exchange rate, or to some general economic index such as the S&P 500. These provide a straightforward example of a liability hedge. The value of the outstanding debt obligation is linked directly to some index that is, in turn, related to firm value. A good example would be a gold mining firm borrowing with principal positively linked to gold prices, or an oil company positively linking its principal to oil prices. An airline with the opposite exposure to oil price movements would need to link its principal negatively to oil prices.

Interest indexed bonds can have a similar hedging features to principal linked bonds. Interest payment can be made to vary directly or inversely with FX rates or commodity prices, depending on the exposure of the issuer and buyers. A variation on this idea is interest forgiveness, which is, really a special case of indexing. If the index reaches a critical level, the interest is forgiven altogether.

Dual currency bonds offer another way of combining debt with a currency hedge. This is essentially a normal bond and a FX swap. The fixed interest payments in the currency issue are exchanged for payment in another currency. Thus, the principal is payable in the currency of issue while the interest payments are made in another currency.

Catastrophe bonds (*insurance-linked bonds*) are a special case of principal- or interest-linked bonds. The principal or interest is linked to some external event that typically is insurable, such as a hurricane or earthquake. The principal or interest may be variable, and the trigger can be the actual losses suffered by the issuer from the event, some index of the overall cost of the event, an index of the cost to the insurance industry, or a physical description of the event (the force of the hurricane or the Richter scale reading for the earthquake). These bonds can be of value to insurers who write a large amount of direct insurance in a vulnerable area or to firms that have assets located in the risky area. These are several unusual features of these bonds. For example, the debt is not used for investment by the firm and the arrangement is "fronted" by the creation of a "one transaction firm" called a "special purpose vehicle." Detailed discussion will be deferred until Chapter 16, where a case study of hedging in the insurance industry is undertaken.

Hedging Unspecified Loss with Hybrid Debt

The hybrid debt instruments described so far allow the issuing firm to hedge against some specific external economic variable that is correlated with its value: interest rates, commodity prices, FX rates, or some natural event. The derivative embodied in the debt is linked to the external event or variable, and the change in the value of the embedded derivative is negatively correlated with firm value. But with callable, puttable, and convertible debt, the value of the embedded derivative was also related to the firm's own value. For example, consider convertible debt. Figure 13–6 shows the gain and loss to the firm from including the conversion option for different changes in the firm value. It is assumed here that the conversion option initially is out of the money. An increase in firm value of $\Delta+$ is just sufficient to increase share prices enough to bring the conversion option at the money. Increases beyond this point cause a loss of value to the firm. Changes below $\Delta+$ will not result in exercise, and the firm will receive the net

F I G U R E   13–6

Hedging Changes in Firm Value. Payoffs to Equity from Options Positions

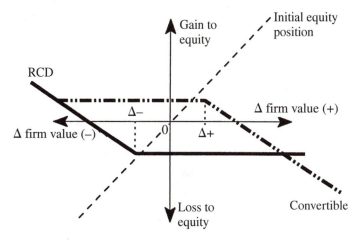

gain of the option premium, which is the lower interest paid to bondholders. The firm has a hedge that is proportional in the upside risk but is capped in the downside. But note that the downwards-sloping part of the line is not 45°; the firm does not give away all increase in value above the striking price. There is a dilution of equity, and increases in value are shared between old and new (ex-bondholders) shareholders.

An alternative hedge profile is to include a derivative in the debt that more closely resembles an insurance policy; that is, is proportional in the downside but capped on the upside. Thus, the firm pays a fixed premium in return for coinsurance on a fall in value below a given attachment point. This payoff can be achieved by allocating the conversion option in the debt to the issuer rather than to the bondholder; that is, by reverse-convertible debt (RCD). The striking price for conversion is denoted as a price fall of $\Delta-$. If the firm value falls by more than $\Delta-$, the conversion option will kick in and its value will increase as firm value continues to decline. Thus, in Figure 13–6, if the fall in firm value is greater than $\Delta-$, the issuer will exercise its conversion option and (say) cancel $1000 debt by exchanging $800 worth of stock. The difference between the exercise price and the bond value is a gain to the issuer and offsets the underlying reduction in share value. If firm value does not fall, the firm is out of pocket by the conversion option premium.

Figure 13–7 shows the effect of hedging with convertible and reverse convertible debt on the value of equity. RCD insures the downside risk, but there is not full insurance of the downside risk. Rather, there is coinsurance, as the downside risk is shared with bondholders. This is shown by the slope of the line marked RCD. At values lower than $\Delta-$, net equity position still falls but by less than the fall in underlying firm value. The fall is partly cushioned by creditors. Nevertheless, the worse the downside outcome, the greater the value of the firm's conversion option and the more of the loss is shared by bondholders. In contrast, convertible debt is like a short position in an insurance policy. The firm receives a premium and in return transfers part of the firm to the bondholders if an adverse event fails to materialize. While convertible does involve some hedging of downside risk, it does so only to the extent that the equity receives a net gain of the option premium

F I G U R E   13–7

Hedged Positions with Convertible and Reverse Convertible Debt

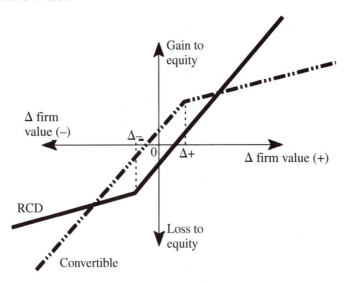

in adverse firm values. This downside compensation to equity is not scaled to firm value.

Resolving Underinvestment with Principal-Indexed Bonds

In previous sections underinvestment arose because new debt, issued after loss, increased the value of the default put option. The other post-loss underinvestment we have considered arose from the default option on existing debt. If productive assets are lost, shareholders are cushioned from the full loss of value by defaulting on existing debt. If the assets are replaced, the value created by the reinvestment accrues partly to creditors by reducing the default put. Shareholders therefore cannot capture all the value created by reinvestment and may thereby reject some positive NPV project.

   Consider a simple representation of this problem. In this illustration we will ignore future investment opportunities and will assume that if reinvestment occurs, it is financed with new equity. Here, C is the cost of reconstruction of damaged assets; $V_R(F)$ is the value of the firm with reconstruction; and $V_N(F)$ is the value if damaged assets are not repaired or replaced. The values of existing equity, with and without reconstruction, are:

$$V_R'(E) = -C + V_R(F) - D + P\{V_R(F); D\} = -C + V_R - D + P_R$$
$$V_N'(E) = V_N(F) - D + P\{V_N(F); D\} \qquad = V_N - D + P_N$$

where $P(V(F); D)$ is the after-loss value of a put option written on $V(F)$ with striking price D. If reinvestment adds value, then $V_R > V_N$, and, assuming no major difference in risk, replacement will reduce the value of the default put option: $P_R < P_N$. But shareholders will be better off if the following rule holds:

$$\text{Shareholder Rule} \qquad (V_R + P_R) - (V_N + P_N) \geq C$$
$$\text{or} \qquad \text{NPV} - P_N + P_R > 0$$

In contrast, the usual capital budgeting rule is that the net present value of the investment, NPV (which is equal to the change in firm value $V_R - V_N$), must be no less than the cost of the project C.

$$\text{Normal rule} \qquad V_R - V_N \geq C \qquad \text{or} \qquad \text{NPV} > 0$$

Thus, a positive NPV investment would be lost if:

$$P_N - P_R > \text{NPV} \geq 0$$

That is, if the reduction in the value of the default put option with investment is greater than the NPV from reinvestment. Suppose that the firm could have a contingent financing instrument in which an investor (possibly an existing creditor) would agree to provide funds for reinvestment at a rate below the cost of capital such that the subsidy in the post-loss capital cost were equal to at least $P_N - P_R - \text{NPV}$. If that guarantee were unconditional on the post-loss investment decision, shareholders would simply "take the money and run." They would take the subsidy and follow their self-interested "shareholder rule" for reinvestment; that is, they would not reconstruct the lost asset. However, if the subsidy could be made *conditional on reinvestment*, the underinvestment problem could, in principle, be resolved. We will discuss the practicality of this instrument after we provide an illustration of the idea.

Consider the following simple post-loss underinvestment problem from Chapter 11. Without a loss the firm is worth 1000. If a loss, such as a fire, occurs and the damage is not repaired, the firm will be worth 200 but the value will restore to 1000 if damage is repaired. The cost of reinvestment is 600 and the NPV = 800 − 600 = 200. The firm has existing debt of 600. Also, suppose that the prior chance the fire will occur is 0.1.

The following table presents the values of the firm and of its debt and equity, under alternative post-loss decisions.

Decision	Firm	Debt	Equity
Reinvest	1000	600	400
Not reinvest	200	200	0
Gain	800	400	400
Cost of Reinvestment			600

The value of equity will rise by 400 from reinvestment. But the cost of reinvestment is 600. Thus, reinvestment would not be selected by shareholders. In the notation used above,

$$P_N - P_R > V_R - V_N - C \geq 0 \qquad \text{or}$$
$$400 - 0 > 1000 - 200 - 600 \geq 0$$

However, we know from working through this example in Chapter 11 that the firm would go bankrupt and the creditors, now owners, would find it in their interest to raise the 600 for reinvestment (e.g., with a new share issue) and undertake the reinvestment.[9] Thus, the values after bankruptcy are:

Decision	Firm	Equity ex-creditors	Equity new creditors
Reinvest	950	350	600
Not reinvest	150	150	
Gain	800	200	

---

9. For example, the firm goes bankrupt. The creditors are now issued 350 shares. They can decide to reinvest. They float a new issue of 600 new shares to pay for reinvestment. Total of 950 shares. Since the value of the firm is 950 (1000 minus 50 bankruptcy cost) and there is no longer any debt, the new share would be worth $600/950 \times 950 = 600$. Thus, the firm could finance the reinvestment with this issue.

We can value this firm prospectively, recognizing the 0.1 change that the fire will occur:

Value of firm	$0.9(1000) + 0.1(950 - 600) = 935$
Value of debt	$0.9(600) + 0.1(350)$ $= 575$
Value of equity	$0.9(400) + 0.1(0)$ $= 360$

Now suppose that existing creditors write the following principal at risk contract. They agree to buy the firm's debt, having a face of 600, but they agree in addition that they will forgive 200 of principal (effectively pay a subsidy to the firm) *conditional on the firm choosing to reinvest.* We can think of this 200 as a subsidy to help pay for the reinvestment; thus, shareholders would only be left to find a net of $600 - 200 = 400$ to pay for the reinvestment. The amount of forgiveness is calculated as follows:

$$(P_N - P_R) - \text{NPV} = (P_N - P_R) - (V_R - V_N - C)$$
$$= (400 - 0) - (1000 - 200 - 600) = 200$$

Thus, we could avoid bankruptcy and reinvest after the loss as shown:

Decision	Firm	Debt	Equity	Net Cost of Reinvestment
Reinvest	1000	600–200 = 400	400	200
Not reinvest	150	150	0	
Gain	850	250	400	
Cost of Reinvestment	600		400	200

First, note that, *ex post,* the shareholders would choose to reinvest. In anticipation of this decision, the firm and its component claims are revalued as follows:

Value of firm	$0.9(1000) + 0.1(1000 - 600) = 940$
Value of debt	$0.9(600) + 0.1(600 - 200)$ $= 580$
Value of equity	$0.9(400) + 0.1(0)$ $= 360$

Notice that the debt is more valuable. Without the commitment for a contingent subsidy for the reinvestment, the debt was worth 575. With the commitment, its value rises to 580. Bondholders are better off forgiving the principal. This paradox is resolved when one considers that the debt forgiveness affects the shareholders' investment choice after the loss and thereby avoids default on the debt. Note that forgiving 200 is better than losing 250 through bankruptcy (recall that creditors only get 350 with bankruptcy); there is a net *ex post* gain of 50, which is the savings in bankruptcy costs. The increase in the *ex ante* value of debt of 5 is simply the bankruptcy cost of 50 times a 0.1 chance of loss. Finally, the *ex ante* equity value is the same either way, that is, 360. However, there is a definite gain for shareholders because bondholders are now willing to pay 580, instead of 575, for debt with this commitment.

So much for the theory. Is such debt feasible in practice? When discussing lines of credit and the asset substitution issue, I suggested that if a firm raising debt after a loss could not commit to use of those funds for particular low-risk investment decisions, it was unlikely to be able to commit before the loss to contingent post-loss investment choices. It is simply difficult to draft contract language that separates future investment alternatives, and even if one could, successful implementation of new investment projects requires flexibility as new information is acquired. This flexibility would be lost if the bond indenture contained very specific project constraints.

But in the current case the issue is reconstruction of existing assets. There are indeed contracts in which a "subsidy" is paid to the owner of an asset if he or she repairs or reconstructs the asset. Many commercial property insurance policies contain such a condition. If the property is rebuilt, the policy covers the cost of reconstruction and the owner benefits by having older construction replaced by new. If the property is not rebuilt, the policy will cover its "actual cash value," which is essentially its pre-loss market value. Such policies are operational because the investment is very specific and it is comparatively easy to monitor whether the condition has been fulfilled. If such specificity leads to a workable arrangement in insurance, it would seem that a reinvestment trigger for principal forgiveness also could be built into a debt contract.

The arrangement could be achieved in various ways. The most straightforward way is for creditors to put their principal at risk conditional on the double trigger (a loss occurs and the asset is replaced). A more complex arrangement is for the original debt to be married to a limited insurance contract that pays off part of the principal only in reinvestment is undertaken.

The underinvestment problem arose because the shareholders could default on their debt obligation. By choosing not to reinvest, shareholders are able to acquire the valuable default put option, P_N, in exchange for the less valuable P_R. This ability to increase the value of the default put changes the incentives for reinvestment. Any strategy that removes this gain to shareholders will restore incentives for shareholders to adopt value-maximizing investment decisions. But, in addition, it is useful if this restoration of value-maximizing incentives is transparent to bondholders so that the *ex ante* bond value will not be discounted by this agency cost. The most direct way of doing this is to return the default put P_N, to the creditors, depending on the shareholders' reinvestment decision. Principal-linked debt can do this. Regular debt will have a post-loss value of

$$D - P_N - C - \text{NPV}$$

This assumes that the shareholders will default without reinvesting (thus, the value is reduced by the default put without reinvestment, P_N, and by the bankruptcy cost, C) but bondholders will choose to reinvest once the firm is passed to them in bankruptcy.

Index-linked debt, with forgiveness of $(P_N - P_R - \text{NPV})$ will have a post-loss value of

(face value) + (principal forgiven) − (default put
  assuming reinvestment)
$$= D - (P_N - P_R - \text{NPV}) - P_R$$
$$= (D - P_N - C - \text{NPV}) + C$$
$$= \text{(value of regular debt)} + \text{(saving in bankruptcy cost)}$$

As can be seen in the final equations, returning the default put effectively increases the after-loss value of debt by the NPV of the reinvestment opportunity. Thus, debt will have a pre-loss of

$$D - \pi(P_N - C - \text{NPV}) + \pi C$$

where π is the probability of loss. The bondholders' gain from the forgiveness provision is a more effective post-loss reinvestment strategy that reduces default risk, and this gain is anticipated in the current value of debt.

REDUCTION IN BANKRUPTCY COSTS

Many of the hybrid bonds considered will reduce the probability of bankruptcy compared with conventional debt. Debt that includes a benefit to the bondholder, such as an option, forward, or swap, will carry a lower interest rate. The benefit often comes in a sharing of upside risk, and this is paid for by the bondholder in receiving lower interest. The inclusion of such derivatives in the debt permits the issuer to reduce its debt obligation and so reduce the probability of bankruptcy. While the inclusion of the option per se does not reduce the cost of debt (i.e., in economist jargon, "there is no free lunch"; the option is priced), the consequent reduction in bankruptcy cost is a net gain to the firm's stakeholders. Bankruptcy costs take the form of direct payments to outsiders (such as lawyers' and accountants' fees) and opportunity costs (which can arise from inefficiencies of court supervision of the firm's operations) and are deadweight costs to the firm's main stakeholders. Prospectively, firm value will rise by the expected reduction in these costs. Given absolute priority, these costs would be borne by bondholders. Consequently, a reduction in the probability of bankruptcy by relieving the debt burden in poor states will raise the value of the debt.

The effect can be illustrated with convertible bonds as shown in Figure 13–2. The conversion option allows the firm to reduce the face value of debt from D to D_c; that is, by the value of the option premium. The reduction in expected bankruptcy costs can be explained by a reduction in the probability that firm value will fall below the lower threshold, D_c. This would be true if the distribution of firm value were unaffected by the substitution of convertible for nonconvertible debt. But there are secondary benefits. Insofar as the issue of convertible changes incentives for project selection, the distribution of firm value will exhibit lower risk and/or shift to the right as less risky, higher-NPV investments are chosen. This further reduces bankruptcy costs and further enhances the value of bonds.

While convertible debt reduces the probability of default, reverse convertible avoids problems of default altogether. Figure

13–2 illustrates the issue. As the value of the firm falls below the striking price for the option, C_R, the fixed debt obligation is replaced by equity participation. The default put is replaced by the conversion put. Exercise of the default put is accompanied by the associated transaction costs, whereas exercise of the conversion put presumably would be relatively cost-free. Thus, RCD promises to be effective in reducing the cost of debt by avoiding any discounting for bankruptcy costs.

Perhaps the most direct way in which bankruptcy costs can be reduced by hybrid debt is by forgiving the principal or interest conditional on an event that decimates the firm's value. While the price of the debt will reflect the expected loss to the bondholder from interest or principal forgiveness, the price should also reflect the prospect that (for severe events) the bondholders would have borne bankruptcy had the debt not been forgiven. Thus, the net loss to the bondholders for events that result in bankruptcy is the difference between the unpaid principal (or interest) and the bankruptcy costs. The saving in expected bankruptcy costs with principal- or interest-linked bonds therefore represents a lowering of the cost of debt.

HYBRID DEBT AND FINANCING POST-LOSS INVESTMENT

One of the main ways in which value can be created by managing risk is by permitting the firm to capture fully the value of post-loss investment opportunities. This can be done by reducing the risk of adverse events or lowering the costs of financing post-loss investment. Thus, insurance protects low-cost internal funds for new investments. Can hybrid debt secure similar benefit? In order for it to do so, the operation of the embedded derivative must

 • Create a hedge in the event of a major loss
 • Lower the cost of access to new funds after the loss

Two forms of hybrid debt score on these dimensions. Principal- or interest-linked debt lowers the debt cost on earnings and preserves internal funds for new investment. There is a liquidity issue. Relieving the firm of the requirement to meet current interest payments is more immediate in its cash impact than relieving principal. With lower interest due, the firm is left with higher net income to finance new investments. Relieving principal is slower in its liquidity impact, unless a payment happens to be due. However, the relief of principal on existing debt will also increase the post-loss debt capacity of the firm.

Reverse-convertible debt would have a similar effect. The conversion of the debt into equity is triggered by an event that causes firm value to fall, such as the occurrence of a major property, liability, or FX loss. By avoiding continuing interest payments, the firm is better able to finance post-loss investments from low-cost internal funds. Reverse-convertible debt also can facilitate post-loss investment by lowering the cost of new money. Suppose that there is an optimal capital structure; that is, that the weighted average cost of capital curve is u-shaped. If the firm is somewhere in the region of this optimum, then suffers a major unhedged loss, it will emerge from the loss with considerably higher, and likely suboptimal, leverage. This is a less than an ideal situation from which to approach the capital market for new money. Equity funding will be particularly expensive. The issue of new equity, and the NPV of the postloss investment, will help redress the capital structure imbalance. But recall from Myers and Majd's pecking order hypothesis that debt financing is more expensive than internal funds but less expensive than new equity. An important reason for this ranking is that the costs of information asymmetry are high for new equity. It seems reasonable to conjecture that this differential between debt and equity costs will not diminish, but increase, in the uncertainty following a major loss event. The cost of new financing for the overlevered, post-loss firm will be high. The cost of new money will be lowered if the loss itself triggered an unlevering. Such is the case with reverse-convertible debt. The firm will face its post-loss investment program with a lowered debt burden and an enhanced capacity to finance reconstruction of lost assets as well as new investment projects.

CONCLUSION

Risk management costs arise in large part from the leverage of the firm. Leverage causes potential for bankruptcy costs and agency costs that give rise to distortions in project selection. These costs increase with risk, or conversely, can be reduced with the management of risk. One way to address this problem is simply to hedge. With any given level of leverage, the bankruptcy and agency costs will be lowered by the reduction of risk. If the risk is caused by changes in interest rates, commodity prices, foreign exchange rates, or insurable perils, the firm can purchase a derivative or insurance policy. The leverage stays the same but the risk is reduced and so are the costs associated with risk.

The approach considered in this chapter exploits the fact that leverage and risk *jointly* cause risk costs. Accordingly, the risk management strategy explored is to build into the debt a derivative that is triggered by the offending peril. Some of these hybrids are well known and widely used (though not always explicitly for risk management ends). For example, debt is often used with a call option or is puttable back to the firm. These embedded options can be triggered by interest rate changes, or changes in the firm's credit risk, and so these forms of hybrid debt can be used to ameliorate the costs of risk and leverage that arise from interest or credit changes. Convertible bonds also are common and also can lower risk costs. Less common are bonds in which the interest, or principal, is linked to some external index such as commodity prices, foreign exchange rates, or even some insurable peril such as earthquake or hurricane. These instruments permit the firm to avail itself of the tax benefits of debt financing, but avoid many of the risk costs because firm effectively unlevers when adverse outcomes cause the debt burden to be costly. The firm can effectively lever in the good times and automatically unlever when things go sour. A more innovative variation on this theme is reverse-convertible debt, debt that is convertible at the option of the firm. This instrument also unlevers when firm value falls and can be designed to address the underinvestment and asset substitution problems. Such is the risk management potential of instruments that they can be shown to have higher value than conventional debt despite the fact that the bondholders hold the short position in the conversion option.

Instruments such as reverse-convertible debt and indexed-linked debt do have some hedging value. They create value for shareholders by relieving a debt obligation at a time when the firm loses value. We will now turn to the other side of the balance sheet. The more conventional form of hedge instruments operates on the asset side of the balance sheet. The more usual hedge instruments and insurance policies increase in value when an adverse outcome occurs. Such asset hedges and insurance policies are the subject of the next chapter.

REFERENCES

Brennan, Michael, and Eduardo Schwartz. 1988. "The Case for Convertibles," *Journal of Applied Corporate Finance* 1:55–64.

Froot, Kenneth, and Jeremy Stein. 1998. "Risk Management, Capital Budgeting and Capital Structure for Financial Institutions." *Journal of Financial Economics* 47:52–82.

Green, Richard C. 1984. "Investment Incentives, Debt and Warrants." *Journal of Financial Economics* 13:115–36.

LeLand, Hayne E. 1998. "Agency Costs, Risk Management and Capital Structure" Journal of Finance, 53:1213–43.

Lewis, C. M., R. J. Rogalski, and J. K. Seward. 1994. "An Empirical Analysis of Convertible Debt Financing by NYSE/AMEX and NASDAQ Firms." Working Paper, Amos Tuck School of Business, Dartmouth College.

Rawls, Waite, and Charles Smithson. 1989. "The Evolution of Risk Management Products." *Journal of Applied Corporate Finance* 1(4).

Smithson, Charles, and Donald Chew. 1998. "The Uses of Hybrid Debt in Managing Corporate Risk." in *The Revolution in Corporate Finance*, 3d ed. ed. J. M. Stein and D. H. Chew. Malden, Mass.: Blackwell Business.

Stein, Jeremy. 1992. "Convertible Bonds as Backdoor Equity Financing." *Journal of Financial Economics* 32:3–21.

Tufano, Peter. 1997. "Financial Innovation and First Mover Advantages." *Journal of Financial Economics* 25:213–40.

CHAPTER 14

Hedging and Insurance

Some of the contingent financing strategies introduced in Chapter 8 embodied a degree of hedging. For example, the loss equity puts could be exercised at a price above the post-loss market value of the equity. The difference between the exercise price and the post-loss market price represents a post-loss hedge against the loss; the counter-party absorbed some of the loss of value and was paid an up-front premium (the put price) for doing so. Similarly, with reverse-convertible debt, the exercise of the conversion option at a time when the share value is low means that the firm is buying out of a fixed obligation at a price that is less than the obligation. The difference is a hedge. The hedge component of these hybrid instruments will secure the benefits of risk reduction, discussed at length in Chapter 13. The earnings and/or value will be partly protected from the impact of the loss event, and this smoothing will lower the chance of bankruptcy, lessen conflicts of interest between stakeholders, favor the financing of new investments, and so on. But while these instruments have some hedge component, they are not naturally characterized as hedges. In this chapter we will focus directly on hedging instruments. We will concentrate mostly on insurance and insurable risks, but derivatives and noninsurable risk also are an integral part of the hedging landscape.

The chapter starts by considering insurance as an instrument for post-loss financing; as such, it is in competition with debt and equity financing. We will do this for two forms of loss: a loss of productive assets that requires a reinvestment decision and a loss of value such as a liability claim or currency loss. This approach gives a basis for comparing insurance with competing post-loss financing sources. But it leaves something out: the benefits of risk transfer and smoothing. Thus, the two examples will be developed to address the gain in value from risk transfer.

REVIEW OF POST-LOSS FINANCING AND THE INTRODUCTION OF INSURANCE

We will start the introduction of insurance with an example using the valuation structure presented in Chapter 10. To recall, the valuation method estimates the share price by discounting future net cash flows at the cost of equity capital. The idea in that chapter was to estimate the share price under alternative reinvestment and financing decisions. If the share value is higher with reinvestment, then one searches for the post-loss financing source that creates most value. We will depart in small ways from the tabular structure to emphasize certain key issues. The main departure is to separate out that part of the share value that reflects the future growth potential of the firm since this component becomes pivotal in the financing decision. Instead of having a row in the table for expected growth of earnings, we will have an item showing how much investors are willing to pay for that growth potential. This will focus attention squarely on the effects of crowding out. As we introduce insurance presently, a more important change will be made. Instead share values after loss for different post-loss financing choices being compared, insurance will be evaluated in anticipation of possible future losses and compared *prospectively* with debt and equity financing. The sequence is as follows. First, we will value the following illustrated firm, New Drugs, without considering potential losses. Then we will pose several loss scenarios and calculate the post-loss values. Finally, we will consider prospective losses and use an *ex ante* valuation framework to compare insurance with post-loss financing alternatives.

The following is relevant and summarized financial data for New Drugs:

♦ *Productive capital with a replacement cost of $10 billion yields expected EBIT of $2 billion per year.*

♦ *Current debt is $5 billion at 7% (treat as perpetuity); thus annual interest is $350m.*

♦ *Shares outstanding 300m—current cost of equity 11%.*

♦ *Tax rate 34%.*

♦ *New Drugs has an R&D program and a history of successful innovation. Investors estimate the value of future investment opportunities as equivalent of $15 per share (note that we could have presented this as a growth opportunity; i.e., net earnings are expected to grow at an annual rate of* x%*). To avail itself of these investment opportunities, the firm must be able to raise and commit new capital. Using crowding out reasoning, we estimated that some of these opportunities might be lost if there are large uninsured losses, and the growth premium investors are willing to pay may fall below $15 per share.*

Valuation of New Drugs

Table 14–1 calculates the share value in the following sequence. Net cash flow from current operations is discounted at the cost of equity capital

T A B L E   14–1

Value of Shares if No Loss Suffered

EBIT per annum	2,000m p.a.
Interest Senior 7% on $5b	350m
Interest Post-loss Debt—8% on Lost Assets	1,650m
Tax @ 34%	561m
Net Income per annum	1,089m
Cost of Equity (reflects leverage)	11%
Equity Value of Current Operations	9,900m
Number of Outstanding Shares	300m
Share Value from Current Operations	$33
Value of Investment Opportunities	$15
Market Value of Shares	$48

to yield a value of equity, which is divided by the number of shares to give a share value from current operations. Finally, investor valuation of future growth of $15 per share is added to give the overall share value. The capital structure of New Drugs is shown below with and without the inclusion of the value of future growth:

With future growth:

$$\frac{\text{debt}}{\text{equity}} = \frac{\$5b}{\$14.4b} = 0.347$$

Without future growth:

$$\frac{\text{debt}}{\text{equity}} = \frac{\$5b}{\$9.9b} = 0.505$$

From this base, we now can see how value will be affected by three different loss scenarios.

Valuation after Three Loss Scenarios

The three scenarios differ in two dimensions. Losses of different relative size are examined, and these will be compared with and without reinvestment. The three scenarios are:

1. A fire destroys $100 million of productive assets (1% of the total $10 billion assets value).
   The assets are replaced and financed with debt at 8%.
   Cost of equity increases to 11.03% because of increased leverage

2. Fire destroys $1 billion of productive assets (10% of productive assets).
   The assets are replaced and financed with debt at 8%.
   Cost of equity increases to 11.5% because of increased leverage

3. Fire destroys $1 billion of productive assets (10% of productive assets).
   Destroyed assets are not replaced—result loss of 10% of EBIT.
   Cost of equity increases to 11.5% because of increased leverage.

It is assumed that uninsured losses are tax-deductible in the year in which they occur.

Scenario 1

In tracing through the effects, we will have to make various judgments. The first of these concerns the effects of the fire on future earnings. The first loss scenario is that $100 million in productive assets are destroyed then replaced. The capacity to return to pre-loss production is replaced, but this does not guarantee that post-loss revenues and earnings will be restored. There may be temporary or permanent interruption loss. If production is down for a short period and the firm cannot cover this with inventory or excess capacity, then sales can be lost. This may be a short-run phenomenon, or customers can be lost permanently thought the failure to deliver. In the working through of this example, it is assumed that there is no permanent loss and the firm can cover temporary production shortfall through inventory and excess capacity. Thus, expected future EBIT remains at $2 billion.

The first column of Table 14–2 below shows the estimate of the post-loss share price of $47.86, reflecting a drop of 14 cents from the pre-loss value. The negative change in share price reflects two factors: the reconstruction of the asset cost $100 million and money was borrowed at 8% to pay for this. The additional interest, shown in the third row, leaves less net income to divide amongst shareholders. To add a little insult to injury, the additional debt, together with the lowering of equity value since net income is lower, increases leverage,[1] which in turn increases the cost of equity. Discounting the net earnings at a higher rate further lowers the value of shares.

The tax treatment here needs a little explanation. The estimated annual EBIT of $2b, less interest, attracts on annual tax liability at 34%, as shown in the fifth row. In addition, the uninsured loss is assumed to be fully tax deductible in the year in which it occurs. Assuming actual EBIT for the year does not fall much below $2 billion, there is enough taxable income to take full advantage of this deductibility. This is a once only deduction. To avoid crediting the tax refund on losses in all future years, it has been shown as a once only refund in the ninth row. The qualification that there is sufficient income to fully deduct the losses can be important. If the expected EBIT for the year is highly variable, there is a chance that deductibility will be lost or become a carry-forward against future income.

---

1. You can verify that the leverage ratio is 0.52 when growth potential is not included in equity value and 0.356 when it is included.

T A B L E   14–2

Share Value under Different Loss Scenarios

	Loss $100m Replaced	Loss $1 billion Replaced	Loss $1 billion Not Replaced
Operating Income: EBIT per annum	2,000m p.a.	2,000m p.a.	1,800m p.a.
Interest: Senior 7% on $5 b	350m	350m	350m
Interest: Post-loss debt 8% on lost assets	8m	80m	
	1,642m	1,570m	1,450m
Tax @ 34%	558m	534m	493m
Income per annum	1,084m	1,036m	957m
Cost of Equity (reflects leverage)	11.03%	11.5%	11.5%
Equity Value of Operations	9,825m	9,009m	8,322m
Tax Deductibility Uninsured Loss	34	340m	340m
Number of Outstanding Shares	300m	300m	300m
Share Value from Operations	$32.86	$31.16	$28.87
Value of Investment Opportunities	$15 ?	?	?
Market Value of Shares	$47.86 ?	?	?
Debt/Equity (absent invest opportunities)	0.52	0.64	0.58

The question mark after the share value reflects the second judgment input. Before the loss, investors placed a $15 value on future growth opportunities. After the loss, the firm may still have the same investment opportunities; the question is whether the loss has made it more difficult to finance them. Consider again the crowding out hypothesis. Has the loss depleted internal funds so that the firm is forced to more costly external financing, or has the loss increased the cost of external financing by increasing leverage and bankruptcy risk? The judgment made here is that the 25-cent fall in share price and the small increase in leverage (from 0.505 to 0.52), together with the fact that reconstruction was paid from new debt (thus leaving cash in the coffers), mean that the firm's capacity to raise new money has hardly changed.

Though the loss cost the firm $100 million in reconstruction, this has had negligible impact on the firm's "financials."

It is important to point out that you do not need to agree with my judgments here. The important thing is to see how decisions are made. What is provided here is a framework for making decisions. If you wish to draw different implications on business interruption loss or on crowding out (i.e., there would be some loss of future growth because the small deterioration in the firm's financial capacity would compromise some marginal future investment), then your alternative judgment can be processed through this framework. The answer may be different, but the process is the same.

Scenario 2

This proceeds in the same fashion as scenario 1. I have again assumed that the replacement of the productive asset is conducted without any long-term loss of earnings. You may feel less comfortable with this judgment because there was now a $1 billion fire. However, the judgment would have to relate to individual circumstances. Imagine the firm was operating at 80% capacity (either because the economy was in a downturn or because the firm deliberately chosen to operate with excess capacity to deter new entrants from the industry) and the undamaged capacity could be cranked up on short notice. In this case, my assumption that EBIT remains at $2 billion seems warranted. But if the firm were at full capacity, or the damaged plant was highly specialized, or there were no inventory, or rival firms were waiting in the wings to steal customers whenever an order was not fulfilled, then replacement of productive capacity might not be sufficient to protect future earnings. An alternative EBIT figure would be needed.

Note again the increase in the cost of equity from the additional leverage and that the growth premium in the share value has been queried. In this case, the share price, exclusive of growth premium, is down to $31.16, some $1.84 below the pre-loss value, and the leverage rate is up from 0.505 to 0.64. The question is, have the financials now deteriorated sufficiently that the firm's ability to finance growth opportunities is now compromised? Now I am a little uncertain what to put in the illustration. The seemingly enormous $1 billion loss has not been devastating to the firm (share value, exclusive of growth, has fallen 9%; the changes have been more than marginal but less than severe). How would the market respond to new debt and equity issues? I have left this growth *premium open. The impact of the loss on share price will depend on how you answer this question.*

Scenario 3

The difference from the previous scenario is that the loss is not replaced and the scale of operations is correspondingly reduced. I have assumed that the $1 billion loss, which constitutes 10% of asset values, causes a proportionate 10% reduction in EBIT. Alternative situations can be assumed, depending on such features as excess capacity, vertical integration, and specialization of the destroyed assets. The loss in EBIT could turn out to be less or more than proportional 10%. Now the (exclusive of growth premium) share value is down to $28.87 (from pre-loss $33). The loss now has a much more significant value effect and the prospects of future growth are now dimmer. This scenario looks worse than scenario 2 because the firm has not recaptured any value through reinvestment; replacing the damaged asset is indeed a positive NPV reinvestment opportunity that is squandered. Thus, there is a significant loss of equity and a corresponding increase in leverage.

$$\frac{\text{debt}}{\text{equity}} = (1)\,\frac{\$5,100m}{\$9,859m} = 0.52 : (2)\,\frac{\$6,000m}{\$9,349b}$$

$$= 0.64 : (3)\,\frac{\$5,000m}{\$8,662m} = 0.58$$

The post-loss analysis reveals several interest issues. First, as seen in earlier examples, the loss of share value depends jointly on the cost of replacement, the source of post-loss financing, and the reinvestment decision. Secondly, the loss of share value is not proportional to the asset value lost. For example, the $100 million loss of productive assets (1% of assets) caused share value to fall from $48 to $47.86 (a 0.3% fall). The effect on share value can be more or less than proportional, depending on the cost of refinancing and on the NPV of the reinvestment project. Thirdly, the example shows that this firm can tolerate large absolute losses of productive assets, perhaps up to $1 billion, without real financial hardship and perhaps without sacrificing much future growth. Of course, this conclusion depends very much on the judgment made about potential interruption loss, how investors would perceive future risk in the firm, and so on.

The Introduction of Insurance: Pre-loss Analysis

Now let us look at the same firm on a prospective basis. For potential future losses, can we anticipate:

+ What reinvestment decisions are likely to be made?
+ What sources of post-loss financing add most value?
+ Does pre-loss financing add more value than post-loss financing?

To answer these questions, the same types of judgments will have to be made as in the post-loss analysis, only now these judgments must be anticipated. We will address these questions using a method sometimes called "dynamic programming." The idea is to work backwards, starting with the decisions that we would choose to make after the loss, then considering the immediate decision as to what pre-loss financing arrangements (if any) should be set in place. To illustrate, this analysis will first ask whether reinvestment will add value, then, conditional on the answer to that question, we will consider whether insurance should be purchased to finance the reinvestment.[2]

The framework we will use for looking at insurance and other hedging instruments is essentially similar to that used for post-loss analysis. The criterion used is to select the strategy that maximizes share value. But here we are concerned not with the share price after the loss but with the pre-loss share price and how that might be affected by risk management decisions. To get started, consider again the New Drugs example.

---

2. This should intuitively be more appealing than the reverse question "should we buy insurance then, when we have decided that, and if we have a loss, should we reinvest?" In this order we can waste money on insurance that is not needed.

PRE-LOSS ANALYSIS OF INSURANCE VERSUS DEBT FINANCING

The following is a summary of data on the loss potential of New Drugs, Actuaries estimate that the expected loss from insurable property losses is $50 million, and a quotation has been received to cover this loss exposure for a premium of $60 million. The premium is tax-deductible, giving an after-tax insurance cost of $39.6m. If losses are uninsured, they are tax-deductible in the year in which they occur (thus the expected deduction on an expected loss of $50m is 0.34 × $50m = $17m).

- *Expected loss of assets E(L) = $50 million per year*
- *Insurance premium $60m (note 20% markup on expected loss) = 60 (1 − 0.34) = 39.6 after tax*
- *Losses can be funded with post loss debt at 8% interest.*

Table 14–3 gives an analysis of the effects of the insurance purchase on the share price.

T A B L E   14–3

Insurance versus Post-loss Debt Financing

	Insurance Coverage	Post-loss Debt Financing
Operating Income: EBIT per year	2,000m p.a.	2,000m p.a.
Interest: Senior 7% on $5b	350m	350m
Expected Interest (8% of $50m) per year		4m
	1,650m	1,646m
Tax @ 34%	561m	560m
Income per annum	1,089m	1,086m
Cost of Equity (reflects leverage)	11%	11.01%
Equity Value of Operations	9,900m	9,867m
Insurance Premium after tax	39.6m	
Tax Deduction of Uninsured Loss		17m
Equity Value of Operations	9,860m	9,884m
Number of Outstanding Shares	300m	300m
Share Value from Operators	$32.87	$32.95
Value of Investment Opportunities	$15	?
Market Value of Shares	$47.87	?

We can talk through this calculation. First, is assumed that insurance will be used to replace destroyed assets and that, as a result, expected EBIT will be preserved at $2 billion; there will be no interruption loss. In the presentation here, the insurance premium is not deducted directly from earnings. The earnings figures are annual earnings. What we wish to decide is whether to buy insurance now for losses that arise within the next year. We do not have to decide now on insurance that might be purchased in 10 or 20 years' time ("sufficient onto the day is the evil thereof").[3] Thus, the table isolates this year's net of tax premium as a single cost of $39.6m that reduces the overall net value of equity, as shown in the ninth row. Because insurance is being used to pay for reconstruction of assets, there are not post-loss financing costs to consider.

To give a point of comparison, the insurance strategy is valued alongside post-loss debt financing. But how do we compare pre-loss financing with insurance with post-loss financing with debt? Isn't this a case of mixing apples and oranges (or, as the English say, chalk and cheese)? The trick here is to be clear that we are comparing the pre-loss valuation of insurance with the pre-loss valuation of a strategy for post-loss debt financing should a loss occur. To put this another way, we are comparing:

1. *The estimated share value today, under the assumption that insurance is purchased, with*
2. *What the share price should be today if it is known that the firm is not insured but plans to reinvest should any loss occur and pay for the reconstruction with debt financing. We are undertaking a pre-loss analysis of post-loss debt.*

Contingent debt financing is shown in the final column. Note that the expected value of loss is $50 million. If a loss occurs, it is most unlikely to be $50 million; it will be more or less. At some future date the firm might borrow more or less than $50 million to pay for some uninsured loss. Prospectively, the expected value of new debt it will have to take

---

3. You may consider that future earnings has netted out the cost of future fires. For example, if insurance were to be purchased in future years, then EBIT would be interpreted as earnings after deduction of insurance premiums. This EBIT value is then adjusted for tax, reflecting the tax deductibility of future premiums. This ensures consistent treatment with this year's premium. The virtue of showing this year's premium as a once only deduction from the market value of equity is that it isolates those cash flows on which a decision has to be made today.

on is equal to the expected value of reconstruction cost of future loss; that is, $50 million. Thus, the expected interest charge is 8% on $50 million, which is $4m. I have made a small adjustment in the cost of equity to reflect the fact that committing to a post-loss debt financing strategy implies a possibility of future increases in leverage. Notice that the tax deductibility of the loss is shown as a once only expected refund of $17m, calculated from the expected loss for the current year of $50m.[4]

With the data and assumptions used, the current share value from committing to the post-loss debt strategy is $32.95 plus any premium investors are willing to pay for future growth potential. Now here's the rub. Does this strategy compromise the firm's ability to finance future investment opportunities? Previous analysis suggests that large losses, relative to the firm's value, can crowd out new investments. If no loss occurs, this is no problem. But if a very large loss occurs, the firm might find it difficult and/or expensive to fund new investment. Prospectively, estimated expected growth will be reduced, and this will lower the premium investors will be willing to pay for this growth potential. If this growth premium is lowered from $15 per share to $14, the estimated share value with prospective debt financing will be $46.95, compared with $47.87 with insurance, and insurance will be preferred.

Insurance: The Benefits of Risk Transfer

The analysis of insurance shown above is incomplete. Much of the earlier analysis of this book was concerned with why risk reduction can add value to firms. If we compare insurance with post-loss financing strategies such as debt or equity financing, we must account for the fact that insurance both permits the firm to finance post-loss investment (like debt or equity) and hedges risk (unlike debt and equity). In the New Drugs example we did address the crowding out hypothesis; when insurance was purchased, the firm was in a stronger position to fund future investment opportunities and therefore the premium investors would pay in the share price for this growth potential remained high. In contrast, this growth

---

4. The expected value of the tax deduction is probably overstated at $17m. While the expected loss is $50m, the actual loss could be much smaller or much larger. With smaller losses the tax deductibility would be preserved. But for much larger losses the firm might find itself with insufficient income to use the tax deduction fully.

potential was in doubt with debt financing. Let us return to the crowding out hypothesis and the other theories of why risk reduction matters and show how they affect the analysis. Recalling the four main shareholder value theories that explain why risk is costly and why risk reduction adds value:

1. Risk transfer reduces expected taxes (as shown by the downwards arrow in the following table) if tax functions are convex. This will increase after-tax income and thereby increase the share value.

2. Risk transfer reduces expected bankruptcy costs. This will reduce the interest burden (as shown by the downwards arrow in the table) paid on debt. This will tend to increase share value.

3. Risk transfer reduces agency costs and thereby improves project selection (increasing operating income) and reduces the cost of debt, as shown by the directional arrows in the table. Both effects should increase share value.

4. Risk transfer will reduce the crowding out problem and facilitate the financing, and therefore the value, of future investment opportunities. The effect on share price should be positive.

How Risk Reduction Through Insurance Can Increase Share Value

	Tax	Bankruptcy	Agency	Crowding Out
Operating Income: EBIT			↑	
Interest		↓	↓	
Tax	↓			
Income per annum				
Cost of Equity (reflects leverage)				
Equity Value of Operations				
Insurance Premium after tax				
Equity Value of Operations				
Number of Outstanding Shares				
Share Value from Operations				
Value of Investment Opportunities				↑
Market Value of Shares				

With this framework at hand, we will work through another example of insurance versus debt financing, but this time we will address a liability exposure.

Hawker Chemicals is worried about its liability for leakages of chemicals that could cause harm to the environment or, more directly, to people. The loss distribution for potential liability settlement is:

Size	Probability
$400m	0.1
Zero	0.9

Hawker is fairly sure that EBIT will be $500m this coming year and that it will be stable at that level in the future, absent any liability losses. However, the management estimates that purchasing insurance would secure various value additive benefits. This would reduce the probability of defaulting on debt, reduce the possibility of an underinvestment problem arising should the firm suffer some future liability loss, and permit orderly financing of new investments from retained earnings. The effect would be to increase the premium paid by investors for future growth from $10 per share to $12 per share. The alternative strategy is to finance future losses by new debt.

The firm has 40 million shares outstanding and its cost of equity capital is 10%. The cost of equity is expected to remain at 10% if insurance is used to hedge losses but would rise to 10.5% if the firm's strategy is to use post-loss debt financing because of the contingent leverage effect. The firm has existing debt of $1,250m at 8% interest but is planning to reissue. The estimated cost of debt will remain at 8% if post-loss debt financing is proposed but will fall to 7.6% if insurance is purchased (reflecting a lowering of the agency and bankruptcy costs).

It is important not to double count the benefits of risk reduction. Resolving underinvestment problems will increase future expected earnings as the firm captures the value of all positive NPV projects. This increases future growth. But lowering the crowding out costs also helps capture the positive NPV of future projects and will ultimately be re-

flected in expected future earnings. In this presentation, both effects have been presented as a premium in the share price for future growth potential. However, we do show a separate effect on the cost of debt to allow for the fact that more risky strategies increase the value of the default put in the debt.

The firm's earnings are taxed at 40% but tax shields allow the firm to shelter from taxes depreciation of $100m as well as interest payments. Earnings below this shield are untaxed and we assume no carry-forwards for simplicity. The firm also can deduct from current income any uninsured loss and interest payments. We will compare post-loss debt financing with the purchase of insurance. However we will go one step further than in the New Drugs case by comparing two strategies; one in which liability insurance is purchased in each of the future years; the other in which debt financing will be used for losses occurring in all future years. The insurance premium is $45m and is tax deductible. If post-loss debt is used, the firm will borrow the $400m and repay in two annual installments; the first being $232m and the second $216m. These are calculated as follows. The loss is assumed to occur, if at all, at the beginning of the year; the firm borrows 400 at this time and repays 200 of principle plus 8% interest, 32, at year end. The firm then repays the remaining 200 principle, at the end of year 2 + 16 in interest, i.e., 8% of the remaining 200. Thus, in any year, debt payment (principal plus interest) could be (joint probabilities in parentheses assuming independence).

216 + 232 if a loss occurred in this and the prior year (0.01)

216 + 0 if a loss occurred in the prior year but not
the current year (0.09)

0 + 232 if there was no loss in the prior year but there was a loss
in the current year (0.09)

0 + 0 if no losses occurred in either prior or current year (0.81)

The figures in parentheses at the end of each loss scenario are the joint probabilities. These reflect the 0.1 chance of a loss and 0.9 chance of no loss in any given year. Because losses are assumed to be independent, the joint probabilities are calculated by multiplication.

Before solving the main problem, the comparison of debt and equity financing, we need to address a preliminary problem: how nonlinear taxes affect the expected tax burden and therefore the expected net of tax cash flow. Because marginal tax rates change from 0 to 40% when the firm's earnings pass $100m, we cannot simply calculate the expected tax by applying the tax rate to the expected income. This is done in the following table. The columns show combinations of the current year's and prior year's loss experience. Note that this analysis does assume that the EBIT is riskless.

Annual Estimated Future Taxes with Post-loss Debt Financing

	Loss Prior Loss Current	Loss Prior No Loss Current	No Loss Prior Loss Current	No Loss Prior No Loss Current
EBIT	500	500	500	500
Loss this year	400	0	400	0
Interest	$100 + 48 = 148$	$100 + 16 = 116$	$100 + 32 = 132$	100
Depreciation	100	100	100	100
Taxable Income	$500 - 400 - 148$ $- 100 = -148$	$500 - 116 - 100$ $= 284$	$500 - 400 - 132$ $- 100 = -132$	$500 - 100 - 100$ $= 300$
Tax	0	$0.4(284) = 113.6$	0	$0.4(300) = 120$

The column headings show the different combinations of loss experience; that is, whether there was a loss in the current and prior years. The first row is simply EBIT, and the second row shows this year's loss. The third row is the total interest, combining interest on existing debt (100) and possible interest on new debt used to pay for losses. The additional interest is 32 if a loss occurs in the current year and 16 for a loss in the prior year. The fifth row shows taxable income, which is EBIT, minus deduction for current year's loss, minus interest, minus depreciation. Tax is shown in the final row. With no carryforward assumed, a tax liability of zero is shown when taxable income is negative.

The expected tax is simply the weighted average of the taxes for each combination of loss experience, as shown in the third row of the next table. Also shown in the next table are the net cash flows that are available to shareholders as dividend payments or retained earnings after meeting obligations for taxes and for interest and principal repayments on debt. The expected value of this net cash flow also is shown.

Annual Estimated Net Cash Flows with Post-loss Debt Financing

	Loss Prior Loss Current	Loss Prior No Loss Current	No Loss Prior Loss Current	No Loss Prior No Loss Current	Expected Value
EBIT	500	500	500	500	500
Repayment	400	200	200	0	40
Interest	148	116	132	100	104.8
Tax	0	113.6	0	120	107.4
Net Cash Flow	−48	70.4	168	280	247.8

We can now perform a comparison of the effects of the two risk management strategies on the firm's share value.

	Insurance Coverage	Post-loss Debt Financing
Operating Income: EBIT per year	500m p.a.	500m p.a.
Expected Debt Repayments		40m
Premium	45m	
Expected Interest	95m	104.8m
	360m	355.2m
Tax at 40%	104m[a]	107.4
Net Cash Flow per annum	256m	247.8m
Cost of Equity (reflects leverage)	10%	10.5%
Equity Value of Operations	2,560m	2,360m
Number of Outstanding Shares	40m	40m
Share Value from Operations	$64	$59
Value of Investment Opportunities	$12	$10
Market Value of Shares	$76	$69

[a] Note: taxable income that reflects depreciation of 100 is 500 − 45 − 95 − 100 = 260.
Tax = 0.4(260) = 104

Insurance leads to the higher share value because:

♦ *It lowers taxes—with debt there is a chance tax shields are not used.*

♦ *It enhances future growth because it preserves liquid funds for new investment and reduces underinvestment and asset substitution problems.*

OTHER HEDGING INSTRUMENTS

Insurance is one of a number of instruments available to hedge specific firm risks. Options, futures, and forward contracts can be used to hedge certain risks. For example, the oil company can hedge its exposure to oil price change by taking a short position in oil futures, and the airline can hedge its exposure by taking a long position. To see this, consider first the oil company. Because it produces oil, it is vulnerable to future price changes; price rises will increase profit and price falls will reduce profit. This endowed long oil position is shown as the solid upwards-sloping line in Figure 14–1. The upwards slope indicates that positive changes in price, shown on the horizontal axis, cause positive changes in profit, as shown on the vertical axis (and vice versa). Suppose the oil firm sells oil futures. This means that it has sold oil for future delivery at a price that is fixed today. If the price falls, the firm gains from the short future position because it will sell at the pre-agreed futures price rather than the depressed spot price at the time of delivery. Contrarily, if the price rises, the firm is still committed to sell at the lower fixed futures prices. Thus, the payoff structure of the short future position is shown as the downwards-

F I G U R E   14–1

Oil Firm Hedges with Oil Future

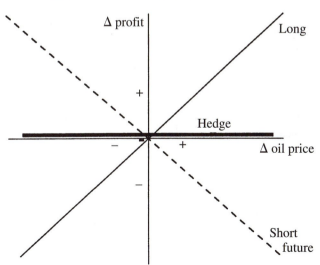

sloping dashed line. If we put these two positions together, the upwards slope of the long oil position and the downwards slope of the future position cancel to give a bold horizontal line (labeled "hedge") that is insensitive to changes in the oil price.

The airline has an opposite profile. Oil is a major cost to airlines and a price rise will reduce profit. The airline's endowed interest in oil prices can be represented as a downwards-sloping solid line, as shown in Figure 14–2. The oil company therefore buys a future contract. The long futures position is shown as the dashed upwards-sloping line. A rise in oil prices will reduce profits but increase the value of the future contract for the airline. Conversely, a fall in prices will increase profits, but this will be offset by a loss on the futures position. Thus, the airline is hedged against price changes.

The following table is summarized from Chapter 8 and shows some of the instruments available to hedge against specific corporate risks. The list is not exhaustive, but it serves to show that a portfolio risk management strategy is often feasible. This portfolio approach is now being built into the design of insurance contracts.

F I G U R E   14–2

Airline Hedges with Oil Future

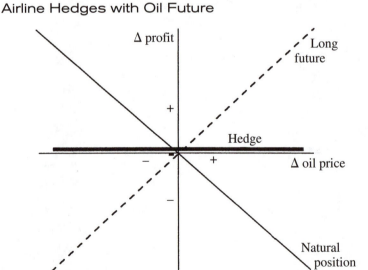

Illustrations of Hedging Strategies

Tool→ Source↓	Property Damage	Liability Loss	Interest Rate Risk	Foreign Exchange Risk	Commodity Risk	Market Risk
Property Insurance	•					
Liability Insurance		•				
Interest Future			•			
FX Forward				•		
Commodity Future					•	
Market Index Future						•

Integrated Products and Coordinated Coverage

For some time, insurers have offered "blanket" or "multi-peril" insurance policies. Often such coverages bundle together risks in a geographical fashion. For example, property or liability insurance is arranged over a number of locations, ultimately under a worldwide basis. Such coverage can be subject to common conditions. For example, an occurrence limit in liability with similar deductibles in each location. Another coordination device is to have a cumulative deductible. However, until recently these blanket policies rarely were much more than a common policy that combined separate coverages in a common folder. Recently several insurers have derived products that address the portfolio risk of the firm more effectively. In this section we will look at the problems of uncoordinated coverage and show how different product innovations are resolving these issues.

In Chapter 8 we discussed how a piecemeal approach to risk management can leave the firm's value exposed to cumulations of risky events. For example, the liability coverage may have a $5m deductible and the property insurance also have a $5m deductible. However, the combination of a couple of property losses followed later in the year by a liability loss would leave the firm exposed up to $15 million in retained losses. This may be too high, given the firm's liquidity, and the firm may realize it is getting into problems when the first two property losses have occurred. At this time its tolerance for another $5m retention on a possible liability claim is stretched, given that it has just suffered two $5m property retentions.

The issues of coordination can become even more important when it comes to upper limits of coverage. For example, a financial institution may have a large credit risk exposure that intensifies when interest rates rise (or when the economy takes a downturn). In times of low credit risk, an upper limit on liability losses of $100m may be acceptable because its cash position will be strong and it will have relatively easy access to new money. But in times of high credit exposure, this level of liability coverage leaves the firm exposed to the potential cumulation of a high credit loss and a liability loss.

STRUCTURING INSURANCE AND HEDGING PROGRAMS

Risk Sharing: Simple Optimality of a Layered Program

In Chapter 2, dealing with expected utility, different forms of risk sharing were examined: deductibles, coinsurance, and upper limits. For an individual who is risk-averse, the form of risk sharing that yields highest expected utility is the deductible. With a deductible the policyholder can cap risk at a level that is tolerable. Losses in the lower layers are often frequent and their overall cost is reasonably predictable. Retaining this layer creates little financial volatility for the policyholder. The higher levels of loss typically have a higher coefficient of variation (ratio of standard deviation to expected value), but these layers can be transferred to the insurer who has greater capacity to bear that risk.

We will now look at risk sharing arrangements typically encountered in commercial insurance and we will see similar principles at work. To set the stage, the following loss distribution is shown to typify the loss profile on many commercial property or casualty exposures. All but the smallest firms can expect smaller losses to happen regularly. Firms typically have several, perhaps many, smaller workers' compensation losses, vehicle accidents, small fires and other property losses, and smaller liability claims. In aggregate, these smaller losses will be a regular annual charge on the firm. Small losses tend to be of high frequency. The overall cost of these "high-frequency—low-severity" losses will normally vary only moderately between years. Large losses, in contrast, tend to be of low frequency. The small probability of a very large loss imposes considerable risk on the firm. Years may go by without anything really bad happening, then suddenly a loss will occur that wipes out many years of profit. The following discrete distribution illustrates this pattern. I have shown only a limited number of loss sizes for simplicity. But the main issue is that smaller losses are quite likely and high losses are of low probability.

Loss	Probability
0	0.5
10	0.2
50	0.15
100	0.1
400	0.05

A typical insurance design for this type of commercial loss exposure is to divide the distribution into layers and assign different layers to different parties. For example, the policyholder may take a deductible up to 10. Losses below 10 are self-insured and this layer is often called a "self-insured retention" (SIR). Above 10, an insurer will pay the loss minus the 10 deductible. However, this insurer may limit its aggregate payout on any loss (or any cumulation of losses within the coverage period). In this illustration the insurer limits its coverage to maximum payout of 100 minus the deductible; that is, the insurer covers a layer of 90 in excess of the deductible 10 (sometimes denoted "90 xs 10"). This does not mean that the insurer does not respond to a loss of 400; rather, its payout is limited to $100 - 10 = 90$. The layer of coverage above the deductible is known as the "primary insurer."

Losses above 100 form the next layer (known as "excess layer"). These can be insured by a second insurer (who may be a specialist in high layer coverage, known as "excess carrier" or "surplus lines carrier") or they can be self-insured. The excess layer will respond only to losses above 100 and will pay the loss minus 100. The layering may continue, with the excess carrier imposing an upper limit and possibly a second excess layer lying above the first excess. For example, if the first excess carrier covered losses between 100 and 300, it would have a layer described as "200 xs 100." The points at which one layer ends and the next layer starts are called "attachment points." Thus, the primary layer attaches at 10 and the excess layer at 100.

The insurance market rarely offers unlimited coverage. This is especially important with liability insurance where the potential loss is open-ended. The coverage plan will usually have some final limit, and beyond this the policyholder is self-insured. In this illustration, if there were only a primary insurer, the layer above 100 would be self-insured.

Consider the three layers of risk. The first layer, up to 10, is a deductible; the second layer is between 10 and 100 and the final layer is above 100. The following calculation shows the expected loss and risk (standard deviation) in each layer.

LAYER 1. DEDUCTIBLE:

Policyholder bears	L if $L \leq 10$ 10 if $L > 10$	
Expected loss	$0.5(0) + 0.5(10)$	= 5
Standard deviation	$[0.5(0 - 5)^2 + 0.5(10 - 5)^2]^{1/2}$	= 5
Coefficient of variation	$5 \div 5$	= 1

LAYER 2. PRIMARY:

Insurer Pays	0 if $L \leq 10$ $L - 10$ if $100 > L > 10$ and 100 if $L \geq 100$	
Expected loss	$0.7(0) + 0.15(50 - 10) + 0.15(100 - 10)$	= 19.5
Standard deviation	$[0.7(0 - 19.5)^2 + 0.15(50 - 19.5)^2 \, 0.15(100 - 19.5)^2]^{1/2}$	= 37.1
Coefficient of variation	$37.1 / 19.5$	= 1.9

LAYER 3. EXCESS:

Insurer Pays	0 if $L \leq 100$ $L - 100$ if $L > 100$	
Expected loss	$0.95(0) + 0.05(400 - 100)$	= 15
Standard deviation	$[0.95(0 - 15)^2 + 0.05(300 - 15)^2]^{1/2}$	= 65.4
Coefficient of variation	$65.4 / 15$	= 4.4

ENTIRE DISTRIBUTION:

$E(L) = 39.5$ $\sigma(L) = 88.5$ Coefficient of variation $= 2.24$

The coefficient of variation (C. of V.) for the entire distribution is 2.24, meaning that the standard deviation is two and a quarter times the expected loss. Roughly, this means that we can be about 68% confident that each dollar of expected loss invested in this activity has a variation of up to ±$2.24. But if the firm retains the layer up to 10, its expected loss is 5 and the standard deviation is also only 5. Each dollar of expected loss is surrounded by an average variation of ±$1. In retaining this layer, the firm is exposed to limited volatility. The next layer, the primary layer, has an expected loss of 19.5 and a standard deviation of 37.1, given a C. of V. approaching 2. The excess layer is much more risky relative to expected loss, with a C. of V. of 4.4. Given the thin tail of the distribution, the higher layers tend to be more volatile relative to expected loss.

Now suppose that the firm could hedge risk at zero transaction costs. This means that it is able to transfer to another party the entire loss distribution for its expected value; that is, the insurance company would fully insure any loss for a premium of 39.5. If this were the case, the expected value of the firm's earnings would (ignoring any tax effects) be unchanged by the insurance purchase, but the earnings would become riskless. If risk is costly due to agency costs, bankruptcy costs, etc., the firm gains value from this insurance hedge. But insurance is rarely available at expected cost, and the firm must balance some transaction costs with the benefit of risk transfer. The optimal solution is usually to insure only part of the loss; that is, to share the risk between the policyholder and the insurer. In our example, the firm should probably focus most on transferring those layers of the loss distribution that are most volatile; that is, the higher layers with the higher coefficients of variation.

To summarize, from a reduction of risk viewpoint, it is usually more efficient for the insured to retain the lower layers and insure the higher layers. This result is the standard rule of thumb in designing commercial insurance programs and echoes the results generated with expected utility analysis in earlier chapters.

Integrated Layered Programs

Basket Insurance (Basket Options)

In the previous section the hedging problem facing the firm was simple. There was apparently only a single source of risk to the firm, and that risk could be hedged by purchasing an insurance policy. In reality, things are more complex: firms face many types of risk. To look at hedging strategies with multiple sources of risk and to introduce some of the bundled instruments that are now appearing on the market, we will consider an example in which the firm faces an insurable liability loss and a foreign exchange risk that can be hedged by purchase of futures. The following table shows a loss distribution in the first two columns. Let us suppose this is the distribution for product liability loss; it is denoted L. The next two columns show that the basic earnings of the firm are themselves risky. Basic earnings (before deducting liability losses) are denoted B and are either 400 or -200, depending on whether the dollar is strong or weak relative to a basket of other currencies. The firm's final earnings, F, must account for the basic earnings and any liability loss, and the final column combines these into a joint distribution. To derive the joint distribution, losses and basic earnings are assumed to be independent. For example, if earnings are 400 and the loss is 50, final earnings will be 350. The probability is simply the probability of the loss being 50 (i.e., 0.2) times the probability that earnings are 400 (0.5).

An Unhedged Position

Liability Loss L	Probability	Basic Earnings	Probability	Final Earnings $F = B - L$	Probability	Summary of Joint Distribution
0	0.5	+400	0.5	400	0.25	
50	0.2	−200	0.5	350	0.1	
200	0.15			200	0.075	
500	0.1			−100	0.05	
1000	0.05			−600	0.025	
				−200	0.25	
				−250	0.1	
				−400	0.075	
				−700	0.05	
				−1200	0.025	$E(F) = -40$
						$\sigma(F) = 389.74$

Without any hedging or insurance, the final earnings have an expected value of −40 and a standard deviation of 389.74, as shown in the bottom right of the table. Now imagine the firm had the following hedging instruments available. First is an insurance policy that covers losses but with a deductible of 200. In this way the firm can limit its liability loss to 100 plus the cost of the insurance premium, which we will say is 70 (note that the expected payout on this policy is 0.1(300) + 0.05(800) = 70; so there is no premium loading). It can also buy a currency hedge that will pay 400 given an adverse exchange rate regime. The cost of this hedge is 200. Note that the basic earnings with this hedge are either 400 − 200 = 200 or −200 − 200 + 400 = 0, each with a probability of 0.5. Thus, the firm has put a floor on its basic earnings of 0 and a limit on its liability loss of 200.

Now look at the possible outcomes with these separate hedges in place. To read the table, consider a loss of 500 and earnings of 400. The net hedged earnings are 400 minus the insurance deductible of 200 minus the insurance premium of 70 minus the cost of the foreign exchange hedge of 200 = 70. Not surprisingly, the separate hedges are able to reduce risk from 389.74 to 132.66, as shown at the bottom right of the table. Since both hedges were priced at expected cost, the expected value of final earnings is unchanged at −40. Normally there would be some transaction cost and the expected earnings would decline as more risk was transferred.

Separate Hedges on Liability Risk and Foreign Exchange Risk

Events	Separately Hedged Earnings	Probability	
Liability Loss = 0 Basic Earnings = 400	400 − 0 − 70 − 200 = 130	0.25	
Liability Loss = 50 Basic Earnings = 400	400 − 50 − 70 − 200 = 80	0.1	
Liability Loss ≥ 200 Basic Earnings = 400	400 − 200 − 70 − 200 = −70	0.15	
Liability Loss = 0 Basic Earnings = −200	−200 + 400 − 0 − 70 − 200 = −70	0.25	
Liability Loss = 50 Basic Earnings = −200	−200 + 400 − 50 − 70 − 200 = −120	0.1	
Liability Loss ≥ 200 Basic Earnings = −200	−200 + 400 − 200 − 70 − 200 = −270	0.15	$E(F) = -40$ $\sigma(F) = 132.66$

Now consider a contract that resembles "basket options" used for hedging FX risk. The idea in a basket option is to write the payoff on the total (or index) of several random variables (such as several foreign currencies) rather than writing separate options on each of the components. Consider such a "basket insurance" or a "basket hedge" product that is written on several sources of risk, such as FX and liability risk. In our example this is basket insurance on final earnings, which are defined as basic earnings minus any liability loss.

$$F = B - L$$

The hedge instrument will pay (the precise parameters will become apparent in a moment):

$$139 - F \quad \text{if } F < -100$$
$$\text{ZERO} \quad \text{if } F \geq -100$$

Thus, if final earnings are -600, the instrument pays $139 - (-600) = 739$. This ensures that F can never fall below 139 less the cost of the hedge. The cost of this hedge turns out to be 270 if it is priced at the expected value of the payout, which you can check. Notice this is the same as the firm were paying for the two separate hedges in the previous illustration. The question is whether spending the same amount of money on a basket hedge on final earnings is more effective in reducing risk than hedging the components separately. The final earnings of the firm with this complete hedge are as shown below:

A Basket Hedge on Final Earnings

Unhedged Final Earnings	Hedged Final Earnings	Probability	
400	400 − 270 = 130	0.25	
350	350 − 270 = 80	0.1	
200	200 − 270 = −70	0.075	
$F \leq -100$	F + (139 − F) − 270 = −131	0.575	E(earnings) = −40 Standard deviation = 116.16

Because the hedge was fairly priced, the expected final earnings are still -40 (identical with the unhedged and separately hedged positions). But now the standard deviation is 116.16, compared with 132.66 with the separate hedge instruments. At the same cost, the firm was able to transfer more risk with the combined hedge than with the separate hedges. The advantage of the basket hedge is fairly intuitive. By focusing the hedge on final earnings, instead of on each component, the basket hedge is able to protect the firm against accumulations of losses. For example, the separate insurance policy with a 200 deductible may provide adequate protection for the firm if the basic earnings are positive. Similarly, the foreign exchange hedge may provide adequate protection against foreign exchange risk as long as the firm does not have a major liability suit. The danger is that both adverse events happen at the same time. Even with the two hedges, final earnings could fall to −270 if the firm suffered both a major liability suite and a foreign exchange hit. In contrast, the basket hedge puts a floor of −131 on final earnings.

This reasoning is embodied in various integrated insurance products. Recent examples are products offered by insurers such as AIG and Swiss Re that include in one contract coverage across various lines of insurance and also include risks that traditionally have not been insurable, such as foreign exchange risk. Moreover, these products can be arranged with common limits and common deductibles. Figure 14–3 and 14–4 illustrate these integrated products. In Figure 14–3 a conventional insurance program is shown with separate coverages for different lines of insurance. The deductibles and the coverage limits differ by line, and there is no coverage for risks such as foreign exchange. In Figure 14–4 the coverages have been combined with a single deductible and single upper limit.

Conditional Coverage: Second Risk Trigger

Another device that has recently appeared is one in which the conditions of coverage (deductibles, upper limits, etc.) depend upon realizations of another risk. Such coverages can be called "second risk triggers" (SRT). The previous example can be used to illustrate the idea. The firm can purchase a liability policy with a deductible of 200 for a fair premium of 70. The problem is that this deductible is fine is basic earnings are 400 but is a problem if basic earnings fall to −200. The idea is to make the deductible on

F I G U R E   14–3

Separate Coverages

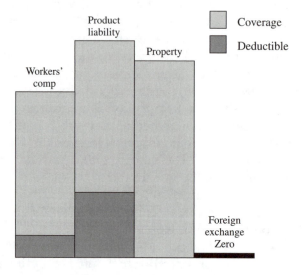

F I G U R E   14–4

An Integrated Program

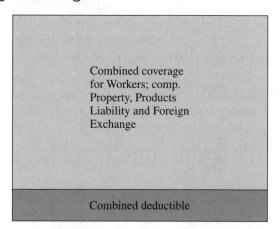

the liability loss conditional on earnings being 400. This could be achieved either by making the deductible conditional on the level of earnings (if earnings are 400, the deductible is 200; if earnings are −200, the deductible is zero) or by making the deductible a function of exchange rates. These could be called respectively an "internal trigger" and an "external trigger" because earnings are internal to and under the control of the firm, whereas exchange rates are not.

There are moral hazard reasons to prefer the external trigger. The policyholder firm is able to control actual and reported earnings and may be tempted to do so if the difference in coverage is significant. In contrast, exchange rates are outside the control of the policyholder and cannot be manipulated. But there is a trade-off in terms of *basis risk*. The ability to absorb a deductible does not depend on exchange rates per se; it depends on the cash and financial strength of the firm. If there is a close correlation between earnings and exchange rates (as in this example), then the exchange rate is a very good proxy for earnings and it makes little difference which trigger is used. This is a situation of little basis risk. Contrarily, if the correlation is weaker, there is more basis risk.[5]

The operation of the second risk trigger will be illustrated in more detail now with the prior example. I would like to find some combination of an SRT deductible policy and a separate foreign exchange hedge that cost the same price as the basket hedge (i.e., 270) and gives comparable overall coverage. This will require a little reverse mathematics.[6] For simplicity, I will assume the trigger

---

5. The concept of basis risk will be discussed in considerable detail in Chapter 16 in connection with catastrophe insurance and reinsurance.

6. To make the example comparable to the integrated hedge, I set the maximum and minimum final wealth at 130 and −131 as with the basket insurance. The values of the deductible, D, the foreign exchange hedge payout, F, and the insurance premium, P, were set by solving a set of simultaneous equations. To ensure that income, when no liability loss is suffered and basic earnings are 400, amounts to 130, and noting that the overall cost of the hedge must be 270 (i.e., $P + 0.5X = 270$), the following must be satisfied:

$$400 - P\ 0.5X = 230$$

and to ensure that the final earnings are −131 when basic earnings are −200 and a liability loss of 1000 occurs, the following equation must hold:

$$-200 + X - 0.5X - P = -131$$

Solving these two equations gives $P = 100.5$ and $X = 339$. We now need to select the deductible such that it disappears when $B = 200$ and the expected insurance payout is 100.5. This is done by setting the expected payout, with deductible of D, to 100.5, i.e., $0.5\{0.2(50) + 0.15(200) + 0.1(500) + 0.05(1000)\}\ 0.5\{0.1(500 - D) + 0.05(1000 - D)\} = 100.5$ which gives $D = 260$.

is activated when basic earnings fall to -200 and the deductible disappears. The hedge strategy includes:

* A second risk trigger liability coverage with a deductible of 260 for a premium of 100.5. The deductible disappears if earnings fall to -200.

plus

* An interest rate hedge that costs 169.5 but offers a payout of 339 when earnings fall to -200.

The foreign exchange hedge clearly is priced at expected payout. So too is the SRT insurance policy, as can be seen from the following calculation:

Expected payout if $B = -200$ 0.2(50) + 0.15(200) + 0.1(500)
$$= 140$$
Expected payout if $B = 400$ 0.1(500 - 260) + 0.05(1000 - 26)
$$= 61$$

If we bear in mind there is a 50–50 chance that basic earnings will be 400 or -200, the expected payout is 0.5(140) + 0.5(61) = 100.5, and we would expect the premium to be at least this value. For comparison with the basket hedge, it is assumed that this premium is exactly equal to the fair price of 100.5.

The final earnings are now plotted with these interactive hedges in place in the following table. You will notice that, as engineered, the distribution of final earnings after the hedge strategy is very similar to that with the fully integrated basket hedge. In both cases final earnings range from 130 to -131. Moreover, the firm pays 270 for each hedge strategy, and thus there is a comparable attempt at risk transfer. While the final earnings are not exactly the same as the basket hedge, the combination of the SRT liability insurance and the separate hedge foreign exchange is an almost exact replica. The expected value and the risk are almost identical at 40 and 116.11.

Second Risk Trigger on Liability Insurance

Events	Separately Hedged Earnings	Probability	
Liability loss = 0 Basic earnings = 400	Earnings position 400 − 169.5 Insurance position −100.5 Final earnings 130	0.25	
Liability loss = 50 Basic earnings = 400	Earnings position 400 − 169.5 Insurance position −100.5 − 50 Final earnings 80	0.1	
Liability loss = 200 Basic earnings = 400	Earnings position 400 − 169.5 Insurance position −100.5 − 200 Final earnings −70	0.075	
Liability loss ≥ 260 Basic earnings = 400	Earnings position 400 − 169.5 Insurance position −100.5 − 260 Final earnings −130	0.075	
Liability loss = ANY Basic earnings = −200	Earnings position −200 + 339 − 169.5 Insurance position −100.5 Final earnings −131	0.5	$E(F) = -40$ $\sigma(F) = 116.11$

Second risk triggered policies have recently appeared in insurance markets. For example, Cigna Insurance Company has introduced such a product where self-insured retentions can be tied directly to interest rates or other economic variables that may affect corporate value. Notice that these are external triggers and should not encounter moral hazard in the activation of the trigger. On the other hand, the hedge value of the second trigger depends on the particular correlation with firm profitability and value. These products should be particularly attractive for firms for whom such correlation is high.

The basket hedge discussed earlier permits common coverage across many risks in a single contract. This has the attractiveness of simplicity, and there may be economies from grouping risks in a single product. Moreover, there is not the potential basis risk problem that arises with SRT policies with an external trigger. On the other hand, the introduction of SRT insurance policies permits bundling of insurable, financial, and economic risk but with more flexibility. The SRT policy, in combination with separate hedges on financial and other risks, can effectively replicate the basket hedge without the necessity of dealing exclusively with one counter-party or insurer. This unbundling can increase the market power of the firm vis-à-vis potential counter-parties and reduces problem of contract "lock in."

A second advantage of unbundling and using the SRT for interlocking is that insurers may differ in their efficiency in providing ancillary services. One insurer may have a comparative advantage in providing product liability insurance (it is efficient at claim defense) whereas another has a comparative advantage in engineering services associated with writing pollution risk. A third advantage is that the unbundled/SRT strategy provides greater flexibility to vary coverage terms across risks, according to the differences in risk and return of each risk. For example, the prices of liability insurance and interest rate hedges (expressed in relation to expected costs) may differ substantially due to moral hazard, adverse selection, or other transaction costs. If so, the optimal hedge strategy may involve higher deductibles for those sources of risk for which transaction costs are higher.

BACKING OFF A FULL BASKET OPTION PROGRAM (THE LIMITS OF INTEGRATION)

Price and Availability by Layer

If insurers incurred no risk-bearing costs, or if they were infinitely diversified so that they could insure any loss without it increasing the relative risk of their portfolios, then policies would probably have no upper limits. The risk that is most troublesome to the policyholder (the highest layers) could be absorbed by the insurer without cost.[7] But insurers are firms with their own ownership and management structure just like policyholders. While insurers are more diversified and have a comparative advantage in bearing risk, risk is still costly to them. All the agency, tax, bankruptcy, and crowding out explanations for why risk is costly to firms apply also to insurers. To the extent that insurers are left with undiversified risk, it diminishes value. Accordingly, insurers will ultimately face layers of coverage that cannot be accommodated

---

7. This means "without cost" above the expected value. The firm would still have to pay for the expected value of loss. But the insurer would not have to charge a risk premium, since risk is not costly under these assumptions.

within their portfolios without increase in relative risk. They will then seek to pass that risk on to another risk bearer (traditionally by reinsurance), retain the risk with a compensating risk premium, or decline coverage. The exercise of this choice will affect price and availability of insurance in the following way:

- ◆ Coverages with any insurer are usually limited. A large corporate exposure will usually be spread over several insurers, often with a broker coordinating the coverage.
- ◆ Multiinsurer coverage can be organized for large risks, but even so, there is usually a limit to the amount of coverage that can be found for individual exposures. For example, in liability insurance, coverage is rarely available for individual losses in excess of about $0.5 billion or for accumulations of such losses within any given year.
- ◆ The price of transferring risk tends to be higher the higher the layer of risk.

Consider the following evidence from reinsurance markets. Kenneth Froot (1997) has examined the catastrophe reinsurance market and plotted price by layer of coverage. While there is much variation in pricing, the pattern seems to be as shown in Figure 14–5. There is considerable anecdotal evidence that this pattern prevails in the direct market, notably for liability coverage, but apparently no formal evidence. Such a pattern would be understandable in the direct liability market since mega-losses could cause financial stress to insurers. There is a further reason to expect that higher layers would be more expensive. There are fewer insurers competing in this layer. This may be due in part to the higher capital needed to write coverages in higher layers and in part to the more specialized skills needed to write higher layers where coverages and claims tend to be more complex.[8]

Bringing together the supply and demand sides of the insurance market leaves the risk manager with something of a conundrum. This is illustrated in Figure 14–6. The layers refer to losses rather than coverage. Losses have been ordered according to their impact on the firm's earnings and value. Small losses (relative to

---

8. See Doherty and Smith (1993) for a discussion of the restrictive supply levels in higher coverage layers.

F I G U R E   14–5

Price By Layer of Coverage

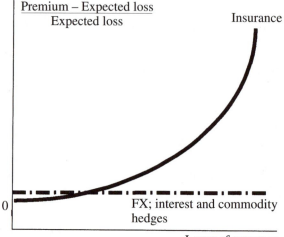

F I G U R E   14–6

Losses by Impact on Firm and by Insurance Capacity

Layer 1. Too small to have significant impact on firm's earnings or value

Layer 2. Large enough to have significant impact on firm's earnings and value

Layer 3. Large enough to affect earnings and value severely, but beyond capacity of insurance market

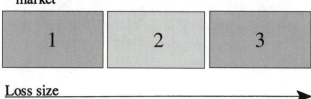

the firm size) have relatively little impact on the firm's earnings and value and can be retained easily. These small losses are shown as layer 1 in Figure 14–6. Whether these losses are uninsured or not does little to change the riskiness of the firm, and realized losses can cause only minor uncertainty to financial numbers such as earnings, leverage, and share price. Accordingly, self-insuring would cause few problems in terms of agency costs, bankruptcy costs, increased taxes, and crowding out costs. But larger losses in the range 2 in Figure 14–6 can impact value significantly, and self-insuring these losses gives rise to the agency, bankruptcy, etc. costs of risk, as seen in the New Drugs example above. At the top end, in range 3 in the figure, the potential of unhedged losses to harm the firm is most severe, but insurance typically is not available.

The problems of high-end availability are unlikely to be the same for different types of risk. The high-end availability issue is likely to be most severe for liability insurance for the larger firm. The multi-billion-dollar firm can face potential liabilities that could cut deep into its net worth yet still be beyond the capacity of the insurance market. Recent litigation on Dow Corning's breast implants, Exxon's *Valdez* oil-spill, and the tobacco companies' liability to the state provide perfect examples of multi-billion-dollar exposure for which available insurance is insufficient to provide indemnity. However, available hedging capacity is effectively unlimited for exposures such as interest rate risk, commodity risk, and foreign exchange risk. Standardized, exchange-traded hedge products can be purchased in very large quantities. Moreover, the price is not likely to be sensitive to the size of the purchase.

Given that the cost of transferring risk with different hedging instruments varies, it is not necessarily optimal to have identical retentions and transfers for each type of risk. Other things being equal, value will be added by transferring less risk with those instruments that are more costly and transferring more risk with those instruments that are less pricy. A simple illustration shown in the middle column of the following table will make the point. Suppose that there are only two uncorrelated exposures, each hedged with a policy having a deductible, or self-insured retention (SIR), of 100. First, consider the cost of hedging that can be measured by the risk premium (which is the price of the hedge net of expected payout). The first hedge has a risk premium of 10 and the unhedged risk below the deductible has a standard deviation of 100. The second has a risk premium of 15 and the unhedged standard deviation is 60. The total hedging cost is 25 and the retained risk is $(100^2 + 60^2)^{0.5} = 116.6$. The deductibles on the both policies can be increased or reduced, and the first and third columns of the table plot out the risk premiums for the two policies together with the levels of risk associated with the self-insured retentions.

	Lower Deductible	Deductible = 100	Higher Deductible
Risk Premium Policy A	15	10	5
Risk Premium Policy B	17	15	12
SIR Standard Deviation A	90	100	110
SIR Standard Deviation B	25	60	100

Should the firm lower or raise the deductible on both policies? The risk premia are plotted together with the total risk from the two exposures below.

Both deductibles are lowered:

Portfolio risk premium	$15 + 17$	$= 32$
Portfolio standard deviation	$(90^2 + 25^2)^{0.5}$	$= 93.4$

Both deductibles stay at 100:

Portfolio risk premium	$10 + 15$	$= 25$
Portfolio standard deviation	$(100^2 + 60^2)^{0.5}$	$= 116.6$

Both deductibles are raised:

Portfolio risk premium	$5 + 12$	$= 17$
Portfolio standard deviation	$(110^2 + 100^2)^{0.5}$	$= 148.7$

There is not a dominant strategy. If the deductibles are lowered, the hedging strategy becomes more expensive (the overall risk premium increases from 25 to 32) but less risky (standard deviation falls from 116.6 to 93.4). Whether this enhances value depend on how the reduced cost of risk bearing stacks up against the saving in the cost of the hedges. But raising the deductible clearly is not a dominant strategy either. There is a saving in costs at the expense of an increase in risk. If one were forced to choose be-tween these three strategies, the choice would depend on how costly risk bearing was to the firm.

But all these strategies are fully coordinated with similar deductibles for both policies. Suppose one now chooses different levels of hedging for the two exposures: raising the deductible on policy A and lowering it on policy B.

Deductible on A is raised; Deductible on B is lowered:

Portfolio risk premium $\quad$ 5 + 17 $\qquad$ = 17
Portfolio standard deviation $\quad (110^2 + 25^2)^{0.5}$ = 112.8

This is a strategy that unambiguously dominates the starting position. Compared with the common deductible of 100, the firm is now able to reduce its cost of hedging risk and reduce the riskiness of its retentions.

The risk–return-incentive trade off is particularly pertinent in the comparison of *core* and *non-core* risk. The case developed for not hedging core risk in Chapter 7 rests on the argument that the firm will accumulate economic profit for assuming core risk but will not do so for assuming non-core risk. This rent accrues from its specialized expertise in controlling this risk. Following through with this logic, the value added per unit of risk assumed should be higher for core risk and low for non-core risk. Accordingly, one would wish to hedge non-core risk where there is no reward to assumption, but retain that core risk where the firm has a comparative advantage over potential counter-parties.

Moral Hazard

Besides price availability issues, there may be other reasons to vary limits and deductibles across different risk exposures. Two reasons will be discussed briefly here but are discussed in more detail elsewhere.

The first is moral hazard,[9] which was discussed in Chapter 3. In that context the treatment of moral hazard was conducted

---

9. Recall that when we talk of moral hazard we are using an economist's definition which refers to the inability of the insurer to monitor safety and loss prevention. We are not using the more casual insurance term which connotes improper behavior.

with expected utility. A risk-averse individual bought insurance and also had some control over safety and loss mitigation. When the risk was transferred, the incentive to invest in costly mitigation was relaxed. If it were simple for the contract terms to be conditioned on the level of care and safety, moral hazard could be easily controlled. The insurance policy would require that certain actions be undertaken or that the coverage terms could be conditional on those actions. But this requires that all relevant actions be observable and that these contract conditions be enforceable after the fact by the courts should there be a dispute. For some forms of loss mitigation, such as installation of sprinklers, this is not a big problem. But other actions, particularly behavior, cannot be recorded and built into contract conditions so easily. Moreover, courts are not always willing to enforce penalistic conditions against policyholders *ex post*. Thus, other remedies are needed to redress moral hazard.

The two methods that have emerged for dealing with moral hazard are deductibles (and other risk-sharing devices) and rating schemes that are based on loss experience. Risk-sharing devices such as deductibles reduce the amount of risk transfer but give the policyholder a larger stake in loss-reducing activities because more of her own money is on the line. The second device has the same effect. By using retrospective rating (a retrospective adjustment is made to this year's premium to reflect actual loss experience during the coverage period) or experience rating (premiums for current coverage are calculated with reference to loss experience prior to the coverage period), the policyholder shares the losses and thus will have a stronger economic interest in safety and loss prevention. In fact, we can make stronger statements about such conditions. Given that moral hazard exists, these types of risk sharing are the best solutions that can be achieved, even though moral hazard is not eliminated. It is better for the policyholder to share some risk and reduce moral hazard than to fully insure risk and increase moral hazard. The reason is that the moral hazard will be anticipated and reflected in the premium. Thus, the policyholder is better off agreeing to a risk-sharing arrangement that will reduce moral hazard and thereby reduce the premium, even if it means some risk sharing.

The message about moral hazard, then, is that it is better for it to be recognized in the policy conditions so that the policyholder can accept a trade-off between the price of the insurance and the degree of risk transferred. Moral hazard is an issue in many insurance contracts since the policyholder usually has some control over the loss distribution but relinquishes responsibility for paying for the loss. For other types of hedges this may not be the case. For example, hedges written on interest rate changes, foreign exchange rates or commodity prices are unlikely to encounter moral hazard since the party buying the hedge cannot influence these underlying prices. These contracts are unlikely to face the same risk sharing–efficiency trade-off, and, other things being equal, one would expect hedge ratios to be higher than for insurance.

Thus, where moral hazard problems differ across risk exposures, we would expect the degree of hedging to differ, with lower hedge ratios for exposures with most moral hazard.

Deep Pockets and Liability Insurance

An argument that will be developed later in Chapter 15 suggests that the purchase of high limits on third party liability insurance (i.e., for liabilities to parties not in a contractual relationship with the firm) increases the *ex ante* costs of risk. The increase arises for two reasons. First, liability insurance increases the net worth of the firm and thereby increases the amount that can be paid for very large claims. In the absence of the insurance, part of the cost would be externalized in the form of unpaid damages. If the liability is fully insured, the cost is fully internalized to the firm. This argument by itself may raise some public policy concerns because it leads to a position where the firm might use limited liability as a risk management tool and thereby "default" on its obligation to injured third parties. This will be taken up later. The second reason is that the net worth of the firm, especially focusing on available insurance limits, becomes a target for plaintiff's in seeking non-compensatory damages. In some jurisdictions punitive damages can be related to net worth. Thus, increasing liability insurance increases the target for punitive damage awards, regardless of the culpability of the defendant or the damage caused.

These considerations suggest that the firm may not wish to choose similar hedge ratios for liability risk as for other exposures.

We have another reason for backing off a full integrated risk management strategy with identical coverage for different risks.

CONFLICT RESOLUTION: HORIZONTAL VERSUS VERTICAL PROGRAMS

Figure 14–7 shows two types of insurance or hedging programs, one vertical and the other horizontal. We have been considering the typical layered insurance program thus far. In this program there is a primary layer, and when this is exhausted by claims, an excess layer kicks in. But the excess layer will normally have a limit of coverage, and when this is exhausted a second excess layer may kick in, and so on. This is *vertical* layering; each layer is stacked on top of the one below. In Figure 14-7 the dark shaded layer is the primary layer and the lighter shaded one is the excess.

An alternative configuration is to structure the program horizontally. Consider the first year in Figure 14-7 in which there only a primary layer. This layer is divided between two (or more) insurers, as shown by the vertical line, and thus the coverages are side by side or *horizontal*. As shown, the line is drawn down the

F I G U R E   14–7

Vertical and Horizontal Layering

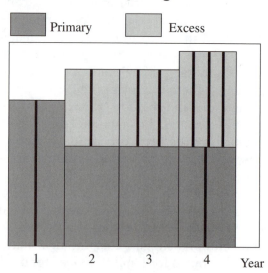

middle of the layer, suggesting that each insurer takes 50% of the losses in that layer. Thus, if the layer is shared, any and all losses are equally divided the two insurers. The division need not be equal and there can be more insurers.

One can combine vertical and horizontal layering, as shown in later years in Figure 14-7. In years 2, 3, and 4 the excess layer (lying vertical above the primary) is divided among two (in year 2) and three (in year 3) and four (in year 4) insurers. Moreover, the primary layer is divided between two insurers in year 4. Such combined, vertical and horizontal, arrangements are not uncommon in many large and complex insurance programs.

The choice between vertical and horizontal layering involves issues of risk sharing and conflict resolution. As we saw earlier in this chapter, the typically skewed nature of loss distributions implies that the higher layers are much more risky (relative to their expected values) than the lower layers. Participation of surplus lines carriers in the high layers exposes them to relatively low expected losses but very high volatility. These insurers must carry high surplus or be very highly diversified in order to remain solvent. This surplus lines is composed partly of specialized carriers who are structured to deal with this level of volatility (together with marginal carriers who come and go).

But the different structures also carry different potential for conflicts of interest to arise between the various parties. This occurs in liability insurance, which is used here to illustrate the problems. With liability insurance a natural tension always exists between the policyholder and the insurer in settling claims with third parties. The insurer typically is concerned with settling the claim for as little as possible. The policyholder has different interests. For example, some policyholders may be anxious to be exonerated and may seek to incur considerable defense costs to fight a case rather than make a low settlement offer. In this way the policyholder's reputation is protected. In contrast, the insurer may be quite willing to settle for as little as possible and pay scant attention to the firm's reputation. This conflict can be especially severe if the policy has unlimited coverage for defense costs. One can imagine other conflicts of interest between the policyholder and insurer.

But our main concern here is with conflicts between different insurers. Consider a vertically layered program with a primary and an excess layer. For illustration, the primary layer is for $5m and the excess layer is for $20m excess of the $5m primary. As is normal in such cases, the primary insurer is responsible for defense costs. A liability case arises and the primary insurer must decide on a defense strategy that might involve negotiations with the plaintiff to settle. Consider the following scenario. The plaintiff's actual losses are probably well above the $5m (say $20m or more), but there is some doubt about liability and therefore some doubt about whether a court would favor the plaintiff or the defendant. The primary insurer reasons that if it fights the suit, it has an even chance of winning, but if it fights and losses, the case may well settle for $25m. The defense costs of fighting are estimated at $1m. However, the primary insurer also reasons that the plaintiff would be willing to settle the case now for $10m and might even settle for as low as $5m. Let us suppose that there is a 0.9 chance of settling for $10m and a 0.5 chance of settling for $5m. If not settled, the case goes to trial and the estimated damages and defense costs are as before (zero or $25m, each with 0.5 chance, and defense costs of $1m). With early settlement, the defense costs are $100,000.

Vertical Coverage (with Primary Covering Defense Costs)

Consider the following defense strategies: "go to trial," "try to settle for $5m," and "try to settle for $10m." From the primary insurer's viewpoint, it bears all the defense costs but only has to pay compensation to the plaintiff up to a maximum of $5m. From the excess carrier's viewpoint, it pays no defense costs but bears the damages in excess of $5m. Thus, the three choices can be examined in terms of their expected values to each carrier

1. Go to trial:

   Primary   0.5(ZERO) + 0.5($5m) + $1m   = $3.5m
   Excess   0.5(ZERO) + 0.5($20m)   = $10m

2. Settlement offer of $5m (with 0.5 chance of acceptance):

   Primary 0.5($5m + $0.1m) + 0.5{0.5(ZERO)
               + 0.5($5m) + $1m)} = $4.3m
   Excess   0.5(ZERO) + 0.5{0.5(ZERO) + 0.5($20m)} = $5m

3. Settlement offer of $10m (with 0.9 chance of acceptance):

Primary 0.9($5m + $0.1m) + 0.1{0.5(ZERO)
         + 0.5($5m) + $1m)} = $4.94m

Excess   0.9($5m) + 0.1{0.5(ZERO) + 0.5($20m)} = $5.5m

From the primary's viewpoint, the best strategy is to fight it out. Despite the primary paying the high defense costs, it can only lose a maximum of $5m (plus $1m defense). Though going to trial is risky because the damages may be high at $25m, the primary is not concerned, since its damages are capped at $5m and the primary would pay at least $5m in a settlement. Going to trial is the worst decision from the excess carrier's view because there is a good chance it will be made to pay $20m. Conversely, the best strategy from the excess carrier's viewpoint is to try to settle, preferably for $5m, because if the plaintiff accepts, the excess carrier will pay nothing. If the primary controls the defense, as is often the case, it will choose to fight. The combined expected costs to the two carriers will be $13.5m. Now let us see how this would play out if the policies were not vertically layered but were horizontal, with each insurer sharing indemnity and defense costs.

Horizontal Coverage (Shared Indemnity and Defense Costs)

With horizontal coverage, the insurers would share the loss and the defense costs so their interests would be aligned. If the primary and excess insurer acted together, they could well do the following comparisons of the expected costs of each of the three strategies (each would share in the following combined expected costs):

1. Go to trial:

0.5(ZERO) + 0.5($25m) + $1m = $13.5m

2. Settlement offer of $5m (with 0.5 chance of acceptance):

0.5($5m + $0.1m) + 0.5{0.5(ZERO) + 0.5($25m) + $1m)} = $9.3m

3. Settlement offer of $10m (with 0.9 chance of acceptance):

0.9($10m + $0.1m) + 0.1{0.5(ZERO)

$$+ 0.5(\$25m) + \$1m)\} = \$10.44m$$

Thus, both insurers would prefer to try to settle at $5m, in which case their combined expected cost would be $9.3m, or $4.65m each. This has two advantages. First, because the interests of the two insurers are aligned, arranging contracts should involve lower frictional costs. Secondly, it would affect the overall price of liability insurance to the policyholder. With horizontal coverage, the incentives of the insurers are to lower the aggregate cost of liabilities, and rationally, the premium will be calculated with this expectation. With vertical coverage, settlements are likely to be made that lower the costs to the primary only. These self-interested settlements for the primary can turn out to be higher in total than for horizontal coverages. Thus, in summary, vertical coverages misalign the interests of the primary and excess carriers, and this can lead to an increase in the overall costs of liability insurance. Horizontal coverage realigns the interests and gives all insurers an incentive to work together in keeping down the overall settlement costs.

TRADING OFF RISK AND RETURN IN HEDGING STRATEGY: THE EFFICIENT FRONTIER

The simple example just presented illustrates the trade-off facing firms between the costs and benefits of hedging risk. This trade-off will now be examined more formally by considering which combination of hedges leads to the preferred attainable combination of overall risk and return.

The efficient frontier for investment portfolios was presented in Chapter 4. This function plotted the maximum expected rate of return that could be achieved for any given level of risk. The different points on the frontier represented different investment portfolios. The frontier was derived by choosing a set of investment weights to maximize a linear combination of expected return and risk (or to minimize a corresponding relationship between risk and return). If we consider the measure of risk as a proxy for the costs that risk imposes on the firm, we can use similar techniques to choose an "efficient portfolio" of hedging instruments for a firm.

Let us suppose that the firm has several sources of risk. Consider the cost of hedging as the C, as price paid for the hedge instrument, P, minus the expected payout, $E(L)$. This "cost" is the risk premium; that is, the amount over and above the expected loss paid for transferring risk. To give effect to the layering issues discussed above, each risk exposure is divided into layers (the first $10m, the second $10m, etc.). The layers will be defined with lower and upper limits, denoted l and h, and coverage in each layer will attach only when the layer is penetrated. If the instrument is an interest rate hedge, we can think of the layer as an option spread with the lower and upper limits being the striking prices on the long and short option positions. The price of buying a hedge on the jth layer of the ith risk is P_{ij}. The probability of any loss of size L on exposure i is $f(L_i)$. We can now state the following expected value, variance, and covariance relationships:

$$C_{ij} = P_{ij} - \int_{l_{ij}}^{h_{ij}} (L_i - l_{ij}) f(L_i) dL_i$$

$$\sigma^2(L_{ij}) = \int_{l_{ij}}^{h_{ij}} ((L_i - l_{ij}) - E(L_i - l_{ij})))^2 \, f(L_i) dL_i$$

$$= \int_{l_{ij}}^{h_{ij}} (L_i - E(L_i))^2 \, f(L_i) dL_i$$

$$\sigma(L_{ij} \, L_{mn}) = \int_{l_{ij}}^{h_{ij}} \int_{l_{mn}}^{h_{mn}} (L_i - E(L_i)(L_m - E(L_m)) \, f(L_i) dL_i \, g(L_m) dL_m$$

The covariances are of particular interest. Different layers of the same exposure will have quite high correlations. For example, an insurance policy that attaches at $20m must be triggered if the next layer is pierced. Thus, attachment of higher layers must involve attachment of lower layers, but the reverse may not be true. Similarly, if an interest rate call option with a high striking price is in the money, so too must be an option with a lower striking price. Correlations between different risk exposures, foreign exchange, insurance, and so on typically are not too high. An obvious exception might be a high correlation between interest rates and exchange rates.

A simple portfolio risk management problem is to choose a set of hedge ratios, h_{ij}, that scale the firm's purchase of the jth layer of the ith risk exposure. These hedge ratios are proportional

F I G U R E   14-8

The Risk Management Efficient Frontier

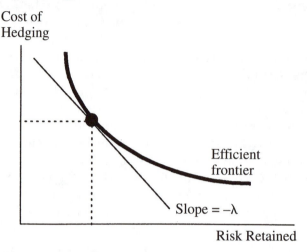

weights. For example, applied to insurance, the hedge ratio is the percentage of the layer transferred to the insurer. Applied to futures or options, the ratio is the number of contracts written on that spread. Choosing proportional rates makes the portfolio problem similar in structure to maximizing the investment efficient frontier.[10] The problem is to minimize the weighted sum of the additional cost of hedging (given by the Cs) and the cost of retained risk (given by the variances and covariances). Here λ measures the cost of bearing risk and will be higher the more costly risk bearing is to the firm. Given the various theories of risk bearing, λ will be higher for firms with higher leverage, more convex tax functions, and so on.

$$\text{Minimize } (h_{ij}): \quad \sum_i \sum_j h_{ij} \, C_{ij}$$

$$+ \lambda \left(\sum_{ij} \sum_{mn} (1 - h_{ij})(1 - h_{mn}) \, \sigma(L_{ij}; L_{mn}) \right)$$

The efficient frontier is illustrated in Figure 14–8. Because the

---

10. A more complex problem is to solve by choosing the weights and the attachment points for the layers. A severe complication of this approach would be that the prices cannot be scaled according to the weights of the positions but would probably be unique to each attachment point.

task is to minimize a combination of undesirable qualities, price and risk, it is better to be close to the origin. In other words, the firm's value will be higher the more southwesterly the firm is. The cost of risk measure, λ, is shown by the slope of the straight line. The tangency point shows the position where the trade-off between price and risk is optimized.

The efficient frontier as outlined here is an exercise in "mean variance analysis." Various techniques are available to conduct such exercises. One conceptually easy approach is to run many simulations of a portfolio, varying the hedge ratios and allowing losses to occur randomly. In this way the performance of different combinations of hedge ratios can be averaged over different loss scenarios and the hedge strategies that perform best can be identified. More direct techniques use mathematical optimization routines to solve the hedge ratios that offer highest return per unit of risk. The best known of these is quadratic programming, which has become a standard tool for calculating investment frontiers. Computer software is available for these exercises. But whatever the technique, data are required on the riskiness of different corporate assets and activities and on the prices at which these can be hedged.

The use of mean variance optimization to derive a hedging strategy rests on the assumption that variances are good proxies for the costs to the firm of bearing risk (the greater the risk, the higher the costs to the firm, and the more risk is reduced, the greater the value added). However, it is possible to extend this type of analysis to focus more directly on the value of the firm. For example, modeling the structure of the firm makes it possible to trace the impact of random events on financial performance. In particular, one can focus on key results such as periodic earnings and leverage and on whether the firm becomes bankrupt. Simulation can be used to show how these results are affected by hedging strategies. The advantage over simple mean variance analysis is that, while variance acts as a crude proxy for the costs of risk on the firm, these financial variables allow us to measure the effect of risk directly.

Commercial risk models are available that trace the impact of risk management strategies on key financial performance measures. The real issue is whether such models pick up the particular costs of risk to the firm described in Chapter 7; this type of modeling is still in its infancy.

CONCLUSION

Several contingent financing and contingent leverage instruments examined in previous chapters provided a partial hedge against specific events. For example, loss equity put options are exercised jointly by some triggering event and a fall in the stock price. Thus, the event is partly financed by the party holding the short position in the put, who recapitalizes the firm at a price above the post-loss value. Similarly, with reverse-convertible debt, part of the loss of equity value is recaptured when shareholders exercise their option to replace debt with an equity claim. Perhaps the most complete hedge instrument considered in early chapters was forgivable debt, in which principal and/or interest was at risk. In this chapter we went further, addressing instruments that directly hedge the risky event. The most apparent is insurance, and we adapted the valuation framework used for post-loss financing to consider how insurance can add value. In particular, judgments made about the effects of risk reduction on the costs of financial distress, agency cost, and the funding of future investments can be placed within a valuation framework. In this way, comparisons can be made between insurance and other loss-financing strategies.

This chapter also looked at the bundling of hedges to cover multiple sources of risk. This can be achieved simply by grouping together separate hedge that operate independently, or by using integrated hedges whose payout is defined on the firm's aggregate loss. Integrated hedges have the advantage of protecting the firm from accumulations of risky events happening in rapid succession. We also showed that the advantages of an integrated hedge can be nearly replicated by separate hedge instruments written on different events but with interlocking triggers (second triggers). These second triggers allowed us to focus risk transfer on the accumulated loss suffered by the firm and thereby increase its effectiveness.

Despite the trend towards more integrated risk management programs, there are limits. The transfer of core risk to an outside risk bearer can be inefficient because the firm usually has a comparative advantage in measuring and controlling such risk. Moreover, some risk transfer is associated with moral hazard, whereas other risks are largely outside the control of the firm. Higher levels of risk retention are appropriate to control moral hazard costs. Finally, for some risks such as liability risk, the firm may wish to limit insurance because the protection itself becomes a target for plaintiffs in seeking compensatory and punitive damages. Heavily insured firms become deep pockets.

The arguments for how much risk to transfer for different types of risk can be examined in terms of a risk–return trade-off. The ratio of the expected profit to risk will vary for different risk types (it should be high for core risks and low for non-core). Similarly, the ratio of the cost of transfer to the amount of risk transferred will differ across types of risk (it will be higher for risks with high moral hazard and adverse selection). The desired hedging program can be framed as a portfolio optimization exercise. We finished the chapter by adapting the investor's portfolio choice problem for financial securities to the risk management problem facing the firm. Such techniques are now being used for insurance and hedging choices.

REFERENCES

Ahn, Dong-Hyun, Jacob Boudoukh, Mathew Richardson, and Robert F. Whitelaw. 1999. "Optimal Risk Management Using Options." *Journal of Finance* 54: 359–75.

Berkman, Henk, and Michael E. Bradbury. 1996. "Empirical Evidence on the Corporate Use of Derivatives." *Financial Management* 25:5–13.

Bodnar, Gordon M., Gregory S. Hayt, and Richard C. Marston. 1998. "Wharton Survey of Financial Risk Management by US Non-financial Firms." *Financial Management* 27:70–91.

Cambell, Tim S., and William A. Kracaw. 1987. "Optimal Managerial Incentive Contracts and the Value of Corporate Insurance." *Journal of Financial and Quantitative Analysis* 22:315–28.

Davidson, Wallace N., Mark L. Cross, and John H. Thornton. 1992. "Corporate Demand for Insurance: Some Empirical and Theoretical Results." *Journal of Financial Services Research* 6:61–72.

Doherty, Neil A, and Clifford W. Smith Jr. 1993. "Corporate Insurance Strategy: The Case of British Petroleum." *Journal of Applied Corporate Finance* 6:4–15.

Froot, Kenneth A. 1997. "The Limiting Financing of Catastrophe Risk." National Bureau of Economic Research Working Paper 6025, Cambridge, Mass.

Grace, Martin, and Michael J. Rebello. 1991. *Financing and the Demand for Corporate Insurance.* Geneva Papers on Risk and Insurance Theory, no. 18. 147–172.

Grillet, Luc. 1992. "Organizational Capital and Corporate Insurance Hedging." *Journal of Risk and Insurance* 59:462–69.

Lamm-Tennant, Joan. 1989. "Asset/Liability Management for the Life Insurer: Situation Analysis and Strategy Formulation." *Journal of Risk and Insurance* 56:501–17.

Main, Brian G. M. 1983. "Corporate Insurance Purchases and Taxes." *Journal of Risk and Insurance* 50:197–223.

Mayers, David, and Clifford W. Smith Jr. 1987. "Corporate Insurance and the Underinvestment Problem." *Journal of Risk and Insurance* 54:45–54.

———. 1990. "On the Corporate Demand for Insurance: Evidence from the Reinsurance Market." *Journal of Business* 63:19–40.

Meyer, Richard L., and Fred B. Power. 1983. "The Investment Value of Corporate Insurance." *Journal of Risk and Insurance* 50:151–56.

Porat, Moshe M., et al. 1991. "Market Insurance versus Self Insurance: The Tax Differential Treatment and its Social Cost." *Journal of Risk and Insurance* 58: 657–69.

Pretty, Deborah. 1988. *Risk Financing Strategies: The Impact on Shareholder Value.* London: Risk and Insurance Research Group Ltd.

Sung, Jaeyoung. 1997. "Corporate Insurance and Managerial Incentives." *Journal of Economic Theory* 74:297–332.

CHAPTER 15

Organizational Form and Risk Management: Limited Liability

Under normal rationality assumptions, the value of a firm is the lower of the expected present value of its cash flows and the disposal value of its assets. The firm has an ongoing option to continue in business, and, if it does so its value is the expected present value of its future cash flows. But the firm also has the real option of winding up its operations and disposing of its assets. If it does wind up, firm value will be the disposal value of assets net of any transaction costs associated with the liquidation. These two options, to continue or to liquidate, are available to the firm now and at all times in the future. Now suppose the firm loses an asset. The cash flows on that asset also will be lost. The valuation statement in the first sentence will still be true after the loss. The loss may deplete the assets and earnings of the firm, but after the loss the firm can still continue in business or liquidate. Rationally, it will choose the higher-value alternative. This logic seems to tell us that the maximum loss the firm can suffer by the occurrence of a risky event is its market value. The firm can lose more than the disposal value of its assets, but not more than the expected value of its cash flows.

There is a strong hidden assumption here. Suppose the risky event is a liability to the firm that exceeds either the value of its cash flows or the disposal value of its assets. Examples could be a class action product liability lawsuit brought by customers or a lawsuit for environmental damage brought by injured parties or by the Environmental Protection Agency. There is no reason at all why the loss suffered by the injured parties should be constrained by the firm's value. The statements made in the previous paragraph will only be true if there is some external constraint on firm value. This is the case for many firms. The joint stock form of organization limits the liability of a firm's owners to the value of their equity. Moreover, even without corporate limited liability, bankruptcy laws constrain individual liabilities. Thus, even if an unlimited liability firm, such as a partnership or a traditional Lloyd's insurance syndicate, faces a liability exceeding the present value of cash flows, liability is truncated by the (normally) higher personal net worth of the firm's owners.

Limited liability gives rise to a number of interesting risk management possibilities. The first is that when a firm faces potential liabilities that exceed net worth, it may choose to limit net worth by spinning off the risky operation or avoiding future growth. The advantage of this strategy can be seen with a recent well-known example and a little hindsight. Dow Corning earned only a tiny fraction of its earnings from breast implants, yet this operation resulted in the firm's bankruptcy. A corollary of this strategy concerns the purchase of liability insurance. Liability insurance increases the net worth of the firm available to liability claimants, and may even be used as a target for plaintiffs and their lawyers in setting damages. On the other hand, insurance is prepaid and the premium is related to the expected value of damages. Whereas limited liability externalizes costs to injured claimants *ex post*, insurance effectively internalizes that cost *ex ante*. This raises interesting questions on how much liability insurance to buy. A third set of risk management questions concerns the level of safety and loss prevention to adopt. Insofar as limited liability externalizes costs, it reduces the payback to the firm from investing in safety and loss prevention. Consequently, one would expect the firm with low net worth to underinvest in safety relative to the highly capitalized firm.

In this chapter we will examine these strategies. In doing so, we will face a crucial distinction: whether claimants on the firm do or do not have a contractual relationship with the firm. Using this distinction, we will examine whether risk management strategies that are optimal from the viewpoint of the firm are also optimal for the society as a whole. For example, if the firm spins off an activity that creates high risk of injury for customers and this enterprise is endowed with minimal capital, then injured customers can be left uncompensated even if they have valid product liability claims. This seems unfair and will undoubtedly be unappealing to the plaintiff's bar. Yet there are circumstances in which this strategy benefits both the firm and its customers. But a similar spinoff motivated by the prospect of environmental injury affecting unrelated parties raises a very different set of policy issues. Accordingly, we will also address some of these public policy issues.

EXTERNALIZING COSTS WITH LIMITED LIABILITY

Recall the agency issue that can arise between shareholders and creditors. Because creditors have a prior claim and the residual claim of shareholders cannot be negative, shareholders will have a natural tendency to select high-risk projects. In doing so, the shareholders get all the upside risk but can rid themselves of part of the downside by defaulting on their obligations to creditors. In more technical language, shareholders own a default put option that will increase in value as risk increases. A very similar set of issues arises with respect to other claimants on the firm. If employees, customers, or third parties are injured, they can be compensated only if the firm has sufficient value. From the shareholders' point of view, liability claimants, like creditors, have a prior claim on the value of the firm. However, the joint recovery of all prior claims cannot exceed the firm value.

The after-loss value of a firm, $V'(F)$, is the after-loss value of the firm's cash flows from existing operations, V_0', plus liquid assets, L, plus the present value of future investment, $-K_t' + V_t'$, minus transaction costs from loss financing, T, minus the cost of settling the loss, C:

$$V'(F) = V_0' + L - K_t' + V_t' - T' - C$$

When we looked at this problem in the chapter on contingent financing, the concern was that the loss of equity from the risky event, and the consequent increase in leverage, would increase the possibility of future default and this would affect the incentive to reinvest after the loss. This effect was shown by considering the value of the default put option embedded in the value of equity. Thus, the post-loss value of equity was:

$$V'(E) = V'(F) - D + P\{V(F); \sigma(F); D\} = V'(F) - D + P'\{.\}$$

where D is the face value of the debt and $P\{.\}$ is the value to shareholders of the option to default on debt due to limited liability.

We now shift our attention to the possibility of immediate bankruptcy as a direct result of a liability claim costing C. To see this, let us denote the postloss firm value, before deduction of C, as $V'(F)$ or more simply as $\underline{V}'$. This means that $V' \equiv \underline{V}' - C$. We can now rewrite the value of equity in the following form:

$$V'(E) = \underline{V}' - C - D + P'\{.\}$$

After the loss, the firm holds obligations both to its creditors, D, and to the liability claimants, C. Thus, we will also redefine the default put, P, as the value of the shareholders' ability to default jointly on the debt and liability obligations. The ranking of these obligations in a bankruptcy is not our immediate concern here, and for simplicity we assume that they rank jointly as general creditors of the firm.

Consider several possibilities in which the liability claimants can be paid in full:

+ The claim, C, plus immediate payments on debt, is less than the firm's liquid assets, L. Thus, the firm can meet all immediate obligations.

+ The claim plus total debt obligations is less than the value of liquid assets plus the disposal value of nonliquid assets. In this case the firm can pay all obligations through liquidation.

+ The claim plus total debt obligations is less than the liquid assets plus the present value of cash flows from current operations. While the firm may not be able to pay all obligations immediately, there exists a possibility to sell claims on future income and use the proceeds to pay debt and liability obligations. Alternatively, the various claimants might accept payment in the form of claims on future income. In fact, several class action liability settlements have been fashioned in this form. The firm faces a liquidity crunch but still has sufficient ongoing value to discharge obligations ultimately.

♦ The claim plus total debt obligations is less than the liquid assets plus the present value of cash flows from current operations and future investment opportunities. While the firm may not be able to pay all obligations immediately, there exists a possibility to use its franchise value to pay debt and liability obligations. The firm faces a liquidity crunch but has sufficient franchise value to discharge obligations.

The last of these possibilities is particular interest here. The firm may be able to settle very large liability claims by using future income. This means that the franchise value to the firm's shareholders is its raw value, $-K_t' + V_t'$, minus any liability claim that is due. Thus, the franchise value is shoring up the liability claim and its net value to shareholders is reduced. If the franchise could have been separated from the operation that generates the liability claim, its value would be higher.

Conglomerate Corp has 2 divisions. One division (Division 1) generates income with present value of 200 and the other (Division 2) generates income with a present value of 100. The firm has no debt. The total net worth of the firm would be 300 absent any possible liabilities for injury to third parties. However, Division 2 generates toxic wastes that could create injuries to the public (potential victims have no contractual relationship with the firm and the firm's revenue is not affected directly by this risk). However, there is a civil liability for such loss. The probability distribution for such loss is:

Loss	Probability
0	0.6
50	0.1
100	0.1
150	0.1
200	0.1

Assume that as long as net worth exceeds the liability loss, there is always some financing device that will permit claimants to be paid in full. What is the value of Conglomerate? If division 2 were a separate firm with limited liability, what would its value be?

The expected loss is 50 and the value of Conglomerate is the sum of the values of the two divisions minus the expected liability cost, i.e., 200 + 100 − 50 = 250. Notice that the firm value is expressed net of the full expected loss of 50. As far as Conglomerate is concerned, it will always have sufficient value to compensate claimants (the combined value of the firm, 300, is higher than the maximum loss of 200) and thus the expected compensation Conglomerate will pay is equal to the expected loss. If Division 2 were separate, it could not pay losses in excess of its value of 100. The expected value of losses Division 2 could actually pay (as a stand alone) is:

$$0.1(50) + 0.1(100) + 0.1(100) + 0.1(100) = 35$$

Thus, the value of Division 2 as a standalone firm is 100 − 35 = 65. Note that the firm could gain by spinning off Division 2 because it is worth only 50 if it stays within the firm but 65 if it is sold.

A standalone division 2 can be said to be (partly) "judgment-proof." Even though a legal judgment might be made against it, it does not have the wherewithal to meet its liabilities in full. It is partly immune from the judgment and is thus judgment-proof.

The example of Conglomerate shows that firms can create value by spinning off risky operations so that the entire firm value is not held at risk by a single operation. The feature that makes this work is that the new entity is itself a limited liability firm and its owners are now liable only to the extent of the net worth of the new firm. Thus, the liability loss can be limited to the net worth of the spun-off firm, rather than to the much larger net worth of the conglomerate. The legal reality is more complex, at least in the United States. Limited liability has been likened to a "corporate veil" (a little gentler than an iron curtain) that is drawn around the firm and shields the owners from liability above their investment. However, cases are known in which the corporate veil is "pierced" and the owners are held liable beyond their equity stake. This is unusual and occurs when there is some particularly egregious behavior that will need to be resolved in individual litigation.

The prospect that a spin-off of a hazardous activity might fail to protect the net worth of the owner is real. The plaintiff's bar is often aggressive in seeking to pierce the corporate veil and is sometimes successful. But other risk management strategies that also work on the principle of limiting the net worth behind hazardous activity may have more legal security. The acquisition of a "safe" firm by a "risky" one exposes the safe firm's net worth to the potential liability arising from the risky firm's activities. Unless there are other compelling reasons for the acquisition, the safe firm would have more value on its own or under alternative ownership. The example also works in reverse, where a risky firm acquires a safe one. In this vein, one may question whether a tobacco company or an asbestos manufacturer facing enormous liabilities would wish to diversify into less risky product lines. Similarly, one might question whether safe firms might choose to enter joint ventures with risk firms.

The idea can also be applied in the case of emerging technologies. For example, consider the research and development for introducing new drugs or genetically engineered products. The potential litigation risks are large, but the probabilities are unknown. Are the initial R&D and product development better handled by a large firm or a startup? There are many dimensions to this problem, but one important consideration is indeed the question of how much capital is exposed to the liability threat. It is interesting to note that a substantial proportion of the development of highly innovative and potentially risky products is undertaken by small firms. Some research by Ringleb and Wiggins (1990) speaks to this issue. After classifying firms by risk levels, and controlling for other features that influence firm size, they do indeed find that a disproportionate amount of high-risk activity is undertaken by small firms.

EXTERNALIZING COSTS— EX ANTE ANALYSIS

Contracting Parties—Employees and Customers

Suppose that the Conglomerate example had described a liability to customers (or to employees) instead of a liability to members of the public. We can choose either customers or employees to make the point. Unlike members of the public who may be injured by an atmospheric discharge of a toxic material, both customers and employees are in a contractual relationship with the firm. If an accident occurs to an employee on the work floor, or to a customer by the faulty operation of a product sold, it is an unfortunate side effect of a well-defined and preexisting economic relationship. It is not unlikely that the conditions of the contractual relationship between the firm and its customers and employees will anticipate such events. Other things being equal, a product that has a higher risk of injuring a customer will be less attractive than a less risky product and should command a lower price. Similarly, controlling for other features, jobs with higher injury risk will be less attractive than jobs with lower injury risk and should command a higher wage. This does, of course, assume that the customers and employees (or those that bargain on their behalf) have some knowledge of the risk factors.

To demonstrate that limited liability will not reduce the expected liability to customers of a firm when customers are aware of the loss potential, we will use some very basic microeconomics. To start, the profit of a firm, Π, is defined as the difference between total revenue and total costs, $\Pi = TR - TC$. Total revenue is price of the good, P, times quantity, Q, that is, $TR = PQ$. The price is normally a downwards-sloping function, which is represented as $P = a - bQ$. Putting this all together,

$$\Pi = PQ - TC = (a - bQ)Q - TC$$

The normal task for the firm is to select the quantity that maximizes profit. This can be illustrated formally using calculus. Intuitively, one can start changing quantity a little at a time to see if this increases profit. If profit does increase, the change in Q is worthwhile. But one can still explore the possibilities for increasing profit even further by another tentative change in Q. When one exhausts possibilities for such profit increases—that is, further changes in Q leave Π unchanged—profit is maximized. This is, in effect, how one solves the problem with calculus. Formally, when the first derivative is zero, profit is maximized.[1]

---

1. The method is a little more complex. One must check that a maximum, rather than a minimum, is reached by examining the second derivative. Moreover, use of calculus does assume that the profit function is continuous in Q.

Now introduce the possibility of consumer injury from using the product:

◆ If any injuries to customers were to be fully compensated, then the demand for the product should be unaffected by the level of risk. This seems to imply that consumers are indifferent between safe and unsafe products, and indeed this is the case. You might be tempted to object to this statement; surely consumers would prefer safe products even if they were compensated. It all depends on how much compensation is given for actual injuries. If customers are really *fully* compensated, in the sense that any disutility from the injury is made good by a cash payment, then, by definition, they are indifferent as to whether the injury occurs. To argue otherwise is simply to argue that the compensation is inadequate to compensate for the injury. Thus, the demand curve with full compensation is:

$$P = a - bQ$$

◆ If the injuries are uncompensated (i.e., there is no law making producers liable for such injuries), the utility obtained from use of the product will be lowered by the disutility of the prospective injury. Let us call the disutility of an actual injury D and the probability of such an injury λ. The expected disutility of a potential injury is λD. Thus, one may assume that the amount the consumer would be willing to pay for the product is now reduced by λD and the demand curve is now:

$$P = a - bQ - \lambda D$$

◆ Now suppose that injuries are partially compensated. There is a legal obligation for producers to pay full compensation, but they have insufficient funds to do so. The maximum that can be paid is M, which is less than the full compensation value of the injury, D. Now the consumer's utility from buying the product is reduced by the expected injury, λD, but this is partly recovered by expected compensation, λM, leaving a net disutility loss of $\lambda(D - M)$. The demand curve is:

$$P = a - bQ - \lambda(D - M)$$

The value $\lambda(D - M)$ is the expected value of the default put option; while the firm is legally liable to pay compensation, it has created for itself a put option to transfer the liability for claims above M to the victims. If the price of the product reflects this default, then the price implicitly includes an option premium paid by the firm to the customer for the default put option; that is, the lower price is discounted in return for the customer assuming part of the liability risk.

Now let us consider the effect of limited liability on the profit of a firm. The revenue of the firm is $PQ = [a - bQ - \lambda (D - M)]Q$ and the costs are now the original costs, TC, plus the expected amount that the firm will pay in compensation given limited liability, λM. Thus, the profit is:

$$\Pi = PQ - TC - \lambda M = [a - bQ - \lambda(D - M)]Q$$
$$- TC - \lambda M$$
$$= [a - bQ]Q - TC - \lambda D$$

Notice that M disappears; profit is independent of the limit on liability. Thus, when calculus is used to select the profit, maximizing level of output, M will have no role to play. This is because the firm ends up paying the full expected value of liability, λD, one way or another. The firm will pay part of the liability, M, if a loss occurs (i.e., with probability λ) and will "pay" the remaining part of the expected liability, $\lambda(D - M)$, as a reduction in the price it receives when selling the product. It will end up paying λD. The only effect of limited liability is determine what portion of the expected liability is paid up front as a price reduction and what portion is paid after the fact as damages.

To illustrate this principle, we can change the example of Conglomerate to make the injuries occur to customers rather than third parties.

Conglomerate Corp. still has its has 2 divisions. One division (Division 1) generates income with present value of 200 and the other (Division 2) income with a present value of 100. The loss distribution for injuries is the same as before, but this now describes injuries to its customers. The income of 100 from division 2 is made by selling a total of 50 units of a product at a price of 12 and an average cost of 10. Earnings are TR *−* TC *= 50(12) −50(10) = 100. We can think of all these values as the present values of future profits, earnings, and so on.*

If Division 2 stays within the corporate umbrella, the firm will be able to meet all liabilities. Thus, demand will be unaffected but costs will reflect the expected compensation payments. The expected compensation payments are (0) + 0.1(50) + 0.1(100) + 0.1(150) + 0.1(200) = 50. Total corporate profit is:

	200	*profits of Division 1*
	+600	*revenue of Division 2 (i.e., 50 units sold at a price of 12)*
	−500	*costs of Division 2 (i.e., 50 units at average production cost of 10)*
	− 50	*expected compensation payment*
TOTAL	250	

If Division 2 is spun off, the maximum the firm can pay is 100 in total to all customers. The expected value of liabilities to be paid is now only 0.6(0) + 0.1(50) + 0.1(100) + 0.1(100) + 0.1(100) = 35. Consumers will now suffer a loss of utility equal to the expected value of uncompensated losses, i.e., 50 − 35 = 15. Prices paid by consumers will be reduced by 15 (i.e., each of the 50 units sold will sell for 11.3, making total revenue of 50 times 11.7 = 585) and total corporate profit will be:

	200	*profits of Division 1*
	+585	*revenue of division 2 (i.e., 50 units sold at a price of 11.7)*
	−500	*costs of division 2 (i.e., 50 units at average production cost of 10)*
	− 35	*expected compensation payment*
TOTAL	250	

If customers are fully informed about the risks involved in products, there is no advantage to a firm from limiting the net worth behind risky products. Any gain secured by limiting compensation payments to net worth will be offset by lower demand and lower prices. It should be apparent that a similar statement can be made about the firm's liability to its employees for work injuries; any gain on the swings of limited liability will be lost on the roundabouts of higher wages. Workers will simply demand an increased wage to compensate them up front for any under-compensation should they be injured. But this conclusion also re-quires that information about potential injuries filters through to the marketplace. For example, will unions and firms have credible information on workplace injuries when negotiating wages and other employment conditions? Will customers be informed about product safety?[2] In the "information age" this condition is not so implausible. Consumer associations test and disseminate infor-mation on product quality and prices (including safety), and con-siderable information on product quality is available electroni-cally.

Now suppose the opposite: market prices do not reflect in-formation about product or employment risks. If this is true, a firm with private information about such risks can benefit from spinning off risky operations. We are covering all bases. The ques-tion of whether consumers are informed, or whether prices reflect available financial information about the firm's ability to pay, is not a theoretical matter but an empirical one. If prices are sensitive to ability to pay, there is no gain from separating high-risk activ-ities; if prices are not so sensitive, there is a gain.

An interesting variation on this issue can arise when prices are determined not by market forces but by regulation. For ex-ample, the state of Florida, like many other states, regulates prices on homeowners insurance. Following Hurricane Andrew in 1992, many insurers considered themselves overexposed to Florida windstorm risk and considered regulated insurance premiums too low. Accordingly, these insurers sought to limit their Florida busi-ness and some to withdraw altogether from the state. Fearing sup-ply shortages, the state severely restricted their ability to cancel coverages. A reaction from some insurers was to establish a lim-ited net worth subsidiary to sell only in Florida. The success of this tactic in controlling insurer risk depends on whether the courts allow claimants to pierce the subsidiary veil, and the suc-

---

2. The requirement is not that every customer have perfect information, but rather that prices reflect information that depends on the much weaker assumption that the marginal consumer is informed.

cess in adding value depends on whether regulated prices reflect net worth. The tactic could backfire altogether if regulators lowered prices for such providers, and, *ex post,* courts did in fact allow claimants access to the parent's capital. In other cases startup insurers have entered the market as one-state providers. These new single-state startups can add value only to the extent that regulated prices do not reflect the value of the default put option.

Noncontracting Parties–Third Party Claimants

The original data given in the Conglomerate illustration described liability claimants that were not engaged in a prior contractual relationship with the firm. Under these circumstances, externalizing liability costs to claimants by limiting net worth can add value. For such firms, the profit function will be increased by the value of the default put.

$$\Pi = PQ - TC - \lambda M = [a - bQ - \lambda(D - M)]Q - TC - \lambda M$$

Notice that the default put option is noted priced (thus the strikeout of this term in the product price), leaving a net price, $a - bQ$, that does not distinguish between highly capitalized firms and those with very low net worth. Despite similar prices, the firm with adequate capital will face an expected liability cost of λD compared with the lower value λM for the firm using limited liability to externalize part of this cost. In such a market, firms with lower net worth will compete successfully with more capitalized firms, other things being equal.

Again a caveat is required if the industry is subject to price or safety regulation. Regulators may anticipate this action in determining prices, and even if prices are not regulated, the regulatory burden of such firms may increase indirectly. For example, regulators might feel inclined to imposed stricter safety requirements on such firms.

LIMITED LIABILITY AND OPTIMAL INSURANCE

If a firm decides to limit its net worth in order to externalize liability costs to claimants, it would seem not to make sense to purchase liability insurance. By buying insurance, the firm is simply increasing the resources potentially available to a liability claimant. In effect, insurance increases net worth in the event that a valid liability claim should arise. Insurance simply reverses the effects of limited liability. The liability cost would no longer be externalized; rather, it would be paid in advance by the purchase of insurance. Somewhat different (but, as we shall see, erroneous) reasoning suggests that the firm wishing to maximize its value should buy insurance only up to the level of its net worth; to buy any more is wasteful because the firm would only pay claims up to its net worth anyway. In this section we will examine the optimal level of insurance for the firm that is able to externalize costs by limited capitalization.

To show what will happen, Figure 15–1 shows a simple diagram in which the value-maximizing level of insurance is shown in a setting where limited liability is not an issue (this will be introduced shortly). The horizontal axis shows the wealth of the firm if no loss occurs, and the vertical axis shows wealth if a loss arises. If the firm were "fully" insured, its wealth would be fully protected from a loss; thus, wealth would be the same in the

F I G U R E   15–1

Optimal Insurance

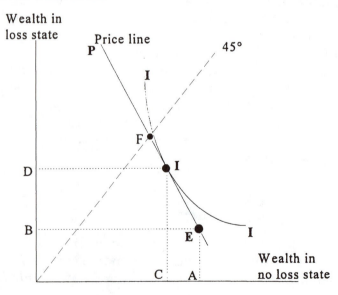

"loss" and "no-loss" states. Such full insurance is therefore shown as a 45° dotted line. To start, the firm has no insurance, and this circumstance is shown as position E. This endowed position shows the wealth as A with no loss and the lower amount B if a loss arises. The difference, $A - B$, is the amount of the loss. The firm can buy insurance by paying a premium. This will reduce the amount of wealth in the no-loss state in exchange for compensation in the loss state. The "price" of insurance in this context can be thought of as number of cents sacrificed in the no-loss state to purchase $1 of compensation should a loss arise. The insurance possibilities are shown as the line EP. The slope indicates the price of insurance; the steeper the line, the lower the price paid in the no-loss state to buy $1 of protection in the loss state. Now the firm can buy as much insurance as it wants at this price. For example, it could full-insure, taking it up the price line to the point at which it meets the full insurance 45° line shown as F.

How much insurance should be purchased? It depends on its risk preferences. These are represented by an indifference curve such as the line II. The convexity of this line to the origin implies that risk is costly. If the insurance is priced above the expected loss (which normally it is), then the optimal insurance will be less than full insurance, such as shown by position N. The fact that N is between the endowed position E and below the 45° line indicates that the firm has bought some insurance but has not bought enough to fully indemnify any loss. Note that the wealth is C if no loss occurs (thus a premium of $A - C$ has been paid) and a payment is made by the insurance company to increase the firm's wealth from B to D should a loss arise.

Now consider what happens when a firm faces a potential loss that is larger than its net worth. Figure 15–2 shows an endowment point, E, in which the firm has positive wealth, A, if no loss occurs, which would fall to negative wealth, $-B$, if it suffers a loss. In other words, the loss exceeds initial wealth, thus giving negative wealth in the loss state. If there were unlimited liability, we could go through a comparable analysis to Figure 15–1. The insurance possibilities line is EP and the firm attains the highest indifference curve available. The value-maximizing level of insurance is shown as point N, which is less than full insurance. However, limited liability restricts the wealth to nonnegative values. If the firm faces a liability award of $A - (-B) = A + B$, then the

F I G U R E   15-2

Optimal Insurance with Limited Liability

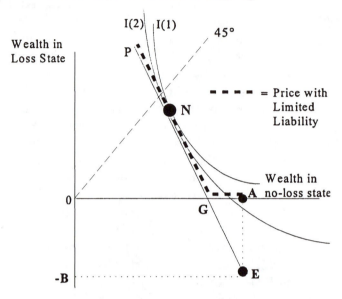

maximum it can lose is *A*, reducing wealth in the no-loss state to zero. Thus, the firm really faces a wealth endowment, shown as point *A*. Buying a little insurance for such a large loss will cost the firm a small premium, but it will have no effect in increasing wealth in the loss state. The reason is that the firm is bankrupt and all insurance proceeds simply go to increase the damages actually paid to the injured party. Thus, the insurance line starting at *A* is initially horizontal and insurance is not a value-enhancing deal for the firm. Only if the insurance payment exceeds *B* (i.e., it is large enough to bring the firm back to a solvent state) will the firm reap any benefit at all. Thus, the complete set of wealth possibilities attainable with insurance is the heavy dashed line *AGP*.

How much insurance is bought depends on the slope of the indifference curve. If the curve is *I*(1), the amount of insurance is identical to that with unlimited liability. The indifference curve is tangential to both the unlimited liability line *EP* and the limited liability line *AGP* at the point *N*. Notice that *N* beats the no-insurance position *A*. But now suppose that the indifference curve is less convex to the origin as shown by $I(2)$. This would signify that the firm is less risk-averse (or that the costs of bearing risk are small). The optimal level of insurance is no longer N. If the firm buys no insurance, it will stay at its (limited liability) endowment point A, which is father from the origin than the indifference curve $I(2)$. This indicates that the firm is better off buying no insurance at all. The prediction on insurance will differ according to the risk-aversion of the firm. With limited liability and limited net worth, more risk-averse firms will continue to buy the same level of insurance as before, but less risk-averse firms will simply buy no insurance. The following example shows how insurance internalizes costs and can lower value.

Low Cap Manufacturing has no debt and has equity of 100. However, it faces a 0.1 chance of a liability suit costing 20 and a further 0.1 chance of a liability suit costing 200. These liabilities can be fully insured at their expected cost (i.e., 22) or can be insured for some proportion, α, of the damage at a premium of 22α. The following table shows the expected value of equity under different assumptions about the level of insurance, α. The equity value with a loss of 20 is $-$ 100 minus the loss of 20 plus the insurance settlement of 20 α minus the premium of 22α. If a loss of 200 is suffered, the value is either zero or (if greater) the original 100 minus the loss of 200 plus the settlement of 200 α minus the premium of 22α.

With α less than 0.6, the insurance settlement for a 200 loss is insufficient to protect the firm from bankruptcy. Accordingly, increasing the amount of insurance from $\alpha = 0$ to $\alpha = 0.5$ reduces the expected value of equity because the additional insurance money simply goes to pay more to the liability claimant without removing the firm from bankruptcy in the high-loss situation. The table also shows the standard deviation of equity value with different levels of insurance. Increasing the level of insurance from 0 to 0.5 does little to reduce equity risk to equity. There is actually a small reduction in risk because the small loss has more coverage. But increasing insurance does nothing to reduce the equity risk from the large loss, because the payment is insufficient to protect from bankruptcy. Indeed, with respect to high losses, insurance below $\alpha = 0.6$ gives no net gain to the shareholders but is paid for in advance.

α	Calculation of Expected Value of Equity	EV	σ
0	(0.8)(100) + (0.1)(80) + (0.1)(0)	88	29.9
0.1	(0.8)(100 − 2.2) + (0.1)(80 + 2 − 2.2) + (0.1)MAX[0; 100 − 200 + 20 − 2.2]	86.22	29.2
0.2	(0.8)(100 − 4.4) + (0.1)(80 + 4 − 4.4) + (0.1)MAX[0; 100 − 200 + 40 − 4.4]	84.44	28.5
0.3	(0.8)(100 − 6.6) + (0.1)(80 + 6 − 6.6) + (0.1)MAX[0; 100 − 200 + 60 − 6.6]	82.66	27.9
0.4	(0.8)(100 − 8.8) + (0.1)(80 + 8 − 8.8) + (0.1)MAX[0; 100 − 200 + 80 − 8.8]	80.88	27.2
0.5	(0.8)(100 − 11) + (0.1)(80 + 10 − 11) + (0.1)MAX[0; 100 − 200 + 100 − 11]	79.1	26.5
0.6	(0.8)(100 − 13.2) + (0.1)(80 + 12 − 13.2) + (0.1)MAX[0; 100 − 200 + 120 − 13.2]	78	23.9
0.7	(0.8)(100 − 15.4) + (0.1)(80 + 14 − 15.4) + (0.1)MAX[0; 100 − 200 + 140 − 15.4]	78	17.9
0.8	(0.8)(100 − 17.6) + (0.1)(80 + 16 − 17.6) + (0.1)MAX[0; 100 − 200 + 160 − 17.6]	78	11.9
0.9	(0.8)(100 − 19.8) + (0.1)(80 + 18 − 19.8) + (0.1)MAX[0; 100 − 200 + 180 − 19.8]	78	6.0
1.0	(0.8)(100 − 22) + (0.1)(80 + 20 − 22) + (0.1)MAX[0; 100 − 200 + 200 − 22]	78	0

Only if the insurance settlement is sufficient to protect against bankruptcy will the shareholders get any benefit from the insurance money paid on a 200 loss. In this range the firm is solvent despite the large liability suit and the shareholders are paying the defendant's damages. Thus additional insurance will compensate them for the damage payments and, as α increases above 0.6, the equity value increases in the high-loss state. As α increases, the expected wealth remains constant (this is only because the premium is equal to the expected loss and the additional premium exactly offsets the expected insurance benefit to shareholders) but the riskiness of equity falls. Accordingly, the decision for Low Cap is whether to buy full insurance or none at all. If the cost of risk bearing is low (Low Cap is tolerant of risk), then it is better off with no liability insurance; expected wealth is 88, compared with 78 when insurance is purchased. Only if Low Cap is sufficiently risk-averse does it make sense to sacrifice the loss of expected wealth that comes with insurance.

As shown by the Low Cap example, value maximizing liability insurance will tend to extreme values; either no insurance or full insurance. This is not a hard and fast rule, but a general inclination. The effect can be seen in Figure 15–3a. There is some value of insurance that is just sufficient to bring the firm back to a solvent position for a given large loss (i.e., that exceeds net worth). This level is shown as α^*. For an insurance level below α^*, the expected value of equity will fall as insurance increases. This is because the firm is paying the premium in advance but receives no incremental benefit from the insurance payment. The incremental insurance payment benefits claimants and creditors. Nor does an increase in insurance protection in this range have much effect on the risk to equity. The standard deviation falls somewhat because there is some reduction of equity risk as the small losses have more insurance coverage.

Only when insurance passes α^* does incremental insurance show a more normal risk–return trade-off. In this range the insured firm is paying the premium and the whole insurance payment accrues to the firm. The value of equity is unchanged as the value as α increases in the Low Cap example, but would normally decline if there is a premium loading as we show in the diagram. Moreover, in this range, increases in α bring a significant reduction in risk. The risk–return profile is depicted again in Figure 15–3b.

F I G U R E   15–3a

Liability Insurance and Equity Value

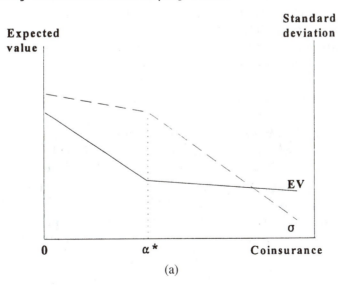

(a)

F I G U R E   15–3b

Risk and Return with Liability Insurance

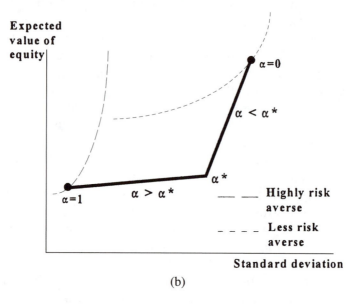

(b)

Here one can see that low levels of α result in a steep risk–return trade-off (increasing α involves a sharp loss of expected equity value, with little reduction in risk), whereas higher levels of α involve a flat risk–return trade-off (increasing α involves a moderate reduction in return with a large reduction in risk). The whole curve is shown as the heavy kinked solid line. The dashed lines are indifference curves for a less risk-averse and more risk-averse firm. Depending on the degree of risk-aversion, either full insurance or no insurance is optimal. The kink in the risk–return curve tends to produce this result. The sharper the kink, the more likely corner result is to emerge.

One can play with this problem some more. For example, we have worked with a loss distribution with two levels of loss, small and large. The firm actually gets the full benefit from insuring small losses, but only benefits, if at all, from insuring losses in excess of net worth if the indemnity exceeds the difference between the size of the loss and net worth. This suggest that different levels of insurance might be purchased on different levels of loss; for example, all small losses are well insured but large loses may or may not be insured.

LIMITED LIABILITY, SAFETY, AND LOSS PREVENTION

Limited liability creates opportunities for shareholders to create value by spinning off activities that involve very large risk to outsiders. A corollary of this strategy is to purchase little or no insurance on very large losses. We will now address another way in which risk management choices are affected by limited liability. The firm must make a series of choices on the safety of its products and operations. These choices will include choices of safety in designing and manufacturing products, safety of the workplace, generation and disposal of pollutants, safety of its vehicles, and so on.

The value-maximizing choice for the firm is that which balances the *private* marginal costs and benefits. "Private" refers only to the marginal costs and benefits faced by the firm: what it spends on safety and the benefit it obtains from this investment. Investing in safety will reduce either the probability or size of such loss. If potential injuries and damages are to be paid in full by the firm, the private benefit from investing in safety is a reduction in all of these costs. On the other hand, safety is not free. Improved designs are often more costly, and quality control can be expensive, as are guards for machines. Safety education for workers costs money. Similarly, substitution of less toxic materials in production and improved methods of disposing of toxic wastes can be expensive. To maximize value, the firm will balance the marginal reduction in cost of paying for injuries with the marginal cost of the investment in safety. This is shown in Figure 15–4. The total costs and benefits of safety are shown in the upper half. The point at which benefits of safety exceed costs by the greatest margin is at safety level s^*. This is where the slopes of the two lines are equal; in other words, where marginal costs and benefits intersect, as shown in the lower half of the diagram.

Now suppose that the firm has limited its exposure to such injury costs by limiting the net worth to a value that is lower than the potential size of the damage award. The firm does not face the prospect of paying for the full cost of the injury to the customer,

F I G U R E   15–4

Costs and Benefits of Safety

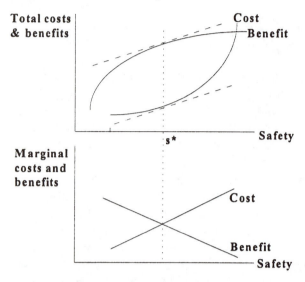

worker, or third party; but only for that part of the damage award it can meet given its financial resources. If it does not pay for the full damages, the firm does not reap the full benefit of the reduction in expected damages from investing in safety. The marginal benefit curve shifts downwards as shown by the arrow, to the dashed line as shown in Figure 15–5. With this reduction in the *private* benefit of safety, the firm will maximize value by investing at level s^p rather than at s^*. Because it does not reap the full rewards of safety, the value-maximizing firm will reduce its investment in safety. The limiting case is somewhat obvious. Suppose that the firm has no responsibility to pay any damages for injured third parties. Investing in safety costs money but brings the firm no benefit; the potential claimants reap all the benefit. Logically, the value-maximizing firm would invest nothing in safety.

Optimal Safety for Injury
to Noncontracting Parties

Having established this base, we can develop the thinking about safety, using the same distinction between contracting and noncontracting parties used in the analysis of net worth. Whether the

F I G U R E   15-5

Limited Liability and Safety

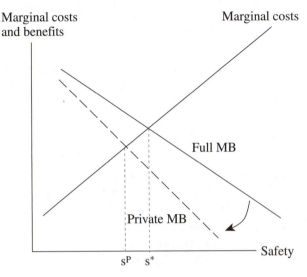

potential claimants are contracting or noncontracting parties, safety will reduce the expected value of liabilities to the firm and these liabilities can be truncated by net worth. Thus, part of the firm's liabilities will remain uncompensated. For noncontracting parties there is no *ex ante* adjustment mechanism to compensate third parties for the fact that the firm might be judgment-proof. Accordingly, the analysis of the previous paragraph seems to be valid.

The following example will show how limited liability affects safety. But it will also show how this effect interacts with the spin-off decision. The example starts with safety fixed and looks at the spin-off decision. Then the optimal safety choice for the firm is calculated with and without spin-off. Finally, it is shown that the value gained from spin-off is modified by compensating reductions in the chosen level of safety.

Associated Industries has two divisions. Division 1 generates a riskless income stream that has a net worth (net present value) of 700. Division 2 makes fertilizers and generates an income stream with a net worth of 300 absent any possible pollution liabilities. However, Division 2 has a

0.3 chance of a pollution accident (a chemical release) that could cost a total of 900. The potential victims are third parties who have no contractual relationship with the firm. The firm has no debt.

a. *What is the total value of Associated after accounting for the potential liability?*

b. *Now assume that the fertilizer division is sold to outsiders as a separate entity and the proceeds of the sale are distributed to Associated shareholders. Lawyers assert that Associated cannot be held liable for any accidents after the sale. What is the gain to Associated shareholders from such a sale?*

c. *Now assume that the safety of the fertilizer plant can be improved. The chance of an accident is now (0.3)/(1 + s), where s is the dollar level of investment in safety chosen by Associated. How much would Associated spend on safety? If the fertilizer division were a separate firm, how much would it choose to spend on safety? In each case, assume that the objective is to maximize the value of the firm.*

d. *Now, recognizing the optimal choices of safety, what is the gain to Associated shareholders from selling the fertilizer division?*

ANSWER

Part a. Total value of the firm $= 700 + 300 - (0.3)(900) = 730$

Part b. Separate value of fertilizer division $= 300 - (0.3)(300) = 210$

Shareholders can keep the firm intact, in which case their equity is worth 730. Or they can sell off the fertilizer division for 210 and retain Division 1, which has value of 700, making a total value of 910. The gain to shareholders is 180 from the spin-off.

Part c. In order to calculate the optimal choice of safety, we will need a little calculus. The sequence is to show the profit of the firm and how this is related to choice of safety. We will then choose the profit-maximizing level of safety by taking the derivative of profit with respect to safety and setting this to zero to obtain a maximum.

For the combined firm, the value, V, is the value of the two divisions, 700 and 300, minus the expected liability that can be paid in full,

900(0.3)/(1 + s), minus the actual expenditure on safety, s. Notice that the expected liability depends on the choice of safety.

$$V = 700 + 300 - 900(0.3)/(1 + s) - s = 1000 - \frac{270}{1 + s} - s$$

The value-maximizing level of safety is calculated by setting the derivative to zero:[3]

$$dV/ds = \frac{270}{(1 + s)^2} - 1 = 0$$

which gives s = 15.43

For the fertilizer division as a standalone, the maximum that can be paid in a liability settlement is 300. The expected liability is 300(0.3)/(1 + s) and the value is:

$$V = 300 - \frac{300(0.3)}{1 + s} - s$$

$$MAX\ profit \quad dV/ds = \frac{90}{(1 + s)^2} - 1 = 0$$

which gives s = 8.48

Because the standalone fertilizer division can pay damages only up to 300, its incentive to reduce expected loss through investment in safety is tempered. The optimal of safety for the firm is 8.48, compared with the investment of 15.43 that would be optimal if the firm were sufficiently capitalized to meet the full liability.

> *Part d. We can now recalculate the value for shareholders with and without the spin-off, but now recognizing that the optimal choice of safety will be 15.43 without the spin-off and 8.48 with a separate fertilizer division.*

Value before spin-off

$$700 + 300 - \frac{900(0.3)}{1 + 15.43} - 15.43 = 968.14$$

---

3. Note the following derivative:

$$\text{If } y = \frac{a}{1 + x}: \text{ then } \frac{dy}{dx} = \frac{-a}{(1 + x)^2}$$

Value after spin-off

value of division 1 + value of division 2

$$\{700\} + \left\{\frac{300 - 300(0.3)}{1 + 8.48} - 8.48\right\} \quad = 982.03$$

GAIN 13.89

Notice that the gain in value was 180 if safety was fixed. But when safety choices can be made according to the organization structure, the gain from spin-off is reduced to a modest 13.89. Why the big difference? Well, without the spin-off, Associated is fully responsible for the full loss if it occurs. However, it is able to reduce the expected liability very considerably by choosing a high level of safety and reducing the probability of that liability considerably. This means that keeping Division 2 inside the firm is not as bad as first appeared. With the spin-off the incentive to invest in safety is much reduced, and while the firm can only pay up to 300, the probability of this payment is relatively high because of the low investment in safety. While there is still a gain from spin-off, it is much smaller than at first appeared.

We can now back off this conclusion a little. Precisely because the firm can be judgment-proof, there are regulatory mechanisms that can induce the firm to choose levels of safety that come close to the social optimum. For example, the firm might be subject to command-and-control-type regulation on safety issues. Government agencies are armed with a set of standards and are charged with enforcing compliance. An indirect mechanism that can have a similar effect on safety choices is compulsory insurance. We will address these regulatory mechanisms in the discussion of social policy presently.

Optimal Safety for Injury to Contracting Parties

For customers, employees, and other potential claimants who have a contractual relationship with the firm, the chosen level of safety can be reflected in the terms of the contract. This will be explored by returning to the example of Conglomerate.

To recall, Conglomerate has two divisions. Division 1 has a riskless value of 200 and Division 2 generates a cash flow from a product that has intrinsic product liability risk. The demand for this product reflects the basic quality of the product but also reflects any uncompensated losses. As before, we set the price equal to 12 minus the expected value of any uncompensated losses. At this price, some 50 units are sold at an average cost of 10. The product liability has the following distribution:

Loss	(Probability after Safety)
L_i	$P_i = p/(1 + s)$
0	$1 - 0.4/(1 + s)$
50	$0.1/(1 + s)$
100	$0.1/(1 + s)$
150	$0.1/(1 + s)$
200	$0.1/(1 + s)$

Notice the change in the final column. The loss probability can be reduced from its original level, p (as shown in the earlier example), by investing s dollars in safety. The redefined loss probability is P_i for any level of safety investment, s. Now consider what the firm would invest in safety if Divisions 1 and 2 are kept within the corporate umbrella. To do this, first note that the expected compensation to be paid is:

$$\frac{\Sigma p}{1 + s} (L) = 50 \frac{0.1}{1 + s} + 100 \frac{0.1}{1 + s} + 150 \frac{0.1}{1 + 2 + s}$$
$$+ 200 \frac{0.1}{1 + s} = \frac{50}{1 + s}.$$

The firm has sufficient net worth that it will not default. Because all losses can be compensated, the value of the joint firm is:

200	*profits of Division 1*
+600	*revenue of Division 2 (i.e., 50 units sold at a price of 12)*
− 0	*expected value of uncompensated losses*
−500	*costs of Division 2 (i.e., 50 units at average production cost of 10)*
−50/(1 + s)	*expected compensation payment*
−s	*the cost of safety*
TOTAL $V = 300 - 50/(1 + s) - s$	

Using the same technique as in Associated to maximize the value by choosing s, we set the derivative to zero:

$$\frac{50}{(1 + s)^2} - 1 = 0 \qquad so \qquad s = 6.07$$

The joint firm would commit to a total investment of 6.07 in safety.

Now suppose that Division 2 were a standalone firm with net worth of 100. The firm would never pay for losses over 100. Expected paid losses are:

$\Sigma p_i/(1 + s)$ (MIN of L_i or 100)

$$= 50 \frac{0.1}{1 + s} + 100 \frac{0.1}{1 + s} + 100 \frac{0.1}{1 + s} + 100 \frac{0.1}{1 + s}$$

$$= \frac{35}{1 + s}$$

But expected losses to customers are 50/(1 + s). Thus, the expected value of uncompensated losses is 50(1 + s) − 35/(1 + s) = 15/(1 + s). Noting that the demand for Division 2's product is reduced by the expected value of uncompensated losses, we can specify the value of the standalone as:

	600	basic revenue of Division 2 (i.e., 50 units sold at a price of 12)
	−15/(1 + s)	reduction in revenue for expected uncompensated losses
	−500	costs of Division 2 (i.e., 50 units at average production cost of 10)
	−35/(1 + s)	expected compensation payment
TOTAL	V = 100 − 50(1 + s) − s	

and the derivative is:

$$\frac{50}{(1 + s)^2} - 1 = 0 \qquad so \qquad s = 6.07$$

The standalone will commit exactly the same investment in safety as the combined firm. The reasoning parallels that for the decision to spin off. Because customers are contracting with the firm ex ante, the demand for the product will reflect any change in the compensation to be paid. If customers are fully informed (both about product risks and about the financial condition of the firm), then the limited net worth firm will have a dual incentive to invest in safety:

1. *To reduce the expected value of compensated damages*
2. *To boost demand by reducing the expected value of uncompensated damages*

The last example does depend on consumers being informed. The requirement is not that all customers have perfect information, but that information about the product risk and the firm's financial condition is reflected in prices.

IMPLICATIONS FOR SOCIAL POLICY

Welfare Implications of Limited Liability with Contracting Parties and Full Information

The preceding analysis shows that with full information and contracting parties, the decision to use limited liability to constrain liability payment will be reflected in the price paid by customers (or the wage paid to employees). Let us return to the case of Conglomerate to illustrate the effects and examine the welfare implications for the various parties. For the moment, consider the Conglomerate case with safety fixed and where injuries can occur to customers. When Division 2 was within the organizational umbrella, this firm secured revenues of 600 (selling 50 units at a unit price of 12), but when this division was spun off, its revenue fell to 585 (selling 50 units at a price of 11.7). The difference in price reflected the change in the expected liability payments that would be made to injured customers; this expectation fell from 50 to 35, revealing an expected uncompensated loss for consumers of 15 due to the very limited net worth of the standalone Division 2. Thus, the price difference of 0.3 per unit reflected the loss to consumers from being unable to recover damages in full. Who has gained and who has lost from the spin-off?

First, consider Conglomerated. As we showed in the example, Conglomerated should be indifferent between spinning off Division 2 and keeping it. If Division 2 is kept, the total value to shareholders is 200 for Division 1 and 100 minus an expected liability of 50 for Division 2, giving a total of 250. If Division 1 is spun off, the total value is 200 for Division 1 plus an expected 50 from the sale of Division 2. This 50 is the value of revenues, 585, minus costs, 500, minus an expected liability of 35. Either way, shareholders have value of 250 and, absent any transactions costs, receive no gain from the spin-off.

What about consumers? In expected value terms, they too should be indifferent. Without the spin-off, they paid a total of 600 (price of 12 per unit) for a product which included expected compensation of 50 for future injury. After spin-off they pay a total of 585 (11.7 per unit), which includes expected compensation of 35. In expected values, it is a wash. But what if consumers are risk-averse? At first sight, it seems that consumers are worse off from the separation of Division 2. When the product is sold by Conglomerate, they have effective insurance for all future injury from product defects. The expected value of this "insurance" is 50. But with the spin-off, the product risk is only insured to the value of 35 and the remaining 15 is self-insured. If the consumer is risk-averse, it seems that this forced self-insurance must make her worse off. But this analysis ignores the possibility of consumers insuring this risk on a first party insurance policy. There is a vital insurance market in which people can insure for accidental injuries and diseases. The consumers could simply buy policies to cover the uncompensated product risk of 15, and if the market were competitive, the price would be 15. Thus, with the spin-off, the risk-averse consumers would pay 585 for the product and 15 for the residual insurance and would have exactly the same coverage for injury as when the product was sold directly by Conglomerate. Thus, with a first party insurance market, consumers should be indifferent as to whether Division 2 is spun off or not. Thus, our preliminary conclusion is that there is no welfare implication to the spin-off.

A further look at consumer preferences and at transaction costs will suggest that there is a possible efficiency *gain* from the spin-off. First, consider transaction costs. With full product liability, there are two main types of transaction costs. The first is legal fees. The mechanism for compensating injured consumers is the civil law system. Injured parties bring suit against producers, each with legal representation, and some of the cases ultimately go to trial. Fees are likely to be high. Contingent fees by plaintiff's law-yers are typically 30% or higher, to which must be added defense legal fees. Total legal costs consume a large portion of the amount paid by defendants in discharge of these claims; in other words, lawyers probably receive an amount not very different from what the injured claimants receive. On top of these costs, producers usually try to avoid the risk associated with product liability by insurance, and third party insurance has its own transaction costs, including insurers' expenses and agency and brokerage commis-sions. In total, the costs associated with distributing compensation to injured consumers by means of the civil law system are very high.

If compensation is made by consumers purchasing first party insurance on their own account, the principle transaction cost is that of providing the insurance; that is, insurer expenses and agents' commissions. One would expect these costs to be lower by far than the costs of product liability. The transaction costs of first party insurance are typically paid by consumers within the premium. The transaction costs of product liability will be shared between consumers (who pay contingent fees from awards) and producers (who pay their own defense costs and the third party insurance charges).[4] Product prices will tend to reflect these costs if the product market is competitive. Regardless of who bears these costs, the lower transaction costs associated with first party insurance suggest that there is an efficiency gain to be shared be-tween consumers and producers from a full substitution of first party insurance for product liability. But spinning off is only a partial substitution. Limited net worth will constrain damage pay-ments, not typically avoid them (unless net worth is close to zero). Thus, the spin-off will lead to some duplication of compensation systems, both product liability and first party insurance. The issue of overall efficiency gain depends on whether there is some dou-bling up of the fixed costs associated with operating two systems and how this compares with the partial replacement of product liability with a lower-cost first party system. This issue can be illustrated quite simply. Suppose that X are to be transferred to

---

4. Though one would expect that anticipated liability costs would be reflected in the
   product price.

injured parties. The transaction costs of doing this, $C_P(X)$, by product liability are:

Cost with product liability $C_P(X) = F_P + V_P(X)$

where F_P is the fixed cost associated with product liability and V_P is a variable cost. Similarly, the transaction costs of transferring the same amount by first party insurance, $C_I(X)$, is:

Cost with insurance $\quad C_I(X) = F_I + V_I(X)$

Evidence seems to suggest that $C_I(X) < C_P(X)$. But the issue with some duplication is whether a transfer of K dollars from product liability to first party insurance results in an efficiency gain.

$$C_P(X - K) + C_I(K) = F_P + V_P(X - K) + F_I + V_I(K) < C_P(X)$$

Casual inspection will show that this inequality does not necessarily hold, especially if fixed costs are high relative to variable costs.

    We cannot be sure that a partial substitution of first party insurance for product liability will be an efficiency gain even if the latter is a more efficient system.[5] But a second argument does suggest an efficiency gain from spinning off. With either system there are transaction costs from providing consumers with compensation for accidents. In product liability the consumer has no choice but to fully insure against product injuries by paying up front for this protection in the product price and then having access to product liability protection should an accident arise. However, we know from economic theory that even if people are risk-averse, full insurance is not optimal when there is a premium loading. Thus, product liability (which involves a very large transaction costs) forces people to overinsure relative to their risk preferences. Lowering the amount of product liability gives consumers a choice in whether they wish to supplement their product liability protection with first party insurance. They can pay an explicit premium for explicit first party insurance. This will enable consumers to address risk–return preferences explicitly.

    The indirect effect of limiting liability lies in how it might change the incentives for the firm to invest in safety. However,

---

5. Though the example suggests that a *full* substitution of first party insurance for product liability would be more efficient in terms of transaction costs.

under the assumptions given here, the firm still has as strong incentives to make the product safe as shown in the previous section. The main difference made by limiting liability is that the producer's payback from investing in safety comes partly in terms of its effect on the product demand (rather than wholly as a reduction in expected liability payments). But a qualification can be made now that transaction costs have been addressed. Suppose, as argued above, that the transaction costs are particularly high for product liability and that the expected value of these costs increases as the expected liability cost increases. The payback from saving $1 in expected payments to injured parties will be accompanied by a saving of $T in transaction cost making a total saving of $(1 + T). Enhancing the payback from safety investment in this way can increase the investment in safety to levels that are too high from a social cost benefit view. Shifting to a compensation structure with lower transaction costs will tend to minimize this distorting tendency to over-invest in safety.

Welfare Implications of Limited Liability with Noncontracting Parties and/or Incomplete Information

When contracting parties do not have access to information on the risks of products or employment, or on the financial condition of the firm, a strategy of constraining future damage payments by limiting net worth will create a wealth transfer from accident victims to the firm. Similarly, if the parties at risk do not have a contractual relationship with the firm, the use of the limited liability strategy can create wealth for the shareholders at the expense of third parties. This can give rise to a "lemons" problem.[6] The capital of firms, and their ability meet large damage settlements, differ. Moreover, the safety of products varies. If consumers are unable to track which firms are adequately capitalized and do

---

6. The name "lemons" comes from the used car market. If buyers do not know the quality of used cars, but sellers do, buyers may assume that all cars offered for sale are average and prices would reflect this quality. If this were true, sellers with better than average cars would get a poor price (relative to the car's quality) and sellers with "lemons" would get a great price. Thus, the cars offered for sale would be disproportionately of poor quality. Thus, the lack of consumer information would largely close down the market for quality used cars. See Ackerloff (1970).

not know which products are safe, they may show a general suspicion of all firms and products. They may assume that all firms have average capitalization and all products are of average quality. Prices will thereby reflect average capitalization and product quality. Because firms with higher capitalization and safer products will not be rewarded by higher demand, they will have an incentive to reduce capital and produce cheaper, riskier products. Thus, there will be a general erosion of the financial backing for product liability and a general decline in product quality. This represents an efficiency loss for the economy as a whole unless firms find some credible way of signaling their product quality and capitalization.

Absent such signaling, there may be a case for regulation. For example, the case for environmental health and safety laws seems compelling because the absence of a contractual relationship denies those at risk the means to influence producer behavior. In contrast, bargaining between employers and workers (and/or unions) can produce optimal safety, and the efficiency case for mandated regulation rests on information problems or monopolistic imperfections. Similar arguments apply to product safety. However we will conclude this chapter by looking at another regulatory mechanism that addresses directly the problems of limited liability.

Compulsory Insurance

Compulsory insurance is often used to internalize a liability cost *ex ante*, especially where the potential victims are contractually unrelated. The most common example of this is automobile liability, for which the states have enacted various compulsory insurance or financial responsibility laws. The fear is that the injured motorist might have a valid tort claim against another, but the claim is worthless because the offending motorist does not have the money to pay. Accordingly, the states have required motorists to demonstrate financial responsibility, most commonly by showing evidence of a minimum amount of third party insurance. Other financial responsibility, or compulsory insurance, laws have been enacted covering the transport of hazardous materials, including the shipping of oil around the coastline, and the operation of nuclear power plants and satellites.

To show the effects of such laws the example of Associated will be revisited.

To recall, Associated Industries has two divisions. Division 1 generates a riskless income stream that has a net worth (net present value) of 700. Division 2 makes fertilizers and generates an income stream with a net worth of 300 absent any possible pollution liabilities. However, Division 2 has a 0.3/(1 + s) chance of a pollution accident that could cost a total of 900. The potential victims are third parties.

Associated is compelled to purchase insurance for the full liability of 900. To see what happens in terms of a possible spin-off, and in terms of safety incentives, requires making some assumptions about the setting of premiums by the insurer. To start, let us assume that the insurer can and does monitor the firm's chosen level of safety, s, and this is reflected in the premium. Also, the premium is simply the expected value of loss, 0.3(900)/(1 + s). In this case the optimal level of safety can be solved by maximizing the value of the firm by an appropriate choice of s. Now firm value is the present value of cash flows minus the premium.

$$\text{Value of firm with Division 2} \quad V = 700 + 300 - \frac{900(0.3)}{1 + s} - s$$

$$\text{Value of standalone Division 2} \quad V = 300 - \frac{900(0.3)}{1 + s} - s$$

It should be immediately apparent that the optimal choice of s is not affected by the spin-off decision. As calculated in the original example, optimal s is 15.43. Consequently, the value available to shareholders by keeping the firm intact, or by spinning off Division 2, should be zero

$$\text{Value before spin-off} \quad 700 + 300 - \frac{900(0.3)}{1 + 15.43} - 15.43 = 968.14$$

Value after spin-off

$$\text{value of division 1 + value of division 2}$$

$$700 + 300 - \frac{900(0.3)}{1 + 15.43} - 15.43 = 968.14$$

Gain zero

The reason there is no gain in value from the spin-off is that the firm does not avoid its full obligation to compensate injured third parties ex ante. *Either way, it pays an insurance premium based on the full expected value of damages.*

Now assume that the insurance premium is insensitive to the level of s. *This may be the case if the insurer is unable to monitor safety. In this case the premium may be treated as a fixed constant, P. Accordingly, there is no incentive to invest in safety (while Associated pays the cost of safety, the insurer reaps all the benefit in terms of reduced claim payments). Thus, there would be underinvestment in safety. However, there would still be no gain from the spin-off, since the premium is unaffected. If the insurer is unable to monitor s directly, there are still mechanisms to induce appropriate investment in safety. A common device for commercial liability insurance is to relate premiums to past loss experience.*

It is of interest that compulsory insurance laws typically do not require insurance of liability between parties who are closely contractually related. Unless there is a significant information asymmetry, it will be difficult to rationalize such laws. The freedom to engage in a contractual relationship in which net worth is limited permits parties to seek mutually beneficial risk sharing solutions that are more efficient than those mandated by product and employment liability laws.

CONCLUSION

Use of limited liability as a risk management tool is clearly a difficult issue. At a purely objective level, limiting net worth does have several material risk management implications. If there is a risk of liability to noncontracting parties, limiting liability will truncate the value of liability, and this will be reflected prospectively in the expected value of loss. In turn, this will reduce the incentive to invest in safety and reduce, though not necessarily eliminate, the need for liability insurance. These risk management strategies do raise concerns of social policy. Some financial responsibility laws do require those engaged in certain high-risk activities to show evidence of insurance or other financial capability to respond to liability loss. Moreover, the tendency to underinvest in safety provides a rationale for regulations controlling safety for the public.

But where the potential victims have a contractual relationship with the firm, the risk management implications are quite different. First, there is little to be gained by spinning off risky operations into new firms with little capital. Because customers of employees can estimate the risk, it will be reflected *ex ante* in wage rates and product prices. Firms will end up paying the full expected cost of injuries, regardless of their capitalization, either in up-front contract prices or in after the fact compensation. Nor is there likely to be underinvestment in safety. Given price sensitivity, low capital firms have an incentive to make products safer because this will have a positive effect on demand, and high capital firms have similar incentives because safety will reduce expected compensation.

These arguments have social policy implications. The first is that when potential victims have little information about risk or no contractual relationship with the firm, use of limited liability transfers wealth from the victims to the firm and exposes them to unnecessarily high risk. Policies such as product liability laws, financial responsibility laws, and health and safety laws may be necessary to control these externalities. But with contractual relationships and access to information, the use of limited liability does not harm customers and workers and the case for protective laws is weak. Firms will voluntarily invest in safety to secure demand. Moreover, the very high transaction costs with product liability, together with its tendency to overcompensate victims relative to their risk preferences, make it an inefficient compensation tool.

REFERENCES

Ackerloff, George. 1970. "The Market for Lemons: Quantitative Uncertainty and the Market Mechanism" *Quarterly Journal of Economics* 488–500.

Banerjee, Anindya, and Timothy Besley. 1990. "Moral Hazard, Limited Liability and Taxation: A Principal–Agent Model." *Oxford Economic Papers* 42:46–60.

Butler, Ann, and Neil A. Doherty. 1991. "Torts and Orbits." *American Economic Review* 81(2):46–49.

DeFusco, Richard, Paul Shoemaker, and Nancy Stara. 1996. "Controlling the Moral Hazard Created by Limited Liability." *Journal of Applied Business Research* 12:9–19.

Endres, Alfred, and Andreas Ludeke. 1998. "Limited Liability and Imperfect Information: On the Existence of Safety Equilibria under Products Liability Law." *European Journal of Law and Economics* 5:153–65.

Garven, James R. 1992. "An Exposition of the Implications of Limited Liability and Asymmetric Taxes for Property-Liability Insurance." *Journal of Risk and Insurance* 59:34–56.

Gollier, Christian, Pierre-Francis Koelh, and Jean-Charles Rochet. 1997. "Risk Taking Behavior with Limited Liability and Risk Aversion." *Journal of Risk and Insurance* 64:347–70.

Jost, Peter-J, 1996. "Limited Liability and the Requirement to Purchase Insurance." *International Review of Law and Economics* 16:259–76.

Huberman, Gur, David Mayers, and Clifford W. Smith Jr. 1982. "Optimal Insurance Policy Indemnity Schedules" *Bell Journal of Economics* 13:415–26.

Laffont, Jean-Jacques. 1995. "Regulation, Moral Hazard and Insurance of Environmental Risks." *Journal of Public Economics* 58:319–36.

Lawarree, Jacques P., and Marc A. Van Audenrode. 1996. "Optimal Contract, Imperfect Output Observation and Limited Liability." *Journal of Economic Theory* 71:514–31.

McMinn, Richard D., and Patrick L. Brockett. 1995. "Corporate Spin Offs as a Value Enhancing Technique when Faced with Legal Liability." *Insurance Mathematics and Economics* 16:63–68.

McMinn, Richard D., and Li-Ming Han. 1990. "Limited Liability, Corporate Value and the Demand for Liability Insurance." *Journal of Risk and Insurance* 57:581–607.

Park, Eun-Soo. 1995. "Incentive Contracting under Limited Liability." *Journal of Economics and Management Strategy* 4:477–90.

Posey, Lisa Lipowski. 1993. "Limited Liability and Incentives when Firms Can Inflict Damage Greater than Net Worth." *International Review of Law and Economics* 13:325–30.

Ringleb, Al H., and Steven N. Wiggins. 1990. "Liability and Large-Scale, Long-Term Hazards." *Journal of Political Economy* 98:574–95.

Shavell, Steven. 1982. "On Liability and Insurance." *Bell Journal of Economics* 13:120–32.

———. 1986. "The Judgment Proof Problem." *International Review of Law and Economics* 6:45–58.

Suen, Wing. 1995. "Risk Avoidance under Limited Liability." *Journal of Economic Theory* 65:627–34.

CHAPTER 16

A Case Study: The Securitization of Catastrophe Risk

An area in which risk management innovation has been particularly dramatic is the hedging and securitization of natural catastrophe risk. The insurance of catastrophe (cat) risk has always been problematic because insurers cannot easily diversify the risk they assume from their policyholders. With automobile or life insurance, losses arise randomly and independently across the population; in contrast, natural hazards affect a large number of policies at the same time. The insurer may go years without any significant claims, and then a single event can write off years of income. To protect against this nondiversifiable risk, insurers have traditionally used the reinsurance market to hedge. Reinsurers insure the insurers and typically operate on a wide geographical scale. Reinsurers can spread their exposure over many insurers and many regions and thus achieve the diversification not available to a more concentrated primary insurer.

Reinsurance seemed to work fairly well for natural hazard risk until the late 1980s and early 1990s, when a number of abnormally large losses shook the industry. Earthquakes such as Loma Prieta, Northridge, and Kobe had a big impact on insurers, as did hurricanes such as Iniki and Andrew. These events triggered a series of responses. First, insurers' surplus was reduced and their ability to write new business was compromised. The losses also affected reinsurer capacity, and reinsurance became scarce and expensive. There was a general realization that previous estimates of the financial impact of such events were too low. Boosted by the increasing use of catastrophe models, estimated loss exposures were generally revised upwards and premiums (primary and reinsurance) were increased. From the other side of the market, public awareness of the impact of disasters was awakened and demand increased. Faced with both a reduction in market supply and an increase in demand, insurers and reinsurers scrambled for ways to expand their supply. The market responded in two ways. First came a wave of new innovations in which insurers sought hedging instruments or innovative forms of post-loss recapitalization directly from investors. Secondly, the capital market provided equity capital directly to existing and startup reinsurers (mainly in Bermuda) in search of high rates of return.

These innovations were stimulated by the shortage of traditional reinsurance, but their growth seems to have been limited by the restoration of much of that reinsurance capacity. This observation could lead to the conclusions that the innovations have been a stopgap response to unusual market circumstances and that the market will return to its reinsurance norm. A counterargument that is often given is that the new instruments are here to stay because the capital market provides a much larger and wider pool in which to diversify insurer catastrophe risk. The net worth of the U.S. property liability insurance industry is approaching $300 billion, whereas U.S. capital markets represent an asset base of $10–$20 trillion. Surely, catastrophe risk can be spread much more effectively in this much wider market. But this argument misses the point that catastrophe risk can be spread effectively through the capital market simply by investors buying reinsurers' equity.

A more convincing argument for the permanence of the new cat instruments is that they are varied and flexible. The variety of instruments (including reinsurance) permits insurers to derive risk management strategies appropriate to their particular needs, and new instruments can be designed to address particular risk management costs. Consider moral hazard. Once protected by reinsurance, insurers may be inclined to be less than careful in underwriting insurance for people in high-risk locations and overly generous in settling claims with policyholders because this buys goodwill and avoids costly disputes. This incentive issue may be particularly severe with cat reinsurance because the event will probably overwhelm the insurer's resources for loss settlement. Reinsurers rely on monitoring, on the reputation of primary insurers, and on long-term relationships to prevent such abuse. Insurers succumbing to such temptations will find it difficult to secure future reinsurance protection. But such controls are constraining and costly. The new innovations include alternative controls against moral hazard, such as indexing the payout on the hedge to aggregate industry losses rather than to the losses of the hedging insurer. Another example of how innovation enhances flexibility relates to credit risk. The prospect of default from a cat reinsurer is real because the same cat event will probably give rise to claims on many of its reinsurance contracts. Some of the new instruments remove this credit risk by effectively collateralizing the reinsurer's liability. This can be done by forming a liability hedge.

Finally, because reinsurance is a risk transfer, the prospect of the parties agreeing on contract terms depends largely on whether they hold similar expectations on the loss distribution. If expectations differ, conventional contracts may not be closed. The many innovations have been possible because of an improvement in information. Not only is intensive modeling of catastrophe risk undertaken in support of most of the new instruments, but the information is generated by independent modeling firms and is available to all parties. But even if information does not meet this standard, there are risk sharing alternatives that can be designed to be mutually acceptable even when expectations differ.

This chapter is essentially a case study of the cat risk management. We will examine the major innovations and show how they are differently configured to address different risk management costs. We will start by looking at reinsurance. This is a conventional hedge instrument that is available to primary insurers to transfer part of their portfolio risk.

CATASTROPHE REINSURANCE

Simple diversification will not always remove risk from a primary insurer's portfolio. For example, liability insurance is subject to significant correlation because changes in liability rules can simultaneously affect all policies in an insurer' portfolio. Catastrophe insurance is subject to even more apparent correlation. The law of large numbers cannot be relied upon to remove relative risk. Reinsurance is the traditional hedging instrument available to primary insurers. However, its use does involve significant transaction costs which are now discussed.

Credit Risk[1]

Catastrophe hedging instruments face design choices that trade off various inefficiencies against each other. Reinsurance can be used to illustrate these trade-offs. First, there is credit risk: the risk that the reinsurer will be unable to pay its obligation to the primary firm. The recent $17 billion Andrew losses and the $12 billion Northridge losses revealed some chinks in the insurance industry's armor and estimates of a repeat of the 1906 San Francisco earthquake have forecast widespread insolvencies amongst primary firms (Doherty et al., 1991). Such insolvencies would be transmitted to reinsurers. Indeed, the defaults could be disproportionately large in the reinsurance industry. A common way in which an insurer can off-load risk to a reinsurer is with a "stop loss" (i.e., the contract contains a deductible with the reinsurer paying only the excess above the deductible). Payoffs from such plans occur only when losses penetrate the right tail of the loss distribution. For such payoffs the coefficient of variation is very high and consequently large catastrophes would probably cause widespread insolvencies. Initial estimates of potential industry payouts for large catastrophes (Cummins and Doherty, 1996) support this conclusion, with the number of insolvencies rising disproportionately with the size of the catastrophic loss.

Basis Risk

Basis risk is the risk that the payout on a hedge contract will not match the loss suffered. If an individual insures fully her home, then any loss, L, is matched by a payment, I, from the insurer. The

---

1. An aspect of credit risk that is not developed in this work is liability risk. Litigation does arise between primary insurers and reinsurers over contract wording or the conduct of the parties. The prospect of nondelivery on a reinsurance contract and the costs of enforcing legal claims against reinsurers are significant costs. The new instruments that are discussed later can be expected to face similar liability risk. For example, one can expect cases in which investors maintain that the dimensions of risk were not properly represented or that the issuer did not act appropriately to control the level of risk.

payment I is exactly equal to L. More formally, there is a perfect negative correlation between the insured's loss and the insurer's payout. This would be a situation in which there is no basis risk; the payout of the insurer I is exactly equal to L, whatever L may be. Now suppose that the insurance contact was written as follows. If your house is damaged by a storm, the insurer will pay you the average of the damage suffered to your house and the house next door, that is, $I = (L_1 + L_2)/2$ where the subscripts 1 and 2 refer to your loss and your neighbor's loss. If, by chance, both houses are damaged to the same extent, you will receive exactly the right amount of compensation for your loss. But this would be most unlikely. Probably the houses would be damaged to a different extent. If your house receives more (less) damage than your neighbor's, then you will be under (over) compensated. The risk that your compensation, I, will not match your loss, L_1, is the basis risk. In this case we could put a measure on the basis risk by looking at the correlation between your loss, L_1, and the average of your and your neighbor's loss, $(L_1 + L_2)/2$, which we will call r_{L1}. If the house could always be guaranteed to be damaged to the same extent, there would be no basis risk and r_{L1} would be 1. The lower the relationship between your loss and your neighbor's, the lower r_{L1} and the higher the basis risk. So let us do one last adjustment. We will measure basis risk as:

$$\text{Basis risk} \quad b = 1 - r_{L1}$$

as this will lead to a positive relationship. The higher b is, the lower the basis risk (because r_{1P} is lower). This measure will be used later when we come back to basis risk and discuss its relationship with moral hazard.

   While credit risk is present with reinsurance, basis risk is resolved. Reinsurance payoffs are geared to losses sustained by the primary insurer. Contracts usually cover the primary firm's portfolio losses on designated lines of business (treaty reinsurance) or specific primary policies (facultative reinsurance). Moreover, policies share risk between primary insurer and reinsurer according to linear or nonlinear formulas. Thus, while the primary firm will retain some risk, there is no mismatch between the asset on which the reinsurance payoff is defined and the asset to be hedged. In other words, there is no basis risk. But, it is possible to imagine a reinsurance contract with basis risk. If an insurer purchased a reinsurance contract with a payoff structured on the industry losses, rather than on the primary firm's own losses, there would be basis risk. The extent of basis risk would depend on the correlation between industry and firm losses; the lower the correlation, the higher the basis risk. The discussion of basis risk is important because it forms an important design element in structuring new hedges and can be used to mitigate another inefficiency, moral hazard.

Moral Hazard

Moral hazard is the lip side of basis risk. Moral hazard arises with all insurance policies, as discussed in Chapter 3. With reinsurance contracts, moral hazard can take two generic forms: *ex ante* and *ex post* moral hazard. *Ex ante* moral hazard arises when, due to reinsurance protection, the primary insurer fails to take actions to reduce future insurance claims or takes actions that increase claims. This occurs because the reinsurer cannot monitor the primary continuously and condition the reinsurance contract on the primary's behavior. Thus, the primary firm may be lax in its underwriting procedures, pay inadequate attention to spread of risk, or fail to provide adequate risk audits for potential new policies.

Naturally, the reinsurer will anticipate this behavior and some level of monitoring will take place. But monitoring is costly and the combination of the costs of monitoring and the excess losses suffered due to inadequate underwriting provides a measure of the costs of moral hazard. These costs are substantial. Industry sources frequently put the transaction cost of reinsurance at 20% of premiums or higher. These direct costs take the form of commissions and premium loading. In addition, many reinsurance relationships are implicitly long-term and experience-rated to compensate for costly monitoring. These temporal relationships constrain the parties and contribute to the costs of moral hazard. It may be noticed that moral hazard arises from the quality of the hedge; that is, from the absence of basis risk. Consequently, the structuring of a catastrophe hedge provides the opportunity for trading off moral hazard and basis risk.

Ex post moral hazard arises when the loss settlement practices of the insurer are relaxed due to reinsurance. This is a particular problem for catastrophic losses. The loss settlement capacity of any insurer (and of the industry) is reasonably geared to the normal levels of loss frequency. When an event such as Hurricane

Andrew arises, primary firms simply do not have the capacity to inspect and negotiate claims settlements thoroughly. And without thorough claim investigation it is difficult to prevent the build-up of claims (policyholders including uninsured damage in the claim or exaggerating the size of the loss) or outright fraud on the part of policyholders. However, the incentive for the primary insurer to control its claims will be relaxed if it has reinsurance protection. The primary may be able to avoid the transaction costs of settling claims, and even buy some goodwill with its policyholders by making generous settlements with policyholders and passing the costs of excess settlements to its reinsurer. Also, insurers are often pressured by regulators to be prompt and generous in settling losses in a highly publicized catastrophe. When protected by re-insurance, the primary insurer can achieve regulatory goodwill and pass the cost to the reinsurers.

Of course, there are constraints on this type of behavior. For moderate losses the primary firm may well consider its reputation in the reinsurance market before engaging in such opportunistic behavior. Primary insurers will seek future reinsurance protection, and a history of moral hazard will hardly stand them in good stead. But with severe catastrophes the normal constraints on such insurer moral hazard will be especially dulled. When insurers are facing financial stress, their reputation in returning to reinsurance markets in the future is unlikely to be so constraining.

A More Formal Look at Moral Hazard and Reinsurance

Let us look at moral hazard a little more formally. I will use a little calculus here, but if you are unfamiliar with this technique, bear with me and I will describe intuitively what is going on. The object is to see how moral hazard affects the design of reinsurance contracts and the structure of reinsurance markets. In particular, I wish to be able to show why reinsurance locks the parties together into long-term relationships and why these relationships appear so costly relative to hedging instruments traded on financial exchanges.

In regard to moral hazard the term "mitigation" will be used generally for those efforts and expenditures undertaken by the primary insurer to reduce its eventual loss payments. Mitigation can include efforts to improve underwriting, inspections of risks, controls against accumulation of risk, and various loss settlement practices aimed at avoiding excessive loss payouts to policyholders (such as post-loss inspections, adequate training and staffing of loss settlement personnel, remedial activity, and avoidance of use of excessive loss settlements as marketing devices).

To start, consider a very simple single-period valuation model of an insurer. At the beginning of the year the insurer contributes equity capital of E and receives premiums, P (net of expenses). The initial funds, $E + P$, are invested at a random rate of return, r_i, for one year. Claims, L (also random), are paid at the end of the year. The terminal value of the insurer's equity, T, is:

$$T = (E + P)(1 + r_i) - L \qquad (16.1)$$

Now add in reinsurance. At the beginning of the year the insurer pays an amount R, as a reinsurance premium. The policy assumed is a treaty stop loss policy that pays the insurer when losses on some underlying insurance portfolio, I (which may or may not be identical to the primary insurer's book of business) exceed a deductible (striking price), S. The payoff to the reinsurance can be represented as a call option, and we use the rotation $C(I; S)$. The term h is the hedge ratio, which may be interpreted here as the proportion of the underlying portfolio I above S that is reinsured. Naturally, the reinsurance premium, R, also depends on I and S (i.e., $R = R(I; S)$). In normal arrangements the reinsurance coverage is based on the ceding insurer's portfolio or some particular lines. There is no inherent basis risk other than that assumed by the ceding company by accepting a deductible. Thus, for reinsurance, we can consider I and L as identical. With other hedging instruments basis risk can be present and we will keep the distinct notation.

The final element is mitigation. The insurer is able to reduce the level of expected claims by spending an amount a on mitigation (better underwriting, loss control, loss adjustment, etc.). While mitigation is a direct cost to the insurer, losses will decline as more is spent on mitigation. The notation $L(a)$ is used to show that losses depend on the level of mitigation, and we assume the relationship is negative. The expected terminal value of equity now can be shown as:

$$E(T) = (E - P - R(I; S))(1 + E(R_i)) - E(L(a))$$
$$+ hC(I; S) - a \qquad (16.2)$$

Now consider that optimal choice of mitigation for the primary insurer.[2] The usual mathematical technique for solving this optimization problem involves calculus. For those familiar with this technique, I will show the solution. For the unfamiliar, I will show that the solution does follow one's intuition. Formally, the optimal level of mitigation for the insurer can be established from the first order condition:

$$\frac{\partial E(T)}{\partial a} = -\frac{\partial E(L(a))}{\partial a} - 1 + h \frac{\partial C}{\partial I} \frac{\partial I}{\partial L} \frac{\partial L}{\partial a} = 0 \qquad (16.3)$$

There are three effects that can be described in words.

+ The first term $(-\partial E(L(a))/\partial a)$ shows a gain to the insurer from mitigation: spending of an extra dollar on mitigation will reduce the primary's expected losses. The reduction of a liability is a gain to the insurer. This term is simply the expected value of the reduction in losses from the additional dollar spent on mitigation.
+ The second term (-1) shows that spending an extra dollar on mitigation is a direct cost of one dollar to the insurer. This is a loss to the insurer.
+ The third term $(h(\partial C/\partial I)(\partial I/\partial L)(\partial L/\partial a))$ shows the effect of additional mitigation (and therefore reduced expected claims for the primary) on the expected recovery under the reinsurance policy. This term picks up a negative effect of mitigation on the insurer. Increasing mitigation reduces expected losses and therefore reduces the amount the insurer can expect to recover from reinsurer.

If there were no reinsurance, the primary insurer would reap all the benefits of mitigation and the third term would drop out, leaving only the first two effects (and Equation (16.3) would be $-\partial E(L(a))/\partial a = 1$). This can be interpreted as follows. Without reinsurance, the primary insurer will balance the costs and benefits of mitigation. The insurer will spend an amount on mitigation until the additional dollar of expenditure on mitigation brings a

---

2. To stress the problem of moral hazard here I assume that the reinsurer cannot monitor the primary's mitigation, a, and therefore the premium, P, is not shown as sensitive to a. A potential solution to this problem is retrospective rating as shown in Chapter 3, but in this chapter we will address different responses to moral hazard.

reduction of one dollar in expected losses. Reinsurance disturbs this balance. With reinsurance, the third term of Equation (16.3) becomes important, and this will serve to reduce the primary's choice of mitigation. Any benefit to the primary in terms of reduced policyholder claims simply reduces the reinsurance recovery. The higher the deductible, the lower the choice of mitigation.

But this reduction in mitigation does not ultimately benefit the primary insurer. Because reinsurers will rationally anticipate this reduction in mitigation in the reinsurance premium, the primary will end up paying in advance for additional incurred losses.

Given that a moral hazard problem exists with reinsurance, how can it be solved? The generic moral hazard problem was tackled in Chapter 3. One solution is to use a deductible. If the reinsurance attaches at a higher value, the primary is fully liable for all smaller losses as well as for a fixed contribution to losses above the deductible. Having some "skin in the game" puts the primary insurer at risk and will provide an incentive to mitigate both prospectively and retrospectively. The second mechanism described in Chapter 3 is to make the terms under which future reinsurance is available conditional on previous reinsurance claims experience.[3] As reinsurance claims become more frequent and more severe, future reinsurance coverage becomes more restricted and more expensive. The rationale here is to bring the consequences of mitigation back to the primary insurer, at least in

---

3. Denote the primary insurer's profit as $\Pi_P = \Pi_P(R, L, S, h) - a$. This is assumed to be a concave function of Π_P to account for costs of bearing risk:

$$V_P = \int U\{\Pi_P(R, L, S, h)\}f(L; a)dL - a \qquad (a)$$

where $f(L; a)$ is the conditional probability of observing losses, L, given a mitigation level of a. The primary's optimal choice of a can now be represented by the following first order condition, which is called the "incentive constraint":

$$\int U\{\Pi_P(R, L, S, h)\}f_a(L; a)dL = 1 \qquad (b)$$

The problem is to minimize V_P subject to the incentive constraint and a second (participation) constraint to ensure that the primary will actually purchase the contract offered. The solution is well known: *the optimal reinsurance premium, R, is a nondecreasing function of the revealed loss, L* (see Kreps, 1990, ch. 16). The optimal design of the reinsurance contract is one with retrospective premiums. The adaptation of the standard one-period principal–agent problem to the design of reinsurance yields retrospective premiums. The single-period model has been extended to many periods (see Lambert, 1986).

a probabilistic manner. Thus, in mitigating to reduce expected losses, the insurer is helping to secure more, and cheaper, reinsurance in the future.

Reinsurers also can address moral hazard by increasing the resources devoted to monitoring the behavior of the ceding firms and conditioning the reinsurance coverage on this behavior. If reinsurers can monitor at low cost, it will be more efficient to do so than to impose risk on the primary through *ex post* rating. In practice, one would expect to see some monitoring and some experience rating. In this case the costs of moral hazard would be incurred partly in monitoring cost, partly in imposing risk on the primary through *ex post* rating, and, to the extent that these did not completely eliminate expropriatory behavior, partly through increased claims.

Do reinsurance contracts actually fit this old? Recent evidence (Doherty and Smetters, 1999) suggests that both experience rating and monitoring are used to encourage appropriate mitigation from the primary insurer. As the theory suggests, the use of these controls is more intensive the greater the proportion of the primary's portfolio that is reinsured. The results gain further credibility from theories of Riordan (1990) and Cremer (1993). These models suggest that contracts written between firms that are vertically integrated would favor monitoring over contractual incentives (such as retrospective and experience rating) to resolve moral hazard problems. In contrast, for contracts between unrelated firms, monitoring is more costly and moral hazard would tend to be redressed through contract incentives. The evidence of Doherty and Smetters does reveal this pattern for almost all lines of property casualty insurance.

The effectiveness of these controls for moral hazard is enhanced by the enduring nature of many reinsurance relationships. The reinsurer benefits from this arrangement by being able to spread the abnormal losses of a single year over time (poor claims experience against the reinsurer can be recovered in future premiums), and the primary insurer benefits by having the security of future reinsurance coverage. Thus, the primary insurer can define how much insurance coverage it can safely commit to its own policyholders. Within this long-term relationship there is a close alignment of the interests of the reinsurer and the primary insurer, and the reinsurer's interest in the primary bears some elements of an equity investment. The long-term arrangement is not usually formalized in a long-term unbreakable contract, and parties are free to dissolve the relationship if either is unsatisfied. But in perpetuating existing relationships, or establishing new ones, the reputation of the primary is important. Reputation, and with it the ability to secure attractive level and terms of future reinsurance coverage, provides a powerful restraint on moral hazard.

Long-term relationships allow implicit experience rating; future premiums can be related to past loss experience. A recent formal approach to establishing a multiyear relationship between premiums and claims is "finite reinsurance." Where experience rating sets premiums relative to claims, finite reinsurance reverses the direction: claims are limited by the amount of premium to be paid. Here, a multiyear "insurance" is arranged in which the amount of coverage is defined in relation to aggregated premiums. For example, the coverage limit in a three-year plan would normally be defined in relation to the sum of the three annual premiums. At a minimum, a plan limiting cover to the summed premium would be essentially a debt instrument (though there would be some limited insurance of timing risk). Plans vary in how much risk transfer is built on top of this debt base. By limiting the degree of risk transfer, the finite risk plan limits the degree of moral hazard.

THE DESIGN SPACE

Reinsurance has some credit risk because performance relies on the financial condition of the reinsurer. Reinsurance, by nature, does not have basis risk. But because it is an indemnity contract, reinsurance does face moral hazard. We will focus on these three properties in discussing new cat instruments. There may indeed be more design features, such as liquidity, regulative acceptance, and comprehensibility by insurers and investors. Our focus is not intended to underplay these features. Rather, it is simply to get us started in specifying design choices by concentrating on some of the more basic issues. Some other design goals may be overlaid.

Figure 16–1 shows the three main design criteria on three axes. Credit risk is on the vertical axis, with higher values indicating higher credit risk. Because reinsurance has an inherent credit risk problem, it is scored poorly on this criterion. Basis risk

F I G U R E   16–1

Design Properties

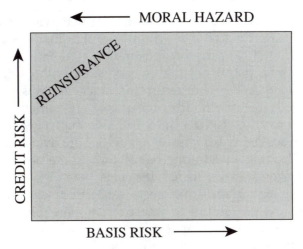

is shown on the lower horizontal axis, with risk increasing as we move to the right. By nature, reinsurance is an indemnity contract and is not subject to basis risk. Thus, reinsurance is shown to perform well on this axis. Moral hazard is shown on the upper horizontal axis, and this increases as we move from right to left. The reason it becomes possible to show basis risk and moral hazard in the left–right space is that there is a definite negative relationship between them: more (less) basis risk means less (more) moral hazard. The trade-off is picked up by showing these two criteria as acting in opposition to each other. Any point to the left of the diagram means less basis risk and therefore more moral hazard. Because reinsurance has little basis risk and therefore is subject to moral hazard, it is shown to the left. Thus, reinsurance occupies the top left corner of the diagram; it is an instrument with potentially high credit risk, low basis risk, and high moral hazard.

The design space represented in Figure 16–1 provides a guide to financial innovation. It is not clear whether any position in this space is universally superior to any other. As the new instruments are introduced, they will be seen to fit different niches in this design space.

CATASTROPHE HEDGE INSTRUMENTS

Catastrophe Options

New types of catastrophe instruments are often explained in terms of the need to provide direct access to capital markets to supplement the limited capacity of reinsurance markets. With it noted that catastrophe risk is not highly correlated with capital market returns, the required rate of return to attract capital is the risk-free rate. Current rates on line for reinsurance are sufficiently high to be able to beat the risk-free rate. But this explanation is incomplete. If attractive investment opportunities are available to investors from shorting catastrophe risk, why is there not an influx of capital into reinsurance firms? It seems that high rates on line support the high transaction costs associated with reinsurance rather than excess returns to reinsurance shareholders. Thus, if new instruments are to compete successfully with reinsurance and be attractive to investors, they must be designed to lower transaction costs. Moreover, because the dominant transaction cost is that due to moral hazard (excess losses, the additional costs of monitoring, and locking parties into long-term relationships), successful securitization of catastrophe risk requires more effective ways of dealing with moral hazard. Also important is the ability of new instruments to address credit risk.

With reinsurance, the source of the moral hazard was the absence of basis risk. This can be seen by the term $\partial I/\partial L$ in Equation (16.3) which is now reproduced:

$$\frac{\partial E(T)}{\partial a} = -\frac{\partial E(L(a))}{\partial a} - 1 + h \frac{\partial C}{\partial I} \frac{\partial I}{\partial L} \frac{\partial L}{\partial a} = 0 \qquad (16.3)$$

The expression $\partial I/\partial L$ in the third part of the equation picks up the impact of a change in the insurer's claims paid to its policyholders, L, on its reinsurance recovery. Because reinsurance is defined on the primary's loss, L, $I = L$ and $\partial I/\partial L = 1$. This means that there is no basis risk and the third term in Equation (16.3) operates to reduce the optimal level of mitigation. But now imagine a hedge instrument in which I is not the same as L but is only loosely correlated with L. This would reduce moral hazard because higher claims settlements by the primary to its policyholders would have only a weak effect on the recovery from the hedge. The weaker the relationship between L and I, the smaller will be

$\partial I / \partial L$ and the larger the basis risk. At the extreme the term $\partial I / \partial L$ would be close to zero and there would be no effective hedge in place, and no moral hazard. One of the major innovations in the new cat instruments is to define indices I to provide acceptable basis risk and low moral hazard.

Catastrophe options are traded on the Chicago Board of Trade. The basic structure of these contracts is similar to those of other options and, except for the difference in basis risk, resembles stop loss reinsurance. The CBOT contracts are defined on various industry (mostly quarterly) indices of property liability under-writing results. The indices are defined by region within the United States. A national index, regional indices (Western, Mid-western, Southeaster, Northeastern, and Eastern), and state indices (California, Florida, and Texas) exist. When index losses exceed the striking price, the contract pays the difference between the index value and the striking price. The basic instrument can be used to derive many trading strategies (spreads, strips, etc.) in much the same fashion as stock options.

The effects of hedging with catastrophe options can be presented in the same formula used for reinsurance.[4] The trading strategy shown is a long position in a call. In Equation (16.3) the term $R(I; S)$ can be reinterpreted as the price of the option. Here h is the number of contracts purchased and $C(I; S)$ is the payout on a standard contract on index, I, with strike price, S. However, because the insurer pays its own losses, L, but receives a payoff based on the chosen index, I, there is basis risk (L does not equal I). The size of the basis risk will vary. First, the insurer's own losses will contribute to the index, but for many insurers this will be modest. Secondly, to the extent that the primary has a portfolio similar to (different from) that of the other insurers comprising the index, the basis risk will be small (large). Indeed, one would expect the hedging demand for CBOT options to be strongest for insurers with representative portfolios.

---

4. Other hedging strategies can be derived. One that offers some continuity with tradi-tional reinsurance strategies is to buy a spread. This involves holding a call option with one striking price and selling another call with a higher striking price. The effect is to obtain a layer of hedge protection between a range of index losses. Apart from the fact that the loss is defined on the index, this arrangement is simi-lar to layered reinsurance arrangements.

The major benefit of defining the option on the index is that it controls moral hazard. The primary insurer that is able to practice *ex ante* or *ex post* mitigation will receive much of the benefit of that activity in the form of reduced claims. However, this benefit will not be offset by a reduction in the payoff to the option, except to the limited extent that the primary's reduced losses affect the index. The idea can be illustrated by a simple example. Suppose that an insurer has a portfolio that represents 5% of the market covered by the index and correspondingly wishes to buy a call option that pays 0.05 times the payoff on the amount by which industry losses exceed a striking price S. Because I is the sum of industry losses ($I \equiv \Sigma L_i$), spending of a_i on safety by insurer i will reduce the index at the rate $\partial L / \partial a_i$. But because the primary is hedging only 5% of changes in the index, the primary's payoff on its call position will be reduced only at the rate $(0.05)\partial L / \partial a_i$.[5] In contrast, spending on mitigation reduces the primary's own claims obligations to its policyholders at the full rate $\partial L / \partial a_i$. Thus, mitigation yields a large marginal net benefit to the primary ($0.95 \times \partial L / \partial a_i$).

Like reinsurance, catastrophe options face credit risk. Many financial instruments use "mark to market" to address credit risk. When the instrument is written on an underlying asset whose price evolves as a smooth process, mark to market offers considerable credit protection. This device prevents the build-up of large liabilities. However, the temporal path of catastrophe insurance liabilities is anything but smooth. With storms, the lead time is at most a few days. With earthquakes, the liability can change from zero to billions of dollars in seconds. Mark to market is of little use. Sellers of catastrophe bonds are required to maintain a margin account. However, this device offers only limited protection unless the account is maintained at a level equal to (or close to) the maximum possible loss. Thus, catastrophe options impose some credit

---

5. The same concepts can be described in the appropriate terminology. CBOT options are denominated in payment of $200 for every $100 million change in the index. Each $100 million in the index is referred to as a "point." The primary wishing to hedge for a 5% of the amount by which the index exceeded a chosen striking price would purchase 25,000 units. If the strike price were 400 and the actual index value turned out to be 450, the payoff on this position would be $(450 - 400) \times 200 \times 25,000 = \$250$ million. Notice that $250 million is exactly 5% of the amount by which industry losses ($45 billion) exceed the strike price ($40 billion).

risk. The CBOT options offer a second line of defense. The CBOT maintains a security fund. However, the scale of this fund is fairly small compared with the multi-billion-dollar liabilities that are plausible with these instruments. This is not to say that the credit risk is severe, only that it is potentially severe. The degree of credit risk depends on the spread of liability amongst investors who take short positions in these instruments. The point is that the structural design of this and other asset hedges introduces credit risk. As we shall see below, the structural design of the liability hedges avoids this problem.

Catastrophe Bonds

Debt forgiveness instruments go by several names, such as insurance-linked bonds, Act of God bonds, catastrophe bonds, and (anciently) bottomry. The idea is very old, dating to the medieval origins of insurance in Italy. A primitive arrangement was for merchants to fund ventures by borrowing to pay for the ship and/or cargo. However, in the event of the loss of ship or cargo, the debt would be forgiven. Thus, the lenders were "insuring" the vessel and its cargo. The idea has recently reappeared in insurance markets. Recently, insurers have announced bond issues that have forgiveness provisions in the event of catastrophic losses, the consideration being a higher interest rate. The generic design can allow for interest and/or principal forgiveness that is scaled to the size of the loss. Moreover, the forgiveness can be triggered either by catastrophic losses to the issuing firm or by catastrophic losses measured on some composite index of insurer losses or some parametric description of the catastrophic event.

The effects of hedging with cat bonds can be analyzed with Equation (16.4) below. To describe the cat bond we will engage in a little fiction. Suppose insurer issues debt with a face value D that must be repaid with interest at a rate r (later we will see that the insurer does not actually issue the bond; it is issued through a separate entity known as a "special purpose vehicle," SPV). However, the debt can be forgiven (here I illustrate with the principal being forgiven, not the interest) according to a loss index I; as the index I gets higher, the amount of the debt is progressively reduced or forgiven. The forgiveness is shown by the term $hC(I; S)$, which indicates that the cat bond is really a simple bond with an embedded call option, $C(I; S)$, written on the catastrophe loss index I with a trigger or striking price S. When I exceeds the trigger S, the amount of debt to be repaid is scaled back from $D(1 + r)$ to $D(1 + r) - hC(I; S)$. The term h is again the hedge ratio, which may be interpreted as the percentage of $I - S$ that is taken from the principal. The insurer's terminal equity with a cat bond is:

$$T = \{E + D\}(1 + E(r)) - E(L(a)) - D(1 + r) - hC(I; S) - a \tag{16.4}$$

The analysis of moral hazard is similar to that for reinsurance and cat options. Equation (16.5) below shows the condition for mitigation for the primary insurer, which is identical to Equation (16.3). The first term shows the effect of mitigation on the primary insurer's losses; the second term shows the increased marginal cost of mitigation; and the third term is the effect of reduced mitigation (and therefore increased losses) on the cat bond forgiveness.

$$\frac{\partial E(T)}{\partial a} = -\frac{\partial E(L(a))}{\partial a} - 1 + h \frac{\partial c}{\partial I} \frac{\partial I}{\partial L} \frac{\partial L}{\partial a} = 0 \tag{16.5}$$

The interpretation of Equation (16.5) depends on whether there is basis risk (i.e., whether i equals L). Consider that the cat bond is forgiven according to the primary's own catastrophic losses, $I = L$. This moral hazard effect is similar to that under reinsurance. If the cat bond is forgiven dollar for dollar against the primary's own catastrophe losses, the primary has little or no incentive to control those losses. Controlling losses simply increases the amount of debt that must be repaid (the first and third terms would cancel out). With no cat bond, the primary would have reaped all the benefit of mitigation and chosen a level of mitigation at which marginal benefit equaled marginal cost.

If the cat bond is forgiven on the basis of some industry index of catastrophe losses, $I \neq L$, the moral hazard is similar to that for the catastrophe option. Mitigation will only reduce the debt forgiveness to the extent of its share of the index. Thus, the primary contracting for forgiveness at the rate of 5% of the index (i.e., $5 of debt is forgiven for every $100 increase in industry losses) will reap a net benefit from mitigation equal to 95% of the reduction in its direct claims.

This analysis shows that cat bonds can be designed to achieve different balances between basis risk and moral hazard. Given freedom to select indices, the primary may well be able to identify some industry portfolio with similar exposure to its own. If it can, the basis risk from writing the cat bond on this index will be small and the moral hazard problem will be largely mitigated. If the primary's portfolio is not well represented by any industry loss index (i.e., its spread of business is unusual), then the hedging properties of an index based cat bond will be poor, even though moral hazard is addressed. In such circumstances a cat bond based on the primary's own losses may be preferable with other controls (e.g., monitoring) used to address the moral hazard.

Cat bonds avoid the credit risk to the issuer that is found with reinsurance or catastrophe options. Bondholders provide the hedge to the insurer by forgiving existing debt. Thus, the value of the hedge is independent of the bondholders' assets and the primary insurer has no risk of nondelivery on the hedge. In essence, the cat bond is similar to a reinsurance contract in which the reinsurer opens a margin account equal to the maximum expected loss. Moreover, the primary insurer has access to the margin account. This avoids all possibility of default to the primary.[6]

The typical structure for implementing this and other cat securitizations is to use a special purpose vehicle, SPV, to stand between the hedging insurer and the investors. The special purpose vehicle is a firm set up as a repository for the transaction. Figure 16–2 describes the structure. The insurer buys insurance from the SPV, a reinsurance contract is written, premiums and losses ($h\text{MAX}(I - S; 0)$) are paid in the normal fashion. However, the SPV backs the transaction by issue of the cat bond with face value D to investors. The proceeds of the bond are held in trust and earn interest r. This trust account collateralizes the reinsurance

---

6. The risk to the bondholder is of interest. Had the primary issued a nonforgiveness bond, it would have been subject to default risk. However, one of the most likely causes for default on such an issue would be that the primary insurer sufferd catastrophic losses. What the cat bond does is to turn the default risk (i.e., the implicit default put) into an explicit embedded forgiveness option.

F I G U R E   16–2

Administration of a CAT Bond

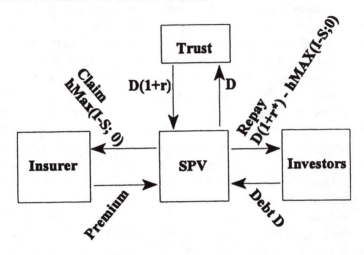

obligation. If a loss occurs, the principal is repaid less the loss paid to the insurer $h\text{MAX}(I - S; 0)$. If no loss is incurred, the bonds are repaid in full with interest r^*, which is unusually high to compensate investors for risking their principal and interest.

Perhaps the most visible of the early issues of cat bonds was that made by the U.S. insurer USAA (see Froot, 1999). The first successful issue by USAA took place in 1997 and was renegotiated in 1998. The structure (as renegotiated in 1998) is as follows. A SPV, Residential Reinsurance Ltd. in the Cayman Islands, issued bonds in two tranches. In one tranche, the principal was at risk for which the investor received 400 basis points above the LIBOR; in the other tranche, interest was at risk and the investor received 180 points above LIBOR (these rates were reduced on reissue). The trigger for forgiveness was USAA's own windstorm losses in excess of $1 billion. Together, the forgiveness of these tranches hedged 90% of the risk to USAA from losses incurred by USAA in the layer between $1 billion and $1.5 billion. The remaining 10% of losses in this layer was retained by USAA. This retention was a response to moral hazard. The debt forgiveness was based on USAA's losses (it was an "indemnity" trigger rather than an indexed trigger) and therefore had the same moral hazard issues as reinsurance. To offset this, their first issue had a 20% coinsurance, and this was reduced to 10% on the 1998 reissue.

The reason the USAA cat bond used an indemnity trigger was that the geographical spread of USAA's book of business was uneven, largely concentrated around military bases. An indexed contract would therefore have had too much basis risk. Other cat bond contracts have been indexed or have been parameterized to the physical dimensions of the of the cat event. For example, a cat bond issue for Tokyo Fire and Marine in 1998 on earthquake risk in the Tokyo region was triggered by the intensity and location of the earthquake. The trigger was nonmanipulable by the insurer, so there was no *ex post* moral hazard. Thus, any saving in loss payouts did not affect the debt repayment. Because the insurer had a high concentration of risk in this area, the basis risk from such a parameterized contract was presumably moderate or low.

Policy Conditions and Mutualization

Perhaps the most direct way in which the insurer can hedge its catastrophe risk is to require that the policyholder bear some of this risk. To explore this further, it is useful to take a small detour into the economics of insurance. Much of intellectual and lay thinking about insurance focuses on an ideal in which the policyholder is fully insured for all loss. At an intellectual level this ideal can be derived by assuming that policyholders are risk-averse but that all risk can be diversified if the insurer holds a large portfolio of independent policies. The law of large numbers asserts that such a portfolio will leave the insurer with a highly predictable per policy average loss, and thus the competitive insurer will charge little or no risk premium. Being risk-averse, individuals will fully insure because they can avoid risk without facing any significant loading of the premium above the expected value of loss.

With catastrophe risk, losses are highly correlated and the law of large numbers is violated. The insurer cannot rely on holding many policies to diversify its risk away. Moreover, if risk is costly to the insurer (why otherwise would we be discussing insurer hedging strategies?), the insurer will be forced to charge a risk premium and the optimal amount of insurance will be less than full coverage. The insured is better off having less insurance (and avoiding part of the risk premium) than being fully insured and facing the full risk premium. In short, the insured is trading off expected wealth against risk, as shown in Chapter 2.

This reasoning can be refined in several ways following the seminal work of Karl Borch (1962). Where risk cannot be fully diversified, the optimal insurance arrangement, from all policyholders' perspectives, is one in which all are fully insured for idiosyncratic (diversifiable) risk but each shares in the common undiversifiable risk. This is tantamount to a mutual insurance arrangement; each policyholder is insured for catastrophe risk, but the proportion of insurance depends on the size of the catastrophe. In practice, this can be accomplished by a mutual that pays everyone's claim but reduces its dividend to all policyholders (or assesses them) by an amount related to total losses.[7,8]

An illustration of this principle is provided by the California Earthquake Authority, which was set up in the state of California to help improve the supply of earthquake insurance. Part of this

---

7. The argument that mutualization of this sort is "optimal" is often misunderstood. Policyholders would certainly be better off if they could fully insure at no risk premium. But this is not an option in a competitive market, since investors would require that the insurer cover any cost of bearing undiversified risk. Thus, the real choice for policyholders is (a) to have a policy with a large risk loading that would induce policyholders to accept a large deductible or coinsurance or (b) to accept a policy that covers idiosyncratic risk but requires the policyholder to contribute in proportion to total losses. The argument here is that option (b) is better for policyholders than option (a). Notice that this argument is identical to the reasoning of the capital asset pricing model. In that model it is shown that the optimal investment strategy is for risk-averse investors to hold a diversified portfolio (i.e., the market portfolio) such that each shares in the total market risk but each diversifies away idiosyncratic risk.

8. The second way in which this reasoning can be refined is to address moral hazard between the policyholder and the primary insurer. This is closely related to the moral hazard occurring between the primary insurer and the reinsurer. For example, the *ex post* moral hazard that can arise between the primary insurer and reinsurer stems from the lack of appropriate actions by the primary to prevent policyholders from "building up" claims or filing fraudulent claims. In short, the moral hazard that arises between the primary insurer and reinsurer is largely a "pass through" of the moral hazard between the policyholder and the primary. Policyholder moral hazard can be addressed by requirng that the policyholder share the loss, normally thorough the use of a deductible or policy limit (see Shavell, 1979, and Stiglitz, 1983). This idea has been extended by Smith and Stultzer (1994), who have shown that sharing risk through dividends also helps control moral hazard.

structure is that in the event of a major earthquake causing catastrophic losses to the industry, insurers will be permitted to surcharge their policyholders to recoup part of the loss. In effect, policyholders are being assessed negative dividends as though they belonged to a mutual insurer.

Catastrophe Equity Puts

Equity put options, described in Chapter 12, have been issued to insurance companies to provide contingent capital in the event of major cat losses. The leader in this field has been the broker Aon, who has been involved in a number of issues of their trademarked "CatEPuts." These instruments follow the general structure described in Chapter 12 but were issued on preferred shares with a cat trigger and a provision for buyback of the shares by the issuer. The insurer issues an option to put preferred shares to a counterparty in the event of a major cat loss. The issue of preferred shares, rather than common, avoids dilution of equity but effectively increases the leverage of the insurer after a loss. The issues made so far have also included a buyback provision permitting the issuing insurer to repurchase the preferred shares within a time period after issue. The cat trigger is one specified in terms of the issuing company's losses.

These instruments do provide some hedging capacity because the exercise of the option to issue preferred shares below their market value results in a wealth transfer from the counterparty to the issuing insurer. However, their main feature is that they provide a recapitalization of the insurer following a major catastrophe loss. Herein lies their particular appeal. A natural catastrophe such as earthquake or hurricane commonly affects all insurers operating in a region. The surplus of each insurer will fall, although to different extents depending on the particular geographical distribution of its book of business. Assuming the cat is severe, there will be a noticeable shortage of capacity to supply insurance after the loss. On the demand side of the market, the loss will probably remind many policyholders of their exposure to future cat losses, and an increase in demand is likely. Basic economics suggests that a reduction of supply, together with an increase in demand, will lead to an increase in price. Thus, the insurance market after a cat loss is a very attractive one for selling insurance. The problem is that each insurer's capacity to sell insurance has been reduced and the opportunity may be lost through lack of capital. The cat puts options are mainly an instrument to restore the insurer's surplus, thus enabling the insurer to exploit the post-loss insurance opportunities. Moreover, because the counter-party provides a hedge only to the difference between the post-loss value of the shares and the exercise price, this instrument should be a cheaper method of recapitalizing than a full indemnity instrument.

REVISITING THE DESIGN SPACE

Now that we have presented the major instruments that have appeared in the emerging cat market, it will be useful to allocate them their due position in the design space considered earlier in Figure 16–1. This is reproduced as Figure 16–3, but here we have added some of the newer instruments that have recently emerged. Reinsurance occupies the top left segment as before. Cat options have inherent credit risk but minimize the *ex post* moral hazard problem by using an index trigger. The index trigger implies that there is some basis risk but little moral hazard. Thus, cat options

F I G U R E   16–3

Design Properties

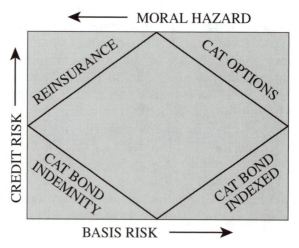

are in the top right of the figure. Cat bonds have no credit risk, since the loss payout is fully collateralized. But they differ in their basis risk/moral hazard trade-off. The indexed bonds are in the bottom right and the indemnity bonds in the lower left. Placing cat equity puts is not quite so clear. They involve some degree of hedging because the counter-party agrees to recapitalize the insurer by purchasing equity at a striking price that is less than the post-loss market value. In contracts seen so far, the main trigger is an indemnity one, the insurer's own loss payouts. But there is not a full hedge and credit risk is present though not so important as with reinsurance. Moreover, the presence of a partial hedge indicates some basis risk and some moral hazard. For these reasons, cat equity puts have been placed in the middle space of Figure 16–3.

Filling out the design space signifies a widening of the solutions available to insurers to manage their cat risk. Different solutions are likely to appeal to different insurers. For example, a small insurer with a geographically undiversified portfolio might find that an indexed product carries too much basis risk and would prefer conventional reinsurance. Such a firm might also benefit from monitoring and technical services provided by a reinsurer. A larger primary insurer with a geographically concentrated portfolio might also prefer an indemnity product but is comfortable supplementing its cat reinsurance by going directly to investors with a cat securitization. Another firm might see its main requirement as having sufficient capital following a major cat loss to maintain its supply of insurance (or even to expand to take advantage of attractive post-loss market opportunities). This firm might not wish to buy an expensive full indemnity hedge but seeks a cheaper way of rebuilding its post-loss capital. For this firm a post-loss recapitalization product such as a cat equity put seems more attractive than conventional reinsurance or other indemnity-based instruments.

It would be difficult to argue that the new products are inherently more efficient than conventional ones. There is not one size to fit all. The new products are expanding the design choices and provide a much richer menu from which insurers can address their particular risk management needs. There are design choices that have not been incorporated. An important one is liquidity. Standardized instruments can be repackaged and resold to appeal to a wider investor community. Some of the nonstandardized issues, such as the USAA cat bond, already have secondary market trades. This liquidity lowers the cost of the instrument. Other issues are regulatory acceptance and tax treatment. These issues are sometimes addressed by use of special purpose vehicles that, to some degree, allow the regulator's concerns to be separated from the insurer's design objectives. For example, in a cat bond issue the regulator's concern for financial stability can be met by allowing the insurer to buy a reinsurance contract from the SPV that holds full collateral for its potential liability in a trust account. But instead of addressing all possible design issues, we will focus on the one innovation that has probably been the hallmark of the cat securitization movement: the use of basis risk to address moral hazard.

TRADING OFF BASIS RISK
AND MORAL HAZARD–INDEXED
AND PARAMETERIZED TRIGGERS

Perhaps the most interesting innovation that has been promoted with the securitization of cat risk has been the use-indexed and parameterized triggers to combat moral hazard. In the earlier parts of this chapter we addressed this subject and showed how different instruments have adopted different triggers. Here we will categorize the triggers that can be used, and in the Appendix we will present a more technical treatment of some of the issues.

In earlier sections we considered index triggers as used in cat options and some cat bonds securitizations. We will now briefly examine some other types of triggers and show how they are likely to perform in offsetting basis risk and moral hazard. An expanded treatment of these trade-offs between basis risk and moral hazard is included in the Appendix.

Complete Market Index

The complete market index is what we have just described: it is the index of all insurers, including the one buying the hedge. The effectiveness of this type of index in providing a good hedge to insurer i with little basis risk and moral hazard depends on two factors: how representative is insurer i's portfolio of the whole index, and what is insurer *i*'s market share. At one extreme, an insurer with a large market share will have a portfolio that differs little from the index of which it is the major part. This implies that there is little basis risk, but high moral hazard. As the market share falls, the moral hazard will fall because the insurer will normally only wish to hedge a small portion of the market index. But basis risk will not necessarily increase as market share falls. One can imagine small insurers with representative portfolios; that is, the geographic spread of their business roughly matches the market as a whole. Such an insurer would have a good hedge with little basis risk and little moral hazard. But another small insurer with a book of business that did not match the market as a whole would have considerable basis risk.

Exclusive Market Index

An alternative can include all insurers *except* that buying the hedge. Hedging with this index presents no moral hazard because any mitigation has no effect on the loss experience of competing insurers. How much basis risk there is depends on how closely the combined book of business of remaining insurers matches that of the hedging firm. The problem with this index design is that it is unique for each hedge contract and cannot be standardized.

Representative Market Index

To overcome the shortcomings of the exclusive index, some standardized index can be constructed with selected representative firms. This lends itself to standardization of contracts, and the moral hazard issues depend on whether the hedging firm is part of the index.

Parametric Trigger

A more radical design is to relate the payoff on the hedge contract to some parametric description of the event that causes the loss to the insurer. For example, if the event is an earthquake, the payoff function can be defined solely in relation to the physical description of the earthquake (e.g., its location, intensity, depth, etc.). Because these data cannot be manipulated by the hedging insurer, there is no moral hazard. But there is basis risk. Other examples of contracts of this type are hedges triggered by the number of inches of rainfall, the number of hours of blackout/brownout in electricity supply, the number of barrels of oil spilled, and so on.

Modeled Trigger

An alternative design that has been contemplated for cat risk is to run a model to estimate what the total claims *should have* been and use this prediction to calculate the payout. For example, consider East Coast hurricane damage to a primary insurer. The various cat modeling firms have models in place in which they can run many thousands of different potential storms and how they would impact a given insurer with a given book of business. The modeling is based on factors such as the parameters of the storm (e.g., intensity, size, and path of the storm), the value and construction standards of property in its path, and the values insured by the insurer in question. With this data the model can estimate what the damage might be for each storm. The same model can be used with one additional storm added; the storm that has just occurred. The model can spill out a damage estimate that can be used to determine the hedge payout.

If the parameters of the model are fixed in advance, there is in principle no moral hazard attached to this type of trigger. But there is basis risk because the model may not predict accurately the actual losses suffered by the insurer. This basis risk arises from the modeling error. Whether this basis risk will be greater or less than that from an indexed trigger cannot be determined as a general proposition. If the model has relatively little error and if the insurer has a book of business that is not well represented by any normal index, the modeled trigger will probably have lower basis risk. But for the insurer with a book of business matching the market, the indexed contract might perform better.

A further interesting feature about the modeled trigger can give rise to offsetting errors. The pricing of most cat bond issues has been based on such simulation models. If the model used has any systematic bias—for example, it tends to underestimate damage from some events and overestimate damage from others—the same bias will creep into the payout when actual events are modeled. Thus, any errors in pricing such contracts are naturally self-correcting.[9] This should offer some comfort to investors who are worried about how to price such radical new types of financial contracts.

CONCLUSION

The types of innovation seen for insurer catastrophe risk can be classified into two types. First and most simple is the placing of insurer cat risk directly to investors who can buy an investment instrument whose performance relates to quite specific catastrophe losses. The investor can take a particular position in a California earthquake, a Japanese typhoon, or a Florida hurricane. Previously, investors could take positions in cat risk but in a much less focused manner; that is, buying insurance and reinsurance stocks. This increased availability of risk management instruments should extend insurance capacity by expanding the pool into which insurance risk can ultimately be spread.

The second type of innovation lies in contract design. In this respect the catastrophe insurance market reveals the whole gamut of contracting innovations that have been described in this book. There are instruments that provide *ex post* financing, contingent financing, and contingent leverage, and, with respect to hedging, there are a variety of trigger alternatives that vary in their credit risk. This enrichment of contractual choices now permits insurers to adopt risk management strategies that match their particular needs.

As mentioned in the introduction to this chapter, the fact that so much innovation has occurred in the cat risk market is not accidental; all the preconditions were met. There was demand for new capacity, the technology to create new instruments had developed, largely through the development of the derivatives market, and there was information from which to price the new instruments. But as mentioned several places in this work, the innovations are not confined to the cat risk arena. The various tests of the theories described in Chapter 7 show that firms are formulating their hedging strategies with respect to their leverage,

---

9. The offsetting error relates solely to the severity risk. The risk of misestimating frequency when pricing contracts remains.

growth potential, and financing needs. This indicates a wide-spread consideration of leverage and financing in formulating risk management strategy. Several surveys of financial hedging behavior of firms and insurers are now increasingly bundling insurance and financial risks into integrated risk management products, and we are now seeing some securitizations of other insurable risks together with innovative options embedded in corporate debt that mitigate the dysfunctional aspects of risk.

But the future is not yet here. Many firms clearly attack risk management as a series of isolated decisions on separate sources of risk. These firms buy insurance separately for different lines, hedging financial risk is a spotty practice, and insurance and financial risk management are undertaken in isolation and with little attention to any credible theory of value added. For many, integrated risk management remains "what might be" rather than "what is."

REFERENCES

Aiuppa, Thomas A., Robert J. Carney, and Thomas M. Krueger. 1993. "An Examination of Insurance Stock Prices Following the 1989 Loma Prieta Earthquake." *Journal of Insurance Issues and Practices* 16:1–14.

Babbel, David F., and Anthony M. Santomero. 1996. "Risk Management by Insurers: An Analysis of the Process." Working Paper, Financial Institutions Center, Wharton School, University of Pennsylvania.

Borch, Karl. 1962. "Equilibrium in a Reinsurance Market." *Econometrica* 30:424–44.

Cheval, S. 1979. "On Moral Hazard and Insurance." *Quarterly Journal of Economics* 11:541–62.

Cummins, J. David, and N. A. Doherty. 1996. "Can Insurers Pay for the 'Big One': Measuring the Capacity of the Insurance Industry to Respond to Catastrophic Losses." Working Paper, Wharton School, University of Pennsylvania.

Doherty, Neil A. 1985. *Corporate Risk Management: A Financial Analysis.* New York: McGraw-Hill.

———. 1996, "Corporate Insurance: Competition from Capital Markets." In *Universal Banking,* ed. A. Saunders and I. Walter. New York: Salomon Center, New York University.

Doherty, Neil, Anne E. Kleffner, and Howard Kunreuther. 1992. "Should Society Deal with the Earthquake Problem?" In *Regulation* 15(2).

Doherty, Neil A., and Kent Smetters. 1999. "Moral Hazard and Contract Innovation in Reinsurance Markets." Working Paper, Wharton School, University of Pennsylvania.

Doherty, Neil, and Seha Tinic. 1981. "A Note on Reinsurance under Conditions of Capital Market Equilibrium." *Journal of Finance* 36:949–53.

Froot, Kenneth. 1998. "The Evolving Market for Catastrophe Event Risk." Working Paper No. 7287, National Bureau of Economic Research, Cambridge, Mass.

———. 1999. "The Limited Financing of Catastrophe Insurance: An Overview." In *The Financing of Catastrophe Risk*. Chicago: University of Chicago Press.

Froot, Kenneth, and Paul O'Connell. 1999. "The Pricing of US Catastrophe Reinsurance." In *The Financing of Catastrophe Risk*. Chicago: University of Chicago Press.

Froot, Kenneth, David Scharfstein, and Jeremy Stein. 1993. "Risk Management: Co-ordinating Investment and Financing Problems." *Journal of Finance* 48: 1629–58.

Garven, James R., and Henri Louberge. 1996. "Reinsurance, Taxes and Efficiency: A Contingent Claims Model of Insurance Market Equilibrium." *Journal of Financial Intermediation* 5:74–93.

Harrington, Scott. 1997. "Insurance Derivatives, Tax Policy, and the Future of the Insurance Industry." *Journal of Risk and Insurance* 64:719–25.

Harrington, Scott, Steven Mann, and Greg Niehaus. 1995. "Insurer Capital Decisions and the Viability of Insurance Derivatives." *Journal of Risk and Insurance* 62:483–508.

Jensen, Michael C., and William H. Meckling. 1976. Theory of the Firm: Managerial Behavior, Agency Costs and Ownership Structure." *Journal of Financial Economics* 3:305–60.

Kreps, David. 1990. *A Course in Microeconomic Theory*. Princeton, N.J.: Princeton University Press.

Lamb, Reinhold P. 1995. "An Exposure Based Analysis of Property Liability Insurer Stock Values Around Hurricane Andrew." *Journal of Risk and Insurance* 62:111–23.

Lambert, R. 1983. "Long Term Contracts and Moral Hazard." *Bell Journal of Economics* 8:441–52.

Lane, Morton. 1998. "Price Risk and the Rating of Insurance Linked Notes." Paper issued by Sedgwick Lane Financial.

Lew, Keun-Ock. 1991. "Reinsurance and the Firm Value." Ph.D. Dissertation, Wharton School, University of Pennsylvania.

Major, John A. 1996. "Index Hedge Performance: Insurer Market Penetration and Basis Risk." Paper presented at National Bureau of Economic Research Conference, Palm Beach, Florida.

Mayers, David, and Clifford W. Smith Jr. 1983. "On the Corporate Demand for Insurance." *Journal of Business* 55:281–96.

———. 1990. "On the Corporate Demand for Insurance: Evidence from Reinsurance Markets." *Journal of Business* 63:19–40.

Myers, Stewart C. 1977. "Determinants of Corporate Borrowing." *Journal of Financial Economics* 5:147–75.

Nance, D. R., C. W. Smith Jr., and C. W. Smithson. 1993. "On the Determinants of Corporate Hedging." *Journal of Finance* 48:267–84.

O'Brien, Thomas. 1997. "Hedging Strategies Using Catastrophe Insurance Options." *Insurance Mathematics and Economics* 21:153–62.

Shapiro, Alan C., and Sheridan Titman. 1985. "An Integrated Approach to Corporate Risk Management." *Midland Corporate Finance Journal* 3(2):41–56.

Shavell, Stephen. 1979. "Risk Sharing and Incentives in the Principal and Agent Relationship." *Bell Journal of Economics* 10:55–73.

Shelor, Roger M., Dwight C. Anderson, and Mark L. Cross. 1992. "Gaining from Loss: Property-Liability Insurer Stock Prices in the Aftermath of the 1989 California Earthquake." *Journal of Risk and Insurance* 5:476–88.

Smith, B. D., and M. J. Stultzer. 1994. "A Theory of Mutual Formation and Moral Hazard." Working Paper, University of Minnesota.

Smith, Clifford W. Jr., and Rene Stulz. 1985. "The Determinants of Firm's Hedging Policies." *Journal of Financial and Quantitative Analysis* 28:391–405.

Stiglitz, J. 1983. *Risk, Incentives and Insurance: The Pure Theory of Moral Hazard.* Geneva Papers on Risk and Insurance, 8(26), 4–33.

A P P E N D I X

In this section on basis risk we will do four things. First, we will consider the use of indices to determine payout on cat instruments. Basis risk can be considered as the correlation between the index and the insurer's loss. Secondly, we will show how the basis risk in an indexed cat product affects the insurer's overall risk position and introduce the idea of an optimal hedge ratio. Thirdly, we will explore how moral hazard can be reduced through an indexed payout. Here we will show that it is not basis risk per se that controls moral hazard, but market share risk. Finally, we will look briefly at other payout triggers that expose the insurer to some basis risk but that can be used to address moral hazard.

Indices and Basis Risk

I have argued that the designers of insurer catastrophe hedges are faced with an important trade off between basis risk and moral hazard. This was captured in the optimal choice of mitigation by the insurer who has purchased a hedge. Equation (16.3) is reproduced

$$\frac{\partial E(T)}{\partial a} = -\frac{\partial E(L(a))}{\partial a} - 1 + h\frac{\partial C}{\partial I}\frac{\partial I}{\partial L}\frac{\partial L}{\partial a} = 0 \qquad (16.3)$$

The derivative $\partial I/\partial L$ is central. The higher this ratio, the more severe is the moral hazard (though the basis risk is correspondingly less severe). As discussed earlier, this derivative is unity with an indemnity contract. But moral hazard is lessened at the expense of basis risk, as this derivative falls. Here we will look at basis risk when the payout under the instrument is indexed to an aggregate measure of losses incurred by some population. In the current context, cat securitizations are often linked to an index of the aggregated cat losses of a number of insurers, such as the regional and national insurance indices used in CBOT cat options. In this Appendix we will focus on a complete market index; that is, one including all insurers in the market.

A simple measure of basis risk discussed earlier in this chapter is (one minus) the correlation between the loss incurred by an insurer holding the hedge instrument and the value of the index (see Major, 1996). It is argued here that simple correlation is too crude to capture the appropriate trade-offs in designing an index and that we need to decompose basis risk into what can be called "representation risk" and "market share risk."

Consider a market with a number of insurers. We focus on one insurer, subscripted i, that has an aggregate loss on its book of business of L_i. All other insurers are considered together as the rest of the market and are subscripted j, and their combined loss is L_j. The market covered by the index is subscripted m and the random aggregate market loss is $L_m = L_i + L_j$. The basis risk will be inversely related to the covariance between L_i and L_m, COV $(L_i L_m)$. To elaborate:

$$\text{COV } (L_i; L_m) = \text{COV } (L_i; L_i + L_j)$$

$$= \text{COV } (L_i; L_i) + \text{COV } (L_i; L_j)$$

$$r_{im}\sigma_i\sigma_m = \sigma_i^2 + r_{ij}\sigma_i\sigma_j$$

where $r_{i,m}$ is the correlation coefficient between firm i's losses and the market index. We can use this relationship to come up with the following measure of basis risk:

$$\text{Basis risk} = 1 - r_{im} = \left(1 - r_{ij}\frac{\sigma_j}{\sigma_m}\right) - \left(\frac{\sigma_i}{\sigma_m}\right)$$

Thus, basis risk has two components. The final part of this equation, σ_i/σ_m, can be called "market share risk." Other things being equal, the larger the market share of insurer i, the closer will σ_i/σ_m be to unity and the smaller the basis risk. The first component, $1 - r_{ij}\sigma_j/\sigma_m$, arises not from i's market share, but from how representative i's portfolio is of the whole market, and is called "representation risk." An insurer that had a small book of business that nevertheless reflected the spread of business in the whole market (i.e., by zip code, by type of risk, etc.), would have representational risk approaching zero (r_{ij} and σ_j/σ_m both close to unity). Thus, it can be seen there are two ways to achieve low basis risk: by having high market share risk (i.e., by dominating the index) and by having low market share but having a spread of exposure resembling other insurers in the market; that is, low representational risk. As we will see presently, moral hazard arises only from market share risk. Thus, the ideal index for a particular contract would have low market share risk (to control moral hazard) and low representational risk (to keep basis risk low).

Basis Risk and Hedge Ratios

A Simple Hedge

To put the notation in place, call the payout on some hedging instrument H. Now look at a simple instrument by which the insurance firm hedges all of its risk by reinsuring 100% of its own losses L_i:

$$\text{Insurer risk} = \text{risk in insurance portfolio}$$
$$+ \text{ risk in hedge instrument} + 2 \text{ COV}$$

$$\text{where COV} = r \ \sigma(L_i) \ \sigma(H)$$

$$\sigma^2 = \sigma^2(L_i) + \sigma^2(H) - 2r \ \sigma(L_i) \ \sigma(H)$$

Because the hedge is based exclusively on the insurer's own loss, L_i, $H = L_i$ and the insurer's risk is:

$$\sigma^2 = \sigma^2(L_i) + \sigma^2(L_i) - 2r \ \sigma(K_i) \ \sigma(L_i)$$

Thus, if $E(L_i) = 100$ and $\sigma(L_i) = 60$, and by definition $r = -1$:

$$\sigma^2 = 60^2 + 60^2 + (2)(-1)(60)(60) = 0$$

There is a perfect hedge that has eliminated all risk.

Hedge on Index or Market

Suppose that the insurance firm i with loss L_i controls a proportion x of market. The aggregate losses of all insurers is the random value L_m which we will call the market index. The firm buys a hedge that pays a portion h of L_m (the term h is the hedge ratio). The cost of the hedge will be related to the expected cost $xE(L)$. For example, with a 10% transaction cost, the price of the hedge is $(1.1)xE(L_m)$, or more generally, $(1 + t)xE(L_m)$, where t is the proportional transaction cost. The value of this hedge will depend on the correlation coefficient between L_i and L_m, which is labeled r. How much risk will the insurer be able to get rid of by buying a hedge on the index?

Adding to the data in the prior example ($E(L_i) = 100$ and $\sigma(L_i) = 60$), suppose $E(L_m) = 1000$ (i.e., firm has $x = 0.1$ of market) and the firm chooses a hedge ratio that reflects its market share: $h = x$. Accordingly, the hedge instrument pays xL_m (10% of market index). Also suppose $\sigma(L_m) = 300$. Finally, suppose that L_i and L_m have a correlation of 0.8.

Insurer's risk $\sigma^2 = \sigma^2(L_i) + \sigma^2(H) - 2r\,\sigma(L_i)\,\sigma(H)$

$\qquad\qquad\quad = \sigma^2(L_i) + x^2\,\sigma^2(L_m) - 2rx\,\sigma(L_i)\,\sigma(L_m)$

$\qquad\quad \sigma^2 = 60^2 + (0.1)^2(200)^2 + (2)(0.1)(-0.8)(60)(300)$

$\qquad\qquad\quad = 1620$

thus $\qquad\quad \sigma = 40.25$

Thus, the insurer started with a risk of 60 and has reduced this to 40.25 by hedging on the market index. The effectiveness of the index hedge depends on correlation. The higher the correlation, the more risk can be reduced for the insurer by an index hedge; that is, there is less basis risk.

Hedge Ratio That Minimizes Insurer Risk

Instead of buying a hedge that pays in proportion to its market share, x, the insurer hedges according to a ratio h that may differ from x. The insurer's risk is now:

$$\sigma^2 = \sigma^2(L_i) + h^2\sigma^2(L_m) - 2rh\,\sigma(L_i)\,\sigma(L_m)$$

The hedge ratio that minimizes insurer risk is determined by setting the derivative to zero:

$$\frac{d\sigma^2}{dh} = 2h\sigma^2(L_m) - 2r\sigma(L_i)\sigma(L_m) = 0$$

$$h = \frac{r\sigma(L_m)\,\sigma(L_i)}{\sigma^2(L_m)} = \frac{(0.8)(60)(300)}{300^2} = 0.16$$

With a hedge ratio of 0.16, the insurer's risk is now calculated:

$$\sigma^2 = 60^2 + (0.16)^2(300))^2 + (2)(0.16)(-0.8)(60)(300)$$
$$= 1296$$

thus $\sigma = 36$

When basis risk is present, the risk-minimizing hedge ratio will not usually be the same as market share. The insurer has a 10% market share but does not reduce risk to its minimum by hedging 10% of the market. The hedge ratio that minimizes risk is somewhat higher at 16%. Increasing the hedge ratio from 0.1 to 0.16 reduces the insurer's risk further from 40.25 to 36, and given the correlation coefficient of 0.8, this is the lowest risk level we can achieve. The remaining risk simply cannot be unloaded with this hedging instrument. The only way to reduce risk further is to find an index H that has a higher correlation with the insurer's own losses, L_i.

Finally, we have calculated that for this insurer, hedging on a market index that has a correlation coefficient of 0.8 with the insurer's own losses, a hedge ratio of 0.16 would reduce the insurer's risk to its minimum level attainable. But this does not mean that a hedge ratio of 0.16 is the best choice for the insurer. We must also take account of moral hazard.

Controlling Moral Hazard with Indexed Hedges

Moral Hazard with No Hedge

To illustrate hedging and moral hazard, we will return to analysis similar to that conducted in Chapter 3. Suppose that insurer can reduce $E(L)$ from 100 to $100/(1 + s)$ by spending s on loss reduction. With no hedge the insurer would choose s to minimize its total costs. We can calculate this cost, minimizing level of s by setting the derivative of costs to zero. The total costs are the sum of the losses it pays, $100/(1 + s)$, and the amount it spends on loss reduction, s.

$$\text{MIN} \frac{100}{1 + s} + s; \quad \frac{dC}{ds} = \frac{-100}{(1 + s)^2} + 1 = 0; \quad s = 9$$

Thus, the insurer would minimize costs by spending 9 on mitigation.

Moral Hazard with Index Hedge

We will now use the same data but allow the firm both to hedge on the market index and to determine its level of loss reduction, s. The insurer's expected loss is still $100/(1 + s)$, and the expected loss of other insurers is $L_j = 900$. As before, $L_m = L_i + L_j$. Assume that the insurer i chooses a risk-minimizing hedge ratio of 16%. The expected recovery on the hedge is now:

$$h \left\{ \frac{EL_i}{1 + s} + E(L_j) \right\} = 0.16 \frac{100}{1 + s} + 900$$

Insurer chooses s to minimize costs:

$$\text{MIN } \frac{100}{1 + s} - 0.16 \left(\frac{100}{1 + s} + 900 \right) + s;$$

$$\frac{dC}{ds} = -0.84 \left(\frac{100}{(1 + s)^2} \right) + 1 = 0; \quad s = 8.17$$

Thus, there is a little reduction in spending on loss prevention—from 9 to 8.17. With this hedge instrument the insurer reduced its risk from 60 to 35. Overall, the insurer reduced its risk level (as measured by the standard deviation) by 42% with only a 9.2% reduction in the spending on mitigation. Compare this with a full indemnity contract in which the risk is reduced by 100% but spending on mitigation also is reduced by 100%, as shown below.

Moral Hazard with Simple Hedge

$$\text{MIN } \frac{100}{1 + s} - 1.0 \left(\frac{100}{1 + s} \right) + s; \quad \frac{dC}{ds} = +1; \quad s = 0$$

These three cases illustrate the trade-off between basis risk and moral hazard. We can have a perfect hedge and high moral hazard (the simple hedge), an intermediate hedge and little moral hazard (the index hedge), or no hedge and no moral hazard. Which of these is best in any given circumstance depends on the rate at which one acquires moral hazard as one hedges. The task facing designers is to find indexes that give a reasonably good hedge (large reduction in risk) with little accumulated moral hazard. As with many trade-offs, the best solutions are often found in the middle rather than at the extremes. For insurers with moderate market share and fairly representative portfolios, indexed triggers might provide respectable hedges yet let them encounter only modest moral hazard.

APPENDIX

STANDARD NORMAL (TABLE SHOWS SHADED AREA) DISTRIBUTION, THREE VALUES

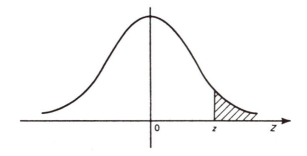

Z	.00	.01	.02	.03	.04	.05	.06	.07	.08	.09
0.0	.5000	.4960	.4920	.4880	.4840	.4801	.4761	.4721	.4681	.4641
0.1	.4602	.4562	.4522	.4483	.4443	.4404	.4364	.4325	.4286	.4247
0.2	.4207	.4168	.4129	.4090	.4052	.4013	.3974	.3936	.3897	.3859
0.3	.3821	.3783	.3745	.3707	.3669	.3632	.3594	.3557	.3520	.3483
0.4	.3446	.3409	.3372	.3336	.3300	.3264	.3228	.3192	.3156	.3121
0.5	.3085	.3050	.3015	.2981	.2946	.2912	.2877	.2843	.2810	.2776
0.6	.2743	.2709	.2676	.2643	.2611	.2578	.2546	.2514	.2483	.2451
0.7	.2420	.2389	.2358	.2327	.2296	.2266	.2236	.2206	.2177	.2148
0.8	.2119	.2090	.2061	.2033	.2005	.1977	.1949	.1922	.1894	.1867
0.9	.1841	.1814	.1788	.1762	.1736	.1711	.1685	.1660	.1635	.1611
1.0	.1587	.1562	.1539	.1515	.1492	.1469	.1446	.1423	.1401	.1379
1.1	.1357	.1335	.1314	.1292	.1271	.1251	.1230	.1210	.1190	.1170
1.2	.1151	.1131	.1112	.1093	.1075	.1056	.1038	.1020	.1003	.0985
1.3	.0968	.0951	.0934	.0918	.0901	.0885	.0869	.0853	.0838	.0823
1.4	.0808	.0793	.0778	.0764	.0749	.0735	.0721	.0708	.0694	.0681
1.5	.0668	.0655	.0643	.0630	.0618	.0606	.0594	.0582	.0571	.0559
1.6	.0548	.0537	.0526	.0516	.0505	.0495	.0485	.0475	.0465	.0455
1.7	.0446	.0436	.0427	.0418	.0409	.0401	.0392	.0384	.0375	.0367
1.8	.0359	.0351	.0344	.0336	.0329	.0322	.0314	.0307	.0301	.0294
1.9	.0287	.0281	.0274	.0268	.0262	.0256	.0250	.0244	.0239	.0233
2.0	.0228	.0222	.0217	.0212	.0207	.0202	.0197	.0192	.0188	.0183
2.1	.0179	.0174	.0170	.0166	.0162	.0158	.0154	.0150	.0146	.0143
2.2	.0139	.0136	.0132	.0129	.0125	.0122	.0119	.0116	.0113	.0110
2.3	.0107	.0104	.0102	.0099	.0096	.0094	.0091	.0089	.0087	.0084
2.4	.0082	.0080	.0078	.0075	.0073	.0071	.0069	.0068	.0066	.0064
2.5	.0062	.0060	.0059	.0057	.0055	.0054	.0052	.0051	.0049	.0048
2.6	.0047	.0045	.0044	.0043	.0041	.0040	.0039	.0038	.0037	.0036
2.7	.0035	.0034	.0033	.0032	.0031	.0030	.0029	.0028	.0027	.0026
2.8	.0026	.0025	.0024	.0023	.0023	.0022	.0021	.0021	.0020	.0019
2.9	.0019	.0018	.0018	.0017	.0016	.0016	.0015	.0015	.0014	.0014
3.0	.0013	.0013	.0013	.0012	.0012	.0011	.0011	.0011	.0010	.0010

INDEX